The Rorty Reader

BLACKWELL READERS

In a number of disciplines, across a number of decades, and in a number of languages, writers and texts have emerged which require the attention of students and scholars around the world. United only by a concern with radical ideas, Blackwell Readers collect and introduce the works of pre-eminent theorists. Often translating works for the first time (Levinas, Irigaray, Lyotard, Blanchot, Kristeva), or presenting material previously inaccessible (C. L. R. James, Fanon, Elias), each volume in the series introduces and represents work which is now fundamental to study in the humanities and social sciences.

The Lyotard Reader
Edited by Andrew Benjamin

The Irigaray Reader
Edited by Margaret Whitford

The Kristeva Reader
Edited by Toril Moi

The Levinas Reader
Edited by Sean Hand

The C. L. R. James Reader
Edited by Anna Grimshaw

The Wittgenstein Reader, Second Edition
Edited by Anthony Kenny

The Blanchot Reader
Edited by Michael Holland

The Lukács Reader
Edited by Arpad Kadarkay

The Cavell Reader
Edited by Stephen Mulhall

The Guattari Reader
Edited by Garry Genosko

The Bataille Reader
Edited by Fred Botting and Scott Wilson

The Eagleton Reader
Edited by Stephen Regan

The Castoriadis Reader
Edited by David Ames Curtis

The Goffman Reader
Edited by Charles Lemert and Ann Branaman

The Frege Reader
Edited by Michael Beaney

The Virilio Reader
Edited by James Der Derian

The Hegel Reader
Edited by Stephen Houlgate

The Norbert Elias Reader
Edited by Johan Goudsblom and Stephen Mennell

The Angela Y. Davis Reader
Edited by Joy James

The Stanley Fish Reader
Edited by H. Aram Veeser

The Žižek Reader
Edited by Elizabeth Wright and Edmond Wright

The Talcott Parsons Reader
Edited by Bryan S. Turner

The Certeau Reader
Edited by Graham Ward

The Adorno Reader
Edited by Brian O'Connor

The Jameson Reader
Edited by Michael Hardt and Kathi Weeks

The Bauman Reader
Edited by Peter Beilharz

The Raymond Williams Reader
Edited by John Higgins

The Kierkegaard Reader
Edited by Jane Chamberlain and Jonathan Rée

The Tocqueville Reader
Edited by Olivier Zunz and Alan S. Kahan

The Nietzsche Reader
Edited by Keith Ansell Pearson and Duncan Large

The Rorty Reader
Edited by Christopher J. Voparil and Richard J. Bernstein

The Rorty Reader

Edited by
Christopher J. Voparil
and
Richard J. Bernstein

A John Wiley & Sons, Ltd., Publication

This edition first published 2010
Editorial material and organization © 2010 Blackwell Publishing Ltd.

Blackwell Publishing was acquired by John Wiley & Sons in February 2007. Blackwell's publishing program has been merged with Wiley's global Scientific, Technical, and Medical business to form Wiley-Blackwell.

Registered Office
John Wiley & Sons Ltd, The Atrium, Southern Gate, Chichester, West Sussex, PO19 8SQ, United Kingdom

Editorial Offices
350 Main Street, Malden, MA 02148-5020, USA
9600 Garsington Road, Oxford, OX4 2DQ, UK
The Atrium, Southern Gate, Chichester, West Sussex, PO19 8SQ, UK

For details of our global editorial offices, for customer services, and for information about how to apply for permission to reuse the copyright material in this book please see our website at www.wiley.com/wiley-blackwell.

The right of Christopher J. Voparil and Richard J. Bernstein to be identified as the authors of the editorial material in this work has been asserted in accordance with the UK Copyright, Designs and Patents Act 1988.

Library of Congress Cataloging-in-Publication Data
The Rorty reader / edited by Christopher J. Voparil and Richard J. Bernstein.
    p.   cm. – (Blackwell readers)
  Includes bibliographical references and index.
   ISBN 978-1-4051-9831-8 (hardcover : alk. paper) – ISBN 978-1-4051-9832-5 (pbk. : alk. paper)   1. Rorty, Richard.   I. Voparil, Christopher J., 1969–   II. Bernstein, Richard J.
   B945.R524R677 2010
   191–dc22

                                                      2009050267

A catalogue record for this book is available from the British Library.

Set in 10.5/12.5pt Bembo
by SPi Publisher Services, Pondicherry, India
Printed in Singapore by Ho Printing Singapore Pte Ltd

01   2010

For our students

Contents

Preface

Richard Rorty (1931–2007) was one of the most provocative and controversial philosophers of the past fifty years. He had the rare ability to combine sophisticated argument with wit, charm, and humor. He was never dull – and he reached a wide public throughout the world. Originally trained in the history of philosophy and the grand tradition of metaphysics, he became fascinated with the linguistic turn in analytic philosophy. During his early years he wrote articles that were at the cutting edge of analytic philosophy. He developed a new approach to the mind–body problem and raised troubling questions about the project of conceptual analysis. But he began to question what he called the "Kantian foundations" of analytic philosophy. In 1979, he published *Philosophy and the Mirror of Nature*, a book that became an immediate sensation and has now been translated into more than twenty languages. Rorty – employing ingenious arguments – questioned the basis of analytic philosophy and, more generally, the very idea of systematic philosophy. He claimed that the metaphor of the "mirror of nature" had misled many philosophers into thinking that the task of philosophy is to "get things right" by correctly representing a world of objective facts. Rorty identified himself with the American pragmatic tradition, especially William James and John Dewey, but his appropriation of pragmatism was idiosyncratic. He was always a gadfly and intellectual provocateur. Rorty critically engaged the leading analytic philosophers of his time, including Quine, Sellars, and Davidson, and Putnam and also the leading continental philosophers, including Heidegger, Gadamer, Habermas, Foucault, and Derrida. He wrote perceptively about Proust, Nabokov, and Orwell. In *Contingency, Irony, and Solidarity* Rorty sketched his vision of a post-philosophical culture, a liberal utopia that would combine the public project of minimizing human cruelty and humiliation with private projects of individual self-creation. In *Achieving our Country: Leftist Thought in Twentieth-Century America*, he set forth his democratic political vision for America. He chided some of the excesses of intellectuals shaped by the New Left for neglecting "real politics" where the poor are exploited by the greedy; he called for a new alliance of the Old and New Left in the tradition of Whitman and Dewey.

In his splendid introduction Christopher Voparil develops a detailed and illuminating overview of Rorty's entire career. The introduction provides the context for appreciating the richness and variety of Rorty's writings. Rorty concluded *Philosophy and Mirror of Nature* by declaring that "the only point on which I would insist is that philosophers' moral concern should be with continuing the conversation of the West." In one of his last articles he returned to the so-called analytic–continental split. He felt that this dichotomy was a crude and misleading one, and he suggested substituting the "analytic–conversational" distinction.

> Substituting analytic-conversational for analytic-continental as a description of the most salient split among today's philosophy professors might help us resist the temptation to treat this split either as dividing those who love truth and reason from those who prefer dramatic effects and rhetorical triumphs, or as dividing the unimaginative clods from the free spirits. It is better understood as a split between two quite different ways of thinking of the human situation. (p. 191, this volume)

Rorty identified himself with the conversational philosophers, but as the following readings show, he contributed to *both* sides of this split – and he looked forward to the day when philosophers might see themselves as "fellow travelers on the same journey." It is our hope that this diverse selection of Rorty's writings will stimulate the ongoing conversation that he encouraged and cherished.

Richard J. Bernstein

Acknowledgments

The making of this book incurred many debts, without which it would be an immeasurably inferior work. The endless stream of encouragement, enthusiasm, and sage advice from Jeff Dean at Wiley-Blackwell, as well as the patient and capable assistance of Tiffany Mok, have been invaluable. Mary Varney Rorty was exceedingly generous in her support of the project, including her willingness to grant permission for a number of essays, share photos, and provide other helpful information only she knows. The unique knowledge and perspective of Rorty's former graduate assistant, Gideon Lewis-Kraus, was pivotal on a number of issues and decisions. His work compiling the comprehensive bibliography of Rorty's writings is a boon to all Rorty scholars. Tess Zimmerman of the Union Institute & University Library tracked down more copies of decades-old, obscure Rorty essays than she probably cares to remember. Absent the painstaking research and insights of Neil Gross into Rorty's early life and career in his *Richard Rorty: The Making of an American Philosopher*, not just the biographical section but the entire Introduction would have been considerably flimsier.

A number of colleagues and friends provided crucial support. Colin Koopman, Alan Malachowski, and Wojciech Malecki graciously read early drafts of the Introduction and nobly endured all of my questions and queries. They furnished much-needed counsel and prevented many missteps and errors of judgment. Conversations and email exchanges at various points with James Campbell, Michael Eldridge, and John McDermott were especially helpful. The members of the Central European Pragmatist Forum offered a great sounding board for ideas and a source of stimulation. I am grateful to the many students at Union Institute & University and Lynn University over the years for their feedback on the numerous Rorty essays inflicted upon them. Their voices were never far from mind throughout this process. My debt to Richard Bernstein goes far beyond the depth of knowledge, history, and care he contributed to the making of this book. The origins of this project and my own interest in Rorty can be traced to the day a decade and a half ago when he brought Rorty himself to his year-long seminar on American pragmatism at The New School for Social Research for his students to interrogate. My understanding of Rorty and pragmatism more generally owes much to Bernstein's teaching, his many incisive readings of Rorty work – beacons in the miasma of unilluminating retorts to Rorty in which one can easily find oneself mired – and his model of careful, critical, engaged Deweyan inquiry overall. I am also grateful for the love and support (and tolerance and patience) bestowed upon me by my family during this project.

Lastly, I must thank the late Richard Rorty for his inspiration, provocation, and commitment to the pragmatist spirit.

Christopher J. Voparil

Source Acknowledgments

The editor and publisher gratefully acknowledge the permission granted to reproduce the copyright material in this book:

CHAPTER 1 INTRODUCTION: METAPHYSICAL DIFFICULTIES OF LINGUISTIC PHILOSOPHY: Richard M. Rorty, "Introduction: Metaphysical Difficulties of Linguistic Philosophy," pp.1–4, 33–9, in Richard M. Rorty (ed.), *The Linguistic Turn: Essays in Philosophical Method,* 2nd edn, © 1967, 1992 by Chicago University Press. Reprinted with permission of Chicago University Press.

CHAPTER 2 DEWEY'S METAPHYSICS: Richard M. Rorty, "Dewey's Metaphysics," pp. 45–74, in Steven M. Cahn (ed.), *New Studies in the Philosophy of John Dewey,* © 1977 by University Press of New England, Lebanon, NH. Reprinted with permission of the publisher.

CHAPTER 3 PHILOSOPHY AND THE MIRROR OF NATURE: "Introduction," and ch.VIII, "Philosophy Without Mirrors" in Richard M. Rorty, *Philosophy and the Mirror of Nature,* © 1979 by Princeton University Press, NJ. Reprinted with permission of Princeton University Press.

CHAPTER 4 PRAGMATISM, RELATIVISM, AND IRRATIONALISM: Richard M. Rorty, "Pragmatism, Relativism and Irrationalism," *Proceedings and Addresses of the American Philosophical Association,* vol. 53 (6), August 1980: 719–38, © 1980 by American Philosophical Association. Reproduced with permission of American Philosophical Association in the format Textbook via Copyright Clearance Center.

CHAPTER 5 NINETEENTH-CENTURY IDEALISM AND TWENTIETH-CENTURY TEXTUALISM: Richard M. Rorty, "Nineteenth-Century Idealism and Twentieth-Century Textualism," *The Monist,* vol. 64 (2), 1981: 155–74, © 1981, *The Monist: An International Quarterly Journal of General Philosophical Inquiry,* Open Court Publishing Company, Chicago, Illinois. Reprinted by permission.

CHAPTER 6 FROM LOGIC TO LANGUAGE TO PLAY: Richard M. Rorty, "From Logic to Language to Play: A Plenary Address to the InterAmerican Congress," *Proceedings and Addresses of the American Philosophical Association* vol. 59 (5), June 1986: 747–53, © 1986 by American Philosophical Association. Reproduced with permission of American Philosophical Association in the format Textbook via Copyright Clearance Center.

Chapter 7 Pragmatism, Davidson, and Truth: Richard M. Rorty, "Pragmatism, Davidson and Truth," pp. 333–55 in Ernest LePore (ed.) *Truth and Interpretation: Perspectives on the Philosophy of Donald Davidson*, © 1986 by Blackwell Publishing Ltd, Oxford. Reproduced with permission of Blackwell Publishing Ltd.

Chapter 8 Twenty-Five Years After: Richard M. Rorty, "Twenty-Five Years After," pp. 371–4 in Richard M. Rorty (ed.), *The Linguistic Turn: Essays in Philosophical Method*, 2nd edn, © 1967, 1992 by Chicago University Press. Reprinted with permission of Chicago University Press.

Chapter 9 Putnam and the Relativist Menace: Richard M. Rorty, "Putnam and the Relativist Menace," *Journal of Philosophy*, vol. 90 (9), September 1993: 443–61, © 1993 The Journal of Philosophy, Inc. Reprinted with permission from the *Journal of Philosophy* and the Estate of Richard Rorty.

Chapter 10 analytic and Conversational Philosophy: Richard M. Rorty, "Analytic and Conversational Philosophy," pp.17–31 from C. G. Prado (ed.), *A House Divided: Comparing Analytic and Continental Philosophy* (Amherst, NY: Humanity Books, 2003), © 2003 by Richard Rorty. Reprinted with permission from the Estate of Richard Rorty.

Chapter 11 Philosophy as Science, as Metaphor, and as Politics: Richard M. Rorty, "Philosophy as Science, as Metaphor, and as Politics," pp.13–33 in Avner Cohen and Marcelo Dascal (eds.), *The Institution of Philosophy: A Discipline in Crisis?* Reprinted with permission of Open Court Publishing Company, a division of Carus Publishing Company, Peru, IL, from *The Institution of Philosophy: A Discipline in Crisis?* by Avner Cohen and Marcelo Dascal (eds.), © 1989 by Open Court Publishing Company.

Chapter 12 Solidarity or Objectivity: Richard M. Rorty, "Solidarity or Objectivity," *Nanzen Review of American Studies*, vol. 6 (1984): 1–19, © 1984 by Nanzen Review of American Studies: A Journal of Center for American Studies, Nanzen University, Nagoya. Reprinted with permission.

Chapter 13 The Priority of Democracy to Philosophy: Richard M. Rorty, "The Priority of Democracy to Philosophy," pp.257–82 in Merrill D. Peterson and Robert C. Vaughn, *The Virginia Statute for Religious Freedom* (Cambridge, 1988), © 1988 by Cambridge University Press. Reprinted with the permission of Cambridge University Press.

Chapter 14 Freud and Moral Reflection: Richard M. Rorty, "Freud and Moral Reflection," pp.1–27 in Joseph H. Smith and William Kerrigan (eds.), *Pragmatism's Freud: The Moral Disposition of Psychoanalysis* (Baltimore: Johns Hopkins University Press, 1986), © 1986 by The Forum on Psychiatry and the Humanities, Washington School of Psychiatry. Reprinted by permission.

Chapter 15 Private Irony and Liberal Hope: chapter 4, pp. 73–95, in Richard M. Rorty, *Contingency, Irony, and Solidarity* (New York, 1989), © 1989 by Cambridge University Press. Reprinted with the permission of Cambridge University Press.

Chapter 16 The Humanistic Intellectual: Eleven Theses: Richard M. Rorty, "The Humanistic Intellectual: Eleven Theses," pp. 9–12 in *ACLS Occasional Papers* no. 10

(November 1989), © 1989 by Richard Rorty. Reprinted with permission from the Estate of Richard Rorty.

CHAPTER 17 HEIDEGGER, KUNDERA, AND DICKENS: Richard M. Rorty, "Philosophers, Novelists, and Intercultural Comparisons: Heidegger, Kundera, and Dickens," pp. 3–20 in Eliot Deutsch (ed.), *Culture and Modernity: East–West Philosophic Perspectives* (Honolulu: University of Hawaii Press, 1991), © 1991 by Eliot Deutsch. Reprinted by kind permission of Eliot Deutsch.

CHAPTER 18 DE MAN AND THE AMERICAN CULTURAL LEFT: pp. 129–39 in Richard M Rorty, *Essays on Heidegger and Others: Philosophical Papers*, vol. 2 (New York, 1991), © 1991 by Cambridge University Press. Reprinted with the permission of Cambridge University Press.

CHAPTER 19 FEMINISM AND PRAGMATISM: Richard M. Rorty, "Feminism and Pragmatism," *Michigan Quarterly Review*, vol. 30 (2), Spring 1991: 231–58. © 1991 by Richard Rorty. Reprinted with permission from the Estate of Richard Rorty.

CHAPTER 20 HUMAN RIGHTS, RATIONALITY, AND SENTIMENTALITY: Richard M. Rorty, "Human Rights, Rationality, and Sentimentality," pp.112–34 in Stephen Shute and Susan Hurley (eds.), *On Human Rights: The Oxford Amnesty Lectures*. © 1993 by Basic Books. Reprinted by permission of Basic Books, a member of Perseus Book Group.

CHAPTER 21 LOOKING BACKWARDS FROM THE YEAR 2096: Richard M. Rorty, "Fraternity Reigns," *The New York Times Magazine,* 28, September 29, 1996: 155–8. © 1996 by Richard Rorty. Reprinted with permission from the Estate of Richard Rorty.

CHAPTER 22 AMERICAN NATIONAL PRIDE: WHITMAN AND DEWEY: reprinted by permission of the publisher from *Achieving Our Country: Leftist Thought in Twentieth-Century America* by Richard Rorty, pp.1–38, Cambridge, MA: Harvard University Press. Copyright © 1998 by the President and Fellows of Harvard College.

CHAPTER 23 REDEMPTION FROM EGOTISM: JAMES AND PROUST AS SPIRITUAL EXERCISES: © Richard Rorty 2001. Reproduced by permission of the Estate of Richard Rorty.

CHAPTER 24 TRUTH WITHOUT CORRESPONDENCE TO REALITY: Richard M. Rorty, "Truth without Correspondence to Reality," excerpts from pp. 23–46 in *Philosophy and Social Hope* (New York: Penguin, 1999), © 1999 by Richard Rorty. Produced by permission of Penguin Books Ltd.

CHAPTER 25 ETHICS WITHOUT PRINCIPLES: Richard M. Rorty, "Ethics without Principles," excerpts from pp. 72–90 in *Philosophy and Social Hope* (New York: Penguin, 1999), © 1999 by Richard Rorty. Reproduced by permission of Penguin Books Ltd.

CHAPTER 26 JUSTICE AS A LARGER LOYALTY: Richard M. Rorty, "Justice as a Larger Loyalty," pp. 9–22 in Ron Bontekoe and Marietta Stpaniants (eds.), *Justice and Democracy: Cross-Cultural Perspectives*, © 1997 by University of Hawaii Press. Reprinted with permission from the University of Hawaii Press.

CHAPTER 27 PRAGMATISM AS ROMANTIC POLYTHEISM: Richard M. Rorty, "Pragmatism as Romantic Polytheism," pp. 21–36 in Morris Dickstein (ed.), *The Revival of Pragmatism:*

New Essays on Social Thought, Law, and Culture, © 1998 by Duke University Press. Reprinted by kind permission of Morris Dickstein.

CHAPTER 28 RELIGION IN THE PUBLIC SQUARE: A RECONSIDERATION: Richard M. Rorty, "Religion in the Public Square: A Reconsideration," *Journal of Religious Ethics*, vol. 31 (1), Spring 2003, © 2003 Journal of Religious Ethics, Inc. Reproduced by permission of Blackwell Publishing Ltd.

CHAPTER 29 IS CULTURAL RECOGNITION A USEFUL CONCEPT FOR LEFTIST POLITICS?: Richard M. Rorty, "Is 'Cultural Recognition' a Useful Concept for Leftist Politics?" *Critical Horizons*, vol. 1 (1), 2000: 7–20, © 2000 by Critical Horizons. Reprinted by permission of Acumen Publishing Ltd.

CHAPTER 30 PHILOSOPHY AS A TRANSITIONAL GENRE: from Benhabib, Seyla, and Nancy Freaser (eds.), *Pragmatism, Critique, Judgment: Essays for Richard J. Bernstein*, pp. 3–28, © 2004 Massachusetts Institute of Technology, by permission of The MIT Press.

CHAPTER 31 FROM PHILOSOPHY TO POST-PHILOSOPHY: "Perspectives on Richard Rorty, I: From Philosophy to Post-Philosophy: An Interview with Richard M. Rorty", conducted by Wayne Hudson and Wim van Reijen, *Radical Philosophy* 32, Autumn 1982: 1–4, © 1982 by Radical Philosophy. Reprinted by permission of the journal, *Radical Philosophy*.

CHAPTER 32 TROTSKY AND THE WILD ORCHIDS: Richard M. Rorty, "Trotsky and the Wild Orchids," *Common Knowledge*, vol. 1 (3), 1992: 140–53, © 1992 by Duke University Press. All rights reserved. Used by permission of the publisher.

CHAPTER 33 BIOGRAPHY AND PHILOSOPHY: "Biography and Philosophy," interview with Richard Rorty by Andrezej Szahaj, pp. 148–60 in Eduardo Mendieta (ed.), *Take Care of Freedom and Truth Will Take Care of Itself* (Stanford: Stanford University Press, 2006), © 2006 by Andrezej Szahaj. Reprinted by kind permission of the author.

CHAPTER 34 THE FIRE OF LIFE: Richard M. Rorty, "The Fire of Life," *Poetry*, November 2007: 129–31, © Richard Rorty. Reprinted with permission from the Estate of Richard Rorty.

Abbreviations

AOC   *Achieving Our Country: Leftist Thought in Twentieth-Century America.* Cambridge, MA: Harvard University Press, 1998.

CIS   *Contingency, Irony, and Solidarity.* New York: Cambridge University Press, 1989.

CP   *Consequences of Pragmatism.* Minneapolis: University of Minneapolis Press, 1982.

EHO   *Essays on Heidegger and Others: Philosophical Papers,* vol. 2. New York: Cambridge University Press, 1991.

FR   *The Future of Religion,* with Gianni Vattimo. New York: Columbia University Press, 2005

LT   *The Linguistic Turn: Essays in Philosophical Method,* 2nd edn, ed. Richard Rorty. Chicago: University of Chicago Press, 1992 [1967].

ORT   *Objectivity, Relativism, and Truth: Philosophical Papers,* vol. 1. New York: Cambridge University Press, 1991.

PCP   *Philosophy as Cultural Politics: Philosophical Papers,* vol. 4. New York: Cambridge University Press, 2007.

PMN   *Philosophy and the Mirror of Nature.* Princeton, NJ: Princeton University Press, 1979.

PSH   *Philosophy and Social Hope.* New York: Penguin Books, 1999.

TCF   *Take Care of Freedom and Truth Will Take Care of Itself: Interviews with Richard Rorty,* ed. Eduardo Mendieta. Stanford, CA: Stanford University Press, 2006.

TP   *Truth and Progress: Philosophical Papers,* vol. 3. New York: Cambridge University Press, 1998.

General Introduction

Christopher J. Voparil

Whether or not one shares Harold Bloom's assessment of Richard Rorty as the most interesting philosopher in the world, that he was for a time "the most-talked about philosopher" is hard to dispute.[1] Catapulted to the intellectual heights by the 1979 publication of his *Philosophy and the Mirror of Nature* – recently called "the most widely discussed philosophy book of the second half of the twentieth century" – Rorty's influence transcends the walls of discipline and culture.[2] Books of his have been translated into over twenty languages and his ideas debated in leading journals in fields as diverse as political theory, sociology, legal studies, international relations, feminist studies, literary theory, business ethics, educational theory, and of course philosophy.[3] His work has spawned a body of secondary literature beyond the limits of a single human being to master and played a pivotal role in the revival of the tradition of American pragmatism.[4] Following his death on June 8, 2007, Rorty was heralded by a chorus of prominent intellectuals as "the most influential philosopher of the last three decades," "the most famous philosopher in the world," and nothing less than "a *great* philosopher, who, daringly swimming against the tide of modern analytic philosophy, single-handedly revived pragmatism, with great impact on a variety of fields."[5]

---

1 Anthony Gottlieb, "The Most-Talked About Philosopher," *New York Times* (June 2, 1991): sec. 7, 30. Harold Bloom's statement appears on the back cover of *Contingency, Irony and Solidarity* (CIS).

2 Richard J. Bernstein, "Rorty's Deep Humanism," *New Literary History* 39 (2008): 17.

3 See Alan Malachowski, *Richard Rorty* (Princeton: Princeton University Press, 2002), pp. 184–6, and *passim*.

4 An annotated bibliography of the secondary literature on Rorty in 2002 lists over 1,200 entries. See Richard Rumana (ed.), *Richard Rorty: An Annotated Bibliography of Secondary Literature* (Amsterdam: Rodopi, 2002). On the pragmatist revival, see Richard J. Bernstein, "The Resurgence of Pragmatism," *Social Research* 59, no. 4 (Winter 1992): 813–40; and Morris Dickstein (ed.), *The Revival of Pragmatism New Essays on Social Thought, Law, and Culture* (Durham: Duke University Press, 1998). Dickstein puts it this way in his introduction, "If pragmatism began with James's strong misreading of Peirce, it came to life again with Rorty's strong misreading of Dewey" (p.11).

5 Danny Postel, "High Flyer: Richard Rorty Obituary," *New Humanist* 122, no. 4 (July/August 2007): 38; Mark Edmundson and Richard Posner, Quoted in Stephen Metcalf, "Richard Rorty: What Made Him a Crucial Philosopher?" *Slate Magazine,* June 18, 2007, http://www.slate.com/

Yet this is of course not the whole story. The publication of *Philosophy and the Mirror of Nature* infuriated then dominant analytic philosophers, who viewed Rorty's tome as a Judas-like betrayal from within.[6] American philosophers were incensed by Rorty's use and abuse of John Dewey and the apparent insouciance with which he embraced or ignored at whim the key ideas and commitments of the pragmatist tradition.[7] As his writings began to engage more explicitly social and political themes in the 1980s, Rorty was vilified from the Right and the Left, as both a dangerous relativist and an apologist for the status quo.[8] Although there were other contributing factors behind his decision to leave Princeton University in 1982 after two decades, he would not hold a post in a philosophy department again for the rest of his life.[9] On the most sympathetic view, as one commentator put it, "Seemingly everyone who is impressed with one facet of Rorty's work harbors severe reservations about another."[10] But even that seems too generous. Of the over 1,200 entries in the annotated bibliography of the secondary literature on Rorty compiled in 2002, only a handful are "friendly to Rorty."[11] Still, whether

---

id/2168488/, accessed May 25, 2009. This piece contains brief eulogies by Jürgen Habermas, Daniel Dennett, Stanley Fish, David Bromwich, Simon Blackburn, Morris Dickstein, and others. See also Habermas, "'And to define America, her athletic democracy'; The Philosophy and the Language Shaper: In Memory of Richard Rorty," *New Literary History* 39, no. 1 (2008): 3–12.

6   Bernstein, "Rorty's Deep Humanism," p. 17.

7   The literature on Rorty's misuse of Dewey was for a time a cottage industry. Noteworthy early forays in this area include, Thomas Alexander, "Richard Rorty and Dewey's Metaphysics of Experience," *Southwest Philosophical Studies* 5 (1980): 24–35; Richard J. Bernstein, "Philosophy in the Conversation of Mankind," *Review of Metaphysics* 33, no. 4 (1980): 745–75; Gary Brodsky, "Rorty's Interpretation of Pragmatism," *Transactions of the Charles S. Peirce Society* 17, no. 4 (1982): 311–38; James Campbell, "Rorty's Use of Dewey," *Southern Journal of Philosophy* 22, no. 2 (1984): 175–87; Abraham Edel, "A Missing Dimension in Rorty's Use of Pragmatism," *Transactions of the Charles S. Peirce Society* 21, no. 1 (1985): 21–38; Konstantin Kolenda, "Rorty's Dewey," *Journal of Value Inquiry* 20 (1986): 84–95; and Ralph Sleeper, "Rorty's Pragmatism: Afloat in Neurath's Boat, But Why Adrift?" *Transactions of the Charles S. Peirce Society* 21, no. 1 (1985): 9–20. For additional references, see Rumana (ed.), *Richard Rorty*. More recent work on the two thinkers has seen the relation more amicably. See for example, Colin Koopman, "Pragmatism as a Philosophy of Hope: Emerson, James, Dewey, Rorty," *Journal of Speculative Philosophy* 20, no. 2 (2006): 106–16; and Ken McClelland, "John Dewey and Richard Rorty: Qualitative Starting Points," *Transactions of the Charles S. Peirce Society* 44, no. 3 (2008): 412–45. For Rorty's extended treatments of Dewey, see esp. Dewey's Metaphysics (chapter 2, this volume); "Dewey Between Hegel and Darwin," in *Truth and Progress* (TP); and "Kant vs. Dewey: The Current Situation of Moral Philosophy," in *Philosophy as Cultural Politics* (PCP).

8   Rorty discusses these reactions in his quasi-autobiographical essay, Trotsky and the Wild Orchids (chapter 30, this volume). Of the many examples of vitriol that could be cited here, one of the most entertaining is John J. Stuhr, "Rorty as Elvis: Dewey's Reconstruction of Metaphysics," in his *Genealogical Pragmatism: Philosophy, Experience, and Community* (Albany, NY: State University of New York Press, 1997), where he writes, "Rorty is the Milli Vanilli of liberalism, merely lip-synching the old Elvis refrain: 'Don't Be Cruel'" (p. 126).

9   For an excellent discussion of this background, see Neil Gross, *Richard Rorty: The Making of an American Philosopher* (Chicago: University of Chicago Press, 2008), pp. 190–233.

10   James Ryerson, "The Quest for Uncertainty: Richard Rorty's Pragmatic Pilgrimage," *Lingua Franca* 10, no. 9 (Dec. 2000/Jan. 2001), p. 42.

11   Rumana, *Richard Rorty*, p. ix. For a more in-depth discussion of the unique nature of the critical reaction to Rorty, see Christopher Voparil, "On the Idea of Philosophy as *Bildungsroman*: Rorty and His Critics," *Contemporary Pragmatism* 2, no.1 (2005): 115–33.

Rorty is a Socratic gadfly – "the bad boy of American philosophy" – stinging the philosophical establishment where it hurts, or a "slipshod iconoclast" who has done more harm than good, there is no getting around the fact that, as Richard Rumana observed, "a lot of people from a wide variety of disciplines and perspectives have something to say about him."[12] Indeed, the massive body of work on Rorty itself has been called "an aid for understanding the philosophical and intellectual issues that have preoccupied thinkers for the past several decades."[13] In the end, though, there remains a suspicion that Rorty's work has been "more influential than understood."[14]

If this is indeed the case, it may be forgivable, given the sheer size of Rorty's oeuvre. Rorty was a prolific writer who in nearly five decades of writing penned three books, two essay collections, four volumes of "philosophical papers," an influential edited volume, and a co-authored book, plus scores of uncollected essays and reviews in academic journals, as well as numerous pieces in newspapers, magazines, and popular publications.[15] Rorty also was a prolific reader, with expansive interests and an uncanny ability to drop names not only from the entire philosophical tradition, but of novelists, poets, literary critics, legal scholars, historians, and political theorists. A mainstay in contemporary intellectual debates for several decades, he traveled to all corners of the globe and engaged with the leading thinkers of the day across many fields. Widely recognized for his collegiality, Rorty himself was a consummate collaborator, enthusiastically promoting the work of others and always willing to engage even his harshest critics in the hope of furthering ongoing debates.[16] One historian called Rorty

> the embodiment of the contemporary, a barometer, perhaps, of intellectual pressures across so many discourses […] Rorty – moving as he does with such ease across the entire intellectual terrain – expresses some of the arguably most vibrant areas of contemporary intellectual life.[17]

This collection of Rorty's writings was assembled to assist those who seek a deeper understanding of Rorty and his philosophical and political projects. His vast oeuvre spans multiple traditions and disciplines; without a roadmap of sorts, it can be daunting. The

---

12   Jonathan Rée, "Strenuous Unbelief," *London Review of Books* 20, October 15, 1998; Malachowski, *Richard Rorty*, p. 1; Rumana, *Richard Rorty*, p. ix.

13   Richard J. Bernstein, "Foreword," in Rumana (ed.), *Richard Rorty*, p. vii.

14   Malachowski, *Richard Rorty*, p. 2. Malachowski later adds this wrinkle: "Rorty's sternest philosophical critics deny his main claims. They think he is wrong on just about every front. But they seem unable to state their denial in terms that do not beg the question or tacitly assume what Rorty himself denies" (p. 168).

15   The best bibliography to date of Rorty's works can be found in *Take Care of Freedom and Truth Will Take Care of Itself* (TCF), pp. 161–205.

16   For examples of Rorty dutifully responding to his critics, see Herman J. Saatkamp, Jr. (ed.), *Rorty and Pragmatism: The Philosopher Responds to his Critics* (Nashville: Vanderbilt University Press, 1995); Robert Brandom (ed.), *Rorty and His Critics* (Oxford: Blackwell, 2000); and Matthew Festenstein and Simon Thompson (eds.), *Richard Rorty: Critical Dialogues* (Cambridge: Polity Press, 2002). Amazingly, in all of these collections, Rorty wrote an individual response to each and every contributor's essay.

17   Keith Jenkins, *On 'What is History?': From Carr and Elton to Rorty and White* (New York: Routledge, 1995), p. 4.

essays that follow were chosen with an eye to illuminating Rorty's own positions and commitments, particularly with regard to the more explicitly political concerns that emerge after *Philosophy and the Mirror of Nature,* while painting as full a picture as possible of the overall development of his thought. Like all such collections, many tough choices were involved. A virtuoso of the essay form, Rorty's many treatments of various prominent intellectuals, though insightful and of interest, could fill an entire volume themselves; most could not be included. The full scope and depth of Rorty's analytic philosophy is not represented, in part because this more specialized work falls outside his broader influence. But also because, while of interest to some, not all of this previous work is essential to grasp his larger project, though, as we shall see, he did occasionally lean on particular figures and ideas from the analytic tradition in articulating his later stances.

With the exception of the first two essays, *The Rorty Reader* covers his work from *Philosophy and the Mirror of Nature* until his death in 2007; the facets of his pre-*Mirror* work that bear on his later stances are discussed in the introduction below, following a brief biographical sketch. The introduction traces the development of his thinking from his influential edited volume, *The Linguistic Turn* (1967), to *Philosophy and the Mirror of Nature* (1979) and the somewhat unexpected defense of political liberalism that follows in its wake. The striking continuities in Rorty's interests and overall orientation are highlighted, while charting the changes in his relation to the pragmatist tradition and to analytic philosophy. Roughly the latter half of the introduction is devoted to exposition and framing of his broader philosophical and political projects, including both their challenges and promise, in the hope of laying the groundwork for subsequent inquiry and engagement.

I. Rorty's Life

Born on October 4, 1931 to James Rorty and Winifred Raushenbush, Richard McKay Rorty was an only child. "Bucko," as his parents affectionately called him, was intellectually precocious from the start, with a clear gift for the written word.[18] He wrote a play about the coronation of Edward, Prince of Wales, at age 6. At 7 he composed a letter to the Harvard College Observatory inquiring about the possibility of his becoming an astronomer, and at 8 penned a note of congratulations to the new Dalai Lama, accompanied by a present, for "a fellow eight-year old who had made good" (p. 502, this volume).[19] Although briefly educated in a private school in Brooklyn, the young Rorty was fonder of the Walpack Township School in rural Flatbrookville, New Jersey, the location of a summer property that his family inhabited full-time in the late 1930s, where he delivered a commencement speech at age 12 and began editing the school's newspaper at 13. Still, he found school life less than challenging. With insightful input from their son, in 1946 his parents made the decision that he would attend the innovative program designed by Robert Hutchins at the University of Chicago, just shy of his 15th birthday.[20]

---

18 Gross, *Richard Rorty*, p. 47. For the details of the biographical sketch that follow I rely heavily on Gross's insightful and exhaustive account, which covers Rorty's life and work up to 1982.
19 Ibid., p. 88.
20 Ibid., pp. 88–90 and chapter 3, *passim.*

A household and upbringing more conducive to the development of a politically engaged intellectual is hard to imagine. Both Rorty's parents were not only fixtures in the New York intellectual scene for several decades, but committed leftist activists. In Rorty's words, they "more or less accepted" the description 'Trotskyites' after breaking with the American Communist Party in 1932 (p. 502, this volume). James Rorty was an accomplished author, poet, and muckraking journalist. Son of an Irish immigrant and a New York schoolteacher, he served as an unarmed stretcher-bearer and ambulance driver in World War I, for which he was awarded a Distinguished Service Cross. After the war, he worked for a period as an advertising copywriter in New York, his work appearing frequently in publications like *The Nation*, with dispatches on his war experiences. He authored several collections of poetry and later wrote an attack on the advertising business, *Our Master's Voice,* which bore the influence of his friend, Thorsten Veblen.[21] Winifred Raushenbush was a graduate of Oberlin College who studied sociology at the University of Chicago, where she worked as a research assistant to Robert Park and took classes with George Herbert Mead. Her father was Walter Rauschenbusch, the theologian and seminal figure in the social gospel movement, from whom she inherited a social and political consciousness that informed, among other things, her notable research on race riots. She also wrote actively, publishing a biography of Park, a book on women's fashion, numerous pieces of social and political criticism in outlets like *Commentary,* and a review of Jane Addams's *The Second Twenty Years at Hull House.* The novel she worked at diligently during the 1950s and 1960s, a political tale situated in the Cold War, never made it to publication.[22]

Taken as a whole, the combination of his parents' intellectualism, the circles in which they moved, and the overall milieu of his upbringing, had an extraordinary effect. As biographer Neil Gross characterizes it, Rorty's childhood "involved constant exposure to settings in which propriety demanded and social approval rested in part on how well one could argue and turn a phrase."[23] As a child, Rorty served sandwiches at a party where John Dewey was present, was bounced on the knee of Sidney Hook, and not infrequently encountered a Robert Penn Warren or Allen Tate or A. Phillip Randolph at the dinner table. When for a few months in 1940 his parents harbored John Frank, a secretary of Trotsky's in flight from Stalin's assassins, Rorty was asked to keep their guest's identity a secret, though he later noted that his schoolmates at Walpack Elementary were unlikely to have cared (p. 502, this volume). Later in life his parents' wide network would afford him the ability to write Daniel Bell with questions about the University of Chicago or turn to Hook for advice on graduate programs in philosophy.[24]

In addition to the cultivation of his intellectual and writing abilities, what Rorty also took from this milieu are his parents' political commitments and deep sense of injustice. In an interview Rorty explains, "I was just brought up a Trotskyite, the way people are brought up Methodists or Jews or something like that. It was just the faith of the household."[25] If he had not already absorbed it from the atmosphere, he knew from the

---

21 Ibid., pp. 33–40. Gross devotes a chapter each to exhaustive accounts of the lives and work of Rorty's parents.

22 Ibid., pp. 16, 64, 75, 81, and chapter 2, *passim.*

23 Ibid., p. 92.

24 Ibid., pp. 91, 93.

25 Quoted in Gross, *Richard Rorty,* p. 93.

Workers' Defense League documents he messengered around Manhattan to places like the Brotherhood of Pullman Car Porters office in the early 1940s for his parents, who themselves would later become champions of civil rights, that "the poor would always be oppressed until capitalism was overcome." A self-described "red-diaper anti-communist baby" and "teenage Cold War liberal" (AOC, p. 58), Rorty flatly stated that "at 12, I knew that the point of being human was to spend one's life fighting social injustice" (p. 502, this volume). However, as he recounts in his quasi-autobiographical essay, "Trotsky and the Wild Orchids," what the young Rorty did more than anything with "the vast amount of spare time given to a clever, snotty, nerdy only child" was to read. Solitude also afforded opportunities to spend time in the mountains around his New Jersey home, where he pursued the elusive wild orchid, a subject on which the young botanist made himself expert, as well as escaped the bullies who he said "regularly beat me up on the playground of my high school" (p. 503, this volume).[26]

Upon arriving at the so-called Hutchins College in 1946, to the extent that the young Rorty had a project in mind, by his own lights it was "to reconcile Trotsky and the orchids." Having fully internalized the political and intellectual identity of his parents, what he sought in his challenging new academic environment was an overall intellectual or aesthetic framework that would in his words, "let me – in a thrilling phrase which I came across in Yeats – 'hold reality and justice in a single vision.'" That is, what he hoped to find was both a philosophical or moral justification for his idiosyncratic pursuit of wild orchids, given the apparent uselessness of this endeavor for the quest for social justice, and a moral identity that would allow him to be both "an intellectual and spiritual snob and a friend of humanity – a nerdy recluse and a fighter for justice" (p. 503, this volume).[27]

The commitment to philosophical absolutes that Mortimer Adler had provided to Hutchins' "Great Snippets" curriculum offered precisely such a framework. Actually, it offered two: religion and absolutist philosophy.[28] As a result of what he called his "prideful inability to believe what I was saying when I recited the General Confession," Rorty gradually gave up his "awkward attempts to get religion." That left the philosophical route – specifically, Plato – whom Rorty read intensively during the summer after his first year. While Rorty said he did convince himself that "Socrates was right – virtue *was* knowledge" and for a time espoused the view that there were indeed timeless truths about human existence that it fell to philosophers to uncover, his attempt, roughly from the time he was 15 until he turned 20, to become a Platonist "didn't pan out" (p. 504, this volume). Nevertheless, despite earning two Cs in philosophy, which were apparently the result of a bout of the depression he shared with his father, the lack of viable options for

---

26   Rorty was an avid bird-watcher as well (TCF, p. 1).

27   Rorty discusses his parents' politics and their view of justice in greater depth in "The Eclipse of the Reformist Left," in *Achieving Our Country* (AOC), pp. 41–71.

28   Rorty believed that it was only for "those lucky Christians for whom the love of God and of other human beings are inseparable, or revolutionaries who are moved by nothing save the thought of social justice" that "whatever idiosyncratic things or persons one loves with all one's heart and soul and mind" (his wild orchids) are united with "one's moral responsibilities to other people" (his Trotsky) (p. 506, this volume).

graduate study that existed in 1949 for this "very serious, shy, sensitive boy"[29] who held a BA at age 18 after only three years of coursework led the young Rorty to decide to remain at the University of Chicago to pursue graduate work in the philosophy department.

The reasons behind the failure of Platonism to take hold as a viable intellectual stance are significant. While the quest for stable absolutes was certainly not derailed by the courses he took, along with classmate Allan Bloom, with Leo Strauss, who had joined the University of Chicago in 1949, Rorty did acquire an interest in social and political philosophy that would continue throughout his life and later emerge more prominently in his own thought.[30] Significantly, he also started to question "how one could get a noncircular justification of any debatable stand on any important issue." As he explains in retrospect,

> The more philosophers I read, the clearer it seemed that each of them could carry their views back to first principles which were incompatible with the first principles of their opponents, and that none of them ever got to that fabled place 'beyond hypotheses.' There seemed to be nothing like a neutral standpoint from which these alternative first principles could be evaluated. But if there were no such standpoint, then the whole idea of 'rational certainty', and the whole Socratic-Platonic idea of replacing passion by reason, seemed not to make much sense. (p. 504, this volume)

As he began his graduate study of philosophy, his inability to take a de-historicized view of philosophy came to the forefront. Drawn to metaphysician Charles Hartshorne, under whom Rorty wrote his masters thesis on the role of potentiality in Alfred North Whitehead's metaphysical thought, he sought out books like Hegel's *Phenomenology of Spirit,* Whitehead's *Adventures of Ideas,* and Arthur Lovejoy's *Great Chain of Being,* that nourished his interest in the history of philosophical ideas. He soon came to the realization, as Gross puts it, that "his *métier* was historically oriented philosophizing."[31]

Despite the overt hostility at Hutchins toward pragmatism, especially toward Dewey, pragmatist ideas and influences had a significant place within Rorty's orbit at this early stage. While Rorty's masters thesis remained in the mold of the metaphysics of Whitehead and Hartshorne, and he himself did not identify with pragmatism explicitly

---

29   This description was offered by the writer James Farrell, a friend of Rorty's father who had attended the University of Chicago as well, and who wrote a letter on the young Rorty's behalf. Gross, *Richard Rorty,* p. 103. On Rorty's depression, see Gross, pp. 98–105.

30   Rorty not only tended to socialize more with the students in the Committee on Social Thought than with fellow philosophy students, on the completion of his MA he seriously considered taking his doctoral degree from the Committee. His having already been at Chicago for some time, combined with doubts about the ability of this new interdisciplinary doctoral program to place its graduates in academic positions, apparently led him to rule out this option. See Gross, *Richard Rorty,* pp. 115, 126–7.

31   Gross, *Richard Rorty,* pp. 112–13. Rorty himself came to appropriate a particular narrative of the history of philosophy himself. On this issue, see Richard J. Bernstein, "One Step Forward, Two Steps Backward: Rorty on Liberal Democracy and Philosophy," in *The New Constellation: The Ethical-Political Horizons of Modernity/Postmodernity* (Cambridge, MA: MIT Press, 1992), esp. pp. 249–53. On Rorty's "grand narrative," see also David L. Hall, *Richard Rorty: Prophet and Poet of the New Pragmatism* (Albany, NY: SUNY Press, 1994), chapter 1.

for some time, in his earliest published essays these pragmatist influences are quite visible.[32] From Richard McKeon, Rorty received a strong grounding in the history of philosophy. Though critical of Dewey, McKeon, who along with Adler was influential in shaping parts of Hutchins' curriculum – as it happens, McKeon was also, as Rorty put it, "the villain of [Robert] Pirsig's *Zen and the Art of Motorcycle Maintenance*" (p. 503, this volume) – was a graduate student at Columbia under Dewey and influenced by the debates between realism and pragmatism going on there in the mid-1920s. In addition to Whitehead, at Harvard Hartshorne had studied with Ralph Barton Perry, a student and scholar of William James, and C. I. Lewis, a student of Josiah Royce. Hartshorne also had worked, along with Paul Weiss, on preparing the papers of Charles Sanders Peirce for publication.[33]

Like the philosophy department at Chicago, at Yale the technicism associated with the prevailing analytic tradition of philosophy was less dominant. When Rorty arrived in 1952 to continue his studies toward a doctorate, it was still possible to adopt the kind of approach characteristic of the broad, speculative metaphysics of Whitehead and Hartshorne. This was much less true at Harvard, which also had granted Rorty admission, where the reliance on symbolic logic characteristic of Lewis and Willard Van Orman Quine was seen as indispensable for philosophical reasoning. The pluralism of Yale's department suited Rorty well. With his interest in the history of philosophy and classical training in the humanities, Rorty exemplified the profile of the broadly educated student of philosophy Yale valued. While he would end up writing his dissertation on the concept of potentiality in Aristotle, the seventeenth-century rationalists, and the logical empiricists, his exposure to pragmatist influences continued at Yale. His dissertation was directed by Paul Weiss, a student of Morris Cohen, who was the mentor of Sidney Hook. Rorty studied Peirce with Rulon Wells and was a teaching assistant for a course on pragmatism taught by John E. Smith.[34]

Rorty defended his 600-page dissertation, "The Concept of Potentiality," in 1956. Now familiar characteristics of Rorty's approach were already apparent: the construction of a sweeping historical narrative, the emphasis on language, the contextualization of philosophical problems, and the appeal to greater dialogue between traditions. Adopting the

32   Rorty's first published essay begins with the line, "Pragmatism is getting respectable again," and posits similarities between Peirce and Wittgenstein. See Rorty, "Pragmatism, Categories, and Language," *Philosophical Review* 70, no. 2 (1961): 197–223. Both Dewey and James are briefly discussed in his "Recent Metaphilosophy," *Review of Metaphysics* 15, no. 2 (1961): 299–318. For a (quite critical) essay by Hartshorne on Rorty, written in 1984, as well as Rorty's response to his former teacher, see Saatkamp (ed.), *Rorty and Pragmatism*, pp. 16–36.

33   Gross, *Richard Rorty*, pp. 107, 119–20.

34   Ibid., pp. 127–9, 132, 137. Rorty himself thought he learned less philosophy at Yale than at Chicago, on account of spending less time at Yale, having less outstanding teachers, and losing himself in his dissertation writing. However, his correspondence at the time suggests he was much happier at Yale. Gross attributes this at least in part to the sense of historic mission alive in the philosophy department, which was united by a commitment to pluralism and aspired to recovering philosophy's broader purposes from the narrowness of the dominant analytic tradition by drawing widely from ancient philosophy, contemporary metaphysics, and recent developments in Continental thought – all of which would be characteristic of Rorty's later oeuvre. His relationship with and marriage in 1954 to Amélie Oksenberg, a philosophy student he had met at Chicago who had been admitted to the program at Yale as well, may also have contributed to his greater happiness.

broad historical perspective to which he was given, the work drew distinctions between philosophical schools, noting the lineage of the ancient Greeks' concern with things, the rationalists' interest in ideas and judgments, and the logical empiricists' preoccupation with words. Though not unsympathetic toward the logical empiricists, he critiqued the narrowness of their understanding of potentiality, as well as the then reigning view that they could solve the problems of philosophy on their own. Instead, he argued that the concept of potentiality demanded a broader approach, informed by the perspectives of other schools. He explained his focus on potentiality as the topic where "the relation between the problems of logical empiricism and the problems of traditional metaphysics and epistemology may be most easily perceived."[35]

Upon completion of his doctorate, Rorty was drafted into the army, arriving at Fort Dix, New Jersey, in early 1957. As he explained in an interview, "I was drafted into the army because I stupidly didn't delay my dissertation until past my twenty-sixth birthday. I have no idea why I was that dumb" (TCF, p. 5). After basic training, Rorty landed a post in the army signal corps, where he worked in computer development, ultimately earning a programming medal for persuading his superiors to adopt the more efficient Polish system of logical notation.[36] Upon his discharge in 1958, with the help of Weiss's connections he secured an instructor position at Wellesley College in 1960 that became an assistant professorship. Before long it became clear that the "conceited and aggressively ambitious twenty-seven-year-old," as Rorty described himself in retrospect, hired by Wellesley would have other options.

In the fall of 1961 he accepted a one-year visiting position at Princeton University.[37] Despite the failure of the initial designs of department chair Gregory Vlastos to hire him to teach Greek philosophy, Rorty nonetheless received a three-year tenure-track appointment the following year. In 1965 he was promoted to associate professor and in 1970 to full professor. His time at Princeton, which extended until his move to the University of Virginia in 1982, had an important impact on Rorty's relation to the analytic tradition. Because it was much more analytical than Chicago or Yale, Rorty initially felt out of place in the Princeton philosophy department. "My first years at Princeton," he recalled, "I was desperately trying to learn what was going on in analytic philosophy. Most of my colleagues had been at Harvard, and you had to know what they were talking about at Harvard in order to be with it." Despite these efforts, before long Rorty's wider interests and training proved an ill fit for the department and his colleagues. As he later described it, "My recollection is that for the first ten years at Princeton, I was one of the boys. But

35 Rorty, "The Concept of Potentiality," quoted in Gross, *Richard Rorty,* pp. 142–3.

36 Gross notes that despite doing relatively interesting work during his nearly two-year peacetime deployment, as "a left-wing anti-Communist and intellectual with refined cultural tastes," Rorty found the experience emotionally trying and generally dehumanizing (*Richard Rorty,* p. 146). Former colleague Mark Edmundson reflected that Rorty's time in the army may have had a bigger impact on him than his time at elite institutions like Princeton and Yale, noting that it was "where he learned to be one guy among a bunch, to look at life from down below, and to distrust posturing in all its forms. That Army hitch no doubt helped Dick to make one of his most important contributions: bringing American intellectual life closer to earth. Socrates, himself an accomplished ironist who did some time as a soldier, would have approved" (quoted in Metcalf, "Richard Rorty").

37 Quoted in Gross, *Richard Rorty,* p. 148. Within a year of accepting the position at Princeton, Rorty would receive offers from Texas, Harvard, Johns Hopkins, Connecticut, and an offer from John Smith, who sought to attract him back to Yale (Gross, pp. 166–9).

for the second ten years, I was seen as increasingly contrarian or difficult" (TCF 6, 8).[38] He put the issue rather more specifically in a letter to Princeton president William Bowen:"Roughly speaking, I tell historical stories and everybody else in the department analyzes arguments."[39]

The almost immediate popularity of *Philosophy and the Mirror of Nature* across the humanities quickly led to multiple job offers not long after its publication in 1979. The combination of his unhappiness at Princeton, his tenuous relationship to mainstream philosophy, the receipt of a MacArthur Prize, and the lure of an interdisciplinary, university professorship with no departmental duties, led Rorty to move to the University of Virginia in 1983, a year after the publication of his essays from the 1970s under the title, *Consequences of Pragmatism*.[40] For the most part, in his new post Rorty taught Continental philosophy to literature students. Although he missed Princeton's top philosophy students and "had to teach in a way that didn't allude to Quine's criticism of the analytic–synthetic distinction," he was generally content. Over time, though, he began to have reservations about the uses to which he observed Derrida and Foucault being put in literature departments (TCF, p. 10).[41]

Rorty's 15 years at Virginia were among his most productive. Confessing in a letter to finding the new vistas opened by his move out of the "disciplinary matrix" of philosophy and transition from a Professor of Philosophy to a Professor of Humanities "both exhilarating and vaguely frightening," he soon published his most ambitious and wide-ranging work, *Contingency, Irony, and Solidarity* (1989).[42] During the same period he wrote enough essays to fill the first two volumes of his philosophical papers, *Objectivity, Relativism, and Truth* and *Essays on Heidegger and Others,* which both appeared in 1991. Before leaving Virginia, he produced material for the third volume, *Truth and Power* (1993), as well as his most accessible collection, *Philosophy and Social Hope* (1999). Following the appearance of the somewhat unexpected *Achieving Our Country,* in 1998 he accepted a position at Stanford University, this time in the department of comparative literature. That he would not be in a philosophy department was to Rorty's mind "of no particular significance," since "nonanalytic philosophy is, in America, more frequently taught outside of philosophy departments than within them." During the last two decades of his career he was largely able to teach what he wanted. For instance, during his first year at Stanford he taught "a course about Nietzsche and William James, one

38   Rorty also noted other complications: "I got divorced and remarried, and because my first wife (Amélie Oksenberg) was a philosopher and a friend of my colleagues, there were problems. It was not a friendly divorce, and I didn't handle it very well." He married Mary Varney, a philosopher with a PhD from Johns Hopkins, in 1970 (Gross, *Richard Rorty,* p. 17).
39   Quoted in ibid., p. 231.
40   Virginia was kind enough to grant Rorty a leave for the 1982/3 academic year so he could complete an already arranged stay at the Center for Advanced Study in the Behavioral Sciences in Palo Alto. The MacArthur grant helped him secure a reduced teaching load. See Gross, *Richard Rorty,* pp. 232–3.
41   In retrospect, Rorty noted that he "did not foresee what has actually happened: that the popularity of philosophy (under the sobriquet 'theory') in our literature departments was merely a transitional stage on the way to the development of what we in America are coming to call the Academic Left," TCF, p. 12. See also, DE MAN AND THE AMERICAN CULTURAL LEFT (chapter 18, this volume).
42   Quoted in Gross, *Richard Rorty,* p. 233.

about Heidegger and Derrida, and another about Foucault and Habermas" (TCF 66). He remained at Stanford until retiring from teaching in 2005. Rorty passed away on June 8, 2007 from complications of pancreatic cancer, just three months after the publication of his fourth volume of philosophical papers, *Philosophy as Cultural Politics*.

II. Early Work: Pragmatism, Technicism, and Fruitful Conversation

What stands out in Rorty's dissertation and early orientation is his proclivity to take the broad view, to work in and amongst different schools of thought, rather than to stay within a particular tradition. His gift was for putting competing perspectives into dialogue, seeing connections, elucidating continuities – that is, doing "very McKeonite, comparative" work, as he termed it, informed by an acute historical consciousness. As he put it an interview conducted a few years after the publication of *Philosophy and the Mirror of Nature*, "My interests until 1960 were historical and metaphysical." While at Wellesley, however, he learned from his colleagues, including his department chair, Virginia Onderdonk, who had a degree from Chicago but had been a student of the later Wittgenstein at Cambridge, that he was "behind the times." So he started reading Wittgenstein, along with "the then fashionable Oxford philosophers (Austin, Ryle, Strawson)." In Rorty's own words, he "changed from being an old-fashioned philosopher to being an up-to-date analytic philosopher partly as a result of pressure from my peers" (pp. 493–4, this volume). When he arrived at Princeton in 1961, this pressure only increased.[43]

Taking for granted the importance of the analytic project, Rorty's earliest published essays involve efforts to put the analytic tradition into dialogue with other modes of philosophical reflection. He did this by highlighting unrecognized shared resonances and suggesting ways the tradition would benefit from the resources of nonanalytic schools.[44] This search for avenues of "fruitful conversation," as he called it, yielded a keen awareness of how rare indeed this commodity was in the history of philosophy.[45] More often than not, incommensurability and stalled impasses seemed to prevail. To describe the work of sorting through these difficulties Rorty adopted the sobriquet 'metaphilosophy,' which in one of his earliest essays he defined as the attempt to address the following "inconsistent triad" of beliefs:

1. A game in which each player is at liberty to change the rules whenever he wishes can neither be won nor lost.
2. In philosophical controversy, the terms used to state criteria for the resolution of arguments mean different things to different philosophers; thus each side can take the rules of the game of controversy in a sense which will guarantee its own success (thus in effect, changing the rules).

43 Gross, *Richard Rorty*, p. 147.
44 See Rorty, "Recent Metaphilosophy"; "The Limits of Reductionism," in I. C. Lieb (ed.), *Experience, Existence, and the Good* (Carbondale: Southern Illinois University Press, 1961), pp. 100–16; and "Realism, Categories, and the 'Linguistic Turn,'" *International Philosophical Quarterly* 2, no. 2 (1962): 307–22.
45 Rorty, "Realism, Categories, and the 'Linguistic Turn,'" p. 309.

3. Philosophical arguments are, in fact, won and lost, for some philosophical positions do, in fact, prove weaker than others.[46]

The central metaphilosophical argument, as Rorty saw it, emanates from the fact that "traditional methods of posing and resolving philosophical questions inevitably lead to dialectic impasses between competing schools."[47] While metaphilosophy "aims at neutrality among philosophical systems," the inconsistencies inherent in the above triad lead to a paradox in that "each system can and does create its own private metaphilosophical criteria, designed to authenticate itself and disallow its competitors." As a result, the existence of this paradox undermines the traditional philosophical assumptions of "absolute neutrality" and "a categorical imperative that would bind all philosophers equally."[48]

Rorty's primary interest was in possible responses to these difficulties. The most promising approach seemed to be linguistic analysis. At the time, he seemed pretty convinced both that "philosophy in the old style – philosophy as 'metaphysics, epistemology, and axiology' – needs to be replaced by metaphilosophy," and that "only by taking the linguistic turn can we escape from such impasses" as metaphilosophy entailed.[49] Using the terminology he employed in his dissertation, he rejects outright what he regarded as retrograde claims that "linguistic philosophy" should be abandoned so that philosophers could "get back to asking questions about things rather than about words," as some critics of the linguistic turn argued.[50] Yet Rorty never fully converts to linguistic philosophy. Despite his belief in the importance of the linguistic turn, he is not blind to its shortcomings; in his view linguistic analysis is vulnerable to the pitfalls of both realism and reductionism. Generally speaking, Rorty praises "the analytic philosophical movement" for "making us self-conscious about metaphilosophical issues." But in his judgment they have too often been "reductionist" metaphilosophers, in that "they have used metaphilosophical analyses to reduce their opponents to absurdity, but they have lacked the courage to apply these analyses to themselves."[51] Rorty offers an original argument about how even ordinary-language theory, which also had taken the linguistic turn, "leads to the adoption of a realistic epistemology" virtually "indistinguishable from Aristotelianism."[52]

Then there was the pragmatist response. What seems most congenial to Rorty when it comes to responding to the impasses identified by metaphilosophy is what he calls in one essay "the 'ideal-language' theory, or, indifferently, the 'pragmatist' theory," and in another, "metaphilosophical *pragmatism*."[53] In the first instance he cites Peirce as the "best example," and praises the "distinctly non-realistic set of categories" and the "ethically-centered epistemology" toward which his work points; in the second he notes that what

46 Rorty, "Recent Metaphilosophy," p. 299.
47 Rorty, "Realism, Categories, and the 'Linguistic Turn,'" p. 322.
48 Rorty, "The Limits of Reductionism," p. 110.
49 Rorty, "Recent Metaphilosophy," p. 301; "Realism, Categories, and the 'Linguistic Turn,'" p. 322.
50 Rorty, "Realism, Categories, and the 'Linguistic Turn,'" p. 308.
51 Rorty, "Recent Metaphilosophy," p. 317.
52 Rorty, "Realism, Categories, and the 'Linguistic Turn,'" pp. 319, 309. Rorty cites Gilbert Ryle, Peter Strawson, and Kurt Baier as representatives of "so-called 'ordinary-language' analysts."
53 Rorty, "Realism, Categories, and the 'Linguistic Turn,'" pp. 309–10; "Recent Metaphilosophy," p. 302. (emphasis in original).

he dubs metaphilosophical pragmatism is "fairly close to the attitude which Dewey adopted toward the history of philosophy."[54] Dewey, and those like him, are dubbed "metaphilosopher's metaphilosophers" for the way they respond to metaphilosophical thesis (1) above. What Rorty finds most attractive about these responses is that rather than despairing of the philosopher's ability to change the rules, they take the stance that "philosophy is the greatest game of all precisely because it is the game of 'changing the rules.'" Alluding to a notion that would emerge in his own thought almost three decades later as "redescription," he explains the inference drawn by these metaphilosophers like this: "since any metaphysical, epistemological, or axiological arguments can be defeated by redefinition, nothing remains but to make a virtue of necessity and to study this process of redefinition itself."[55]

What is striking about Rorty's orientation to these issues is his disinclination to regard philosophy's failure to offer lasting solutions to traditional problems as a cause for lament. This fundamental stance is what makes pragmatism so appealing. The upshot of the pragmatist responses is that they displace the function of philosophy from the pursuit of truth or certainty to simply "making communication possible."[56] The reason for this relates back to the central paradox of metaphilosophy noted above. The insight perceived by this young philosopher, only a few years beyond his dissertation defense and just shy of his 30th birthday, is that what distinguishes the pragmatist response and keeps it from falling prey to reductionism is the way it frames the problem of philosophers always being able to change the rules as "a progress rather than a regress." In other words, pragmatists understood that "to keep communication going is to win the game."[57] All they can offer is "advice about what has to be done in order to stay in the dialogue."[58]

Although it was not central to his purposes at the time, Rorty also perceives the important moral dimension of the pragmatists' stance. On the one hand, he recognizes that an appeal to pragmatic justification always threatens to end the dialogue by demonstrating success at "getting a job done, and refus[ing] to discuss the relation of this job to other jobs" – that is, it entails "a request for the appreciation of new values" that "calls in question the value of remaining within the dialogue which we call 'philosophy'." Yet he also sees that the "appeal to practice transfers the question of the acceptability of a philosophical program out of metaphilosophy and into the realm of moral choice." He called this "the dependence of criteriology on ethical norms."[59] For instance, Peirce, on

---

54 Rorty, "Realism, Categories, and the 'Linguistic Turn,'" pp. 311, 317; "Recent Metaphilosophy," p. 302. Though unsurprising, given Rorty's contact with Peirce scholars like Hartshorne, Weiss, and Rulon Wells, the centrality of Peirce to Rorty's earliest writings, especially "Pragmatism, Categories, and Language," has not received as much attention as one would expect. As Gross noted, when Rorty turned away from Peirce later in his career, "it was not a turn born of ignorance," *Richard Rorty*, p. 142.

55 Rorty, "Recent Metaphilosophy," p. 301.

56 Ibid.

57 Ibid., p. 302. He continues, "the plausibility of [metaphilosophical thesis] (1) is due only to a narrow, and ethically objectionable, interpretation of 'game,' and 'losing'."

58 Rorty, "The Limits of Reductionism," p. 111.

59 Ibid., pp. 111; 116n11. Rorty explains that this "transference" to the ethical realm can be seen in the critiques of "objectivity" as the goal of philosophizing by Dewey and Kierkegaard, who both learned of this "dependence of criteriology upon ethical norms" from Hegel.

Rorty's view, responds by appealing to "self-control" – "a moral virtue rather than a theoretical insight" – as the only thing that "can save inquiry from anarchy."[60] Likewise, the metaphilosophical pragmatism Rorty associates with Dewey suggests that "it becomes a moral duty to keep the series [the "infinite series" of philosophers changing the rules] going, lest communication cease."[61] When nearly twenty years later Rorty insists in the closing sentence of *Philosophy and the Mirror of Nature* that "philosophers' moral concern should be with continuing the conversation of the West, rather than with insisting upon a place for the traditional problems of modern philosophy," he appeals to this same capacity for moral choice (p. 110, this volume). He knew even in this early period that "every philosophy will contrive to present a self-justificatory account of the criteria for choice between philosophies."[62]

Rorty's earliest essays, then, demonstrate the extent to which pragmatist issues and perspectives are present in his work from the outset.[63] While brief moments of discussion of James and Dewey are common, not unsurprisingly, given his teachers at Chicago and Yale, by a large margin it is Peirce who receives the most sustained engagement in his early work. While Rorty finds aspects of Peirce's stances attractive in themselves, for instance what he called Peirce's "anti-realistic approach to knowledge," for the most part his interest in Peirce, as the classical pragmatist with the most in common with the analytic tradition, seems driven primarily by the potential for Peirce to be a bridge – a basis for fruitful conversation – to other schools, most prominently by relating Peirce to Wittgenstein.[64] Following this line of thought emphasizing Peirce's relevance to analytic philosophy, Rorty starts building a case for the relevance of pragmatism. However, the thinkers to which he turns to advance this argument at this point are Quine, Morton White, Wilfrid Sellars, Rudolph Carnap, Nelson Goodman, and others, rather than James and Dewey.

Understanding the motives behind the technicism that characterizes Rorty's engagement with analytic and linguistic philosophy during the 1960s enables us to see the pragmatist bent driving even this dimension of his work. Without this technical side of philosophy, philosophical dialogue would be "simply an exchange of claims and counterclaims," with no genuine dialogue capable of moving us beyond impasses. Beginning with essays that appeared in print in 1963, discussion of metaphilosophy and pragmatism, grounded in a wide historical perspective, is displaced by highly technical analyses of topics like "the subject-property categoreal frame," "mind-body identity theory," and

---

60   Rorty, "Realism, Categories, and the 'Linguistic Turn,'" p. 317.

61   Rorty, "Recent Metaphilosophy," p. 302.

62   Rorty, "The Limits of Reductionism," p. 111. Rorty also sees that "it is nevertheless by and through such contrivance that philosophical controversy is made possible, and the dialogue permitted to continue." If nothing else, his own contrivances over the years have succeeded in prompting a continuation of the dialogue.

63   Rorty's fluency with the pragmatist tradition is also visible in his early reviews. See, for example, his reviews of *Experience and the Analytic: A Reconsideration of Empiricism,* by Alan Pasch, *Ethics* 70 (October 1959): 75–7; of *John Dewey: His Thought and Influence,* ed. John Blewett, *Teacher's College Record* 62 (October 1960): 88–9; and of *American Pragmatism: Peirce, James, and Dewey,* by Edward C. Moore, *Ethics* 72, no. 2 (1962): 146–7.

64   Rorty, "Realism, Categories, and the 'Linguistic Turn,'" p. 316. Rorty argues that, "Veridical knowledge is never a starting point of inquiry for Peirce, but only its ideal end." For his discussion of Peirce and Wittgenstein, see "Pragmatism, Categories, and Language."

"'topic-neutral' translations of mentalistic statements."[65] In these essays Rorty appears quite comfortable with the methods of linguistic philosophy. However, the underlying values informing these linguistic analyses, which stem from "the lack of any clear criterion for 'progress' or for 'discovery' in philosophy," change little. In "The Philosopher as Expert," an essay written before Rorty arrived at Princeton that remained unpublished until 2009, he explains the importance of logic, rigor, and "methodical care" to the philosophical endeavor: "the questioning of presuppositions will not be effective unless one can show that there exist genuine alternatives to these presuppositions, and to show this takes time, patience, and attention to detail."[66] On this view, to philosophize is "to raise questions about questions," particularly new questions about "unexpressed assumptions" and "presuppositions." This approach implies the primacy of "imaginative vision," a notion that would reemerge in Rorty's thought several decades later. Most importantly, when done well the work of technicians "may actually show, once and for all, that a certain promising line of thinking is in fact a dead end."[67]

III. From *The Linguistic Turn* to *Philosophy and the Mirror of Nature*

As we have seen, from his earliest published essays Rorty was preoccupied with the problem in the history of philosophy of "dialectical impasses between competing schools" and, as a result, with how to "distinguish good from bad regresses and vicious from fruitful circles."[68] Written in 1965, his introduction to *The Linguistic Turn*, a volume that brings together thirty years of prominent linguistic philosophy from England and America, once again begins with "the spectacle of philosophers quarreling endlessly over the same issues." Rorty's aim is to evaluate the promise of "the most recent philosophical revolution" – linguistic philosophy – as a way out of these quarrels. By linguistic philosophy he understands, "the view that philosophical problems are problems which may be solved (or dissolved) either by reforming language, or by understanding more about the language we presently use" (pp. 60, 62, this volume). Any legitimate means of escaping the endless quarrels over philosophical theses must entail two things: a presuppositionless starting point that is not dependent upon a substantive philosophical thesis itself, and a criterion for success in solving a philosophical problem that admits of rational agreement (*LT* 4). Despite holding only five years earlier that "only by

---

65   See, respectively, Rorty, "The Subjectivist Principle and the Linguistic Turn," in *Alfred North Whitehead: Essays on His Philosophy*, ed. George L. Kline, 134–57; "Mind–Body Identity, Privacy, and Categories," *Review of Metaphysics* 19, no. 1 (1965): 24–54; "Incorrigibility as the Mark of the Mental," *Journal of Philosophy* 67, no. 12 (1970): 399–429.

66   Rorty, "The Philosopher as Expert," included in the 30th anniversary edition of *Philosophy and the Mirror of Nature* (Princeton, NJ: Princeton University Press, 2009), p. 407. The essay was discovered by Gross, who believes the undated manuscript was written while Rorty was at Wellesley and revised after arriving at Princeton.

67   Ibid., pp. 406–9. Rorty sums up this way: "Philosophies, to repeat, aren't killed off, but they are modified almost (but never entirely) beyond recognition as the dialogue continues. This process of modification is the work not of great thinkers, but of the technicians" (p. 410).

68   Rorty, "Realism, Categories, and the 'Linguistic Turn,'" p. 322; "Recent Metaphilosophy," p. 299.

taking the linguistic turn can we escape from such [unbridgeable] impasses," the results of Rorty's assessment are given in his introduction's subtitle, which highlights the "metaphilosophical difficulties" of linguistic philosophy.[69] In the final analysis, painstakingly detailed in nearly thirty pages of careful argument, he concludes that linguistic philosophy falls short of offering either a presuppositionless method or agreed-upon criteria for success in dissolving philosophical problems.

To those versed in the history of philosophy, this should come as no surprise. Citing Descartes, Kant, Hegel, Husserl, and the early and later Wittgensteins as examples, Rorty notes that "the history of philosophy is punctuated by revolts against the practices of previous philosophers." These revolts all failed for the same reason: while each offered a "new method" that would remove the sources of philosophical error by replacing opinion with knowledge and promised "presuppositionless" procedures and criteria for adjudicating competing philosophical theses, none of these philosophical rebels succeeded in doing so. Like Friedrich Nietzsche and William James before him, Rorty understood that there are no presuppositionless choices: "To know what method to adopt, one must already have arrived at some metaphysical and some epistemological conclusions" – conclusions that cannot be acknowledged as presuppositions.[70] To do so would involve either defending those conclusions by the use of one's new method, thereby courting the charge of circularity, or not defending them, holding that the need to adopt the proposed method follows from those very conclusions. Either way, the new method fails as a decision-procedure for settling disputes about the conclusions themselves because there is no neutral standpoint from which to decide (pp. 60–1, this volume).

But this is not cause for despair on Rorty's part. On the contrary, "despite the failure of all philosophical revolutions to achieve their ends," he assures, "no such revolution is in vain." He continues, delivering helpful insights into his own conception of the philosophical enterprise,

> If nothing else, the battles fought during the revolution cause the combatants on both sides to repair their armor, and these repairs eventually amount to a complete change of clothes [...] Philosophers who do not change (or at least re-tailor) their clothes to suit the times always have the option of saying that current philosophical assumptions are false and that the arguments for them are circular or question-begging. But if they do this too long, or retreat to their tents until the winds of doctrine change direction, they will be left out of the conversation. No philosopher can bear *that*, and this is why philosophy makes progress. (p. 61, this volume)

In the rest of his introduction, Rorty both repairs some armor and, by the end, calls for a new change of clothes. In the first endeavor, he suggests linguistic philosophy can be redeemed from its failure to provide agreed-upon criteria for success in the dissolution

---

69   For the earlier statement, see Rorty, "Realism, Categories, and the 'Linguistic Turn,'" p. 322, which was presented in 1960.

70   As James puts it, "Of whatever temperament a professional philosopher is, he tries, when philosophizing, to sink the fact of his temperament. Temperament is no conventionally recognized reason, so he urges impersonal reasons only for his conclusions. Yet his temperament really gives him a stronger bias than any of his strictly objective premises." "The Present Dilemma of Philosophy," in John J. McDermott (ed.), *The Writings of William James: A Comprehensive Edition* (Chicago: University of Chicago Press, 1967), p. 363.

of philosophical problems by adopting a more limited conception of its function. The linguistic philosophers only fail, he points out, if by 'dissolution of a philosophical problem' one means "a demonstration that there is, *tout court,* 'no problem' about, for example, perception, free will, or the external world." If instead all that is offered is "a demonstration that a *particular formulation* of a given problem involves a use of a linguistic expression which is sufficiently unusual to justify our asking the philosopher who offers the formulation to restate his problem in other terms," then indeed the linguistic turn is capable of achieving success.[71] While Rorty admits this second position seems "rather wishy-washy," his point is that "deviant" and "*prima facie* silly" uses of language, like that in questions such as, 'How do we know that we are in pain?', can be interpreted in "an interesting and fruitful way." What this demands is asking the philosopher who employs such usages to explain why he does so, such that we are able to decide whether "we assent to the premises which generate his problems, and see some point in playing his game" (LT, pp. 32–3).

Rorty calls for a complete change of clothes because the catch of adopting this "limited notion of the function of linguistic philosophy" is that it enables us to see its value for "forcing those who wish to propound the traditional problems to admit that they can no longer be put forward in the traditional formulations" (LT, pp. 32–3). Although he does not yet identify his own position with the "metaphilosophical pragmatism" that he associates with Carnap in this introduction and elsewhere with Dewey, one can see the pragmatic thrust of the conclusions he starts to draw from his metaphilosophical reflections in his realization that "the only presupposition which we must make is that if we have no criteria for evaluating answers to certain questions, then we should stop asking those questions until we do" (LT, p. 14).[72] In the course of Rorty's discussion, it emerges that the difficulties he identifies in linguistic philosophy's analyses of statements are equally applicable to traditional philosophy's "attempts to offer necessary truths" (LT, p. 31). This insight helps us understand how only a few pages after calling the linguistic period a "great age," he stakes out the following position, worth quoting at length:

> I wish to argue that the most important thing that has happened in philosophy during the last thirty years is not the linguistic turn itself, but rather the beginning of a thoroughgoing

71   This call for a more limited function indicates the extent to which Rorty's understanding of the linguistic endeavor differed markedly from the major figures of this school in its assumptions about the tools of linguistic philosophy and the ends to which he put them, despite the fact that he continued to publish essays in an analytic mode fairly consistently until roughly the mid-1970s, and then well beyond that in his intermittent debates with those working in the analytic tradition, both identifying with and explicitly employing these same tools. One of the ways Rorty charts this path is through distinguishing his alternative reading of the later Wittgenstein from that of noteworthy analysts. See, for example, "Wittgenstein, Privileged Access, and Incommunicability," *American Philosophical Quarterly* 7, no. 3 (1970): 192–205; "Verificationism and Transcendental Arguments," *Noûs* 5, no. 1 (1971): 3–14; and "Criteria and Necessity," *Noûs* 7, no. 4 (1973): 313–29. The origins of this reading of Wittgenstein in relation to the "dissolution" of philosophical problem date to his attempt to reconcile Wittgenstein and Peirce in his first published essay, "Pragmatism, Categories, and Language."

72   For more on metaphilosophical pragmatism, see p. 67, this volume; and "Recent Metaphilosophy," p. 302.

rethinking of certain epistemological difficulties which have troubled philosophers since Plato and Aristotle. I would argue that if it were not for the epistemological difficulties created by this account, the traditional problems of metaphysics (problems, for example, about universals, substantial form, and the relation between the mind and the body) would never have been conceived. If the traditional "spectatorial" account of knowledge is overthrown, the account of knowledge which replaces it will lead to reformulations everywhere else in philosophy. (pp. 69–70, this volume)[73]

Striking an odd note for an introduction, Rorty closes with the prediction that the essays in the volume will likely be rendered "obsolete" by these larger developments, given the historicity of the vocabularies in which they are written. Nevertheless, the linguistic turn has instrumental value for making philosophers more self-conscious about what Rorty calls the "pattern of creeping obsolescence" in the history of philosophy, and for identifying particular dead ends, even if linguistic analysis itself turns out to be one (p. 70, this volume).[74]

A few years later in the 1970 essay "Cartesian Epistemology and Changes in Ontology," Rorty again probes the issue of the lack of fixed, agreed-upon criteria. This time the impasses under consideration, which are just as inconclusive, are those between "Absolute Idealists and Physical Realists, interactionists and epiphenomenalists, process philosophers and substance philosophers."[75] Turning to Descartes and to the ontological question, 'What is really real?', Rorty points out, once again, that the ways of answering this question have differed by epochs. Noting that one can trace these different answers back to the Greeks and to medieval philosophers, he decides to focus on what he calls "the 'Cartesian' period of philosophy – the one that stretches from the end of the seventeenth to the middle of the twentieth centuries." His point is that "the criteria for a satisfactory answer to this question changed in the seventeenth century, and are changing now."[76] Why these changes take place is primarily a result of specific controversies losing their interest on account of particular conceptions losing their appeal. With a nod to Sellars'

73   Even though it would not appear in print until 1979, within a decade of penning these lines in the mid-1960s, the bulk of *Mirror* had been written. See Gross, *Richard Rorty*, pp. 204–5, where he notes that most of the writing for the book had been completed by 1974 while Rorty had been on leave from teaching thanks to a Guggenheim fellowship.

74   Twenty years hence, Rorty interpreted the contribution of the linguistic turn to philosophy as initiating "a shift from talk about experience as a medium of representation to talk of language as such a medium" that made it easier to "set aside the notion of representation itself" (p. 178, this volume). For a very helpful discussion of the linguistic turn and its relevance for pragmatism and contemporary philosophy more generally, see Colin Koopman, "Language is a Form of Experience: Reconciling Classical Pragmatism and Neopragmatism," *Transactions of the Charles S. Peirce Society* 43, no. 4 (2007): 694–727.

75   Rorty, "Cartesian Epistemology and Changes in Ontology," in John E. Smith (ed.), *Contemporary American Philosophy* (New York: Humanities Press, 1970), p. 273.

76   Ibid., p. 274. More specifically, he argues that "the Cartesian tradition jumped on the fact that knowledge must be belief in what is true, and thought that by learning more about knowledge we could learn more about what is true. Thus we got a priori ontological conclusions deduced from sheer reflection on the nature of knowledge. The post-Cartesian tradition (exemplified by Wittgenstein, Austin, Sellars, Dewey, and Quine) rallies around the principle that empirical knowledge needs no foundation, emphasizes 'justified' rather than 'true', recognizes that 'justified' does not mean 'justified now and forever, beyond the possibility of revision'"(p. 283).

"Principle that the Given is a Myth," Rorty terms this "the Principle of the Relativity of Incorrigibility," which holds:

> That a given sentence is used to express incorrigible knowledge is not a matter of a special relation which holds between knowers and some object referred to by this sentence, but a matter of the way in which the sentence fits into the language of a given culture, and the circumstances of its user, at a given time.[77]

Lamenting that a full understanding of these changes in the history of ontology would require "a much broader historical account of cultural change – an account on the Hegelian scale," he notes that the popularity of "picture-thinking," or "thinking of the mind as an 'inner eye' which was capable of seeing only inner entities," played a role. The conclusion he draws here, which offers a rationale for the technicism that still would characterize Rorty's work for some time, is that

> a priori 'overcomings', or defenses, of ontology should be replaced by an attempt to go through the traditional 'problems of ontology' one-by-one, examine the premises which generate the problems, and see whether there is any reason to believe these premises.

The linguistic turn, in his view, already has begun this work; however, while "a necessary first step," the "analytical jobs being done by linguistic philosophers will certainly not be enough to let us understand what happened in history."[78]

IV. A Post-Philosophical Culture

Rorty's allusion in 1970 to the need for a broad account of cultural change on a Hegelian scale is instructive.[79] His references to the possibility of a "post-philosophical" culture in *The Linguistic Turn* and to a "post-Kantian culture" in *Philosophy and the Mirror of Nature* signal what he takes to be the advent of a new "historical epoch" (pp. 65, 86, 88, this volume). While Rorty does not offer a complete map of this new epoch, he does point out a few signposts in the early twentieth century: the outstripping of the religious by the secular, the declining role of scientists in intellectual culture, and the displacement of preachers and philosophers by poets and novelists as "the moral teachers of the youth" (p. 85, this volume). Like Nietzsche's madman, Rorty is in the midst of his philosophical brethren with a lantern and a message, trying to open their eyes to momentous changes that have rendered their most deeply cherished assumptions absurd.[80]

---

77   Ibid., p. 282. Rorty makes a similar argument in the much more technical essay, "Incorrigibility as the Mark of the Mental," where he nonetheless concludes, "When ontological issues boil down to matters of taste, they cease to be ontological issues […] Insistence on the 'identity' of the mental and the physical would seem an unnecessary rhetorical flourish" (p. 424).
78   Ibid., pp. 284, 292.
79   Rorty, "Cartesian Epistemology and Changes in Ontology," p. 292.
80   Friedrich Nietzsche, *The Gay Science,* trans. Walter Kaufmann (New York: Vintage Books, 1974 [1887]), para. 125. To be clear, as Rorty put it in "Cartesian Epistemology and Changes in Ontology," all this is not simply a matter of "a few mistaken epistemological or methodological premises. (That would be like saying that Western religion is a result of a failure to understand that existence is not a predicate and that there can be no atemporal causes)" (p. 292).

Evidence of this historical awareness is apparent in Rorty's essays of the early to mid-1970s, which are often characterized by an odd mix of broad, sweeping claims about the history of philosophy, followed by pages and pages of tightly argued, point-by-point technical analysis of others' positions, frequently cast in the terms of symbolic logic.[81] He continues to do the essential work he called for back in 1970 of examining the "problems" of traditional philosophy, and the premises behind them, one by one, in order to determine if there is any reason to continue believing in these premises. Yet increasingly one encounters Rorty telling a story – constructing a broad narrative – about the history of philosophy, as way to orient us toward the larger cultural shift. This approach emanates from a deeply held belief, with obvious parallels to his own experience: "The self-image of a philosopher – his identification of himself as such (rather than as, perhaps, an historian or a mathematician or a poet) – depends almost entirely," Rorty held, "upon how he sees the history of philosophy" (CP, p. 41). Rather than evince point-by-point arguments to undermine persistent philosophical premises, Rorty begins offering alternative viewpoints or 'redescriptions' as a result of which we might situate ourselves differently in relation to philosophical tradition and to key thinkers. And by situating the philosophical endeavor within these alternative historical narratives, a new – or least non-Cartesian – conception of what philosophers might do starts to emerge.[82]

This stance yields the two-pronged enterprise that defines Rorty's project. On one front, there is the attempt to grasp the full implications of what it would mean to move beyond "the entire cultural tradition which made truth […] a central virtue" (CP, p. 35). Thinking through the implications of this shift for politics, ethics, justice, and religion, in addition to philosophy, as well as giving positive expression to lineaments of a culture that no longer sees itself as in need of philosophical justification or support, constitutes the bulk of Rorty's efforts for the next three decades. On the other, lies the negative or "therapeutic" work required to assist philosophers, and ultimately everyone else, in letting go of the conceptions and assumptions rendered obsolete as a result of the larger shift. As he states in the preface to *Philosophy and the Mirror of Nature,* from his earliest exposure to philosophy, he was "impressed by the way in which philosophical problems appeared, disappeared, or changed shape, as a result of new vocabularies." Given his

81   See, for example, "The World Well Lost," "Keeping Philosophy Pure," and "Is There a Problem about Fictional Discourse?", collected in *Consequences of Pragmatism* (CP), as well as others of the time, like "Realism and Reference," *The Monist* 59, no. 3 (1976): 321–40. The latter, which opens with the claim: "Our ancestors believed in many things which did not exist – gods, witches, the luminiferous ether, phlogiston, reincarnated souls, sense-data, conceptual analysis, and the like," poses the question, "If we feel entitled to say that our ancestors quite literally did not know what they were talking about […] why should we assume we are any better off?" (327, 329), before turning to issues raised by "Donnellan and Kripke between 'cluster-concept' theories of what names refer to and 'causal' theories" in order to argue that "the causal Meinongianisn of common sense does not need correction nor supplementation by theories of reference."

82   For early examples of this, see the following essays, all in CP: "Overcoming the Tradition," where Rorty proposes to "offer sketches of Dewey as he would presumably look to Heidegger and of Heidegger as he would presumably look to Dewey" (p. 42); "Philosophy as a Kind of Writing"; "Method, Social Science, and Social Hope," where Rorty tells us the moral seventeenth-century philosophers "*should* have drawn" from Galileo (193); and "Philosophy in America Today," which explicitly defends "learning to tell a story about what one is doing" and asserts that constructing an argument or a story are "both good things to do"(CP, p. 223).

historical sensibility, Rorty knew that a "philosophical problem" was "a product of the unconscious adoption of assumptions built into the vocabulary in which the problem was stated – assumptions which were to be questioned before the problem itself was taken seriously." If he could get back to these "assumptions," and make clear that they are "optional," he believed, it "would be 'therapeutic' in the way that Carnap's original dissolution of the standard textbook problems was 'therapeutic.'" *Philosophy and the Mirror of Nature,* he tells us, is the result of this project (PMN, pp. xiii–xiv).[83]

More specifically, what turns out to be "optional" in the account Rorty presents in *Mirror* is "the notion of knowledge as the assemblage of accurate representations" (p. 88, this volume). While this may not seem like much at first glance, the implications are revolutionary. As Rorty explains in the introduction, if culture is comprised of various claims to knowledge by science, morality, art, and religion, and if philosophy understands itself to be "a general theory of representation" whose business it is to "divide culture up into the areas which represent reality well, those which represent it less well, and those which do not represent it at all (despite their pretense of doing so)," then a decline in the importance of how accurate our representations need to be will leave philosophers with a lot less to do (p. 84, this volume). Nevertheless, despite his talk, going back to *The Linguistic Turn,* of a "post-philosophical culture," he consistently affirms that this spells not an end to philosophy as such, but to a particular tradition characterized by a need to answer unanswerable questions.[84]

That the heroes of *Mirror* – Wittgenstein, Heidegger, and Dewey – are exalted for having perceived the cultural changes under way and, as a result, abandoning their initial efforts to find new ways to breathe life into shopworn philosophical categories and assumptions, is not coincidental. All three "glimpse the possibility of a form of intellectual life in which the vocabulary of philosophical reflection inherited from the seventeenth century would seem as pointless as the thirteenth-century philosophical vocabulary had seemed to the Enlightenment" (p. 86, this volume). Like these thinkers in their later work, *Mirror* aims to be "therapeutic rather than constructive, edifying rather than systematic, designed to make the reader question his own motives for philosophizing rather than to supply him with a new philosophical program." The aims of edifying philosophy involve helping not only readers of philosophy, but "society as a whole," to "break free

83 Although he would continue his dialogue with select analytic philosophers for the rest of his life, his landmark 1979 tome would be the last major foray on the latter front. As he indicated in a 1982 letter to the president of the MacArthur Foundation, which had granted him a so-called "genius grant," his hopes were to become "a sort of all-around intellectual, or man of letters, or something of the sort." It seemed that "writing lots of stuff on what was wrong with the self-image of the Philosophical Establishment" had run its course for him. Quoted in Gross, *Reading Rorty,* p. 233.

84 See, for example, his statement on the last page of *Mirror,* assuring that "there is no danger of philosophy's 'coming to an end,'" (p. 110, this volume) See also, for an extended discussion, "Keeping Philosophy Pure" in CP, esp. pp. 29–36, where he states, "Philosophy resembles space and time: it is hard to imagine what an 'end' to any of the three would look like" (p. 29); and more specifically, "So to say that the [Wittgenstein's] *Investigations* might bring philosophy to an end can only mean that this book might somehow rid us of 'the picture which held us captive' – the picture of man which generates the traditional problems. To say that philosophy might end is not to say that holding large views might become unfashionable, or that philosophy departments might be plowed under, but rather to say that a certain cultural tradition might die out" (p. 32).

from outworn vocabularies and attitudes, rather than to provide 'grounding' for the intuitions and customs of the present" (p. 89, this volume). As he explains in the final chapter,
"Philosophy Without Mirrors," the goal of this "edification" – helping us "become different people" – can be accomplished in two ways: Rorty's métier, making connections
between our own culture or historical period and other ones; and the "poetic" activity of
imagining new possibilities. Because edifying discourse is "abnormal" or "revolutionary"
discourse, in Thomas Kuhn's sense, it will "take us out of our old selves by the power of
strangeness, to aid us in becoming new beings" – change that would enable us to catch
up with the larger cultural shift (p. 91, this volume).[85]

V. The Return to Pragmatism and Break
with Analytic Philosophy

The principal implications of the stance Rorty adopts by the late 1970s are a more decisive break with the analytic tradition and a deeper embrace of pragmatism. If in 1970
Rorty viewed the analytic work being done by linguistic philosophers as "a necessary
first step," in *Philosophy and the Mirror of Nature* he calls analytic philosophy just "one
more variant of Kantian philosophy" whose substitution of linguistic categories for
mental ones "does not essentially change the Cartesian-Kantian problematic."[86] His turn
to broader historical narratives of cultural change creates an opening into which the
tradition of American thinkers he had been aware of since he was a child soon moves.
The richness of the pragmatist tradition, not just along a philosophical plane but in its
political, moral, and cultural resources, affords Rorty the kind of thematically-engaged
intellectual language he needs to move beyond the problems of philosophers and take
up the social and political issues to which he had been committed since he started thinking at the age of twelve that "the point of being human was to spend one's life fighting
social injustice" (p. 502, this volume). It would take some time for the full extent of his
identification with the pragmatist tradition to take hold, but as early as the 1976 essay

85   Although he is not included in Rorty's trinity of the three most important philosophers of
the twentieth century, Gross has noted that Thomas Kuhn is cited as often in *Mirror* as Dewey.
Kuhn's influence on Rorty is apparent in "Cartesian Epistemology and Changes in Ontology,"
where explicitly drawing on Kuhn, Rorty notes that "scientific epochs are defined by the solutions they take as paradigmatic, whereas philosophical epochs are defined by the problems they
take as paradigmatic" (p. 275n1). For an insightful discussion of Kuhn's importance for Rorty, see
Gross, *Richard Rorty,* pp. 202–11. Kuhn joined the Princeton faculty in 1964, only a few years after
Rorty. Gross posits that along with the later Wittgenstein, Kuhn "provided Rorty with the symbolic resources he needed to argue his way out of mainstream analytic philosophy and into a
broader conception of the philosophical enterprise" (ibid., p. 209). For Rorty's own take on his
indebtedness to Kuhn, see "Thomas Kuhn, Rocks and the Laws of Physics," in *PSH,* pp. 175–89;
as well as, "Science as Solidarity," in *Objectivity, Relativism, and Truth* (ORT), pp. 35–45, where he
calls pragmatism "left-wing Kuhnianism" (p. 38).
86   Rorty, "Cartesian Epistemology and Changes in Ontology," p. 292; (p. 87, this volume).
While he admits that his critique in *Mirror* is "parasitic" upon the efforts of the very analytic philosophers whose "frame of reference" is being called into question – like Sellars, Quine, Davidson,
Ryle, Malcolm, Kuhn, and Putnam – he suggests that the reason for his use of the analytic
vocabulary is "merely autobiographical," as it is the philosophical language and literature with
which he is most familiar.

"Professionalized Philosophy and Transcendentalist Culture," delivered on the occasion of a Bicentennial Symposium of Philosophy, it is apparent.[87]

In Rorty's story, the rise of the post-metaphysical culture is set in motion by inadvertent moves by Kant and Hegel that authorize the advent of an autonomous, secular, nonscientific, literary culture. Rorty uses the terms "literary criticism" or "culture criticism" for what follows, describing it in this way:

> Beginning in the days of Goethe and Macauley [sic] and Carlyle and Emerson, a kind of writing has developed which is neither the evaluation of the relative merits of literary productions, nor intellectual history, nor moral philosophy, nor epistemology, nor social prophecy, but all these things mingled together into a new genre. (CP, p. 66)[88]

Not yet ready to identify his own work as pragmatist, he affirmatively cites Sidney Hook's conception of pragmatism, the philosopher on whose knees he was bounced as a boy, as "the theory and practice of enlarging human freedom in a precarious and tragic world by the arts of intelligent social control" (CP, pp. 69–70). In NINETEENTH-CENTURY IDEALISM AND TWENTIETH-CENTURY TEXTUALISM, Rorty draws links between the culture criticism of the nineteenth century and the twentieth century "textualism" characteristic of post-structuralists and Yale school literary critics. The common denominators of these intellectual movements are anti-scientism and anti-realism. Although he does not explicitly affiliate himself with textualism, its primary tenet of seeking "to place literature in the center [of the culture], and to treat both science and philosophy as, at best, literary genres," is the view he espouses (p. 123, this volume).

The broad contours of the *Weltanschauung* expressed in "Nineteenth Century Idealism and Twentieth Century Textualism" did not change fundamentally over the next two and half decades of Rorty's life. Combined with his important 1979 address as president of the American Philosophical Association's Eastern Division (chapter 4, this volume, PRAGMATISM, RELATIVISM AND IRRATIONALISM), these two essays contain the bulk of the ideas and commitments Rorty would continue to work on for the remainder of his career.[89] In these essays there are no traces of the finely wrought technical analyses that were his stock-in-trade and the style of philosophizing that helped him earn tenure and

87   In CP, pp. 60–71. Although there is an appearance in the 1984 essay SOLIDARITY AND OBJECTIVITY? (p. 234, this volume), it is not until a decade after the publication of *Mirror* that Rorty's use of "we Deweyans" and "we pragmatists" becomes commonplace. See for example, PSH, p. 124; TP, p. 211n.

88   For another description of this culture, see also p. 129, this volume. In DEWEY'S METAPHYSICS, written the year before, he describes Dewey's view of philosophy as "the criticism of culture" (p. 72, this volume). In PHILOSOPHY AS A TRANSITIONAL GENRE, written almost 25 years later, Rorty presents his thesis in more pat form: "the intellectuals of the West have, since the Renaissance, progressed through three stages," roughly from religion through philosophy to literature p. 476, this volume. The additional wrinkle Rorty adds to his historical account here is that philosophy was "a transitional stage in the development of increased self-reliance" (p. 479, this volume).

89   For a more specific discussion of these ideas and commitments, see the introduction to Part I of this volume below pp. 58–9. Although its themes overlap with material covered in the aforementioned two pieces, one might also add "Method, Social Science, and Social Hope," in CP, pp. 191–210.

a full professorship. Although he states in his address that nothing he offers is "an argument in favor of pragmatism," only an attempt to answer "various superficial criticisms which have been made about it," it marks his most direct engagement and positive affirmation of pragmatism itself, where this tradition is not simply marshaled to achieve some other end but framed as a salutary intellectual orientation that we would do well to make "central to our culture and our self-image" (p. 121, this volume). In one of the address's most memorable passages, Rorty offers a particularly evocative statement of the consequences of accepting this pragmatism:

> If we give up this hope, we shall lose what Nietzsche called "metaphysical comfort," but we may gain a renewed sense of community. Our identification with our community – our society, our political tradition, our intellectual heritage – is heightened when we see this community as *ours* rather than *nature's, shaped* rather than *found,* one among many which men have made. In the end, the pragmatists tell us, what matters is our loyalty to other human beings clinging together against the dark, not our hope of getting things right. (p. 115, this volume)

Interestingly, the note on which the essay ends honors James and Dewey, not for any particular philosophical arguments, but for giving us "a hint of how our lives might be changed" (p. 121, this volume).[90]

Aligning himself with James and Dewey, rather than Peirce, enables Rorty to turn pragmatism against analytic philosophy.[91] While his first published essay brought Peirce, the classical pragmatist whose assumptions and approach were most amenable to the analysts, into dialogue with the later Wittgenstein, here Rorty warns of "a tendency to overpraise Peirce," dubbing him, "the most Kantian of thinkers" for his support for an historical frame of philosophical inquiry.[92] Without identifying whom, he reports that "many" philosophers see pragmatism as offering various "holistic corrections" to the atomistic doctrines of the early logical empiricists. His point here is that this assumption, while not wrong in itself, permits one to overlook the fact that logical empiricism is

90   A decade and a half later, Rorty starts referring to pragmatism as "an attempt to alter our self-image." See ETHICS WITHOUT PRINCIPLES (p. 425, this volume).

91   Here James, who was mentioned affirmatively but mostly in passing in *Mirror*, becomes more prominent, though often merely lumped in with Dewey in imprecise encomia. Rorty's most sustained engagements with the thought of James do not come until "Religious Faith, Intellectual Responsibility, and Romance," in PSH, pp. 148–67; and PRAGMATISM AS ROMANTIC POLYTHEISM, (chapter 27, this volume). James is discussed in relation to Davidson in PRAGMATISM, DAVIDSON, AND TRUTH (chapter 7, this volume).

92   Rorty's revised sense of Peirce's relevance now holds that his contribution to pragmatism was "merely to have given it a name, and to have stimulated James" (p. 112, this volume). Although Rorty's later work contains fleeting allusions to Peirce, often positive ones – e.g., citing Peirce's admonition not to block the road of inquiry (see, for example, PCP, p. 5; CP, p. xlvii) – Rorty does not engage Peirce in the kind of depth he did in his early work. Rorty was also fond of citing Peirce's notion of beliefs as habits of action; see, for example, ORT, pp. 93, 118. The few later essays where Peirce receives more than passing mention include, "Dewey Between Hegel and Darwin," in TP, pp. 290–306; "Two Meanings of 'Logocentrism': A Reply to Norris," in *Essays on Heidegger and Others* (EHO), pp. 107–18, where he (briefly) discusses Derrida's revival of Peirce's anti-Cartesianism; and PRAGMATISM, DAVIDSON, AND TRUTH, (chapter 7, this volume), esp. ORT, pp. 127–32.

itself but "one variety of standard, academic, neo-Kantian, epistemologically centered philosophy," presumably as he may have overlooked at one time himself. The consequences of pragmatism cut much deeper than this: "The great pragmatists should not be taken as suggesting a holistic variation of this variant, but rather as breaking with the Kantian epistemological tradition altogether." In a thinly veiled remark, he continues, "The pragmatist tells us that it is useless to hope that objects will constrain us to believe the truth about them, if only they are approached with an unclouded mental eye, or a rigorous method, or a perspicuous language" (pp. 111,115, this volume).

His break with the analytic tradition is solidified two years later in "Philosophy in America Today," the piece that closes *Consequences of Pragmatism*. Here Rorty presents a new "story" on the "rise and fall of 'Oxford philosophy'" and in the process charts a new course for himself. Taking up the analytic–Continental split in contemporary philosophy, Rorty eschews the language of dialogue and rapprochement he employed in the past. Instead, he suggests we "put aside wistful talk of bridge-building and joining forces" and accept this split as "both permanent and harmless." What accounts for this shift is Rorty himself taking a more radical view of his own philosophical assumptions. He does not mean to signal the "fall" of analytic philosophy; on the contrary, most philosophers today, he points out, are "more or less 'analytic.'"[93] However, there is no "agreed-upon list of 'central problems'" for analytic philosophers to take up, leaving only a "stylistic and sociological unity." What has changed since his analysis in *The Linguistic Turn* is that he now sees this as evidence of a much larger cultural shift. "Whether it likes it or not," he asserts, analytic philosophy is now much like everywhere else in the humanities in "*not* knowing in advance what our problems are, and in not needing to provide criteria of identity which will tell us whether our problems are the same as those of our predecessors." Once the assumptions that unified the community of analytic inquirers no longer hold, as with Kuhn's analysis of the move from normal to revolutionary science, a new paradigm is in the offing. The old paradigm – the dream of philosophy as *scientia scientiarum,* one shared by both Plato and the analysts – shall pass:

> We should renounce the idea that we have access to some superconcepts which are the concepts of no particular historical epoch, no particular profession, no particular portion of culture, but which somehow necessarily inhere in all subordinate concepts, and can be used to "analyze" the latter. (CP 222)

What we are left with is the more vast conception of intellectual inquiry, which Rorty sums up with Sellars's "bland" definition of philosophy: "seeing how things, in the largest sense of the term, hang together, in the largest sense of the term." With that shift securely established, analytic and Continental philosophers can "agree to differ on whether finding interesting new problems about which to argue, or telling sweeping historical stories, is the more profitable residual enterprise" (CP, pp. 216, 226–7).[94]

93 In the Introduction to CP, though, he is less ambiguous: "I think that analytic philosophy culminates in Quine, the later Wittgenstein, Sellars, and Davidson – which is to say that it transcends and cancels itself" (p. xviii).
94 It is interesting to note here that after leaving Princeton in 1982 Rorty taught almost exclusively nonanalytic – mostly Continental and pragmatist – philosophy. As he stated in an interview, "By that time, I wasn't teaching in a way that required students to keep up with philosophical journals" (TCF, p. 10).

Continuing the dialogue with analytic philosophy

Despite intimating an end to his engagement with the analytic tradition, Rorty continued to converse regularly with analytic philosophers in their preferred style and approach for the rest of his career.[95] Specifically, he resumed the work of bridging the pragmatist and analytic traditions, only now it was his particular version of pragmatism and only select analytic thinkers that on his reading contained elements congenial to his pragmatist project. Perhaps the reasons for this lasting engagement are, as he puts it in the introduction to *Mirror,* "merely autobiographical" – they are the vocabulary and the literature with which he is most familiar, to which he owes his grasp of philosophical issues. Perhaps it permitted him to retain a fixed pole within his intellectual identity, as he increasingly found himself before all manner of audiences and disciplines around the world. Or perhaps, as Bernstein has suggested, despite repudiating the obsessions of philosophers "there is a sense in which Rorty himself is obsessed. It is almost as if he cannot quite 'let go' and accept the force of his own critique." In any case, it is clear that even if Rorty abandoned his identification with analytic philosophy, he never gave up his engagement with it.[96]

Still, if the "Wittgenstein–Sellars–Quine–Davidson attack," as he dubbed it, indeed has been successful and there are no more philosophical problems to dissolve, and if the broader cultural shift away from traditional philosophy has eroded the assumptions that authorized a distinctive role for this kind of specialized philosophical inquiry anyway, then Rorty's more expansive humanistic conception of post-philosophical culture criticism would seem to have no use for the analytic tradition or methods.[97] For the most part, it

95 To give a quick overview, other than Part III of ORT, the bulk of the essays in that volume engage the analytic tradition. With the exception of "Wittgenstein, Heidegger, and the Reification of Language," the pieces in EHO, also from the 1980s, are much more wide-ranging, discussing an array of thinkers that includes Milan Kundera, Charles Dickens, Derrida, Paul de Man, Habermas, Lyotard, Freud, Foucault, Felix Unger, Cornelius Castoriadis, and Roberto Unger. The essays of the 1990s collected in *TP* are split roughly equally between pieces on individual analytic thinkers and Rorty's attempts to advance his own notion of progress and to relate his pragmatism to human rights, the fall of Communism, and cultural difference. The third part of his final volume of philosophical papers, PCP, which gathers essays from the late 1990s until 2005, is dedicated to "Current Issues with Analytic Philosophy."

96 Bernstein, *Philosophical Profiles: Essays in a Pragmatic Mode* (Philadelphia: University of Pennsylvania Press, 1986), p. 47. Gross notes that Rorty went through a "significant transition" in the early 1960s from being primarily a metaphilosopher to an active participant in analytic debates. He suggests that by 1966 "Rorty's transition from Whiteheadian metaphysician and McKeonesque historian of philosophy to mainstream analytic philosopher was complete" (*Richard Rorty,* p. 189). In Gross's view, Rorty's work of the mid-1960s is best understood as "a distinct piece of his oeuvre," which he interprets as part of Rorty's attempt to establish himself within mainstream philosophy for the purposes of getting tenure at Princeton, which was granted in 1965. I think Gross is right about the context at that time, but as we move beyond 1982, where Gross's book ends, it is hard to conclude that Rorty's engagement with the analytic tradition is a distinct piece and not a lasting strand of his oeuvre.

97 In "Philosophy in America Today," written for a 1981 conference, Rorty identifies two particular fronts on which the analytic approach is inadequate for his emergent purposes: it fails to offer "a story about the present and the future which describes a significant cultural function for

did not; in *Contingency, Irony, and Solidarity,* Rorty's most original, nonderivative presentation of his own substantive views, the analytic tools and debates that were once a mainstay are virtually absent. Generally speaking, then, Rorty's primary focus for the rest of his career was writing in the kind of broadly humanistic, interdisciplinary mode characteristic of audiences outside of philosophy departments, where his works most widely resonated. However, there is a key caveat. Even in *Contingency,* Rorty continually mines individual analytic thinkers for particular conceptions or stances that comport with his positive pragmatist vision: for instance, Davidson's conception of language, Sellars's notion of "we-intentions," Daniel Dennett's idea of the self as "a center of narrative gravity," and Mary Hesse's concept of "metaphorical redescriptions." While these thinkers were not always pleased with Rorty's selective interpretations and appropriations of their work, the debates spurred by his attempts to identify what he viewed as their latent pragmatist leanings and to link them with the Wittgenstein–Sellars–Quine–Davidson line of argument – indeed, that there existed such a coherent lineage at all – mark an important chapter in the development of analytic and pragmatist thought over the last few decades.[98]

VI. From Anti-representationalism to Political Liberalism

Few were prepared for the explicit championing of the political and moral virtues of bourgeois liberal democracy that surfaced in the wake of *Philosophy and the Mirror of Nature.*[99] Recalling the highly political milieu of Rorty's upbringing and the precociousness of his own political sensibilities perhaps makes these political commitments less surprising.[100] Yet the relation of this political turn to the two decades of philosophical

---

philosophy to perform, a continuing task"; and it writes off the resources of the Continental tradition, "writers like Heidegger, Foucault, and their nineteenth-century precursors" (CP, p. 214). In the introduction to CP, Rorty notes that he will capitalize the term "philosophy" when referring to the conception that holds we can "believe more truths or do more good or be more rational by knowing more about Truth or Goodness or Rationality." The point he wants to make is: "Pragmatists are saying that to best hope for philosophy is not to practice Philosophy" (CP, p. xv).

98   Some of these thinkers, like Sellars, Putnam, and Michael Dummett, had been showing up in Rorty's essays since the 1960s; others, like Dennett, Davidson, and Rorty's former student, Robert Brandom, emerged in the early and mid-1970s. TP includes essays devoted to each of these thinkers. For Rorty's engagement with these and other analytical philosophers, see Brandom (ed.), *Rorty and His Critics* (Oxford: Blackwell, 2000). For his part, Rorty sympathized with the philosophers who repeatedly claimed that he had distorted their views: "It's a natural reaction. They think of themselves as having made a quite specific point, and with a wave of my hand I seem to subsume their specific point as part of some great cultural movement, or something like that." Nevertheless, he defended his approach: "I don't see anything wrong with doing that. Regardless of how they feel about it, if you think there's a common denominator or a trend, then why not say so?" (TCF, p. 9).

99   On this point see Bernstein, *The New Constellation,* p. 260. Ian Shapiro describes Rorty's work in the decade after *Mirror* as a "journey from philosophical diagnosis to political prescription," *Political Criticism* (Berkeley: University of California Press, 1990), p. 20. The most conspicuous early example is Rorty's brief 1983 piece in ORT: "Postmodernist Bourgeois Liberalism" (pp. 197–202).

100   Indeed, Rorty's political identity remained remarkably static throughout his entire lifetime. Gross depicts how Rorty's "intellectual self-concept of leftist American patriot," as he calls it,

argument that precede it is not immediately apparent. The introduction to *Objectivity, Relativism, and Truth,* the first of two volumes that collect Rorty's essays of the 1980s, merely offers that the connection between the section of that book on anti-representationalism and the section on political liberalism is the same connection Dewey saw between "the abandonment of what he called 'the spectator theory of knowledge' and the needs of a democratic society" – namely, that "it suits such a society to have no views about truth save that it is more likely to be obtained in Milton's 'free and open encounter' of opinions than in any other way" (ORT, p. 1).

Although he had long been sympathetic to the tradition, Rorty's own explicit iden-tification with American pragmatism in the 1980s provides a vehicle for expressing his longstanding commitments to liberal democracy and social justice in a way that supports his critique of traditional philosophy. More specifically, his turn toward the political is a function of his perception that both the institutions and the culture of liberal democracy would be "better served" by an alternative "vocabulary" of moral and political reflection than one structured around notions of truth, rationality, objectivity, and moral obligation (CIS, p. 44). What does he mean by "better served"? For Rorty it all comes down to "a question of efficiency": how best to bring about the "global democratic utopia," as he describes it, bequeathed to us by the Enlightenment: "a planet on which all members of the species are concerned about the fates of all the other members" (p. 356, this vol-ume; TP 12).[101]

Careful readers of *Philosophy and the Mirror of Nature* may recall that after grandly praising Wittgenstein, Heidegger, and Dewey for their collective therapeutic efforts, Rorty notes that what distinguishes Dewey from the other two is how he "wrote his polemics against traditional mirror-imagery out of a vision of a new kind of society" (p. 89, this volume). Despite their shared rejection of Kantian assumptions, in his 1979 APA address Rorty similarly distinguishes James and Dewey from Nietzsche and Heidegger on the basis of the former pair doing so "in a spirit of social hope." That is, James and Dewey "asked us to liberate our new civilization by giving up the notion of 'grounding' our culture, our moral lives, our politics, our religious beliefs, upon 'philo-sophical bases'" (p. 112, this volume).[102] Linking his philosophical stance to a distinctly American Emersonian spirit, Rorty later frames his own emergent pragmatism as

---

remained unchanged through both his embrace of and his disenchantment with Platonism while a student at Chicago, and argues that Rorty "acquired this identity from his parents, that it became reactivated in the 1970s in response to their deaths, the rise of the New Left, and other historical developments, and that its effect was to renew Rorty's commitment to American pragmatism, which he saw as giving expression to the same values" (*Richard Rorty,* pp. 97, 322). While I think Gross is persuasive regarding the origins of this political identity and the role these factors played in its reactivation, my own sense is that his account underestimates the influence of Rorty's underlying orientation or "temperament," in William James's sense, in terms of the way Rorty approached philosophical problems and intellectual issues more generally, which seemed to have a pragmatist bent long before he started calling it that. For this argument, see Christopher J. Voparil, *Richard Rorty: Politics and Vision* (Lanham, MD: Rowman & Littlefield Press, 2006), esp. pp. 18–25.

101   In "Justice as a Larger Loyalty," he expands this circle of concern to include "all living crea-tures on our home planet." See p. 433, this volume.

102   See also the final section of "Method, Social Science, and Social Hope," where Rorty defends his claim that "[a]lthough Foucault and Dewey are trying to do the same thing, Dewey

consistent with his sense that Dewey's efforts to repudiate representationalist doctrines were motivated by "the thought that these doctrines had become impediments to human beings' sense of self-reliance" (ORT, p. 17).[103]

By appropriating the resources of the pragmatist tradition via his somewhat idiosyncratic reading, Rorty is able to transpose his notion of philosophical change through the adoption of new vocabularies to society as a whole, and to move from a conception of inquiry to a program of social and political change. However, marshaling the pragmatist tradition in concert with his broad concept of culture criticism and understanding of moral progress generated through linguistic novelty means framing pragmatism in a particular way. Baldly put, it entails reading out the 'scientistic' aspects of pragmatism while highlighting its connections to romanticism.[104] What Rorty wanted to avoid was "having the natural scientist step into the cultural role which the philosopher-as-superscientist vacated."[105] While James's pragmatism is more consistent with this effort than Dewey's, Rorty nevertheless sees essential resources in Dewey's thought, including what he took to be Dewey's grasp of the importance of changes in human beings' self-image, specifically "the change from a sense of their dependence upon something antecedently present to a sense of the utopian possibilities of the future, the growth of their ability to mitigate their finitude by a talent for self-creation" (ORT, p. 17).[106]

By the late 1980s, Rorty's depiction of a poeticized, post-metaphysical culture is in full swing. The literary culture with origins in the nineteenth century alluded to in a couple of essays a decade earlier gives way to an entire political vision, culminating in his claim that "the novel is the characteristic genre of democracy, the genre most closely associated with the struggle for freedom and equality" (p. 309, this volume). His essays of this period increasingly are characterized by allusions to what he calls "a general turn against theory and toward narrative." While Rorty was always cognizant of the role of narrative in structuring our apprehension of the history of philosophy, his defenses of

seems to me to have done it better, simply because his vocabulary allows room for unjustifiable hope, and an ungroundable but vital sense of human solidarity"(CP, p. 208).

103 Rorty goes on to describe the essays collected in ORT as "largely devoted to arguing, against Heidegger and others, that such a sense of self-reliance is a good thing to have." The idea of self-reliance would become increasingly important in Rorty's work. See TRUTH WITHOUT CORRESPONDENCE TO REALITY; ETHICS WITHOUT PRINCIPLES; and PHILOSOPHY AS A TRANSITIONAL GENRE (chapters 24, 25 and 30, this volume).

104 As he puts it, "The basic motive of pragmatism, like that of Hegelianism, was [...] a continuation of the Romantic reaction to the Enlightenment's sanctification of natural science" (p. 219, this volume). Pragmatism's relation to romanticism comes increasingly to the forefront in Rorty's later work. See, for example, PRAGMATISM AS ROMANTIC POLYTHEISM (chapter 27, this volume); and "Pragmatism and Romanticism" and "Grandeur, Profundity, and Finitude," both in PCP. On the relation of pragmatism and the Romantic tradition more generally, see Russell B. Goodman, *American Philosophy and the Romantic Tradition* (New York: Cambridge University Press, 1990).

105 "Pragmatism without Method" (ORT, p. 75). This essay marks Rorty's most in-depth defense of this reading of pragmatism. Rorty's turn to romanticism is motivated in part by this desire to curb the ascendancy of science, which he took to be responsible for many of the assumptions that ultimately undid analytic philosophy.

106 In the preface to his final collection of essays, he reiterates this view: "From Dewey's point of view, the history of philosophy is best seen as a series of efforts to modify people's sense of who they are" (PCP, p. ix).

narrative and stories now take on an explicitly political cast. And his embrace of the romanticist paradigm is now less about getting traction against scientism than about a particular forward-looking orientation toward political and social change.

The broad contours of the political vision that take shape during this period change little over the rest of his career. The general direction of this constellation of ideas elaborates the Romantic, literary, and imaginative strands of his thought into a more concrete strategy of self-criticism and reform of Western societies for making them more responsive to suffering and injustice, both at home and abroad. What was until now merely a rough outline of the poeticized culture that follows in the wake of our waning commitments to rationalism, realism, and the correspondence theory of truth is more fully fleshed out. Hope replaces transcendental knowledge, a lightly sketched possible future takes the place of appeals to an independent reality, stories supplant rational arguments, proto-pragmatist Hume supersedes Kant, and abstract notions of humanity and rights are abandoned for felt, emotional identifications with particular communities. Rorty offers nothing short of a full-blown program for "sentimental education" designed to cultivate the kind of inclusive moral identity that not only would alter orientations of citizens and the self-image of Western societies, but reinvigorate the ability of democratic institutions to serve social justice.[107]

What is essential to understand about Rorty's fundamental orientation, including his reaction to the postmoderns, is that he sees "the culture of the liberal democracies as still providing a lot of opportunities for self-criticism and reform" (ORT, p. 15). Indeed, Rorty seems never to have wavered in his "hunch," as he put it, that "Western social political thought may have had the last *conceptual* revolution it needs" – namely, "J. S. Mill's suggestion that governments devote themselves to optimizing the balance between leaving people's private lives alone and preventing suffering" (CIS, p. 63).[108] Virtually all of Rorty's work since the late 1980s not devoted to specific debates with particular analytic philosophers is dedicated to deepening and defending this claim and rebutting suggestions to the contrary that Western liberal democracies are in need of some more radical transformation.

While this stance, not unfairly, has led some to see Rorty's project as a defense of the status quo, there also is a deeply democratic impulse at work here, which Rorty refers to as pragmatism's "anti-authoritarianism."[109] Although he never states it this flatly, for

---

107   In addition to the essays collected in this volume, see also "Unger, Castoriadis, and the Romance of a National Future" in EHO; "Movements and Campaigns" and "The Inspirational Value of Great Literature" in AOC; and "Who are We? Moral Universalism and Economic Triage," *Diogenes* 173 (Spring 1996): 3–15. During the early 1990s, Rorty wrote countless brief pieces on these topics outside of academic journals, particularly as they relate to education; see the comprehensive bibliography in TCF. "Education as Socialization and as Individualization" in *PSH* is a good representative example of his stance that "if pre-college education produces literate citizens and college education produces self-creating individuals, then questions about whether students are being taught the truth can safely be neglected," *PSH*, p. 118. See also, THE HUMANISTIC INTELLECTUAL, chapter 16, this volume.

108   In a footnote, Rorty clarifies, writing in the mid-1980s, that this does not mean "that the world has had the last *political* revolution it needs. It is hard to imagine a diminution of cruelty in countries like South Africa, Paraguay, and Albania without violent revolution," CIS, p. 63n21.

109   For the most direct presentation of this stance, see "Pragmatism as Anti-Authoritarianism," in John R. Shook and Joseph Margolis (eds.), *A Companion to Pragmatism* (Malden, MA: Blackwell

Rorty the commitments of traditional philosophy to realism, rationality, and truth, that ground its claim to epistemic privilege are simply anti-democratic, in the sense that they appeal to something outside of the necessarily ethnocentric web of beliefs and desires of any particular community in order to trump claims to pluralism and difference. Addressing the relation of his philosophical stance to democracy in the 1995 essay "Pragmatism as Romantic Polytheism," Rorty puts it this way:

> Although I do not think that there is an inferential path that leads from the antirepresenta-
> tionalist view of truth and knowledge common to Nietzsche, James, and Dewey either to
> democracy or antidemocracy, I do think there is a plausible inference from democratic
> convictions to such a view. (p. 449, this volume)

The reason why Rorty believes this inference is possible is because "devotion to democracy is unlikely to be wholehearted if you believe, as monotheists typically do, that we can have knowledge of an 'objective' ranking of human needs that can overrule the result of democratic consensus" (p. 449, this volume). Also a function of the "anti-authoritarian motif" he associates with Dewey and with pragmatism more generally is what Rorty calls the "pragmatist objection to fundamentalism." The pragmatist objection is not so much an intellectual but a moral objection to "attempting to circumvent the process of achieving democratic consensus about how to maximize happiness" by appealing to "the authority of something 'not ourselves'" (pp. 450, 454, this volume). This objection lies at the heart of his critique of foundationalism in philosophy and fundamentalism in religion.[110]

From changing philosophical vocabularies to changing society

A fundamental idea informing Rorty's understanding of the relation of philosophy to issues of democracy and social change is the notion that all of our commitments, philosophical and otherwise, are interwoven with our identity or "self-image," as individuals and as members of a community. The principal locus of change in Rorty's worldview is our self-image, understood as the way in which we give sense to our historical rootedness through narratives of self-understanding. In *Contingency, Irony, and Solidarity,* he terms this a person's "final vocabulary" – the "set of words" or "story of our lives" that we employ to justify our beliefs and actions (p. 279, this volume). If we can succeed in altering that self-image, particularly in ways more consistent with our political ideals, like equality, freedom, and justice, then anything can be changed. As early as his introduction to *The Linguistic Turn,* he had written of philosophy's function after the linguistic turn being primarily about changing our consciousness. As we have seen, Rorty's essays of the mid-1970s suggest the importance of narrative in constituting philosophers' identities: "the self-image of a philosopher," he held, "depends almost entirely on how he sees the history of philosophy" (CP, p. 41). Indeed, the traditional problems of philosophy, along with conceptions of philosophy as the discipline distinctively qualified to address them,

---

Publishing, 2006), pp. 257–66. Bernstein offers a good account of the points at which Rorty's defense of liberalism is "little more than an *apologia* for the status quo," *The New Constellation,* p. 233.

110   What Rorty espouses is a society where "both monotheism and the kind of metaphysics or science that purports to tell you what the world is *really* like are replaced with democratic politics" (p. 447, this volume). See also RELIGION IN THE PUBLIC SQUARE (chapter 28, this volume).

persist because of the fact that the professional philosopher's self-image depends upon his professional preoccupation with the image of the Mirror of Nature (p. 109, this volume). Similarly, Rorty appeals to "Dewey's version of the history of philosophy" because it is "designed to purify our self-image of all the remnants of the previous epochs in the history of metaphysics" (CP, p. 51).[111]

The problem facing philosophers, Rorty wrote in 1981, is that "we no longer have a story to tell about the relation between our problems and those of the past" (CP, p. 217).[112] In the decade after *Philosophy and the Mirror of Nature,* this is precisely what Rorty sought to do for Western culture: to tell a new story about its past in order to alter its members' self-image in the present. In line with his larger historical narrative about a broad cultural shift, his essays of the mid-1980s highlight the work of "liberating the culture" from metaphors that have been rendered "obsolete," not unlike the optical metaphors he critiqued in *Mirror.* The need for imaginative generation of new metaphors to take their place is what authorizes the prominent role of the poet in Rorty's post-metaphysical culture (p. 219, this volume). However, we will not be able to do this work until we get to "the point where we no longer worship *anything,* where we treat *nothing* as a quasi divinity, where we treat *everything* – our language, our conscience, our community – as a product of time and chance" (CIS, p. 22).[113] This is the stance he adopts in *Contingency, Irony, and Solidarity* and never abandons.

Rorty had already envisioned this larger project of social change at the close of his 1979 APA address, where he intimates the need to sketch out more fully what things would look like "if pragmatism became central to our culture and our self-image" (p. 121, this volume).[114] In "Solidarity or Objectivity?", he begins more explicitly "putting the issue in such moral and political terms, rather than epistemological or metaphilosophical terms" to make clear that "the question is not about how to define words like 'truth' or 'rationality' or 'knowledge' or 'philosophy', but about what self-image our society should have of itself" (p. 233, this volume). The only catch is that this involves going outside of the discipline of philosophy proper. As we have seen, to construct this story Rorty goes back in his essays of the mid-1970s to the nineteenth

---

111   Rorty's most grandiose statement on this topic comes in an essay on Robert Brandom: "But rhetoric matters, especially if one sees, as I do, the pragmatist tradition not just as clearing up little messes left behind by the great dead philosophers, but as contributing to a world-historical change in humanity's self-image" (TP, p. 132).

112   Interestingly, Rorty laments that the overriding shortcoming of the analytic tradition, despite its salutary emphasis on language, is that it "does not really give philosophy a new self-image" (p. 87, this volume).

113   Bernstein calls this the "dark side" of Rorty's stance: once we get to the point where everything is treated as contingent, then "anything can be made to look good or bad by redescription." So the flipside of Rorty's liberal hope is "the acute awareness that there is nothing we can rely on to determine which scenario will be our future" (*The New Constellation,* pp. 274–5). For Rorty's response to some of Bernstein's criticisms of his position, see "Thugs and Theorists: A Reply to Bernstein," *Political Theory* 15, no. 4 (1987): 564–80, where he argues that it is best if we treat "thugs as thugs and theorists as theorists," instead of appealing to philosophy or theory as a guard against inhumanity and evil. Because theories are not rooted in fixed essences, in Rorty's view they can offer no such assistance.

114   Interestingly, a decade and a half later Rorty would suggest that we think of pragmatism itself as "an attempt to alter our self-image" (p. 425, this volume).

century to identify a much broader conception of intellectual activity – namely, culture criticism. The moral of his new story is unambiguous: "Novels and poems are now the principal means by which a bright youth gains a self-image" (CP, p. 66). As we have seen, a decade later he makes a case for the novel's importance in "the struggle for freedom and equality" (p. 309, this volume).

Yet philosophy still has a role to play. The more expansive form of culture criticism that he saw developing out of the nineteenth century entails the work of "weaving" these new metaphors into "our communal web of beliefs and desires" (p. 219, this volume). The chief way in which philosophy serves social or cultural change is this kind of reweaving of beliefs. Philosophers can help us "to get past common sense, past common ways of speaking, past vocabularies; modifying them in order to take account of new developments like Enlightenment secularism, democratic governments, Newton, Copernicus, Darwin, Freud" (TCF, p. 47).[115] In the mid-1980s, Rorty describes what he was up to in this way: "I shall try to show that the vocabulary of Enlightenment rationalism, although it was essential to the beginnings of liberal democracy, has become an impediment to the preservation and progress of democratic societies." Better suited to the latter endeavor is a vocabulary organized around "metaphor and self-creation rather than around notions of truth, rationality, and moral obligation" (CIS, p. 44). Rorty's work aims to provide such a vocabulary.

Redescription as inquiry, as politics, and as alternative to argument

One of the corollaries of Rorty's vision of a post-philosophical culture no longer demarcated by Kantian–Weberian autonomous spheres is a change in the nature of inquiry toward what he calls 'redescription'. Like so much else in his oeuvre, this change is informed by his longstanding views about the unavailability of fixed, widely accepted criteria. "A poeticized, or post-metaphysical, culture," he explains in an interview, "is one in which the imperative that is common to religion and metaphysics – to find an ahistorical, transcultural matrix for one's thinking, something into which everything can fit, independent of one's time and place – has dried up and blown away" (TCF, p. 46).[116] If for historicist reasons universal transcultural criteria are unavailable to us as culturally constituted beings, the task, then, is to reconceive of inquiry as a "criterionless muddling through" – or more formally, "a Quinean picture of inquiry as the continual reweaving of a web of beliefs rather than as the application of criteria to cases" (p. 231, this volume).[117]

Under different names this work of redescribing was a part of Rorty's thinking since his earliest published work, where he calls attention to the fact that "any metaphysical, epistemological, or axiological arguments can be defeated by redefinition" – the philosopher's ability to "change the rules" of the game largely by altering the relevant

---

115   Here Rorty refers to this work as "what William James called 'weaving the old and the new together', in order to assimilate weird things like Freudian psychology with moral common sense." For Rorty's own attempt to do this, see FREUD AND MORAL REFLECTION (chapter 14, this volume).

116   Getting rid of this imperative, he asserts, would make it a lot easier to think of "the entire culture, from physics to poetry, as a single, continuous, seamless activity in which the divisions are merely institutional and pedagogical" (ORT, p. 76).

117   As we shall see below, this notion of "criterionless muddling through" characterizes what he refers to as "cultural politics" in his most recent work.

criteria.[118] As he later establishes in "Philosophy as Science, as Metaphor, and as Politics," this approach looks to the imagination, rather than to inference, for the kind of "recontextualization," as he once called it, that happens at certain points in the reweaving process, not unlike what takes place in Kuhnian periods of revolutionary science.[119] Kuhn is important here because taking what Rorty calls a "post-Kuhnian" view of science gets us beyond the notion of "sticking within a logical space which forms an intrinsically privileged context" (ORT, pp. 95–6). The need to give up the idea that there exist such privileged contexts outside of the webs of belief that constitute us is central to Rorty's pragmatism. There is no getting outside of these webs for Rorty; the notion that we can is a function of a conception of rational inquiry authorized by the assumption that everything can be translated into a single, widely available context and vocabulary accepted by any rational inquirer. Without privileged contexts and accepted criteria, all we can do is redescribe things and compare one redescription to another.[120]

In "Nineteenth Century Idealism and Twentieth Century Textualism," Rorty takes both "Kuhn's romantic philosophy of science" and "[Harold] Bloom's philosophy of romantic poetry" to be consistent with the pragmatist insight of Nietzsche and James that "a new and useful vocabulary is just *that,* not a sudden unmediated vision of things or texts as they are." To the pragmatist, he asserts, "there is no interesting difference between tables and texts, between protons and poems […] these are *all* just permanent possibilities for use, and thus for redescription, reinterpretation, manipulation" (p. 132, this volume). This is the context of Rorty's embrace of Bloom's notion of "strong misreading." Once we are outside the realm of privileged contexts where the application of criteria can settle issues, argumentation loses its traction, as does representationalism and

118   Rorty, "Recent Metaphilosophy," pp. 299–301. Here Rorty states that "philosophical argumentation is not a search for truth, but an occasion for inspiration." Prefiguring what he would do in his later work, he points out that "nothing remains but to make a virtue of necessity and to study this process of redefinition itself." Rorty's first use of the actual term "redescription" seems to have been the 1970 essay "Cartesian Epistemology and Changes in Ontology," where in good historicist fashion he shows how various insights in ontology consisted in a "redescription" that had been brought about by the acceptance or nonacceptance of certain contingent premises. While he does not yet use the term to describe his own approach, he establishes the importance of the primary idea he espouses in the essay, the Principle of the Relativity of Incorrigibility, noting that he has "not yet given arguments for its truth." He then admits, "I do not know how to do this save by rebutting objections." Intimating what seems a very pragmatic approach, he continues, "Instead of dreaming up some objections and then knocking them down, I want to introduce a new topic into the discussion – one which provides an illustration of the way in which this Principle can be put to work in practice" (pp. 278–9, 284).

119   On the idea of recontextualization, a term which Rorty seems to have abandoned for "redescription," see "Inquiry as Recontextualization," in ORT, pp. 93–110. Part of the reason he thinks it appropriate to refer to our culture as an increasingly poeticized one is because "the desire to dream up as many new contexts as possible" for our beliefs in his view happens more in art and literature than in the natural sciences (p. 110).

120   To be clear, Rorty holds that "there is nothing wrong with science, there is only something wrong with the attempt to divinize it, the attempt characteristic of realistic philosophy." What such realism amounts to in this context is "the idea that inquiry is a matter of find out the nature of something which lies outside the web of beliefs and desires" that constitute human beings (p. 238, this volume).

the correspondence theory of truth. As Rorty explains, a strong misreading is when a critic "asks neither the author nor the text about their intentions but simply beats the text into a shape which will serve his own purpose." Whether it is a "great physicist or a great critic," from time to time this process yields "a new vocabulary which enables us to do a lot of new and marvelous things" (pp. 131, 133, this volume).

To illustrate this criterion-less view of intellectual progress, Rorty gives examples from the history of philosophy:

> Hobbes did not have theological arguments against Dante's world-picture; Kant had only a very bad scientific argument for the phenomenal character of science; Nietzsche and James did not have epistemological arguments for pragmatism. Each of these thinkers presented us with a new form of intellectual life, and asked us to compare its advantages with the old. (p. 135, this volume)

By *Contingency, Irony, and Solidarity*, redescription is virtually a bona fide method for Rorty himself. "Conforming to my own precepts," he tells readers early on,

> I am not going to offer arguments against the vocabulary I want to replace. Instead, I am going to try to make the vocabulary I favor look attractive by showing how it may be used to describe a variety of topics. (CIS, p. 9)

His strategy is "changing the subject, rather than granting the objector his choice of weapons and terrain by meeting his criticisms head-on" (CIS, p. 44).

Redescription for Rorty is now much more than a method of inquiry: "speaking differently, rather than arguing well," on his view is "the chief instrument of cultural change" (CIS, p. 7). In a word, redescription is political; redescriptions have the power to change our minds. In a more recent essay, he sums up the limits of argument via Shelley: "the sort of truth that is the product of successful argument cannot, Shelley thought, improve our moral condition" (p. 484, this volume). The human use of the imagination as "the cutting edge of cultural evolution" is what enables us to make the future richer than the past. Indeed, the "ability to redescribe the familiar in unfamiliar terms" is what unites Newton and Christ, Freud and Marx (p. 432, this volume). When it comes to social change, then, if we only work toward those programs that can be supported by arguments, in Rorty's view we are limited to that which can be made sense of within existing assumptions via currently accepted criteria. Without the political equivalent of the moves of Kuhnian revolutionary science, we will never alter our self-image, and thus will close off the possibility of a previously unimagined future.[121]

The problem with argument as a means of spurring belief change is that it gets its traction through appeals to antecedently accepted criteria, by "working according to the rules of some familiar language-game, some familiar way of describing the current situation." Because of this recourse to familiar vocabularies, Rorty thought that arguments "often just get in the way of attempts to create an unfamiliar vocabulary, a new *lingua franca* for those trying to transform what they see around them" (EHO, pp.189, 181). This is why he appealed to the imagination as the engine of moral and intellectual

---

121 On this issue see the under-appreciated essay, "Unger, Castoriadis, and the Romance of a National Future" (EHO, pp. 177–92). As we have seen above, it is not coincidental that Rorty once referred to pragmatism as "left-wing Kuhnianism" (ORT, p. 38).

progress. In ways that recall the breaking of the crust of convention that Dewey thought so essential, for Rorty the fruits of the imagination – something "unforeseeable and passionate" – are capable of disrupting what Roberto Unger calls "frozen politics," which Rorty glosses as familiar language-games that "serve to legitimate, and make seem inevitable, precisely the forms of social life [...] from which we hope to break free." Argumentative procedures, in Rorty's view, are "not relevant to the situation in which nothing familiar works and in which people are desperately (on the couch, on the barricades) looking for something, no matter how familiar, which might work" (EHO, pp. 189–90).[122]

Rorty's defense of the imagination over reasoned argument emanates from his view that social change is constrained by the appeal to "rational acceptability by the standards of the existing community" that argument entails. Acts of "courage and imagination," then, become "the only recourse" for moral progress beyond the limits of present beliefs (pp. 340–1, this volume). In essays of the 1990s, such as "Feminism and Pragmatism," Rorty links this stance more directly to the pursuit of social justice. He defends pragmatism for its receptivity toward appeals "to courage and imagination rather than to putatively neutral criteria" (p. 343, this volume). By contrast, "universalist philosophers," he argues, "assume, with Kant, that all the logical space necessary for moral deliberation is now available – that all important truths about right and wrong can not only be stated but made plausible, in language already to hand." Without expanding this logical space through new metaphors and ways of talking, "a voice saying something never heard before" may be heard, but it will lack resonance because it falls outside of the established meanings that delimit this space, particularly in cases where this space is defined by "the language of the oppressor" (p. 331, this volume). Philosophy's specific role, as he sees it at this point, is simply "to clear the road for prophets and poets, to make intellectual life a bit simpler and safer for those who have visions of new communities." Only once this space has been cleared can the formation of new moral identities no longer linked to injustice and oppression be forged from "terms not presently available" to those who are suffering (pp. 340, 347, this volume).

The notion of philosophy as "cultural politics" that comes to the foreground in Rorty's last collection of essays puts an explicitly political label on the work that he saw philosophy doing for some time. Cultural politics aims to subvert the idea inherent in Enlightenment rationalism that "persistent argument will lead all inquirers to the same set of beliefs" (p. 478, this volume). In this new connotation, which differs from the pejorative meaning attributed to the phrase in *Achieving Our Country,* cultural politics amounts to a catch-all phrase for the conversation or inquiry that takes place in the absence of agreed-upon criteria to govern argument. The difference that makes a difference is that the lack of agreed-upon criteria means there can be no final resolution of any problem. Instead, for philosophy to "intervene" in cultural politics means to join poets and other intellectuals in offering novel vocabularies and new ways of looking at the world, but also to reconcile seemingly incompatible existing visions. In the process, all it

122   Here Rorty is responding to Habermas's claim that "[c]ommunicative reason finds its criteria in the argumentative procedures for directly or indirectly redeeming claims to propositional truth, normative rightness, subjective truthfulness, and aesthetic harmony," quoted in EHO, p. 189n41. For his part, Dewey cited as the function of art and the imagination "to break through the crust of conventionalized and routine consciousness." *The Public and its Problems* (Athens, OH: Swallow Press, 1954), p. 183.

can hope to do is to change the course of humanity's ongoing conversation about "what to do with itself." Those forms of intellectual endeavor not engaged in helping along this process of cultural change by asking what difference, if any, an idea or vocabulary or proposal will make to our "social hopes, programs of action, and prophecies of a better future," simply may not be worth doing (PCP, pp. ix–x).

VII. The Challenges and the Promise of Rorty's Poetic, Post-Metaphysical Liberalism

One of the greatest challenges of Rorty's project is liberating Enlightenment liberalism and its lofty political ideals from their unwieldy foundations in rationality and objectivity in such a way that "our traditional liberal habits and hopes" survive. This effort of recovery is what animates his unexpected defense of the virtues of liberal democracy in his first round of post-*Mirror* essays in the mid-1980s. As we have seen, the primary way he does this is by turning to pragmatism – in particular to Dewey. Because of his critique of presuppositionless inquiry in the service of rationally agreed-upon criteria, he cannot justify his turn to pragmatism or the liberal habits and hopes he espouses in traditional fashion via transcultural rationality. The only tenable justification is a circular one – that is, a pragmatist justification. The example Rorty offers is Winston's Churchill's defense of democracy as the worst form of government except for all the other forms that have been tried so far. This justification, Rorty tells us,

> is not by reference to a criterion, but by reference to various detailed practical advantages. It is circular only in that the terms of praise used to describe liberal societies will be drawn from the vocabulary of the liberal societies themselves. (p. 234, this volume)

In the rest of this section I outline a number of areas where Rorty's attempt to retain a conception of Enlightenment politics without its philosophical justification has been vulnerable to critique: his defense of a public–private split, his account of contingent moral obligation and program of sentimental education, his attempt to reconcile ethnocentrism and pluralism, and the tension between cultural and "real" politics. These areas reveal not only the challenges of his post-metaphysical liberalism but its promise as well; even when problematic or imperfectly resolved, the fundamental issues Rorty tackles underscores areas in need of greater attention by intellectuals, particularly in the West.

A firm distinction between public and private

A popular target of Rorty's critics has been his insistence on the need for a "firm distinction" between public and private.[123] Although he had examined arguments about public and private in the context of philosophy of language debates twenty years earlier,

---

123   See, among others, Richard J. Bernstein, "Rorty's Liberal Utopia," *Social Research* 57, no. 1 (1990): 31–72; Nancy Fraser, "Solidarity or Singularity? Richard Rorty between Romanticism and Technology," *Praxis International* 8, no. 3 (1988): 257–72; Thomas McCarthy, "Private Irony and Public Decency: Richard Rorty's New Pragmatism," *Critical Inquiry* 16, no. 2 (1990): 355–70; Scott Roulier, "Beyond Richard Rorty's Public: Relegitimizing the Quest for Transcendence," *Journal of Interdisciplinary Studies* 9, no. 1/2 (1997): 19–38; Richard Shusterman, "Pragmatism and

his first explicit defenses of the need to maintain this divide appear in the mid-1980s. The importance of this divide comes to the forefront in *Contingency, Irony, and Solidarity* and remains present throughout his work.[124] The public–private split occupies a substantive place in Rorty's political theory, if you will, embodied in his combination of "private irony and liberal hope." Being an ironist when it comes to our "final vocabulary" – the set of words through which we make our actions and beliefs cohere – means recognizing and accepting the contingency of this vocabulary, along with its openness to continual revision and "redescription." Keeping irony private ensures that our ongoing projects of self-creation do not cause us to lose sight of the importance of working to diminish cruelty and suffering in the world, given the contingent nature of such public liberal commitments. The possibility that one can fully embrace the radicalism of postmodern philosophical critiques and still be a reformist liberal becomes the linchpin of Rorty's project – namely, that we can divide ourselves up into "a private self-creator and a public liberal," such that we can be "in alternate moments, Nietzsche and J. S. Mill" (pp. 279, 288, this volume).[125]

The need to insist upon this divide is a manifestation of a deeper tension in Rorty's thought, a tension that emanates from his desire to defend both Enlightenment liberalism and a poeticized culture that continually threatens to undermine the primacy of its political goals. On the one hand, Rorty seeks to mobilize what he refers to in his last collection of essays as "pragmatism's potential for producing radical cultural change" (PCP, p. ix) and to embrace the possibility of an undefined future open to the advent of imaginatively-generated new vocabularies, new conceptions of community – even "a new culture" (p. 382, this volume). On the other hand, he wants to protect the liberal values and practices to which he is deeply committed by insisting that "Western social and political thought may have had the last *conceptual* revolution it needs." When it comes to those who seem to suggest otherwise, like a Foucault or Derrida, Rorty makes it a point to establish that their critiques are counterproductive: "contemporary liberal society already contains the institutions for his own improvement" (CIS, p. 63). Specifically, he asserts that "J. S. Mill's suggestion that governments devote themselves to optimizing

---

Liberalism Between Dewey and Rorty," *Political Theory* 22, no. 2 (1994): 391–413; Keith Topper, "Richard Rorty, Liberalism, and the Politics of Redescription," *American Political Science Review* 89, no. 4 (1995): 945–75; John R. Wallach, "Liberals, Communitarians, and the Tasks of Political Theory," *Political Theory* 15, no. 4 (1987): 581–611; Sheldon S. Wolin, "Democracy in the Discourse of Postmodernism," *Social Research* 57, no. 1 (1990): 5–30; and essays by Jo Burrows, and Charles B. Guignon, and David R. Hiley, in Malachowski (ed.), *Reading Rorty*.

124   See "Mind–Body Identity, Privacy, and Categories." For references to this split in his later work, see, for example, PHILSOPHY AS A TRANSITIONAL GENRE (p. 485, this volume).

125   Rorty's softest statement of this public–private split comes in a 1995 interview: "I don't think private beliefs can be fenced off; they leak through, so to speak, and influence the way one behaves toward other people. What I had in mind in making the distinction was this: the language of citizenship, of public responsibility, of participation in the affairs of the state, is not going to be an original, self-created language. Some people, the ones we think of as poets or makers, want to invent a new language – because they want to invent a new self. And there's a tendency to try to see that poetic effort as synthesizable with the activity of taking part in public discourse. I don't think the two are synthesizable, but that doesn't mean that the one doesn't eventually interact with the other" (TCF, p. 50). See also, TROTSKY AND THE WILD ORCHIDS (chapter 32, this volume).

the balance between leaving people's private lives alone and preventing suffering seems to me pretty much the last word" (CIS, p. 63).

The problem is that Rorty employs the public–private divide itself to ensure that there will be no new conceptual revolutions that might challenge Mill's "last word." His admonition to liberal societies in an early chapter of *Contingency, Irony, and Solidarity*, previously published in 1986, is this: "*Privatize* the Nietzschean–Sartrean–Foucauldian attempt at authenticity and purity, in order to prevent yourself from slipping into a political attitude which will lead you to think that there is some social goal more important than avoiding cruelty" (CIS, p. 65). From this point forward Rorty becomes more explicit about his attempts, as he describes them, "to separate what is sometimes called 'post-modernism' from political radicalism" – that is, to "disengage polemics against 'the metaphysics of presence' from polemics against 'bourgeois ideology', and criticisms of Enlightenment rationalism and universalism from criticisms of liberal, reformist political thought."[126] In this way he can insulate liberal reformism from the more radical implications of postmodern theory, allowing him to cordon off not only Derrida, Foucault, and de Man, but also to demarcate Kierkegaard, Nietzsche, Baudelaire, Proust, Heidegger, and Nabokov, on the one hand, from Marx, Mill, Dewey, Habermas, and Rawls, on the other (CIS, p. xiv). The logic of this firm distinction between public and private allows him to embrace all that was anti-Cartesian and antirepresentationalist in Nietzsche, Derrida, and Foucault, while at the same time safeguarding his commitment to liberal culture and values, including his Deweyan sense of the importance of fellow-feeling.[127]

For his part, Rorty was aware of this tension almost a decade before *Contingency, Irony, and Solidarity*. In "Nineteenth Century Idealism and Twentieth Century Textualism" he perceptively identifies the problem facing both textualism and pragmatism as this: "the stimulus to the intellectual's private moral imagination provided by his strong misreadings [...] is purchased at the price of his separation from his fellow-humans." The pragmatist claim, which is shared by textualism, that "all vocabularies, even that of our own liberal imagination, are temporary historical resting places" means that there is no "antecedent morality" or "common vocabulary" to which we can appeal to translate the fruits of the private moral imagination to public discourse. Because he embraces the historical contingency of such vocabularies, Rorty concludes that the primary

---

126   Rorty, "Thugs and Theorists," p. 564. Responding to critics of these attempts, in this essay he outlines eight theses of a political credo that he believes "we" liberals share.

127   Rorty's reading of Derrida, whose approach he found interesting and imaginative from his first reading in the mid-1970s for manifesting so many of the qualities he valued himself, highlights his blurring the line between philosophy and literature, his generating new metaphors, and of course his insouciance toward traditional philosophy. See, for example, "Derrida on Language, Being, and Abnormal Philosophy," *Journal of Philosophy* 74, no. 11 (1977): 673–81; and "Philosophy as a Kind of Writing," CP, pp. 90–109. Even into the mid-1980s Rorty remains on the whole positive toward Derrida, though he distinguishes the "constructive, bad side" from the "deconstructive, good side" of his work (CP, p. 99) – see "Deconstruction and Circumvention" and "Two Meanings of 'Logocentrism'" in EHO. By the late 1980s, Rorty is insisting that Derrida be treated as "a private writer – writing for the delight of us insiders who share his background, who find the same rather esoteric things as funny or beautiful or moving as he does," rather than "a writer on a public mission, someone who gives us weapons with which to subvert 'institutionalized knowledge' and thus social institutions," EHO, p. 120. See also DE MAN AND THE CULTURAL LEFT (CHAPTER 18, this volume).

objection to textualism is "moral" rather than "epistemological" in nature (p. 135, this volume). Indeed, as he moves outside the analytic and pragmatist traditions in the mid-1970s and starts reading Continental thinkers sympathetic to the spirit of his own epistemological critiques of the Plato–Kant tradition, like Derrida and Foucault, his familiar method of highlighting parallels and shared resonances between apparently disparate traditions leads him to the similarities between Nietzsche and James, and between Dewey and Foucault, particularly on epistemological grounds.[128] Yet as his focus turns to sketching the political consequences of his philosophical critiques, these thinkers become strange bedfellows.[129] So he draws a distinction that cuts across the pragmatism–textualism continuity, between the pragmatism of James and Bloom, on the one hand, and the pragmatism of Nietzsche and Foucault, on the other. In sum, "Bloom's way of dealing with texts preserves our sense of a common human finitude," while Foucault's does not. Rorty ends "Nineteenth Century Idealism and Twentieth Century Textualism" on this note:

> But I do not know how to back up this preference with argument, or even with a precise account of the relevant differences. To do so would involve a full-scale discussion of the possibility of combining private fulfillment, self-realization, with public morality, a concern for justice. (p. 137, this volume)

The publication of his next book nine years later offers this full-scale discussion. Picking up precisely where he left off in "Nineteenth Century Idealism and Twentieth Century Textualism," CIS opens with the following sentence:

> The attempt to fuse the public and the private lies behind both Plato's attempt to answer the question "Why is it in one's interest to be just?" and Christianity's claim that perfect self-realization can be attained through service to others.

---

128   See for example, "On my view, James and Dewey were not only waiting at the end of the dialectical road which analytic philosophy traveled, but are waiting at the end of the road which, for example, Foucault and Deleuze are currently traveling" (CP, p. xviii). Rorty goes on to put it this way: "textualism adds nothing save an extra metaphor to the romanticism of Hegel and the pragmatism of James and Nietzsche" (p. 134, this volume). In general, the two key essays here are NINETEENTH CENTURY IDEALISM AND TWENTIETH CENTURY TEXTUALISM (chapter 5, this volume) and "Method, Social Science, and Social Hope," in CP.
129   The most obvious instance of this dissonance is the somewhat jarring title of his 1983 essay, "Postmodernist Bourgeois Liberalism," a label he soon disavowed. In the introduction to EHO, he notes dryly that while he had sometimes used the term 'postmodern' himself "in the rather narrow sense defined by Lyotard as 'distrust of metanarratives […] I now wish that I had not." Because the term had been "so over-used that it is causing more trouble than it is worth," he now proposes "post-Nietzschean" instead to describe Heidegger, Derrida, and others. But at this point (1990) he leaves no ambiguity: while Nietzsche "was as good an anti-Cartesian, antirepresenta-tionalist, and antiessentialist as Dewey," Nietzsche's version of pragmatism "had, to be sure, little to do with the social hopes characteristic of James and Dewey" (EHO, pp. 1–2). A few years later he laments, "I seem doomed to be referred to as a 'postmodernist', even though the only time I used that term – in the title of an article called 'Postmodernist Bourgeois Liberalism' – I was trying to make a joke. No matter how much I squirm, I now cannot get the label off" (Rorty and His Critics, p. 214n1).

Two paragraphs later he gives us the conclusion at which he had arrived, introducing a stance that would become a mainstay of his political thought:

> ...there is no way to bring self-creation together with justice at the level of theory. The vocabulary of self-creation is necessarily private, unshared, unsuited to argument. The vocabulary of justice is necessarily public and shared, a medium for argumentative exchange. (CIS, pp. xiii–xiv)[130]

One of the things that had intervened in the interim is Rorty's engagement with Freud, who has an unexpected significance in the development of Rorty's understanding of morality and moral reflection. It is in his discussion of Freud that Rorty first distinguishes between "public morality," which entails "the attempt to be just in one's treatment of others" and refers to the morality that is "codifiable in statutes and maxims," and "private morality," which is about the development of character, "the search for perfection in oneself" (p. 268, this volume).[131] The ultimate conclusion Rorty takes from his reflection on Freud is that this morality of character has nothing to do with politics or our relations with others. On the contrary, he observes that Freud "diminishes our ability to take seriously much of the traditional jargon of both liberalism and radicalism – notions such as 'human right' and 'autonomy' and slogans such as 'man will prevail' and 'trust the instincts of the masses'," since they rest on the Aristotelian attempt to establish a center for the self (p. 277, this volume). So while Rorty warmly welcomes Freud's decentering of the essential self, he warns of the dangers associated with this decentering for public life.

Whether they come from Freud, Nietzsche, Foucault, or Derrida, delimiting public from private is Rorty's way of controlling for threats to solidarity and "common human concerns." At the same time, because the private imagination is the creative engine of the new metaphors and novel vocabularies his project invites, some transaction between private and public seems necessary. This tension, which is even more pronounced in the idea of philosophy as cultural politics, remains largely unresolved in Rorty's thought. Pinning the hope for social and political change on a rather slim reed, all he is able to claim, given his strictures on the public and the private, is that "poetic, artistic, philosophical, scientific, or political progress results from the accidental coincidence of a private obsession with a public need" (CIS, p. 37).

Contingent moral obligation and sentimental education

At times, Rorty's poeticized, post-metaphysical culture seems to promote irony and aesthetic play without much else.[132] Defending not only the philosophical but the political viability of contingent, nonfoundational commitments is the *sine qua non* of his political project.

130   See also TROTSKY AND THE WILD ORCHIDS (chapter 32, this volume).

131   While FREUD AND MORAL REFLECTION (chapter 14, this volume) marks his deepest engagement, the first appearances of Freud in Rorty's published work come in his early essays on Derrida: "Derrida on Language, Being, and Abnormal Philosophy," *Journal of Philosophy* 74, no. 11 (1977): 673–81; and "Philosophy as a Kind of Writing," CP, pp. 90–109. In *Mirror*, Rorty praises both Marx and Freud for helping us see "the change in behavior which results from change in self-description" (p. 389, this volume).

132   See, for example, the criticisms of Richard J. Bernstein, "One Step Forward, Two Steps Backward: Rorty on Liberal Democracy and Philosophy," *Political Theory* 15, no. 4 (1987): 538–63;

By Rorty's own lights, the "fundamental premise" of CIS, his most original and constructive book, is that "a belief can still regulate action, can still be thought worth dying for, among people who are quite aware that this belief is caused by nothing deeper than contingent historical circumstance" (CIS, p. 189).[133] What this defense requires is accounting for a strong sense of responsibility and moral obligation with no grounding save an historicist, contingent, ethnocentric sense of "us" (p. 229, this volume).[134] This endeavor generates the most ambitious dimensions of Rorty's vision – nothing short of "recreating human beings," as we shall see – which prompts questions about the viability and limits of his project.

Rorty takes up these issues most explicitly in the mid-1990s, where accounting for a sense of moral obligation within an anti-essentialist and anti-metaphysical culture comes to the forefront.[135] The particular language of "edification" Rorty adopts in *Philosophy and the Mirror of Nature,* where he argues that "edifying discourse is *supposed* to be abnormal, to take us out of our old selves by the power of strangeness, to aid us in becoming new beings," never quite takes hold in his thought (p. 91, this volume). Yet the theme persists, emerging most visibly in "Ethics Without Principles" where Rorty suggests that "we think of pragmatism as an attempt to alter our self-image" (p. 425, this volume). As we have seen, changing the way we understand ourselves through the stories we weave to make sense of our lives is at the heart of Rorty's conception of human progress. What authorizes this malleability is Rorty's understanding of the self, following Daniel Dennett, as "a center of narrative gravity," rather than a fixed essence or essential human nature. Rorty explicitly links such change to the moral realm: "Moral development in the individual, and moral progress in the human species as a whole, is a matter of re-marking human selves so as to enlarge the variety of the relationships which constitute those selves." This process of "recreating human beings" obtains not by making people more rational, but by "increasing sensitivity, increasing responsiveness to the needs of a larger and larger variety of people and things." For pragmatists, the appeal to nonhuman notions

---

Ronald Beiner, "Richard Rorty's Liberalism," *Critical Review* 7, no. 1 (1993): 15–31; Robert Kane, "The Ends of Metaphysics," *International Philosophical Quarterly* 33, no. 132 (1993): 413–28; Berel Lang, "Rorty Scrivener," *Salmagundi* no. 88–89 (1990/1991): 127–48; Alexander Nehamas, "A Touch of the Poet," *Raritan* 10, no. 1 (1990): 104–25; Jacques Poulain, "Irony Is Not Enough: The Limits of the Pragmatist Accommodation of Aesthetics to Human Life," *Poetics Today* 14 (1993): 165–80; Charlene Haddock Seigfried, "Weaving Chaos into Order: A Radically Pragmatic Aesthetics," *Philosophy and Literature* 14, no. 1 (1990): 108–16; and Richard Shusterman, "Postmodern Ethics and the Art of Living," in his *Pragmatist Aesthetics: Living Beauty, Rethinking Art* (Cambridge, MA: Blackwell, 1992), pp. 236–61.

133   Bernstein notes that "Without this 'fundamental premise' his entire project falls apart" (*The New Constellation,* p. 280).

134   As he sums up in an interview, "I think we ought to be able to be responsible to our interlocutors without being responsible to reason or the world or the demand of universality or anything else" (TCF, p. 48). For Rorty's attempts to defend this notion of community, see chapters 12, 13, and 26 in this volume: SOLIDARITY OR OBJECTIVITY?; THE PRIORITY OF DEMOCRACY TO PHILOSOPHY; and JUSTICE AS A LARGER LOYALTY. See also "The Contingency of Community" and "Solidarity" in CIS. For a critique of the limits of Rorty's conception of community, see Voparil, *Richard Rorty,* chapter 4.

135   See for example, ETHICS WITHOUT PRINCIPLES and JUSTICE AS A LARGER LOYALTY (chapters 25 and 26, this volume). For a sustained discussion of his antiessentialism see "A World without Substances or Essences" in PSH.

of Truth or Moral Goodness should be replaced with this idea of "getting more and more human beings into our community" (p. 429, this volume; PSH 82).

The series of lectures Rorty gave in Vienna and Paris in 1993 entitled "Hope in Place of Knowledge," which sketch his mature "version of pragmatism," as he termed it, contain his most suggestive phrase for this conception of social and political change: "Emerson self-creation on a communal scale" (p. 421, this volume).[136] For the first time, Rorty highlights the particularly American quality of pragmatism, using this as a basis for distinguishing James and Dewey from Peirce. These lectures present the recognizable motifs of substituting hope for knowledge, imagination for certainty, and the idea of a better human future for notions of reality, reason, and nature (PSH, p. 27).[137] Drawing on Dewey, he describes both pragmatism and America as "expressions of a hopeful, melioristic, experimental frame of mind" (PSH, p. 24). From this point forward, both Emerson and Whitman become fixtures in Rorty's writing. Contrasting the European "metaphysics of presence" with Dewey's "new" metaphysic of democracy as a "relation of man and his experience in nature," Rorty argues that "philosophy should stop trying to provide reassurance and instead encourage what Emerson called 'self-reliance'" (PSH, pp. 28, 34). The spirit of these lectures aligns with Dewey's view in *Reconstruction in Philosophy* of philosophy as an instrument of change rather than conservation of the status quo, repudiating the idea of philosophy as, in Dewey's words, "a substitute for custom as the source and guarantor of higher moral and social values," as well as James's notion that "a philosophy is the expression of a man's intimate character."[138] Within this tradition, the power of ideas emanates not from foundational or metaphysical grounding, but from being embodied in a concrete life and lived. In other words, what gives our convictions weight and makes them more than randomly-arrived-at groundless assertions is that they are *our* convictions, rooted in our personal vision of the world and its possibilities.[139]

136   The three lectures are "Truth Without Correspondence to Reality," "A World without Substances or Essences," and "Ethics Without Principles." He refers to it as "my own version of pragmatism" since it "makes no pretense of being faithful to the thoughts of either James or Dewey (much less Peirce, whom I barely mention). Rather, it offers my own, sometimes idiosyncratic, restatements of Jamesian and Deweyan themes" (PSH, p. xiii).
137   See also "Philosophy and the Future," in Saatkamp (ed.), *Rorty & Pragmatism,* pp. 197–205.
138   Rorty quotes this passage from Dewey (p. 419, this volume); James's phrase is from *A Pluralistic Universe,* John J. McDermott (ed.), *The Writings of William James: A Comprehensive Edition* (Chicago: University of Chicago Press, 1977), p. 489. See also James, "The Present Dilemma in Philosophy," in McDermott, *Writings,* pp. 362–76. When I once asked Rorty directly about this, he replied, "I never had much use for James' claim that 'a philosophy is an expression of a man's intimate character'. To be sure, people choose philosophers, as they choose lovers, spouses, music and poems, because of the idiosyncrasies of their own genes and circumstances. But some people have no philosophies, just as some people don't read poetry and some never fall in love. If one extends the term 'philosophy' so widely that everybody gets to have one, the connection between 'philosophy' in that extended sense and the topics that we philosophy professors talk about becomes so thin as to be invisible" (email correspondence with the author, October 31, 2006).
139   For more on this idea, and on this Emersonian dimension of pragmatism, see Amanda Anderson, "Pragmatism and Character," *Critical Inquiry* 29, no. 2 (2003): 282–301; Cornel West, *The American Evasion of Philosophy: A Genealogy of Pragmatism* (Madison: University of Wisconsin Press, 1989); Richard Shusterman, *Practicing Philosophy: Pragmatism and the Philosophical Life* (New York: Routledge, 1997); Russell B. Goodman, *American Philosophy and the Romantic*

Broadly speaking, Rorty tackles the contingency of moral obligation by outlining three areas of moral and ethical life in need of cultivation: an ability to identify with others, an emotional attachment to the societies and cultures of which we are a part (whether pride or shame), and a sense of self-reliance. In "Human Rights, Rationality, and Sentimentality," he establishes the importance of sympathetic identification, holding that:

> The best, and probably the only, argument for putting foundationalism behind us is the one I have already suggested: it would be more efficient to do so, because it would let us concentrate our energies on manipulating sentiments, on sentimental education. (p. 358, this volume)

Here too Rorty's defends this approach on pragmatic grounds of "efficiency" and "causal efficacy"; the cultivation of sympathy simply produces better results than appeals to Kantian ideas of "unconditional moral obligation" (pp. 355, 362, this volume). Sentimental education is Rorty's term for the work done by narrative rather than theory. If philosophy's job is to clear the road, the constructive work that this makes possible is accomplished in Rorty's view not through increased moral knowledge – hence not traditional philosophy – but through "sad and sentimental stories" (p. 355, this volume). The vehicles of sentimental education include "genres such as the ethnography, the journalist's report, the comic book, the docudrama, and especially the novel" (CIS, p. xvi). These forms manipulate sentiments simply by getting us to imagine ourselves in the shoes of the oppressed. The goal is to make our moral identities more inclusive by expanding the reference of what we mean by "our kind of people" and "people like us." For Rorty, "everything turns on who counts as a fellow human being" (p. 359, this volume).

In the absence of universal norms with transcultural moral validity, on Rorty's view justice too is best understood in terms of our moral identities. As with moral progress, becoming more just means cultivating a "new and larger loyalty" to an even more inclusive "global moral community," ideally as wide as "all living creatures on our home planet." Because of our ethnocentrism, this project must build "a community of trust between ourselves and others" beginning from where we are (pp. 441, 443, this volume). The way to do so is by minimizing one difference at a time:

> ...the difference between Christians and Muslims in a particular village in Bosnia, the difference between blacks and whites in a particular town in Alabama, the difference between gays and straights in a particular Catholic congregation in Quebec. The hope is to sew such groups together with a thousand little stitches – to invoke a thousand little commonalities between their members, rather than specify one great big one, their common humanity. (pp. 431–2, this volume)

As before, what is required is "imaginative power" – the ability to redescribe the familiar in familiar terms so as to create "new conceptions of possible communities" – rather than getting closer to "the True or the Good or the Right" (p. 432, this volume).

Tradition (New York: Cambridge University Press, 1992); and Richard Poirier, *The Renewal of Literature* (New York: Random House, 1987).

Community, ethnocentrism, and pluralism

As we have seen, the quasi-communitarian dimension of Rorty's thinking dates to his 1979 APA address. There he defends the idea of a culture that gives up the ambition of transcendence – one that accepts "our inheritance from, and our conversation with, our fellow-humans as our only source of guidance" – as central to pragmatism. Abandoning the hope of escaping the contingency of human existence may spell a loss of "meta-physical comfort," he tells us, using one of Nietzsche's phrases, but our gain is "a renewed sense of community" (p. 115, this volume). Using the label 'communitarian' is somewhat misleading, since, as he establishes in "The Priority of Democracy to Philosophy," Rorty rejects the basic premises of most communitarians, primarily on philosophical grounds, even though he concedes that if one wants a theory of the self that "comport[s] well with liberal democracy," the communitarian view of the community as constitutive of the self is "pretty much the right view" (p. 242, this volume). Yet if we restrict it to the sense in which Dewey's thought is communitarian, it can be helpful – that is, one in which the identities of citizens are defined to some extent by the communities of which they are a part, rather than a merely instrumental or sentimental conception. Rorty's claim that "our glory is in our participation in fallible and transitory human projects" comes pretty close (p. 115, this volume).[140]

Often overshadowed by Rorty's effort to cultivate a shared moral identity and invocation of national pride is the extent to which his vision entails an embrace of pluralism and difference.[141] A contributing factor here is his naked, unabashed ethnocentrism. In the late 1980s, this ethnocentrism surfaces as one of the links between Rorty's antirepresentationalism and political liberalism. That is, the antirepresentationalist conception of inquiry Rorty advocates leaves us "without a skyhook" from which to escape from the ethnocentrism produced by acculturation (ORT, p. 2). In the absence of an Archimedean standpoint from which to stand objectively apart from this ethnocentrism, there can be no noncircular justifications of our beliefs. In this sense, "everybody is ethnocentric when engaged in actual debate, no matter how much realistic rhetoric about objectivity" (p. 235, this volume)[142] To say everybody is ethnocentric, it is worth noting, is not to put us on the

140 My discussion here has benefited from Bernstein, *The New Constellation*, pp. 233–8. Although Rorty does not deem Dewey a communitarian in "The Priority of Democracy to Philosophy," he calls him "a fervent communitarian" elsewhere. See Rorty, "The Communitarian Impulse," *Colorado College Studies* 32 (1999): 58. Here Rorty also notes that "The communitarian–individualist quarrel is about abstractions that cannot be made relevant to any actual political choices." Leaving aside these stale debates about abstractions, as Rorty's notion of "Emersonian self-creation on a communal scale" suggests, like Dewey he sought to do justice to the claims both of the individual and of the community. See also 256–7, this volume.

141 Such pluralism is the chief virtue of the secular "polytheism" Rorty offers as a redescription of pragmatism. "You are a polytheist," he tells us, in a conception that covers not only Nietzsche and James but John Stuart Mill and Isaiah Berlin, "if you think that there is no actual or possible object of knowledge that would permit you to commensurate and rank all human needs" (p. 446, this volume).

142 Rorty clarifies that what he means here is not reference to a particular *ethnos*, in the sense of "loyalty to the sociopolitical culture of what Marxists used to call 'bourgeois democracies,'" but rather ethnocentrism as "an inescapable condition – roughly synonymous with 'human finitude'" (ORT, p. 15).

slippery slope of relativism. As Rorty explains in "Postmodernist Bourgeois Liberalism," there is a difference between "saying that every community is as good as every other [relativism] and saying that we have to work out from the networks we are, from the communities with which we presently identify [ethnocentrism]" (ORT, p. 202).[143]

If everybody is ethnocentric in this sense, it is no longer possible to claim "that a single moral vocabulary and a single set of moral beliefs are appropriate for every human community" (p. 253, this volume). Such a stance would require the kind of rational agreement on criteria that, as he has shown, philosophers routinely have failed to attain; that such agreement would be forthcoming in moral or political realms seems even less likely. The obstacle, of course, is that not everyone agrees on "who counts as a decent human being and who does not" (ORT, p. 209). This lack of agreement mirrors the problem of interminable philosophical quarrels between schools that had long preoccupied Rorty. He keenly observes that one's "ethnos" is comprised of "those who share enough of one's beliefs to make fruitful conversation possible" (p. 235, this volume). When we deem people "irredeemably crazy, stupid, base, or sinful," we fail to see these people as "possible conversation partners" (ORT, p. 203). This is a key insight. The remedy he proposes in the context of politics is the same he proposed for philosophers: conversation. Liberal culture's only redress for ethnocentrism, other than turning back to metaphysics, is to make a virtue of necessity and avoid the disadvantages of this condition: "to be open to encounters with other actual and possible cultures, and to make this openness central to its self-image." Liberal culture can then take pride in "its ability to increase the freedom and openness of encounters, rather than on its possession of truth" (ORT, p. 2).

What makes such encounters so essential is that perspectives which do not fit into "the scheme of beliefs and desires which we [currently] would claim as ours" are needed for the self-criticism of cultures to take place. As we have seen, for Rorty moral progress is "the ability to think of people wildly different from ourselves as included in the range of 'us'" (CIS, p. 192). His appeal to novels, particularly social-realist novels or "the novel of moral protest," offers a basis for telling a contingent story about the progress of the West, rather than a metanarrative of the gradual realization of some antecedent truth that the West has "gotten right." Inspired by reflections of Franco-Czech novelist Milan Kundera on the relevancy of the tradition inaugurated by Cervantes, in "Heidegger, Kundera, and Dickens," Rorty posits the centrality of "narrative, detail, diversity, and accident" in the novel as a way to subvert the essentialism grounded in traditional philosophy's privileging of "theory, simplicity, structure, abstraction, and essence." Importantly, rather than culminating in a stance that amounts to saying "what matters for me takes precedence over what matters for you, entitles me to ignore what matters to you, because I am in touch with something – reality – with which you are not," in what Rorty frames as the "democratic utopia" implicit in Kundera's vision of the novel, "it is comical to believe that one human being is more in touch with something nonhuman than another human being" (p. 314, this volume). Moving effortlessly from Kundera to Dickens, Rorty calls attention to "the unsubsumable, uncategorizable idiosyncrasy" of the

143   See also p. 253, this volume, where Rorty notes that "it is not clear how to argue for the claim that human beings ought to be liberals rather than fanatics without being driven back on a theory of human nature, on philosophy." For a more in-depth presentation of Rorty's views on ethnocentrism, see his "On Ethnocentrism: A Reply to Clifford Geertz," ORT, pp. 203–10.

characters that populate Dickens' novels as symbolic of the rich, irreducible diversity and plurality of moral viewpoints traditional philosophy never came to terms with:

> A society which took its moral vocabulary from novels rather than from ontotheological or ontico-moral treatises would not ask itself questions about human nature, the point of human existence, or the meaning of human life. Rather, it would ask itself what we can do so as to get along with each other, how we can arrange things so as to be comfortable with one another, how institutions can be changed so that everyone's right to be understood has a better chance of being gratified. (p. 317, this volume)

One of Rorty's most suggestive statements of his ideal of pluralism and diversity comes, strangely enough, in "American National Pride."[144] Against what he saw as an unhelpful multiculturalism of "a morality of live-and-live" and "side-by-side development in which members of distinct cultures preserve and protect their own culture against the incursions of other cultures," Rorty advocates the idea of a "poetic agon," in which "jarring dialectical discords would be resolved in previously unheard harmonies." Without the "competition and argument between alternative forms of life" he believed necessary for the criticism of culture from within, citizens would be unable to see the limitations of the belief-systems into which they have been acculturated (p. 382, this volume). Although perhaps not asserted enough, for Rorty "[t]he value of free discussion of possible changes by participants in a culture should always take precedence over the value of preserving cultural identity." Without such discussion, "nobody will ever know which cultural traditions are excuses for the strong to oppress the weak and which are traditions that even the weak would, given the option, prefer to preserve."[145]

If ethnocentric, it is a cosmopolitan ethnocentrism that Rorty seeks, where individuals are "articulate and reflective enough to make intercultural comparisons without much strain."[146] The flipside of our ethnocentric condition is that human beings are "centerless webs of beliefs and desires" whose "vocabularies and opinions are determined by historical circumstance" and therefore are contingent and alterable. Belief-change and altering our self-image are central to Rorty's project, their ethnocentrism notwithstanding, because he believes not only that cultures are capable of self-criticism and self-improvement, but that this cultural criticism must be actively fostered. The rub is that enough overlap must exist for fruitful conversation to be possible (pp. 253–4, this volume). Since there is no transcending our ethnocentrism, all we can do is to "reweave" and "recontextualize" the beliefs we happen to have in light of the new people or new beliefs we encounter. Whether this reweaving is adequate to address the injustices and conflicts of the twenty-first century is the question. Rorty's point, though, is that once we see the ethnocentrism of putatively universal appeals to Reason or a core human essence or categorical imperative, this reweaving is all we have.

144 Rorty was fond of noting the lineage running from Mill's invocation in *On Liberty*'s epigraph of Wilhelm von Humboldt's commitment to "the absolute and essential importance of human development in its richest diversity" to Whitman's discussion of Mill and call for "full play for human nature to expand itself in numberless and even conflicting directions" in the opening paragraph of *Democratic Vistas* to James's dedication of his *Pragmatism* lectures to Mill. See (pp. 381–2, this volume; and PCP, p. 28.

145 Rorty, "The Communitarian Impulse," p. 60.

146 Ibid., p. 58.

Cultural politics, real politics, and the postmodern Left

Rorty's appeals to identities and self-images sound a lot like the kind of cultural politics he railed against in *Achieving Our Country*. Generally speaking, two distinct registers of politics exist in Rorty's thought that are usefully distinguished, although Rorty himself does not always do so. One is the immediate, organized efforts to rectify concrete forms of injustice and suffering, primarily along economic lines of basic needs and making people's lives better in banal ways, that he once dubbed "real politics." This politics is the province of what he calls the "Old" or "reformist" Left, which existed roughly from 1900 to 1964, and entails reducing economic inequality and insecurity in the hope that prejudice too would gradually disappear, mostly through labor unions, coalitions, and changing laws.[147] The other conception is contained in the notion of politics alluded to in the title of Rorty's final collection of philosophical papers, *Philosophy as Cultural Politics*: the broad, generational cultural change that takes place through "gradual inculcation of new ways of speaking" prompted by the advent of new metaphors, new vocabularies, and new stories that are then woven into the larger culture and promulgated, primarily through changing the books read by the young (PSH, p. xix). More akin to a Kuhnian paradigm shift than a concrete series of reforms, this second conception is impelled by a lightly sketched utopian vision of a society and a culture that is more tolerant and just and thus characterized by less suffering and greater happiness for all its members (PCP, pp. ix–x).

As we have seen, this latter conception has been present as part of the Romantic backdrop of Rorty's thinking for almost three decades.[148] However, in the past he referred to this kind of social change as "moral progress," "altering our self-image," or "modify[ing] people's sense of who they are," rather than cultural politics. Indeed, in *Achieving Our Country,* the phrase "cultural politics" has a distinctly pejorative connotation aimed at those in the "academic, cultural Left" who are dismissive of "real politics" because of their view that "the system, and not just the laws, must be changed. Reformism is not good enough" (AOC, p. 78). Even in the 2000 essay, "Is 'Cultural Recognition' a Useful Concept for Leftist Politics?" he confesses his "scepticism" about "the recent vogue of 'cultural studies' in departments of literature," pointing out that "the growing 'cultural studies' literature does not amount to much as a form of leftist

---

147   See IS "CULTURAL RECOGNITION" A USEFUL CONCEPT FOR LEFTIST POLITICS? (chapter 29, this volume); and "The Eclipse of the Reformist Left" and "A Cultural Left" in AOC.

148   For example, he refers to "the romantic sense that everything can be changed by talking in new terms" in NINETEENTH CENTURY IDEALISM AND TWENTIETH CENTURY TEXTUALISM, (p. 130, this volume). One could argue that his recent idea of "philosophy as cultural politics" comes full circle from a claim in the 1976 essay "Professionalized Philosophy and Transcendentalist Culture," where he speculates, "It may be that American philosophy will continue to be more concerned with developing a disciplinary matrix than with its antecedents or its cultural role," CP, p. 69. At the time, he was rather sanguine that philosophy "may or may not" take up this cultural role, insisting only that philosophy "not try to beat" the genres doing this cultural work by claiming epistemological privilege. Not only the title of his final volume, but his assertion in the preface, suggest Rorty may have been less sanguine about philosophy's role toward the end of his life: "The more philosophy interacts with other human activities – not just natural science, but art, literature, religion, and politics as well – the more relevant to cultural politics it becomes, and thus the more useful," PCP, p. x.

political activity." That said, he also admits to having "the feeling of just not getting it" and the possibility that this lack of appreciation might just be a blind spot (p. 463, this volume).

Plausible as this admission is, his account of the "extraordinary success" of the cultural Left in *Achieving Our Country* suggests that on some level he does get it. There he asserts, "Except for a few Supreme Court decisions, there has been little change for the better in our country's laws since the Sixties [when the Old Left was supplanted by the New Left]. But the change in the way we treat another has been enormous." He attributes the decrease in "sadism" that resulted to, in a word, education:

> This change is largely due to the hundreds of thousands of teachers who have done their best to make their students understand the humiliation which previous generations of Americans have inflicted on their fellow citizens. By assigning Toni Morrison's *Beloved* instead of George Eliot's *Silas Marner* in high school literature classes, and by assigning stories about the suicides of gay teenagers in freshman composition courses, these teachers have made it harder for their students to be sadistic than it was for those students' parents. (AOC, p. 81)

It would probably be more accurate to say that Rorty's problem is less with cultural politics in this sense than with the cultural academic Left itself. For one, as he states in "Is 'Cultural Recognition' a Useful Concept," this Left's overestimation of the utility of philosophy – "that terms like 'deconstruction', 'subject-position', and 'power'" are essential for rectifying injustices – has inured it to the belief that spinning out increasingly sophisticated theoretical critiques itself amounts to valuable political work in Rorty's first sense of alleviating concrete forms of suffering. For another, as a result of becoming enamored of a certain brand of radical critique, the rhetoric of the cultural Left is revolutionary rather than reformist, longing for "magical transformations" that spell a collapse of "the system" instead of working to realize a concrete platform of reforms (AOC, pp. 102–5).

What most troubles Rorty is the degree to which this Left is unable to engage in "national politics." In *Achieving Our Country*, Rorty offers an historical narrative to contextualize this "semiconscious anti-Americanism," locating it in the New Left's perception that "the Vietnam War, and the endless humiliation inflicted on African-Americans, were clues to something deeply wrong with their country, and not just mistakes correctable by reforms." No longer believing that social justice is possible by working within the system, these intellectuals underwent a change in their moral identity or self-image, but not for the better; on the contrary, it made it easier "to stop thinking of oneself as a member of a community, as a citizen with civic responsibilities." As he explains, "For if you turn out to be living in an evil empire (rather than, as you had been told, a democracy fighting an evil empire), then you have no responsibility to your country; you are accountable only to humanity" (AOC, pp. 65–6). As a result, for the cultural Left connecting with those outside of academia – namely, the "voting public" that "must be won over if the Left is to emerge from the academy into the public square" – is abandoned (AOC, p. 104).

For Rorty, absent an emotional attachment to the targets of social and political criticism, like pride, the transformative potential of projects of democratic self-renewal is lost, leaving us with detached, spectatorial critiques whose theoretical sophistication offers a false sense of engagement. On the one hand, his call for national pride is an effort to counterbalance the tone of pessimistic self-mockery dominant among those on the Left who have read Foucault and Heidegger and are eager to participate in the "America Sucks Sweepstakes." Despite the attempts of Paul de Man and other deconstructionists to "reinvigorate leftist social criticism by deploying new philosophico-literary weapons," what resulted instead, in Rorty's view, is a "spectatorial, disgusted, mocking Left rather than a Left which dreams of achieving our country," in the phrase he borrows from James Baldwin's *The Fire Next Time*, who have succeeded in making a "principled, theorized, philosophical hopelessness" fashionable (pp. 321, 387, this volume).[149] On the other, the emotional attachment inherent in pride – and shame – becomes a central ingredient in Rorty's political theory. We learn in the opening sentence of "American National Pride," that national pride is "a necessary condition for [collective] self-improvement." He continues:

> Those who hope to persuade a nation to exert itself need to remind their country of what it can take pride in as well as what it should be ashamed of." This commitment to America, via a shared moral identity, as an ongoing project is the essential ingredient in the stances of Whitman and Dewey, but also Baldwin, who in Rorty's view combined "an unwillingness to forgive with a continuing identification with the country that brought over his ancestors in chains. (pp. 372, 376, this volume)[150]

To be sure, this effort was never simply an exercise in nostalgia for Rorty. One of his more trenchant criticisms of the post-Sixties cultural Left is that during the same period when sadism declined, economic inequality increased. Citing data that has since worsened, he discusses how the decline in real wages since the early 1970s, combined with the rising costs of day care, health insurance, and college tuition, have contributed to the what he calls "the formation of hereditary castes" – all of which is being insufficiently addressed by the academic Left, if at all (AOC, pp. 83–7). Often lost amidst his polemics against the cultural Left is Rorty's longstanding concern with the costs of globalization, particularly on the economic side, both at home and abroad. While he did call for an international legal structure and "global polity" that would make it possible to address these costs through his first kind of politics, for the most part his response to globalization led him to the realm of cultural politics in its second iteration, where "encouraging people to have a self-image in which their real or imagined citizenship in a democratic republic is central" is the most promising path to change.[151] In the end, the relationships between cultural and real politics, and between national pride and international sympathetic identification, were never adequately worked out.

---

149   As Rorty puts it in an interview, "I was surrounded by what seemed to me an idiot Left in the literature departments, people who claimed to be politically involved but who, as far as I could see, weren't" (TCF, p. 11). See also "A Cultural Left" and "The Eclipse of the Reformist Left" in AOC. Rorty attributes the phrase "America Sucks Sweepstakes" to Jonathan Yardley. See p. 501, this volume.

150   In addition to pride and shame, Rorty also discusses the "generous anger" that fueled the concern for social justice in Dickens, Orwell, Stowe, and Martin Luther King, Jr. See pp. 318–19, this volume.

151   Rorty, "Globalization, the Politics of Identity and Social Hope," PSH, p. 238. See also his "Can American Egalitarianism Survive a Globalized Economy," in Patricia H. Werhane (ed.), *New Approaches to Business Ethics* (Ruffin Series in Business Ethics, vol. 1, 1998), pp. 1–6.

VIII. Looking Forward

Taken as a whole, Rorty's work bequeaths us a compelling picture of a post-metaphysical culture, including novel metaphors and vocabularies that prompt ways to reimagine ourselves and our relations to others. It is a vision still oriented toward the fundamental political goals inherited from the democratic revolutions of the late eighteenth century. In that sense, Rorty's ideals are not postmodern, though his critiques of traditional philosophy may have this quality. Despite his emphasis on novelty and proliferating forms of inquiry, Rorty never gave up "the search for a single utopian form of political life – the good global society" (p. 486, this volume). Yet his embrace of historicity, contingency, and pluralism opens multiple, revisable paths and urges more inclusive conversations about how to get there. To conceive of a society where there are no privileged standpoints or ways of knowing, and where the desire to escape time and chance is no longer woven into the way we understand ourselves, is in many ways to move beyond prevailing modernisms.[152]

Rorty helped initiate a sea-change in our thinking, prompting us to realize that our deepest and most cherished beliefs and values and ways of life are contingent. His role in spurring a renewal of interest in American pragmatism, propelled by his attention to previously unseen connections between pragmatist concerns and an array of other traditions, altered the intellectual landscape of the late twentieth century. If our intellectual discourses prove unwilling or unable to engage and ameliorate social problems, he tirelessly taught, they should be abandoned for others that do. More broadly, his example of clear yet complex and engaged interdisciplinary writing, in the words of a former colleague, "established a standard for a whole generation of younger writers" and "invited people into the discussion who had been sidelined for not knowing all the key terms," effectively democratizing intellectual life in the process.[153] By all accounts, Rorty lived his commitments to conversation and democratic discourse; for all of his ability to play the stinging gadfly and to provoke, his openness, modesty, and indefatigable willingness to engage each and every critic and interlocutor will not soon be surpassed.

Whether the metaphors and redescriptions Rorty offers find a resonance and a use or collect dust at the bottom of the twenty-first century's toolbox remains to be seen. As he himself asserted, "poetic, artistic, philosophical, scientific, or political progress" comes down to "the accidental coincidence of a private obsession with a public need" (CIS, p. 37). Only time and chance will tell if his obsessions will spur the kind of progress toward a global democratic utopia he envisioned, progress spurred by his own hopes for

---

152   Michael Berubé captures the implications of this stance very nicely: "One of the reasons Rorty's view of the world seemed so attractive was that it offered us humans a useful way to think about why it is that we disagree with each other about what those moral truths actually are: If you think you are acting in accordance with the eternal moral truths of the universe, after all, it is likely that you will think of people who think and act differently as being defective, deluded, or downright dangerous. On the other hand, if you think that morality is a matter of contingent vocabularies, you don't have to become a shallow relativist – you can go right on believing what you believe, except that you have to give up the conviction that there's no plausible way another rational person could think differently." Quoted in Metcalf, "Richard Rorty."

153   Mark Edmundson, quoted in Metcalf, "Richard Rorty."

"a global, cosmopolitan, democratic, egalitarian, classless, casteless society" (PSH, p. xii). Although he did not live to see the election of America's forty-fourth president, the commitments, orientation, and rhetoric of Barack Obama, with their invocation not only of a pragmatist spirit but of the need to fulfill the unfinished project of America outlined in *Achieving Our Country,* suggest Rorty's vision may have not yet outlived its usefulness.[154]

For his part, Rorty confessed toward the end of his life to being "very pessimistic" about the chances of achieving the kind of democratic utopia he espoused (p. 519, this volume) His greatest fear after September 11 was that democratic institutions would prove too fragile to withstand the threats to liberty that accompany the national security state.[155] Nevertheless, as he once quipped, "what else have we got except hope?"[156] Indeed, this undying hope for a better human future may be Rorty's defining quality and perhaps his greatest legacy. Of his many expressions of this hope, few surpass this one:

> My sense of the holy, insofar as I have one, is bound up with the hope that someday, any millennium now, my remote descendants will live in a global civilization in which love is pretty much the only law. In such a society, communication will be domination-free, class and caste would be unknown, hierarchy would be a matter of temporary pragmatic convenience, and power would be entirely at the disposal of the free agreement of a literature and well-education electorate.[157]

Other times, though, he put it much more simply: "if we can work together, we can make ourselves into whatever we are clever and courageous enough to imagine ourselves becoming" (p. 358, this volume).

154   See, for example, Christopher Hayes, "The Pragmatist," *The Nation* (Dec. 10, 2008): http://www.thenation.com/doc/20081229/hayes.; and Mitchell Aboulafia, "Obama's Pragmatism (or Move Over Culture Wars, Hello Political Philosophy)," Dec. 17, 2008: http://tpmcafe.talkingpointsmemo.com/talk/blogs/mitchell_a/2008/12/obamas-pragmatism-or-move-over.php. For additional resources, see the website, "Barack Obama's Pragmatism," http://www.obamaspragmatism.info/

155   See for example, "Fighting Terrorism with Democracy," *The Nation* (Oct. 21, 2002): 11–14; "Post-Democracy," *London Review of Books* (April 1, 2004): 10–11; and his brief contribution to a symposium on the 2004 presidential election, *The Nation* (Dec. 20, 2004): 17–18. Rorty gives a more comprehensive account of the reasons for his doubt in *PSH*, pp. 271–6.

156   Interview by Gideon Lewis-Kraus, "Richard Rorty," *The Believer* (June 2003): http://www.believermag.com/issues/200306/?read=interview_rorty, accessed July 31, 2009 – one of Rorty's most open and revealing interviews. The full quote is "If I had to lay bets, my bet would be that everything is going to go to hell, but, you know, what else have we got except hope?"

157   "Anticlericalism and Atheism," in *The Future of Religion*, p. 40.

Part I

Toward Philosophy Without Mirrors

Introduction

The essays in this section are among the most important for understanding Rorty's fundamental philosophical orientation. Covering roughly the period from 1965 to 1980, these pieces illustrate how the constellation of 'metaphilosophical' concerns established in his first series of published essays from the early 1960s are brought to bear, first on linguistic philosophy in his introduction to *The Linguistic Turn* (LT), and then in *Philosophy and the Mirror of Nature* (PMN) on the broader Cartesian–Kantian conception of philosophy as a foundational discipline. At the forefront of these concerns is Rorty's preoccupation with identifying and distinguishing fruitful and unfruitful responses to philosophical impasses and suggesting ways we might move beyond them by drawing on other traditions. By 1980 he explicitly and self-consciously defends pragmatism, specifically James and Dewey, as offering the most useful tools for navigating such metaphilosophical difficulties, even as he calls attention to unresolved tensions he sees in Dewey's own thought.

Of the many strands running through the background of these essays is the prospect of being "post-philosophical," in the specific sense of moving beyond Philosophy with a capital "P." This possibility exists for philosophy itself, as an abandoning of the Plato–Kant tradition with its claims to privileged access to Truth, Goodness, and Rationality, but also for the entire culture erected upon these philosophical foundations. If pragmatism is "post-philosophical philosophy," as he puts it below (p. 125, this volume), then it remains for Rorty not only to outline a post-Philosophical culture – what would happen "if pragmatism became central to our culture and our self-image" (p. 121, this volume) – but to highlight ways for us to get from here to there, which is precisely what he begins to do in these essays. Importantly, such cultural developments are "not going to be resolved by any sudden new discovery of how things really are," only by "slow and painful choice between alternative self-images" (CP, p. xliv). In these essays, we also see that Rorty's skepticism about the utility of argument was present even in this early work. One of the ways this manifests itself is in his attraction to thinkers like Wittgenstein, who he took to be doing effective philosophical work without recourse to direct argument.[1] As early as 1965, one

---

1 See, for example, *Linguistic Turn* (LT), p. 10. In *Mirror*, Rorty praises Wittgenstein, Dewey, and Heidegger for the fact that they "set aside" rather than "argue against" epistemology and metaphysics" (p. 86, this volume).

of the possibilities he outlines for the future is that philosophy would "cease to be an argumentative discipline, and grow closer to poetry" (p. 64, this volume).

As Rorty describes in its preface, the anthology *The Linguistic Turn* (1967) collects roughly 35 years of linguistic philosophy, including classic essays by Moritz Schlick, Rudolf Carnap, Gustav Bergmann, Gilbert Ryle, and others, that establish the thesis that philosophical questions are questions of language, as well as subsequent reassessments of these works.[2] Rorty's introduction is divided into five sections; only the first and fifth have been excerpted here. The second section, "The Search for a Neutral Standpoint," opens with the two questions that guided his selection of the essays for the volume, questions that need to be answered, he tells us, before one can evaluate the so-called methodological revolution of linguistic philosophy:

1.   Are the statements of linguistic philosophers about the nature of philosophy and about philosophical methods actually presuppositionless, in the sense of being dependent upon no substantive theses for their truth?
2.   Do linguistic philosophers actually have criteria for philosophical success which are clear enough to permit rational agreement? (LT, p. 4).

A primary aim of Rorty's is to underscore what he calls "the progressive character of philosophy," the fact that dominant philosophical conceptions once held dear are no longer entertained. If it is not progress – without criteria of success in solving a philosophical problem, how can we say? – it is at least change.[3] What is clear though is that in some cases philosophical problems, rather than being solved, just seem to lose the interest of philosophers. The more interesting question for Rorty is, "why philosophers *think* they have made progress," specifically, why the vanguard of each subsequent philosophical revolution believes they have finally succeeded in becoming "presuppositionless." This is the context in which Rorty approaches the most recent philosophical revolution: linguistic analysis. In the nearly thirty pages of close analysis we have omitted, he sets himself to "uncovering the presuppositions of those who think they have none" (p. 62, this volume).[4]

After noting in the last section of the introduction that it is "too soon to answer" the question of whether a "post-philosophical culture" is conceivable, Rorty outlines six possibilities for the future of philosophy after the dissolution of its traditional problems. Most striking, though, is his startling statement on the final page that the most important event in the last thirty years is not the linguistic turn but "the beginning of a thorough-going rethinking of certain epistemological difficulties which have troubled philosophers

2   Following the classic essays in Part I, there is a section each on ideal-language philosophy and ordinary-language philosophy. The final section of the book offers reconsiderations and forecasts for the future of philosophy after the linguistic turn.

3   Rorty calls this the "pattern of creeping obsolescence" in philosophy (p. 61, this volume). Philosophers who refuse to change with the times, Rorty claims, risk being "left out of the conversation." Philosophy makes progress because "no philosopher can bear *that*" (p. 70, this volume).

4   He covers the answers to the first question provided by the essays that follow in section two of LT; section four, "Criteria for Success in Analytic Philosophy," outlines the answers to the second question. The third section compares the answers from the ideal-language and ordinary-language camps. Because they get fairly technical, Rorty's summary and analysis of these essays presuppose a background in analytic philosophy and for that reason were omitted.

since Plato and Aristotle." In the span of a few sentences, Rorty intimates what would become the focus of his work over the next decade. Specifically, what he has in mind is a rethinking of the traditional "spectatorial" account of knowledge that, he tells us in a footnote, has been "the common target of philosophers as different as Dewey, Hampshire, Sartre, Heidegger, and Wittgenstein."

In a 1974 letter, Rorty suggests an apt description of the mix of historicist and technical analysis marshaled in his work of this period to dissolve traditional philosophical problems that no longer require the attention of philosophers: "therapeutic positivism laced with historicism and *Schwarmerei.*"[5] Although not published until 1979, Rorty began outlining "the plot" of *Philosophy and the Mirror of Nature* in 1969–70 and wrote a draft in 1973–4 while on a Guggenheim Fellowship (PMN, p. xiv). During this time the historically oriented dimension of his approach comes to the forefront and, along with it, attention to the impact of cultural change on philosophical conceptions and positions. On this view, what counts as a philosophical problem is historically contingent. Thus, as the contexts and motivations for philosophizing change, so do the problems themselves; rather than seeing them as perennial, developments in philosophy should be regarded as "events in a certain stage in a conversation" (p. 108, this volume).[6] Rorty frequently refers to Hegel and wonders whether "a genuine world-historical change" is taking place in philosophy.[7]

He also turns to Dewey who, he argues in "Dewey's Metaphysics," sought "to sketch a culture that would not continually give rise to new versions of the old problems, because it would no longer make the distinctions between Truth, Goodness, and Beauty which engender those problems" (p. 83, this volume).[8] Rorty affirms Dewey's understanding of philosophy as "an instrument of social change" and, foreshadowing the direction his own work would take thirty years later, the way Dewey thought philosophy could function as "the criticism of culture." At the same time, Rorty identifies what he sees as a deep tension in Dewey's thought between the Hegelian historicist side and the Lockean naturalistic side. Attempting to read out of Dewey's oeuvre the places where "he was sidetracked into doing 'metaphysics,'" he offers criticisms of Dewey's "naturalistic metaphysics" and his "metaphysics of experience" as remnants of the Kantian notion that the criticism of culture requires a philosophical basis. Although it helped spark a renewal of interest in Dewey, "Dewey's Metaphysics" marks the first salvo

---

5   Quoted in Neil Gross, *Richard Rorty: The Making of an American Philosopher* (Chicago: University of Chicago Press, 2008), p. 197, an excellent book that covers Rorty's life and work until 1982.

6   For example, "Without the spectator model of knowledge we should never have had a mind-body problem in the first place" (p. 81, this volume); "Without the notion of mind as mirror, the notion of knowledge as accuracy of representation would not have suggested itself" (p. 89, this volume).

7   "Cartesian Epistemology and Changes in Ontology," in *Contemporary American Philosophy,* ed. John E. Smith (New York: Humanities Press, 1970), p. 274. This is a key essay in the period between *The Linguistic Turn* and *Philosophy and the Mirror of Nature* for, among other things, the way Rorty establishes his critical focus on the "Cartesian" period of philosophy. For a more in-depth discussion, see the general introduction above (pp. 18–22).

8   Rorty also claims that Dewey is "just the philosopher one might want to reread if one were turning from Kant to Hegel, from a 'metaphysics of experience' to a study of cultural development" (p. 75, this volume).

in Rorty's battle with prominent American philosophers over what we might call his strong misreading of Dewey.[9]

The selections from *Philosophy and the Mirror of Nature* included below – the introduction and the final chapter, "Philosophy without Mirrors" – bookend the more technical analysis and argument that constitute the bulk of the book. In the relatively brief introduction Rorty situates what is otherwise a highly specialized and very technical work in a compelling grand narrative of sorts, bestowing a sense of world-historical importance on the endeavor.[10] He not only establishes the historical origins in Locke, Descartes, and Kant of the vocabularies or metaphors that have given rise to philosophy's sense of its perennial aims; taken together, these propositions undergird a larger "conception of culture" that needs philosophy to provide it with an ahistorical grounding or non-human foundation. Already in the nineteenth century, he tells us, "a new form of culture" had arisen, in which poets and novelists displace not only philosophers but preachers at the moral center of the culture, only now without all the philosophical and foundational backup. From this new vantage, justification is not, as he puts it later in the book, "a matter of a special relation between ideas (or words) and objects, but of conversation, of social practice." If the justification of belief is social rather than ahistorical and foundational, then the standard of accuracy of representation, the notion of mind as Mirror of Nature, and the conception of philosophy with privileged access, all lose their relevance (PMN, p. 170). Philosophy can find its *raison d'être* elsewhere.

Despite perceptions to the contrary, Rorty does not see this as spelling the end of philosophy.[11] The three philosophers heralded in the introduction – Wittgenstein, Heidegger, and Dewey – are singled out for the "therapeutic rather than constructive, edifying rather than systematic" quality of their later work (p. 85, this volume). "Philosophy without Mirrors" develops what Rorty has in mind here, explaining these labels and linking them to the romantic notion of self-creative individuals he sees in Hans-Georg Gadamer's hermeneutics and Michael Oakeshott's ideal of cultural and intellectual development as "conversation." What is striking is how far Rorty goes beyond simply signaling this larger cultural shift. The goal of therapeutic or edifying discourse entails nothing less than "to take us out of our old selves by the power of strangeness, to aid us in becoming new beings" (p. 91, this volume).

Although present in the background of *Philosophy and the Mirror of Nature,* it is not until "Pragmatism, Relativism, and Irrationalism," Rorty's 1979 presidential address to the Eastern Division of the American Philosophical Association, that he explicitly offers

---

9   For some of the responses this essay provoked, see the General Introduction above, note 7. The primary fault line in these debates is between language and experience as the most central category of pragmatism. For more on this issue, see Colin Koopman, "Language is a Form of Experience: Reconciling Classical Pragmatism and Neopragmatism," *Transactions of the Charles S. Peirce Society* 43, no. 4 (2007): 694–727. For Rorty's other major discussions of Dewey, see PRAGMATISM AS ROMANTIC POLYTHEISM (chapter 27, this volume); "Dewey Between Hegel and Darwin," in *Truth and Progress* (TP); and "Kant vs. Dewey: The Current Situation of Moral Philosophy," in *Philosophy as Cultural Politics* (PCP).

10   Indeed, Gross recounts how the book almost failed to be published because a reviewer thought it too technical (*Richard Rorty,* p. 315). In the final chapter, Rorty describes *Mirror* as "a sort of prolegomenon to a history of epistemology-centered philosophy as an episode in the history of European culture" (p. 108, this volume).

11   See for example the final page of the book (p. 110, this volume).

pragmatism as the leading candidate for what might become "central to our culture and our self-image" (p. 121, this volume).[12] After outlining three "sloganistic" characterizations of pragmatism's central doctrine,[13] he defends pragmatism against charges of relativism and irrationalism, pointing out that once the need for a "Platonic–Kantian notion of grounding" of culture goes, so does the force of these criticisms. Familiar Rortyan ideas that make their appearance in this address include: his commitment to social hope; his orientation against "method"; his embrace of contingency of human life; a brief appeal to loyalty; an acceptance of our inescapable ethnocentrism; his critique of a narrowly professionalized philosophical profession; and other key themes evident in *Mirror* and in essays of this time regarding the edifying role of philosophy, the move away from argumentation, and the importance of our connections with fellow-humans.

Written for a conference in 1980, NINETEENTH-CENTURY IDEALISM AND TWENTIETH-CENTURY TEXTUALISM (chapter 5, this volume) fleshes out the idea of a "new form of culture" alluded to in the introduction to *Philosophy and the Mirror of Nature,* placing it in a larger narrative. It contains seeds of virtually all of the substantive stances Rorty would adopt in the years and decades ahead, most notably in *Contingency, Irony, and Solidarity*: the idea that truth is made rather than found and the critique of the correspondence theory of truth; the notion that science and philosophy should be treated as "at best, literary genres"; the attachment to romanticism; the view that belief change comes about through the creation of new vocabularies, rather than argumentation; the idea that pragmatism is "post-philosophical philosophy"; his attraction to Harold Bloom's notion of "strong misreading"; his important sense that the primary difference between the pragmatists and the textualists (read, postmodernists) is moral, not epistemological; his appeal to community; his view of the tension between public and private; and his claim that we should give up the idea of "getting something right."[14]

12   In *Mirror,* Rorty espouses "epistemological behaviorism," which he notes parenthetically "might be called simply 'pragmatism', were this term not a bit overladen" (PMN, p. 176).
13   In summary form, the three are: anti-essentialism toward objects of philosophical theorizing, like truth, knowledge, language, and morality, supported by an appeal to the "vocabulary of practice" for saying something useful about truth; a leveling of hierarchies between normative and empirical truth, facts and values, and morality and science, such that all inquiry is about "the relative attractions of various concrete alternatives" and not about getting things right according to unambiguous criteria; and the idea that "there are no constraints on inquiry save conversational ones," which amounts to an acceptance of the contingency of our concepts and an abandonment of the hope of transcending this contingency (pp. 112–15, this volume).
14   On the implications of the latter, see Christopher Voparil, "The Problem with Getting it Right: Richard Rorty and the Politics of Antirepresentationalism," *Philosophy and Social Criticism* 30, no. 2 (2004): 221–46.

1

Introduction to *The Linguistic Turn*

The history of philosophy is punctuated by revolts against the practices of previous philosophers and by attempts to transform philosophy into a science – a discipline in which universally recognized decision-procedures are available for testing philosophical theses. In Descartes, in Kant, in Hegel, in Husserl, in Wittgenstein's *Tractatus*, and again in Wittgenstein's *Philosophical Investigations*, one finds the same disgust at the spectacle of philosophers quarreling endlessly over the same issues. The proposed remedy for this situation typically consists in adopting a new method: for example, the method of "clear and distinct ideas" outlined in Descartes' *Regulae*, Kant's "transcendental method," Husserl's "bracketing," the early Wittgenstein's attempt to exhibit the meaninglessness of traditional philosophical theses by due attention to logical form, and the later Wittgenstein's attempt to exhibit the pointlessness of these theses by diagnosing the causes of their having been propounded. In all of these revolts, the aim of the revolutionary is to replace opinion with knowledge, and to propose as the proper meaning of "philosophy" the accomplishment of some finite task by applying a certain set of methodological directions.

In the past, every such revolution has failed, and always for the same reason. The revolutionaries were found to have presupposed, both in their criticisms of their predecessors and in their directives for the future, the truth of certain substantive and controversial philosophical theses. The new method which each proposed was one which, in good conscience, could be adopted only by those who subscribed to those theses. Every philosophical rebel has tried to be "presuppositionless," but none has succeeded. This is not surprising, for it would indeed be hard to know what methods a philosopher ought to follow without knowing something about the nature of the philosopher's subject matter, and about the nature of human knowledge. To know what method to adopt, one must already have arrived at some metaphysical and some epistemological conclusions. If one attempts to defend these conclusions by the use of one's chosen method, one is open to a charge of circularity. If one does not so defend them, maintaining that

Richard M. Rorty, "Introduction: Metaphysical Difficulties of Linguistic Philosophy," pp. 1–4, 33–9, in Richard M. Rorty (ed.), *The Linguistic Turn: Essays in Philosophical Method,* 2nd edn, © 1967, 1992 by Chicago University Press. Reprinted with permission of Chicago University Press.

given these conclusions, the need to adopt the chosen method follows, one is open to the charge that the chosen method is inadequate, for it cannot be used to establish the crucial metaphysical and epistemological theses which are in dispute. Since philosophical method is in itself a philosophical topic (or, in other words, since different criteria for the satisfactory solution of a philosophical problem are adopted, and argued for, by different schools of philosophers), every philosophical revolutionary is open to the charge of circularity or to the charge of having begged the question. Attempts to substitute knowledge for opinion are constantly thwarted by the fact that what *counts* as philosophical knowledge seems itself to be a matter of opinion. A philosopher who has idiosyncratic views on criteria for philosophical success does not thereby cease to be accounted a philosopher (as a physicist who refused to accept the relevance of empirical disconfirmation of his theories would cease to be accounted a scientist).

Confronted with this situation, one is tempted to *define* philosophy as that discipline in which knowledge is sought but only opinion can be had. If one grants that the arts do not seek knowledge, and that science not only seeks but finds it, one will thus have a rough-and-ready way of distinguishing philosophy from both. But such a definition would be misleading in that it fails to do justice to the progressive character of philosophy. Some philosophical opinions which were once popular are no longer held. Philosophers do argue with one another, and sometimes succeed in convincing each other. The fact that in principle a philosopher can always invoke some idiosyncratic criterion for a "satisfactory solution" to a philosophical problem (a criterion against which his opponent cannot find a non-circular argument) might lead one to think of philosophy as a futile battle between combatants clad in impenetrable armor. But philosophy is not really like this. Despite the failure of all philosophical revolutions to achieve their ends, no such revolution is in vain. If nothing else, the battles fought during the revolution cause the combatants on both sides to repair their armor, and these repairs eventually amount to a complete change of clothes. Those who today defend "Platonism" repudiate half of what Plato said, and contemporary empiricists spend much of their time apologizing for the unfortunate mistakes of Hume. Philosophers who do not change (or at least re-tailor) their clothes to suit the times always have the option of saying that current philosophical assumptions are false and that the arguments for them are circular or question-begging. But if they do this too long, or retreat to their tents until the winds of doctrine change direction, they will be left out of the conversation. No philosopher can bear *that*, and this is why philosophy makes progress.

To say that philosophy makes progress, however, may itself seem to beg the question. For if we do not know what the goal is – and we do not, as long as we do not know what the criteria for a "satisfactory solution" to a philosophical problem are – then how do we know that we are going in the right direction? There is nothing to be said to this, except that in philosophy, as in politics and religion, we are naturally inclined to define "progress" as movement toward a contemporary consensus. To insist that we cannot know whether philosophy has been progressing since Anaximander, or whether (as Heidegger suggests) it has been steadily declining toward nihilism, is merely to repeat a point already conceded – that one's standards for philosophical success are dependent upon one's substantive philosophical views. If this point is pressed too hard, it merely becomes boring. It is more interesting to see, in detail, why philosophers *think* they have made progress, and what criteria of progress they employ. What is particularly interesting is to see why those philosophers who lead methodological revolts think that they have, at last, succeeded in becoming "presuppositionless," and why their opponents think that they have not. Uncovering the presuppositions of those who think they have none is one of the principal means by which philosophers find new issues to debate. If this is not progress, it is at least change, and to understand such changes is to understand why philosophy, though fated to fail in its quest for knowledge, is nevertheless not "a matter of opinion."

The purpose of the present volume is to provide materials for reflection on the most recent philosophical revolution, that of linguistic philosophy. I shall mean by "linguistic philosophy" the view that philosophical problems are problems which may be solved (or dissolved) either by reforming language, or by understanding more about the language we presently use. This view is considered by many of its proponents to be the most important philosophical discovery of our time, and, indeed, of the ages. By its opponents, it is interpreted as a sign of the sickness of our souls, a revolt against reason itself, and a self-deceptive attempt (in Russell's phrase) to procure by theft what one has failed to gain by honest toil.[1] Given the depth of feeling on both sides, one would expect to find a good deal of explicit discussion of whether it is in fact the case that philosophical problems can be solved in these ways. But one does not. A metaphilosophical question at so high a level of abstraction leaves both sides gasping for air. What one does find is: (a) linguistic philosophers arguing against any *non*-linguistic method of solving philosophical problems, on the basis of such substantive philosophical theses as "There are no synthetic *a priori* statements," "The linguistic form of some sentences misrepresents the logical form of the facts which they signify," "All meaningful empirical statements must be empirically disconfirmable," "Ordinary language is correct language," and the like; (b) other linguistic philosophers, as well as opponents of linguistic philosophy, arguing against these theses; (c) linguistic philosophers pointing with pride to their own linguistic reforms and/or descriptions of language, and saying "Look, no problems!"; (d) opponents of linguistic philosophy replying that the problems may have been disingenuously (or self-deceptively) evaded.

The situation is complicated by the fact, noted in (b) above, that many of the substantive philosophical theses which for some linguistic philosophers count as reasons for adopting linguistic methods, are repudiated by other linguistic philosophers, who nevertheless persist in using these methods. There is a growing tendency among linguistic philosophers to abandon the sort of argument mentioned under (a), to fall back on (c), and to ask to be judged solely by their fruits. This tendency goes along with a tendency to say that either one *sees*, for example, that Wittgenstein has dissolved certain traditional problems, or one does not. Some linguistic philosophers who adopt this attitude are fond of the analogy with psychoanalysis: either one sees that one's actions are determined by unconscious impulses, or one does not.[2] (The psychoanalyst's claim that one's actions are so determined can always be countered by the patient's statements of his reasons for his actions. The psychoanalyst will insist that these reasons are merely rationalizations, but if the patient is good at rationalizing, the difference between rationalizations and reasons will remain invisible to him; he may therefore leave as sick as he came.) The irritation which this analogy creates in opponents of linguistic philosophy is intense

---

1   See, for example, Blanshard [2], especially Chapters 1, 7, 8; Gellner [5]; Mure [1]; Adler [1], especially Chapters 1, 16. Numbers in square brackets refer to chapters in LT – ed.
2   See Wisdom [9], [10]; Cavell [2] (especially the concluding pages), and also his "Aesthetic Problems of Modern Philosophy" in *Philosophy in America*, ed. Max Black (Ithaca, 1965).

and natural. Being told that one holds a certain philosophical position because one has been "bewitched by language" (Wittgenstein's phrase), and that one is unsuited for serious philosophical conversation until one has been "cured," results in attempts by such critics of linguistic philosophy as Gellner and Mure to turn the tables. These critics try to explain away linguistic philosophy as a psychologically or sociologically determined aberration.

A further source of confusion and complication is the tendency of more recent linguistic philosophers to drop the anti-philosophical slogans ("All philosophical questions are pseudo-questions!" and the like) of a somewhat earlier period, and to remark blandly that they are doing exactly what the philosophers of the past were doing – that is, trying to find out the nature of knowledge, freedom, meaning, and the like. Since these philosophers, however, tacitly equate "discovering the nature of X" with "finding out how we use (or should use) 'X' (and related words),"[3] opponents of linguistic philosophy remain infuriated. The linguistic philosopher's claim of continuity with the Great Tradition can be substantiated only by saying that insofar as the philosophers of the past attempted to find out the nature of X by doing something *other* than investigating the uses of words (postulating unfamiliar entities, for example), they were misguided. The opponents of linguistic philosophy therefore demand an account of *why* they were misguided, but they get little response save "Since they could never agree, they *must* have been misguided; a method which does not lead to a consensus cannot be a good method."

This is hardly a conclusive argument. One can always rejoin that the lack of consensus is a function of the difficulty of the subject matter, rather than the inapplicability of the methods. It is easy, though not really very plausible, to say that philosophers do not agree, while scientists do, simply because philosophers work on more difficult problems.[4] Conclusive or not, however, this argument has had a decisive historical importance. As a sociological generalization, one may say that what makes most philosophers in the English-speaking world linguistic philosophers is the same thing that makes most philosophers in continental Europe phenomenologists – namely, a sense of despair resulting from the inability of traditional philosophers to make clear what could count as evidence for or against the truth of their views. The attraction of linguistic philosophy – an attraction so great that philosophers are, *faute de mieux*, willing to stoop even to the highly un-Socratic tactic of saying "Well, either you see it or you don't" is simply that linguistic analysis (like phenomenology) *does* seem to hold out hope for clarity on this methodological question, and thus for eventual agreement among philosophers. As long as this hope remains, there is little likelihood that linguistic philosophers will change their ways.

[…]

5. Prospects for the Future: Discovery versus Proposal

I have now done all that I can, within the restricted compass of an introduction to an anthology, to answer the two questions posed at the beginning of Section 2. In doing so, I have implicitly raised certain other questions which I have not tried to answer. I cannot

3   See, for example, the opening paragraphs of P. F. Strawson, "Truth," in *Philosophy and Analysis*, ed. M. MacDonald (Oxford, 1954), and J. L. Austin, "Truth," in *Philosophical Papers* (Oxford, 1961).
4   See Adler [1], Chapter 10.

do so now, but I shall try to point out where some of the unanswered questions lie by taking up, once again, the very general question raised at the outset: Is the linguistic turn doomed to suffer the same fate as previous "revolutions in philosophy"? The relatively pessimistic conclusions reached in the preceding sections entail that linguistic philosophers' attempts to turn philosophy into a "strict science" must fail. How far does this pessimism carry? If linguistic philosophy cannot be a strict science, if it has a merely critical, essential dialectical, function, then what of the future? Suppose that all the traditional problems are, in the fullness of time, dissolved – in the sense that no one is able to think of any formulations of these questions which are immune to the sort of criticisms made by linguistic philosophers. Does that mean that philosophy will have come to an end – that philosophers will have worked themselves out of a job? Is a "post-philosophical" culture really conceivable?

The only sensible thing to say about most of these questions is that it is too soon to answer them. But it may be useful to list some of the alternative standpoints from which they might be answered. One can envisage at least six possibilities for the future of philosophy, after the dissolution of the traditional problems.

(1)   Since the single substantive philosophical thesis that unites the various branches of linguistic philosophy is methodological nominalism, a repudiation of this thesis would open new horizons. If there were a way of agreeing upon answers to the traditional philosophical questions which would not involve the reduction of questions about the nature of things either to empirical questions (to be turned over to the sciences) or to questions about language, then the linguistic turn would probably be treated as having led to a dead end. Many contemporary philosophers think that phenomenology offers such a way.

(2)   A second possibility is that *both* methodological nominalism *and* the demand for clear-cut criteria for agreement would be dropped. Philosophy would then cease to be an argumentative discipline, and grow closer to poetry. Heidegger's later essays can be seen as an attempt to do philosophy in an entirely new way – one which rejects the *traditional* problems as spurious, yet insists that there *are* problems to be solved which are not simply problems about how it would be best to talk. The fact that these problems are all but unstatable, and consequently are such that no agreement about criteria for their solution is available, would be cheerfully accepted. This would be taken as signifying the difficulty of the subject matter, rather than (as Heidegger's critics take it) the perversity of the methods employed.

(3)   Another possibility is that methodological nominalism would be retained, but that the demand for clear-cut criteria of agreement about the truth of philosophical theses would be dropped. Philosophers could then turn toward creating Ideal Languages, but the criterion for being "Ideal" would no longer be the dissolution of philosophical problems, but rather the creation of new, interesting and fruitful ways of thinking about things in general. This would amount to a return to the great tradition of philosophy as system-building – the only difference being that the systems built would no longer be considered *descriptions* of the nature of things or of human consciousness, but rather *proposals* about how to talk. By such a move, the "creative" and "constructive" function of philosophy could be retained. Philosophers would be, as they have traditionally been supposed to be, men who gave one a *Weltanschauung* – in Sellars' phrase, a way of

"understanding how things in the broadest possible sense of the term hang together in the broadest possible sense of the term."[5]

(4) It might be that we would end by answering the question "Has philosophy come to an end?" with a resounding "Yes," and that we would come to look upon a post-philosophical culture as just as possible, and just as desirable, as a post-religious culture. We might come to see philosophy as a cultural disease which has been cured, just as many contemporary writers (notably Freudians) see religion as a cultural disease of which men are gradually being cured. The wisecrack that philosophers had worked themselves out of a job would then seem as silly a sneer as a similar charge leveled at doctors who, through a breakthrough in preventive medicine, had made therapy obsolete. Our desire for a *Weltanschauung* would now be satisfied by the arts, the sciences, or both.[6]

(5) It might be that empirical linguistics can in fact provide us with non-banal formulations of the necessary and sufficient conditions for the truth of statements, and non-banal accounts of the meaning of words. Granted that these formulations and accounts would apply only to our present linguistic practices, it might be that the discovery of such formulations and accounts would satisfy at least some of the instincts which originally led men to philosophize. Linguistic philosophy, instead of being lexicography pursued for an extrinsic purpose, would become lexicography pursued for its own sake. Such a vision of the future of philosophy is put forward, though with many qualifications and reservations, by Urmson's description of the Austinian "fourth method of analysis" .... Though such a project would be related to the tradition neither through sympathy (as in [3]), nor through repudiation (as in [4]), it might nevertheless reasonably be called "philosophy" simply because its pursuit filled part (although obviously not all) of the gap left in the cultural fabric by the disappearance of traditional philosophy.

(6) It might be that linguistic philosophy could transcend its merely critical function by turning itself into an activity which, instead of inferring from facts about linguistic behavior to the dissolution of traditional problems, discovers necessary conditions for the possibility of language itself (in a fashion analogous to the way in which Kant purportedly discovered necessary conditions for the possibility of experience). Such a development is envisaged by Strawson, when he says that the goal of "descriptive metaphysics" is to show "how the fundamental categories of our thought hang together, and how they relate, in turn, to those formal notions (such as existence, identity, and unity) which range through all categories." A discipline of this sort would perhaps emerge with very general conclusions, such as "It is a necessity in the use of language that we should refer to persisting objects, employing some criteria of identity through change."[7]

---

5 Sellars [6], p. 1.
6 Goethe said that if you had science and art you thereby had religion, but that if you had neither, you had better go out and get religion ("*Wer Wissenschaft und Kunst besitzt/ Hat auch Religion/ Wer jene beiden nicht besitzt/ Der habe Religion,*" Zahme Xenien, Neuntes Buch). Substituting "philosophy" for "religion," I suggest that this expresses the view of many followers of Wittgenstein.
7 Hampshire [13], p. 66. See below for a more complete quotation from this passage.

Positions (1) through (6) may be associated respectively with six names: Husserl, Heidegger, Waismann, Wittgenstein, Austin, and Strawson. This is not to say that any of these men would embrace one of these alternatives without many qualifications and restrictions, but rather that those who opt for one of these alternatives often cite one of these six philosophers as a good example of the sort of philosophical attitude and program which they have in mind. For our present purposes, it would be impracticable to take up (1) and (2), the Husserlian and Heideggerian alternatives. Whether orthodox Husserlian phenomenology is in fact a presuppositionless method offering criteria for the accuracy of phenomenological descriptions is too large a question to be discussed. All that can be said is that linguistic philosophers are perennially puzzled by the question of whether Husserlian methods differ, other than verbally, from the methods practiced by linguistic philosophy – whether, in other words, a phenomenological description of the structure of X is more than an Austinian account of our use of "X," phrased in a different idiom.[8] When we turn to "existential phenomenologists" – heretical disciples of Husserl, among them Sartre and the Heidegger of *Sein und Zeit* – we find that linguistic philosophers are tempted to assimilate such efforts to the sort of proposals for an Ideal Language mentioned in (3). This temptation extends even to the work of the later Heidegger. A Waismann-like view of philosophy as "the piercing of that dead crust of tradition and convention, the breaking of those fetters which bind us to inherited preconceptions, so as to attain a new and broader way of looking at things"[9] is able to welcome even such quasi-poetic efforts as Heidegger's "Bauen Wohnen Denken." Once philosophy is viewed as proposal rather than discovery, a methodological nominalist can interpret both the philosophical tradition, and contemporary attempts to break free of this tradition, in equally sympathetic ways.

If we restrict ourselves to alternatives (3) through (6), which all adhere to methodological nominalism, we can see that (3) and (4) share a common ground not shared by (5) and (6). Both (3) and (4) repudiate the notion that there are philosophical truths to be discovered and demonstrated by argument. Waismann says that "To seek, in philosophy, for rigorous proofs is to seek for the shadow of one's voice,"[10] and Wittgenstein that "If one tried to advance *theses* in philosophy, it would never be possible to debate them, because everyone would agree with them."[11] What difference there is between these two positions lies in Wittgenstein's apparent feeling that philosophers' attempts to "break the fetters" by inventing new, specifically philosophical, language-games are bound to result only in exchanging new fetters for old. Whereas Waismann thought that philosophical system-building had, and could again, crystallize a "vision," the mystical strain in Wittgenstein led him to strive for an "unmediated vision" – a state in which things could be seen as they are, without the mediation of a new way of thinking about them. Such a difference is not an appropriate topic for argument. It must suffice to say that Waismann and Wittgenstein share the view that philosophy, apart from its critical and dialectical function, can be *at most* proposal, never discovery.

The view that philosophy should aim at proposing better ways of talking rather than at discovering specifically philosophical truths is, of course, the direct heir of the Ideal

---

8   See Downes [1], and the articles by Chappell, Turnbull, and Gendlin in the same issue of *The Monist* (XLIX, No. 1). See also Schmitt [1], Taylor [2], and Ayer [10].

9   Waismann [2], p. 483.

10   Waismann [2], p. 482.

11   Wittgenstein [1], Part I, Section 128.

Language tradition in linguistic philosophy. There is not a great difference between the metaphilosophical pragmatism of an article like Carnap's "Empiricism, Semantics and Ontology" and Waismann's vision of philosophy-as-vision. In contrast to this attitude, which contemplates with equanimity the lack of a strict decision-procedure for judging between alternative proposals, the Oxford tradition of Ordinary Language analysis has tended to hold out for the view that there are specifically philosophical truths to be discovered. Hampshire says of Austin that

> Since it was a constant point of difference between us, he often, and over many years, had occasion to tell me that he had never found any good reason to believe that philosophical inquiries are essentially, and of their very nature, inconclusive. On the contrary he believed that this was a remediable fault of philosophers, due to premature system-building and impatient ambition, which left them neither the inclination nor the time to assemble the facts, impartially and cooperatively, and then to build their unifying theories, cautiously and slowly, on a comprehensive, and therefore secure, base.[12]

Such a view, which serves as the point of departure for much contemporary work, suggests that lexicography, pursued for its own sake and apart from its critical function, will in the end give us something rather like a traditional philosophical system. The body of truths about how we speak, ordered by a complex but precise taxonomic theory, will present itself as a *Weltanschauung*. The claim that this is the *right* world view will be based simply on the fact that it is the one built in our language, and is therefore more likely to be correct than (to quote a phrase which Austin used in another context) "any that you or I are likely to think up in our armchairs of an afternoon."[13] Insofar as Austin had in mind a model for such a system, the model was Aristotle. Like Aristotle's, such a hypothetical system would not consist of answers to all the questions posed by philosophers of the past, but would instead dismiss many (if not all) of these questions as ill-formed, and would proceed to make distinctions which, once explicitly recognized, would free us from the temptation to answer these questions. It would thus accomplish the critical aims which were, for Wittgenstein, the sole justification of continued philosophical inquiry, as a by-product of a search for truths. *Pace* Wittgenstein, it *would* be "possible to question" these truths, but such questions could be answered. They could be answered in the same way as a theorist in any other empirical science answers questions about the truth of his theory – by pointing to its superior ability to account for the facts.

At the present time, this Austinian alternative – (5) above – is (in English-speaking lands) the most widespread conception of what the philosophy of the future will be like. Its strongest rival is neither (3) nor (4), but (6) – the Strawsonian view that we need not restrict ourselves to a theory which accounts for our linguistic behavior, but that we can get a theory about language as such – about any possible language, rather than simply about the assemblage of languages presently spoken. Such a project, which suggests that the study of language can lead us to certain necessary truths as well as to an Austinian empirical theory, holds out the hope that linguistic philosophy may yet satisfy our Platonic, as well as our Aristotelian, instincts – the instincts which impelled Wittgenstein

---

12   Hampshire [6], p. vii (Reprinted below.)
13   *Philosophical Papers*, p. 130.

to write the *Tractatus*. It is far from clear how exponents of this project hope to avoid the usual difficulties arising from the gap between contingent truths about linguistic behavior and necessary truths about language as such, but the general strategy may be glimpsed in the following quotation from Hampshire.

> The argument of this chapter has been that it is a necessity in the use of language that we should refer to persisting objects, employing some criteria of identity through change: it is a necessity that the speaker should have the means of indicating his own point of view or standpoint, since he is himself one object among others; that every object must exhibit different appearances from different points of view: and that every object, including persons who are language-users, agents and observers, has a history of changing relations to other things in its environment. These truisms entail consequences in the theory of perception, the theory of mind, the theory of action … *We cannot claim an absolute and unconditional finality for these truisms, since the deduction of them is always a deduction within language as we know it. But the deduction only shows that we are not in a position to describe any alternative forms of communication between intentional agents which do not exemplify these truisms.*[14]

Hampshire seems to suggest that a language which we cannot imagine being used is not a language, and that the sort of language we can imagine being used is determined by the language we ourselves use. Consequently, we can fairly infer from features of our own language to features of anything that we shall ever describe as a "language." To put it crudely, if the Martians speak a language which does not exemplify the truisms cited, we shall never know that they do; therefore the suggestion that they do is not one which we can really understand. If we put aside the question of whether Hampshire's "truisms" are in fact true, there remains one obvious difficulty: philosophers are constantly doing something which they describe as "sketching a possible language" – a language which does not exemplify some or all of these truisms.[15] Unless some criteria are developed to test the suggestion that such languages could not be used by someone who did not already know a language which embodied the truisms in question (that such languages are, in Strawson's phrase, "parasitic" upon ordinary language),[16] the strategy will not work. Granted that the limits of the language a man can speak are, in some sense, the limits of his thought and his imagination, it seems nevertheless that our language is so rich that we can pull our imagination up by its own bootstraps. Thus, the difficulty presented to traditional Ordinary Language philosophy by science-fiction-like examples of exotic linguistic behavior remains a difficulty for a project such as (6).

14   Hampshire [13], pp. 66–67. [Italics added].
15   As an example of such a language, consider the "canonical notation," characterized by an absence of singular terms, which Quine develops in *Word and Object*. Another example to be considered is the language which Sellars suggests might come into existence if people stopped thinking of themselves as *persons*, and began thinking only about, say, molecules and their behavior. (See Sellars [6], especially pp. 32–40.) Sellars has Hampshire-like reservations about the possibility of such a language (see pp. 39–40), but the basis for these reservations is not clear.
16   For this notion of "parasitism," see Strawson's "Singular Terms, Ontology and Identity," *Mind*, LXV (1956), 433–54. See also Quine's dismissal of Strawson's point as irrelevant in *Word and Object*, p. 158 n., and Manley Thompson's "On the Elimination of Singular Terms," *Mind*, LXVIII (1959), 361–76. For another example of the use of the notion of one language's being "parasitic" on another, see Wilfrid Sellars, "Time and the World-Order," *Minnesota Studies in the Philosophy of Science*, III, especially Sections 1 and 9.

It is, however, far too soon to pass judgment on this project. It is presently exemplified by only a few documents – notably Strawson's *Individuals* and Hampshire's *Thought and Action* – and can hardly be said to have had a fair run.[17]

This brief sketch of some possible futures must suffice. The only moral that may be drawn, I think, is that the metaphilosophical struggles of the future will center on the issue of reform versus description, of philosophy-as-proposal versus philosophy-as-discovery – the issue between the least common denominator of (2), (3), and (4) on the one hand, and the least common denominator of (1), (5), and (6) on the other. We have seen, in the course of the preceding sections, a certain oscillation between these two metaphilosophical alternatives. Once the linguistic turn had been taken, and once methodological nominalism had taken hold, it was natural for philosophers to suggest that the function of their discipline is to *change* our consciousness (by reforming our language) rather than to describe it, for language – unlike the intrinsic nature of reality, or the transcendental unity of apperception – is something which, it would seem, *can* be changed. But it was equally natural for philosophers to resist abandoning the hope that their discipline could be a science, an activity in which the principal criterion of success is simply accurate description of the facts. Ever since Plato invented the subject, philosophy has been in a state of tension produced by the pull of the arts on one side and the pull of the sciences on the other. The linguistic turn has not lessened this tension, although it has enabled us to be considerably more self-conscious about it. The chief value of the metaphilosophical discussions included in this volume is that they serve to heighten this self-consciousness.

A final cautionary word: an important (although, I believe, inevitable) defect of this anthology, and of this introduction, is that they do not adequately exhibit the interplay between the adoption of a metaphilosophical outlook and the adoption of substantive philosophical theses. This interplay is exceedingly complex, and often subliminal, and the relations involved more often causal than logical. I have discussed the degree to which linguistic philosophy is "presuppositionless," but I have not tried to discuss the more difficult topic of how changes in the vocabulary used in formulating substantive theses produce changes in the vocabulary of metaphilosophy. Nor do I know how to do this. I should wish to argue that the most important thing that has happened in philosophy during the last thirty years is not the linguistic turn itself, but rather the beginning of a thoroughgoing rethinking of certain epistemological difficulties which have troubled philosophers since Plato and Aristotle.[18] I would argue that if it were not for the epistemological difficulties created by this account, the traditional problems of metaphysics (problems, for example, about universals, substantial form, and the relation between the mind and the body) would never have been conceived. If the traditional "spectatorial"

17   For criticisms of (6), see Black [4] (reprinted at pp. 331–39 below); Julius Moravscik, "Strawson and Ontological Priority," in *Analytical Philosophy, Second Series*, ed. R. J. Butler (Oxford, 1965), pp. 109–19; Burtt [1]; and Mei [1] and [3] and Price [1] (on whether Ordinary Language philosophers need study Chinese).

18   These difficulties exist only if one holds that the acquisition of knowledge presupposes the presentation of something "immediately given" to the mind, where the mind is conceived of as a sort of "immaterial eye," and where "immediately" means, at a minimum, "without the mediation of language." This "spectatorial" account of knowledge is the common target of philosophers as different as Dewey, Hampshire, Sartre, Heidegger, and Wittgenstein.

account of knowledge is overthrown, the account of knowledge which replaces it will lead to reformulations everywhere else in philosophy, particularly in metaphilosophy. Specifically, the contrast between "science" and "philosophy" – presupposed by *all* the positions (1) through (6) which I have described – may come to seem artificial and point-less. If this happens, most of the essays in this volume will be obsolete, because the vocabulary in which they are written will be obsolete. This pattern of creeping obsoles-cence is illustrated by the fate of the notions of "meaninglessness" and "logical form" (and by my prediction that their successors, the notions of "misuse of language" and "conceptual analysis," will soon wither away). The notions which the metaphilosophers of the future will use in the struggle between philosophy-as-discovery and philosophy-as-proposal almost certainly will not be the notions used in the debates included in the present volume. But I do not know what they will be. The limits of metaphilosophical inquiry are well expressed in the following quotation from Hampshire.

> The rejection of metaphysical deduction, and the study of the details of linguistic usage, are sometimes supported by the suggestion that all earlier philosophers have been mistaken about what philosophy is, about its necessary and permanent nature. This is an inconsist-ency. If we have no final insight into the essence of man and of the mind, we have no final insight into the essence of philosophy, which is one of men's recognisable activities: recog-nisable, both through the continuity of its own development, each phase beginning as a partial contradiction of its predecessor, and also by some continuity in its gradually chang-ing relation to other inquiries, each with their own internal development.[19]

19   Hampshire [13], p. 243.

2

Dewey's Metaphysics

Very near the end of his life, Dewey hoped to write a new edition of *Experience and Nature*, "changing the title as well as the subject matter from *Nature and Experience* [sic] to *Nature and Culture*." In a letter to Bentley, he says

> I was dumb not to have seen the need for such a shift when the old text was written. I was still hopeful that the philosophic word "Experience" could be redeemed by being returned to its idiomatic usages – which was a piece of historic folly, the hope I mean.

Around the same time, Dewey formally abjured his attempts to rehabilitate the word "metaphysics."[1] As he came to recognize, it is hard to say in what sense *Experience and Nature*, which is often called his "principal work on metaphysics,"[2] is to be assimilated to the genre which includes the central books of Aristotle's *Metaphysics*, Spinoza's *Ethics*, Royce's *The World and the Individual*, and similar paradigms. Dewey's book consists, very roughly, of accounts of the historical and cultural genesis of the problems traditionally dubbed "metaphysical," interspersed with recommendations of various pieces of jargon which, Dewey thinks, will help us to see the irreality (or, at least, the evitability) of these problems. It is easier to think of the book as an explanation of why nobody needs a metaphysics, rather than as itself a metaphysical system. If one thinks of it as a book which ought to have been called *Nature and Culture*, one will be tempted to assimilate it with what, for lack of a better name, we can call the history of ideas: works such as *Metaphysics A*, Kant's "Amphiboly of the Concepts of Reflection," Hegel's *Phenomenology*, Lovejoy's *Great Chain of Being*, and Foucault's *The Order of Things*. Given such an assimilation, one can see the book not as an "empirical metaphysics" but as a historico-sociological study

Richard M. Rorty, "Dewey's Metaphysics," pp. 45–74, in Steven M. Cahn (ed.), *New Studies in the Philosophy of John Dewey*, © 1977 by University Press of New England, Lebanon, NH. Reprinted with permission of the publisher.

1   Cf. John Dewey and Arthur F. Bentley, *A Philosophical Correspondence 1932–1951*, ed. S. Ratner and J. Altman (New Brunswick, Rutgers University Press, 1964), p. 643, for the suggested title change. Cf. "Experience and Existence: A Comment," *Philosophy and Phenomenological Research*, 9 (1949), 712 ff., for a renunciation of "metaphysics."

2   E.g. by Arthur E. Murphy, in "Dewey's Epistemology and Metaphysics" in *The Philosophy of John Dewey*, ed. P. A. Schilpp (Evanston and Chicago, Tudor Publishing Co., 1939), p. 219.

of the cultural phenomenon called "metaphysics." It can be seen as one more version of the polemical critique of the tradition offered in *Reconstruction in Philosophy* and *The Quest for Certainty*.

For most of his life, however, Dewey would not have relished this assimilation. For better or worse, he *wanted* to write a metaphysical system. Throughout his life, he wavered between a therapeutic stance toward philosophy and another, quite different, stance – one in which philosophy was to become "scientific" and "empirical" and to do something serious, systematic, important, and constructive. Dewey sometimes described philosophy as the criticism of culture, but he was never quite content to think of himself as a kibitzer or a therapist or an intellectual historian. He wanted to have things both ways. When Santayana, reviewing *Experience and Nature*, remarked that "naturalistic metaphysics" was a contradiction in terms,[3] Dewey responded as follows:

> This is the extent and method of my "metaphysics": – the large and constant features of human sufferings, enjoyments, trials, failures and successes together with the institutions of art, science, technology, politics, and religion which mark them, communicate genuine features of the world within which man lives. The method differs no whit from that of any investigator who, by making certain observations and experiments, and by utilizing the existing body of ideas available for calculation and interpretation, concludes that he really succeeds in finding out something about some limited aspect of nature. If there is any novelty in *Experience and Nature*, it is not, I should say, this "metaphysics" which is that of the common man, but lies in the use made of the method to understand a group of special problems which have troubled philosophy.[4]

In this passage, Dewey wants to say simultaneously "I am just clearing away the dead wood of the philosophical tradition" and "I am using my own powerful invention – the application of scientific and empirical method in philosophy – to do so." But two generations of commentators have been puzzled to say what method might produce "a statement of the generic traits manifested by existences of all kinds without regard to their differentiation into mental and physical"[5] while differing "no whit" from that employed by the laboratory scientist. Nor has it been any clearer how displaying such generic traits could either avoid banality or dissolve traditional philosophical problems.

Yet another way of putting this tension in Dewey's thought is suggested by some remarks of Sidney Hook, describing Dewey's view of the place of philosophy in culture:

> Traditional metaphysics has always been a violent and logically impossible attempt to impose some parochial scheme of values upon the cosmos in order to justify or undermine a set of existing social institutions by a pretended deduction from the nature of Reality. ... But once crack the shell of any metaphysical doctrine, what appears is not verifiable knowledge but a directing bias ... the preeminent subject matter of philosophy has been the relation between things and *values*.[6]

3   "Dewey's Naturalistic Metaphysics," reprinted in Schilpp, p. 245.
4   Dewey, "Half-Hearted Naturalism," *Journal of Philosophy*, 24 (1927), 59.
5   Dewey, *Experience and Nature* (New York, W. W. Norton, 1929), p. 412.
6   Sidney Hook, *John Dewey* (New York, John Day, 1939), pp. 34–35.

Given this view, one has a dilemma: either Dewey's metaphysics differs from "traditional metaphysics" in not having a directing bias concerning social values because Dewey has found an "empirical" way of doing metaphysics which abstracts from any such biases and values, or else when Dewey falls into his vein of talking of the "generic traits manifested by existences of all kinds" he is in slightly bad faith. The first horn of this dilemma is not one which any Deweyan would want grasped. The best thing about Dewey, one may well feel, is that he did not, like Plato, pretend to be a "spectator of all time and eternity," but used philosophy (even that presumably highest and purest form of philosophy – metaphysics itself) as an instrument of social change. Even if, somehow, one could explain what "empirical method" in metaphysics came down to, it *ought* not (on Dewey's own principles) to be something with the magisterial neutrality which traditionally belongs to a discipline that offers us "generic traits of existents of all kinds." Even if Dewey *could* explain what is "observational and experimental" about *Experience and Nature*, his own remarks about observation and experiment always being tools in aid of some project involving social values should be brought to bear upon his own work. If, as I have said, the actual content of *Experience and Nature* is a series of analyses of how such pseudo-"problems of philosophy" as subject–object and mind-versus-matter arose and how they can be dissolved, the nature of that project is clear. But it is also clear that the talk of "observations and experiment" is as irrelevant to the accomplishment of the project as it was to the great predecessor of all such works of philosophy-as-criticism-of-culture, Hegel's *Phenomenology*.

This point is well brought out by Hook's contrast between the logical positivists' attitude toward philosophical problems and Dewey's own:

> Dewey had shown that most of the traditional problems of philosophy were pseudo-problems, i.e., they could not be solved even in their own terms. In a much more formal way the logical empiricists did the same thing and stopped. But instead of stopping with the demonstration of the logical futility of continuing the controversy over formulations which in principle could never be adequate to any concrete problems, Dewey went on to inquire what the genuine conflicts were which lay at the bottom of fruitless verbal disputes.[7]

This seems to me an accurate account of the relevant differences, and also to help explain various changes of fashion in the last forty years or so of the history of American philosophy. Deweyan naturalism, after a period of dominance, was shoved off the American philosophical scene for a couple of decades, during the heyday of logical empiricism. This can easily be explained if one is willing to grant that writers like Russell, Carnap, Ayer, and Black were doing a better job of showing the "pseudoness" of pseudo-problems than Dewey had been able to do. They could do so because they had the virtues of their vices. What now seems to us (in the light of, for example, Quine's and Sellars' criticisms of its assumptions) the dogmatism and artificiality of the logical empiricist movement was precisely what permitted this movement to criticize the tradition so sharply and so effectively. Following Kant in wishing to put philosophy upon the secure path of a science, and writing as if Hegel had never lived, the logical empiricists carried assumptions common to Descartes, Locke, and Kant to their logical conclusion and thus reduced the traditional problematic of philosophy to absurdity. By exhibiting the implications of the quest for certainty, and the inability to resist Hume's conclusions

7   Ibid., p. 44.

once one had adopted Descartes' spectatorial account of knowledge and what Austin called "the ontology of the sensible manifold," they made clear what Dewey had been unable to make clear: just why the pictures common to the great philosophers of the modern period had to be abandoned.

But in doing this, the logical empiricists encompassed their own destruction, as Austin pointed out against Ayer, and Wittgenstein against Russell, Moore, and his earlier self. "Oxford philosophy," an even shorter-lived movement than logical empiricism, helped us see how logical empiricism had been the *reductio ad absurdum* of a tradition, not the criticism of that tradition from the standpoint of magisterial "logical" neutrality which it had thought itself to be. The narrowness and artificiality of the dualisms which logical empiricism presupposed enabled them to do what Dewey, precisely because of his broader scope and his ability to see the tradition in perspective, had not. Dewey's inquiry into "the genuine conflicts which lay at the bottom of fruitless verbal disputes" had the vices of its virtues: it distracted attention from the way in which, *in their own terms*, the Cartesian-Humean-Kantian assumptions were self-refuting. The positivists and later the "Oxford philosophers" brought these internal contradictions to much sharper focus than had Dewey and his followers, just because their vision was so much narrower.

Hook's account also helps explain the current revival of interest in Dewey. The working out of the pseudoness of pseudo-problems is by now familiar. Philosophers would like something new to do. As usual when their fountains of inspiration dry up, English-speaking philosophers are looking to the Continent for some new ideas, and what they find there is just what Dewey hoped for. In 1930, Dewey wrote:

> Intellectual prophecy is dangerous; but if I read the signs of the times aright, the next synthetic movement in philosophy will emerge when the significance of the social sciences and arts has become the object of reflective attention in the same way that mathematical and physical sciences have been made the objects of thought in the past, and when their full import is grasped.[8]

In such writers as Habermas and Foucault, we find just the sort of attention Dewey wanted paid to the cultural matrix in which "the idea of a social science" arose and to the problems which the dubious self-understanding of the social sciences engenders in debates on social and political questions. In writers like Dérrida (and some American philosophers who admire Dérrida's work, like Cavell and Danto), one finds questions about the relation between philosophy and novels, philosophy and theater, philosophy and film, emerging to replace the traditional Kantian, Husserlian, and Carnapian questions about the relation between philosophy on the one hand, and mathematical physics and introspective psychology on the other. This is not, obviously, the first time in the history of philosophy that such questions have been raised; one need only think of Nietzsche, Dilthey, and Cassirer. So I do not want to prophesy that, having finally overcome the Kantian obsession with modeling philosophy on "the mathematical and physical sciences" and with the data and methods of these sciences as principal loci of philosophical inquiry, we are now about to enter a golden age of philosophy under the

8   "From Absolutism to Experimentalism" (1930), reprinted in *John Dewey on Experience, Nature and Freedom*, ed. Richard J. Bernstein (New York, The Library of Liberal Arts, 1960), p. 18.

aegis of Hegelian historicism. I confess I *hope* that that is the case, but the hope may be idle. For present purposes, I simply note that Dewey is just the philosopher one might want to reread if one were turning from Kant to Hegel, from a "metaphysics of experience" to a study of cultural development.

This contrast brings me back from an excursus on recent philosophical fashions to the tension in Dewey's thought which I want to discuss. To give one more illustration of this tension, consider Dewey's devastating remark about the tradition that "Philosophy has assumed for its function a knowledge of reality. This fact makes it a rival instead of a complement to the sciences."[9] To pursue this line of thought consistently, one must renounce the notion of an "empirical metaphysics" as wholeheartedly as one has already renounced a "transcendental account of the possibility of experience." I see no way to reconcile such passages as this, which I think represent Dewey at his best, with his best answer to Santayana – his talk of "generic traits." Sympathetic expositors of Dewey-as-metaphysician – such as Hofstadter, who describes "the aim of metaphysics, as a general theory of existence" as "the discovery of the basic types of involvements and their relationships"[10] – cannot, I think, explain why we *need* a discipline at that level of generality, nor how the results of such "discoveries" can be anything but trivial. Would anyone – including Dewey himself – really believe that there is a discipline that could somehow do for "the basic types of involvement" something left undone by novelists, sociologists, biologists, poets, and historians? All one might want a philosopher to do is to synthesize the novels, poems, histories, and sociologies of the day into some larger unity. But such syntheses are, in fact, offered us on all sides, in *every* discipline. To be an intellectual, rather than simply to "do research," is precisely to reach for some such synthesis. Nothing save the myth that there is something special called "philosophy" that provides the paradigm of a synthetic discipline, and a figure called "the philosopher" who is the paradigm of the intellectual, suggests that the professional philosopher's work is incomplete unless he has drawn up a list of the "generic traits of all existents" or discovers "the basic types of involvements."[11]

So far I have been saying that it is unlikely that we shall find, in *Experience and Nature*, anything which can be called a "metaphysics of experience" as opposed to a therapeutic treatment of the tradition – on the ground that Dewey's own view of the nature and

9   *The Quest for Certainty* (New York, Minton, Balch, 1929), p. 309. I pursue the analogies between this strand in Dewey's thought and Heidegger's criticism of "metaphysics" in "Overcoming the Tradition: Heidegger and Dewey," *Review of Metaphysics*, 30, December 1976. The comparison, I think, helps one see the interplay between what British and American philosophers have made of Hegel's criticism of Kant and what Continental philosophers have made of it.

10   Albert Hofstadter, "Concerning a Certain Deweyan Conception of Metaphysics," in *John Dewey: Philosopher of Science and Freedom*, ed. Sidney Hook (New York, Dial Press, 1949), p. 269. For criticism of this sort of view, see Hook's discussion of Randall in *The Quest for Being* (New York, St. Martins Press, 1961), pp. 163 ff.

11   Here again there is a useful analogy to be drawn with Heidegger. The notion that one should discover "the basic types of involvements" is just what led Heidegger to draw up a list of *Existentiale* in *Sein und Zeit*. The realization that this was part of the "humanist" tradition of metaphysics which he wished to set aside led him, in his later work, to renounce any such project. I discuss the relation between the professional philosopher and the all-purpose intellectual in "Keeping Philosophy Pure," *The Yale Review*, 65 (1976) and in "Professionalized Philosophy and Transcendentalist Culture," *The Georgia Review*, 30 (1976).

function of philosophy precludes it. To confirm this, one needs to look at what Dewey actually says about experience in this book, and I shall do so shortly. But first I want to insert an account of one of Dewey's earlier views–the notion of "philosophy as psychology" which he held in the 1880's and which became the center of a controversy with Shadworth Hodgson. Turning back the pages to the beginnings of Dewey's philosophical career will show us, I think, both why he thought it was so important to "redescribe experience" and will also suggest why he was tempted to describe that redescription as "the whole of philosophy." Dewey was a hedgehog rather than a fox; he spent his life trying to articulate and restate a single vision, and in the writings of his third decade he already exhibits the tension I have claimed to find in the later writings.

Hodgson reacts indignantly to Dewey's youthful claim that "Psychology is the completed method of philosophy, because in it science and philosophy, fact and reason, are one." He writes:

> The passage [in Dewey's articles] which comes nearest to a description of the method of psychology is the following:
>> But the very essence of psychology as method is that it treats of experience in its absolute totality, not setting up some one aspect of it to account for the whole, as, for example, our physical evolutionists do, nor yet attempting to determine its nature from something outside and beyond itself, as, for example our so-called empirical psychologists have done.
> The method is here described by negatives only. It consists in the precepts to avoid the faults exemplified by the physical evolutionists on the one hand and the empirical psychologists on the other. But as to any positive direction how to go to work in investigation, there is a blank. This is quite what we should expect from the identification of psychology with transcendental philosophy.[12]

Hodgson's criticism is, I think, entirely justified. It parallels Santayana's criticism of the possibility of a "naturalistic metaphysic," and neatly singles out a recurrent flaw in Dewey's work: his habit of announcing a bold new positive program when all he offers, and all he needs to offer, is criticism of the tradition. "Psychology as method" was only the first of a series of resounding but empty slogans that Dewey employed, but it is important to see why this particular slogan attracted him. He ends one of the articles attacked by Hodgson by saying:

> The conclusion of the whole matter is that a "being like man," since self-conscious, is an individualized universe, and hence that his nature is the proper material of philosophy, and in its wholeness the only material. Psychology is the science of this nature, and no dualism in it, or in ways of regarding it, is tenable.[13]

In this passage, and in the pages leading up to it, we get the following doctrines: (a) most of the troubles philosophy has encountered stem from untenable dualisms; (b) traditional

---

12   Shadworth Hodgson, "Illusory Psychology," an attack on Dewey originally published in *Mind* for 1886, and reprinted in *The Early Works of John Dewey*, Vol. 1 (Carbondale, Southern Illinois University Press, 1969). This passage appears in that volume at p. lvi, and the two passages cited from Dewey at pp. 157–158 and pp. 161–162 respectively.
13   From "Psychology as Philosophic Method," *Early Works*, 1, pp. 166–167.

empiricism (as represented by Hume, Bain, and Hodgson) puts forward a "partial account of experience" which separates percepts from concepts;[14] (c) the way to overcome such dualisms as those produced by empiricism's separation of percepts from concepts, and thus of consciousness from self-consciousness, is "psychology," the discipline which tells us that no such separations are possible. In his reply to Hodgson, Dewey never really answers Hodgson's question about what the method of psychology might be, but blandly says

> I speak, not as a Germanizing transcendentalist, but according to my humble lights as a psychologist, when I say that I know nothing of a perceptual order apart from a conceptual, and nothing of an agent or bearer apart from the content which it bears. As a psychologist, I see the possibility of abstractly analyzing each from the other, and if I were as fond of erecting the results of an analysis into real entities as Mr. Hodgson believes me to be, I should suppose that they were actually distinct as concrete experiences. But, sticking fast to what Psychology teaches me, I must hold that they are aspects, analytically arrived at, of the one existing reality – conscious experience.[15]

It was not, of course, "psychology" which taught Dewey this, but rather T. H. Green, who had spent a great deal of energy reiterating Kant's criticism of Hume, viz. that no set of percepts juggled about could produce self-consciousness, and who drew the moral that the British empiricist notion of a sensory impression was a confusion between a physiological causal process and a self-conscious perceptual belief.[16] Dewey, however, is not content to let Green's analysis of experience be a better one than Bain's and Hodgson's Humean account: he needs to insist that what Green tells us is also told us by experience itself:

> We may see how the matter stands by inquiring what would be the effect upon philosophy if self-consciousness were not an *experienced fact*, i.e., if it were not one actual stage in that realization of the universe by an individual which is defined as constituting the sphere of psychology. The result would be again, precisely, that no such thing as philosophy, under any theory of its nature whatever, is possible. Philosophy, it cannot be too often repeated, consists simply in viewing things *sub specie aeternitatis* or *in ordine ad universum*.... To deny, therefore, that self-consciousness is a matter of psychological experience is to deny the possibility of any philosophy.[17]

Though Dewey was soon to recant this definition of philosophy, he was never to escape the notion that what he himself said about experience described what experience

---

14 For the notion of an "empiricism" as the view in which a "partial account of experience, or rather account of partial experience, is put forward as the totality," see *Early Works*, 1, p. 161.

15 *Early Works*, 1, pp. 171–172.

16 Cf. T. H. Green, *Works*, 1 (London, 1885), pp. 13–19. Green's point in this passage is made explicitly by Dewey in one of the essays which Hodgson is criticizing ("The Psychological Standpoint," *Early Works*, 1, pp. 125–126). Note also Dewey's often cited tribute to Green (*Early Works*, 1, p. 153). For Green's and Dewey's central point against Hume clothed in modern dress, see Sellars, "Empiricism and the Philosophy of Mind," sec. VI (reprinted in his *Science Perception and Reality* [London, Routledge and Kegan Paul, 1963]) and J. Bennett, *Locke, Berkeley, Hume* (Oxford, Oxford University Press, 1971), sec. 4).

17 *Early Works*, 1, p. 152.

itself looked like, whereas what others said of experience was a confusion between the data and the products of their analyses. Others might be transcendentalizing metaphysicians, but he was a "humble psychologist." Other philosophers produced dualisms, he was to insist throughout his life, because they "erected the results of an analysis into real entities." But a non-dualistic account of experience, of the sort Dewey himself proposed, was to be a true return to *die Sache selbst*. Though he gave up the term "psychology" for his own "philosophical method," replacing it with still vaguer notions like "scientific method in philosophy" and "experimentalism in metaphysics," he was always to insist that his opponents were those who erected dualisms because they "abandoned the acknowledgement of the primacy and ultimacy of gross experience – primary as it is given in an uncontrolled form, ultimate as it is given in a more regulated and significant form – a form made possible by the methods and results of reflective experience."[18] What exasperated Hodgson in the 1880's was to exasperate another generation of critics in the 1930's. These critics welcomed with enthusiasm Dewey's suggestions about the cause and cure of traditional empiricisms and rationalisms, but were unable to see much point in Dewey's own "constructive" attempts to produce a philosophical jargon that was dualism-free, nor in his claim to be more "empirical" in method than his opponents.

To conclude this look at Dewey's earliest formulation of a program and method, I think we can see from the passages I have cited how easy it would have been for him, once he had, as he put it, "drifted away from Hegelianism,"[19] to have tried to do justice both to his earlier belief that the Kant–Hegel–Green critique of empiricism was the key to an understanding of man, and to his growing distrust of philosophy as a view of the universe *sub specie aeternitatis*. His resolution of the conflict amounted to saying: there must be a standpoint from which experience can be seen in terms of some "generic traits" which, once recognized, will make it impossible for us to describe it in these misleading ways which generate the subject-object and mind-matter dualisms that have been the dreary topics of traditional philosophical controversy. This viewpoint would not be *sub specie aeternitatis*, since it would emphasize precisely the temporality and contingency which Augustine and Spinoza used the notion of "eternity" to exclude. But it would resemble traditional metaphysics in providing a permanent neutral matrix for future inquiry. Such a naturalistic metaphysics would say, "Here is what experience is really like, before dualistic analysis has done its fell work." Such a philosophy would thus enjoy the benefit of that "immense release and liberation"[20] which young Dewey had found in Hegel, while spurning all temptations toward "German transcendentalizing."

Some such notion of doing equal justice to Hegel and to "naturalism" lies behind the project Dewey set himself in *Experience and Nature*, and I hope this backward look at the young Dewey may have helped lend additional plausibility to the criticisms I now want to make of that book. The first and most general criticism just repeats Santayana's claim that "naturalistic metaphysics" is a contradiction in terms. One can put this point best, perhaps, by saying that no man can serve both Locke and Hegel. Nobody can claim to

18   *Experience and Nature*, p. 15.
19   The phrase is from the autobiographical essay "From Absolutism to Experimentalism," reprinted in Bernstein, p. 12. On the same page he remarks that "I should never think of ignoring, much less denying, what an astute critic occasionally refers to as a novel discovery – that acquaintance with Hegel has left a permanent deposit in my thinking."
20   "From Absolutism to Experimentalism," p. 10.

offer an "empirical" account of something called "the inclusive integrity of 'experience,'" nor take this "integrated unity as the starting point for philosophic thought,"[21] if he also agrees with Hegel that the starting point of philosophic thought is bound to be the dialectical situation in which one finds oneself caught in one's own historical period–the problems of the men of one's time. Only someone who thought, with Locke, that we can free ourselves from the problems of the day and pursue a "plain, historical, method" in examining the emergence of complex experiences out of simple ones would have written the following:

> That the physiological organism with its structure, whether in man or in the lower animals, is concerned with making adaptations and uses of material in the interest of maintenance of the life-process, cannot be denied. The brain and nervous system are primarily organs of action-undergoing; biologically it can be asserted without contravention that primary experience is of a corresponding type. Hence, unless there is breach of historic and natural continuity, cognitive experience must originate within that of a non-cognitive sort.[22]

Again, only someone who thought that a proper account of the "generic traits" of experience could cross the line between physiology and sociology – between causal processes and the self-conscious beliefs and inferences that they make possible – would have written the chapter in *Experience and Nature* called "Nature, Life and Body-Mind," or have attempted to develop a jargon that would apply equally to plants, nervous sytems, and physicists.[23] But this return to Lockean modes of thought, under the aegis of Darwin, betrayed precisely the insight which Dewey owed to Green: that nothing is to be gained for an understanding of human knowledge by running together the vocabularies in which we describe the causal antecedents of knowledge with those in which we offer justifications of our claims to knowledge. Dewey's naturalistic metaphysics hoped to eliminate epistemological problems by offering an up-to-date version of Locke's "plain, historical method." But what Green and Hegel had seen, and Dewey himself saw perfectly well except when he was sidetracked into doing "metaphysics," was that we can eliminate epistemological problems by eliminating the assumption that justification must repose on something other than social practices and human needs. To say, as Dewey wants to, that to gain knowledge is to solve problems, one does not need to find "continuities" between nervous systems and people, or between "experience" and "nature." One does not need to justify our claim to know that, say, a given action was the best we could take by noting that the brain is an "organ of action-undergoing," any more than by pointing out that the particles which make up the brain are undergoing some actions themselves. Dewey, in short, confuses two ways of revolting against philosophical dualisms. The first way is to point out that the dualism is imposed by a tradition for specific cultural reasons, but has now outlived its usefulness. This is the Hegelian way – the way Dewey adopts in "An Empirical Survey of Empiricisms." The second is to describe the phenomenon in a nondualistic way which emphasizes "continuity between lower and higher processes." This is the Lockean way – the way which

21 *Experience and Nature,* p. 9.
22 Ibid., p. 23.
23 The sort of jargon which Dewey and Bentley were still aiming for in *Knowing and the Known.*

led Locke to assimilate all mental acts to raw feels, thus paving the way for Humean skepticism. It was this assimilation which provoked Kant's remark that whereas Leibniz "intellectualized" appearances, "Locke sensualized all concepts of the understanding"[24] and which led German thought to turn away from the "naturalism" which Locke seemed to represent. Its reappearance in *Experience and Nature* led the logical empiricists to accuse Dewey of confusing "psychological" with "conceptual" issues.

Dewey wanted to be as naturalistic as Locke and as historicist as Hegel. This can indeed be done. One can say with Locke that the causal processes that go on in the human organism suffice, without the intrusion of anything non-natural, to explain the acquisition of knowledge (moral, mathematical, empirical, and political). One can also say, with Hegel, that rational criticism of knowledge-claims is always in terms of the problems that human beings face at a particular epoch. These two lines of thought neither intersect nor conflict. Keeping them separate has the virtue of doing just what Dewey wanted to do – preventing the formulation of the traditional, skeptically motivated "problems of epistemology." But it also leaves "systematic philosophy" or "metaphysics" with little to do. Dewey never quite brought himself to adopt the Bouwsma-like stance that philosophy's mission, like that of therapy, was to make itself obsolete. So he thought, in *Experience and Nature*, to show what the discovery of the *true* "generic traits" of experience could do.

To make this line of criticism a bit more specific, consider Dewey's treatment of the mind-body problem. He thought to "solve" this problem by avoiding both the crudity and paradox of materialism and the "unscientific" theorizing offered by traditional dualisms. The solution is to say that

> Feelings make sense; as immediate meanings of events or objects, they are sensations, or more properly, sensa. Without language, the qualities of organic action that are feelings are pains, pleasures, odors, noises, tones, only potentially and proleptically. With language, they are discriminated and identified. They are then "objectified"; they are immediate traits of things. This "objectification" is not a miraculous ejection from the organism or soul into external things, nor an illusory attribution of psychical entities to physical things. The qualities never were "in" the organism; they always were qualities of interactions in which both extra-organic things and organisms partake.[25]

Such phrases as "qualities of interactions" soothe those who do not see a mind–body problem and provoke those who do. Tell us more, the latter say, about these interactions: are they interactions between people and tables, say? Is my *interaction* with this table brown, rather than, as I had previously thought, the *table* being brown? Is Dewey saying something more than that nobody would know that the table was brown unless he understood what the word "brown" meant? Is *that*, in turn, to make the Kantian point that there are no divisions between objects, or between objects and their qualities, until concepts have been used to give sense to feelings? But can that point be made without committing oneself to transcendental idealism? Have we solved the problem of the relation between the empirical self and the material world only to wind up once again with a transcendental ego constituting both?

24   *Kritik der reinen Vernunft*, A271 = B327.
25   *Experience and Nature*, pp. 258–259.

This sequence of rhetorical questions expresses the exasperation which readers of Dewey often feel at his attempt to be as commonsensically realistic as Aristotle while somehow sounding as idealistic as Kant and Green. There is obviously *some* sense in which Dewey agrees with Kant that only the transcendental idealist can be an empirical realist. I think the sense is this: Dewey believed that only someone who broke with Humean empiricism in the way in which Kant and Green did, who recognized that intuitions without concepts were blind, and that no data were ever "raw," could say that both brown tables and swirls of colorless atoms were equally "given in experience." That is, he thought that what Sellars has called "the clash between the scientific and the manifest images of man" could be resolved only by taking commonsense concepts like "brown" and "ugly" and "painful" and "table" as qualities of one sort of interaction and scientific concepts like "atom" and "mass" as qualities of another. What Kant had called "the constitution of the empirical world by synthesis of intuitions under concepts," Dewey wanted to call "interactions in which both extra-organic things and organisms partake." But he wanted this harmless-sounding naturalistic phrase to have the same generality, and to accomplish the same epistemological feats, which Kant's talk of the "constitution of objects" had performed. He wanted phrases like "transaction with the environment" and "adaptation to conditions" to be simultaneously naturalistic and transcendental – to be common-sensical remarks about human perception and knowledge viewed as the psychologist views it and also to be expressions of "generic traits of existence." So he blew up notions like "transaction" and "situation" until they sounded as mysterious as "prime matter" or "thing-in-itself." He made it sound as if what the table *really* was was neither an ugly brown thing whose hard edges bumped people, nor yet a swirl of particles, but something common to both–sheer potentiality, ready to be transformed in a situation. He wanted, in a way, just what he had wanted in the 1880's – that psychology and metaphysics should be one. But the way in which they were to be made one consisted merely in lifting the vocabulary of the evolutionary biologist out of the laboratory and using it to describe everything that could ever count as "Knowledge." It can, of course, be so used. But no problems are solved by doing so, any more than they were solved by Locke's "sensualization" of concepts.

To return to the mind–body problem, the passage I quoted about secondary qualities as "qualities of interactions in which both extra-organic things and organisms partake" leads one naturally to ask: what qualities do those two sorts of things have when they are not interacting? And here Dewey always turns naturalistic and common-sensical on us. Suddenly dropping talk of the "generic traits of existence," we are told that what is interacting is just the good old table, and the good old human body of common sense, or else two swirls of particles, or any other nongeneric description you like. If Dewey had, like Ryle and Sellars and Wittgenstein and Heidegger, confined himself to remarking that without the spectator model of knowledge we should never have had a mind–body problem in the first place, he would have been on firm ground, and would (I think) have said all that needs to be said. But, once again, he wanted not merely skeptical diagnosis but also constructive metaphysical system-building. The system that was built in *Experience and Nature* sounded idealistic, and its solution to the mind-body problem seemed one more invocation of the transcendental ego, because the level of generality to which Dewey ascends is the same level at which Kant worked, and the model of knowledge is the same – the constitution of the knowable by the cooperation of two unknowables. Sounding like Kant is a fate that will overtake *any* systematic account of human knowledge which purports to supplant both physiological Lockean accounts and sociological Hegelian accounts by something still more generic. The "ontology of the sensible manifold" is the common destiny of all philosophers who try for an account of subject-and-object, mind-and-body, which has this generic quality.

I have now made all the criticisms of Dewey's "naturalistic metaphysics" which I have to make, and I should like to end by offering a brief encomium on what Dewey accomplished, sometimes despite himself. Dewey set out to show the harm which traditional philosophical dualisms were doing to our culture, and he thought that to do this job he needed a metaphysics – a description of the generic traits of existence that would solve (or dissolve) the traditional problems of philosophy, as well as open up new avenues for cultural development. I think that he was successful in this latter, larger, aim; he is one of the few philosophers of our century whose imagination was expansive enough to envisage a culture shaped along lines different from those we have developed in the West during the last three hundred years. Dewey's mistake – and it was a trivial and unimportant mistake, even though I have devoted most of this essay to it – was the notion that criticism of culture had to take the form of a redescription of "nature" or "experience" or both. Had Dewey written the book called *Nature and Culture*, which was to replace *Experience and Nature*, he might have felt able to forget the Aristotelian and Kantian models and simply have been Hegelian all the way, as he was in much of his other (and best) work.

By being "Hegelian" I mean here treating the cultural developments which Kant thought it was the task of philosophy to preserve and protect as simply temporary stopping-places for the World-Spirit. Kant thought that there were three permanent data of philosophy: (1) Newtonian physics and the resulting conception of a unified science centering on mathematical descriptions of micro-structures; (2) the common moral consciousness of a North German Pietist; (3) the sense of delicacy, of playful freedom from the imperatives of scientific inquiry and moral duty, offered by the eighteenth-century aesthetic consciousness. The aim of philosophy was to preserve these cultural accomplishments by drawing the lines between them (preferably writing a separate book about each) and showing how they could be rendered compatible with one another and made "necessary." Philosophy, for Kant, as it had been for Aristotle, was a matter of drawing boundaries to keep scientific inquiry from interfering with morals, the aesthetic from interfering with the scientific, and so on. For Hegel, on the other hand, Newtonian physics, the contrite consciousness, and the delight in landscape gardens were brief episodes in the development of spirit: stepping-stones on the way to a culture that would encompass all of these without dividing them from one another. For Dewey, the quests for truth, for moral virtue, and for aesthetic bliss are seen as distinct and potentially competing activities only if one thinks of truth as "accuracy of representation," of moral virtue as purity of heart, and of beauty as "purposiveness without purpose." He did not question the accuracy of Kant's description of the eighteenth-century's ways of thinking of these things, but, with Hegel, he questioned the necessity of staying in the eighteenth century.

If one abandons the Kantian distinctions, one will not think of philosophy as a matter of solving philosophical problems (for example, of having a theory of the relation between sense-experience and theoretical knowledge which will reconcile rationalists and empiricists, or a theory of the relation between mind and body which will reconcile materialists and panpsychists). One will think of it as a matter of putting aside the distinctions that permitted the formulations of the problems in the first place. Dewey, I suggested earlier, was not as good at dissolving philosophical problems as the followers of either the early or the latter Wittgenstein–but he had a larger aim in view. He wanted to sketch a culture that would not continually give rise to new versions of the old problems, because it would no longer make the distinctions between Truth, Goodness, and Beauty which engender such problems.

In doing this larger job, his chief enemy was the notion of Truth as accuracy of representation, the notion later to be attacked by Heidegger, Sartre, and Foucault. Dewey thought that if he could break down this notion, if scientific inquiry could be seen as adapting and coping rather than copying, the continuity between science, morals, and art would become apparent. We would no longer ask ourselves questions about the "purity" of works of art or of our experience of them. We would be receptive to notions like Dérrida's – that language is not a device for representing reality, but a reality in which we live and move. We would be receptive to the diagnosis of traditional philosophy which Sartre and Heidegger offer us – as the attempt to escape from time into the eternal, from freedom into necessity, from action into contemplation. We would see the social sciences not as awkward and unsuccessful attempts to imitate the physicists' elegance, certainty, and freedom from concern with "value," but as suggestions for ways of making human lives into works of art. We would see modern physics both as Snow sees it – as the greatest human accomplishment of the century – and as Kuhn sees it, as one more episode in a series of crises and intervening claims, a series that will never terminate in "the discovery of the truth," the finally accurate representation of reality.

Finally, we might move out from under the shadow of Kant's notion that something called a "metaphysics of experience" is needed to provide the "philosophical basis" for the criticism of culture, to the realization that philosophers' criticisms of culture are not more "scientific," more "fundamental," or more "deep" than those of labor leaders, literary critics, retired statesmen, or sculptors. Philosophers would no longer seem spectators of all time and eternity, or (like social scientists) unsuccessful imitators of the physical sciences, because the scientists themselves would not be seen as spectators or representers. Philosophers could be seen as people who work with the history of philosophy and the contemporary effects of those ideas called "philosophic" upon the rest of the culture – the remnants of past attempts to describe the "generic traits of existence." This is a modest, limited enterprise – as modest and limited as carving stones into new shapes, or finding more basic elementary particles. But it sometimes produces great achievements, and Dewey's work is one of those achievements. It is great not because it provides an accurate representation of the generic traits of nature or experience or culture or anything else. Its greatness lies in the sheer provocativeness of its suggestions about how to slough off our intellectual past, and about how to treat that past as material for playful experimentation rather than as imposing tasks and responsibilities upon us. Dewey's work helps us put aside that spirit of *seriousness* which artists traditionally lack and philosophers are traditionally supposed to maintain. For the spirit of seriousness can only exist in an intellectual world in which human life is an attempt to attain an end beyond life, an escape from freedom into the atemporal. The conception of such a world is still built into our education and our common speech, not to mention the attitudes of philosophers toward their work. But Dewey did his best to help us get rid of it, and he should not be blamed if he occasionally came down with the disease he was trying to cure.

3

Philosophy and the Mirror of Nature: Introduction and Chapter VIII

Introduction

Philosophers usually think of their discipline as one which discusses perennial, eternal problems – problems which arise as soon as one reflects. Some of these concern the difference between human beings and other beings, and are crystallized in questions concerning the relation between the mind and the body. Other problems concern the legitimation of claims to know, and are crystallized in questions concerning the "foundations" of knowledge. To discover these foundations is to discover something about the mind, and conversely. Philosophy as a discipline thus sees itself as the attempt to underwrite or debunk claims to knowledge made by science, morality, art, or religion. It purports to do this on the basis of its special understanding of the nature of knowledge and of mind. Philosophy can be foundational in respect to the rest of culture because culture is the assemblage of claims to knowledge, and philosophy adjudicates such claims. It can do so because it understands the foundations of knowledge, and it finds these foundations in a study of man-as-knower, of the "mental processes" or the "activity of representation" which make knowledge possible. To know is to represent accurately what is outside the mind; so to understand the possibility and nature of knowledge is to understand the way in which the mind is able to construct such representations. Philosophy's central concern is to be a general theory of representation, a theory which will divide culture up into the areas which represent reality well, those which represent it less well, and those which do not represent it at all (despite their pretense of doing so).

We owe the notion of a "theory of knowledge" based on an understanding of "mental processes" to the seventeenth century, and especially to Locke. We owe the notion of "the mind" as a separate entity in which "processes" occur to the same period, and especially to Descartes. We owe the notion of philosophy as a tribunal of pure reason, upholding or denying the claims of the rest of culture, to the eighteenth century and especially to Kant, but this Kantian notion presupposed general assent to Lockean notions of mental processes and Cartesian notions of mental substance. In the nineteenth century, the notion of philosophy as a foundational discipline which "grounds" knowledge-claims was consolidated in the writings of the neo-Kantians. Occasional protests against this conception of culture as in need of "grounding" and against the pretensions of a theory of knowledge to perform this task (in, for example, Nietzsche and William James) went largely unheard. "Philosophy" became, for the intellectuals, a substitute for religion. It was the area of culture where one touched bottom, where one found the vocabulary and the convictions which permitted one to explain and justify one's activity *as* an intellectual, and thus to discover the significance of one's life.

At the beginning of our century, this claim was reaffirmed by philosophers (notably Russell and Husserl) who were concerned to keep philosophy "rigorous" and "scientific." But there was a note of desperation in their voices, for by this time the triumph of the secular over the claims of religion was almost complete. Thus the philosopher could no longer see himself as in the intellectual avant-garde, or as protecting men against the forces of superstition.[1] Further, in the course of the nineteenth century, a new form of culture had arisen – the culture of the man of letters, the intellectual who wrote poems and novels and political treatises, and criticisms of other people's poems and novels and treatises. Descartes, Locke, and Kant had written in a period in which the secularization of culture was being made possible by the success of natural science. But by the early twentieth century the scientists had become as remote from most intellectuals as had the theologians. Poets and novelists had taken the place of both preachers and philosophers as the moral teachers of the youth. The result was that the more "scientific" and "rigorous" philosophy became, the less it had to do with the rest of culture and the more absurd its traditional pretensions seemed. The attempts of both analytic philosophers and phenomenologists to "ground" this and "criticize" that were shrugged off by those whose activities were purportedly being grounded or criticized. Philosophy as a whole was shrugged off by those who wanted an ideology or a self-image.

It is against this background that we should see the work of the three most important philosophers of our century – Wittgenstein, Heidegger, and Dewey. Each tried, in his early years, to find a new way of making philosophy "foundational" – a new way of formulating an ultimate context for thought. Wittgenstein tried to construct a new theory of representation which would have nothing to do with mentalism, Heidegger to construct a new set of philosophical categories which would have nothing to do with science, epistemology, or the Cartesian quest for certainty, and Dewey to construct a naturalized version of Hegel's vision of history. Each of the three came to see his earlier effort as self-deceptive, as an attempt to retain a certain conception of philosophy after the notions needed to flesh out that conception (the seventeenth-century notions of knowledge and mind) had been discarded. Each of the three, in his later work, broke free of the Kantian conception of philosophy as foundational, and spent his time warning us against those very temptations to which he himself had once succumbed. Thus their later work is therapeutic rather than constructive, edifying rather than systematic, designed to make the reader question his own motives for philosophizing rather than to supply him with a new philosophical program.

Wittgenstein, Heidegger, and Dewey are in agreement that the notion of knowledge as accurate representation, made possible by special mental processes, and intelligible

1   Terms such as "himself" and "men" should, throughout this book, be taken as abbreviations for "himself or herself," "men and women," and so on.

through a general theory of representation, needs to be abandoned. For all three, the notions of "foundations of knowledge" and of philosophy as revolving around the Cartesian attempt to answer the epistemological skeptic are set aside. Further, they set aside the notion of "the mind" common to Descartes, Locke, and Kant – as a special subject of study, located in inner space, containing elements or processes which make knowledge possible. This is not to say that they have *alternative* "theories of knowledge" or "philosophies of mind." They set aside epistemology and metaphysics as possible disciplines. I say "set aside" rather than "argue against" because their attitude toward the traditional problematic is like the attitude of seventeenth-century philosophers toward the scholastic problematic. They do not devote themselves to discovering false propositions or bad arguments in the works of their predecessors (though they occasionally do that too). Rather, they glimpse the possibility of a form of intellectual life in which the vocabulary of philosophical reflection inherited from the seventeenth century would seem as pointless as the thirteenth-century philosophical vocabulary had seemed to the Enlightenment. To assert the possibility of a post-Kantian culture, one in which there is no all-encompassing discipline which legitimizes or grounds the others, is not necessarily to argue against any particular Kantian doctrine, any more than to glimpse the possibility of a culture in which religion either did not exist, or had no connection with science or politics, was necessarily to argue against Aquinas's claim that God's existence can be proved by natural reason. Wittgenstein, Heidegger, and Dewey have brought us into a period of "revolutionary" philosophy (in the sense of Kuhn's "revolutionary" science) by introducing new maps of the terrain (viz., of the whole panorama of human activities) which simply do not include those features which previously seemed to dominate.

This book is a survey of some recent developments in philosophy, especially analytic philosophy, from the point of view of the anti-Cartesian and anti-Kantian revolution which I have just described. The aim of the book is to undermine the reader's confidence in "the mind" as something about which one should have a "philosophical" view, in "knowledge" as something about which there ought to be a "theory" and which has "foundations," and in "philosophy" as it has been conceived since Kant. Thus the reader in search of a new theory on any of the subjects discussed will be disappointed. Although I discuss "solutions to the mind-body problem" this is not in order to propose one but to illustrate why I do not think there is a problem. Again, although I discuss "theories of reference" I do not offer one, but offer only suggestions about why the search for such a theory is misguided. The book, like the writings of the philosophers I most admire, is therapeutic rather than constructive. The therapy offered is, nevertheless, parasitic upon the constructive efforts of the very analytic philosophers whose frame of reference I am trying to put in question. Thus most of the particular criticisms of the tradition which I offer are borrowed from such systematic philosophers as Sellars, Quine, Davidson, Ryle, Malcolm, Kuhn, and Putnam.

I am as much indebted to these philosophers for the means I employ as I am to Wittgenstein, Heidegger, and Dewey for the ends to which these means are put. I hope to convince the reader that the dialectic within analytic philosophy, which has carried philosophy of mind from Broad to Smart, philosophy of language from Frege to Davidson, epistemology from Russell to Sellars, and philosophy of science from Carnap to Kuhn, needs to be carried a few steps further. These additional steps will, I think, put us in a position to criticize the very notion of "analytic philosophy," and indeed of "philosophy" itself as it has been understood since the time of Kant.

From the standpoint I am adopting, indeed, the difference between "analytic" and other sorts of philosophy is relatively unimportant – a matter of style and tradition rather than a difference of "method" or of first principles. The reason why the book is largely written in the vocabulary of contemporary analytic philosophers, and with reference to problems discussed in the analytic literature, is merely autobiographical. They are the vocabulary and the literature with which I am most familiar, and to which I owe what grasp I have of philosophical issues. Had I been equally familiar with other contemporary modes of writing philosophy, this would have been a better and more useful book, although an even longer one. As I see it, the kind of philosophy which stems from Russell and Frege is, like classical Husserlian phenomenology, simply one more attempt to put philosophy in the position which Kant wished it to have – that of judging other areas of culture on the basis of its special knowledge of the "foundations" of these areas. "Analytic" philosophy is one more variant of Kantian philosophy, a variant marked principally by thinking of representation as linguistic rather than mental, and of philosophy of language rather than "transcendental critique," or psychology, as the discipline which exhibits the "foundations of knowledge." This emphasis on language, I shall be arguing in chapters four and six, does not essentially change the Cartesian-Kantian problematic, and thus does not really give philosophy a new self-image. For analytic philosophy is still committed to the construction of a permanent, neutral framework for inquiry, and thus for all of culture.

It is the notion that human activity (and inquiry, the search for knowledge, in particular) takes place within a framework which can be isolated prior to the conclusion of inquiry – a set of presuppositions discoverable a priori – which links contemporary philosophy to the Descartes–Locke–Kant tradition. For the notion that there is such a framework only makes sense if we think of this framework as imposed by the nature of the knowing subject, by the nature of his faculties or by the nature of the medium within which he works. The very idea of "philosophy" as something distinct from "science" would make little sense without the Cartesian claim that by turning inward we could find ineluctable truth, and the Kantian claim that this truth imposes limits on the possible results of empirical inquiry. The notion that there could be such a thing as "foundations of knowledge" (*all* knowledge – in every field, past, present, and future) or a "theory of representation" (*all* representation, in familiar vocabularies and those not yet dreamed of) depends on the assumption that there is some such a priori constraint. If we have a Deweyan conception of knowledge, as what we are justified in believing, then we will not imagine that there are enduring constraints on what can count as knowledge, since we will see "justification" as a social phenomenon rather than a transaction between "the knowing subject" and "reality." If we have a Wittgensteinian notion of language as tool rather than mirror, we will not look for necessary conditions of the possibility of linguistic representation. If we have a Heideggerian conception of philosophy, we will see the attempt to make the nature of the knowing subject a source of necessary truths as one more self-deceptive attempt to substitute a "technical" and determinate question for that openness to strangeness which initially tempted us to begin thinking.

One way to see how analytic philosophy fits within the traditional Cartesian-Kantian pattern is to see traditional philosophy as an attempt to escape from history – an attempt to find nonhistorical conditions of any possible historical development. From this perspective, the common message of Wittgenstein, Dewey, and Heidegger is a historicist one. Each of the three reminds us that investigations of the foundations of knowledge or morality or language or society may be simply apologetics, attempts to eternalize a certain contemporary language-game, social practice, or self-image. The moral of this book is also historicist, and the three parts into which it is divided are intended to put the notions of "mind," of "knowledge," and of "philosophy," respectively, in historical perspective. Part I is concerned with philosophy of mind, and in chapter one I try to show that the so-called intuitions which lie behind Cartesian dualism are ones which have a historical origin. In chapter two, I try to show how these intuitions would be changed if physiological methods of prediction and control took the place of psychological methods.

Part II is concerned with epistemology and with recent attempts to find "successor subjects" to epistemology. Chapter three describes the genesis of the notion of "epistemology" in the seventeenth century, and its connection with the Cartesian notions of "mind" discussed in chapter one. It presents "theory of knowledge" as a notion based upon a confusion between the justification of knowledge-claims and their causal explanation – between, roughly, social practices and postulated psychological processes. Chapter four is the central chapter of the book – the one in which the ideas which led to its being written are presented. These ideas are those of Sellars and of Quine, and in that chapter I interpret Sellars's attack on "givenness" and Quine's attack on "necessity" as the crucial steps in undermining the possibility of a "theory of knowledge." The holism and pragmatism common to both philosophers, and which they share with the later Wittgenstein, are the lines of thought within analytic philosophy which I wish to extend. I argue that when extended in a certain way they let us see truth as, in James's phrase, "what it is better for us to believe," rather than as "the accurate representation of reality." Or, to put the point less provocatively, they show us that the notion of "accurate representation" is simply an automatic and empty compliment which we pay to those beliefs which are successful in helping us do what we want to do. In chapters five and six I discuss and criticize what I regard as reactionary attempts to treat empirical psychology or philosophy of language as "successor subjects" to epistemology. I argue that only the notion of knowledge as "accuracy of representation" persuades us that the study of psychological processes or of language – qua media of representation – can do what epistemology failed to do. The moral of part II as a whole is that the notion of knowledge as the assemblage of accurate representations is optional – that it may be replaced by a pragmatist conception of knowledge which eliminates the Greek contrast between contemplation and action, between representing the world and coping with it. A historical epoch dominated by Greek ocular metaphors may, I suggest, yield to one in which the philosophical vocabulary incorporating these metaphors seems as quaint as the animistic vocabulary of pre-classical times.

In part III I take up the idea of "philosophy" more explicitly. Chapter seven interprets the traditional distinction between the search for "objective knowledge" and other, less privileged, areas of human activity as merely the distinction between "normal discourse" and "abnormal discourse." Normal discourse (a generalization of Kuhn's notion of "normal science") is any discourse (scientific, political, theological, or whatever) which embodies agreed-upon criteria for reaching agreement; abnormal discourse is any which lacks such criteria. I argue that the attempt (which has defined traditional philosophy) to explicate "rationality" and "objectivity" in terms of conditions of accurate representation is a self-deceptive effort to eternalize the normal

discourse of the day, and that, since the Greeks, philosophy's self-image has been dominated by this attempt. In chapter eight I use some ideas drawn from Gadamer and Sartre
to develop a contrast between "systematic" and "edifying" philosophy, and to show how
"abnormal" philosophy which does not conform to the traditional Cartesian-Kantian
matrix is related to "normal" philosophy. I present Wittgenstein, Heidegger, and Dewey
as philosophers whose aim is to edify – to help their readers, or society as a whole, break
free from outworn vocabularies and attitudes, rather than to provide "grounding" for
the intuitions and customs of the present.

I hope that what I have been saying has made clear why I chose "Philosophy and the
Mirror of Nature" as a title. It is pictures rather than propositions, metaphors rather
than statements, which determine most of our philosophical convictions. The picture
which holds traditional philosophy captive is that of the mind as a great mirror, containing various representations – some accurate, some not – and capable of being
studied by pure, nonempirical methods. Without the notion of the mind as mirror, the
notion of knowledge as accuracy of representation would not have suggested itself.
Without this latter notion, the strategy common to Descartes and Kant – getting more
accurate representations by inspecting, repairing, and polishing the mirror, so to speak –
would not have made sense. Without this strategy in mind, recent claims that philosophy could consist of "conceptual analysis" or "phenomenological analysis" or
"explication of meanings" or examination of "the logic of our language" or of "the
structure of the constituting activity of consciousness" would not have made sense. It
was such claims as these which Wittgenstein mocked in the *Philosophical Investigations*,
and it is by following Wittgenstein's lead that analytic philosophy has progressed toward
the "post-positivistic" stance it presently occupies. But Wittgenstein's flair for deconstructing captivating pictures needs to be supplemented by historical awareness –
awareness of the source of all this mirror-imagery – and that seems to me Heidegger's
greatest contribution. Heidegger's way of recounting history of philosophy lets us see
the beginnings of the Cartesian imagery in the Greeks and the metamorphoses of this
imagery during the last three centuries. He thus lets us "distance" ourselves from the
tradition. Yet neither Heidegger nor Wittgenstein lets us see the historical phenomenon of mirror-imagery, the story of the domination of the mind of the West by ocular
metaphors, within a social perspective. Both men are concerned with the rarely favored
individual rather than with society – with the chances of keeping oneself apart from
the banal self-deception typical of the latter days of a decaying tradition. Dewey, on the
other hand, though he had neither Wittgenstein's dialectical acuity nor Heidegger's
historical learning, wrote his polemics against traditional mirror-imagery out of a
vision of a new kind of society. In his ideal society, culture is no longer dominated by
the ideal of objective cognition but by that of aesthetic enhancement. In that culture,
as he said, the arts and the sciences would be "the unforced flowers of life." I would
hope that we are now in a position to see the charges of "relativism" and "irrationalism" once leveled against Dewey as merely the mindless defensive reflexes of the philosophical tradition which he attacked. Such charges have no weight if one takes
seriously the criticisms of mirror-imagery which he, Wittgenstein, and Heidegger
make. This book has little to add to these criticisms, but I hope that it presents some of
them in a way which will help pierce through that crust of philosophical convention
which Dewey vainly hoped to shatter.

Philosophy Without Mirrors

1. Hermeneutics and Edification

Our present notions of what it is to be a philosopher are so tied up with the Kantian attempt to render all knowledge-claims commensurable that it is difficult to imagine what philosophy without epistemology could be. More generally, it is difficult to imagine that any activity would be entitled to bear the name "philosophy" if it had nothing to do with knowledge – if it were not in some sense a theory of knowledge, or a method for getting knowledge, or at least a hint as to where some supremely important kind of knowledge might be found. The difficulty stems from a notion shared by Platonists, Kantians, and positivists: that man has an essence – namely, to discover essences. The notion that our chief task is to mirror accurately, in our own Glassy Essence, the universe around us is the complement of the notion, common to Democritus and Descartes, that the universe is made up of very simple, clearly and distinctly knowable things, knowledge of whose essences provides the master-vocabulary which permits commensuration of all discourses.

This classic picture of human beings must be set aside before epistemologically centered philosophy can be set aside. "Hermeneutics," as a polemical term in contemporary philosophy, is a name for the attempt to do so. The use of the term for this purpose is largely due to one book – Gadamer's *Truth and Method*. Gadamer there makes clear that hermeneutics is not a "method for attaining truth" which fits into the classic picture of man: "The hermeneutic phenomenon is basically not a problem of method at all."[2] Rather, Gadamer is asking, roughly, what conclusions might be drawn from the fact that we have to practice hermeneutics – from the "hermeneutic phenomenon" as a fact about people which the epistemological tradition has tried to shunt aside. "The hermeneutics developed here," he says, "is not ... a methodology of the human sciences, but an attempt to understand what the human sciences truly are, beyond their methodological self-consciousness, and what connects them with the totality of our experience of the world."[3] His book is a redescription of man which tries to place the classic picture within a larger one, and thus to "distance" the standard philosophical problematic rather than offer a set of solutions to it.

For my present purposes, the importance of Gadamer's book is that he manages to separate off one of the three strands – the romantic notion of man as self-creative – in the philosophical notion of "spirit" from the other two strands with which it became entangled. Gadamer (like Heidegger, to whom some of his work is indebted) makes no concessions either to Cartesian dualism or to the notion of "transcendental constitution" (in any sense which could be given an idealistic interpretation).[4] He thus helps reconcile

---

2   Hans-Georg Gadamer, *Truth and Method* (New York, 1975), p. xi. Indeed, it would be reasonable to call Gadamer's book a tract against the very idea of method, where this is conceived of as an attempt at commensuration. It is instructive to note the parallels between this book and Paul Feyerabend's *Against Method*. My treatment of Gadamer is indebted to Alasdair MacIntyre; see his "Contexts of Interpretation," *Boston University Journal* 24 (1976), 41–46.

3   Gadamer, *Truth and Method*, p. xiii.

4   Cf. ibid., p. 15. "But we may recognize that *Bildung* is an element of spirit without being tied to Hegel's philosophy of absolute spirit, just as the insight into the historicity of consciousness is not tied to his philosophy of world history."

the "naturalistic" point I tried to make in the previous chapter – that the "irreducibility of the *Geisteswissenschaften*" is not a matter of a metaphysical dualism – with our "existentialist" intuition that redescribing ourselves is the most important thing we can do. He does this by substituting the notion of *Bildung* (education, self-formation) for that of "knowledge" as the goal of thinking. To say that we become different people, that we "remake" ourselves as we read more, talk more, and write more, is simply a dramatic way of saying that the sentences which become true of us by virtue of such activities are often more important to us than the sentences which become true of us when we drink more, earn more, and so on. The events which make us able to say new and interesting things about ourselves are, in this nonmetaphysical sense, more "essential" to us (at least to us relatively leisured intellectuals, inhabiting a stable and prosperous part of the world) than the events which change our shapes or our standards of living ("remaking" us in less "spiritual" ways). Gadamer develops his notion of *wirkungsgeschichtliches Bewusstsein* (the sort of consciousness of the past which changes us) to characterize an attitude interested not so much in what is out there in the world, or in what happened in history, as in what we can get out of nature and history for our own uses. In this attitude, getting the facts right (about atoms and the void, or about the history of Europe) is merely propaedeutic to finding a new and more interesting way of expressing ourselves, and thus of coping with the world. From the educational, as opposed to the epistemological or the technological, point of view, the way things are said is more important than the possession of truths.[5]

Since "education" sounds a bit too flat, and *Bildung* a bit too foreign, I shall use "edification" to stand for this project of finding new, better, more interesting, more fruitful ways of speaking. The attempt to edify (ourselves or others) may consist in the hermeneutic activity of making connections between our own culture and some exotic culture or historical period, or between our own discipline and another discipline which seems to pursue incommensurable aims in an incommensurable vocabulary. But it may instead consist in the "poetic" activity of thinking up such new aims, new words, or new disciplines, followed by, so to speak, the inverse of hermeneutios: the attempt to reinterpret our familiar surroundings in the unfamiliar terms of our new inventions. In either case, the activity is (despite the etymological relation between the two words) edifying without being constructive – at least if "constructive" means the sort of cooperation in the accomplishment of research programs which takes place in normal discourse. For edifying discourse is *supposed* to be abnormal, to take us out of our old selves by the power of strangeness, to aid us in becoming new beings.

The contrast between the desire for edification and the desire for truth is, for Gadamer, not an expression of a tension which needs to be resolved or compromised. If there is a

5   The contrast here is the same as that involved in the traditional quarrel between "classical" education and "scientific" education, mentioned by Gadamer in his opening section on "The Significance of the Humanist Tradition." More generally, it can be seen as an aspect of the quarrel between poetry (which cannot be omitted from the former sort of education) and philosophy (which, when conceiving of itself as super-science, would like to become foundational to the latter sort of education). Yeats asked the spirits (whom, he believed, were dictating *A Vision* to him through his wife's mediumship) why they had come. The spirits replied, "To bring you metaphors for poetry." A philosopher might have expected some hard facts about what it was like on the other side, but Yeats was not disappointed.

conflict, it is between the Platonic–Aristotelian view that the *only* way to be edified is to know what is out there (to reflect the facts accurately – to realize our essence by know-ing essences) and the view that the quest for truth is just one among many ways in which we might be edified. Gadamer rightly gives Heidegger the credit for working out a way of seeing the search for objective knowledge (first developed by the Greeks, using mathematics as a model) as one human project among others.[6] The point is, however, more vivid in Sartre, who sees the attempt to gain an objective knowledge of the world, and thus of oneself, as an attempt to avoid the responsibility for choosing one's project.[7] For Sartre, to say this is not to say that the desire for objective knowledge of nature, his-tory, or anything else is bound to be unsuccessful, or even bound to be self-deceptive. It is merely to say that it presents a temptation to self-deception insofar as we think that, by knowing which descriptions within a given set of normal discourses apply to us, we thereby know ourselves. For Heidegger, Sartre, and Gadamer, objective inquiry is per-fectly possible and frequently actual – the only thing to be said against it is that it pro-vides only some, among many, ways of describing ourselves, and that some of these can hinder the process of edification.

To sum up this "existentialist" view of objectivity, then: objectivity should be seen as conformity to the norms of justification (for assertions and for actions) we find about us. Such conformity becomes dubious and self-deceptive only when seen as something more than this – namely, as a way of obtaining access to something which "grounds" current practices of justification in something else. Such a "ground" is thought to need no justification, because it has become so clearly and distinctly perceived as to count as a "philosophical foundation." This is self-deceptive not simply because of the general absurdity of ultimate justification's reposing upon the unjustifiable, but because of the more concrete absurdity of thinking that the vocabulary used by present science, moral-ity, or whatever has some privileged attachment to reality which makes it *more* than just a further set of descriptions. Agreeing with the naturalists that redescription is not "change of essence" needs to be followed up by abandoning the notion of "essence" altogether.[8] But the standard philosophical strategy of most naturalisms is to find some way of showing that our own culture has indeed got hold of the essence of man – thus making all new and incommensurable vocabularies merely "noncognitive" ornamenta-tion.[9] The utility of the "existentialist" view is that, by proclaiming that we have no

6   See the section called "The Overcoming of the Epistemological Problem …" in *Truth and Method*, pp. 214ff., and compare Martin Heidegger, *Being and Time,* trans. John Macquarrie and Edward Robinson (New York, 1962), sec. 32.

7   See Jean-Paul Sartre, *Being and Nothingness*, trans. Hazel Barnes (New York, 1956), pt. two, chap. 3, sec. 5, and the "Conclusion" of the book.

8   It would have been fortunate if Sartre had followed up his remark that man is the being whose essence is to have no essence by saying that this went for all other beings also. Unless this addition is made, Sartre will appear to be insisting on the good old metaphysical distinction between spirit and nature in other terms, rather than simply making the point that man is always free to choose new descriptions (for, among other things, himself).

9   Dewey, it seems to me, is the one author usually classified as a "naturalist" who did not have this reductive attitude, despite his incessant talk about "scientific method." Dewey's peculiar achievement was to have remained sufficiently Hegelian not to think of natural science as having an inside track on the essences of things, while becoming sufficiently naturalistic to think of human beings in Darwinian terms.

essence, it permits us to see the descriptions of ourselves we find in one of (or in the unity of) the *Naturwissenschaften* as on a par with the various alternative descriptions offered by poets, novelists, depth psychologists, sculptors, anthropologists, and mystics. The former are not privileged representations in virtue of the fact that (at the moment) there is more consensus in the sciences than in the arts. They are simply among the repertoire of self-descriptions at our disposal.

This point can also be put as an extrapolation from the commonplace that one cannot be counted as educated – *gebildet* – if one knows *only* the results of the normal *Naturwissenschaften* of the day. Gadamer begins *Truth and Method* with a discussion of the role of the humanist tradition in giving sense to the notion of *Bildung* as something having "no goals outside itself."[10] To give sense to such a notion we need a sense of the relativity of descriptive vocabularies to periods, traditions, and historical accidents. This is what the humanist tradition in education does, and what training in the results of the natural sciences cannot do. Given that sense of relativity, we cannot take the notion of "essence" seriously, nor the notion of man's task as the accurate representation of essences. The natural sciences, by themselves, leave us convinced that we know both what we are and what we can be – not just how to predict and control our behavior, but the limits of that behavior (and, in particular, the limits of our significant speech). Gadamer's attempt to fend off the demand (common to Mill and Carnap) for "objectivity" in the *Geisteswissenschaften* is the attempt to prevent education from being reduced to instruction in the results of normal inquiry. More broadly, it is the attempt to prevent abnormal inquiry from being viewed as suspicious solely because of its abnormality.

This "existentialist" attempt to place objectivity, rationality, and normal inquiry within the larger picture of our need to be educated and edified is often countered by the "positivist" attempt to distinguish learning facts from acquiring values. From the positivist point of view, Gadamer's exposition of *wirkungsgeschichtliche Bewusstsein* may seem little more than reiteration of the commonplace that even when we know all the objectively true descriptions of ourselves, we still may not know what to do with ourselves. From this point of view, *Truth and Method* (and chapters six and seven above) are just overblown dramatizations of the fact that entire complaince with all the demands for justification offered by normal inquiry would still leave us free to draw our own morals from the assertions so justified. But from the viewpoints of Gadamer, Heidegger, and Sartre, the trouble with the fact-value distinction is that it is contrived precisely to blur the fact that alternative descriptions are possible in addition to those offered by the results of normal inquiries.[11] It suggests that once "all the facts are in" nothing remains except "noncognitive" adoption of an attitude – a choice which is not rationally discussable. It disguises the fact that to use one set of true sentences to describe ourselves is already to choose an attitude toward ourselves, whereas to use another set of true sentences is to adopt a contrary attitude. Only if we assume that there is a value-free vocabulary which renders these sets of "factual" statements commensurable can the positivist distinction between facts and values, beliefs and attitudes, look plausible. But the philosophical fiction that such a vocabulary is on the tips of our tongues

10   Gadamer, *Truth and Method*, p. 12.
11   See Heidegger's discussion of "values" in *Being and Time*, p. 133, and Sartre's in *Being and Nothingness*, pt. two, chap. 1, sec. 4. Compare Gadamer's remarks on Weber (*Truth and Method*, pp. 461 ff.).

is, from an educational point of view, disastrous. It forces us to pretend that we can split ourselves up into knowers of true sentences on the one hand and choosers of lives or actions or works of art on the other. These artificial diremptions make it impossible to get the notion of edification into focus. Or, more exactly, they tempt us to think of edification as having nothing to do with the rational faculties which are employed in normal discourse.

So Gadamer's effort to get rid of the classic picture of man-as-essentially-knower-of-essences is, among other things, an effort to get rid of the distinction between fact and value, and thus to let us think of "discovering the facts" as one project of edification among others. This is why Gadamer devotes so much time to breaking down the distinctions which Kant made among cognition, morality, and aesthetic judgment.[12] There is no way, as far as I can see, in which to *argue* the issue of whether to keep the Kantian "grid" in place or set it aside. There is no "normal" philosophical discourse which provides common commensurating ground for those who see science and edification as, respectively, "rational" and "irrational," and those who see the quest for objectivity as one possibility among others to be taken account of in *wirkungsgeschichtliche Bewusstsein*. If there is no such common ground, all we can do is to show how the other side looks from our own point of view. That is, all we can do is be hermeneutic about the opposition – trying to show how the odd or paradoxical or offensive things they say hang together with the rest of what they want to say, and how what they say looks when put in our own alternative idiom. This sort of hermeneutics with polemical intent is common to Heidegger's and Derrida's attempts to deconstruct the tradition.

2. Systematic Philosophy and Edifying Philosophy

The hermeneutic point of view, from which the acquisition of truth dwindles in importance, and is seen as a component of education, is possible only if we once stood at another point of view. Education has to start from acculturation. So the search for objectivity and the self-conscious awareness of the social practices in which objectivity consists are necessary first steps in becoming *gebildet*. We must first see ourselves as *en-soi* – as described by those statements which are objectively true in the judgment of our peers – before there is any point in seeing ourselves as *poursoi*. Similarly, we cannot be educated without finding out a lot about the descriptions of the world offered by our culture (e.g., by learning the results of the natural sciences). Later perhaps, we may put less value on "being in touch with reality" but we can afford that only after having passed through stages of implicit, and then explicit and self-conscious, conformity to the norms of the discourses going on around us.

I raise this banal point that education – even the education of the revolutionary or the prophet – needs to begin with acculturation and conformity merely to provide a cautionary complement to the "existentialist" claim that normal participation in normal discourse is merely one project, one way of being in the world. The caution amounts to

---

12 See Gadamer's polemic against "the subjectivization of the aesthetic" in Kant's Third Critique (*Truth and Method*, p. 87) and compare Heidegger's remarks in "Letter on Humanism" on Aristotle's distinctions among physics, logic, and ethics (Heidegger, *Basic Writings*, ed. Krell [New York, 1976], p. 232).

saying that abnormal and "existential" discourse is always parasitic upon normal dis-course, that the possibility of hermeneutics is always parasitic upon the possibility (and perhaps upon the actuality) of epistemology, and that edification always employs materi-als provided by the culture of the day. To attempt abnormal discourse *de novo*, without being able to recognize our own abnormality, is madness in the most literal and terrible sense. To insist on being hermeneutic where epistemology would do – to make our-selves unable to view normal discourse in terms of its own motives, and able to view it only from within our own abnormal discourse – is not mad, but it does show a lack of education. To adopt the "existentialist" attitude toward objectivity and rationality com-mon to Sartre, Heidegger, and Gadamer makes sense only if we do so in a conscious departure from a well-understood norm. "Existentialism" is an *intrinsically reactive* move-ment of thought, one which has point only in opposition to the tradition. I want now to generalize this contrast between philosophers whose work is essentially constructive and those whose work is essentially reactive. I shall thereby develop a contrast between philosophy which centers in epistemology and the sort of philosophy which takes its point of departure from suspicion about the pretensions of epistemology. This is the contrast between "systematic" and "edifying" philosophies.

In every sufficiently reflective culture, there are those who single out one area, one set of practices, and see it as the paradigm human activity. They then try to show how the rest of culture can profit from this example. In the mainstream of the Western philo-sophical tradition, this paradigm has been *knowing* – possessing justified true beliefs, or, better yet, beliefs so intrinsically persuasive as to make justification unnecessary. Successive philosophical revolutions within this mainstream have been produced by philosophers excited by new cognitive feats – e.g., the rediscovery of Aristotle, Galilean mechanics, the development of self-conscious historiography in the nineteenth century, Darwinian biology, mathematical logic. Thomas's use of Aristotle to conciliate the Fathers, Descartes's and Hobbes's criticisms of scholasticism, the Enlightenment's notion that reading Newton leads naturally to the downfall of tyrants. Spencer's evolutionism, Carnap's attempt to overcome metaphysics through logic, are so many attempts to refashion the rest of culture on the model of the latest cognitive achievements. A "mainstream" Western philosopher typically says: Now that such-and-such a line of inquiry has had such a stunning success, let us reshape all inquiry, and all of culture, on its model, thereby permitting objectivity and rationality to prevail in areas previously obscured by conven-tion, superstition, and the lack of a proper epistemological understanding of man's ability accurately to represent nature.

On the periphery of the history of modern philosophy, one finds figures who, with-out forming a "tradition," resemble each other in their distrust of the notion that man's essence is to be a knower of essences. Goethe, Kierkegaard, Santayana, William James, Dewey, the later Wittgenstein, the later Heidegger, are figures of this sort. They are often accused of relativism or cynicism. They are often dubious about progress, and especially about the latest claim that such-and-such a discipline has at last made the nature of human knowledge so clear that reason will now spread throughout the rest of human activity. These writers have kept alive the suggestion that, even when we have justified true belief about everything we want to know, we may have no more than conformity to the norms of the day. They have kept alive the historicist sense that this century's "superstition" was the last century's triumph of reason, as well as the relativist sense that the latest vocabulary, borrowed from the latest scientific achievement, may not express privileged representations of essences, but be just another of the potential infinity of vocabularies in which the world can be described.

The mainstream philosophers are the philosophers I shall call "systematic," and the peripheral ones are those I shall call "edifying." These peripheral, pragmatic philosophers are skeptical primarily *about systematic philosophy*, about the whole project of universal commensuration.[13] In our time, Dewey, Wittgenstein, and Heidegger are the great edifying, peripheral, thinkers. All three make it as difficult as possible to take their thought as expressing views on traditional philosophical problems, or as making constructive proposals for philosophy as a cooperative and progressive discipline.[14] They make fun of the classic picture of man, the picture which contains systematic philosophy, the search for universal commensuration in a final vocabulary. They hammer away at the holistic point that words take their meanings from other words rather than by virtue of their representative character, and the corollary that vocabularies acquire their privileges from the men who use them rather than from their transparency to the real.[15]

The distinction between systematic and edifying philosophers is not the same as the distinction between normal philosophers and revolutionary philosophers. The latter distinction puts Husserl, Russell, the later Wittgenstein, and the later Heidegger all on the same ("revolutionary") side of a line. For my purposes, what matters is a distinction between two kinds of revolutionary philosophers. On the one hand, there are revolutionary philosophers – those who found new schools within which normal, professionalized philosophy can be practiced – who see the incommensurability of their new vocabulary with the old as a temporary inconvenience, to be blamed on the shortcomings of their predecessors and to be overcome by the institutionalization of their own vocabulary. On the other hand, there are great philosophers who dread the thought that their vocabulary should ever be institutionalized, or that their writing might be seen as commensurable with the tradition. Husserl and Russell (like Descartes and Kant) are of the former sort. The later Wittgenstein and the later Heidegger (like Kierkegaard and

13   Consider the passage from Anatole France's "Garden of Epicurus" which Jacques Derrida cites at the beginning of his "La Mythologie Blanche" (in *Marges de la Philosophie* [Paris, 1972], p. 250):
      ... the metaphysicians, when they make up a new language, are like knife-grinders who grind coins and medals against their stone instead of knives and scissors. They rub out the relief, the inscriptions, the portraits, and when one can no longer see on the coins Victoria, or Wilhelm, or the French Republic, they explain: these coins now have nothing specifically English or German or French about them, for we have taken them out of time and space; they now are no longer worth, say, five francs, but rather have an inestimable value, and the area in which they are a medium of exchange has been infinitely extended.

14   See Karl-Otto Apel's comparison of Wittgenstein and Heidegger as having both "called into question Western metaphysics as a theoretical discipline" (*Transformation der Philosophie* [Frankfurt, 1973], vol. 1, p. 228). I have not offered interpretations of Dewey, Wittgenstein, and Heidegger in support of what I have been saying about them, but I have tried to do so in a piece on Wittgenstein called "Keeping Philosophy Pure" (*Yale Review* [Spring 1976], pp. 336–356), in "Overcoming the Tradition: Heidegger and Dewey" (*Review of Metaphysics* 30 [1976], 280–305), and in "Dewey's Metaphysics" in *New Studies in the Philosophy of John Dewey*, ed. Steven M. Cahn (Hanover, N.H., 1977).

15   This Heideggerean point about language is spelled out at length and didactically by Derrida in *La Voix et le Phénomène*, translated as *Speech and Phenomenon* by David Allison (Evanston, 1973). See Newton Garver's comparison of Derrida and Wittgenstein in his "Introduction" to this translation.

Nietzsche) are of the latter sort.[16] Great systematic philosophers are constructive and offer arguments. Great edifying philosophers are reactive and offer satires, parodies, aphorisms. They know their work loses its point when the period they were reacting against is over. They are *intentionally* peripheral. Great systematic philosophers, like great scientists, build for eternity. Great edifying philosophers destroy for the sake of their own generation. Systematic philosophers want to put their subject on the secure path of a science. Edifying philosophers want to keep space open for the sense of wonder which poets can sometimes cause – wonder that there is something new under the sun, something which is *not* an accurate representation of what was already there, something which (at least for the moment) cannot be explained and can barely be described.

The notion of an edifying philosopher is, however, a paradox. For Plato defined the philosopher by opposition to the poet. The philosopher could give reasons, argue for his views, justify himself. So argumentative systematic philosophers say of Nietzsche and Heidegger that, whatever else they may be, they are not *philosophers*. This "not really a philosopher" ploy is also used, of course, by normal philosophers against revolutionary philosophers. It was used by pragmatists against logical positivists, by positivists against "ordinary language philosophers," and will be used whenever cozy professionalism is in danger. But in that usage it is just a rhetorical gambit which tells one nothing more than that an incommensurable discourse is being proposed. When it is used against edifying philosophers, on the other hand, the accusation has a real bite. The problem for an edifying philosopher is that qua philosopher he is in the business of offering arguments, whereas he would like simply to offer another set of terms, *without* saying that these terms are the new-found accurate representations of essences (e.g., of the essence of "philosophy" itself). He is, so to speak, violating not just the rules of normal philosophy (the philosophy of the schools of his day) but a sort of metarule: the rule that one may suggest changing the rules only because one has noticed that the old ones do not fit the subject matter, that they are not adequate to reality, that they impede the solution of the eternal problems. Edifying philosophers, unlike revolutionary systematic philosophers, are those who are abnormal at this meta-level. They refuse to present themselves as having found out any objective truth (about, say, what philosophy is). They present themselves as doing something different from, and more important than, offering accurate representations of how things are. It is more important because, they say, the notion of "accurate representation" itself is not the proper way to think about what philosophy does. But, they then go on to say, this is not because "a search for accurate representations of … (e.g., 'the most general traits of reality' or 'the nature of man')" is an *in*accurate representation of philosophy.

Whereas less pretentious revolutionaries can afford to have views on lots of things which their predecessors had views on, edifying philosophers have to decry the very notion of having a view, while avoiding having a view about having views.[17] This is an awkward, but not impossible, position. Wittgenstein and Heidegger manage it fairly well. One reason they manage it as well as they do is that they do not think that when we say something we

---

16   The permanent fascination of the man who dreamed up the whole idea of Western philosophy – Plato – is that we still do not know which sort of philosopher he was. Even if the *Seventh Letter* is set aside as spurious, the fact that after millenniums of commentary nobody knows which passages in the dialogues are jokes keeps the puzzle fresh.

17   Heidegger's "*Die Zeit des Weltbildes*" (translated as "The Age of the World-View" by Marjorie Grene in *Boundary II* [1976]) is the best discussion of this difficulty I have come across.

must necessarily be expressing a view about a subject. We might just be *saying something* – participating in a conversation rather than contributing to an inquiry. Perhaps saying things is not always saying how things are. Perhaps saying *that* is itself not a case of saying how things are. Both men suggest we see people as saying things, better or worse things, without seeing them as externalizing inner representations of reality. But this is only their entering wedge, for then we must cease to see ourselves as *seeing* this, without beginning to see ourselves as seeing something else. We must get the visual, and in particular the mirroring, metaphors out of our speech altogether.[18] To do that we have to understand speech not only as not the externalizing of inner representations, but as not a representation at all. We have to drop the notion of correspondence for sentences as well as for thoughts, and see sentences as connected with other sentences rather than with the world. We have to see the term "corresponds to how things are" as an automatic compliment paid to successful normal discourse rather than as a relation to be studied and aspired to throughout the rest of discourse. To attempt to extend this compliment to feats of *ab*normal discourse is like complimenting a judge on his wise decision by leaving him a fat tip: it shows a lack of tact. To think of Wittgenstein and Heidegger as having views about how things are is not to be wrong about how things are, exactly; it is just poor taste. It puts them in a position which they do not want to be in, and in which they look ridiculous.

But perhaps they *should* look ridiculous. How, then, do we know when to adopt a tactful attitude and when to insist on someone's moral obligation to hold a view? This is like asking how we know when someone's refusal to adopt our norms (of, for example, social organization, sexual practices, or conversational manners) is morally outrageous and when it is something which we must (at least provisionally) respect. We do not know such things by reference to general principles. We do not, for instance, know in advance that if a given sentence is uttered, or a given act performed, we shall break off a conversation or a personal relationship, for everything depends on what leads up to it. To see edifying philosophers as conversational partners is an alternative to seeing them as holding views on subjects of common concern. One way of thinking of wisdom as something of which the love is not the same as that of argument, and of which the achievement does not consist in finding the correct vocabulary for representing essence, is to think of it as the practical wisdom necessary to participate in a conversation. One way to see edifying philosophy *as* the love of wisdom is to see it as the attempt to prevent conversation from degenerating into inquiry, into a research program. Edifying philosophers can never end philosophy, but they can help prevent it from attaining the secure path of a science.

3. Edification, Relativism, and Objective Truth

I want now to enlarge this suggestion that edifying philosophy aims at continuing a conversation rather than at discovering truth, by making out of it a reply to the familiar charge of "relativism" leveled at the subordination of truth to edification. I shall be claiming that the difference between conversation and inquiry parallels Sartre's distinction

---

18   Derrida's recent writings are meditations on how to avoid these metaphors. Like Heidegger in "Aus einem Gespräch von der Sprache zwischen einem Japaner und einem Fragenden" (in *Unterwegs zur Sprache* [Pfullingen, 1959]), Derrida occasionally toys with the notion of the superiority of Oriental languages and of ideographic writing.

between thinking of oneself as *pour-soi* and as *en-soi*, and thus that the cultural role of the edifying philosopher is to help us avoid the self-deception which comes from believing that we know ourselves by knowing a set of objective facts. In the following section, I shall try to make the converse point. There I shall be saying that the wholehearted behaviorism, naturalism, and physicalism I have been commending help us avoid the self-deception of thinking that we possess a deep, hidden, metaphysically significant nature which makes us "irreducibly" different from inkwells or atoms.

Philosophers who have doubts about traditional epistemology are often thought to be questioning the notion that at most one of incompatible competing theories can be true. However, it is hard to find anyone who actually does question this. When it is said, for example, that coherentist or pragmatic "theories of truth" allow for the possibility that many incompatible theories would satisfy the conditions set for "the truth," the coherentist or pragmatist usually replies that this merely shows that we should have no grounds for choice among these candidates for "the truth." The moral to draw, they say, is not that they have offered inadequate analyses of "true," but that there are some terms – for example, "the true theory," "the right thing to do" – which are, intuitively and grammatically, singular, but for which no set of necessary and sufficient conditions can be given which will pick out a unique referent. This fact, they say, should not be surprising. Nobody thinks that there are necessary and sufficient conditions which will pick out, for example, the unique referent of "the best thing for her to have done on finding herself in that rather embarrassing situation," though plausible conditions can be given which will shorten a list of competing incompatible candidates. Why should it be different for the referents of "what she should have done in that ghastly moral dilemma" or "the Good Life for man" or "what the world is really made of"?

To see relativism lurking in every attempt to formulate conditions for truth or reality or goodness which does not attempt to provide uniquely individuating conditions we must adopt the "Platonic" notion of the transcendental terms which I discussed above. We must think of the true referents of these terms (the Truth, the Real, Goodness) as conceivably having no connection whatever with the practices of justification which obtain among us. The dilemma created by this Platonic hypostatization is that, on the one hand, the philosopher must attempt to find criteria for picking out these unique referents, whereas, on the other hand, the only hints he has about what these criteria could be are provided by current practice (by, e.g., the best moral and scientific thought of the day). Philosophers thus condemn themselves to a Sisyphean task, for no sooner has an account of a transcendental term been perfected than it is labeled a "naturalistic fallacy," a confusion between essence and accident.[19] I think we get a clue to the cause of this self-defeating obsession from the fact that even philosophers who take the intuitive impossibility of finding conditions for "the one right thing to do" as a reason for repudiating "objective values" are loath to take the impossibility of finding individuating conditions for the one true theory of the world as a reason for denying "objective physical reality." Yet they should, for formally the two notions are on a par. The reasons for and against adopting a "correspondence" approach to moral truth are the same as those regarding truth about the physical world. The giveaway comes, I think, when we find that the usual excuse for invidious treatment is that we are shoved around by

---

19   On this point, see William Frankena's classic "The Naturalistic Fallacy," *Mind* 68 (1939).

physical reality but not by values.[20] Yet what does being shoved around have to do with objectivity, accurate representation, or correspondence? Nothing, I think, unless we confuse *contact* with reality (a causal, non-intentional, non-description-relative relation) with *dealing with* reality (describing, explaining, predicting, and modifying it – all of which are things we do under descriptions). The sense in which physical reality is Peircean "Secondness" – unmediated pressure – has nothing to do with the sense in which one among all our ways of describing, or of coping with, physical reality is "the one right" way. Lack of mediation is here being confused with accuracy of mediation. The absence of description is confused with a privilege attaching to a certain description. Only by such a confusion can the inability to offer individuating conditions for the one true description of material things be confused with insensitivity to the things' obduracy.

Sartre helps us explain why this confusion is so frequent and why its results are purveyed with so much moral earnestness. The notion of "one right way of describing and explaining reality" supposedly contained in our "intuition" about the meaning of "true" is, for Sartre, just the notion of having a way of describing and explaining *imposed* on us in that brute way in which stones impinge on our feet. Or, to shift to visual metaphors, it is the notion of having reality unveiled to us, not as in a glass darkly, but with some unimaginable sort of immediacy which would make discourse and description superfluous. If we could convert knowledge from something discursive, something attained by continual adjustments of ideas or words, into something as ineluctable as being shoved about, or being transfixed by a sight which leaves us speechless, then we should no longer have the responsibility for choice among competing ideas and words, theories and vocabularies. This attempt to slough off responsibility is what Sartre describes as the attempt to turn oneself into a thing – into an *être-en-soi*. In the visions of the epistemologist, this incoherent notion takes the form of seeing the attainment of truth as a matter of *necessity*, either the "logical" necessity of the transcendentalist or the "physical" necessity of the evolutionary "naturalizing" epistemologist. From Sartre's point of view, the urge to find such necessities is the urge to be rid of one's freedom to erect yet another alternative theory or vocabulary. Thus the edifying philosopher who points out the incoherence of the urge is treated as a "relativist," one who lacks moral seriousness, because he does not join in the common human hope that the burden of choice will pass away. Just as the moral philosopher who sees virtue as Aristotelian self-development is thought to lack concern for his fellow man, so the epistemologist who is merely behaviorist is treated as one who does not share the universal human aspiration toward objective truth.

Sartre adds to our understanding of the visual imagery which has set the problems of Western philosophy by helping us see why this imagery is always trying to transcend itself. The notion of an unclouded Mirror of Nature is the notion of a mirror which would be indistinguishable from what was mirrored, and thus would not be a mirror at all. The notion of a human being whose mind is such an unclouded mirror, and who *knows* this, is the image, as Sartre says, of God. Such a being does *not* confront something alien which makes it necessary for him to choose an attitude toward, or a description of, it. He would have no need and no ability to choose actions or descriptions. He can be called "God" if we think of the advantages of this situation, or a "mere machine" if we

20   What seems to be a sense of being shoved around by values, they reductively say, is just physical reality in disguise (e.g., neural arrangements or glandular secretions programmed by parental conditioning).

think of the disadvantages. From this point of view, to look for commensuration rather than simply continued conversation – to look for a way of making further redescription unnecessary by finding a way of reducing all *possible* descriptions to one – is to attempt escape from humanity. To abandon the notion that philosophy must show all possible discourse naturally converging to a consensus, just as normal inquiry does, would be to abandon the hope of being anything more than merely human. It would thus be to abandon the Platonic notions of Truth and Reality and Goodness as entities which may not be even dimly mirrored by present practices and beliefs, and to settle back into the "relativism" which assumes that our only useful notions of "true" and "real" and "good" are extrapolations from those practices and beliefs.

Here, finally, I come around to the suggestion with which I ended the last section – that the point of edifying philosophy is to keep the conversation going rather than to find objective truth. Such truth, in the view I am advocating, is the normal result of normal discourse. Edifying philosophy is not only abnormal but reactive, having sense only as a protest against attempts to close off conversation by proposals for universal commensuration through the hypostatization of some privileged set of descriptions. The danger which edifying discourse tries to avert is that some given vocabulary, some way in which people might come to think of themselves, will deceive them into thinking that from now on all discourse could be, or should be, normal discourse. The resulting freezing-over of culture would be, in the eyes of edifying philosophers, the dehumanization of human beings. The edifying philosophers are thus agreeing with Lessing's choice of the infinite *striving for* truth over "all of Truth."[21] For the edifying philosopher the very idea of being presented with "all of Truth" is absurd, because the Platonic notion of Truth itself is absurd. It is absurd either as the notion of truth about reality which is not about reality-under-a-certain-description, or as the notion of truth about reality under some privileged description which makes all other descriptions unnecessary because it is commensurable with each of them.

To see keeping a conversation going as a sufficient aim of philosophy, to see wisdom as consisting in the ability to sustain a conversation, is to see human beings as generators of new descriptions rather than beings one hopes to be able to describe accurately. To see the aim of philosophy as truth – namely, the truth about the terms which provide ultimate commensuration for all human inquiries and activities – is to see human beings as objects rather than subjects, as existing *en-soi* rather than as both *pour-soi* and *en-soi*, as both described objects and describing subjects. To think that philosophy will permit us to see the describing subject as itself one sort of described object is to think that all possible descriptions can be rendered commensurable with the aid of a single descriptive vocabulary – that of philosophy itself. For only if we had such a notion of a universal description could we identify human-beings-under-a-given-description with man's "essence." Only with such a notion would that of a man's *having* an essence make sense, whether or not that essence is conceived of as the knowing of essences. So not even by saying that man is subject as well as object, *pour-soi* as well as *en-soi*, are we grasping our essence. We do not escape from Platonism by saying that "our essence is to have no essence" if we then try to use this insight as the basis for a constructive and systematic attempt to find out further truths about human beings.

21   Kierkegaard made this choice the prototype of his own choice of "subjectivity" over "system." Cf. *Concluding Unscientific Postscript*, trans. David Swenson and Walter Lowrie (Princeton, 1941), p. 97.

That is why "existentialism" – and, more generally, edifying philosophy – can be *only* reactive, why it falls into self-deception whenever it tries to do more than send the conversation off in new directions. Such new directions may, perhaps, engender new normal discourses, new sciences, new philosophical research programs, and thus new objective truths. But they are not the point of edifying philosophy, only accidental byproducts. The point is always the same – to perform the social function which Dewey called "breaking the crust of convention," preventing man from deluding himself with the notion that he knows himself, or anything else, except under optional descriptions.

4. Edification and Naturalism

I argued that it would be a good idea to get rid of the spirit-nature distinction, conceived as a division between human beings and other things, or between two parts of human beings, corresponding to the distinction between hermeneutics and epistemology. I want now to take up this topic again, in order to underline the point that the "existentialist" doctrines I have been discussing are compatible with the behaviorism and materialism I advocated earlier. Philosophers who would like to be simultaneously systematic and edifying have often seen them as incompatible, and have therefore suggested how our sense of ourselves as *pour-soi*, as capable of reflection, as choosers of alternative vocabularies, might itself be turned into a philosophical subject matter.

Much recent philosophy – under the aegis of "phenomenology" or of "hermeneutics," or both – has toyed with this unfortunate idea. For example, Habermas and Apel have suggested ways in which we might create a new sort of transcendental standpoint, enabling us to do something like what Kant tried to do, but without falling into either scientism or historicism. Again, most philosophers who see Marx, Freud, or both as figures who need to be drawn into "mainstream" philosophy have tried to develop quasi-epistemological systems which center around the phenomenon which both Marx and Freud throw into relief – the change in behavior which results from change in self-description. Such philosophers see traditional epistemology as committed to "objectivizing" human beings, and they hope for a successor subject to epistemology which will do for "reflection" what the tradition did for "objectivizing knowledge."

I have been insisting that we should not try to have a successor subject to epistemology, but rather try to free ourselves from the notion that philosophy must center around the discovery of a permanent framework for inquiry. In particular, we should free ourselves from the notion that philosophy can explain what science leaves unexplained. From my point of view, the attempt to develop a "universal pragmatics" or a "transcendental hermeneutics" is very suspicious. For it seems to promise just what Sartre tells us we are not going to have – a way of seeing freedom as nature (or, less cryptically, a way of seeing our creation of, and choice between, vocabularies in the same "normal" way as we see ourselves *within* one of those vocabularies). Such attempts start out by viewing the search for objective knowledge through normal discourse in the way I have suggested it should be viewed – as one element in edification. But they then often go on to more ambitious claims. The following passage from Habermas is an example:

> ... the functions knowledge has in universal contexts of practical life can only be successfully analyzed in the framework of a reformulated transcendental philosophy. This, incidentally, does not entail an empiricist critique of the claim to absolute truth. As long as

cognitive interests can be identified and analyzed through reflection upon the logic of inquiry in the natural and cultural sciences, they can legitimately claim a "transcendental" status. They assume an "empirical" status as soon as they are analyzed as the result of natural history – analyzed, as it were, in terms of cultural anthropology.[22]

I want to claim, on the contrary, that there is no point in trying to find a general synoptic way of "analyzing" the "functions knowledge has in universal contexts of practical life," and that cultural anthropology (in a large sense which includes intellectual history) is all we need.

Habermas and other authors who are impelled by the same motives see the suggestion that empirical inquiry suffices as incorporating an "objectivistic illusion." They tend to see Deweyan pragmatism, and the "scientific realism" of Sellars and Feyerabend, as the products of an inadequate epistemology. In my view, the great virtue of Dewey, Sellars, and Feyerabend is that they point the way toward, and partially exemplify, a nonepistemological sort of philosophy, and thus one which gives up any hope of the "transcendental." Habermas says that for a theory to "ground itself transcendentally" is for it to '

> become familiar with the range of inevitable subjective conditions which both make the theory possible *and* place limits on it, for this kind of transcendental corroboration tends always to criticize an overly self-confident self-understanding of itself.[23]

Specifically, this overconfidence consists in thinking that

> there can be such a thing as truthfulness to reality in the sense postulated by philosophical realism. Correspondence-theories of truth tend to hypostatize facts as entities in the world. It is the intention and inner logic of an epistemology reflecting upon the conditions of possible experience as such to uncover the objectivistic illusions of such a view. Every form of transcendental philosophy claims to identify the conditions of the objectivity of experience by analyzing the categorical structure of objects of possible experience.[24]

But Dewey, Wittgenstein, Sellars, Kuhn, and the other heroes of this book all have their own ways of debunking "truthfulness to reality in the sense postulated by philosophical realism," and none of them think that this is to be done by "analyzing the categorical structure of objects of possible experience."

The notion that we can get around overconfident philosophical realism and positivistic reductions only by adopting something like Kant's transcendental standpoint seems to me the basic mistake in programs like that of Habermas (as well as in Husserl's notion of a "phenomenology of the life-world" which will describe people in some way "prior" to that offered by science). What is required to accomplish these laudable purposes is not

---

22   Jürgen Habermas, "Nachwort" to the second edition of *Erkenntnis und Interesse* (Frankfurt: Surkamp, 1973), p. 410; translated as "A Postscript to *Knowledge and Human Interests*," by Christian Lenhardt in *Philosophy of the Social Sciences* 3 (1973), 181. For a criticism of the line Habermas takes here – a criticism paralleling my own – see Michael Theunissen, *Gesellschaft und Geschichte: Zur Kritik der Kritischen Theorie* (Berlin, 1969), pp. 20 ff. (I owe the reference to Theunissen to Raymond Geuss.)

23   Habermas, "Nachwort," p. 411; English translation, p. 182.

24   Ibid., pp. 408–409; English translation, p. 180.

Kant's "epistemological" distinction between the transcendental and the empirical standpoints, but rather his "existentialist" distinction between people as empirical selves and as moral agents.[25] Normal scientific discourse can always be seen in two different ways – as the successful search for objective truth, or as one discourse among others, one among many projects we engage in. The former point of view falls in with the normal practice of normal science. There questions of moral choice or of edification do not arise, since they have already been preempted by the tacit and "self-confident" commitment to the search for objective truth on the subject in question. The latter point of view is one from which we ask such questions as "What is the point?" "What moral is to be drawn from our knowledge of how we, and the rest of nature, work?" or "What are we to do with ourselves now that we know the laws of our own behavior?"

The primal error of systematic philosophy has always been the notion that such questions are to be answered by some new ("metaphysical" or "transcendental") descriptive or explanatory discourse (dealing with, e.g., "man," "spirit," or "language"). This attempt to answer questions of justification by discovering new objective truths, to answer the moral agent's request for justifications with descriptions of a privileged domain, is the philosopher's special form of bad faith – his special way of substituting pseudo-cognition for moral choice. Kant's greatness was to have seen through the "metaphysical" form of this attempt, and to have destroyed the traditional conception of reason to make room for moral faith. Kant gave us a way of seeing scientific truth as something which could never supply an answer to our demand for a point, a justification, a way of claiming that our moral decision about what to do is based on *knowledge* of the nature of the world. Unfortunately, Kant put his diagnosis of science in terms of the discovery of "inevitable subjective conditions," to be revealed by reflection upon scientific inquiry. Equally unfortunately, he thought that there really was a decision procedure for moral dilemmas (though not based on *knowledge*, since our grasp of the categorical imperative is not a *cognition*).[26] So he created new forms of philosophical bad faith – substituting "transcendental" attempts to find one's true self for "metaphysical" attempts to find a world elsewhere. By tacitly identifying the moral agent with the constituting transcendental self, he left the road open to ever more complicated post-Kantian attempts to reduce freedom to nature, choice to knowledge, the *pour-soi* to the *en-soi*. This is the road I have been trying to block by recasting ahistorical and permanent distinctions between nature and spirit, "objectivizing science" and reflection, epistemology and hermeneutics, in terms of historical and temporary distinctions between the familiar and the unfamiliar, the normal and the abnormal. For this way of treating these distinctions lets us see them not as dividing two areas of inquiry but as the distinction

25   Wilfrid Sellars uses this latter Kantian distinction to good effect in his insistence that personhood is a matter of "being one of us," of falling within the scope of practical imperatives of the form "Would that we all ...," rather than a feature of certain organisms to be isolated by empirical means. I have invoked this claim several times in this book, particularly in chapter four, section 4. For Sellars's own use of it, see *Science and Metaphysics* (London and New York, 1968), chap. 7, and the essay "Science and Ethics" in his *Philosophical Perspectives* (Springfield, Ill., 1967).

26   See Kant's distinction between knowledge and necessary belief at *K.d.r.V.*, A824–B852 ff., and especially his use of *Unternehmung* as a synonym for the latter. This section of the First Critique seems to me the one which gives most sense to the famous passage about denying reason to make room for faith at Bxxx. At many other points, however, Kant inconsistently speaks of practical reason as supplying an enlargement of our *knowledge*.

between inquiry and something which is *not* inquiry, but is rather the inchoate questioning out of which inquiries – new normal discourses – may (or may not) emerge.

To put this claim in another way, which may help bring out its connections with naturalism, I am saying that the positivists were absolutely right in thinking it imperative to extirpate metaphysics, when "metaphysics" means the attempt to give knowledge of what science cannot know. For this is the attempt to find a discourse which combines the advantages of normality with those of abnormality – the intersubjective security of objective truth combined with the edifying character of an unjustifiable but unconditional moral claim. The urge to set philosophy on the secure path of a science is the urge to combine Plato's project of moral choice as ticking off the objective truths about a special sort of object (the Idea of the Good) with the sort of intersubjective and democratic agreement about objects found in normal science.[27] Philosophy which was utterly unedifying, utterly irrelevant to such moral choices as whether or not to believe in God would count not as *philosophy*, but only as some special sort of science. So as soon as a program to put philosophy on the secure path of science succeeds, it simply converts philosophy into a boring academic specialty. Systematic philosophy exists by perpetually straddling the gap between description and justification, cognition and choice, getting the facts right and telling us how to live.

Once this point is seen, we can see more clearly why epistemology emerged as the essence of systematic philosophy. For epistemology is the attempt to see the patterns of justification within normal discourse as *more* than just such patterns. It is the attempt to see them as hooked on to something which demands moral commitment – Reality, Truth, Objectivity, Reason. To be behaviorist in epistemology, on the contrary, is to look at the normal scientific discourse of our day bifocally, both as patterns adopted for various historical reasons and as the achievement of objective truth, where "objective truth" is no more and no less than the best idea we currently have about how to explain what is going on. From the point of view of epistemological behaviorism, the only truth in Habermas's claim that scientific inquiry is made possible, and limited, by "inevitable subjective conditions" is that such inquiry is made possible by the adoption of practices of justification, and that such practices have possible alternatives. But these "subjective conditions" are in no sense "inevitable" ones discoverable by "reflection upon the logic of inquiry." They are just the facts about what a given society, or profession, or other group, takes to be good ground for assertions of a certain sort. Such disciplinary matrices are studied by the usual empirical-cum-hermeneutic methods of "cultural anthropology." From the point of view of the group in question these subjective conditions are a combination of commonsensical practical imperatives (e.g., tribal taboos, Mill's Methods) with the standard current theory about the subject. From the point of view of the historian of ideas or the anthropologist they are the empirical facts about the beliefs, desires, and practices of a certain group of human beings. These are incompatible points of view, in the sense that we cannot be at both viewpoints simultaneously. But there is no reason and no need to subsume the two in a higher synthesis. The group in question may itself shift from the one point of view to the other (thus "objectivizing" their past selves through a process of "reflection" and making new sentences true of their present selves). But this is not a mysterious

27   The positivists themselves quickly succumbed to this urge. Even while insisting that moral questions were noncognitive they thought to give quasi-scientific status to their moralistic attacks on traditional philosophy – thus making themselves subject to self-referential criticisms concerning their "emotive" use of "noncognitive."

process which demands a new understanding of human knowledge. It is the common-place fact that people may develop doubts about what they are doing, and thereupon begin to discourse in ways incommensurable with those they used previously.

This goes also for the most spectacular and disturbing new discourses. When such edify-ing philosophers as Marx, Freud, and Sartre offer new explanations of our usual patterns of justifying our actions and assertions, and when these explanations are taken up and inte-grated into our lives, we have striking examples of the phenomenon of reflection's chang-ing vocabulary and behavior. But as I argued in chapter seven, this phenomenon does not require any new understanding of theory-construction or theory-confirmation. To say that we have changed ourselves by internalizing a new self-description (using terms like "bour-geois intellectual" or "self-destructive" or "self-deceiving") is true enough. But this is no more startling than the fact that men changed the data of botany by hybridization, which was in turn made possible by botanical theory, or that they changed their own lives by inventing bombs and vaccines. Meditation on the possibility of such changes, like reading science fiction, does help us overcome the self-confidence of "philosophical realism." But such meditation does not need to be supplemented by a transcendental account of the nature of reflection. All that is necessary is the edifying invocation of the fact or possibility of abnormal discourses, undermining our reliance upon the knowledge we have gained through normal discourses. The objectionable self-confidence in question is simply the tendency of normal discourse to block the flow of conversation by presenting itself as offering the canonical vocabulary for discussion of a given topic – and, more particularly, the tendency of normal epistemologically centered philosophy to block the road by putting itself forward as the final commensurating vocabulary for all *possible* rational discourse. Self-confidence of the former, limited sort is overthrown by edifying philosophers who put the very idea of universal commensuration, and of systematic philosophy, in doubt.

Risking intolerable repetitiveness, I want to insist again that the distinction between normal and abnormal discourse does not coincide with any distinction of subject matter (e.g., nature versus history, or facts versus values), method (e.g., objectivation versus reflec-tion), faculty (e.g., reason versus imagination), or any of the other distinctions which systematic philosophy has used to make the sense of the world consist in the objective truth about some previously unnoticed portion or feature of the world. *Anything* can be discoursed of abnormally, just as anything can become edifying and anything can be sys-tematized. I have been discussing the relation between natural science and other disci-plines simply because, since the period of Descartes and Hobbes, the assumption that scientific discourse was normal discourse and that all other discourse needed to be mod-eled upon it has been the standard motive for philosophizing. Once we set this assump-tion aside, however, we can also set aside the various anti-naturalisms about which I have been complaining. More specifically, we can assert all of the following:

Every speech, thought, theory, poem, composition, and philosophy will turn out to be completely predictable in purely naturalistic terms. Some atoms-and-the-void account of micro-processes within individual human beings will permit the prediction of every sound or inscription which will ever be uttered. There are no ghosts.

Nobody will be able to predict his own actions, thoughts, theories, poems, etc., before deciding upon them or inventing them. (This is not an interesting remark about the odd nature of human beings, but rather a trivial consequence of what it means to "decide" or "invent.") So no hope (or danger) exists that cognition of oneself as *en-soi* will cause one to cease to exist *pour-soi*.

The complete set of laws which enable these predictions to be made, plus complete descriptions (in atoms-and-the-void terms) of all human beings, would not yet be the whole "objective truth" about human beings, nor the whole set of true predictions about them. There would remain as many other distinct sets of such objective truths (some useful for prediction, some not) at there were incommensurable vocabularies within which normal inquiry about human beings could be conducted (e.g., all those vocabularies within which we attribute beliefs and desires, virtues and beauty).

Incommensurability entails irreducibility but not incompatibility, so the failure to "reduce" these various vocabularies to that of "bottom-level" atoms-and-the-void science casts no doubt upon their cognitive status or upon the metaphysical status of their objects. (This goes as much for the aesthetic worth of poems as for the beliefs of persons, as much for virtues as for volitions.)

The assemblage, *per impossible*, of all these objective truths would still not necessarily be edifying. It might be the picture of a world without a sense, without a moral. Whether it seemed to point a moral to an individual would depend upon that individual. It would be true or false that it so seemed, or did not seem, to him. But it would not be objectively true or false that it "really did," or did not, have a sense or a moral. Whether his knowledge of the world leaves him with a sense of what to do with or in the world is itself predictable, but whether it *should* is not.

The fear of science, of "scientism," of "naturalism," of self-objectivation, of being turned by too much knowledge into a thing rather than a person, is the fear that all discourse will become normal discourse. That is, it is the fear that there will be objectively true or false answers to every question we ask, so that human worth will consist in knowing truths, and human virtue will be merely justified true belief. This is frightening because it cuts off the possibility of something new under the sun, of human life as poetic rather than merely contemplative.

But the dangers to abnormal discourse do not come from science or naturalistic philosophy. They come from the scarcity of food and from the secret police. Given leisure and libraries, the conversation which Plato began will not end in self-objectivation – not because aspects of the world, or of human beings, escape being objects of scientific inquiry, but simply because free and leisured conversation generates abnormal discourse as the sparks fly upward.

5. Philosophy in the Conversation of Mankind

I end this book with an allusion to Oakeshott's famous title,[28] because it catches the tone in which, I think, philosophy should be discussed. Much of what I have said about epistemology and its possible successors is an attempt to draw some corollaries from Sellars's doctrine that

> in characterizing an episode or a state as that of *knowing*, we are not giving an empirical description of that episode or state; we are placing it in the logical space of reasons, of justifying and being able to justify what one says.[29]

28   C. Michael Oakeshott, "The Voice of Poetry in the Conversation of Mankind," in his *Rationalism and Politics* (New York, 1975).
29   Wilfrid Sellars, *Science, Perception and Reality* (London and New York, 1963), p. 169.

If we see knowing not as having an essence, to be described by scientists or philosophers, but rather as a right, by current standards to believe, then we are well on the way to seeing *conversation* as the ultimate context within which knowledge is to be understood. Our focus shifts from the relation between human beings and the objects of their inquiry to the relation between alternative standards of justification, and from there to the actual changes in those standards which make up intellectual history. This brings us to appreciate Sellars's own description of his mythical hero Jones, the man who invented the Mirror of Nature and thereby made modern philosophy possible:

> Does the reader not recognize Jones as Man himself in the middle of his journey from the grunts and groans of the cave to the subtle and polydimensional discourse of the drawing room, the laboratory, and the study, the language of Henry and William James, of Einstein and of the philosophers who, in their efforts to break out of discourse to an ἀρχή beyond discourse, have provided the most curious dimension of all? (p. 196)

In this book I have offered a sort of prolegomenon to a history of epistemology-centered philosophy as an episode in the history of European culture. Such philosophy goes back to the Greeks, and goes sideways into all sorts of non-philosophical disciplines which have, at one time or another, proposed themselves as substitutes for epistemology, and thus for philosophy. So the episode in question cannot simply be identified with "modern philosophy," in the sense of the standard textbook sequence of great philosophers from Descantes to Russell and Husserl. But that sequence is, nevertheless, where the search for foundations for knowledge is most explicit. So most of my attempts to deconstruct the image of the Mirror of Nature have concerned these philosophers. I have tried to show how their urge to break out into an ἀρχή beyond discourse is rooted in the urge to see social practices of justification as more than just such practices. I have, however, focused mainly on the expressions of this urge in the recent literature of analytical philosophy. The result is thus no more than a prolegomenon. A proper historical treatment would require both learning and skills which I do not possess. But I would hope that the prolegomenon has been sufficient to let one see contemporary issues in philosophy as events in a certain stage of a conversation – a conversation which once knew nothing of these issues and may know nothing of them again.

The fact that we can continue the conversation Plato began without discussing the topics Plato wanted discussed, illustrates the difference between treating philosophy as a voice in a conversation and treating it as a subject, a *Fach*, a field of professional inquiry. The conversation Plato began has been enlarged by more voices than Plato would have dreamed possible, and thus by topics he knew nothing of. A "subject" – astrology, physics, classical philosophy, furniture design – may undergo revolutions, but it gets its self-image from its present state, and its history is necessarily written "Whiggishly" as an account of its gradual maturation. This is the most frequent way of writing the history of philosophy, and I cannot claim to have avoided such Whiggery entirely in sketching the sort of history which needs to be written. But I hope that I have shown how we can see the issues with which philosophers are presently concerned, and with which they Whiggishly see philosophy as having always (perhaps unwittingly) been concerned, as results of historical accident, as turns the conversation has taken.[30] It has taken this turn

---

30   Two recent writers – Michel Foucault and Harold Bloom – make this sense of the brute factuality of historical origins central to their work. Cf. Bloom, *A Map of Misreading* (New York,

for a long time, but it might turn in another direction without human beings thereby losing their reason, or losing touch with "the real problems."

The conversational interest of philosophy as a subject, or of some individual philosopher of genius, has varied and will continue to vary in unpredictable ways depending upon contingencies. These contingencies will range from what happens in physics to what happens in politics. The lines between disciplines will blur and shift, and new disciplines will arise, in the ways illustrated by Galileo's successful attempt to create "purely scientific questions" in the seventeenth century. The notions of "philosophical significance" and of "purely philosophical question," as they are currently used, gained sense only around the time of Kant. Our post-Kantian sense that epistemology or some successor subject is at the center of philosophy (and that moral philosophy, aesthetics, and social philosophy, for example, are somehow derivative) is a reflection of the fact that the professional philosopher's self-image depends upon his professional preoccupation with the image of the Mirror of Nature. Without the Kantian assumption that the philosopher can decide *quaestiones juris* concerning the claims of the rest of culture, this self-image collapses. That assumption depends on the notion that there is such a thing as understanding the essence of knowledge – doing what Sellars tells us we cannot do.

To drop the notion of the philosopher as knowing something about knowing which nobody else knows so well would be to drop the notion that his voice always has an overriding claim on the attention of the other participants in the conversation. It would also be to drop the notion that there is something called "philosophical method" or "philosophical technique" or "the philosophical point of view" which enables the professional philosopher, *ex officio*, to have interesting views about, say, the respectability of psychoanalysis, the legitimacy of certain dubious laws, the resolution of moral dilemmas, the "soundness" of schools of historiography or literary criticism, and the like. Philosophers often do have interesting views upon such questions, and their professional training as philosophers is often a necessary condition for their having the views they do. But this is not to say that philosophers have a special kind of knowledge about knowledge (or anything else) from which they draw relevant corollaries. The useful kibitzing they can provide on the various topics I just mentioned is made possible by their familiarity with the historical background of arguments on similar topics, and, most importantly, by the fact that arguments on such topics are punctuated by stale philosophical clichés which the other participants have stumbled across in their reading, but about which professional philosophers know the pros and cons by heart.

1975), p. 33: "All continuities possess the paradox of being absolutely arbitrary in their origins and absolutely inescapable in their teleologies. We know this so vividly from what we all of us oxymoronically call our love lives that its literary counterparts need little demonstration." Foucault says that his way of looking at the history of ideas "permits the introduction, into the very roots of thought, of notions of *chance, discontinuity* and *materiality*." ("The Discourse on Language," included in the *Archaeology of Knowledge* [New York, 1972], p. 231) It is hardest of all to see brute contingency in the history of *philosophy*, if only because since Hegel the historiography of philosophy has been "progressive," or (as in Heidegger's inversion of Hegel's account of progress) "retrogressive," but never without a sense of inevitability. If we could once see the desire for a permanent, neutral, ahistorical, commensurating vocabulary as itself a historical phenomenon, then perhaps we could write the history of philosophy less dialectically and less sentimentally than has been possible hitherto.

The neo-Kantian image of philosophy as a profession, then, is involved with the image of the "mind" or "language" as mirroring nature. So it might seem that epistemological behaviorism and the consequent rejection of mirror-imagery entail the claim that there can or should be no such profession. But this does not follow. Professions can survive the paradigms which gave them birth. In any case, the need for teachers who have read the great dead philosophers is quite enough to insure that there will be philosophy departments as long as there are universities. The actual result of a widespread loss of faith in mirror-imagery would be merely an "encapsulation" of the problems created by this imagery within a historical period. I do not know whether we are in fact at the end of an era. This will depend, I suspect, on whether Dewey, Wittgenstein, and Heidegger are taken to heart. It may be that mirror-imagery and "mainstream," systematic philosophy will be revitalized once again by some revolutionary of genius. Or it may be that the image of the philosopher which Kant offered is about to go the way of the medieval image of the priest. If that happens, even the philosophers themselves will no longer take seriously the notion of philosophy as providing "foundations" or "justifications" for the rest of culture, or as adjudicating *quaestiones juris* about the proper domains of other disciplines.

Whichever happens, however, there is no danger of philosophy's "coming to an end." Religion did not come to an end in the Enlightenment, nor painting in Impressionism. Even if the period from Plato to Nietzsche is encapsulated and "distanced" in the way Heidegger suggests, and even if twentieth-century philosophy comes to seem a stage of awkward transitional backing and filling (as sixteenth-century philosophy now seems to us), there will be something called "philosophy" on the other side of the transition. For even if problems about representation look as obsolete to our descendants as problems about hylomorphism look to us, people will still read Plato, Aristotle, Descartes, Kant, Hegel, Wittgenstein, and Heidegger. What roles these men will play in our descendants' conversation, no one knows. Whether the distinction between systematic and edifying philosophy will carry over, no one knows either. Perhaps philosophy will become purely edifying, so that one's self-identification as a philosopher will be purely in terms of the books one reads and discusses, rather than in terms of the problems one wishes to solve. Perhaps a new form of systematic philosophy will be found which has nothing whatever to do with epistemology but which nevertheless makes normal philosophical inquiry possible. These speculations are idle, and nothing I have been saying makes one more plausible than another. The only point on which I would insist is that philosophers' moral concern should be with continuing the conversation of the West, rather than with insisting upon a place for the traditional problems of modern philosophy within that conversation.

4

Pragmatism, Relativism, and Irrationalism

Part I: Pragmatism

"Pragmatism" is a vague, ambiguous, and overworked word. Nevertheless, it names the chief glory of our country's intellectual tradition. No other American writers have offered so radical a suggestion for making our future different from our past, as have James and Dewey. At present, however, these two writers are neglected. Many philosophers think that everything important in pragmatism has been preserved and adapted to the needs of analytic philosophy. More specifically, they view pragmatism as having suggested various holistic corrections of the atomistic doctrines of the early logical empiricists. This way of looking at pragmatism is not wrong, as far as it goes. But it ignores what is most important in James and Dewey. Logical empiricism was one variety of standard, academic, neo-Kantian, epistemologically-centered philosophy. The great pragmatists should not be taken as suggesting an holistic variation of this variant, but rather as breaking with the Kantian epistemological tradition altogether. As long as we see James or Dewey as having "theories of truth" or "theories of knowledge" or "theories of morality" we shall get them wrong. We shall ignore their criticisms of the assumption that there ought to *be* theories about such matters. We shall not see how radical their thought was – how deep was their criticism of the attempt, common to Kant, Husserl, Russell, and C. I. Lewis, to make philosophy into a foundational discipline.

One symptom of this incorrect focus is a tendency to overpraise Peirce. Peirce is praised partly because he developed various logical notions and various technical problems (such as the counterfactual conditional) which were taken up by the logical empiricists. But the main reason for Peirce's undeserved apotheosis is that his talk about a general theory of signs looks like an early discovery of the importance of language. For all his genius, however, Peirce never made up his mind what he wanted a general theory

Presidential Address delivered before the Seventy-Sixth Annual Eastern Meeting of the American Philosophical Association in New York City, December 29, 1979. Richard M. Rorty, "Pragmatism, Relativism and Irrationalism," *Proceedings and Addresses of the American Philosophical Association,* vol. 53 (6), August 1980: 719–38, © 1980 by American Philosophical Association. Reproduced with permission of American Philosophical Association in the format Textbook via Copyright Clearance Center.

of signs *for*, nor what it might look like, nor what its relation to either logic or epistemology was supposed to be. His contribution to pragmatism was merely to have given it a name, and to have stimulated James. Peirce himself remained the most Kantian of thinkers – the most convinced that philosophy gave us an all-embracing ahistorical context in which every other species of discourse could be assigned its proper place and rank. It was just this Kantian assumption that there was such a context, and that epistemology or semantics could discover it, against which James and Dewey reacted. We need to focus on this reaction if we are to recapture a proper sense of their importance.

This reaction is found in other philosophers who are currently more fashionable than James or Dewey – for example, Nietzsche and Heidegger. Unlike Nietzsche and Heidegger, however, the pragmatists did not make the mistake of turning against the community which takes the natural scientist as its moral hero – the community of secular intellectuals which came to self-consciousness in the Enlightenment. James and Dewey rejected neither the Enlightenment's choice of the scientist as moral example, nor the technological civilization which science had created. They wrote, as Nietzsche and Heidegger did not, in a spirit of social hope. They asked us to liberate our new civilization by giving up the notion of "grounding" our culture, our moral lives, our politics, our religious beliefs, upon "philosophical bases." They asked us to give up the neurotic Cartesian quest for certainty which had been one result of Galileo's frightening new cosmology, the quest for "enduring spiritual values" which had been one reaction to Darwin, and the aspiration of academic philosophy to form a tribunal of pure reason which had been the neo-Kantian response to Hegelian historicism. They asked us to think of the Kantian project of grounding thought or culture in a permanent ahistorical matrix as *reactionary*. They viewed Kant's idealization of Newton, and Spencer's of Darwin, as just as silly as Plato's idealization of Pythagoras, and Aquinas' of Aristotle.

Emphasizing this message of social hope and liberation, however, makes James and Dewey sound like prophets rather than thinkers. This would be misleading. They had things to say about truth, knowledge, and morality, even though they did not have *theories* of them, in the sense of sets of answers to the textbook problems. In what follows, I shall offer three brief sloganistic characterizations of what I take to be their central doctrine.

My first characterization of pragmatism is that it is simply anti-essentialism applied to notions like "truth," "knowledge," "language," "morality," and similar objects of philosophical theorizing. Let me illustrate this by James' definition of "the true" as "what is good in the way of belief." This has struck his critics as not to the point, as unphilosophical, as like the suggestion that the essence of aspirin is that it is good for headaches. James' point, however, was that there *is* nothing deeper to be said: truth is not the sort of thing which *has* an essence. More specifically, his point was that it is no use being told that truth is "correspondence to reality." Given a language and a view of what the world is like, one can, to be sure, pair off bits of the language with bits of what one takes the world to be in such a way that the sentences one believes true have internal structures isomorphic to relations between things in the world. When we rap out routine undeliberated reports like "This is water," "That's red," "That's ugly," "That's immoral," our short categorical sentences can easily be thought of as pictures, or as symbols which fit together to make a map. Such reports do indeed pair little bits of language with little bits of the world. Once one gets to negative universal hypotheticals, and the like, such pairing will become messy and *ad hoc*, but perhaps it can be done. James' point was that carrying out this exercise will not enlighten us about why truths are good to believe, or offer any clues as to why or whether our present view of the world is, roughly, the one we should hold. Yet nobody would have asked for a "theory" of truth if they had not wanted answers to these latter questions. Those who want truth to have an essence want knowledge, or rationality, or inquiry, or the relation between thought and its object, to have an essence. Further, they want to be able to use their knowledge of such essences to criticize views they take to be false, and to point the direction of progress toward the discovery of more truths. James' thinks these hopes are vain. There are no essences anywhere in the area. There is no wholesale, epistemological, way to direct, or criticize, or underwrite, the course of inquiry.

Rather, the pragmatists tell us, it is the vocabulary of practise rather than of theory, of action rather than contemplation, in which one can say something useful about truth. Nobody engages in epistemology or semantics because he wants to know how "This is red" pictures the world. Rather, we want to know in what sense Pasteur's views of disease picture the world accurately and Paracelsus's inaccurately, or what exactly it is that Marx pictured more accurately than Machiavelli. But just here the vocabulary of "picturing" fails us. When we turn from individual sentences to vocabularies and theories, critical terminology naturally shifts from metaphors of isomorphism, symbolism, and mapping to talk of utility, convenience, and likelihood of getting what we want. To say that the parts of properly analyzed true sentences are arranged in a way isomorphic to the parts of the world paired with them sounds plausible if one thinks of a sentence like "Jupiter has moons." It sounds slightly less plausible for "The earth goes round the sun," less still for "There is no such thing as natural motion," and not plausible at all for "The universe is infinite." When we want to praise or blame assertions of the latter sort of sentence, we show how the decision to assert them fits into a whole complex of decisions about what terminology to use, what books to read, what projects to engage in, what life to live. In this respect they resemble such sentences as "Love is the only law" and "History is the story of class struggle." The whole vocabulary of isomorphism, picturing, and mapping is out of place here, as indeed is the notion of being true *of objects*. If we ask what objects these sentences claim to be true of, we get only unhelpful repetitions of the subject terms – "the universe", "the law", "history". Or, even less helpfully we get talk about "the facts," or "the way the world is". The natural approach to such sentences, Dewey tells us, is not "Do they get it right?", but more like "What would it be like to believe that? What would happen if I did? What would I be committing myself to?" The vocabulary of contemplation, looking, *theoria*, deserts us just when we deal with theory rather than observation, with programming rather than input. When the contemplative mind, isolated from the stimuli of the moment, takes large views, its activity is more like deciding what to *do* than deciding that a representation is accurate. James' dictum about truth says that the vocabulary of practise is uneliminable, that no distinction of kind separates the sciences from the crafts, from moral reflection, or from art.

So a second characterization of pragmatism might go like this: there is no epistemological difference between truth about what ought to be and truth about what is, nor any metaphysical difference between facts and values, nor any methodological difference between morality and science. Even non-pragmatists think Plato was wrong to think of moral philosophy as discovering the essence of goodness, and Mill and Kant wrong in trying to reduce moral choice to rule. But every reason for saying that they were wrong is a reason for thinking the epistemological tradition wrong in looking for the essence of science and in trying to reduce rationality to rule. For the pragmatists, the pattern of all inquiry – scientific as well as moral – is deliberation concerning the relative attractions of various concrete alternatives. The idea that in science or philosophy we can substitute "method" for deliberation between alternative results of speculation is just wishful thinking. It is like the idea that the morally wise man resolves his dilemmas by consulting his memory of the Idea of the Good, or by looking up the relevant article of the moral law. It is the myth that rationality consists in being constrained by rule. According to this Platonic myth, the life of reason is not the life of Socratic conversation but an illuminated state of consciousness in which one never needs to ask if one has exhausted the possible descriptions of, or explanations for, the situation. One simply arrives at true beliefs by obeying mechanical procedures.

Traditional, Platonic, epistemologically-centered philosophy is the search for such procedures. It is the search for a way in which one can avoid the need for conversation and deliberation and simply tick off the way things are. The idea is to acquire beliefs about interesting and important matters in a way as much like visual perception as possible – by confronting an object and responding to it as programmed. This urge to substitute *theoria* for *phronesis* is what lies behind the attempt to say that "There is no such thing as natural motion" pictures objects in the same way as does "The cat is on the mat." It also lies behind the hope that some arrangement of objects may be found which is pictured by the sentence "Love is better than hate", and the frustration which ensues when it is realized that there may be no such objects. The great fallacy of the tradition, the pragmatists tell us, is to think that the metaphors of vision, correspondence, mapping, picturing and representation which apply to small routine assertions will apply to large and debatable ones. This basic error begets the notion that where there are no objects to correspond to we have no hope of rationality, but only taste, passion, and will. When the pragmatist attacks the notion of truth as accuracy of representation he is thus attacking the traditional distinctions between reason and desire, reason and appetitie, reason and will. For none of these distinctions make sense unless reason is thought of on the model of vision, unless we persist in what Dewey called "the spectator theory of knowledge."

The pragmatist tells us that once we get rid of this model we see that the Platonic idea of the life of reason is impossible. A life spent representing objects accurately would be spent recording the results of calculations, reasoning through sorites, calling off the observable properties of things, construing cases according to unambiguous criteria, getting things right. Within what Kuhn calls "normal science", or any similar social context, one can, indeed, live such a life. But conformity to *social* norms is not good enough for the Platonist. He wants to be constrained not merely by the disciplines of the day, but by the ahistorical and nonhuman nature of reality itself. This impulse takes two forms – the original Platonic strategy of postulating novel *objects* for treasured propositions to correspond to, and the Kantian strategy of finding *principles* which are definatory of the essence of knowledge, or representation, or morality, or rationality. Insofar as there is a distinction between "Continental" and "analytic" philosophy, it is that mainstream "Continental" philosophy is a watered-down Platonism and mainstream "analytic" philosophy a watered-down Kantianism. But this difference is unimportant compared to the common urge to escape the vocabulary and practises of one's own time and finding something ahistorical and necessary to cling to. It is the urge to answer questions like "Why believe what I take to be true?" "Why do what I take to be right?" by appealing to something *more* than the ordinary, retail, detailed, concrete, reasons which have brought one to one's present view. This urge is common to nineteenth-century idealists and contemporary scientific realists, to Russell and to Husserl; it is definatory of the Western philosophical tradition, and of the culture for which that tradition speaks. James and Dewey stand with Nietzsche and Heidegger in asking us to abandon that tradition, and that culture.

Let me sum up by offering a third and final characterization of pragmatism: it is the doctrine that there are no constraints on inquiry save conversational ones – no whole-sale constraints derived from the nature of the objects, or of the mind, or of language, but only those retail constraints provided by the remarks of our fellow-inquirers. The way in which the properly-programmed speaker cannot help believing that the patch before him is red has *no* analogy for the more interesting and controversial beliefs which provoke epistemological reflection. The pragmatist tells us that it is useless to hope that objects will constrain us to believe the truth about them, if only they are approached with an unclouded mental eye, or a rigorous method, or a perspicuous language. He wants us to give up the notion that God, or evolution, or some other underwriter of our present world-picture, has programmed us as machines for accurate verbal picturing, and that philosophy brings self-knowledge by letting us read our own program. The only sense in which we are constrained to truth is that, as Peirce suggested, we can make no sense of the notion that the view which can survive all objections might be false. But objections – conversational constraints – cannot be anticipated. There is no method for knowing *when* one has reached the truth, or when one is closer to it than before.

I prefer this third way of characterizing pragmatism because it seems to me to focus on a fundamental choice which confronts the reflective mind: that between accepting the contingent character of starting points, and attempting to evade this contingency. To accept the contingency of starting-points is to accept our inheritance from, and our conversation with, our fellow-humans as our only source of guidance. To attempt to evade this contingency is to hope to become a properly-programmed machine. This was the hope which Plato thought might be fulfilled at the top of the divided line, when we passed beyond hypotheses. Christians have hoped it might be attained by becoming attuned to the voice of God in the heart, and Cartesians that it might be fulfilled by emptying the mind and seeking the indubitable. Since Kant, philosophers have hoped that it might be fulfilled by finding the apriori structure of any possible inquiry, or lan-guage, or form of social life. If we give up this hope, we shall lose what Nietzsche called "metaphysical comfort," but we may gain a renewed sense of community. Our identifi-cation with our community – our society, our political tradition, our intellectual heritage – is heightened when we see this community as *ours* rather than *nature's, shaped* rather than *found*, one among many which men have made. In the end, the pragmatists tell us, what matters is our loyalty to other human beings clinging together against the dark, not our hope of getting things right. James, in arguing against realists and idealists that "the trail of the human serpent is over all," was reminding us that our glory is in our participation in fallible and transitory human projects, not in our obedience to perma-nent non-human constraints.

Part II: Relativism

"Relativism" is the view that every belief on a certain topic, or perhaps about *any* topic, is as good as every other. No one holds this view. Except for the occasional cooperative freshman, one cannot find anybody who says that two incompatible opinions on an important topic are equally good. The philosophers who get *called* "relativists" are those who say that the grounds for choosing between such opinions are less algorithmic than had been thought. Thus one may be attacked as a relativist for holding that familiarity of terminology is a criterion of theory-choice in physical science, or that coherence with the institutions of the surviving parliamentary democracies is a criterion in social philosophy. When such criteria are invoked, critics say that the resulting philosophical position assumes an unjustified primacy for "our conceptual framework", or our purposes, or our institutions. The position in question is criticized for not having done what philosophers are employed to do: explain why our framework, or culture, or interests, or language, or whatever, is at last on the right track – in touch with physical reality, or the moral law, or the real numbers, or some other sort of object patiently waiting about to be copied. So the real issue is not between people who think one view as good as another and people who do not. It is between those who think our culture, or purpose, or intuitions cannot be supported except conversationally, and people who still hope for other sorts of support.

If there *were* any relativists, they would, of course, be easy to refute. One would merely use some variant of the self-referential arguments Socrates used against Protagoras. But such neat little dialectical strategies only work against lightly-sketched fictional characters. The relativist who says that we can break ties among serious and incompatible candidates for belief only by "non-rational" or "non-cognitive" considerations is just one of the Platonist or Kantian philosopher's imaginary playmates, inhabiting the same realm of fantasy as the solipsist, the sceptic, and the moral nihilist. Disillusioned, or whimsical, Platonists and Kantians occasionally play at being one or another of these characters. But when they do they are never offering relativism or scepticism or nihilism as a serious suggestion about how we might do things differently. These positions are adopted to make *philosophical* points – that is, moves in a game played with fictitious opponents, rather than fellow-participants in a common project.

The association of pragmatism with relativism is a result of a confusion between the pragmatists' attitude toward *philosophical* theories with his attitude towards *real* theories. James and Dewey are, to be sure, metaphilosophical relativists, in a certain limited sense. Namely: they think there is no way to choose between incompatible philosophical theories of the typical Platonic or Kantian type. Such theories are attempts to ground some element of our practises on something external to these practices. Pragmatists think that any such philosophical grounding is, apart from elegance of execution, pretty much as good or as bad as the practise it purports to ground. They regard the project of grounding as a wheel that plays no part in the mechanism. In this, I think, they are quite right. No sooner does one discover the categories of the pure understanding for a Newtonian age than somebody draws up another list that would do nicely for an Aristotelian or an Einsteinian one. No sooner does one draw up a categorical imperative for Christians than somebody draws up one which works for cannibals. No sooner does one develop an evolutionary epistemology which explains why our science is so good than somebody writes a science-fiction story about bug-eyed and monstrous evolutionary epistemologists praising bug-eyed and monstrous scientists for the survival value of their monstrous theories. The reason this game is so easy to play is that none of these philosophical theories have to do much hard work. The real work has been done by the scientists who developed the explanatory theories by patience and genius, or the societies which developed the moralities and institutions in struggle and pain. All the Platonic or Kantian philosopher does is to take the finished first-level product, jack it up a few levels of abstraction, invent a metaphysical or epistemological or semantical vocabulary into which to translate it, and announce that he has *grounded* it.

"Relativism" only seems to refer to a disturbing view, worthy of being refuted, if it concerns *real* theories, not just philosophical theories. Nobody really cares if there are incompatible alternative formulations of a categorical imperative, or incompatible sets of categories of the pure understanding. We *do* care about alternative, concrete, detailed, cosmologies, or alternative concrete, detailed, proposals for political change. When such an alternative is proposed, we debate it, not in terms of categories or principles but in terms of the various concrete advantages and disadvantages it has. The reason relativism is talked about so much among Platonic and Kantian philosophers is that they think being relativistic about philosophical theories – attempts to "ground" first-level theories – leads to being relativistic about the first-level theories themselves. If anyone really believed that the worth of a theory depends upon the worth of its philosophical grounding, then indeed they would be dubious about physics, or democracy, until relativism in respect to philosophical theories had been overcome. Fortunately, almost nobody believes anything of the sort.

What people do believe is that it would be good to hook up our views about democracy, mathematics, physics, God, and everything else, into a coherent story about how everything hangs together. Getting such a synoptic view often does require us to change radically our views on particular subjects. But this holistic process of readjustment is just muddling through on a large scale. It has nothing to do with the Platonic-Kantian notion of grounding. That notion involves finding constraints, demonstrating necessities, finding immutable principles to which to subordinate oneself. When it turns out that suggested constraints, necessities, and principles are as plentiful as blackberries, nothing changes except the attitude of the rest of culture towards the philosophers. Since the time of Kant, it has become more and more apparent to non-philosophers that a really professional philosopher can supply a philosophical foundation for just about anything. This is one reason why philosophers have, in the course of our century, become increasingly isolated from the rest of culture. Our proposals to guarantee this and clarify that have come to strike our fellow-intellectuals as merely comic.

Part III: Irrationalism

My discussion of relativism may seem to have ducked the real issues. Perhaps nobody is a relativist. Perhaps "relativism" is *not* the right name for what so many philosophers find so offensive in pragmatism. But surely there *is* an important issue around somewhere. There is indeed an issue, but it is not easily stated, nor easily made amenable to argument. I shall try to bring it into focus by developing it in two different contexts, one microcosmic and the other macrocosmic. The microcosmic issue concerns philosophy in one of its most parochial senses – namely, the activities of the American Philosophical Association. Our Association has traditionally been agitated by the question of whether we should be free-wheeling and edifying or argumentative and professional. For my purposes, this boils down to an issue about whether we can be pragmatists and still be professionals. The macrocosmic issue concerns philosophy in the widest sense – the attempt to make everything hang together. This is the issue between Socrates on the one hand and the tyrants on the other – the issue between lovers of conversation and lovers of self-deceptive rhetoric. For my purposes, it is the issue about whether we can be pragmatists without betraying Socrates, without falling into irrationalism.

I discuss the unimportant microcosmic issue about professionalism first because it is sometimes confused with the important issues about irrationalism, and because it helps focus that latter issue. The question of whether philosophy professors should edify agitated our Association in its early decades. James throught they should, and was dubious about the growing professionalization of the discipline. Arthur Lovejoy, the great opponent of pragmatism, saw professionalization as an unmixed blessing. Echoing what was being said simultaneously by Russell in England and by Husserl in Germany, Lovejoy urged the 16th annual meeting of the APA to aim at making philosophy into a science. He wanted the APA to organize its program into well-structured controversies on sharply defined problems, so that at the end of each convention it would be agreed who had won.[1] Lovejoy insisted that philosophy could either be edifying and visionary *or* could produce "objective, verifiable, and clearly communicable truths," but not both. James would have agreed. He too thought that one could *not* be both a pragmatist and a professional. James, however, saw professionalization as a failure of nerve rather than as a triumph of rationality. He thought that the activity of making things hang together was *not* likely to produce "objective, verifiable, and clearly communicable truths", and that this did not greatly matter.

Lovejoy, of course, won this battle. If one shares his conviction that philosophers should be as much like scientists as possible, then one will be pleased at the outcome. If one does not, one will contemplate the APA in its seventy-sixth year mindful of Goethe's maxim that one should be careful what one wishes for when one is young, for one will get it when one is old. Which attitude one takes will depend upon whether one sees the problems we discuss today as permanent problems for human thought, continuous with those discussed by Plato, Kant, and Lovejoy – or as modern attempts to breathe life into dead issues. On the Lovejoyan account, the gap between philosophers and the rest of high culture is of the same sort as the gap between physicists and laymen. The gap is not created by the artificiality of the problems being discussed, but by the development of technical and precise ways of dealing with real problems. If one shares the pragmatists' anti-essentialism, however, one will tend to see the problems about which philosophers are now offering "objective, verifiable, and clearly communicable" solutions as historical relics, left over from the Enlightenment's misguided search for the hidden essences of knowledge and morality. This is the point of view adopted by many of our fellow-intellectuals, who see us philosophy professors as caught in a time-warp, trying to live the Enlightenment over again.

I have reminded you of the parochial issue about professionalization not in order to persuade you to one side or the other, but rather to exhibit the source of the anti-pragmatist's passion. This is his conviction that conversation necessarily aims at agreement and at rational consensus, that we converse in order to make further conversation

1   See A. O. Lovejoy, "On Some Condition of Progress in Philosophical Inquiry," *The Philosophical Review* XXVI, pp. 123–163 (especially the concluding pages). I owe the reference to Lovejoy's paper to Daniel J. Wilson's illuminating "Professionalization and Organized Discussion in the American Philosophical Association, 1900–1922", *Journal of the History of Philosophy* XVII, pp. 53–69.

unnecessary. The anti-pragmatist believes that conversation only makes sense if something like the Platonic theory of Recollection is right – if we all have natural starting-points of thought somewhere within us, and will recognize the vocabulary in which they are best formulated once we hear it. For only if something like that is true will conversation have a natural goal. The Enlightenment hoped to find such a vocabulary – nature's own vocabulary, so to speak. Lovejoy – who described himself as an "unredeemed *Aufklärer*" – wanted to continue the project. Only if we had agreement on such a vocabulary, indeed, could conversation be reduced to argumentation – to the search for "objective, verifiable, and clearly communicable" solutions to problems. So the anti-pragmatist sees the pragmatist's scorn for professionalism as scorn for consensus, for the Christian and democratic idea that every human has the seeds of truth within. The pragmatist's attitude seems to him elitist and dilettantish, reminiscent of Alcibiades rather than of Socrates.

Issues about relativism and about professionalization are awkward attempts to formulate this opposition. The real and passionate opposition is over the question of whether loyalty to our fellow-humans presupposes that there is something permanent and unhistorical which explains *why* we should continue to converse in the manner of Socrates, something which guarantees convergence to agreement. Because the anti-pragmatist believes that without such an essence and such a guarantee the Socratic life makes no sense, he sees the pragmatist as a cynic. Thus the microcosmic issue about how philosophy professors should converse leads us quickly to the macrocosmic issue: whether one can be a pragmatist without being an irrationalist, without abandoning one's loyalty to Socrates.

Questions about irrationalism have become acute in our century because the sullen resentment which sins against Socrates, which withdraws from conversation and community, has recently become articulate. Our European intellectual tradition is now abused as "merely conceptual" or "merely ontic" or as "committed to abstractions." Irrationalists propose such rubbishy pseudo-epistemological notions as "intuition" or "an inarticulate sense of tradition" or "thinking with the blood" or "expressing the will of the oppressed classes." Our tyrants and bandits are more hateful than those of earlier times because, invoking such self-deceptive rhetoric, they pose as intellectuals. Our tyrants write philosophy in the morning and torture in the afternoon; our bandits alternately read Hölderlin and bomb people into bloody scraps. So our culture clings, more than ever, to the hope of Enlightenment, the hope that drove Kant to make philosophy formal and rigorous and professional. We hope that by formulating the *right* conceptions of reason, of science, of thought, of knowledge, of morality, the conceptions which express their *essence*, we shall have a shield against irrationalist resentment and hatred.

Pragmatists tell us that this hope is vain. On their view, the Socratic virtues – willingness to talk, to listen to other people, to weigh the consequences of our actions upon other people – are *simply* moral virtues. They cannot be inculcated nor fortified by theoretical research into essence. Irrationalists who tell us to think with our blood cannot be rebutted by better accounts of the nature of thought, or knowledge, or logic. The pragmatists tell us that the conversation which it is our moral duty to continue is *merely* our project, the European intellectual's form of life. It has no metaphysical nor epistemological guarantee of success. Further, and this is the crucial point, *we do not know what "success" would mean except simply "continuance."* We are not conversing because we have a goal, but because Socratic conversation is an activity which is its *own* end. The anti-pragmatist who insists that agreement is its goal is like the basketball player who thinks that the reason for playing the game is to make baskets. He mistakes an essential moment in the course of an activity for the end of the activity. Worse yet, he is like a basketball fan who argues that all men by nature desire to play basketball, or that the nature of things is such that balls can go through hoops.

For the traditional, Platonic or Kantian, philosopher, on the other hand, the possibility of *grounding* the European form of life – of showing it to be more than European, more than a contingent human project – seems the central task of philosophy. He wants to show that sinning against Socrates is sinning against our nature, not just against our community. So he sees the pragmatist as an irrationalist. The charge that pragmatism is "relativistic" is simply his first unthinking expression of disgust at a teaching which seems cynical about our deepest hopes. If the traditional philosopher gets beyond such epithets, however, he raises a question which the pragmatist must face up to: the *practical* question of whether the notion of "conversation" *can* substitute for that of "reason." "Reason", as the term is used in the Platonic and Kantian traditions, is interlocked with the notions of truth as correspondence, of knowledge as discovery of essence, of moral-ity as obedience to principle, all the notions which the pragmatist tries to deconstruct. For better or worse, the Platonic and Kantian vocabularies are the ones in which Europe has described and promised the Socratic virtues. It is not clear that we know how to describe these virtues without those vocabularies. So the deep suspicion which the pragmatist inspires is that, like Alcibiades, he is essentially frivolous – that he is com-mending uncontroversial common goods while refusing to participate in the only activ-ity which can preserve those goods. He seems to be sacrificing our common European project to the delights of purely negative criticism.

The issue about irrationalism can be sharpened by noting that when the pragmatist says "All that can be done to explicate 'truth,' 'knowledge,' 'morality,' 'virtue' is to refer us back to the concrete details of the culture in which these terms grew up and developed, the defender of the Enlightenment takes him to be saying "Truth and virtue are simply what a community agrees that they are." When the pragmatist says "We have to take truth and virtue as whatever emerges from the conversation of Europe", the traditional philosopher wants to know what is so special about Europe. Isn't the pragmatist saying, like the irrationalist, that *we* are in a privileged situation simply by being *us*? Further, isn't there something terribly dangerous about the notion that truth can only be character-ized as "the outcome of doing more of what we are doing now"? What if the "we" is the Orwellian state? When tyrants employ Lenin's blood-curdling sense of "objective" to describe their lies as "objectively true," what is to prevent them from citing Peirce in Lenin's defense?[2]

The pragmatist's first line of defense against this criticism has been created by Habermas, who says that such a definition of truth works only for the outcome of *undis-torted* conversation, and that the Orwellian state is the paradigm of distortion. But this is *only* a first line, for we need to know more about what counts as "undistorted." Here Habermas goes transcendental and offers principles. The pragmatist, however, must remain ethnocentric and offer examples. He can only say: "undistorted" means employ-ing *our* criteria of relevance, where *we* are the people who have read and pondered Plato, Newton, Kant, Marx, Darwin, Freud, Dewey, etc. Milton's "free and open encounter", in which truth is bound to prevail, must itself be described in terms of examples rather than

2   I am indebted to Michael Williams for making me see that pragmatists have to answer this question.

principles – it is to be more like the Athenian market-place than the council-chamber of the Great King, more like the twentieth century than the twelfth, more like the Prussian Academy in 1925 than in 1935. The pragmatist must avoid saying, with Peirce, that truth is *fated* to win. He must even avoid saying that truth *will* win. He can only say, with Hegel, that truth and justice lie in the direction marked by the successive stages of European thought. This is not because he knows some "necessary truths" and cites these examples as a result of this knowledge. It is simply that the pragmatist knows no better way to explain his convictions than to remind his interlocutor of the position they both are in, the contingent starting points they both share, the floating, ungrounded, conversations of which they are both members. This means that the pragmatist cannot answer the question "What is so special about Europe?" save by saying "Do you have anything non-European to suggest which meets *our* European purposes better?" He cannot answer the question "What is so good about the Socratic virtues, about Miltonic free encounters, about undistorted communication?" save by saying "What else would better fulfill the purposes *we* share with Socrates, Milton and Habermas?"

To decide whether this obviously circular response is enough is to decide whether Hegel or Plato had the proper picture of the progress of thought. Pragmatists follow Hegel in saying that "philosophy is its time grasped in thought." Anti-pragmatists follow Plato in striving for an escape from conversation to something atemporal which lies in the background of all possible conversations. I do not think one can decide between Hegel and Plato save by meditating on the past efforts of the philosophical tradition to escape from time and history. One can see these efforts as worthwhile, getting better, worth continuing. Or one can see them as doomed and perverse. I do not know what would count as a non-circular metaphysical or epistemological or semantical argument for seeing them in either way. So I think that the decision has to be made simply by reading the history of philosophy and drawing a moral.

Nothing that I have said, therefore, is an argument in favor of pragmatism. At best, I have merely answered various superficial criticisms which have been made of it. Nor have I dealt with the central issue about irrationalism. I have not answered the deep criticism of pragmatism which I mentioned a few minutes ago: the criticism that the Socratic virtues cannot, as a practical matter, be defended save by Platonic means, that without some sort of metaphysical comfort nobody will be able *not* to sin against Socrates. William James himself was not sure whether this criticism could be answered. Exercising his own right to believe, James wrote: "If this life be not a real fight in which something is eternally gained for the universe by success, it is no better than a game of private theatricals from which we may withdraw at will." "It *feels*," he said, "like a fight."

For us, footnotes to Plato that we are, it *does* feel that way. But if James' own pragmatism were taken seriously, if pragmatism became central to our culture and our self-image, then it would *no longer* feel that way. We do not know how it *would* feel. We do not even know whether, given such a change in tone, the conversation of Europe might not falter and die away. We just do not know. James and Dewey offered us no guarantees. They simply pointed to the situation we stand in, now that both the Age of Faith and the Enlightenment seem beyond recovery. They grasped our time in thought. We did not change the course of the conversation in the way they suggested we might. Perhaps we are *still* unable to do so; perhaps we *never* shall be able to. But we can nevertheless honor James and Dewey for having offered what very few philosophers have succeeded in offering: a hint of how our lives might be changed.

5

Nineteenth-Century Idealism and Twentieth-Century Textualism

I

In the last century there were philosophers who argued that nothing exists but ideas. In our century there are people who write as if there were nothing but texts. These people, whom I shall call "textualists," include for example, the so-called Yale school of literary criticism centering around Harold Bloom, Geoffrey Hartmann, and Paul De Man, "post-structuralist" French thinkers like Jacques Derrida and Michel Foucault, historians like Hayden White, and social scientists like Paul Rabinow. Some of these people take their point of departure from Heidegger, but usually the influence of philosophers is relatively remote. The center of gravity of the intellectual movement in which these people figure is not philosophy, but literary criticism. In this paper I want to discuss some similarities and differences between this movement and nineteenth-century idealism.

The first similarity is that both movements adopt an antagonistic position to natural science. Both suggest that the natural scientist should not be the dominant cultural figure, that scientific knowledge is not what really matters. Both insist that there is a point of view other than, and somehow higher than, that of science. They warn us against the idea that human thought culminates in the application of "scientific method." Both offer to what C.P. Snow called "the literary culture" a self-image, and a set of rhetorical devices.

The second similarity is that both insist that we can never compare human thought or language with bare, unmediated, reality. The idealists started off from Berkeley's claim that nothing can be like an idea except another idea. The textualists start off from the claim that all problems, topics, and distinctions are language-relative – the results of our having chosen to use a certain vocabulary, to play a certain language-game. Both use this point to put natural science in its place. The concepts of natural science, idealists pointed out, were shown by Kant to be merely instruments which the mind uses to synthesize sense-impressions; science, therefore, can know only a phenomenal world. In

Richard M. Rorty, "Nineteenth-Century Idealism and Twentieth-Century Textualism," *The Monist*, vol. 64 (2), 1981: 155–74, © 1981, *The Monist: An International Quarterly Journal of General Philosophical Inquiry*, Open Court Publishing Company, Chicago, Illinois. Reprinted by permission.

textualist terms, this becomes the claim that the vocabulary of science is merely one among others – merely the vocabulary which happens to be handy in predicting and controlling nature. It is not as physicalism would have us think, Nature's Own Vocabulary. Both use the same point to exalt the function of art. For the idealists, art could put us in touch with that part of ourselves – the noumenal, free, spiritual part – which science cannot see. For the textualists, the literary artist's awareness that he is making rather than finding, and more specifically the ironic modernist's awareness that he is responding to texts rather than to things, puts him one up on the scientist. Both movements treat the scientist as naive in thinking that he is doing something *more* than putting together ideas, or constructing new texts.

I hope that these two similarities are enough to justify my attempt to view textualism as the contemporary counterpart of idealism – of the textualists as spiritual descendants of the idealists, the species having adapted to a changed environment. The differences in environment, I shall claim, are due to the fact that in the early nineteenth century there was a well-defined and well-regarded discipline, philosophy, which had claims to be architectonic for culture, and within which metaphysical theses could be argued. In our culture there is no such discipline. Idealism was based upon a metaphysical thesis, but textualism is not. When philosophers like Derrida say things like "there is nothing out-side the text" they are not making theoretical remarks, remarks backed up by epistemo-logical or semantical arguments. Rather, they are saying, cryptically and aphoristically, that a certain framework of inter-connected ideas – truth as correspondence, language as picture, literature as imitation, for example – ought to be abandoned. They are not, however, claiming to have discovered the *real* nature of truth or language or literature. Rather, they say that the very notion of discovering the *nature* of such things is part of the intellectual framework which we must abandon – part of what Heidegger calls "the metaphysics of presence," or "the onto-theological tradition."

If one repudiates that tradition, one repudiates the notion which once held realists and idealists together in a single enterprise called "philosophy" – the notion that there is a non-empirical quasi-science which can weigh the considerations for and against a certain view of what reality or knowledge is like. When textualists claim that issues such as those between nineteenth-century idealists and positivists were created by an out-dated vocabulary, and are to be dismissed rather than (as some contemporary analytic philosophers would wish to do) reformulated and made precise, they do not attempt to defend this claim by anything one could call a "philosophical argument." Textualists sometimes, it is true, simply claim that Heidegger ended metaphysics, just as positivists used to smugly claim that Carnap had. Smugness, however, is all the cases have in com-mon. Heidegger did not announce a new philosophical discovery, in the way in which Carnap claimed to have discovered something about language. The whole idea of adopt-ing a new vocabulary because *something has been discovered to be the case* is just one more element in that "metaphysics of presence" which Heidegger wants to deconstruct.

I have been saying, first, that idealism and textualism have in common an opposition to the claim of science to be a paradigm of human activity, and, second, that they differ in that one is a philosophical doctrine and the other an expression of suspicion about philosophy. I can put these two points together by saying that whereas nineteenth-century idealism wanted to substitute one sort of science (philosophy) for another (nat-ural science) as the center of culture, twentieth-century textualism wants to place literature in the center, and to treat both science and philosophy as, at best, literary genres.

The rest of my paper will be an attempt to refine this crude formula and to make it plausible. I shall begin by defining its component terms in the senses in which I wish to use them.

By "science" I shall mean the sort of activity in which argument is relatively easy – in which one can agree on some general principles which govern discourse in an area, and then aim at consensus by tracing inferential chains between these principles and more particular and more interesting propositions. Philosophy since Kant has purported to be a science which could sit in judgment on all the other sciences. As the science of knowledge, the science of science, *Wissenschaftslehre, Erkenntnistheorie*, it claimed to discover those general principles which made scientific discourse scientific, and thus to "ground" both the other sciences and itself.

It is a feature of a science that the vocabulary in which problems are posed is accepted by all those who count as contributing to the subject. The vocabulary may be changed, but that is only because a new theory has been discovered which explains the phenomena better by invoking a new set of theoretical terms. The vocabulary in which the *explananda* are described has to remain constant. It is a feature of what I shall "literature" that one can achieve success by introducing a quite new genre of poem or novel or critical essay without argument. It succeeds simply by its success, not because there are good reasons why poems or novels or essays should be written in the new way rather than the old. There is no constant vocabulary in which to describe the values to be defended or objects to be imitated, or the emotions to be expressed, or whatever, in essays or poems or novels. The reason "literary criticism" is "unscientific" is just that whenever somebody tries to work up such a vocabulary he makes a fool of himself. We don't *want* works of literature to be criticizable within a terminology we already know; we want both those works and criticism of them to give us *new* terminologies. By "literature," then, I shall mean the areas of culture which, quite self-consciously, forego agreement on an encompassing critical vocabulary, and thus forego argumentation.

Though obviously crude, this way of separating science and literature has at least the merit of focusing attention on a distinction which is relevant to both idealism and textualism – the distinction between finding out whether a proposition is true and finding out whether a vocabulary is good. Let me call "romanticism" the thesis that what is most important for human life is not what propositions we believe but what vocabulary we use. Then I can say that romanticism is what unites metaphysical idealism and literary textualism. Both, as I said earlier, remind us that scientists do not bring a naked eye to nature, that propositions of science are not simple transcriptions of what is present to the senses. Both draw the corollary that the current scientific vocabulary is one vocabulary among others, and that there is no need to give it primacy, nor to reduce other vocabularies to it. Both see the scientists' claim to discover the ways things really are as needing qualification, as a pretension which needs to be curbed. The scientist, they say, is discovering "merely scientific" or "merely empirical" or "merely phenomenal" or "merely positive" or "merely technical" truths. Such dismissive epithets express the suspicion that the scientist merely goes through mechanical procedures, checking off the truth-value of propositions – behaving like a glorified stock-room clerk inventorying the universe in accord with a predetermined scheme. The sense that science is banausic, except perhaps in those rare creative moments when a Galileo or a Darwin suddenly imposes a new scheme, is the essence of romanticism. Romanticism inverts the values which, in the third *Critique*, Kant assigned to the determinate and the reflective judgment. It sees the determinate judgment – the activity which ticks off instances of concepts by invoking common, public, criteria – as producing merely *agreement*. Kant thought "knowledge," the name for the result of such activity, was a term of praise. Romanticism accepts Kant's point that objectivity is conformity to rule, but changes the emphasis, so that objectivity becomes *mere* conformity to rule, merely going along with the crowd, merely consensus. By contrast, romanticism sees the reflective judgment – the activity of operating without rules, of searching for concepts under which to group particulars (or, by extension, of constructing new concepts which are "transgressive" in that they do not fit under any of the old rules) – as what really matters. Kant, in saying that aesthetic judgment is noncognitive, because it cannot be brought under rules, is assigning it a second-best status – the status which the scientific culture has always assigned to the literary culture. Romanticism, on the other hand, when it says that science is *merely* cognitive, is trying to turn the tables.

I can sum up by saying that post-Kantian metaphysical idealism was a specifically philosophical form of romanticism whereas textualism is a specifically post-philosophical form. In the next section I shall argue that philosophy and idealism rose and fell together. In section III I shall discuss the relation between textualism as post-philosophical romanticism and pragmatism, arguing that pragmatism is, to speak oxymoronically, post-philosophical philosophy. Finally, in section IV, I shall take up some criticisms which apply equally to textualism and to pragmatism.

II

Maurice Mandelbaum, in his *History, Man and Reason*, tells us that in the post-Enlightenment period "there arose significantly new forms of thought and standards for evaluation" and that throughout this period of about one hundred years – roughly, though not exactly, coincident with the nineteenth century – "there existed only two main streams of philosophic thought, each of which possessed a relatively high degree of continuity ... metaphysical idealism and positivism." He defines metaphysical idealism as the view that

> within natural human experience one can find the clue to an understanding of the ultimate nature of reality, and this clue is revealed through those traits which distinguish man as a spiritual being.[1]

As Mandelbaum stresses, to take this seriously one has to think that there might *be* such a thing as "the ultimate nature of reality." One also has to think that science might not be the last word on the subject, even though one does remain "within natural human experience" and does not look for super-natural sources of information. Why would anyone hold either of those beliefs? Why did anyone think that in addition to science there might also be something called "metaphysics"?

If you just spring the question "what is the ultimate nature of reality?" on somebody, he won't know where to begin. One needs a sense of what some possible answers might be. The Enlightenment had had a simple contrast with which to explain and give sense to the question, the contrast between the world-picture offered by Aquinas and Dante and that

---

1 Maurice Mandelbaum, *History. Man and Reason* (Baltimore: John Hopkins University Press, 1971), p. 6.

offered by Newton and Lavoisier. The one was said to have been produced by superstition and the other by reason. Nobody before Kant suggested that there could be a discipline called "philosophy" which might offer you a third alternative. The so-called "modern philosophers" prior to Kant were not doing something clearly distinguishable from science. Some were psychologists in the manner of Locke and Hume – providing what Kant called a "physiology of the human understanding" in the hope of doing for inner space what Newton had done for outer space, giving a quasi-mechanical account of the way in which our minds worked. But this was a matter of extending the scientific world-picture, rather than of criticizing or grounding or replacing it. Others were scientific apologists for the religious tradition in the manner of Leibniz, trying to smuggle enough Aristotelian vocabulary back into Cartesian science to have things both ways. But this was, once again, not a matter of criticizing or grounding or replacing science but of tinkering with it in the hope of squeezing in God, Freedom, and Immortality. Hume's and Leibniz's conceptions of science were like those of, respectively, B. F. Skinner and LeComte de Noüy. Neither thought that some autonomous discipline, distinct in subject and method from natural science, might demonstrate the truth of a third view about the ultimate nature of reality.

In order to have such a notion one needs an idea of what such an alternative view might be. Idealism – the view that the ultimate nature of reality is "revealed through those traits which distinguish man as a spiritual being" is not just *a* possibility; it is pretty much the *only* possibility which has ever been offered. But, in Berkeley and Kant, idealism becomes something very different from the tradition which goes back to Anaxagoras and runs through Plato and various forms of Platonism. None of these various suggestions that the material world is unreal were presented as the outcome of scientific argumentation – as a solution to an outstanding scientific difficulty. For Berkeley, however, this is just what idealism was – a neat way of coping with the difficulty which had been created by the new and "scientific" doctrine that the mind perceives only its own ideas. As George Pitcher says, the "beautiful and extravagant" Berkeleian philosophy has among its roots a "sober, well-informed account of … sense-perception."[2] The problem which Berkeley confronted was raised by the fact that, as Hume put it "'tis universally allowed by philosophers that nothing is ever really present with the mind but its perceptions or impressions and ideas, and that external objects become known to us only by those perceptions they occasion."[3] The "philosophers" in question were people like Locke, who were doing what we would call psychology, and especially perceptual psychology. Berkeley took himself out of the running as a psychologist by proposing too "quick and dirty" a solution to the puzzle about which ideas resembled their objects – namely, that "*nothing can be like an idea except an idea.*" This struck his contemporaries as the panpsychist suggestion that all matter is alive strikes present-day evolutionary biologists. The problem is not that it's a silly idea, but that it is so abstract and empty that it simply doesn't *help*.

Berkeley, however, is important for an understanding of why idealism was taken seriously, even though his own version is only a curiosity. In Berkeley idealism is not Platonic other-worldliness but a sober answer to a scientific question, Locke's question about the resemblance of ideas to their objects. Hume proceeded to generalize Locke's question into the question of whether we were entitled to speak of "objects" at all, and this enabled

2   George Pitcher, *Berkeley* (London: Routledge, Kegan Paul, 1977), p. 4.
3   David Hume, *Treatise of Human Nature* I, ii, 2.

Kant to change a scientific question about psychophysiological mechanisms into a question about the legitimacy of science itself. He did so by making three points:

(a) one can solve the problem of the nature of scientific truth only by saying that science corresponds to a world which is transcendentally ideal, made rather than found

(b) one can explain the contrast between making and finding, transcendental ideality and transcendental reality, only by contrasting the use of *ideas* to *know* with the use of the *will* to *act* – science with morality

(c) transcendental philosophy, as the discipline which can rise above both science and morality to allot their respective spheres, replaces science as telling one about the ultimate nature of reality.

Kant thus finessed the Enlightenment notion of an opposition between science and religion, reason and superstition, by taking over an unsolved scientific problem – the nature of knowledge – and transmuting it into an issue about the *possibility* of knowledge. This transmutation was made possible by taking Berkeley's suggestion that "nothing can be like an idea except an idea" seriously, while revising it to read "no idea can be true of anything except a world made of ideas." But this latter notion of a world made of ideas needs to be backed up with an explanation of whose ideas these are. Since Berkeley's God was not available to Kant, he had to create the transcendental ego to do the job. As Kant's successors were quick to point out, the only way we could make sense of the transcendental ego was to identify it with the thinkable but unknowable self who is a moral agent – the autonomous noumenal self.

At this point idealism ceases to be a mere intellectual curiosity. For now it offers us not *just* Berkeley's gimmicky *ad hoc* solution to the problem of the relation between sensations and external objects, but a solution to the problem of how to fit art, religion, and morality into the Galilean world-picture. Once one could see a solution to this slightly shamefaced spiritual difficulty as a corollary to the solution of a perfectly respectable scientific problem, one could see the discipline which offered both solutions as *replacing science*, and making respectable Rousseau's distrust of the Enlightenment. Philosophy thus gets to be both a *science* (for has it not solved a problem science was unable to solve?) and a way to regain what science had seemed to take away – morality and religion. Morality and religion could now be encompassed within the bounds of reason alone. For reason had been discovered by philosophy to be wider than science, and philosophy had thus shown itself to be a *super*-science.

So far I have been arguing that transcendental idealism was necessary to make sense of the notion that a discipline called "philosophy" could transcend both religion and science by giving you a third, decisive, view about the ultimate nature of reality. The Kantian system, on my account, began by borrowing the prestige of science through its solution to a scientific problem, and then proceeded to demote science to the second rank of cultural activities. It promoted philosophy to the first rank by showing you how to have the best of both religion and science, while looking down on both. Idealism seemed a scientific thesis – a thesis for which one might actually *argue* – because of what Berkeley and Kant had in common, namely, a concern with Locke's psychological problem about the relation of sensations to their objects. Philosophy came to look like a super-science because of what Kant and Hegel had in common – namely, a solution to the problem of the relation of science to art, morality and religion. One side of transcendental idealism is turned toward Newton, Locke, the way of ideas, and the problem of perception. The other faces toward Schiller, Hegel and romanticism. This ambivalence helps explain why, in the first decades of the nineteenth century, transcendental idealism could look like demonstrable truth. It also helps explain why transcendental philosophy could seem as dramatically new and permanent an addition to culture as Newtonian science had seemed a century earlier. Both illusions were possible only because the prestige of one side of Kant was borrowed by the other side. The argumentative character which the first *Critique* shares with Newton's *Principia* and Locke's *Essay* created an aura of *Wissenschaftlichkeit* which stretched over the second and third *Critiques*, and even over Fichte.

The next step in the development of idealism, however, was the beginning of the end for both idealism and philosophy. Hegel decided that philosophy should be speculative rather than merely reflective, changed the name of the Transcendental Ego to "the Idea," and began treating the vocabulary of Galilean science as simply one among dozens of others in which the Idea chose to describe itself. If Kant had survived to read the *Phenomenology* he would have realized that philosophy had only managed to stay on the secure path of a science for about twenty-five years. Hegel kept the name of "science" without the distinctive mark of science – willingness to accept a neutral vocabulary in which to state problems, and thereby make argumentation possible. Under cover of Kant's invention, a new super-science called "philosophy," Hegel invented a literary genre which lacked any trace of argumentation, but which obsessively captioned itself *System der Wissenschaft* or *Wissenschaft der Logik*, or *Encyklopädie der philosophischen Wissenschaften*.

By the time of Marx and Kierkegaard, everybody was saying that the emperor had no clothes – that whatever idealism might be it was not a demonstrable, quasi-scientific thesis. By the end of the century (the time of Green and Royce) idealism had been trimmed back to its Fichtean form – an assemblage of dusty Kantian arguments about the relation between sensation and judgment, combined with intense moral earnestness. But what Fichte had been certain was both demonstrable truth and the beginning of a new era in human history, Green and Royce disconsolately knew to be merely the opinion of a group of professors. By the end of the century the word "philosophy" had become what it remains today – merely the name, like the words "classics" and "psychology", for an academic department where memories of youthful hope are cherished, and wistful yearnings for recapturing past glories survive. We philosophy professors stand to Kant and Fichte as our colleagues in classics stand to Scaliger and Erasmus, or our colleagues in psychology to Bain and Spencer. Philosophy is an autonomous academic discipline with pretensions to be architectonic for culture as a whole not because we can justify either the autonomy or the pretension but because the German idealists told us that such a discipline was the hope of mankind. But now that idealism is no longer *anybody's* opinion, now that realism-vs.-idealism is something one learns about only in history books, philosophers have lost the conviction that they can tell one about the ultimate nature of reality, or of anything else. They vaguely feel that it is their birthright to preside over the rest of culture, but they cannot figure out how to justify their claim. If I am right in my historical account, philosophers will not regain their old position unless they can once again offer a view about the ultimate nature of reality to compete with that of science. Since idealism is the only interesting suggestion along these lines they have come up with, only if they can resurrect idealism will the rest of culture take their pretensions seriously. The one event seems as unlikely as the other.

III

What survived from the disappearance of metaphysical idealism as a scientific, arguable, thesis was, simply, romanticism. In section I, I defined 'romanticism', unromantically, as the thesis that the one thing needful was to discover not which propositions are true but rather what vocabulary we should use. This may sound both vague and innocuous, but I think that nevertheless it is the best formula to express the sense of liberation from science which was Hegel's legacy to the nineteenth century. Hegel left Kant's ideal of philosophy-as-science a shambles, but he did, as I have said, create a new literary genre, a genre which exhibited the relativity of significance to choice of vocabulary, the bewildering variety of vocabularies from which we can choose, and the intrinsic instability of each. Hegel made unforgettably clear the deep self-certainty given by each achievement of a new vocabulary, each new genre, each new style, each new dialectical synthesis – the sense that now, at last, for the first time, we have grasped things as they truly are. He also made unforgettably clear why such certainty lasts but a moment. He showed how the passion which sweeps through each generation serves the cunning of reason, providing the impulse which drives that generation to self-immolation and transformation. He writes in that tone of belatedness and irony which, as Snow rightly says, is characteristic of the literary culture of the present day.

Hegel's romantic description of how thought works is appropriate for post-Hegelian politics and literature and almost entirely inappropriate for science. One can respond to this difference by saying "So much the worse for Hegel," or by saying "So much the worse for science." The choice between those responses is a choice between Snow's "two cultures" (and between "analytic" and "Continental" philosophy, which are, so to speak, the public relations agencies for those two cultures). From Hegel on, intellectuals who wished to transform the world or themselves, who wished for more than science could give, felt entitled simply to *forget* about science. Hegel had put the study of nature in its place – a relatively low one. Hegel had also shown that there can be a kind of rationality without argumentation, a rationality which works outside the bounds of what Kuhn calls a "disciplinary matrix," in an ecstasy of spiritual freedom. Reason cunningly employed Hegel, contrary to his own intentions, to write the charter of our modern literary culture. This is the culture which claims to have taken over and reshaped whatever is worth keeping in science, philosophy, and religion – looking down on all three from a higher standpoint. It claims to be the guardian of the public weal – Coleridge's "clerisy of the nation." This culture stretches from Carlyle to Isiah Berlin, from Matthew Arnold to Lionel Trilling, from Heine to Sartre, from Baudelaire to Nabokov, from Dostoievsky to Doris Lessing, from Emerson to Harold Bloom. Its luxuriant complexity cannot be conveyed simply by conjoining words like "poetry," "the novel," and "literary criticism." This culture is a phenomenon the Enlightenment could not have anticipated. Kant has no place for it in his threefold division of possible human activities into scientific cognition, moral action, and the free play of the cognitive faculties in aesthetic enjoyment. But it is as if Hegel knew all about this culture before its birth.

I would claim, then, that the principal legacy of metaphysical idealism is the ability of the literary culture to stand apart from science, to assert its spiritual superiority to science, to claim to embody what is most important for human beings. Kant's suggestion that using the vocabulary of *Verstand*, of science, was simply *one* of the good things human beings could do, was a first and absolutely crucial step in making a secular but non-scientific culture respectable. Hegel's inadvertent exemplification of what such a culture could offer – namely, the historical sense of the relativity of principles and vocabularies to a place and time, the romantic sense that everything can be changed by talking in new terms – was the second, no less necessary step. The romanticism which Hegel brought to philosophy reinforced the hope that literature might be the successor subject to philosophy – that what the philosophers had been seeking, the inmost secrets of the spirit, were to be discovered by the new literary genres which were emerging.

There was, however, a third step in the process of establishing the autonomy and supremacy of the literary culture. This was the step taken by Nietzsche and William James. Their contribution was to replace romanticism by pragmatism. Instead of saying that the discovery of vocabularies could bring hidden secrets to light, they said that new ways of speaking could help get us what we want. Instead of hinting that literature might succeed philosophy as discoverer of ultimate reality, they gave up the notion of truth as a correspondence to reality. Nietzsche and James said, in different tones of voice, that philosophy *itself* had only the status which Kant and Fichte had assigned to science – the creation of useful or comforting pictures. Nietzsche and James interpreted metaphysical idealism, and, more generally, the metaphysical urge to say something about "the ultimate nature of reality," in psychological terms. Marx, of course, had already done this, but, unlike Marx, James and Nietzsche did not attempt to formulate a new philosophical position from which to look down on idealism. Instead, they self-consciously abandoned the search for an Archimedean point from which to survey culture. They abandoned the notion of philosophy as super-science. They applied Kant's and Hegel's metaphors of making (as opposed to traditional realist metaphors of finding) not only to Kant and Hegel but to *themselves*. As Nietzsche said, they were the first generation not to believe that they had the truth. So they were content to have *no* answer to the question "Where do you stand when you say all these terrible things about other people?" They were content to take the halo off words like "truth" and "science" and "knowledge" and "reality" rather than offering a view about the nature of the things named by these words.

This replacement of romanticism by pragmatism within philosophy was paralleled by a change in the literary culture's self-conception. The great figures of that culture in our century – the great "modernists," if you like – have tried to show what our lives might be like if we had no hope of what Nietzsche called "metaphysical comfort." The movement I am calling "textualism" stands to pragmatism and to this body of literature as the nineteenth-century attempt to make literature a discoverer of ultimate truth stood to metaphysical idealism and to Romantic poetry. I think we shall best understand the role of textualism within our culture if we see it as an attempt to think through a thorough-going pragmatism, a thorough-going abandonment of the notion of *discovering the truth* which is common to theology and to science.

M. H. Abrams, in an essay about what he calls "Newreading" and I am calling "textualism," opposes it to the traditional "humanistic" conception. He states that conception as follows:

> the author actualizes and records in words what he undertakes to signify of human beings
> and actions about matters of human concern, addressing himself to those readers who are

competent to understand what he has written. The reader sets himself to make out what the author has designed and signified, through putting into play a linguistic and literary expertise that he shares with the author. By approximating what the author undertook to signify the reader understands what the language of the work means.[4]

The textualist conception of criticism, however, brushes aside what the author undertook to signify and takes one or the other of two quite different tacks. The first tack is, to quote Edward Said, to treat the text

> as working alone within itself, as containing a privileged, or, if not privileged, then unexamined and a priori, principle of internal coherence; on the other hand, the text is considered as in itself a sufficient cause for certain very precise effects it has on a (presumed) ideal reader.[5]

Alternatively, however, the textualist may brush aside the notion of the text as machine which operates quite independently of its creator, and offer what Bloom calls a "strong misreading." The critic asks neither the author nor the text about their intentions but simply beats the text into a shape which will serve his own purpose. He makes the text refer to whatever is relevant to that purpose. He does this by imposing a vocabulary – a "grid," in Foucault's terminology – on the text which may have nothing to do with any vocabulary used in the text or by its author, and seeing what happens. The model here is not the curious collector of clever gadgets taking them apart to see what makes them work and carefully ignoring any extrinsic end they may have, but the psychoanalyst blithely interpreting a dream or a joke as a symptom of homicidal mania.

It is important for an understanding of textualism to see both the similarities and the differences between these two models of criticism. The chief similarity is that both start from the pragmatist refusal to think of truth as correspondence to reality. The kind of textualist who claims to have gotten the secret of the text, to have broken its code, prides himself on not being distracted by anything which the text might previously have been thought to be about or anything its author says about it. The strong misreader, like Foucault or Bloom, prides himself on the same thing, on being able to get more out of the text than its author or its intended audience could possibly have found there. Both break with the realism illustrated by the passage I have cited from Abrams. But they differ in that the first kind of critic is only a half-hearted pragmatist. He thinks that there really is a secret code and that once it's discovered we shall have gotten the text right. He believes that criticism is discovery rather than creation. The strong misreader doesn't care about the distinction between discovery and creation, finding and making. He doesn't think this is a useful distinction, anymore than Nietzsche or James did. He is in it for what he can get out of it, not for the satisfaction of getting something right.

4   M. H. Abrams, "How to Do Things with Texts," *Partisan Review* vol. 46 (1979).
5   Edward Said, "Roads Taken and Not Taken in Contemporary Criticism," *Contemporary Literature* vol. 17 (Summer, 1976): 337. In this article Said draws a distinction between Bloom and Foucault (and others such as Bate and Lukacs) on the one hand and textualist critics who exemplify the approach described in the passage I have quoted. This roughly parallels my distinction between strong and weak textualists, but Said puts the difference in terms of "formality vs. materiality," rather than in terms of a half-hearted and a whole-hearted pragmatism.

I can restate this contrast in another way which may make somewhat clearer what I have in mind. Abram's "humanistic" critic thinks that there is a large, overarching, communal vocabulary in which one can describe what various works of literature are about. The first sort of textualists – the weak textualist – thinks that each work has its own vocabulary, its own secret code, which may not be commensurable with that of any other. The second sort of textualist – the strong textualist – has his own vocabulary and doesn't worry about whether anybody shares it. On the account I am offering, it is the strong textualist who is the true heir of Nietzsche and James, and thus of Kant and Hegel. The weak textualist – the decoder – is just one more victim of realism, of the "metaphysics of presence." He thinks that if he stays within the boundaries of a text, takes it apart, and shows how it works, then he will have "escaped the sovereignty of the signifier," broken with the myth of language as mirror of reality, and so on. But in fact he is just doing his best to imitate science – he wants a *method* of criticism, and he wants everybody to agree that he has cracked the code. He wants all the comforts of consensus, even if only the consensus of readers of the literary quarterlies, just as the microbiologist wants the comfort of consensus, if only that of the other three hundred microbiologists who understand his jargon and care about his problem. The strong textualist is trying to live without that comfort. He recognizes what Nietzsche and James recognized, that the idea of *method* presupposes that of a *privileged vocabulary*, the vocabulary which gets to the essence of the object, the one which expresses the properties which it has in itself as opposed to those which read into it. Nietzsche and James said that the notion of such a vocabulary was a myth – that even in science, not to mention philosophy, we simply cast around for a vocabulary which lets us get what we want.

I can summarize what I've been saying as follows. Metaphysical idealism was a momentary, though important, stage in the emergence of romanticism. The notion that philosophy might replace science as a secular substitute for religion was a momentary, though important, stage in the replacement of science by literature as the presiding cultural discipline. Romanticism was *aufgehoben* in pragmatism, the claim that the significance of new vocabularies was not their ability to decode but their mere utility. Pragmatism is the philosophical counterpart of literary modernism, the kind of literature which prides itself on its autonomy and novelty rather than its truthfulness to experience or its discovery of pre-existing significance. Strong textualism draws the moral of modernist literature and creates genuinely modernist criticism.

This summary puts me in a position to return to the somewhat artificial parallel I drew at the beginning of this paper – between the claim that there are only ideas and the claim that there are only texts. The only textualists who make the latter, metaphysical-sounding sort of claim, are the weak ones – the critics who think that they have now found the true method for analyzing literary works because they have now found the fundamental problematic with which these works deal. This sort of claim gets made because such critics have not grasped that, from a full-fledged pragmatist point of view, there is no interesting difference between tables and texts, between protons and poems. To a pragmatist, these are *all* just permanent possibilities for use, and thus for redescription, reinterpretation, manipulation. But the weak textualist thinks, with Dilthey and Gadamer, that there is a great difference between what scientists do and what critics do.[6]

6   On this point, see my remarks directed at Charles Taylor's Diltheyan views in a symposium called "What Is Hermeneutics?" forthcoming in *The Review of Metaphysics*, vol. 33 (1980).

He thinks that the fact that the former often agree and the latter usually don't shows something about the natures of their respective subject-matters, or about the special epistemological difficulties encountered by their respective methods. The strong textualist simply asks himself the same question about a text which the engineer or the physicist asks himself about a puzzling physical object: how shall I describe this in order to get it to do what I want? Occasionally a great physicist or a great critic comes along and gives us a new vocabulary which enables us to do a lot of new and marvelous things. Then we may exclaim that we have now found out the true nature of matter, or poetry, or whatever. But Hegel's ghost, embodied in Kuhn's romantic philosophy of science or Bloom's philosophy of romantic poetry, reminds us that vocabularies are as mortal as men. The pragmatist reminds us that a new and useful vocabulary is just *that*, not a sudden unmediated vision of things or texts as they are.

As usual with pithy little formulae, the Derridean claim that "There is nothing outside the text" is right about what it implicitly denies and wrong about what it explicitly asserts. The *only* force of saying that texts do not refer to non-texts is just the old pragmatist chestnut that any specification of a referent is going to be in some vocabulary. Thus one is really comparing two descriptions of a thing rather than a description with the thing-in-itself. This chestnut, in turn, is just an expanded form of Kant's slogan that "Intuitions without concepts are blind," which, in turn, was just a sophisticated restatement of Berkeley's ingenuous remark that "nothing can be like an idea except an idea." These are all merely misleading ways of saying that we shall not see reality plain, unmasked, naked to our gaze. Textualism has nothing to add to this claim except a new misleading image – the image of the world as consisting of everything written in all the vocabularies used so far. The practices of the textualists have nothing to add save some splendid examples of the fact that the author of a text did not know a vocabulary in which his text can usefully be described. But this insight – that a person's own vocabulary of self-description is not necessarily the one which helps us understand him – does not need any metaphysical or epistemological or semantic back-up. It is the sort of claim which becomes convincing only through the accumulation of examples of the practices it inspires. Strong textualists like Bloom and Foucault are busy providing us with such examples.

I conclude, therefore, that textualism has nothing to add to romanticism and pragmatism save instances of what can be achieved once one stops being bothered by realistic questions such as "Is that what the text really *says*?" or "How could one *argue* that that is what the poem is really *about*?" or "How are we to distinguish between what is in the text from what the critic is imposing upon it?" The claim that the world is nothing but texts is simply the same sort of light-hearted extravagance as the claim that it is nothing but matter in motion, or a permanent possibility of sensation, or the sensible material of our duty. Taken in a strong and ironic sense, the claim that everything is texts can be read as saying: "It makes as much sense to say that atoms are simply Democritean texts as to say that Democritus is merely a collection of atoms. That is because both slogans are attempts to give one vocabulary a privileged status, and are therefore equally silly." Taken in a weakly literal-minded sense, however, this claim is just one more metaphysical thesis. There are, alas, people nowadays who owlishly inform us "philosophy has *proved*" that language does not refer to anything non-linguistic, and thus that everything one can talk about is a text. This claim is on a par with the claim that Kant proved that we cannot know about things-in-themselves. Both claims rest on a phony contrast between some sort of non-discursive unmediated vision of the real and the way we actually talk and think. Both falsely infer from "We can't think without concepts, or talk without words" to "We can't think or talk except about what has been created by our thought or talk."

The *weakest* way to defend the plausible claim that literature has now displaced religion, science and philosophy as the presiding discipline of our culture is by looking for a philosophical foundation for the practises of contemporary criticism.[7] That would be like defending Galilean science by claiming that it can be found in the Scriptures, or defending transcendental idealism as the latest result of physiological research. It would be acknowledging the authority of a deposed monarch in order to buttress the claims of a usurper. The claims of a usurping discipline to preside over the rest of culture can only be defended by an exhibition of its ability to put the other disciplines in their places. This is what the literary culture has been doing recently, with great success. It is what science did when it displaced religion and what idealist philosophy did when it briefly displaced science. Science did not *demonstrate* that religion was false, nor philosophy that science was merely phenomenal, nor can modernist literature or textualist criticism *demonstrate* that the "metaphysics of presence" is an out-dated genre. But each in turn has managed, without argument, to make its point.

IV

In saying that textualism adds nothing save an extra metaphor to the romanticism of Hegel and the pragmatism of James and Nietzsche, I am agreeing with critics of textualism, like Gerald Graff. Graff rightly says that current fashions in literary criticism continue to develop the themes already stated in New Criticism – "modernist assumptions about language, knowledge, and experience"[8] – assumptions he opposes to the older view that literature can "contribute to man's understanding of how things really are, not merely how they appear to our consciousness."[9] He is also right in saying that only rarely is any argument given to support these assumptions. But I think he is wrong in saying that

> from the thesis that language cannot correspond to reality, it is a short step to the current revisionist mode of interpretation that specializes in reading all literary works as commentaries on their own epistemological problematics.[10]

It is in fact a rather long step, and a step backward. The tendency Graff speaks of is real enough, but it is a tendency to think that literature can take the place of philosophy by *mimicking* philosophy – by being, of all things, *epistemological*. Epistemology still looks classy to weak textualists. They think that by viewing a poet as having an epistemology

---

7   Thus when Geoffrey Hartman says, in the preface to *Deconstruction and Criticism* (New York: The Seabury Press, 1979, p. 6) that it would be fruitful for literary criticism and philosophy to interact, he strikes me as simply being courteous to a defeated foe. But perhaps he may be read simply as saying, quite rightly, that it would be useful if people who had read a lot of philosophy books would join with people who had read a lot of poetry and novels in relating these two streams of texts to one another.

8   Gerald Graff, *Literature Against Itself* (Chicago: University of Chicago Press, 1979), p. 5.

9   Ibid., p. 7.

10   Ibid., p. 9.

they are paying him a compliment. They even think that in criticizing his theory of knowledge they are being something more than a mere critic – being, in fact, a philosopher. Thus conquering warriors might mistakenly think to impress the populace by wrapping themselves in shabby togas stripped from the local senators. Graff and others who have pointed to the weirdly solemn pretentiousness of much recent textualist criticism are right, I think, in claiming that such critics want to have the supposed prestige of philosophy without the necessity of offering arguments.

Where I chiefly differ from Graff, however, is in his claim that

> writing, to be effective, has to spring from a coherent and convincing philosophy of life – or at least of that part of life with which the writer deals. There seems no way of getting away from the fact that literature must have an ideology – even if this ideology is one that calls all ideologies into question. The very act of denying all "naive" realisms presupposes an objective standpoint.[11]

This seems to me wrong as a statement about effective writing. It would force one to say either that Baudelaire and Nabokov did not write effectively or that their ironism expressed a "coherent and convincing philosophy of life." Neither alternative is attractive. It also seems wrong about what is required to deny the truth of realism. One *can* do that without proposing an "objective" theory about the real nature of reality or knowledge or language. It is just not the case that one need adopt one's opponents' vocabulary or method or style in order to defeat him. Hobbes did not have theological arguments against Dante's world-picture; Kant had only a very bad scientific argument for the phenomenal character of science; Nietzsche and James did not have epistemological arguments for pragmatism. Each of these thinkers presented us with a new form of intellectual life, and asked us to compare its advantages with the old. Strong textualists are currently presenting us with such another new form of life. There is as little point in asking for epistemological arguments in its favor as in pretending that it gives us a new and better way of doing epistemology.

The serious objections to textualism, I think, are not epistemological but moral. Writers such as Lionel Trilling and M. H. Abrams would join Graff in offering such objections. Abrams sympathizes with Bloom in his protests against Derrida's and Foucault's attempt to eliminate the author of a text, and to substitute inhuman intertextuality for human influence. But he is unable to accept Bloom's self-descriptions of his books on Yeats and Stevens as "strong misreadings." He thinks Bloom often gets Yeats and Stevens right, in a good old-fashioned realist sense of "right," and he wants Bloom to admit it. He wants this, I think, because he wants Yeats and Stevens to be more than grist for their successors' mills. He thinks their moral integrity is impugned by Bloom's treatment. Further, he wants literary criticism to be a field in which one can argue, and thus one in which one is *not* free to lay down any grid one pleases in the hope of getting "creative or interesting misreadings."[12]

Though Abrams admits that what he calls "Newreading" can provide "new and exciting things to say about a literary work which has been again and again discussed," he thinks that the "choice between a radical Newreading and the old way of reading is a matter of cultural cost-accounting":

11   Ibid., p. 11.
12   Cf. Abrams, "How to …," pp. 584–85.

> What we lose is access to the inexhaustible variety of literature as determinably meaningful texts by, for and about human beings, as well as access to the enlightening things that have been written about such texts by the humanists and critics who were our precursors, from Aristotle to Lionel Trilling.[13]

Implicit in this remark is the moral outlook which Abrams shares with Trilling: the view that, in the end, when all the intellectuals have done all their tricks, morality remains widely shared and available to reflection – something capable of being discovered rather than created, because already implicit in the common consciousness of everyone. It is this Kantian conviction, I think, which leads Trilling to protest against one of the most distinctive features of romanticism and of our literary culture, its ability to make what Trilling called "figures" out of writers – a term which he defines as follows:

> figures – that is to say, creative spirits whose work requires an especially conscientious study because in it are to be discerned significances, even mysteries, even powers, which carry it beyond what in a loose and general sense we call literature, beyond even what we think of as very good literature, and bring it to as close an approximation of a sacred wisdom as can be achieved in our culture.[14]

Here Trilling echoes what Kant said about the "metaphysics of the schools" – about learned men who claim to know more of morality and its supposed "foundations" than the ordinary decent citizen. This is the side of Kant which is turned towards the Enlightenment rather than towards Hegel and romanticism. It is the side which is democratic rather than elitist, which regards culture as in the service of the people (rather than, as with Hegel, conversely.) Trilling and Abrams and Graff do not want there to *be* a sacred wisdom which takes precedence over the common moral consciousness. Therefore they resist the romantic attempt to make a "figure" out of a poet and also the suggestion that a misreader has no obligation to argue with those who disagree with his reading. Because they want criticism to bring an antecedent morality to light, enlarge upon it and enrich it, they resist the suggestion that there is no common vocabulary in terms of which critics can argue with one another about how well this task has been performed.

This moral objection to textualism is also a moral objection to pragmatism's claim that all vocabularies, even that of our own liberal imagination, are temporary historical resting-places. It is also an objection to the literary culture's isolation from common human concerns. It says that people like Nietzsche and Nabokov and Bloom and Foucault achieve their effects at a moral cost which is too much to pay. Put in the pragmatist's own preferred cost-accounting terms, it says that the stimulus to the intellectual's private moral imagination provided by his strong misreadings, by his search for sacred wisdom, is purchased at the price of his separation from his fellow-humans.[15]

I think that this moral objection states the really important issue about textualism and about pragmatism. But I have no ready way to dispose of it. I should like to do so

---

13   Ibid., p. 588.

14   Lionel Trilling, "Why We Read Jane Austen" in *The Last Decade* (New York: Harcourt, Brace, Jovanovich, 1979), pp. 206–07.

15   I have discussed, inconclusively, the claim that pragmatism is morally dangerous in "Pragmatism, Relativism, and Irrationalism," forthcoming in *Proceedings of the American Philosophical Association*, vol. 53 (1980).

by drawing a further distinction among strong textualists – a distinction between, for example, Bloom and Foucault. Bloom is a pragmatist in the manner of James, whereas Foucault is a pragmatist in the manner of Nietzsche. Pragmatism appears in James and Bloom as an identification with the struggles of finite men. In Foucault and Nietzsche it appears as contempt for one's own finitude, as a search for some mighty inhuman force to which one can yield up one's identity. Bloom's way of dealing with texts preserves our sense of a common human finitude by moving back and forth between the poet and his poem. Foucault's way of dealing with texts is designed to eliminate the author – and indeed the very idea of "man" – altogether. I have no wish to defend Foucault's inhumanism, and every wish to praise Bloom's sense of our common human lot. But I do not know how to back up this preference with argument, or even with a precise account of the relevant differences. To do so, I think, would involve a full-scale discussion of the possibility of combining private fulfillment, self-realization, with public morality, a concern for justice.

Part II
Conversations with Analytic Philosophy

Introduction

By the time *Philosophy and the Mirror of Nature* appears, Rorty views analytic philosophy simply as "one more variant of Kantian philosophy." Despite its move from mental to linguistic categories, because still committed to the idea of a permanent, neutral framework for inquiry, the linguistic turn ultimately "does not essentially change the Cartesian–Kantian problematic, and thus does not really give philosophy a new self-image" (p. 87, this volume). With "Pragmatism, Relativism, and Irrationalism" he establishes his stance that the pragmatism he associates with James and Dewey, with its aim to "liberate" us from the "reactionary" project of grounding our culture, our politics, our beliefs in a permanent ahistorical matrix and its message of social hope, is required to bring about his self-image (p. 112, this volume). Yet as he admits in the introduction to *Mirror,* the kind of edifying or therapeutic discourse he expounds is nevertheless "parasitic upon the constructive efforts of the very analytic philosophers whose frame of reference" is being called into question (p. 86, this volume). More specifically, he appeals to what he calls "the holistic, 'pragmatizing' strain in analytic philosophy" that he identifies in the work of the later Wittgenstein, Sellars, Quine, and Davidson. Through Davidson's attack on the scheme–content distinction, Sellars's debunking of the "Myth of the Given," and Quine's criticisms of Carnap, on Rorty's reading this particular strand of analytic philosophy of language was able to transcend the Kantian project and adopt "a naturalistic, behavioristic attitude toward language" (CP, pp. xviii–xxi).[1]

These views on language play a central role in Rorty's developing position, both negatively, in terms of repudiating particular Cartesian assumptions, and positively, as he begins to sketch the kind of social and political vision that comports with a post-Philosophical culture. His reading of the pragmatizing strain of analytic philosophy also forms the basis of the bridge he sees between the analytic and Continental traditions; in their critiques of Platonism and of the idea that humans

---

1 Rorty's highly original framing of these stances is developed in the crucial chapters 4 and 6 of *Philosophy and the Mirror of Nature* (PMN). For a good brief summary, as well as discussion of the anti-pragmatist backlash to this strain of analytic philosophy, see the introduction to *Consequences of Pragmatism* (CP), esp. pp. xvii–xxxvii.

can stand apart from the language they use, in Rorty's estimation the post-positivistic analytic thinkers cited above occupy shared territory with the "Nietzsche–Heidegger–Derrida tradition."[2]

In "From Logic to Language to Play," Rorty offers a helpful account of these connections. Marking off previously unnoticed shared ground between different schools, he sketches a narrative of the development of twentieth-century philosophy that highlights the way "an internal dialectic common to so-called 'Anglo-Saxon' and so-called 'Continental' philosophy" has eroded philosophy's "hyper-professionalism." What has resulted, in his view, is "a more playful, more cosmopolitan, less professional tone in which to philosophize" (p. 146, this volume). More substantively, he makes the case that "Human inquiry – in all areas, literature as well as science, politics as much as in physics – is a matter of reweaving our fabric of belief and desire, our attitudes toward various sentences of our language," rather than putting our practices in touch with "the way things really are" (pp. 148, 151 this volume). This epistemological leveling leaves us with the generation of new metaphors and "experimental self-creation" as the primary engines of not only social and political but theoretical change. Importantly, Rorty also avers that, unlike Heidegger and Derrida, who suggest that some radical or revolutionary impact follows from the undermining of the "sovereignty of the signified" or the "Western metaphysics of presence," the pragmatist analytic philosophers see no such connection to "drastic cultural or political change" (p. 149, this volume).

Emblematic of Rorty's appropriation of the pragmatist strain of analytic philosophy is his work on Donald Davidson.[3] Initially attracted to Davidson's particular view of

---

2   See, for example, CP, pp. xix–xxi, where Rorty substantiates this claim by aligning a series of strikingly similar quotes from Peirce, Derrida, Sellars, Wittgenstein, Gadamer, Foucault, and Heidegger. The introduction to ORT offers Rorty's most concise summary of the Darwinian understanding of language he gleans from these two traditions of thought, worth quoting despite its length:

> If one treats it simply as a reminder, rather than as a metaphysics, then I think the following is a good way of bringing together the upshot of both the Quinean-Putnam–Davidson tradition in analytic philosophy of language and the Heidegger–Derrida tradition of post-Nietzschean thought. Consider sentences as strings of marks and noises emitted by organisms, strings capable of being paired off with the strings we ourselves utter (in the way we call 'translating'). Consider beliefs, desires, and intentions – sentential attitudes generally – as entities posited to help predict the behavior of these organisms. Now think of those organisms as gradually evolving as a result of producing longer and more complicated strings, strings which enable them to do things they had been unable to do with the aid of shorter and simpler strings. Now think of *us* as examples of such highly evolved organisms, of our highest hopes and deepest fears as made possible by, among other things, our ability to produce the peculiar strings we do. Then think of the four sentences that precede this one as further examples of such strings. Penultimately, think of the five sentences that precede this one as a sketch for a redesigned house of Being, a new dwelling for us shepherds of Being. Finally, think of the last six sentences as yet another example of the play of signifiers, one more example of the way in which meaning is endlessly alterable through the recontextualization of signs (p. 5).

3   Other discussions of Davidson, a name peppered throughout Rorty's writings, can be found in: "The World Well Lost," in CP; chapter 6 of PMN; "Transcendental Arguments, Self-Reference, and Pragmatism," in Peter Bieri, Rolf-P. Hortsmann, and Lorenz Kruger (eds.), *Transcendental Arguments and Science* (Dordrecht: D. Reidel, 1979), pp. 77–103; "Non-Reductive Physicalism," in *Objectivity, Relativism and Truth* (ORT); and "Is Truth a Goal of Inquiry? Donald Davidson versus

language, which he interprets as providing a useful wedge against Cartesian epistemological assumptions because "it lets us see language not as a *tertium quid* between Subject and Object, nor as a medium in which we try to form pictures of reality, but as part of the behavior of human beings," Rorty discerns that the implications of Davidson's critique of "the scheme-content distinction" entail dissolving the traditional role for philosophy as providing a neutral medium for the epistemological exchange between subject and object (CP xviii).[4] While in "Pragmatism, Davidson, and Truth," Rorty merely evinces Davidson's connections to the pragmatist tradition, both to James and, via Quine, to Dewey – connections that Davidson himself resisted – in "Twenty-Five Years After" he asserts that "Davidson largely succeeds where Dewey failed – succeeds in the attempt to replace a representationalist picture of knowledge and inquiry with a non-representationalist one," primarily as a result of supplanting the notion of experience with that of sentences (p. 177, this volume).

Rorty's reassessment of the linguistic turn twenty-five years after the appearance of his original volume takes a more sober view of its significance, dubbing his early enthusiasm little more than "the attempt of a thirty-three-year-old philosopher to convince himself that he had had the luck to be born at the right time" (p. 175 this volume). While the introduction to *The Linguistic Turn* emphasizes the metaphilosophical relevance of this work, Rorty now highlights the essay's bearing on the debate within pragmatism, sparked in part by Rorty's "Dewey's Metaphysics," over experience vs. language: "Its contribution was, instead, to have helped shift talk about experience as a medium of representation to talk of language as such a medium – a shift which, as it turned out, made it easier to set aside the notion of representation itself" (p. 178 this volume).[5] He closes the piece by reiterating his thoughts on why philosophy is not likely to come to an end.

Rorty's exchanges with Hilary Putnam, another longtime interlocutor, are useful for understanding the resistance on the analytic side to Rorty's appropriation of the "pragmatizing" strain of analytic philosophy.[6] Written in part as a response to Hilary Putnam's charge that he is a "cultural relativist," "Putnam and the Relativist Menace" sheds light

---

Crispin Wright" and "Antiskeptical Weapons: Michael Williams versus Donald Davidson," both in *Truth and Progress* (TP).

4   One way of seeing the shift Rorty advocates is as the move from a conception of language as a system of representations to a view of language as a social practice. Although less obvious than his use of Davidson, Rorty's engagement with Brandom, a former student of his, is crucial here as well. See "Representation, Social Practise, and Truth" (ORT, pp. 151–61); and "Robert Brandom on Social Practices and Representations" (TP, pp. 122–37). When an interviewer informed Rorty that, along with Davidson, Putnam, and Quine, he was one of the "Great Four of American Philosophy," Rorty replied that "the Big Four in post-war analytic philosophy are Quine, Sellars, Davidson, and Brandom" (p. 513 this volume).

5   For the background of this debate see James T. Kloppenberg, "Pragmatism: An Old Name for Some New Ways of Thinking?" *Journal of American History* 83, no. 1 (1986): 100–138. As Rorty puts it elsewhere, he seeks to "graft" the "later, linguistified pragmatists" – Quine, Putnam, Davidson – onto Dewey, such that we "switch over from Deweyan talk of experience to Quinean-Davidsonian talk of sentences" (EHO, p. 3).

6   Despite their efforts to distance themselves from his interpretations, Rorty has said that "the actual substantive differences in philosophical doctrine between either me and Davidson, or me and Putnam, are pretty hard to detect. Whenever I try to write about these differences I find them

on more specialized philosophical issues, such as Rorty's stances on warranted assertibility and non-reductive physicalism. It also shows Rorty in his shoulder-shrugging, "dismissive" mode, as he himself called it, side-stepping the attempts of critics to draw him into controversies and debates that he regards as leading nowhere in the hope of discouraging further attention to such "unfruitful" topics (TP, p. 11).[7] Rorty explains his "Darwinianism," his ethnocentrism, why a sense of solidarity with a particular community may be all we have, and why he is not a relativist. Most importantly, he conveys how his eschewal of appeals to categories that purport to transcend the contingent particulars of our language and culture emanates from a Deweyan grounding in social and political concerns – what Rorty elsewhere calls "moral seriousness" (TP, p. 83).[8]

Returning over two decades later to the analytic–Continental divide he first raised in the introduction to *Consequences of Pragmatism*, in "Analytic and Conversational Philosophy," Rorty suggests that the term "continental" should be dropped in favor of "conversational" philosophy, thus casting the contrast between conversational and analytical approaches in even bolder relief (p. 198, this volume).[9] Attributing the analytic–continental distinction primarily to geographic and sociological differences, he takes the analytic–conversational distinction to be one of differing self-images. If philosophers think of themselves as "enlarging our repertoire of individual and cultural self-descriptions," rather than getting us closer to the way things really are, they will be best situated to spark cultural progress. Instead of trying to get it right, philosophers should try to contribute to humanity's ongoing conversation about what to do with itself. "The point of philosophy," he asserts, is "to make us happier, freer, and more flexible" (p. 198 this volume).

---

disappearing under my eyes" (TCF, p. 144). See also his comments on Putnam below (p. 513, this volume).

7   He concedes that his strategy for escaping many of these criticisms from fellow-philosophers is "to move everything over from epistemology and metaphysics to cultural politics, from claims to knowledge and appeals to self-evidence to suggestions about what we should try" (p. 191, this volume).

8   See for instance the way he disarms Putnam's insistence that he clarify his understanding of "warrant" – as in a standard of warranted assertibility – by pointing out that "many (praiseworthy and blame-worthy) social movements and intellectual revolutions get started by people making *un*warranted assertions" (p. 186, this volume). See also his discussion of Putnam's statements about tolerance and Rorty's "political" stance on p. 191 of this volume.

9   Rorty calls the "Kantian transcendental turn" and the linguistic turn "inevitably unsuccessful attempts to step out of the conversation" (PCP, p. 175).

6

From Logic to Language
to Play

An occasion such as this Congress reminds us that philosophy has, in our century, become more "national" in character than it was in the past. I think that this can be accounted for, in large part, simply by the increase in the number of professors of philosophy. In all countries, the rise in the number and size of universities since 1900 has been spectacular. When a scholar was one of only a few dozen fellow-nationals specializing in a certain subject, his links with fellow-specialists in other countries were bound to be as important as his links with those close at hand. But when there are hundreds of fellow-specialists within his own national borders, and when his speciality becomes self-consciously professionalized, this will no longer be true. The founding of national philosophical societies tends to coincide with a struggle for power to control those societies, a struggle among professors to make sure that their students will also be their successors – a struggle to construct a career ladder for those students. This, in turn, leads to attempts to construct barriers between philosophy and other academic disciplines, to make philosophy more self-enclosed.

Since such attempts proceed nation by nation, the effect is to make philosophy something rather different on each side of each national border. Despite rather awkward attempts to justify such differences by speaking of the "spirit" of English, or French, or North American, or Latin American philosophy, I suspect that none of us is really comfortable with such national differences. We are all, I think, aware that our discipline makes no sense unless it is thought of in cosmopolitan terms. Philosophy was, after all, invented to be what religion and ideology are not: an interchange which has no limits, and no purpose, except those set by the free agreement of participants in a dialogue. We should all be grateful if there were no links between our choice of philosophical topics to pursue, or texts on which to comment, and the power-structures of academic life. We all resent, or should resent, the fact that our relatively parochial educations and careers have restricted our sense of relevance, our familiarity with texts, and our ability to talk

Richard M. Rorty, "From Logic to Language to Play: A Plenary Address to the InterAmerican Congress," *Proceedings and Addresses of the American Philosophical Association* vol. 59 (5), June 1986: 747–53, © 1986 by American Philosophical Association. Reproduced with permission of American Philosophical Association in the format Textbook via Copyright Clearance Center.

to colleagues in other countries. The inevitability of some such restrictions – the inevitability of what Foucault called "links between truth and power" – should not diminish our struggle against any particular example of such a restriction.

In my paper today I should like to argue that the development of philosophy in our century has made it easier to break down such restrictions. In my view, this development has made possible a more playful, more cosmopolitan, less professional tone in which to philosophize. I want to sketch an account of twentieth-century philosophy according to which the hyper-professionalism characteristic of the beginning of the century has been gradually mitigated by an internal dialectic common to so-called "Anglo-Saxon" and so-called "Continental" philosophy.

It may seem premature to attempt to sketch the course of philosophy in our century, if only because the century still has fifteen years to go. But my hunch is that when historians of philosophy (writing in the year 2085, in Santiago or Jakarta) tell the story of what happened in philosophy during the 20th century they may see it as more unified and directed than it appears to us who have lived through some portion of that century. When we look back on the philosophy of the nineteenth century, it seems to us to fall into a fairly clear shape. We think of it as beginning in a romantic idealism and ending in a worship of the posivite sciences. I suspect that a hundred years from now philosophy in our century may also seem to exhibit a fairly clear design. I think that it will be seen as beginning with a revolt against a narrowly empiricist positivism – a revolt conducted in the name of "logic" by Russell and Husserl – and as ending with a return to something reminiscent of Hegel's sense of humanity as an essentially historical being, one whose activities in all spheres are to be judged not by its relation to non-human reality but by comparison and contrast with its earlier achievements and with utopian futures. This return will be seen as having been brought about by philosophers as various as Heidegger, Wittgenstein, Quine, Gadamer, Derrida, Putnam and Davidson.

Nineteenth-century philosophical thought began with a reaction against the scientism of the Enlightenment – against the notion that mathematical demonstration was a model for inquiry and the positive sciences a model for culture. It ended with a general acquiesence in scientism, with a willinghess to see scientific progress and political progress (in the direction of social democracy) as parallel and inseparable aspects of the triumph of rationality over superstition and prejudice. This outcome represented a triumph of the Enlightenment over those counter-Enlightenment tendencies which had given rise to the Romantic Movement and to German Idealism. The latter tendencies were, for the most part, shunted off into literature. By the beginning of our century a clear-cut opposition between a scientific and a literary culture was in place – quite a different cultural situation than had existed in the time of Goethe and Hegel.

Faced with this choice, philosophy allied itself with the scientific culture. In part this was because of the need to establish a professional identity – to have a place within the power-structure of academic institutions. But it was also because philosophers saw themselves as aiding the cause of human freedom. Typically, they saw the literary culture as a kind of privatized aestheticism which contained disturbing strains of irrationalism. (Think of the encounters with D. H. Lawrence recounted in Russell's autobiography, and of how exceptional the young Gadamer was in his ability to move back and forth between Husserl's circle and that of Stefan George.) Philosophers became concerned to model their own discipline on the sciences, to give it "scientific status."

This concern led Russell and Husserl to turn towards mathematics and logic. In Husserl's case, this turn did not last long. It was submerged in his attempt to invent a brand-new discipline – phenomenology – which would share the apodicticity of mathematics but lack its deductive structure. Heidegger successfully subverted this attempt in *Being and Time*, and philosophy in France and Germany then turned away from apodicitity, and, more generally, from the rhetoric of scientism. But Russell's slogan that "logic is the essence of philosophy" persisted in Anglo-Saxon countries. Its effect is still seen in the pattern of philosophic education in those countries – where an ability to follow completeness proofs for formal systems has taken the place, as an academic requirement, of an ability to read foreign languages.

It would be a mistake, however, to think that Anglo-Saxon philosophers' attachment to formal logic was or is a mere scientistic shibboleth. This would be to ignore the importance of Frege, Peirce and, especially, *Principia Mathematica* in providing new alternatives to Aristotelian ways of thinking. Russell's and Whitehead's joint campaign against "Aristotelian subject-predicate logic" blended with various elements of the new physics to produce what Cassirer called a shift from "substance" to "function". It lent comfort to such projects as Carnap's *Aufbau*, by making it seem possible to dissolve the familiar things of this world, and even the unobservables posited by physical theory, into "constructions". By providing an apparatus which made it easy to dissolve substances into congeries of relations, and by making us aware that there might be many ways of effecting this dissolution, just as there were many ways of building up logic from different primitive notions, the "logic of relations" smoothed the way for a kind of pragmatic pluralism. I do not think it far-fetched to see such different books as the *Logische Aufbau der Welt*, Cassirer's *Philosophy of Symbolic Forms*, Whitehead's *Process and Reality*, C.I. Lewis' *Mind and the World-Order*, Langer's *Philosophy in a New Key*, Hartshorne's *The Divine Relativity*, Quine's *Word and Object*, Nelson Goodman's *Ways of Worldmaking* and his *Languages of Art*, Putnam's *Reason, Truth and History*, and Davidson's *Essays on Truth and Interpretation* as developments of the anti-Aristotelian and anti-substantialist, anti-essentialist implications common to *Principia Mathematica* and to the development of non-Euclidean geometries.

For my purposes, the importance of the anti-essentialism which became characteristic of so much philosophical thought in the wake of *Principia* was the way in which it blended with other tendencies to produce a gradual move away from scientism and positivism. The return to Enlightenment ways of thinking characteristic of philosophy at the beginning of our century had been, broadly speakings, naively realistic and Aristotelian. It assumed that science was gradually becoming "unified" (in the sense to be made familiar by the Vienna Circle) under the hegemony of the physicists, and that discoveries in the hard sciences were discoveries of the way the world was in itself. But the possibilities for counter-intuitive redescription, for relativization to choice of primitives, which had been made vivid by non-Euclidean geometry and the "logic of relations" made this sort of realism hard to hold on to. The Kantian suggestion that we create a phenomenal world to suit our faculties was reinforced by Cassirer's and C.I. Lewis' suggestion that the categories, the ground-plans for constructing such worlds, were not fixed by the nature of our faculties but were susceptible of historical and cultural change. The anti-essentialism of such writers became blended with Wordsworthian and Darwinian motifs taken from such writers as Bergson, Dewey, and the later Whitehead to produce an instrumentalistic anti-realist view of physical science. So, for example, by 1960, when Quine's *Word and Object* was published, the recrudesence of the idea that physics "limns the true and ultimate structure of reality" seemed hopelessly out of tune with the aestheticism and pragmatism of the work as a whole.

The most important change which took place within analytic philosophy, however, was not a change of attitude toward physics, but a change in attitude toward logic. In this development the anti-essentialism of the early period of analytic philosophy was turned against the idea of "logical structure", as in Quine's suggestion that the distinction between meaning and fact was an unfortunate holdover from the Aristotelian distinction between essence and accident. Quine's "Two Dogmas" and Wittgenstein's *Investigations* helped philosophers ask themselves Wittgenstein's question: "why did we think that logic was something sublime?" They began to question the attempt to give philosophy "scientific status" by making it "logical" or "formal" or "exact." Metaphilosophical questions about "the method of analytic philosophy" or "the nature of philosophical analysis" which had been popular from the thirties through the fifties were no longer asked – for Quine's attack on analytic truth made "analysis" seem the wrong word for what philosophers were doing. An anthology called *The Linguistic Turn*, published in 1967 and filled with articles on such questions, was obsolete almost before it was printed.

One result of this change was to liberate philosophy of language. The attempt to show that expressions in a natural language could be translated into "the language of unified science" was replaced by Davidson's modest claim that it would be helpful if we could describe features of linguistic usage in an extensional metalanguage. Davidson followed up on Quinean holism and pragmatism by giving us a theory of meaning which dispenses with entities called "meanings", and which replaces the question "what is the meaning of the expression?" with "what is the place of this expression in the language-game? what are the inferential relations between this expression and other expressions in the same game?" This de-logicizing and naturalization of language gives us a sense of language as a variety of human behavior, continuous with the rest of human beings' attempts to cope with the world, rather than as a "structure" or a body of rules, even the sort of changeable and temporary structures of rules which Lewis and Cassirer contemplated. It makes it hard to think of "language" as the name of the special subject-matter of philosophy, just as Quine and Wittgenstein had made it hard to think of "logic" as the "essence of philosophy."

Davidsonian philosophy of language centers around the repudiation of what Davidson calls "the scheme-content distinction" – the idea that we can divide up discourse into the "formal" or "structural" elements and the other "material" elements, and take philosophy as the study of the former. This repudiation can be thought of as one more way of breaking with the traditional Cartesian subject-object model of knowing. This is the model on which one entity reproduces within itself the essence, or the structure, or some intrinsic characteristics, of another entity by the help of, or despite the interference of, a medium or scheme such as "the categories of human thought" or "the structure of consciousness" or "the structure of language". On this model, which is the central feature of what Derrida calls "the metaphysics of presence," the task of philosophical reflection is to explain the nature of this medium.

On a Davidsonian view, there is no such medium, no such scheme. Human inquiry – in all areas, literature as well as science, politics as much as in physics – is a matter of reweaving our fabric of belief and desire, our attitudes toward various sentences of our language. To understand the various techniques used in this rewarding process is to understand human knowledge. The various sciences can explain causal interactions between brain cells and tables and stars, but when one speaks in intentional, belief-and-desire, terms, such causal accounts are not to the point. At that level of discourse, to understand the relation between all actual sentences using the term "X" and the other sentences of the language will give us what philosophers once hoped to discover by investigating the relation between human cognitive faculties and the intrinsic nature of X itself. There is no way to underwrite or criticize the ongoing, self-modifying know-how of the user of language by a philosophical account of the nature of the relation of his mind or his language to the object. There is no way to reach outside our language-game to an account of the relation between that language-game as scheme to "the world" as "content."

The similarity of this view of knowledge and language to Heidegger's suggestion that we break with Cartesian conceptions and think of being-in-the-world in non-subject–object terms is obvious, and by now tediously familiar. Commentators on Heidegger such as Dreyfus, Brandom and Guignon have spelled it out in detail. Arthur Danto has remarked that the doctrines about language common to Heidegger, Gadamer and Derrida differ from those which have become commonplaces of post-Quinean analytic philosophy only in the tone in which they are expressed. There is, in Heidegger and Derrida at least, a hint of crisis and apocalypse – a suggestion that the end of what Derrida calls "the sovereignty of the signified" will have some revolutionary impact upon our lives, or that the end of the "Western metaphysics of presence" is somehow involved with the end of present modes of social existence, the "end of the modern." But even the most radical holists and pragmatists among the analytic philosophers see no such implications. Putnam, it is true, has written that "we are at the beginning of post-modernism in philosophy", but he does not thereby suggest any path from Quinean and Davidsonian holism and naturalism to drastic cultural or political change.

Heidegger's revolt against Husserl's scientism, followed up by Gadamer's rightwing and Derrida's left-wing Heideggerianism, give us, so to speak, the Continental version of the break with scientism which came to analytic philosophy with Quine and Wittgenstein. Both movements repudiated the idea of philosophy as a super-science which, by dealing with "logic" or "form" or "scheme," would provide a permanent neutral matrix for inquiry, one which was indifferent between historical epochs. But only on the Continent did this repudiation lead philosophers to align themselves with the literary as opposed to the scientific culture. Gadamer's attempt to overcome Kant's spectatorial notion of "the aesthetic" complements Derrida's attempt to see language as a seamless intertextual web. Both philosophers help blur the distinction between philosophy and literature, the serious and the playful, the cognitive and the non-cognitive, the aesthetic and the moral. Schiller's claim that "man is truly man only when he is at play" finds obvious echoes both in Gadamer's *Truth and Method* and Derrida's *Margins of Philosophy*.

As we near the close of the century, we can think of the internal dialectic of analytic philosophy as having carried it toward a position which is no longer scientistic, but is not anti-scientistic either. Nor is it linked, in any clear manner, with the literary culture. With a few exceptions (as in the work of Iris Murdoch and Stanley Cavell) analytic philosophy and that culture ignore each other completely. By contrast the internal dialectic of the tradition which began with Husserl has carried it toward a position which is not only linked with the literary culture but is explicitly anti-scientistic. Heidegger's distrust of the "technological" character of our age, his diagnosis of it as "nihilistic", persists not only in Gadamer but even in Habermas' attempt to distinguish between the interests served by the physical sciences and those served by the "sciences of communicative competence."

Yet I think the resulting isolation of "Continental" philosophy from the sciences is, by this time, as artificial—as much the result of mere habit, rather than reflection – as the isolation of analytic philosophy from literature. The conception of language which has come to be common to both traditions should lead both to see culture, as well as language, as a seamless web. Neither has any principled reason to take seriously the traditional distinctions between science and art, between the desire for truth and the desire for goodness and beauty. There is no longer any philosophical excuse for the break between the scientific and the literary cultures, a break which arose during the nineteenth century and has marked the culture of the twentieth. We need to abandon the anti-scientism of Heidegger and Gadamer as well as the scientism of Russell, Husserl and Quine. We should abandon both in favor of a conception of philosophy which is no closer to science than to art, and no farther from either than it is from any other sphere of human self-creation.

My hope is that now, at the end of the century, we philosophers may be in a position to regain Hegel's sense of cultures and languages as matching themselves against past and future cultures and languages rather than against such extra-human forces as God, the moral law, or "the real world". This sense of outselves as engaged in a process of reweaving our beliefs and desires rather than trying to bring these into conformity with something else lets us reappropriate Schiller's sense of play as the highest possibility for human life. In particular, it lets us see the creation of physical or moral or social theories in the same way we see the creations of works of art—as what the British philosopher of science Mary Hesse has called "metaphorical redescriptions of the explicandum."

So much for my speculations about how twentieth-century philosophy may look to our descendants. Let me end by remarking on what I have left out: namely, politics. I have spoken as if philosophy were concerned simply with the arts and the sciences. I have made no reference to philosophy as the source of social theory or of ideology. Further, I have spoken as if human society were at peace, as if there were no war between the rich and the poor, as if we were all leisured citizens of what the Brazilian political philosopher Roberto Unger calls "the rich North Atlantic democracies." Since our congress includes representatives from many countries in which social conflict is intense and growing, countries whose only hope may lie in social revolution, my speculations may seem both parochial and inappropriate.

In the minutes that remain, I can only state briefly and dogmatically a view for which I have argued elsewhere. This is that philosophy, even though it is often inspired by politics, should not be thought of as a foundation for politics nor as a weapon of politics. I agree with anti-Marxist writers such as Popper and Kolakowski that the attempt to ground political theory on overarching theories of the nature of man or the goal of history has done more harm than good. We should not assume that it is our task, as professors of philosophy, to be the avant-garde of political movements. We should not ask, say, Davidson or Gadamer for the "political implications" of their view of language, nor spurn their work because of its lack of such implications. We should think of politics as one of the experimental rather than of the theoretical disciplines. We should discard the last traces of the Marxist idea that a philosophical super-science can tell the working class their true situation, and of Heidegger's idea that the fortunes of philosophy determine the fortunes of mankind as a whole.

It may seem foolish to speak of "play," as I have done, in the midst of a political struggle that will decide whether civilization has a future, whether our descendants will have any *chance* to play. But philosophy should try to express our political hopes rather than to ground our political practices. On the view I am suggesting, nothing grounds our practices, nothing legitimizes them, nothing shows them to be in touch with the way things really are. The sense of human languages and practices as the results of experimental self-creation rather than of an attempt to approximate to a fixed and ahistorical ideal – the position in which I am claiming the philosophy of our century culminates – makes it less plausible than ever to imagine that a particular theoretical discipline will rescue or redeem us. But we do not need such hopes of redemption, or such fantasies of power, to continue our work.

7

Pragmatism, Davidson, and Truth

I Less Is More

Davidson has said that his theory of truth 'provides no entities with which to compare sentences', and thus is a 'correspondence' theory only in 'an unassuming sense'.[1] His paper 'A Coherence Theory of Truth and Knowledge' takes as its slogan 'correspondence without confrontation'.[2] This slogan chimes with his repudiation of what he calls the 'dualism of scheme and content' – the idea that something like 'mind' or 'language' can bear some relation such as 'fitting' or 'organizing' to the world. Such doctrines are reminiscent of pragmatism a movement which has specialized in debunking dualisms and in dissolving traditional problems created by those dualisms. The close affiliations of Davidson's work to Quine's and of Quine's to Dewey's make it tempting to see Davidson as belonging to the American pragmatist tradition.

Davidson, however, has explicitly denied that his break with the empiricist tradition makes him a pragmatist.[3] He thinks of pragmatism as an identification of truth with assertibility, or with assertibility under ideal conditions. If such an identification is essential to pragmatism, then indeed Davidson is as anti-pragmatist as he is anti-empiricist. For such an identification would merely be an emphasis on the 'scheme' side of an unacceptable dualism, replacing the emphasis on the 'content' side represented by traditional empiricism. Davidson does not want to see truth identified with anything. He also does not want to view sentences as 'made true' by anything – neither knowers or speakers on the one hand nor 'the world' on the other. For him, any 'theory of truth' which analyses a relation between bits of language and bits of non-language is already on the wrong track.

Richard M. Rorty, "Pragmatism, Davidson and Truth," pp. 333–55 in Ernest LePore (ed.) *Truth and Interpretation: Perspectives on the Philosophy of Donald Davidson,* © 1986 by Blackwell Publishing Ltd, Oxford. Reproduced with permission of Blackwell Publishing Ltd.

1   Donald Davidson, *Inquiries into Truth and Interpretation* (Oxford University Press, Oxford, 1984), p. xviii.
2   This article appears in *Kant oder Hegel?*, ed. Dieter Henrich (Kleft-Cotta, Stuttgart, 1983). It is reprinted in the present volume. The quoted slogan is on p. 423 of the original publication.
3   *Inquiries*, p. xviii.

On this last, negative, point, Davidson agrees with William James. James thought that no traditional theory of truth had come close to explaining 'the particular go'[4] of such a special relation, and that it was a hopeless quest. On his view, there was no point in trying to give sense to a notion of 'correspondence' which was neutral between, e.g., perceptual, theoretical, moral and mathematical truths. He suggested that we settle for 'the true' as being 'only the expedient in our way of thinking'.[5] When his critics chorused that 'truths aren't true because they work; they work because they are true', James thought they had missed his point, viz., that 'true' was a term of praise used for endorsing, rather than one referring to a state of affairs the existence of which explained e.g., the success of those who held true beliefs. He thought that the moral of philosophers' failures to discover, as it were, the micro-structure of the correspondence relation was that there was nothing there to find, that one could not use truth as an *explanatory* notion.

James, unfortunately, did not confine himself to making this negative point. He also had moments in which he inferred from the false premise that

> If we have the notion of 'justified', we don't need that of 'truth'

to

> 'True' must mean something like 'justifiable'.

This was a form of the idealist error of inferring from

> We can make no sense of the notion of truth as correspondence

to

> Truth must consist in ideal coherence.

The error is to assume that 'true' needs a definition, and then to infer from the fact that it cannot be defined in terms of a relation between beliefs and non-beliefs to the view that it must be defined in terms of a relation among beliefs. But, as Hilary Putnam has pointed out in his 'naturalistic fallacy' argument, 'it might be true but not X' is always sensible, no matter what one substitutes for X (the same point G. E. Moore made about 'good').[6]

Suppose that we prescind from the moments in which James fell into this error, as well as from Peirce's unfortunate attempt (of which more later) to define truth in terms of 'the end of inquiry'. Suppose that we follow up James's negative point – his polemic against the notion of 'correspondence' – and forget his occasional attempts to say something constructive about truth. We can then, I think, isolate a sense for the term 'pragmatism' which will consist *simply* in the dissolution of the traditional problematic about truth, as opposed to a constructive 'pragmatist theory of truth'. This dissolution would start from the claim that 'true' has no explanatory use, but merely the following uses:

4   William James, *Pragmatism* (Hackett, Indiaospolis, 1981), p. 92.
5   Ibid., p. 100.
6   Hilary Putnam, *Meaning and the Moral Sciences* (Cambridge University Press, Cambridge, 1978), p. 108.

(a)   an endorsing use
(b)   a cautionary use, in such remarks as 'Your belief that S is perfectly justified, but perhaps not true' – reminding ourselves that justification is relative to, and no better than, the beliefs cited as grounds for S, and that such justification is no guarantee that things will go well if we take S as a 'rule for action' (Peirce's definition of belief)
(c)   A disquotational use: to say metalinguistic things of the form 'S' is true iff – .[7]

The cautionary use of the term was neglected by James, as was the disquotational use. The neglect of the former led to the association of pragmatism with relativism. The misleading association of the latter (by Tarski) with the notion of 'correspondence' has led people to think that there must have been more to this notion than James realized. Davidson, on my view, has given us an account of truth which has a place for each of these uses while eschewing the idea that the expediency of a belief can be explained by its truth.

In the sense of 'pragmatism' in which Davidson and James are both pragmatists, the term signifies adherence to the following theses:

(1)   'True' has no explanatory uses.
(2)   We understand all there is to know about the relation of beliefs to the world when we understand their causal relations with the world; our knowledge of how to apply terms such as 'about' and 'true of' is fallout from a 'naturalistic' account of linguistic behavior.[8]
(3)   There are no relations of 'being made true' which hold between beliefs and the world.
(4)   There is no point to debates between realism and anti-realism, for such debates presuppose the empty and misleading idea of beliefs 'being made true'.[9]

---

7   There is much to be said about the relations between these three uses, but I shall not try to say it here. The best attempt to do so which I have seen is found in an unpublished paper by Robert Brandom called 'Truth Talk'. Brandom shows how the 'primitive pragmatism' which tries to define truth as assertibility is defeated by the use of 'true' in such contexts as the antecedents of conditionals. But he then suggests a way of developing a sophisticated pragmatism which, invoking Frege and the Grover-Camp-Belnap prosentential theory of truth, saves Dewey's intentions. Brandom not only shows how 'anaphoric or prosentential theories' can, as be says 'retain the fundamental anti-descriptive thrust of the pragmatist position, while broadening it to account also for the embedded uses on which primitive pragmatism founders', but suggests ways of reconciling these theories with Davidsonian disquotationalism.
8   This thesis does not, of course, entail that you can define intentional terms in non-intentional terms, nor that a semantic metalanguage can somehow be 'reduced' to Behaviorese. It is one thing to say 'You learn which sentences using the term "X" are true by finding out which sentences using the term "Y" are true' and another to say 'You can explain the meaning of "X" in terms of "Y"' or 'You can reduce "X"s to "Y"s'. Our intentional concepts are not fall-out from our observation of causal relationships, but our knowledge of how to apply them is. See Section IV below for a discussion of Davidson's non-reductive brand of physicalism.
9   Jamesian pragmatists heartily agree with Dummett's claim that lots and lots of the traditional 'problems of philosophy' (including the problems which Peirce thought to solve with his "Scotistic realism") are best seen as issues between realists and anti-realists over whether there are "matters of fact" in, e.g., physics, ethics, or logic. But whereas Dummett sees himself as having rehabilitated

Notice that, so defined, pragmatism offers no 'theory of truth'. All it gives us is an explanation of why, in this area, less is more – of why therapy is better than system-building.

Both James and Davidson would urge that the only reason philosophers thought they needed an 'explanation of what truth consists in' was that they were held captive by a certain picture – the picture which Davidson calls 'the dualism of scheme and content' and which Dewey thought of as 'the dualism of Subject and Object'. Both pictures are of disparate ontological realms, one containing beliefs and the other non-beliefs. The picture of two such realms permits us to imagine truth as a relation between particular beliefs and particular non-beliefs which (a) is non-causal in nature, and (b) must be 'correctly analyzed' before one can rebut (or concede victory to) the epistemological skeptic. To adopt (1)–(4) above is to erase this picture, and thereby to erase most of the traditional philosophical dualisms which Dewey thought ought to be erased. It is also to drop the picture which the epistemological skeptic needs to make his skepticism interesting and arguable – to make it more than the philosopher's pursuit of *Unheimlichkeit* of a sense of the strangeness of the world.

II Peirce's Half-Way Measure

Before turning to the question of whether Davidson in fact adheres to (1)–(4), it may be helpful to say something about Peirce's 'end of inquiry' pragmatism. This is the version of the so-called 'pragmatist theory of truth' (a misleading textbook label for a farrago of inconsistent doctrines) which has received most attention in recent years. It represents, on my view, a half-way house between idealist and physicalist theories of truth on the one hand, and (1)–(4) on the other.

Idealism and physicalism have in common the hope that

(A)   'There are rocks' is true

is true if and only if

(B)   At the ideal end of inquiry, we shall be justified in asserting that there are rocks

This suggestion requires them, however to say that

(C)   There are rocks

is implied by (B) as well as by (A). This seems paradoxical, since they also wish to assert

(D)   'There are rocks' is linked by a relation of correspondence – accurate representation – to the way the world is

and there seems no obvious reason why the progress of the language-game we are playing should have anything in particular to do with the way the rest of the world is.

---

these fine old problems by semanticizing them, the pragmatist sees him as having conveniently bagged them for disposal.

Idealism and physicalism are attempts to supply such a reason. The idealists suggest that

(E)   The world consists of representations arranged in an ideally coherent system

thus permitting them to analyse (C) as

(F)   'There are rocks' is a member of the ideally coherent system of representations.

Idealists support this move by saying that the correspondence relation of (D) cannot be a relation whose existence could be established by confronting an assertion with an object to see if a relation called 'corresponding' holds. Nobody knows what such a confrontation would look like. (The relation of 'customary response to' which holds between tables and assertions of the presence of tables is clearly not what is wanted.) Since the only criterion of truth is coherence among representations, they say, the only way of saving (D) while avoiding skepticism is (E).

The physicalists, on the other hand, analyse (A) as (D) and then argue that playing the language-games we play will eventually lead us to correspond with reality. It will do so because, so to speak, the world takes a hand in the game. This is the view of philosophers like Friedrich Engels, Jerry Fodor, Michael Devitt, Jay Rosenberg and Hartry Field. They reject the possibility of a priori discovery of the nature of reality, illustrated by the idealists' (E), but they think that one or another empirical science (or the 'unified' ensemble of them all) will provide an answer to the skeptic. These philosophers think that, although there are no entailments, there are deeply buried connections between the conditions of the truth of (B) and of (C). These connections will not be discovered by an analysis of meanings but by empirical scientific work which will pry out the causal connections between, e.g., rocks and representations of rocks.

Peirce, in his earlier period, wanted to avoid both the revisionary metaphysics of idealism and the promissory notes of physicalism. He tried for a quick fix by analysing (D) as (B). He shared with the idealist and the physicalist the motive of refuting the skeptic, but he thought it enough to say that 'reality' means something like 'whatever we shall still be asserting the existence of at the end of inquiry'. This definition of reality bridges the gap the skeptic sees between coherence and correspondence. It reduces coherence to correspondence without the necessity either for metaphysical system-building or for further empirical inquiry. A simple reanalysis of the term 'reality' does the trick.

I do not think (though I once did)[10] that Peircian pragmatism is defensible, but before transcending it I want to remark that Peirce was moving in the right direction. The Peircian pragmatist is right in thinking that the idealist and the physicalist share a common fallacy – namely that 'correspondence' is the name of a relation between pieces of

---

10   As, for instance, when I said, falsely, that 'we can make no sense of the notion that the view which can survive all objections might be false' (*Consequences of Pragmatism* (University of Minnesota Press, Minneapolis, 1982), p. 165 – passage written in 1979). I started retracting this Peircianism in the Introduction to that book (e.g., p. xiv, written in 1981) and am still at it. I was persuaded of the untenability of Peircianism view by Michael Williams' 'Coherence, Justification and Truth' (*Review of Metaphysics* XXXIV (1980) pp. 243–72) in particular by his claim (p. 269) that 'we have no idea what it would be for a theory to be ideally complete and comprehensive ... or of what it would be good for inquiry to have an end'. Cf. his suggestion that we drop the attempt to think of truth as 'in some sense an epistemic notion' (p. 269). Davidson spells out what happens when the attempt is dropped.

thought (or language) and pieces of the world, a relation such that the relata [sic] must be ontologically homogenous. The idealist generalizes Berkeley's point by saying: nothing can correspond to a representation except a representation. So he saves us from skepticism by redescribing reality as consisting of representations. The physicalist thinks that nothing can correspond to a bit of spatio-temporal reality except by being another bit linked to the first by appropriate causal relationships. So he saves us from skepticism by offering a physicalistic account of the nature of our representations – one which shows that, as Fodor once said, the correspondence theory of truth corresponds to reality. The Peircian rises above this debate by saying that the 'about' and 'true of' relations can link utterly disparate relata, and that problems of ontological homogeneity need not arise.[11] All that is necessary is to redefine 'reality' as what the winners of the game talk about, thus insuring that the conditions laid down by (B) and (D) coincide.

The Peircian redefinition, however, uses a term – 'ideal' – which is just as fishy as 'corresponds'. To make it less fishy Peirce would have to answer the question 'How would we know that we were at the end of inquiry, as opposed to merely having gotten tired or unimaginative?' This is as awkward as 'How do we know we are corresponding to reality, rather than merely making conventionally correct responses to stimuli?' Peirce's idea of 'the end of inquiry' might make sense if we could detect an asymptotic convergence in inquiry, but such convergence seems a local and short-term phenomenon.[12] Without such a clarification of 'ideal' or 'end', the Peircian is merely telling that the conditions laid down by (B) and (D) coincide without giving us any reason for thinking they do. Nor is it clear what such a reason could consist in.

Peirce went half-way towards destroying the epistemological problematic which motivated the metaphysical quarrels between idealists and physicalists. He did so by leaving out 'mind' and sticking to 'signs'. But he went *only* half-way because he still thought that (D) was an intuition which any philosophy had to assimilate. James went the rest of the way by saying that not only was 'true of' not a relation between ontologically homogenous relata, but was not an analyzable relation at all, not a relation which could be clarified by a scientific or metaphysical description of the relation between beliefs and non-beliefs. Deciding that no reason could be given for saying that the constraints laid down by (B) and (D) would coincide, he simply dropped (D), and with it the problematic of epistemological skepticism. He thereby set the stage for Dewey's argument that it is only the attempt to supplement a naturalist account of our interaction with our

11   Peircian pragmatism is often criticized on the ground that, like idealism, it raises problems about ontological homogeneity and heterogeneity through a counter-intuitive claim Kantian claim that 'objects in the world owe their fundamental structure – and, if they couldn't exist without displaying that structure, their existence – to our creative activity' (Alvin Plantings, 'How To Be An Anti-Realist', *Proceedings of the American Philosophical Association*, 56 (1982), p. 52). But this confuses a criterial claim with a causal one: the Peircian claim that 'If there are rocks, they will display their structure at the end of inquiry' and the idealist claim that 'If there were no inquiry, there would be no rocks.'

12   See Mary Hesse's distinction between 'instrumental progress' – increase in predicative ability – and 'convergence of concepts' (*Revolutions and Reconstructions in the Philosophy of Sciences* (Indiana University Press, Bloomington, 1980), pp. x–xi). The possibility of scientific revolutions endangers conceptual convergence, which is the only sort of convergence which will do the Peircian any good. To insure against the indefinite proliferation of such revolutions in the future one would need something like Peirce's 'metaphysics of evolutionary love', or Putnam's attempt to certify contemporary physics as 'mature'.

environment with a non-naturalist account (involving some third thing, intermediate between the organism and its environment – such as 'mind' or 'language') which makes that problematic seem interesting.

III Davidson and the Field Linguist

What justification is there for attributing (1)–(4) to Davidson? He has asserted (3) on various occasions. But it may seem odd to attribute (4) to him, since he has often been treated as a prototypical 'realist'. (2) may also sound unDavidsonian, since he has had no truck with recent 'causal theories' in semantics. Further, his association with Tarski, and Tarski's with the notion of 'correspondence', may seem to make him an unlikely recruit for the pragmatist ranks – for pragmatism, as I have defined it, consists very largely in the claim that only if we drop the whole idea of 'correspondence with reality' can we avoid pseudo-problems.

Nevertheless, I propose to argue that all four pragmatist theses should be ascribed to Davidson. To defend this claim, I shall begin by offering an account of what I shall call 'the philosophy of language of the field linguist'. I shall claim that this is all the philosophy of language (and, in particular, all the doctrine about truth) which Davidson has, and all that he thinks anybody needs.

Davidson, like the traditional philosopher who wants an answer to the epistemological skeptic, wants us to step out of our language-game and look at it from a distance. But his outside standpoint is not the metaphysical standpoint of the idealist, looking for an unsuspected ontological homogeneity between beliefs and non-beliefs invisible to science, nor the hopeful standpoint of the physicalist, looking to future science to discover such an homogeneity. Rather, it is the mundane standpoint of the field linguist trying to make sense of our linguistic behavior. Whereas traditional theories of truth asked 'what feature of the world is referred to by "true"?', Davidson asks 'how is "true" used by the outside observer of the language-game?'

Davidson is surely right that Quine 'saved philosophy of language as a serious subject' by getting rid of the analytic-synthetic distinction.[13] Quine's best argument for doing so was that the distinction is of no use to the field linguist. Davidson follows upon this argument by pointing out that, *pace* Dummett and Quine himself,[14] the distinction between the physical objects the natives react to and their neural stimulations is of no use either. The linguist cannot start with knowledge of native meanings acquired prior to knowledge of native beliefs, not with translations of native observation sentences which have been certified by matching them with stimulations. He must be purely coherentist in his approach, going round and round the hermeneutic circle until he begins to feel at home.

All the linguist has to go on is his observation of the way in which linguistic is aligned with non-linguistic behavior in the course of the native's interaction with his environment,

13   'A Coherence Theory ...', p. 431.
14   See 'A Coherence Theory ...', p. 430: 'Quine and Dummett agree on a basic principle, which is that whatever there is to meaning must be traced back somehow to experience, the given, or patterns of sensory stimulation, something intermediate between belief and the usual objects our beliefs are about. Once we take this step, we open the door to skepticism ... When meaning goes epistemological in this way, truth and meaning are necessarily divorced.'

an interaction which he takes to be guided by rules for action (Peirce's definition of 'belief'). He approaches this data armed with the regulative principle that most of the native's rules are the same as ours, which is to say that most of them are true. The latter formulation of the principle is an extension of Quine's remark that any anthropologist who claims to have translated a native utterance as '*p* and not-*p*' just shows that she has not yet put together a good translation manual. Davidson generalizes this: any translation which portrays the natives as denying most of the evident facts about their environment is automatically a bad one.

The most vivid example of this point is Davidson's claim that the best way to translate the discourse of a brain which has always lived in a vat will be as referring to the vat-cum-computer environment the brain is actually in.[15] This will be the analogue of construing most native remarks as about, e.g., rocks and diseases rather than about trolls and demons. In Davidson's words:

> What stands in the way of global skepticism of the senses is, in my view, the fact that we must, in the plainest and methodologically most basic cases, take the objects of a belief to be the causes of that belief. And what we, as interpreters, must take them to be is what they in fact are. Communication begins where causes converge: your utterance means what mine does if belief in its truth is systematically caused by the same events and objects.[16]

In this passage, Davidson weds the Kripkean claim that causation must have *something* to do with reference to the Strawsonian claim that you figure out what somebody is talking about by figuring out what object most of his beliefs are true of. The wedding is accomplished by saying that Strawson is right if construed holistically – if one prefaces his claim with Aristotle's phrase 'on the whole and for the most part'. You cannot, however, use Strawson's criterion for individual cases and be sure of being right. But if *most* of the results of your translation-scheme, and consequent assignment of reference, do not conform to Strawson's criterion, then that scheme must have something terribly wrong with it. The mediating element between Strawson and Kripke is the Quinean insight that knowledge *both* of causation *and* of reference is (equally) a matter of coherence with the field linguist's own beliefs.

Thesis (2) above can be construed in either a Kripkean or a Davidsonian way. On the former, building-block, approach to reference, we want to trace causal pathways from objects to individual speech-acts. This approach leaves open the possibility that speakers may get these pathways all wrong (e.g., by being largely wrong about what there is) and thus that they may never know to what they are referring. This allows the possibility of a wholesale divorce between referents and intentional objects – just the kind of scheme-content gap which Davidson warns us against. By contrast, Davidson is suggesting that we maximize coherence and truth first, and then let reference fall out as it may.

This guarantees that the intentional objects of lots of beliefs – what Davidson calls 'the plainest cases' – will be their causes. Kripkean slippage (e.g., the Goedel-Schmidt case)

---

15 As far as I know, Davidson has not used this example in print. I am drawing upon unpublished remarks at a colloquium with Quine and Putnam, Heidelberg, 1981.
16 'A Coherence Theory…', p. 436. This line of argument – together with Davidson's account of reference as fallout from translation (as at *Inquiries*, pp. 219ff., 236ff.) – is my chief textual evidence for imputing (2) to Davidson.

must be the exception. For if we try to imagine that a split between entities referred to and intentional objects is the rule we shall have drained the notion of 'reference' of any content. That is: we shall have made it, like 'analytic', a notion which the field linguist has no use for. The linguist can communicate with the natives if he knows most of their intentional objects (i.e., which objects most of their rules for action are good for dealing with, which objects most of their beliefs are true of). But he can make as little sense of the skeptical claim that this is not 'really' communication (but just accidentally felicitous cross-talk) as of the suggestion that the 'intended interpretation' of some platitudinous native utterance is 'There are no rocks.'

Davidson's application of this view of the job of the field linguist to epistemological skepticism is as follows. Unless one is willing to postulate some intermediary between the organism and its environment (e.g., 'determinate meanings', 'intended interpretations', 'what is before the speaker's mind', etc.) then radical interpretation begins at home. So, like all other natives, we turn out to have mostly true beliefs. The argument is neat, but does it *answer* the skeptic, as the idealist and the physicalist want to do? Or does it simply tell the skeptic that his question, 'Do we ever represent reality as it is in itself?' was a bad one, as the Jamesian pragmatist does?

A skeptic is likely to reply to Davidson that it would take a lot more than an account of the needs of the field linguist to show that belief is, as Davidson says, 'in its nature veridical'.[17] He will think that Davidson has shown no more than that the field linguist must assume that the natives believe mostly what we do, and that the question of whether most of *our* beliefs are true is still wide open. Davidson can only reply, once again, that radical interpretation begins at home – that if we want an outside view of our own language-game, the only one available is that of the field linguist. But that is just what the skeptic will not grant. He thinks that Davidson has missed the philosophical point. He thinks that Davidson's outside standpoint is not, so to speak, far enough outside to count as philosophical.

As far as I can see, the only rejoinder readily available to Davidson at this point is to remark on the intuitive appeal of (2): the naturalistic thesis, which he shares with Kripke, that there is nothing more to be known about the relation between beliefs and the rest of reality than what we learn from an empirical study of causal transactions between organisms and their environment. The relevant result of this study is the field linguist's translation-manual-cum-ethnographic-report.[18] Since we already have (in dictionaries) a translation manual for ourselves, as well as (in encyclopedias) an auto-ethnography, there is nothing more for us to know *about our relation to reality* than we already know. There is no further job for philosophy to do. This is just what the pragmatist has been telling the skeptic all the time. Both the pragmatist and Davidson are saying that if 'correspondence' denotes a relation between beliefs and the world which can vary though nothing else varies – even if all the causal relations remain the same – then 'corresponds' cannot be an explanatory term. So if truth is to be thought of as 'correspondence', then 'true' cannot be an explanatory term. Pressing (2) to the limit, and freeing it, from the atomistic presuppositions which Kripkean 'building-block' theories of reference add to it, results in (1).

17 'A Coherence Theory …, p. 432.
18 That such a manual cannot be separated from such a report is entailed by the Quine-Davidson argument that you cannot figure out beliefs and meanings independently of one another.

Thus Davidson's strategy with the skeptic would seem to give him reason to subscribe to (1) as well as to (2). Whereas the physicalist invokes (2) with an eye to finding something for 'correspondence' to refer to, Davidson takes the absence of such a thing in the field linguist's results as a reason for thinking that there is nothing to look for. Like Dewey's (and unlike Skinner's) his is a *non-reductive* naturalism, one which does not assume that every important semantical term must describe a physical relationship.[19] He thinks that there will be lots of terms used by theorists who study causal relations (e.g., field linguists, particle physicists) which do not themselves denote causal relations.

On my interpretation, then, Davidson joins the pragmatist in saying that 'true' has no explanatory use.[20] His contribution to pragmatism consists in pointing out that it has a disquotational use in addition to the normative uses seized upon by James. The traditional philosophical attempt to conflate these two kinds of use, and to view them both as explained by the use of 'true' to denote a non-causal relation called 'correspondence', is, on this account, a confused attempt to be inside and outside the language-game at the same time.

My interpretation, however, must deal with the fact that Davidson, unlike the pragmatist, does not present himself as repudiating the skeptic's question, but as answering it. He says that 'even a mild coherence theory like mine must provide a skeptic with a reason for supposing coherent beliefs are true.'[21] Again, he says 'the theory I defend is not in competition with a correspondence theory, but depends for its defense on an argument that purports to show that coherence yields correspondence.'[22] This sounds as if Davidson were not only adopting something like (D) above, but claiming to deduce (D) from (B), in the manner of idealism and Peircean pragmatism. In wanting 'correspondence without confrontation', he shows that he shares with these latter 'isms' the view that we cannot compare a belief with a non-belief to see if they match. But what does Davidson suppose is left of correspondence after confrontation is taken away? What is it that he thinks the skeptic wants? What is it that he proposes to give the skeptic by making coherence yield it?

Davidson says that the skeptical question he wishes to answer is: 'how, given that we "cannot get outside our beliefs and our language so as to find some test other than coherence" we nevertheless can have knowledge and talk about an objective public world which is not of our making?'[23] But this does not help us much. Only if one held some view which made it mysterious that there could be such knowledge and such talk (e.g., one which required ontological homogeneity between beliefs and non-beliefs, or

---

19 Davidson's 'Mental Events' illustrates his strategy of combining identity-with-the-physical with irreducibility-to-the-physical.

20 One might object, as Alan Donagan has suggested to me, that the fact that both the linguist's and the native's beliefs are mostly true is an explanation of the fact that they are able to communicate with one another. But this sort of explanation does not invoke a causally efficacious property. It is like explaining the fact of communication by saying that the two inhabit the same space-time continuum, We do not know what it would be like for them not to, any more than we know what it would be like for one or the other to have mostly false beliefs. The only candidates for causally efficacious properties are properties which we can imagine away.

21 'A Coherence Theory …', p. 426.

22 'A Coherence Theory …', p. 423.

23 'A Coherence Theory …', pp. 426–7. Davidson correctly says, in this passage, that I do not think this is a good question. I am here trying to explain what is wrong with it, and why I think Davidson too should regard it as a bad question.

one which thought that there was an intermediary 'scheme' which 'shaped' the non-beliefs before they became talkable-about), would this be a challenging question. If there is to be a problem here, it must be because the skeptic has been allowed to construe 'objective' in such a way that the connection between coherence and objectivity has become unperspicuous.[24] What sense of 'correspondence' will both preserve this lack of perspicuity and yet be such that Davidson can argue that coherence will yield it?

To make a start, we can note that Davidson thinks 'correspondence' is not, as correspondence-to-*fact* theorists believe, a relation between a sentence and a chunk of reality which is somehow isomorphic to that sentence. In 'True to the Facts', he agrees with Strawson that facts − sentence-shaped chunks of the world − are *ad hoc* contrivances which do not answer to the skeptic's needs. What does, he thinks, is the more complex notion of correspondence made intelligible by Tarski's notion of satisfaction. Rather than thinking of the correspondence of language to reality as symbolized by the relation between two sides of a T-sentence, Davidson says, we should attend to word–world rather than sentence–world mappings, and in particular to the constraints on such mappings required for 'the elaboration of a nontrivial theory capable of meeting the test of entailing all those neutral snowbound trivialities' (viz., the T-sentences).[25]

These constraints are what guide the field linguist who tries to guess the causes of the native's behavior, and then goes around the hermeneutic circle long enough to come up with T-sentences which maximize the truth of the native's beliefs. The eventual theory will link native words with bits of the world by the satisfaction-relation, but these links will not be the basis for the translations. Rather, they will be fallout from the translations. Going around this circle means not attempting (in the manner of building-block theories of reference) to start with some 'secure' links, but rather going back and forth between guesses at translations of occasion-sentences and of standing sentences until something like Rawlsian 'reflective equilibrium' emerges.

The correspondence between words and objects provided by the satisfaction-relations incorporated in a T-theory are thus irrelevant to the sort of correspondence which was supposed to be described by 'true of', and which is supposed to be revealed by 'philosophical analysis', culminating in a 'theory of truth'. So whatever the skeptic's desired correspondence may be, it is not something which is captured in Tarski's account of satisfaction. For 'true' does not offer material for analysis. As Davidson says

> Truth is beautifully transparent compared to belief and coherence and I take it as primitive. Truth, as applied to utterances of sentences, shows the disquotational feature enshrined in Tarski's Convention T, and that is enough to fix its domain of application.[26]

So we cannot define 'true' in terms of satisfaction, nor of anything else. We can only explain our sense that, as Davidson says, 'the truth of an utterance depends on just two

---

24   I think that Davidson may be worrying, in this passage, about the sort of identification of criterial and causal relations for which I criticized Plantinga in note 11 above. This is the sort of identification which is characteristic of idealism, and which generates fear that coherence theories will result in human beings having 'constituted the world'. On my interpretation, he has already disposed of that identification, and thus of the need for worry.

25   *Inquiries*, p. 51.

26   'A Coherence Theory …', p. 425.

things, what the words mean and how the world is arranged' by explaining how we go about finding out these two things, and by pointing out that these two inquiries cannot be conducted independently.

I think Davidson should be interpreted as saying that the plausibility of the thesis just cited – that there is no third thing relevant to truth besides meanings of words and the way the world is – is the best explanation we are going to get of the intuitive force of (D): the idea that 'truth is correspondence with reality.' This thesis is all there is to the 'realistic' intuition which idealists, physicalists, and Peirceans have been so concerned to preserve. But, so construed, (D) makes the merely *negative* point that we need not worry about such *tertia* as, in Davidson's words, 'a conceptual scheme, a way of viewing things, a perspective' (or a transcendental constitution of consciousness, or a language, or a cultural tradition). So I think that Davidson is telling us, once again, that less is more: we should not ask for more detail about the correspondence relation, but rather realize that the *tertia* which have made us have skeptical doubts about whether most of our beliefs are true are just not there.

To say that they are not there is to say, once again, that the field linguist does not need them – and that therefore philosophy does not need them either. Once we understand how radical interpretation works, and that the interpreter can make no good use of notions like 'determinate meaning', 'intended interpretation', 'constitutive act of the transcendental imagination', 'conceptual scheme', and the like, then we can take the notion of 'correspondence to reality' as trivial, and not in need of analysis. For this term has now been reduced to a stylistic variant of 'true'.

If this is indeed what Davidson is saying, then his answer to the skeptic comes down to: you are only a skeptic because you have these intentionalistic notions floating around in your head, inserting imaginary barriers between you and the world. Once you purify yourself of the 'idea idea' in all its various forms, skepticism will never cross your enlightened mind. If this is his response to the skeptic, then I think he is making exactly the right move, the same move which James and Dewey were trying, somewhat more awkwardly, to make. But I also think Davidson was a bit misleading in suggesting that he was going to show us how coherence yields correspondence. It would have been better to have said that he was going to offer the skeptic a way of speaking which would prevent him from asking his question, than to say that he was going to answer that question. It would have been better to tell him that when confrontation goes, so does representation, and thus the picture which made possible both the fears of the skeptic and the hopes of the physicalist, the idealist and the Peircean.

Davidson's favorite characterization of the picture which the skeptic should abjure is 'the dualism of scheme and content'. A common feature of all the forms of this dualism which Davidson lists is that the relations between the two sides of the dualism are non-causal. Such *tertia* as a 'conceptual framework' or an 'intended interpretation' are non-causally related to the things which they organize or intend. They vary independently of the rest of the universe, just as do the skeptic's relations of 'correspondence' or 'representation'. The moral is that if we have no such *tertia*, then we have no suitable items to serve as representations, and thus no need to ask whether our beliefs represent the world accurately. We still have beliefs, but they will be seen from the outside as the field linguist sees them (as causal interactions with the environment) or from the inside as the pre-epistemological native sees them (as rules for action). To abjure *tertia* is to abjure the possibility of a third way of seeing them – one which somehow combines the outside view and the inside view, the descriptive and the normative attitudes. To see language in the same way as we see beliefs – not as a 'conceptual framework' but as the causal interaction with the environment described by the field linguist, makes it impossible to think of language as something which may or may not (how could we ever tell?) 'fit the world'. So once we give up *tertia*, we give up (or trivialize) the notions of representation and correspondence, and thereby give up the possibility of formulating epistemological skepticism.

If my understanding of Davidson is right, then – apart from his appeal to physicalistic unified science, the appeal formulated in the pragmatist's (2) – his only arguments for the claim that the philosophy of language of the field linguist is all we need will be the arguments offered in 'On the Very Idea of a Conceptual Scheme' to the effect that various 'confrontationalist' metaphors are more trouble than they are worth. All that we might add would be further arguments to the same point drawn from the history of philosophy – illustrations of the impasses into which the attempts to develop those metaphors drew various great dead philosophers. It will not be an empirical or a metaphysical discovery that there is no *tertium quid* relevant to the truth of assertions, nor a result of 'analysis of the meaning' of 'true' or 'belief' or any other term. So, like James (though unlike Peirce) Davidson is not giving us a new 'theory of truth'. Rather, he is giving us reasons for thinking that we can safely get along with less philosophizing about truth than we had thought we needed. On my interpretation, his argument that 'coherence yields correspondence' comes down to: From the field linguist's point of view, none of the notions which might suggest that there was more to truth than the meaning of words and the way the world is are needed. So if you are willing to assume this point of view you will have no more skeptical doubts about the intrinsic veridicality of belief.

IV Davidson as Non-Reductive Physicalist

Before turning to a well-known set of objections to the claim that the philosophy of the field linguist is all the philosophy of language we need – those of Michael Dummett – it will be useful to compare Davidson with a philosopher to whom he is, beneath a few superficial differences in rhetoric, very close: Hilary Putnam. Putnam is a proponent of many familiar pragmatist doctrines. He makes fun, as James and Dewey did, of the attempt to get an outside view – a 'God's-eye-view' of the sort which the traditional epistemologist, and the skeptic, have tried for. But when he confronts disquotationalist theories of truth he is troubled. They smell reductionist to him, and he sees them as symptoms of a lingering positivism, a 'transcendental Skinnerianism'. Putnam says:

> If a philosopher says that *truth* is different from *electricity* in precisely this way: that there is room for a theory of electricity but *no room* for a theory of truth, that knowing the assertibility conditions is *all there is to know* about truth, then, in so far as I understand him at all, he is denying that there is a *property* of truth (or a property of rightness or correctness), not just in the realist sense, but in *any* sense. But this is to deny that our thoughts and assertions are *thoughts* and *assertions*.[27]

27   Hilary Putnam, *Realism and Reason* (Cambridge University Press, Cambridge, 1983), p. xv.

Putnam is here assuming that the only reason why one might disclaim the need for a theory of the nature of X is that one has discovered that Xs are 'nothing but' Ys, in good reductivist fashion. So he thinks that Davidson's abjuration of 'an account of what it is for an assertion to be correct and what it is for it to be incorrect' must be made on the basis of a reduction of true assertions to conventionally accepted noises.[28] On this view, to assume the point of view of the field linguist is to reduce actions to movements. But Davidson is not saying that assertions are nothing but noises. Rather he is saying that truth, unlike electricity, is not an explanation of anything.

The idea that the property of truth can serve as an explanation is a product of the misleading picture which engenders the idea that its presence requires an explanation. To see this, notice that it would be a mistake to think of 'true' as having an explanatory use on the basis of such examples as 'He found the correct house because his belief about its location was true' and 'Priestley failed to understand the nature of oxygen because his beliefs about the nature of combustion were false.' The quoted sentences are not explanations but promissory notes for explanations. To get them cashed, to get real explanations, we need to say things like 'He found the correct house because he believed that it was located at …' or 'Priestley failed because he thought that phlogiston …'. The explanation of success and failure is given by the details about what was true or what was false, not by the truth or falsity itself – just as the explanation of the praiseworthiness of an action is not 'it was the right thing to do' but the details of the circumstances in which it was done.[29]

If truth *itself* is to be an explanation of something, that explanandum must be of something which can be caused by truth, but not caused by the content of true beliefs. The function of the *tertia* which Davidson wishes to banish was precisely to provide a mechanism outside the causal order of the physical world, a mechanism which could have or lack a quasi-causal property with which one might identify truth. Thus to say that our conceptual scheme is 'adequate to the world', is to suggest that some cogs and gears are meshing nicely – cogs and gears which are either non-physical or which, though physical, are not mentioned in the rest of our causal story. To suggest, with the skeptic, that our language-game may have nothing to do with the way the world is, is to call up a picture of a gear-wheel so out of touch with the rest of the mechanism as to be spinning idly.[30]

Given his distaste for intentionalist notions, Putnam should have no relish for such pictures, and thus no inclination to regard truth as an explanatory notion. But because he still retains the idea that one should give an 'account of what it is for an assertion to be correct', he demands more than Davidson is in a position to give. He retains this idea, I think, because he is afraid that the inside point of view on our language-game, the point of view where we use 'true' as a term of praise, will somehow be weakened if it receives no support from 'a philosophical account'. Consider the following passage:

28   Ibid., p. xiv.

29   The line of argument I have been employing in this paragraph may also be found in Michael Levin, 'What Kind of Explanation is Truth?' (in *Scientific Realism*, ed. Jarrett Leplin (Berkeley, University of California Press, 1984) pp. 124–39) and in Michael Williams, 'Do We Need a Theory of Truth for Epistemological Purposes?', forthcoming in an issue of *Philosophical Topics* devoted to epistemology.

30   Davidson's position, as Alan Donagan has pointed out to me, is the same as Wittgenstein's; no gears are necessary, for the sentences in which our beliefs are expressed touch the world directly. See *Tractatus Logico-Philosophicus*, 2.1511–2.1515.

> If the cause-effect-description [of our linguistic behavior qua production of noises] is complete from a philosophical as well as from a behavioral-scientific point of view: if all there is to say about language is that it consists in the production of noises (and subvocalizations) according to a certain causal pattern; *if the causal story is not to be and need not be supplemented by a normative story* ... then there is no way in which the noises we utter ... are more than mere 'expressions of our subjectivity' ...[31]

The line I have italicized suggests that disquotationalist theorists of truth think that there is only one story to be told about people: a behavioristic one. But why on earth should such theorists not allow for, and indeed insist upon, supplementing such stories with 'a normative story'? Why should we take the existence of the outside point of view of the field linguist as a recommendation never to assume the inside point of view of the earnest seeker after truth? Putnam, I think, still takes a 'philosophical account of X' to be a synoptic vision which will somehow synthesize every other possible view, will somehow bring the outside and the inside points of view together.

It seems to me precisely the virtue of James and of Dewey to insist that we cannot have such a synoptic vision – that we cannot back up our norms by 'grounding' them in a metaphysical or scientific account of the world. Pragmatism, especially in the form developed by Dewey, urges that we not repeat Plato's mistake of taking terms of praise as the names of esoteric things – of assuming, e.g., we would do a better job of being good if we could get more theoretical knowledge of The Good. Dewey was constantly criticized, from the Platonist right, for being reductionistic and scientistic, inattentive to our needs for 'objective values'. This is the kind of criticism Davidson is currently getting from Putnam. He was also constantly criticized, from the positivist left, for a light-minded relativistic instrumentalism which paid too little attention to 'hard facts', and for trivializing the notion of 'truth' by this neglect.[32] This is the kind of criticism Davidson gets from physicalists such as Field.

Attack from both sides is the usual reward of philosophers who, like Dewey and Davidson, try to stop the pendulum of philosophical fashion from swinging endlessly back and forth between a tough-minded reductionism and a high-minded anti-reductionism. Such philosophers do so by patiently explaining that norms are one thing and descriptions another. In Davidson's case, this comes down to saying that the understanding you get of how the word 'true' works by contemplating the possibility of a Tarskian truth-theory for your language is utterly irrelevant to the satisfaction you get by saying that you know more truths today than you did yesterday, or that truth is great, and will prevail. Putnam's insistence that there is more to truth than disquotationalism can offer is not based on having looked at 'true', or at the language-games we play, and having seen more than Davidson saw. Rather, it is based on a hope that there is more to the notion of a 'philosophical account' than Dewey or Davidson think there can be.

This parallel between Dewey and Davidson seems to me reinforced by Stephen Leeds' formulation of what he calls 'Naturalistic Instrumentalism': the Quine-like combination of the view that 'the only goal relative to which our methods of theory construction and

---

31   Hilary Putnam, 'On Truth', in *How Many Questions*, ed. Leigh S. Caulman et al. (Indianapolis, Hackett, 1983), p. 44.

32   So, simultaneously, was Neurath – who is beginning to get a better press these days.

revision fall into place as a rational procedure is the goal of predicting observations'[33] with the claim that the world is, really and truly *is*, made up of the entities of current science. As Leeds says, this new 'ism' may sound like an oxymoron (as a similar 'ism' did to Dewey's critics.) But it only sounds that way if, as Leeds says, one thinks that 'a theory of truth is needed to explain why our theories work'[34] – if one thinks, that 'truth' can be an explanatory notion. Leeds and Arthur Fine[35] have pointed out the circularity of attempts to use semantics to explain our predictive successes. Such circularity is the natural consequence of trying to be both outside our inquiries and inside them at the same time – to describe them both as motions and as actions. As Davidson has reiterated in his writings on the theory of action, there is no need to choose between these two descriptions: there is only a need to keep them distinct, so that one does not try to use both at once.

V Davidson and Dummett

The question of whether 'truth' is an explanatory property encapsulates the question of whether the philosophy of the field linguist is philosophy of language enough or whether (as Michael Dummett thinks) we need a philosophy of language which links up with epistemology, and with traditional metaphysical issues. Dummett says that a theory of meaning should tell us how:

> an implicit grasp of the theory of meaning, which is attributed to a speaker, issues in his employment of the language and hence ... in the content of the theory. Holism in respect of how one might, starting from scratch, arrive at a theory of meaning for a language, on the other hand, has no such implications, and is, as far as I can see, unobjectionable and almost banal. It is certain that Davidson intends his holism as a doctrine with more bite than this.[36]

Dummett thinks that what you get out of Davidsonian radical interpretation does not include 'the content' of a theory of meaning – 'the specific senses speakers attach to the words of the language'. But on the interpretation of Davidson I have been offering, what Dummett calls a 'sense' is just the sort of *tertium quid* which Davidson wants us to forget about. So the bite of Davidson's theory is not the sort Dummett wants. Dummett wants a theory that bites down on the problems which he thinks can only be formulated when one has a theory of 'sense' – e.g., epistemological and metaphysical issues. Davidson wants a theory of meaning which will serve the field linguists' purposes and to which such problems are irrelevant.

Dummett's argument that more is needed than Davidson gives us is that somebody could know the ensemble of truth-conditions produced by a Davidsonian interpreter

---

33   Stephen Leeds, 'Theories of Reference and Truth', *Erkenntnis*, 13 (1978), p. 117.

34   Dewey would not have restricted theory construction and revision to the sciences which aim at prediction and control, but this difference between Dewey and Leeds is not relevant to the point at hand.

35   In his 'The Natural Ontological Attitude', in *Essays on Scientific Realism*, ed. J. Leplin.

36   Michael Dummett, 'What Is a Theory of Meaning?' in *Mind and Language*, ed. Samuel Guttenplan (Oxford University Press, Oxford, 1975), p. 127.

without knowing the content of the right-hand, metalinguistic, portions of the T-sentences. He thinks that 'a T-sentence for which the metalanguage contains the object-language is obviously unexplanatory' and that if this is so then 'a T-sentence for an object-language disjoint from the metalanguage is equally unexplanatory.'[37] Davidson will reply that no single T-sentence – no single 'neutral snowbound triviality' – will tell you what it is to understand any of the words occurring on the left-hand sides, but that the whole body of such sentences tells you *all* there is to know about this. Dummett regards that reply as an admission of defeat. He says:

> On such an account, there can be no answer to the question what constitutes a speaker's understanding of any one word or sentence: one can say only that the knowledge of the entire theory of truth issues in an ability to speak the language, and, in particular, in a propensity to recognize sentences of it as true under conditions corresponding, by and large, to the T-sentences.[38]

And again:

> no way is provided, even in principle, of segmenting his ability to use the language as a whole into distinct component abilities.[39]

Now it is of the essence of Davidson's position, as of the positions of Wittgenstein and Sellars, that there are no such distinct component abilities.[40] For when you get rid of such *tertia* as 'determinate meanings', 'intended interpretations', 'responses to stimuli', and the like, you are left with nothing to split up the overall know-how into component bits – nothing to reply to 'How do you know that that's called "red"?' save Wittgenstein's: 'I know English.' Davidson has, to insist that the individual T-sentences do not replicate any inner structures, and that any attempt to provide such structures will pay the price of reintroducing *tertia*, entities which will get between our words and the world.

Dummett notes that Davidson tries 'to make a virtue of necessity', but insists that doing so 'is an abnegation of what we are entitled to expect from a theory of meaning'.[41] For Dummett thinks that we are entitled to a theory of meaning which will preserve the traditional notions of empiricist epistemology. He thinks that any such theory must grant that 'an ability to use a given sentence in order to give a

---

37   Ibid., p. 108. Dummett actually says 'M-sentence' (i.e., a sentence of the form '"–" means –') rather than 'T-sentence'. I have changed the quotation for the sake of perspicacity. As Dummett rightly says, for Davidson's purposes the two sorts of sentence are interchangeable.
38   Ibid., p. 115.
39   Ibid., p. 116.
40   A similar position is adopted by Ernst Tugendhat in his *Traditional and Analytical Philosophy* (Cambridge University Press, Cambridge, 1983). Tugendhat thinks of this position as the only alternative to the 'objectualist' account of the understanding of language which has dominated the philosophical tradition up through Husserl and Russell.
41   Ibid., p. 117. Some of the complaints about Davidson I have been citing from Dummett are modified to the appendix to 'What is a Theory of Meaning' (ibid., pp. 123ff.). But the insistence on the point that Davidson 'can make no sense of knowing part of the language' (p. 138) and the unargued-for presumption that philosophy of language must preserve an unQuinean language-fact distinction (p. 137) remain.

report of observation may reasonably be taken, as a knowledge of what has to be the case for that sentence to be true.'[42]

Dummett's paradigm case of grasping the content of an expression is what you do when you observe that something is red. He thinks that the contrast between 'That's red!' and cases like 'Caesar crossed the Rubicon', 'Love is better than hate', and 'There are transfinite cardinals' is something which any adequate philosophy of language must preserve. But for Davidson's and Wittgenstein's holism there simply is no contrast. On their view, to grasp the content is, in *all* these cases, to grasp the inferential relationships between these sentences and the other sentences of the language.[43]

The same point can be made in reference to Dummett's presentation of the issue about realism and anti-realism in terms of bivalence. Dummett seems to think that the question of bivalence, of whether statements are 'determinately true or false, independently of our knowledge or our means of knowing'[44] arises only for statements made by means of sentences 'belonging to the less primitive strata of our language'.[45] He has no doubt that for the 'lower storeys' – e.g., for statements like 'That's red!' – bivalence obtains. Our inarticulable knowledge of what it is for such a statement to be true, presumably, is enough to make us realists about redness. For these types of statements we can have a strong sense of 'correspondence to reality' – 'strong' in that we are confident that what makes the statement true is 'reality' rather than merely ourselves. Here we have the empiricist picture, shared by Quine and Dummett, according to which language stands as a veil between us and reality, with reality punching its way through (or being known to punch its way through) only at the tips of a few sensory receptors. The farther into the upper storeys we get, on the other hand, the more doubt there is that we are in touch with the world, and the more temptation to be an 'anti-realist' in regard to certain entities – that is, to adopt a theory of meaning which explains the truth of such statements 'in terms of our capacity to recognize statements as true, and not in terms of a condition which transcends human capacities'.[46]

By contrast, if one follows Davidson, one will not know what to make of the issue between realist and anti-realist. For one will feel in touch with reality *all the time*. Our language – conceived as the web of inferential relationships between our uses of

42   Dummett, 'What Is a Theory of Meaning? (II)' in Gareth Evans and John McDowell (eds), *Truth and Meaning* (Oxford University Press, Oxford, 1976), p. 95.

43   Dummett thinks that Wittgenstein's view that 'acceptance of any principle of inference contributes to determining the meaning of words' – a view which Davidson shares – is unacceptably holistic. (See 'What Is A Theory of Meaning? (II)', p. 105). Elsewhere Dummett has said that this sort of holism leads to the view that 'a systematic theory of meaning for a language is an impossibility' and thus to the view that philosophy 'seeks to remove, not ignorance or false beliefs but conceptual confusion, and therefore has nothing positive to set in place of what it removes' (*Truth and Other Enigmas* (Harvard University Press, Cambridge, Massachusetts, 1978), p. 453). By 'a systematic theory of meaning for a language' Dummett means one which gives him 'what we are entitled to expect', viz., a handle on traditional philosophical problems. But he begs the question against Davidson when he rebuts the holism shared by Davidson and Wittgenstein on the ground that it leads to the therapeutic approach to traditional problems shared by Dewey and Wittgenstein.

44   'What Is a Theory of Meaning?' (II), p. 101.

45   Ibid., p. 100.

46   What Is a Theory of Meaning? (II), p. 116.

vocables – is not, on this view, something 'merely human' which may hide something which 'transcends human capacities'. Nor can it deceive us into thinking ourselves in correspondence with something like that when we really are not. On the contrary, using those vocables is as direct as contact with reality can get (as direct as kicking rocks, e.g.). The fallacy comes in thinking that the relationship between vocable and reality has to be piecemeal (like the relation between individual kicks and individual rocks), a matter of discrete component capacities to get in touch with discrete hunks of reality.

If one thinks that, one will, for example, agree with Plato and Dummett that there is an important philosophical question about whether there really are moral values 'out there', For Davidson, on the other hand, there is goodness out there in exactly the same trivial sense in which there is redness out there. The relevant sense is explicated by saying that the field linguist will come up with a T-sentence whose right-hand side is 'that's morally right' in just the same manner as he comes up with one whose right-hand side is 'that's red'. He will assume that insofar as the natives fail to find the same things red, or morally right, as we do, our disagreements with them will be explicable by various differences in our respective environments (or the environments of our respective ancestors).

I conclude that for Dummett no philosophy of language is adequate which does not permit the perspicuous reformulation of the epistemological and metaphysical issues discussed by the philosophical tradition. For Davidson this ability is not a desideratum. For James and Dewey, the *inability* to formulate such issues was a desideratum. I should like to attribute this latter, stronger, view to Davidson, but I have no good evidence for doing so. I commend it to him, because I think that his only recourse in arguing with those who think they have a right to expect more philosophy of language than he offers is to adopt this therapeutic stance. More specifically, all he can do is point out that Dummett's expectations stem from the habit of construing correspondence as confrontation, and then exhibit the unhappy history of this construal, a history which stretches from Plato through Locke to Quine. In the end, the issue is going to be decided on a high metaphilosophical plane – one from which we look down upon the philosophical tradition and judge its worth.

VI Davidson, Realism and Anti-Realism

If the argument of the preceding section is right, then Davidson has been put in a false position by Dummett's attempts to place him on the 'realist' side of a distinction between realism and anti-realism. That distinction, stated in terms of a distinction between truth-conditions and assertibility-conditions, will seem a plausible way of classifying philosophical doctrines only if one accepts what Michael Devitt has called Dummett's 'propositional assumption': the assumption that 'an L-speaker's understanding of a sentence of L consists in his knowing that the sentence is true-in-L in such and such circumstances.'[47] Davidson, however, thinks it hopeless to isolate such circumstances. His holism makes him reject the idea of such knowledge. Yet Dummett gives an account of Davidsonian 'truth-conditions' which is radically non-holistic. As Devitt rightly says, Dummett tries to infer from 'X knows the meaning of S' and 'The meaning of S = the truth-conditions of X' to 'S knows that the truth-conditions of X are TC', an inference

---

47   Michael Devitt, 'Dummett's Anti-Realism', *Journal of Philosophy*, 80 (1983), p. 84.

which only goes through if we construe 'S knows the meaning of S' as 'there exists an entity which is the meaning of S and X is acquainted with it.'[48] The latter construal will be made only by someone who accepts the propositional assumption.

Davidson would not accept it,[49] and therefore cannot be seen as a theorist of 'truth-conditions' in Dummett's sense. Davidson thinks that one great advantage of his view is that it gives you a theory of meaning without countenancing such things as 'meanings'. Since he agrees with Quine that a theory of meaning for a language is what comes out of empirical research into linguistic behavior, Davidson would be the first to agree with Devitt, against Dummett, that 'any propositional knowledge of a language that a person has is something over and above his competence, something gained from theorizing about the language.'[50] If we bear Davidson's holism and behaviorism in mind, he will seem the last philosopher to believe that users of S are typically able to envisage acquaintance with sets of circumstances which would conclusively verify S.

Dummett misconstrues Davidson because he himself believes that (in Devitt's words), 'The only sort of behavior that could manifest the speaker's understanding of S is that behavior which brings him into the position in which, if the condition obtains that conclusively justifies the assertion of S, he recognizes it as so doing.'[51] As Devitt says, this expresses Dummett's commitment to 'anti-holist epistemology.'[52] Dummett thinks that there are some familiar cases (e.g., so-called 'observation sentences') where there are indeed such conditions, and such acts of recognition. But for Davidson there are never any of either. So the contrast which Dummett draws between, e.g., realism about tables and anti-realism about values makes no sense for Davidson. For holists, so to speak, truth is *always* evidence-transcendent. But that is to say that X's understanding of S is *never* manifested in the kind of recognitional abilities which Dummett envisages.[53]

48   Ibid., p. 86.
49   Devitt disagrees. He says 'Davidson is open to [Dummett's] argument because he accepts the propositional assumption' (ibid., p. 90). This willingness to accept Dummett's description of Davidson seems to me a blemish in Devitt's incisive criticism of Dummett's attempt to semanticize metaphysics. (Though, as I say below, I also disagree with Devitt's claim that desemanticizing metaphysics restores the purity of that discipline. I think that doing so merely exposes its barrenness.) I suspect the reason why Devitt thinks of Davidson as accepting the propositional assumption is that Davidson, in his earlier articles, identified a theory of meaning for L with what a speaker of L understands, so identification which suggests that the speaker *does* have 'distinct component abilities' corresponding to the various T-sentences. But this identification is, as far as I can see, either incompatible with the holism I have described in the previous section or as misleading a metaphor as that billiard balls have 'internalized' the laws of mechanics.
50   Ibid., pp. 89–90.
51   Ibid., p. 91.
52   Ibid., p. 92.
53   See Paul Horwich, 'Three Forms of Realism', *Synthese*, 51 (1982), p. 199: '[Dummett's] inference from not being able to establish when *p* is true to not being able to manifest knowledge of its truth-conditions is not at all compelling. All it takes to know *p*'s truth–conditions is to understand it, and all it takes to understand *p* is the ability to use it in accordance with community norms, implicit in linguistic practice, for judging in various circumstances, the degree of confidence it should be given.' Horwich's own suggestion that we combine what he calls 'semantic realism' (the claim that truth may extend beyond our capacity to recognize it) with a 'use theory of meaning and a redundancy account of truth' (p. 186) seems to me a succinct description of

Dummett takes the upshot of Frege's linguistification of philosophy to be that the only way to make sense of a metaphysical disagreement is by semantic ascent – jacking up the old metaphysical issue into a new semantical issue. Davidson, on my interpretation, thinks that the benefit of going linguistic is that getting rid of the Cartesian mind is a first step toward eliminating the *tertia* which, by seeming to intrude between us and the world, created the old metaphysical issues in the first place. We can take the final step, and dissolve those issues for good, by not letting philosophy of language recreate the factitious contrasts in terms of which those issues were formulated, e.g., the contrast between 'objective realities' and 'useful fictions', or that between the 'ontological status' of the objects of, respectively, physics, ethics and logic. For Davidson, Quine's idea of 'ontological commitment' and Dummett's idea of 'matter of fact' are both unfortunate relics of metaphysical thought; they are among the ideas which metaphysics wove together to form the scheme-content dualism.

These ideas form such a large, mutually reinforcing, network that it is hard to pick one out as crucial. But the best candidate for being at the center of this network may be the idea repudiated in the pragmatists' thesis (3): the idea that sentences can be 'made true'. Davidson says that 'all the evidence there is is just what it takes to make our sentences or theories true. Nothing, however, no thing, makes sentences or theories true: not experience, not surface irritations, not the world, can make a sentence true.'[54] I interpret this passage as saying that the inferential relations between our belief that S and our other beliefs have nothing in particular to do with the aboutness relation which ties S to its objects. The lines of evidential force, so to speak, do not parallel the lines of referential direction. This lack of parallelism is the burden of epistemological holism. To know about the former lines is to know the language in which the beliefs are expressed. To know about the latter is to have an empirical theory about what the people who use that language mean by what they say – which is also the story about the causal roles played by their linguistic behavior in their interaction with their environment.

The urge to coalesce the justificatory story and the causal story is the old metaphysical urge which Wittgenstein helped us overcome when he told us to beware of entities called 'meanings' - or, more generally, of items relevant to the fixation of belief which are, in Davidson's words, 'Intermediate between belief and the usual objects which beliefs are about'.[55] For such entities are supposed to be *both* causes *and* justifications: entities (like sense-data or surface irritations or clear and distinct ideas) which belong both to the story which justifies me in believing that S and to the story which the observer of my linguistic behavior tells us about the causes of my belief that S. Devitt succumbs to this pre-Wittgensteinian urge when he follows Field in suggesting that we can explicate the 'intuitive idea of correspondence to a "world out there"' by making truth dependent on 'genuine reference relations between words and objective reality'.[56] Dummett succumbs to it when he thinks of a given state of the world as capable of 'conclusively

---

Davidson's strategy. (For an earlier statement of Horwich's anti-Dummett point, see P. F. Strawson's criticism of Crispin Wright: 'Scruton and Wright on Anti-Realism', *Proceedings of the Aristotelian Society*, 1977, p. 16.)

54   *Inquiries*, p. 194.
55   'A Coherence Theory…', p. 430.
56   Devitt, p. 77.

verifying' a belief. The latter notion embodies just the idea of bits of the world making a belief true which Davidson rejects.

Devitt is, I think, right in saying that, once we drop Dummett's anti-holism, the issue about 'realism' is de-semanticized. But it is also trivialized. For there is now nothing for 'realism' to name save the banal anti-idealist thesis which Devitt formulates as 'Common-sense physical entities objectively exist independently of the mental.'[57] Devitt thinks this an interesting and controversial thesis. It is an embarrassment for my interpretation of Davidson as a pragmatist that he apparently does too: witness his pledge of allegiance, cited above, to the idea of 'an objective public world which is not of our making'.[58] This formula strikes me as no more than out-dated rhetoric. For on my view the futile metaphysical struggle between idealism and physicalism was superseded, in the early years of this century, by a metaphilosophical struggle between the pragmatists (who wanted to dissolve the old metaphysical questions) and the anti-pragmatists (who still thought there was something first-order to fight about).[59] The latter struggle is *beyond* realism and anti-realism.[60]

So, despite his occasional pledges of realist faith, is Davidson.[61] On my version of the history of twentieth-century philosophy, logical empiricism was a reactionary development, one which took one step forward and two steps back. Davidson, by subverting the

---

57   Devitt, p. 76.

58   See also *Inquiries into Truth and Interpretation*, p. 198: 'In giving up the dualism of scheme and world, we do not give up the world, but re-establish unmediated touch with the familiar objects whose antics make our sentences and opinions true or false.' Yet surely these familiar objects are simply not the world which anti-idealist philosophers have tried to underwrite. The idealists had these objects too. The world which their opponents were concerned about was one which could vary independently of the antics of the familiar objects; it was something rather like the thing-in-itself. (I developed this distinction between two senses of 'world', the familiar objects on the one hand and the contrived philosophical counterpart of 'scheme' on the other, in an earlier (1972), and rather awkward, attempt to latch on to Davidson's arguments; see 'The World Well Lost', reprinted in *Consequences of Pragmatism*.)

59   I should try to account for this change by reference to (a) Hegel's demonstration that idealism eventually eats its itself up (like the Worm Ourouboros) by deconstructing the mind-matter distinction which it started out with and (b) the disenchantment with that distinction brought about by the theory of evolution. Dewey's importance, I think, lies in having brought Hegel and Darwin together. But this is a long and controversial story.

60   Current debates about Heidegger's 'destruction of the Western metaphysical tradition' and Derrida's 'deconstruction of the metaphysics of presence' form another wing of the same struggle. For some connections between Davidson and Derrida, see the essay by Samuel Wheeler in the present volume, and also his 'The Extension of Deconstruction,' forthcoming in *The Monist*. For parallels between Heidegger's attempt to get beyond both Plato and Nietzsche and Fine's and Davidson's attempts to get beyond realism and anti-realism see my 'Beyond Realism and Anti-Realism', forthcoming in the first volume ("Wo steht die sprachanalytische Philosophie heute?") of *Weiner Riche: Theimen der Philosophie*, ed. Herta Nagl-Docekal, Richard Heinrich, Ludwig Nagl and Helmet Vetter (Vienna: Oldenbourg, 1986, pp. 103–15)

61   Arthur Fine has offered the best recent account of why we ought to get beyond this struggle. See the anti-realist polemic of his 'The Natural Ontological Attitude' (cited in note 35 above) and the anti-anti-realist polemic of 'And Not Anti-Realism Either', *Nous*, 18 (1984), pp. 51–65. The latter paper (p. 54) makes the point that 'The anti-realism expressed in the idea of truth-as-acceptance is just as metaphysical and idle as the realism expressed by a correspondence theory.'

scheme-content dualism which logical empiricism took for granted, has, so to speak, kept the logic and dropped the empiricism (or better, kept the attention to language and dropped the epistemology). He has thus enabled us to use Frege's insights to confirm the holistic and pragmatist doctrines of Dewey. His work makes possible the kind of synthesis of pragmatism and positivism which Morton White foresaw as a possible 'reunion in philosophy'.[62] From the point of view of such a synthesis, the Peirce–Frege turn from consciousness to language (and from transcendental to formal logic) was a stage in the dissolution of such traditional problems as 'realism vs. anti-realism', rather than a step towards a clearer formulation of those problems.[63]

On my interpretation of Davidson, his position pretty well coincides with Fine's 'Natural Onfological Attitude'.

Frederick Stoutland ('Realism and Anti-Realism in Davidson's Philosophy of Language', Part I in *Critica* XIV (August, 1982) and Part II in *Critica* XIV (December, 1982)) has given excellent reasons for resisting attempts (by, e.g., John McDowell and Mark Platts) to construe Davidson as a realist. However, I think that he is wrong in construing him as an anti-realist who holds that 'sentences are not true in virtue of their extra-linguistic objects: they are true in virtue of their role in human practise' (Part I, p. 21). To repeat, Davidson thinks that we should drop the question 'In virtue of what are sentences true?' Therefore, as I said earlier, he does not wish to be associated with pragmatism, for too many people calling themselves 'pragmatists' (including myself) have said things like 'a sentence is true in virtue of its helping people achieve goals and realize intentions' (Stoutland, Part II, p. 36). Despite my disagreement with Stoutland, however, I am much indebted to his discussion. In particular, his remark (Part II, p. 22) that Davidson opposes the idea that it is the 'intentionality of thoughts – their being directed to objects, independently of whether they are true or false – which accounts for the relation of language to reality' seems to me an admirably clear and succinct expression of the difference between Davidson's holism and the 'building-block' approach common to Russell, Husserl, Kripke and Searle.

62   See Morton White, *Toward Reunion in Philosophy* (Harvard University Press, Cambridge, Massachusetts, 1956).

63   I am very grateful to Robert Brandom, Alan Donagan and Arthur Fine for comments on the penultimate version of this paper. I made substantial changes as a result of their comments, but have not tried to acknowledge my indebtedness in every case.

8

Twenty-Five Years After

I wrote "Metaphilosophical Difficulties of Linguistic Philosophy" in 1965. In 1975 I took up some of the same topics in a review of Ian Hacking's *Why Does Language Matter to Philosophy?* It is now 1990, and I have taken the occasion of the translation of these two earlier essays into Spanish to reread them.

What I find most striking about my 1965 essay is how seriously I took the phenomenon of the "linguistic turn," how portentous it then seemed to me. I am startled, embarrassed, and amused to reread the following passage:

> Linguistic philosophy, over the last thirty years, has succeeded in putting the entire philosophical tradition, from Parmenides through Descartes and Hume to Bradley and Whitehead, on the defensive. It has done so by a careful and thorough scrutiny of the ways in which traditional philosophers have used language in the formulation of their problems. This achievement is sufficient to place this period among the great ages of the history of philosophy.

That last sentence now strikes me as merely the attempt of a thirty-three-year-old philosopher to convince himself that he had had the luck to be born at the right time – to persuade himself that the disciplinary matrix in which he happened to find himself (philosophy as taught in most English-speaking universities in the 1960s) was more than just one more philosophical school, one more tempest in an academic teapot.

It now seems to me to have been little more than that. The controversies which I discussed with such earnestness in 1965 already seemed quaint in 1975. By now they seem positively antique. The most eminent of the philosophers now teaching at Oxford, Bernard Williams, writes of "'linguistic analysis', that now distant philosophical style..."[1] The slogan that "the problems of philosophy are problems of language" now strikes me as confused, for two reasons. The first is that I am no longer inclined to view "the problems of philosophy" as naming a natural kind – no longer inclined to think of "philosophy" as (in the words I quoted from Stuart Hampshire at the end of my 1965 essay) "one of man's recognizable activities." The second is that I am no longer inclined to think that there is

Richard M. Rorty, "Twenty-Five Years After," pp. 371–4 in Richard M. Rorty (ed.), *The Linguistic Turn: Essays in Philosophical Method*, 2nd edn, © 1967, 1992 by Chicago University Press. Reprinted with permission of Chicago University Press.

1 Williams, "The Need to Be Sceptical," *Times Literary Supplement*, February 16–22, 1990, 163.

such a thing as "language" in any sense which makes it possible to speak of "problems of language." In what follows, I shall briefly discuss each of these two reasons.

The only natural kind which might usefully be designated by the term "the problems of philosophy" is, I think, the set of interlinked problems posed by representationalist theories of knowledge – the problems connected with what Hacking called "interfacing." These are problems about the relation between mind and reality, or language and reality, viewed as the relation between a medium of representation and what is purportedly represented. In my review of Hacking, I suggested that the Quine-Davidson assault on the distinctions between analytic and synthetic judgments, conceptual questions and empirical questions, language and fact, had made it difficult to formulate such problems – difficult to think of the relation between sentences and the world as a representational one.[2] But at that time (1975) I had not yet realized how radical Davidson's attack on traditional conceptions of language was – even though Davidson had by then published his remarkable paper "On the Very Idea of a Conceptual Scheme."[3]

In that seminal paper, Davidson urged that we give up the "dualism of scheme and world," and thus the idea that different languages represent the world from different perspectives. In later papers, he has made his attack on representationalism more explicit – saying, for example:

> Beliefs are true or false, but they represent nothing. It is good to be rid of representations, and with them the correspondence theory of truth, for it is thinking that there are representations that engenders thoughts of relativism.[4]

If one gives up thinking that there are representations, then one will have little interest in the relation between mind and the world or language and the world. So one will lack interest in either the old disputes between realists and idealists or the contemporary quarrels within analytic philosophy about "realism" and "anti-realism." For the latter quarrels presuppose that bits of the world "make sentences true," and that these sentences in turn represent those bits. Without these presuppositions, we would not be interested in trying to distinguish between those true sentences which correspond to "facts of the matter" and those which do not (the distinction around which realist-vs.-antirealist controversies revolve).[5]

---

2   In this piece, however, I was still representationalist enough to say that "we *made* languages to represent reality." This was a mistake. I should not have said that the notion of language representing reality was unproblematic, but rather that it was unnecessary.

3   This essay was published in *Proceedings and Addresses of the American Philosophical Association* 47 (1974), and reprinted in Davidson's *Inquiries into Truth and Interpretation* (Oxford, Clarendon Press, 1984).

4   Davidson, "The Myth of the Subjective," in *Relativism: Interpretation and Confrontation*, ed. Michael Krausz (Notre Dame: University of Notre Dame Press, 1989), 165–66.

5   I discuss the relations between representationalism and the realist-vs.-antirealist controversies which dominate contemporary analytic philosophy in more detail in the Introduction to my *Objectivity, Relativism and Truth* (Cambridge: Cambridge University Press, 1990), and also in my Introduction to Joseph Murphy, *Pragmatism: From Peirce to Davidson* (Boulder: Westview Press, 1990).

Davidson shows us how to give up the notion of "truth-makers" as well as the notion of representation.[6] He has shown how to escape from one of the pictures which, as Wittgenstein put it, "hold us captive" – where "us" means "most philosophers from Descartes to the present." But the problems produced by the notion that true sentences are representations of reality and are made true by reality cannot be identified with "the problems of philosophy." They are, at best, the majority of the problems of philosophy discussed by the nineteenth-century philosophy textbooks. There are lots of thinkers – e.g., Plato, Aristotle, Vico, Hegel, Marx, Nietzsche, Heidegger – who have discussed lots of problems which can be only tenuously and tangentially connected with representationalist problems. There is, I think, no way to bring all these thinkers together with Descartes, Kant, and Frege into a common enterprise called "philosophy" – a "recognizable human activity" with a continuous history.

If there was ever any truth in the slogan "the problems of philosophy are problems of language" it was that the particular problems *about representation* which philosophers have discussed were pseudo-problems, created by a bad description of human knowledge, one that turned out to be optional and replaceable. I argued in my *Philosophy and the Mirror of Nature* (1979) that these problems were characteristic of post-Cartesian rather than of pre-Cartesian philosophy, and that it was only after Kant that they achieved sufficient prominence to be taken as central to an autonomous academic discipline called "philosophy." Though Heidegger is certainly right that the Greeks paved the way for Descartes, nevertheless what Heidegger calls "the transformation of man into a *subiectum*" is a distinctively Cartesian accomplishment, and only with that transformation do problems of representation come to seem central.

I should now want to argue that the philosophers of the twentieth century – Dewey, Heidegger, and Wittgenstein above all, but also Quine, Sellars, and Davidson – have shown us how to avoid representationalism. But they did so not by "dissolving" old problems, not by showing that they rested upon "conceptual confusions" or upon a "misunderstanding of language," but rather by suggesting a new way of describing knowledge and inquiry. The only sense in which this suggestion was "linguistic" is the sense in which the change from a Ptolemaic–Aristotelian cosmology to a Copernican–Newtonian one was a change in "language." This sense is very attenuated, for in both cases one could as easily speak of a change in theory as of a change in language. (Indeed, it is central to Davidson's position that it does not matter which of the two one says – that it is a matter of indifference whether one speaks of "a better theory" or of "a more perspicuous language.")

The idea that philosophical problems can be dissolved by detecting the "logic of our language" already seemed to me, in 1965, untenable. But I was still, alas, attached to the idea that there was something called "linguistic method in philosophy." I now find it impossible to isolate such a method – to specify a procedure of inquiry (a "logical" or "linguistic" as opposed to a "phenomenological" or "ontological" procedure) which distinguishes late Wittgenstein from early Heidegger, or Davidson's *Inquiries into Truth and Interpretation* from Dewey's *Experience and Nature*. Nevertheless, I should claim that Davidson largely succeeds where Dewey largely failed – succeeds in the attempt to replace a representationalist picture of knowledge and inquiry with a non-representationalist one.

---

6   I try to spell out the way in which he has done this in various essays included in *Objectivity, Relativism and Truth*, in particular in "Non-Reductive Physicalism" and "Pragmatism, Davidson and Truth."

So, insofar as the linguistic turn made a distinctive contribution to philosophy I think that it was not a metaphilosophical one at all. Its contribution was, instead, to have helped shift from talk about experience as a medium of representation to talk of language as such a medium – a shift which, as it turned out, made it easier to set aside the notion of representation itself. Dewey's attempt to set aside the problematic of realism and idealism had involved him in an obscure and dubious attempt to see "experience" and "nature" as two descriptions of the same events and in the idea that "experience become true." But philosophers like Davidson, who speak of sentences instead of experiences, have an easier time.

The term "experience," as used by philosophers such as Kant and Dewey, was, like Locke's term "idea," ambiguous between "sense-impression" and "belief." The term "sentence," used by philosophers in the Fregean tradition, lacks this ambiguity. Once the philosophy of language was freed from what Quine and Davidson call "the dogmas of empiricism" with which Russell, Carnap, and Ayer (though not Frege) had entangled it, sentences were no longer thought of as expressions of experience nor as representations of extra-experiential reality. Rather, they were thought of as strings of marks and noises used by human beings in the development and pursuit of social practices – practices which enabled people to achieve their ends, ends which do not include "representing reality as it is in itself."[7]

Developing this picture of the role which sentences and sentential attitudes play in human life leads Davidson to say that

> We have erased the boundary between knowing a language and knowing our way around in the world generally.
> ... there is no such thing as a language, not if a language is anything like what many philosophers and linguists have supposed.... We must give up the idea of a clearly defined shared structure to which language-users appeal and then apply to cases.... We should give up the attempt to illuminate how we communicate by appeal to conventions.[8]

Davidson here brings to its logical conclusion the naturalism, the holism, and the antidualism characteristic of both Dewey and Quine. He gives up the idea of "a language" as a structured medium of representation, capable of standing in determinate relations to a distinct entity called "the world." He thereby shows that the basic idea of linguistic philosophy as I defined it in 1965 – the idea that philosophy could be advanced by studying a topic called "language" or "our language" – was deeply flawed, deeply implicated in a *non*-naturalistic picture of human knowledge and inquiry, one which still incorporated a "scheme-content" distinction, the distinction which Davidson calls the "third, and perhaps the last, dogma of empiricism."

This completes my sketch of my reasons for believing that neither "philosophy" nor "language" names anything unified, continuous, or structured, and thus of why I should

---

7   On the relation between representationalist and social-practice theories of truth and knowledge, see Robert Brandom, "Truth and Assertibility," *Journal of Philosophy* 73 (1976), and "Heidegger's Categories in *Being and Time*," *The Monist* 66 (1983), as well as my "Representation, Social Practise, and Truth," *Philosophical Studies* 54 (1988) (reprinted in my *Objectivity, Relativism and Truth*).

8   Davidson, "A Nice Derangement of Epitaphs," in *Truth and Interpretation: Perspective on the Philosophy of Donald Davidson,* ed. Ernest LePore (Oxford, Blackwell, 1986), 445–46.

now resist talk of "the problems of philosophy" or of "linguistic problems." I am often accused of being an "end of philosophy" thinker, and I should like to take this occasion to reemphasize (as I tried to do on the final page of *Philosophy and the Mirror of Nature*) that philosophy is just not the sort of thing that can have an end – it is too vague and amorphous a term to bear the weight of predications like "beginning" or "end." What does have a beginning, and may now be coming to an end, is three hundred years' worth of attempts to bridge the gap which the Cartesian, representationalist picture of knowledge and inquiry led us to imagine existed.

I said in my review of Hacking:

> It may be that what Hacking calls the death of meaning at the hands of Quine, Wittgenstein, Davidson and Feyerabend brings with it the death of philosophy as a discipline with a method of its own.

I still believe something like this. Though I do not think that philosophy can end, centuries-old philosophical research programs can end, and have in the past. (Think of Thomism.) So might the idea that philosophy is a special field of inquiry distinguished by a special method. The end of this latter idea would, as far as I can see, do culture no harm. If "philosophy" comes to be viewed as continuous with science (as Quine wishes it to be) on the one hand and as continuous with poetry (as Heidegger and Derrida often suggest it is) on the other, then our descendants will be less concerned with questions about "the method of philosophy" or about "the nature of philosophical problems." The fifty-year history of linguistic philosophy, a history which is now behind us, suggests that such questions are likely to prove unprofitable.[9]

9 To say that linguistic philosophy is now behind us is of course not to say that analytic philosophy is behind us, but only to say that most of those who call themselves "analytic philosophers" would now reject the epithet "linguistic philosophers" and would not describe themselves as "applying linguistic methods." Analytic philosophy is now the name not of the application of such methods to philosophical problems, but simply of the particular set of problems being discussed by philosophy professors in certain parts of the world. These problems, at the moment, center around problems of "realism" and "antirealism" – a fact which we Davidsonians, of course, deplore. What they will center around a decade from now, I should not wish to predict. Since analytic philosophers are typically trained to pay little attention to the history of thought, and since their own sense of the function and cultural role of their discipline therefore lacks an anchor to windward, the direction of their inquiries tends to shift from decade to decade.

9

Putnam and the Relativist Menace

In his *Realism with a Human Face*, Hilary Putnam[1] says that he is "often asked just where I disagree with Rorty" (RHF 20). I am often asked the converse question. We are asked these questions because we agree on a lot of points that a lot of other philosophers do not accept.

I

Here are five points on which I whole-heartedly concur with Putnam:

(I)   … elements of what we call 'language' or 'mind' *penetrate so deeply into what we call "reality" that the very project of representing ourselves as being 'mapper's of something 'language-independent' is fatally compromised from the start.* Like Relativism, but in a different way, Realism is an impossible attempt to view the world from Nowhere (RHF 28).

(II)   [We should] accept the position we are fated to occupy in any case, the position of beings who cannot have a view of the world that does not reflect our interests and values, but who are, for all that, committed to regarding some views of the world – and, for that matter, some interests and values – as better than others (RHF 178).

(III) What Quine called 'the indeterminacy of translation' should rather be viewed as the *'interest relativity of translation'* … '[I]nterest relativity' contrasts with absoluteness, not with objectivity. It can be objective that an interpretation or an explanation is the correct one, *given* the interests which are relevant in the context (RHF 210).

(IV)   The heart of pragmatism, it seems to me – of James' and Dewey's pragmatism, if not of Peirce's – was the insistence on the supremacy of the agent point of view. If we find that we must take a certain point of view, use a certain 'conceptual

Richard M. Rorty, "Putnam and the Relativist Menace," *Journal of Philosophy*, vol. 90 (9), September 1993: 443–61, © 1993 The Journal of Philosophy, Inc. Reprinted with permission from the *Journal of Philosophy* and the Estate of Richard Rorty.

1   Cambridge: Harvard, 1990. Hereafter referred to as RHF.

system', when we are engaged in practical activity, in the widest sense of 'practical activity', then we must not simultaneously advance the claim that it is not really 'the way things are in themselves'.[2]

(V)   To say, as [Bernard] Williams sometimes does, that convergence to one big picture is required by the very concept of knowledge is sheer dogmatism. ... It is, indeed, the case that ethical knowledge cannot claim absoluteness; but that is because the notion of absoluteness is incoherent (RHF 171; roman numerals added).

Since we agree on all this, I have long been puzzled about what keeps us apart – and in particular about why Putnam thinks of me as a "cultural relativist."[3] I am grateful to Putnam for taking up this question explicitly in the pages of *Realism with a Human Face* (pages 18–26). He begins as follows:

> For Rorty, as for the French thinkers whom he admires, two ideas seem gripping. (1) The failure of our philosophical 'foundations' is a failure of the whole culture, and accepting that we were wrong in wanting or thinking that we could have a foundation requires us to be *philosophical revisionists*. By this I mean that, for Rorty or Foucault or Derrida, the failure of foundationalism makes a difference to how we are allowed to talk in ordinary life – a difference as to whether and when we are allowed to use words like 'know', 'objective', 'fact', and 'reason'. The picture is that philosophy was not a reflection *on* the culture, a reflection some of whose ambititious projects failed, but a *basis*, a sort of pedestal, on which the culture rested, and which has been abruptly yanked out. Under the pretense that philosophy is no longer 'serious' there lies hidden a gigantic seriousness. If I am right, Rorty hopes to be a doctor to the modern soul (RHF 19–20).

I do not think that I have ever written anything that suggests that I wish to alter ordinary ways of using 'know', 'objective', 'fact', and 'reason'. Like Bishop Berkeley, William James, Putnam, and most other paradox-mongering philosophers (except maybe Alfred Korzybski; see RHF 120), I have urged that we continue to speak with the vulgar while offering a different philosophical gloss on this speech than that offered by the realist tradition.[4] I have written at tedious length *against* the idea that philosophy has been a pedestal on which our culture rested. In particular, I have complained over and over again about Martin Heidegger's and Jacques Derrida's overestimation of the cultural importance of philosophy.[5] So on this first point I think Putnam is just wrong about what I say.

2   *The Many Faces of Realism* (La Salle, IL: Open Court, 1987), p. 83.
3   For Putnam's use of this term, see his "Why Reason Can't Be Naturalized," in *Realism and Reason* (New York: Cambridge, 1983), pp. 229–47.
4   This suggestion does not conflict with (IV) above. The distinction between the vulgar and the philosophical way of speaking is not an appearance–reality distinction, but a distinction between contexts in which a word is used. Contexts are individuated by the questions regarded as relevant in regard to statements made using the word. Some questions about the sun's motion are asked in astrophysics which are not asked when admiring dawns or sunsets; some questions about truth are asked in philosophy which are not asked in the market place.
5   See, especially, the closing pages of "Philosophy as Science, as Metaphor and as Politics," a lecture given in 1985, and of "Deconstruction and Circumvention," in *Critical Inquiry* (1984). Both are reprinted in my *Essays on Heidegger and Others* (New York: Cambridge, 1991), pp. 21–6, 104–6.

I doubt that my writings evince any more, or any less, desire to be a doctor to the modern soul than do Putnam's own. Both of us think that getting rid of the idea of "the view from Nowhere" – the idea of a sort of knowing that has nothing to do with agency, values, or interests – might have considerable cultural importance. It would probably not change our day-to-day ways of speaking, but it might well, in the long run, make some practical differences. For changes of opinion among philosophical professors sometimes do, after a time, make a difference to the hopes and fears of non-philosophers.

The second idea which Putnam says I find gripping, one which reveals what he calls my "analytic past," is evinced by the fact that:

> (2) when he [Rorty] rejects a philosophical controversy, as for example, he rejects the "realism/antirealism" controversy, or the "emotive/cognitive" controversy, his rejection is expressed in a Carnapian tone of voice – he *scorns* the controversy (RHF 20).

Here I think Putnam has a good point. There *is* a tone of Carnapian scorn in some of my writings (particularly in *Philosophy and the Mirror of Nature*[6]), and there should not be. I should not speak, as I sometimes have, of "pseudo-problems," but rather of problematics and vocabularies that might have proven to be of value, but in fact did not. I should not have spoken of "unreal" or "confused" philosophical distinctions, but rather of distinctions whose employment has proved to lead nowhere, proved to be more trouble than they were worth. For pragmatists like Putnam and me, the question should always be "What use is it?" rather than "Is it real?" or "Is it confused?" Criticism of other philosophers' distinctions and problematics should charge relative inutility, rather than "meaninglessness" or "illusion" or "incoherence."

On the other hand, I think that Putnam is too kind to the problematic and vocabulary of modern philosophy when he follows Stanley Cavell in saying that "the illusions that philosophy spins are illusions that belong to the nature of human life itself" (RHF 20). This notion appears prominently in James Conant's long, helpful, introduction to *Realism with a Human Face*. Conant says, for example:

> unless one carefully examines the character of a given philosophical position's seductiveness to those who are attracted to it, as well as the character of the disappointment it provokes in those who reject it – what allows for it to appear initially so innocent and yet the implications of its failure so precipitous – one's gesture of rejecting the picture will inevitably represent a further form of participation in it and victimization by it (RHF lv).

I do not see how Putnam, Cavell, or Conant could tell whether, for example, the distinction between "our experience" and "the external world" is among "the illusions that belong to the nature of human life itself," or is as ephemeral as the distinction between the superlunary quintessence and the four sublunary elements has proved to be (or as I hope the distinction between the divine and the human, or that between realism and antirealism, may prove to be). The *nature* of human life? For all the ages to come? Talk about *the* nature of human life does not fit in well with the pragmatism sketched in (i)–(v) above, nor with Putnam's view (cited below) that "our norms and standards of

6   Princeton: University Press, 1980.

warranted assertibility … evolve in time." As those norms and standards evolve, so does our notion of what constitutes a live philosophical option, as well as our sense of the difference between such options and futile, "scholastic," quibbles.

When Conant speaks of the "inevitability" of participation and victimization, he is drawing on an analogy between philosophical therapy and psychoanalysis – an analogy which turns on the notion of "the return of the repressed," a notion invoked by both Cavell and Derrida. The idea is that it is terribly difficult, and probably impossible, to avoid "complicity" with phallogocentrism (Derrida), or skepticism (Cavell), or some other leitmotif of the philosophical tradition. These themes are supposed to be as hard to stop harping on as are beliefs about one's parents acquired in early childhood.

This analogy with psychoanalysis strikes me as a symptom of professional deformation – of the same urge to exalt the importance of the topics listed in the "Philosophy 101" syllabus as is evinced by the suggestion that philosophy has been the pedestal on which culture rests.[7] Cavell and Derrida of course *might* be right: maybe these philosophical themes *will* always creep back in disguise, maybe they *are* ineradicable kinks, maybe they *will* always hunt us down the arches of the years. But we shall never find out whether this is the case unless we do our level best to give them the slip, to forget them actively by getting involved with new themes, and by talking in ways that make it hard for those old themes to come up.[8] Questions of whether we are unconsciously participating in, and being victimized by, the old, or instead have succeeded in making it new, should I think be referred to future intellectual historians.[9] There is not much point in trying to answer these questions now.

7   There is a difference between hoping for the end of "Philosophy 101" and hoping for the end of philosophy. I am still thought of (as by Putnam, RHF 19) as recommending "the end of philosophy," despite my explicit rejection of this label on the last page of *Philosophy and the Mirror of Nature*, and my attempts in subsequent writings to scrape it off. Perhaps it may clarify matters if I say that I hope that we never stop reading, e.g., Plato, Aristotle, Kant, Hegel, Dewey, and Heidegger, but also hope that we may, sooner or later, stop trying to sucker the freshmen into taking an interest in "the problem of the external world" and "the problem of other minds."

8   Conant, in his gloss on Putnam's remarks about my Carnapian scorn, says that my "over-whelming emotion, when faced with the traditional problems of philosophy, is one of impatience – a desire to get on to something more fruitful" (RHF li) and that "Rorty's recommendation appears to be that one should leave the fly in the fly-bottle and get on with something more interesting." Conant here gets me exactly right. Despite my regret for my tone of Carnapian scorn, I have no apology to make for my impatience. For some examples of this impatience, see the remarks at pp. 2 and 12 of my *Objectivity, Relativism and Truth* (New York: Cambridge, 1991) about British and American philosophers' continued preoccupation with issues about realism and antirealism, a preoccupation I see as a symptom of cultural lag and parochial education. I am impatient to see what culture would look like when these issues come to seem as obsolete as do controversies about the nature of the elements of the Eucharist. The thing I like best about contemporary "Continental" philosophy is that our colleagues beyond the Channel seem to be glimpsing such a culture.

9   For an example of the sort of debate between intellectual historians I have in mind, see Hans Blumenberg's criticisms of Karl Löwith's claim that the problems of contemporary secular culture are simply the return of repressed theological problems; *The Legitimacy of the Modern Age*, Robert Wallace, trans. (Cambridge: MIT, 1983).

II

So much for my doubts that Putnam, in his description of these two ideas, gets at the underlying difference between us. But before leaving those ideas, let me offer a preliminary suggestion about what this underlying difference is. This suggestion has to do with the fervent physicalism which he and I once shared, and of which, as he rightly says, I still retain a trace.

What I retain is the conviction that Darwinism provides a useful vocabulary in which to formulate the pragmatist position summarized in (i)–(v) above. By 'Darwinism' I mean a story about humans as animals with special organs and abilities: about how certain features of the human throat, hand, and brain enabled humans to start developing increasingly complex social practices, by batting increasingly complex noises back and forth. According to this story, these organs and abilities, and the practices they made possible, have a lot to do with who we are and what we want, but they no more put us in a *representational* relation to an intrinsic nature of things than do the anteater's snout or the bower-bird's skill at weaving. I see Dewey as having used this story to start freeing us from representationalist notions, and I see Putnam and Donald Davidson as continuing this Deweyan initiative.[10] I regard Putnam's continuing insistence on using the term 'representation' as a mistake. I follow Davidson in thinking that "It is good to be rid of representations, and with them the correspondence theory of truth, for it is thinking that there are representations which engenders thoughts of relativism."[11]

Putnam, however, does not feel comfortable with this picture of humans-as-slightly-more-complicated-animals. It strikes him, as does physicalism, as scientistic and reductionist. But these latter epithets would only apply to someone who argued, "Because Darwin tells us how things really and truly are, it behooves us to adjust our self-image to suit." I do not wish to argue in this way. Rather, I am suggesting, in the spirit of Deweyan experimentalism, that it behooves us to give the self-image Darwin suggested to us a try, in the hope of having fewer philosophical problems on our hands.

The antinaturalist self-images that were suggested to us by, among others, Plato and Kant have served us well, but they are hard to reconcile with Darwin's account of our origins. I think Dewey was right in suggesting that we should try to get along without the remnants of those earlier self-images. We should see what happens if (in Jean-Paul

10   Davidson, unlike Putnam, explicitly repudiates representationalism. I discuss this difference between them in my introduction to Joseph Murphy, *Pragmatism: From Peirce to Davidson* (Boulder: Westview, 1990). I suggest there that Dewey's unhappy attempt to construct a "metaphysics of experience" held him back from following out the implications of his pragmatism and of his Darwinism, but that Davidson has now enabled us to drop James's and Dewey's claim to have "described experience as it really is" (as opposed to the – supposedly inaccurate – way in which John Locke and David Hume described it). He has done this by showing how we can eliminate the middle man ("experience") that was supposed to intervene between language and the world, and also by showing how to drop the notion of language as a medium that intervenes between "subject" and "object." This view of Davidson is developed in my "Non-Reductive Physicalism," included in *Objectivity, Relativism and Truth*. I discuss the relation between Darwin and Dewey at some length in my "Dewey Between Hegel and Darwin," in *Modernism and the Human Sciences*, Dorothy Ross, ed. (Baltimore: Johns Hopkins UP, 1993).

11   Davidson, "The Myth of the Subjective," in *Relativism: Interpretation and Confrontation*, Michael Krausz, ed. (Notre Dame: University Press, 1989), pp. 165–6.

Sartre's words) "we attempt to draw the full conclusions from a consistently atheist position," a position in which such phrases as 'the nature of human life' no longer distract us from the absence of a God's-eye view. The first step in conducting this experiment should be to set aside the shards of the subject–object, scheme–content, and reality–appearance distinctions, and to think of our relation to the rest of the universe in purely causal, as opposed to representationalist, terms (the same way in which we think of the anteater's and the bower-bird's relation to the rest of the universe). I think that my differences with Putnam come down, in the end, to his unhappiness with such a purely causal picture. I shall return to this point at the end of this article.

III

After listing the two leading ideas I have already discussed, Putnam suggests that he and I have different concepts of warrant, and that it would help if I indicated "which of the following principles ... he [Rorty] can accept." His list of principles goes like this:

(1)   In ordinary circumstances, there is usually a fact of the matter as to whether the statements people make are warranted or not.
(2)   Whether a statement is warranted or not is independent of whether the majority of one's cultural peers would *say* it is warranted or unwarranted.
(3)   Our norms or standards of warranted assertibility are historical products; they evolve in time.
(4)   Our norms and standards always reflect our interests and values. Our picture of intellectual flourishing is part of, and only makes sense as part of, our picture of human flourishing in general.
(5)   Our norms and standards of *anything* – including warranted assertibility – are capable of reform. There are better and worse norms and standards (RHF 21).

I have no trouble with (3)–(5), but Putnam says that I am "certain to disagree" with (1). I am not sure whether I do or not, and I am equally unsure about (2). As to (1), I certainly agree that it is usually as "objective" (in the sense of 'objective' which – in (III) above – Putnam distinguishes from 'absolute') whether or not S is warranted in asserting p as whether or not she is over five feet tall. This is because I view warrant as a sociological matter, to be ascertained by observing the reception of S's statement by her peers. But the term 'matter of fact' gives me pause. Does 'There is a matter of fact about ...' just mean that we can observe the behavior of S's peers and determine whether. ...? If so, I can happily embrace (1). But it must mean something more than that, or Putnam would not be so sure that I would disagree with it. There being a fact of the matter about warranted assertibility must, for Putnam, be something *more* than our ability to figure out whether S was in a good position, given the interests and values of herself and her peers, to assert p.

But what more, given (i)–(v) above, can it be? Presumably it is whatever makes it possible for a statement not to be warranted even though a majority of one's peers say it is. *Is* that possible? Is (2) true? Well, maybe a *majority* can be wrong. But suppose everybody in the community, except for one or two dubious characters notorious for making assertions even stranger than p, thinks S must be a bit crazy. They think this even after patiently sitting through S's defense of p, and after sustained attempts to talk her out of it. Might S still be *warranted* in asserting *p*? Only if there were some way of determining warrant *sub specie aeternitatis,* some natural order of reasons which determines, quite apart from *S*'s ability to justify *p* to those around her, whether she is *really* justified in holding *p*.[12] I do not see how one could reconcile the claim that there is this nonsociological sort of justification with (I)–(v).

P might of course be *true*. For *S* may be the unhonored prophet of some social movement or intellectual revolution whose time has not yet come. But *warranted*? I cannot see how Putnam could support (2) except by running 'warranted' together with 'true' – running together a claim supported by examining the behavior of *S*'s peers and a claim to which this behavior is irrelevant. He and I presumably agree that lots of (praiseworthy and blameworthy) social movements and intellectual revolutions get started by people making *un*warranted assertions, assertions which only begin to get warranted as (in Putnam's words) "our norms and standards of warranted assertibility … evolve."

Putnam's discussion of his five principles (RHF 22) is a bit confusing because he switches targets, substituting "the Relativist" for me. I entirely agree with, and fervently applaud, his relativist-bashing remark: "Relativism, just as much as Realism, assumes that one can stand within one's language and outside it at the same time" (RHF 23). But I do not see how this remark is relevant to my own, explicitly ethnocentric, position.[13]

Things get clearer, however, when Putnam, later on the same page, zeroes in on my claim that reforms in our standards of warranted assertibility are not "better by reference to a previously known standard, but just better in the sense that they come to seem clearly better than their predecessors."[14] He says this passage amounts "to a rejection, rather than a clarification, of the notion of 'reforming' the ways we are doing and thinking invoked in my fifth principle" (RHF 23). Putnam sees me as relativistic because I can appeal to no "fact of the matter" to adjudicate between the possible world in which the Nazis won, inhabited by people for whom the Nazis' racism seems common sense and our egalitarian tolerance crazy, and the world in which we won and the Nazis' racism seems crazy.

I cannot, indeed, appeal to such a "fact of the matter," any more than a species of animal that is in danger of losing its ecological niche to another species, and thus faces

---

12   On the skepticism-inducing role of the belief that there is such a natural order of reasons – a pattern of justification or warranting which is that of no particular human community but is somehow nature's own – see the sustained polemic against the very idea of "context-independent relations of epistemological priority" in Michael Williams, *Unnatural Doubts: Epistemological Realism and the Basis of Scepticism* (Cambridge: Blackwell, 1991).

13   For the difference between relativism and ethnocentrism, see my 1984 paper "Solidarity or Objectivity?" reprinted in *Objectivity, Relativism and Truth*, pp. 21–34. See especially fn. 13 at p. 30: "there is no truth in relativism, but this much truth in ethnocentrism: we cannot justify our beliefs (in physics, ethics, or any other area) to everybody, but only to those beliefs overlap ours to some appropriate extent." This paper was, in part, a reply to Putnam's criticism of my "relativism" in his *Reason, Truth and History*. My reply was based on taking seriously Putnam's famous rhetorical question, "We should use somebody *else's* conceptual scheme?"

14   This quote is from the following passage in my *Consequences of Pragmatism* (Minneapolis: Minnesota UP, 1982): " [the pragmatist] does think that in the process of playing vocabularies and cultures off against each other, we produce new and better ways of talking and acting – not better by reference to a previously known standard, but just better in the sense that they come to *seem* clearly better than their predecessors" (p. xxxvii).

extinction, can find a "fact of the matter" to settle the question of which species has the right to the niche in question. But neither, as far as I can see, can Putnam.

The problem for Putnam is that he must both maintain his anticonvergence thesis ((v) above) and make sense of the notion of "truth as idealized rational acceptability." He has invoked the latter notion as a defense against my evil twin, "the Relativist," for years, and does so again in *Realism with a Human Face* (page 41). But I cannot see what 'idealized rational acceptability' can mean except "acceptability to an ideal community." Nor can I see how, given that no such community is going to have a God's eye view, this ideal community can be anything more than *us* as we should like to be. Nor can I see what 'us' can mean here except: us educated, sophisticated, tolerant, wet liberals,[15] the people who are always willing to hear the other side, to think out all the implications, etc. – the sort of people, in short, who both Putnam and I hope, at our best, to be. Identifying 'idealized rational acceptability' with 'acceptability to *us* at our best' is just what I had in mind when I said that pragmatists should be ethnocentrists rather than relativists.[16]

If this is not the ideal community Putnam has in mind, then he must either propose another one or give some sense to 'idealized rational acceptability' which is not acceptability to an ideal community. I cannot see any promise in the latter alternative. The former alternative seems to leave him with no option but to fall back on Peirce and the notion of "the community of inquirers at the ideal end of inquiry" – the speakers of Peircish, the people whose norms and standards of warranted assertibility embody what Wilfrid Sellars called "CSP" (short for "Conceptual System Peirce"). But his refusal to grant to Williams that the notion of knowledge entails that of convergence to a single result forbids Putnam to make this Peirce-like move.[17] For once we strip 'idealized' of reference to some process built into any and every inquiry – something like Peirce's own "growth of Thirdness," something which will guide us toward CSP along convergent lines – 'idealized' adds nothing to 'rational acceptability'. If there is no such guidance system built into human beings qua human then the terms 'warranted', 'rational acceptable', etc., will always invite the

---

15 Putnam grants that I am as wet a liberal as they come, but adds that I seem, at times, "ever so slightly decadent"; "Liberation Philosophy," *London Review of Books*, 8/5 (March 1986), p. 5. I am here concerned to show that, as far as decadence goes, there is little to choose between us. Our common commitment to (i)–(iv) makes it impossible for either of us to find an Archimedean fulcrum. Our commitment to (v) makes it impossible to substitute a Peircean *focus imaginarius* for such a fulcrum.

16 See the passage cited in fn. 6 above. The same point comes out in my discussion of Davidson's explication of 'true' in terms of "language I know," and of the ineluctability of self-referential indexicals; *Objectivity, Relativism and Truth*, pp. 157–9. It comes out yet again when I argue that Jürgen Habermas's term 'ideal communication situation' is just an abbreviation for "the way of deciding public issues characteristic of free twentieth-century constitutional democracies, when they are at their rare best"; see my *Contingency, Irony and Solidarity* (New York: Cambridge, 1989), p. 84; and my "Habermas, Derrida and the Functions of Philosophy," forthcoming in *Revue Internationale de Philosophie*.

17 For details about the problems encountered by such a Peirce-like move (a move Putnam and I both made in our salad days), see Michael Williams, "Coherence, Justification and Truth," *Review of Metaphysics*, XXXIV (1980): 243–72. I agree with Davidson that Putnam should apply his own "naturalistic fallacy argument" to his own definition of truth as idealized rational acceptability. The only way in which this argument would not apply would be if 'such as to hit the truth' were built into 'idealized', thereby denaturalizing Putnam's definition at the cost of making it circular.

question 'to whom?' This question will always lead us back, it seems to me, to the answer '*Us*, at our best'. So all 'a fact of the matter about whether *p* is a warranted assertion' can mean is "a fact of the matter about our ability to feel solidarity with a community that views *p* as warranted."

Putnam says that in the possible world in which the Nazis win, "Rorty himself would not feel 'solidarity' with the culture that results." Neither would Putnam, nor the rest of the 'us' described above. The presence or absence of such a sense of solidarity is, on my view, the heart of the matter. Part of the force of the Darwinian picture I am suggesting is that the spirit of Sartre's famous remark about a Nazi victory was right, though the letter is a bit off. Sartre[18] said:

> Tomorrow, after my death, some men may decide to establish Fascism, and the others may be so cowardly or slack as to let them do so. If so Fascism will then be the truth of man, and so much the worse for us (*ibid.*, p. 358).

Sartre should not have said that Fascism will be "the truth of man." There is no such thing. What he should have said is that the truth (about certain very important matters) might be forgotten, become invisible, get lost – and so much the worse for *us*. 'Us' here does not mean "us humans" (for Nazis are humans too). It means something like "us tolerant wet liberals."

So much the worse for truth too? What does that question mean? I take the force of the antiabsolutism embodied in (i)–(v) to be that it does not mean *anything* – that we cannot find a purpose for this additional lament. When we go, so do our norms and standards of rational assertibility. Does truth go too? Truth neither comes nor goes. That is not because it is an entity that enjoys an atemporal existence, but because it is not an entity at all. The word 'truth', in this context, is just the reification of an approbative and indefinable adjective.

IV

Applying what I have been saying to the phrase Putnam finds objectionable, I want to gloss 'come to seem clearly better than their predecessors' as 'come to seem *to us* clearly better than their predecessors'. But 'us' here does not mean "us humans – Nazis or not," any more than it means "whatever otherworlders take over Earth from the humans" or "whatever nonhuman dominant species evolution next throws up to rule the Earth." Rather, it means "language users whom we can recognize as better versions of ourselves."

Is this circular? That is: Does 'recognize them as better versions of ourselves' require recognizing them as people who still agree with us on the central issue in question

18   "Existentialism is a Humanism," in *Existentialism from Dostoevsky to Sartre*, Walter Kaufmann, ed. (New York: New American Library, 1975). I have quoted this passage in the past, leading Jeffrey Stout to remark that he usually takes it "as a sign of backsliding or an invitation to misreading when favorable references to Sartre and existentialism appear in Rorty's work"; *Ethics after Babel* (Boston: Beacon, 1988), p. 260. Stout thinks (see p. 259) that the absence of a third thing, a neutral tribunal, to render judgment on us and the Nazis, does not imply "that there is no moral truth of the matter." As a good ethnocentrist, I quite agree. But Putnam does not; his argument is based on the presupposition that no third thing means no truth.

(e.g., racism)? No. It means, rather: recognize them as people who have come to hold different beliefs from ours by a process that we, by *our present* notions of the difference between rational persuasion and force, count as rational persuasion.[19] Among the interests and values that we have recently evolved into having are an interest in avoiding brainwashing and a positive valuation of literacy, liberal education, a free press, free universities, and genial tolerance of Socratic gadflies and Feyerabendian tricksters. When we picture a better version of ourselves we build into this picture the evolution of this better version out of our present selves through a process in which actualizations of these values played an appropriate part.[20] If we did not build this process into the picture, we should not call the result "a version of ourselves," but something like "an unfortunate replacement for ourselves."

Putnam suggests that I am proposing a different, novel, concept of "better" to replace our present concept. He says that

> *this* concept of 'coping better' is not the concept of there being *better* and *worse* norms or standards at all. … it is internal to our picture of warrant that warrant is logically independent of the majority of our cultural peers … (RHF 24).

Again, this last sentence would have been paradoxical if 'the majority of' had been omitted; I do not recall that I have ever, even at my worst, spoken of either warrant or truth being determined by *majority* vote. Putting aside Quinean doubts (of the sort Putnam and I share) about notions like "internal" and "logically independent" for the moment, I claim that, as non-Quineans use these notions, they would *not* say that *warrant* is like truth in being logically independent of the opinion of our peers, any more than they would say that weight is logically independent of pressure exerted on surrounding objects.

But I shall waive this point. I shall also set aside the problem of how Putnam, who thirty years ago popularized the notion of "cluster concepts," can be so confident about the self-identity of concepts. Let me just grant that, in some suitably broad sense, I *do* want to substitute new concepts for old. I want to recommend explaining 'better' (in the context 'better standards of warranted assertability') as 'will come to seem better to *us*' not as a piece of "meaning-analysis," but as an answer to 'what do you mean by 'better'? which is more in accord with (I)–(v) than, for example, 'closer to the way the world really is' or 'closer to the way God sees it' or 'closer to the facts of the matter' or 'closer to idealized rational acceptability'.

For the usual "naturalistic fallacy" reasons, neither these latter explications, nor my preferred alternative, will do as statements of necessary and sufficient conditions for a view, theory, policy, or practice being better. But once we give up the quest for such conditions – once we recognize that normative terms like 'true' and 'better' are not

19   The importance of 'our present standards of what constitutes rational persuasion' is that we need to cover the possibility that the Nazis, or the nonhuman Galactics, have different ways of distinguishing persuasion and force than ours. It is our ways that count in deciding whether to apply the term 'came to seem better' rather than, for example, 'were brainwashed into'.

20   Does this mean that we have to hold open the possibility that we might come to be Nazis by a process of rational persuasion? Yes. This is no more dangerous than holding open the possibility that we might revert to an Aristotelian–Ptolemaic cosmology by a process of rational persuasion. Neither possibility is very plausible, but to close off either of them is – as the American Civil Liberties Union keeps reminding us – part of what we mean by "intolerance."

susceptible to analysis – there is still plenty of room for debate about which explications raise more problems than they solve. I see my explication of 'better' (as applied to standards of warranted assertibility) in terms of 'us at our best' (where 'us' and 'best' are spelled out along the lines suggested above) as raising fewer problems than Putnam's in terms of 'idealized rational acceptability'.

Putnam considers the possibility that my metaphilosophical stance might be: sure my concept is new and different, but the old feature of our old concept which you prize is a *bad* feature (RHF). His reaction to 'But it is a bad feature' is to ask "But what can 'bad' possibly mean here but 'based on a wrong metaphysical picture'? And how can a Relativist speak of *right* or *wrong* metaphysical pictures?" (RHF 22). I quite agree that the relativist cannot, and that I cannot either. But why should either I, or this patsy called "the Relativist," explicate 'bad' in terms of metaphysical pictures? There are all sorts of occasions on which we say that our concept of X needs to be changed, and old intuitions thrown overboard, not for metaphysical reasons, but for reasons that are called, depending on context, "ethical" or "practical" or "political." Consider, for example, the feminists' suggestion that we change, in initially counterintuitive ways, the concepts we use in alloting social roles, for the sake of a richer, fuller, happier, nonsexist society. Or consider any other social movement that meets the objection, "But what you are saying conflicts with our customary ways of thinking!" with "So what? Let's try some new ways of thinking! We might like them! Our interests and values – both old familiar interests and values and some new ones that we may not yet be quite conscious of having – may turn out to be better served by these new ways."[21]

This analogy to social movements that suggest shoving old concepts aside is my reply to an anti-Rorty argument attributed to Putnam by Bernard Williams:

> [Rorty's views] simply tear themselves apart. If as Rorty is fond of putting it, the correct description of the world (for us) is a matter of what we find it convenient to say, and if, as Rorty admits, we find it convenient to say that science discovers a world that is already there, there is simply no perspective from which Rorty can say, as he also does, that science does not really discover a world that is already there, but (more or less) invents it.[22]

Williams here, of course, runs the Goodman-Putnam claim that there is no "way the world is" together with the straw-man claim that there were no dinosaurs or atoms before we "invented" them; the latter claim is not entailed by anything in (i)–(v) above. But that conflation is a separate issue. I want to speak, instead, to the question Williams raises about convenience. It seems to me that all that his point requires me to do is to distinguish between what has so far been found convenient to say and what might prove still more convenient to say. The convenience of the idea that there is a "way the

---

21   My reference to interests and values of which we are not yet conscious is an invocation of Dewey's doctrine of "the means–end continuum" – the idea that you change what you want as you find out what happens when you try getting what you thought you wanted. Putnam and I are both enthusiastic proponents of this doctrine.

22   Review of *Realism with a Human Face* in *London Review of Books*, 11 November 1989. This passage from Williams is said by Ronald Dworkin to summarize "Hilary Putnam's devastating critique [of Rorty]." For Dworkin's additional reasons for thinking my view "philosophically a dog's dinner," see his "Pragmatism, Right Answers and True Banality," in *Pragmatism in Law and Politics*, Michael Brint and William Weaver, eds. (Boulder: Westview, 1991), pp. 359–88.

world is" would, in a culture convinced of (i)–(v), be superseded by the still greater convenience of the idea that there is not.

The perspective from which I can say that the latter idea might be still more convenient is the familiar one of the tinkerer or the pragmatic social reformer: the person who says "Let's see what happens if we try it this way." The metaphilosophical question about pragmatism is whether there is something other than convenience to use as a criterion in science and philosophy. Williams and (at least in the passage I am discussing) Putnam both seem to assume that the only lever that could pry us out of present convenience is something that has nothing to do with convenience – something like a "metaphysical picture." But what pries us out of present convenience is just the hope of greater convenience in the future. 'Convenience' in this context means something like: ability to avoid fruitless, irresolvable, disagreements on dead-end issues.

In short, my strategy for escaping the self-referential difficulties into which "the Relativist" keeps getting himself is to move everything over from epistemology and metaphysics to cultural politics, from claims to knowledge and appeals to self-evidence to suggestions about what we should try. This seems to me just the strategy one would want to adopt if one is a pragmatist in a sense contextually defined by (i)–(v) above. But Putnam does not adopt it, and I honestly do not see why he does not. At the last moment, it seems to me, he turns intuitionist. Even though he rejects, for the same reasons I should, appeals to intuition as a way of reinvigorating metaphysics (see his criticisms of Saul Kripke and David Lewis, RHF 38–40[23]), he seems quite happy with such appeals when he confutes "the Relativist."

In one passage (RHF 24–25), Putnam acknowledges the possibility that we might "behave better if we became Rortians – we may be more tolerant, less prone to fall for various varieties of religious intolerance and political totalitarianism." This is exactly the possibility I have in mind. It is also, if I read Dewey correctly, Dewey's pragmatic justification of pragmatism – and, specifically, of the views summarized in (i)–(v). But Putnam does not take this "political" stance seriously. He asks: "If our aim is tolerance and the open society, would it not be better to argue for these directly, rather than to hope that these will come as the by-product of a change in our metaphysical picture?" But surely I cannot, any more than Dewey, be accused of thinking that fiddling around with concepts like "fact of the matter," "better," "rational acceptability," etc. – doing the sort of thing we philosophy professors do – is the only, or even a principal, means of commending, or helping to bring about, tolerance and the open society. It is just one more nudge in the right direction – the sort of modest little contribution to social progress to which a somewhat peripheral academic discipline may aspire. Surely, only someone who thought of philosophy as the pedestal on which culture rests would ask for more?

Putnam concludes, on what seems to me very little evidence, that it is "more likely" that

> most of the time anyway, Rorty really thinks that metaphysical realism is *wrong*. We will be better off if we listen to him in the sense of having fewer false beliefs; but this, of course, is something he cannot admit he really thinks. I think, in short, that the attempt to say that *from a God's-Eye View there is no God's-Eye View* is still there, under all that wrapping (RHF 25).

---

23   See also my own remarks on Lewis's notion of "elite objects," *Objectivity, Relativism and Truth*, pp. 7–12.

I cannot figure out what the difference in metaphilosophical status between what I say (e.g., about 'better', in the passage Putnam finds so wildly counterintuitive) and Putnam's own (I)–(v) is supposed by Putnam to be. Why is the former an attempt to give a God's-eye view and the latter not? Is Putnam painting a "metaphysical picture" when he puts forward (I)–(v)? I should have thought that he was doing what he calls "criticizing accepted cultural norms and standards" by suggesting some alternative cultural norms and standards: suggesting, e.g., that we clean out the last remnants of metaphysical realism from our conversational and pedagogical practices. I should have thought I was doing much the same thing.

Putnam, however, says that when I recommend a new cultural practice, and claim that these new practices are more rational, or enable us to hold more true beliefs, than their predecessors, I am using "these semantic and epistemic adjectives ... *emotively*" (RHF 24). For, he says, when I argue that my own views "are more helpful philosophically" than the views I criticize, I am engaging in "hermeneutic discourse (which is to say, in rhetoric)." Again, I can only ask what the difference between his metaphilosophical stance and mine is supposed to be. We seem, both to me and to philosophers who find both our views absurd, to be in much the same line of business. But Putnam sees us as doing something quite different, and I do not know why.

V

So far I have been picking apart Putnam's *ipsissima verba* – a strategy which has its uses, but which distracts from larger, less precise, but more important issues. So I shall conclude by returning to my earlier suggestion that what lurks in the background of Putnam's criticisms of me is his dislike of, and my enthusiasm for, a picture of human beings as just complicated animals. I can develop this suggestion by looking back to Putnam's 1983 essay "Why Reason Can't be Naturalized."

In this essay, Putnam takes as one example of "a naturalistic account of reason" the "appeal to Darwinian evolution." What he has in mind is the idea that we are constructed by evolution so as to be capable of tracking truth – that nature has cleverly contrived an organism that represents it accurately, as opposed to merely coping with it cleverly. Putnam dismisses this idea for same reasons ((I)–(v) again) as I should. My sense of 'Darwinian' has nothing to do either with the notion of truth-tracking or with that of arriving at some goal that nature has set for us.[24]

But after disposing of the evolutionary epistemologists, Putnam goes on to criticize Michel Foucault and me as cultural relativists, people who want to reduce 'better' to consensus, and thus are unable to offer rational criticism of a prevailing consensus. I shall not take up the question of whether this gets Foucault or me right, but instead turn quickly to the morals which Putnam draws in the final paragraphs of his essay, morals

---

24   Dewey effectively criticized Spencer's doctrine that there was such a goal in his "The Philosophical Work of Herbert Spencer": "Since his [Spencer's] 'environment' was but the translation of the 'nature' of the metaphysicians, its workings had a fixed origin, a fixed quality, and a fixed goal. Evolution still tends in the minds of Spencer's contemporaries to 'a single, far-off, divine event' – to a finality, a fixity"; *The Middle Works of John Dewey, vol. 3 (1903–1906)*, p. 208. In this respect, Peirce (and perhaps Bernard Williams also) can be counted among "Spencer's contemporaries."

which sum up the view that results once one rejects the error common to evolutionary epistemologism and cultural relativism, to both "reductionism and historicism."

Putnam says:

> Let us recognize that one of our fundamental self-conceptualizations, one of our fundamental 'self-descriptions', in Rorty's phrase, is that we are *thinkers*, and that *as* thinkers we are committed to there being *some* kind of truth, some kind of correctness which is substantial and not merely 'disquotational'. That means that there is no eliminating the normative.[25]

The idea of "some kind of correctness which is substantial" is the point at which I break off from Putnam. I have no use for either evolutionary epistemology or reductionism, but I think that Putnam runs together the question 'Can we give necessary and sufficient conditions for the application of normative expressions?' with the question 'Does our familiar use of normative expressions show that there is "some kind of correctness which is substantial" (or that, as Putnam goes on to say, "the rightness or wrongness of what we say is not *just* for a time and a place")' (*ibid.*, p. 247)?

My answer to *both* questions is "no." I think that nothing about the substantiality or atemporality of correctness follows from the irreducibility of a set of expressions to one another. Further, I think that the rightness or wrongness of what we say, in the sense of what we are warranted or unwarranted in saying, *is* just for a time and a place. Without falling back into metaphysical realism – into the denial of one or more of propositions (I)–(v) – I cannot give any content to the idea of nonlocal correctness of assertion. If we shift from correctness and warrant to truth, then I suppose we might say, noncontroversially if pointlessly, that the *truth* of what we say is not just for a time or place. But that high-minded platitude is absolutely barren of consequences, either for our standards of warranted assertibility or for any other aspect of our practices. So it is the sort of vacuity that pragmatists like Putnam and I should avoid.

As I see it, the only aspect of our use of 'true' which is captured neither by a common-sensical account of its approbative force nor by a disquotational account is what I have previously called the "cautionary" use of 'true'.[26] This is the use found in such sentences as

---

25 *Realism and Reason*, p. 246. For a criticism of Putnam's criticism of disquotational accounts of truth, and Putnam's reply to this criticism, see the exchange between us in *Philosophy and Phenomenological Research*, LII, 2 (June 1992): 415–8, 431–47.

26 See my "Pragmatism, Davidson and Truth," in *Objectivity, Relativism and Truth*, p. 128. Davidson has said (in "The Structure and Content of Truth," this JOURNAL, LXXXVII, 6 (June 1990): 287–8) that in my paper I misconstrued him as being a disquotationalist. He also objects to my suggestion that there is little to be said about truth, and urges that I, and other fans of disquotationalism, miss that part of "the content of the concept of truth" which is captured by T-theories. While agreeing with Davidson about the importance of theories "for describing, explaining, understanding and predicting a basic aspect of verbal behavior" (*ibid.*, p. 313) – theories of the sort from which T-sentences are a fallout – I am not sure why it is important to call such theories "truth-theories," nor why Davidson thinks that "the concept of truth" is "central" to such theories. I am puzzled by this notion of centrality, and unsure why Davidson thinks "truth" is more central to explanations of verbal behavior than any of the other concepts ("meaning," "belief," "assent," etc.) used in formulating such explanations. I am also puzzled about Davidson's seemingly unQuinean notion of "conceptual content," and by the conceptual-empirical distinction which he draws throughout his Dewey Lectures.

'Your arguments satisfy all our contemporary norms and standards, and I can think of nothing to say against your claim, but still, what you say might not be true'. I take this cautionary use not to be a gesture toward "the way the world might be anyway" but toward possible future generations – toward the "better us" to whom the contradictory of what now seems unobjectionable may have come, via appropriate means, to seem better. Putnam takes it as something more than that – the same mysterious "something more" which causes him to take seriously realistic talk about the presence or absence of a "matter of fact."[27]

I see no problem about either the irreducibility of the normative or about the place of norms in a world of fact. The emergence of language-using organisms, and the development of norm-governed practices by those organisms, is readily explicable in Darwinian terms. This explicability, and the consequent naturalization of reason, has nothing to fear from irreducibility, any more than the utility of taking what Daniel Dennett calls "the intentional stance" toward certain organisms and machines has anything to fear from the irreducibility of intentional to nonintentional discourse. (Or, to use Putnam's famous example, than the utility of talking about square pegs and round holes has anything to fear from particle physics.) So Putnam's claim that "reason can't be naturalized" seems to me ambiguous between an uncontroversial but inconsequential truth about irreducibility and a false claim that the Darwinian story leaves a gap in the fabric of causal explanation.

When Putnam says that "reason is both transcendent and immanent," I can agree with him. This is because all I can mean by 'transcendent' is "pointing beyond our present practices, gesturing in the direction of our possibly different future practices." But this is not what Putnam means, for he takes this claim to entail that "philosophy, as culture-bound reflection and argument about eternal questions, is both in time and eternity."[28]

I see Putnam, in making this inference, as running together a possible transcendence of the present by the future with the necessary transcendence of time by eternity. More generally, I see him as running together our ability to use tensions with our present body of beliefs of desires to put anything (including our present norms and standards for warranted assertibility) up for grabs with our ability to achieve a rightness that is "not just for a time and a place."

This is how I would try to confirm my preliminary suggestion that what Putnam and I really disagree about is how much can be saved from the realist tradition once we affirm positions (I)–(v). Putnam thinks that these positions leave room for something like the Apel–Habermas notion of a "universal validity claim," something like the sense of nonlocal and nontransient rightness with which religion and realist philosophy provided us. I think that these positions are of interest only insofar as as they call on us to do without that notion and that sense, and to experiment with an image of ourselves (i.e., us wet liberals) as as local and transient as any other species of animals, yet none the worse for that.

Putnam, a philosopher from whose writings I have benefited immeasurably for some thirty years, generously calls our debates "a very fruitful ongoing exchange" (RHF 19). I hope that this article may help continue that exchange.

27 The popularity of Michael Dummett's question 'is there a matter of fact about …?' has, alas, reinvigorated the flabby old controversy between realism and antirealism. Since I regret the survival of the controversy, I regret the popularity of the term 'matter of fact'. Explaining the nature of the old controversy by the use of that new term seems to me a striking case of the obscure being explained by the more obscure.
28 *Realism and Reason*, p. 247.

10

Analytic and Conversational Philosophy

The distinction between "analytic" and "Continental" philosophy is very crude, but provides a rough-and-ready way to start sorting out the philosophy professors. To tell which pigeonhole to put a professor in, look at the books and journal issues on her shelves. If she has quite a lot of books by and about Hegel and Heidegger, and none by Davidson or Rawls, she will probably be content to be described as Continental, or at least not described as analytic. If her desk is strewn with marked-up offprints from the *Journal of Philosophy*, the *Philosophical Quarterly*, and *Philosophical Review*, she can safely be typed as analytic.

Sometimes, however, you meet a philosophy professor who takes part in the debates conducted in those journals and also can discourse learnedly on, for example, the adequacy of Habermas's account of the motives for Heidegger's "turn." Quite a few people, both Anglophones and non-Anglophones, move easily back and forth between Rawls and Carl Schmitt, or between Derrida and Wittgenstein, or between Foucault and Cristine Korsgaard. But this ambidexterity, illustrated by the work of the contributors to this volume, is still confined to a relatively small fraction of the world's philosophers. Taking an unverifiable guess, though one based on visits to lots of philosophy departments in many different countries, I would put the proportion at around 10 percent.

The main reason ambidexterity is rare is that graduate students trying to shape themselves into plausible job candidates for teaching positions in philosophy only have time to read so much. They can please only so many potential employers. In most European countries, candidates for such positions have to learn quite a lot of intellectual history before they go on the market. They cannot afford to look blank when somebody asks them what they think about the relation between Hobbes and Machiavelli, or about Nietzsche's preference for Sophocles over Socrates. In Anglophone countries, they can. But then they cannot afford to be ignorant of the issues being debated in recent volumes of the leading Anglophone philosophy journals – or at least some particular subset of these issues.

Richard M. Rorty, "Analytic and Conversational Philosophy," pp.17–31 from C. G. Prado (ed.), *A House Divided: Comparing Analytic and Continental Philosophy* (Amherst, NY: Humanity Books, 2003), © 2003 by Richard Rorty. Reprinted with permission from the Estate of Richard Rorty.

No matter how much intellectual curiosity a student has, and however much she would like to have views about Kierkegaard as well as about Kripke, or about David Lewis as well as Schelling, there just is not enough time. So if she develops ambidexterity, it will often be only in later life – usually after she gets tenure. Then she can afford to start following her nose rather than pleasing interviewers or senior colleagues.

As long as these differences between how to get jobs in various places persist, philosophy will continue to be "split" along roughly analytic-vs-Continental lines. But it is not clear that this split is something to worry about. The academic study of philosophy has, like the academic study of literature and unlike that of the natural sciences, always been fairly parochial. Just as graduate training in the study of literature is typically study of a single national literature, so graduate training in philosophy is typically study of the books and issues currently being discussed in the philosophy departments of the student's own country.

Few Germans took the time to read Léon Brunschvicg during a period when no French student of philosophy could afford to be ignorant of him, or Croce when his Hegel book was being read by every philosopher in Italy. In the 1930s in the United States, most philosophy students at Harvard read quite different books than those that were being read by their counterparts in Heidelberg, Pisa, Oxford, or even Columbia. A student's notion of the frontiers of philosophy – of the urgent issues – will be quite different depending on the country, and indeed the particular university, in which she received her training.

The majority of philosophy professors in every country never move far beyond the horizons that were set for them by their teachers. So if one's teachers at Michigan assured one that Derrida is a charlatan, or if one's teachers at Tuebingen suggested that formal semantics is just a mystification and cognitive science just a boondoggle, one may well believe these propositions for the rest of one's life. Ideally, we philosophers are supposed to be constantly questioning our own presuppositions. In fact, we are no better at doing so than anybody else. Most analytic philosophers feel a vague contempt for Continental philosophy without ever having read much of it. Many Continental philosophers sneer at analytic philosophy without trying to figure out what the analytic philosophers think they are doing.

But if the analytic-Continental split is just the most conspicuous example of familiar, and pretty much inevitable, academic parochialism, why should it be so much more productive of distrust and contempt than the "split" between astrophysics and physical chemistry, or between civil and criminal legal practice, or between Italian and German literature? Why not view it simply as a matter of different people being attracted by different specialties within a single discipline?

The answer is that the differences in professional formation that I have described give rise to different accounts of what philosophy professors are good for, and of philosophy's place in culture. People trained in one way acquire a very different self-image than people trained in the other way. The contempt they frequently feel for people whose training was different results from a suspicion that those people are freeloaders, profiting from the prestige of a discipline whose nature and function they fail to understand. This failure leads them to indulge in various forms of intellectual vice.

The biggest difference in self-image is that the model of the natural sciences remains much more important for most analytic philosophers than it does for most Continental philosophers. Much of what is done by philosophers in France and Germany looks to analytic philosophers like, at best, "mere" intellectual history – something quite different from the kind of problem solving that is the philosopher's proper business. Much of what is published in *Nous, Mind*, and the *Journal of Philosophy* looks like bombination in a pseudoscientific vacuum to most people teaching philosophy in Spain, Japan, Poland, and Brazil. They view the rather miscellaneous group of issues that the analytic philosophers group under the heading "metaphysics and epistemology" as, for the most part, examples of what Berkeley called "kicking up the dust and then complaining that they cannot see." Discussion of those topics, which constitute what the Anglophones call "the core areas" of philosophy, strike them as quite irrelevant to the interests that initially led them to study philosophy.

The question of whether philosophy should think of itself as a science, like that of whether it can be assimilated to intellectual history, might seem discussable without reference to substantive philosophical doctrines. But in fact metaphilosophical issues – issues about what, if anything, philosophy is good for and about how it is best pursued – are inseparable from issues about the nature of knowledge, truth, and meaning. In what follows I shall outline one such issue to show how different responses to it might produce, and be produced by, different metaphilosophical views.

The issue is: Are concepts simply uses of words, or are they entities which are capable of being understood better than the vulgar grasp them – understood in such a way that "conceptual confusion" is eliminated and clarity is achieved? Debate concerning these two alternatives leads one to reflect on such questions as: Is there such an activity as "conceptual analysis," or can philosophers do no more than describe usage and, perhaps, make recommendations for change in usage? Was Wittgenstein right to give up on the idea of a systematic theory of meaning, and Quine right to suggest that the very notion of "meaning" was a hangover of Aristotelian essentialism? If they were, can we preserve the idea that "conceptual clarity" is a goal of philosophical inquiry? Can we repudiate the analytic-synthetic and language-fact distinctions and still cling to the idea that philosophers investigate "conceptual" rather than "empirical" issues? If not, can we find some other way to put philosophy on the secure path of a science?

Metaphilosophical issues hover in the wings of debate about whether the content of an assertion varies from utterer to utterer and from audience to audience. If it does not, if something remains invariable – the concepts expressed by the words that make up the sentence – then perhaps there really are entities with intrinsic properties which philosophical analysis can hope to pin down. But if content does vary in this way, then concepts are like persons – never quite the same twice, always developing, always maturing. You can change a concept by changing usage, but you cannot get a concept right, once and for all.

Robert Brandom has argued that treating concepts on the model of persons is central both to Hegel's thought and to pragmatism.[1] Brandom's own inferentialist philosophy of language is built around the claim that the content of a sentence is in constant flux, and

---

1   See Robert Brandom, "Some Pragmatist Themes in Hegel's Idealism: Negotiation and Administration in Hegel's Account of the Structure and Content of Conceptual Norms," *European Journal of Philosophy* 7, no. 2 (August 1999): 164–89. Brandom identifies "the idealist thesis" as the view that "the structure and unity of the *concept* is the same as the structure and unity of the *self*" (p. 164).

that sentences are none the worse for that. For, on his view, the inferences drawn from and assertions made with the sentence constitute the only content the sentence has. Inferential proprieties are not built into the structure of the language, but are always up for grabs as individuals and communities go about revising their patterns of behavior, linguistic and nonlinguistic.[2] Adopting Brandom's view would force one to give up the notion that concepts such as "knowledge" or "morality" or "mind" or "justice" have permanent, structural features that philosophers can discern but that the vulgar may not have noticed.

In the absence of that notion, it is hard to see the history of philosophy as most analytic philosophers would prefer to see it – as a continuing examination of the same data as were examined by Plato and Aristotle, in the hope of finally getting knowledge, or morality, or mind, or justice, *right*. The hope to get *something* right, once and for all, just as natural scientists do, is very precious to most analytic philosophers. Those whose self-image is built around that hope accuse philosophers who think that there are no stable entities called "concepts" or "meanings" of reducing philosophy to "mere conversation."

In my case, at least, this accusation is quite correct (or would be if "mere" were omitted). Because I do not think that philosophy is ever going to be put on the secure path of a science, nor that it is a good idea to try to put it there, I am content to see philosophy professors as making contributions to culture by suggesting changes in the uses of words, and by putting new words in circulation – thereby breaking down impasses and making conversation more fruitful.[3] I am quite willing to give up the goal of getting things right, and to substitute that of enlarging our repertoire of individual and cultural self-descriptions. The point of philosophy, on this view, is not to find out what anything is "really" like, but to help us grow up – to make us happier, freer, and more flexible. The maturation of our concepts, and the increasing richness of our conceptual repertoire, constitute cultural progress.

As an example of a change in usage that might facilitate philosophical controversy, I suggest we drop the term "Continental" and instead contrast analytic philosophy with *conversational* philosophy. This change would shift attention from the differences between the job requirements imposed on young philosophers in different regions of the world to the issue I have just sketched: whether there is something that philosophers can get right.

The term "getting it right," I would argue, is appropriate only when everybody interested in the topics draws pretty much the same inferences from the same assertions. That happens when there is consensus about the aim of inquiry in the area, and when a problem can be pinned down in such a way that everybody concerned is clear about what it would take to solve it. Common sense provides such consensus on many of the topics

2   See Robert Brandom, *Making It Explicit* (Cambridge: Harvard University Press, 1944), p. 587. "The relativity of explicit inferential endorsements to the deontic repertoires of various score-keepers reflects the underlying relativity of the inferential endorsements implicit in the concepts expressed by particular words, according to various scorekeepers. A word – 'dog,' 'stupid,' 'Republican' – has a different significance in my mouth than it does in yours, because and insofar as what follows from its being applicable, its consequences of application, differ for me, in virtue of my different collateral beliefs [and similarly for circumstances of application – consider 'murder,' 'pornographic,' 'lyrical.']"

3   In the version of this essay published in PCP three years later, this sentence was changed to read, "I am content to see philosophy professors as practicing cultural politics" (p. 124).

we discuss, and expert cultures provide it for many others. Within such cultures there is agreement, for example, on when a gene has been located, a chemical compound analyzed into its component elements, or a theorem proved. The members of such cultures all use the relevant referring expressions ("gene" "element" "proof") in pretty much the same way. They are also pretty much agreed about what exists, for shared confidence in the existence of a certain sort of entity is indistinguishable from consensus on the utility of certain referring expressions.[4]

Analytic philosophy as a whole is not, and has never been, an expert culture characterized by such long-term, near-universal consensus. What consensus has existed has been local and transitory. The problems about which the full professors in analytic philosophy departments wrote their dissertations often look merely quaint to their newly hired junior colleagues. The spectacle of the hungry analytic generations treading each other down is, to my mind, the strongest argument in favor of conversational philosophy. The failure of the analytic philosophers to develop a transgenerational problematic – yet another in the sequence of such failures that is a salient feature of the two-hundred-year history of professionalized philosophy – provides the best reason to think that the slogan "let's get it right!" needs to be replaced by something like "let's try something different!"

Contemplating two hundred years of failure helps one realize that philosophy is what is left over after one has bracketed both common sense and all the various expert cultures.[5] It was never supposed to be such a culture. Whenever it has attempted to transform itself into one it has degenerated into scholasticism, into controversies which are of no interest to anyone outside the philosophical profession. The idea that either literary criticism or philosophy should become an expert culture is a result of unfortunate attempts to squeeze these areas of culture into a university system tailored to the needs of lawyers, physicians, and natural scientists.[6]

4   Brandom has discussed the nature of existence in *Making It Explicit* at pp. 440ff. I gloss his views on this topic, and apply them to a special case, in "Cultural Politics and the Question of the Existence of God," included in *Radical Interpretation in Religion*, ed. Nancy Frankenberry (Cambridge and New York: Cambridge University Press, 2002), pp. 53–77. Some philosophers (including, alas, Quine) think that ontological questions should be distinguished from questions of utility. Antimetaphysicians like Brandom and myself, however, have no use for the notion of "ontological commitment," nor for the project of, as Quine put it, "limning the true and ultimate structure of reality."

5   For a good account of the distinction between philosophers and members of expert cultures, see Isaiah Berlin, "Does Political Theory Still Exist?" included in a collection of his essays edited by Henry Hardy: *The Proper Study of Mankind* (New York: Farrar, Strauss, and Giroux, 1998), pp. 69–90. See especially the arguments leading up to Berlin's claim that "one of the surest hallmarks of a philosophical question … is that we are puzzled from the very outset, that there is no automatic technique, no universally recognized expertise, for dealing with such questions" (p. 62).

6   This is not to deny that a specialized course of reading is necessary in order to produce, or to appreciate, original work in either philosophy or literary criticism. But there is a difference between being learned and being "scientific," in a sense of the latter term which is narrower than the German *wissenschaftlich* – a sense in which physics is taken as paradigmatic of science. It is instructive, in this connection, to compare the results of hyperprofessionalization in American departments of literature with those in American departments of philosophy. The recent popularity of "literary theory" in departments of literature is a result of the fact that you have to produce a book to get tenure. The fastest way to do so is to learn a theory and then apply it to a literary

Once one gives up on the notion that certain things are "natural explananda" – topics of concern to any reflective mind at any era and in any society – one will cease to see Kant, Hegel, Wittgenstein, Austin, or Brandom as "doing" metaphysics or epistemology or semantics, as getting (or failing to get) reality or knowledge or meaning *right*. One will instead think of them as expressing impatience with a certain familiar mind-set, and as attempting to entrench a new vocabulary, one which uses old words in new ways.

Hegel was expressing impatience with the vocabulary used by philosophers who, like Kant, insisted on the irreducibility of the subject–object distinction. In order to persuade people to stop talking in Cartesian and Kantian ways, he offered a wholesale redescription of knowledge, of moral and intellectual progress, and of a whole range of other things. He gave many of the old terms used to discuss these matters new, specifically Hegelian, senses. The later Wittgenstein was expressing impatience with his own *Tractatus* and with the philosophical mind-set shared by Moore and Russell. Austin trashed Ayer because he got impatient with his Oxford colleagues' attempts to find something worth saving in British empiricism. Brandom is not saying: Everybody has been getting concepts wrong, and I am getting them right. He is saying something more like: Representionalist accounts of semantic content have become familiar, and the problems they raise have become increasingly tedious, so let us try an inferentialist account and see whether things go better. *The Phenomenology of Spirit* and *Making It Explicit*, like *Philosophical Investigations* and *Sense and Sensibilia*, are not books of which it is useful to ask "what exactly do they get right?" – nor even "what are they *trying* to get right?" It is more useful to ask: would it help to start talking that way?

Whereas the analytic–Continental distinction is primarily a geographic and sociological one, the analytic–conversational distinction which I should like to substitute distinguishes between differing self-images – images produced by adopting differing metaphilosophical attitudes. These in turn are both cause and effect of the answers one gives to such first-order philosophical questions as those concerning the nature of concepts.

I prefer conversational to analytic philosophy, so defined, because I prefer philosophers who are sufficiently historicist as to think of themselves as taking part in a conversation rather than as practicing a quasi-scientific discipline. I am dubious about analytic philosophy because philosophers in this tradition tend to take for granted that the problems that they were taught to discuss in graduate school are, simply by virtue of that very fact, important. So they are tempted to evaluate other philosophers, past and present, by the relevance of their work to those problems. This sort of professional deformation seems to me more damaging than any similar phenomenon found among the conversational philosophers.

One reason why there is a rough correlation between a philosophy professor's geographical location and her self-image is that conversational philosophy is more popular in those countries in which Hegel is a required text for advanced students of philosophy. It is less popular in countries in which candidates for teaching positions in philosophy can afford to look blank at the mention of his name, and in which the historicism he introduced

---

text. Most such books are unprofitable hack work. The same goes for most of the articles generated by the need to contribute to one or more currently fashionable controversies in order to get tenure in a philosophy department. The good people in both fields do what they have to do to get tenure, and then go on to do something more relevant to whatever interests brought them into the field in the first place.

into philosophy is viewed with considerable suspicion. In those countries, students still tend to go straight from Kant to Frege. Skipping Hegel helps them to retain the Kantian idea that there are permanent structures of thought, or consciousness, or rationality, or language or *something*, for philosophers to reveal, and about which the vulgar may well be confused. Those who believe in such structures tend to think of analytic philosophy as continuous with the Descartes-to-Kant sequence. They often treat the Hegel–Nietzsche–Heidegger sequence as an unfortunate divagation, one that can safely be neglected.

In contrast, philosophers who have spent a lot of time thinking about those latter three figures are usually sympathetic to Hegel's suggestion that "philosophy is its time held in thought." They are inclined to think that philosophy makes progress not by solving problems but by replacing old problems with new problems – that is, problems created by one use of words with problems created by another use of words. This historicist outlook makes them dubious about Wittgenstein's suggestion that philosophy's goal is *"complete clarity"* – that is, an unproblematic grasp of the way things really are, one which will give philosophy perpetual peace (not just Aristotelian philosophy, or Cartesian philosophy, or Fregean philosophy, but philosophy itself). Philosophy, they suspect, cannot cease as long as there is cultural change – as long as the arts, the sciences, and politics come up with things that do not seem happily described when the old words are used in the old ways.[7] It also makes them suspicious of Wittgenstein's incautious use of the term "nonsense," and sympathetic to his alternative suggestion that everything has a sense if you give it a sense. So they see their task not as replacing nonsense with sense but rather as replacing a sensible and coherent use of certain terms with something even better.

Philosophers who adopt this Hegelian outlook tend to be sympathetic to "social constructivist" ideas and in particular to the view (which I have already put forward in passing) that questions about the existence of kinds of objects boil down to questions about the utility of certain referring expressions. They also tend to see philosophy as making progress by imaginative leaps, performed by individuals of genius, rather than by teamwork.

Substituting analytic–conversational for analytic–Continental as a description of the most salient split among today's philosophy professors might help us resist the temptation to regard this split either as dividing those who love truth and reason from those who prefer dramatic effects and rhetorical triumphs, or as dividing the unimaginative clods from the free spirits. It is better seen as a split between two quite different ways of thinking of the human situation – a split as deep as that between religious and secular outlooks. This split has been deepening ever since Hegel challenged Kant's version of the Platonic idea that philosophy could be like mathematics – that it could offer conclusive demonstrations of truths about structural features of human life, rather than simply summaries of the way human beings have conducted their lives so far.

Those who are on the neo-Kantian side of this split take for granted that Plato was right to postulate a permanent ahistorical matrix for human thought: to attempt

---

7   I enlarge on this point in "Im Dienste der Welterschliessung," included in *Was ist ein 'philosophisches' Problem?* ed. Joachim Schulte and Uwe Justus Wenzel (Frankfurt: Fischer Taschenbuch Verlag, 2001), pp. 148–54. I argue there that nonscholastic philosophical problems are created by such events as the rediscovery of the texts of Aristotle, the emergence of corpuscularian mechanics, the French Revolution, evolutionary biology, and the nineteenth-century novel.

to cut things at their joints by making such distinctions as knowledge–opinion, reality–appearance, reason–passion, and logic–rhetoric. Those on the other side follow Hegel in thinking that those distinctions and many others (e.g., mind–body, subjective–objective, transcendental–empirical, realist–antirealist, representationalist–inferentialist, Kantian–Hegelian, analytic–conversational) are temporary expedients that will sooner or later, like most other tools, become obsolete.

Hegelians think that blurring old distinctions (an exercise first systematically performed in *The Phenomenology of Spirit*) is one of the most effective ways to make the future an improvement over the past. Whereas the neo-Kantians like to quote Bishop Butler's maxim, "a thing is what it is and no other thing," the neo-Hegelians think that a thing (and, a fortiori, an academic discipline) is what it is by virtue of its relations to everything else, just as a word has its use by virtue of the uses of all the other words in the language. All such relations are in constant flux.

Those who take this view of both things and words (which might be called "relationalism" but is usually called "holism") include many people who think of themselves as working, as they put it, "within the analytic tradition." (Brandom himself is an obvious example.) But the majority of people who would so describe themselves still distrust holism deeply. These include not just most Anglophone teachers of philosophy, but most of the non-Anglophones who belong to such organizations as *Die Gesellschaft fuer analytische Philosophie in Deutschland*. They correctly perceive that a thoroughgoing holism will sooner or later lead to a conversational view of philosophy, and thereby lead it away from the sciences and in the direction of the humanities. They regard proper philosophical professionalism as inseparable from some form of atomism – some account of philosophy's method and subject-matter which will make it possible to preserve Plato's image of cutting things at the joints.

Those who would like to preserve that image include not just people self-identified as "analytic," but also many of the European and Asian philosophy teachers who have little use for what Anglophones describe as "metaphysics and epistemology." Some of these people cling to the conviction that transcendental phenomenology has finally put philosophy on the secure path of a science. But many who have long since given up on Husserl are still convinced that there is something "out there" to be gotten right – something, for example, that Heidegger was trying to get right when he talked about the *die ontologische Differenz*, and that Derrida was still trying to get right when he talked about *différance*. They still believe in something like an overarching a historical framework of human existence that philosophers should try to describe with greater and greater accuracy. They just think that the Anglophones have been looking for this framework in the wrong places.

Neo-Hegelian holists like myself do not think that the sociological conditions outlined above, the ones that permit one usefully to talk about getting an entity right, are fulfilled in the case of *différance*, or of any other specifically philosophical topic. So we prefer to describe Heidegger and Derrida as offering us imaginative neologisms that help us hold our time in thought. We see no need to distinguish sharply between the imaginative creations offered by philosophers and those offered by nonphilosophers. So we do not worry about which academic department should take responsibility for the study of Hegel, Freud, Heidegger, Nietzsche, or Derrida.

This insouciance leads us to seek out the company of intellectual historians and students of literature, since they too often find these latter figures of interest. We do so, not because we think that the humanities offer truth and the natural sciences do not, but because study of the history of philosophy leads us to try to fit that history into a larger historical context. The history of algebraic topology or of molecular biology does not, we presume, require such contextualization. But the history of philosophy, like the history of the novel, does. Whereas the neo-Kantians think that one can be a well-trained philosopher without any particular knowledge of literary or political history, we disagree. Just as the value of a philosopher's work, in our eyes, is not a matter of its relation to *die Sache Jelbst*, but to the work of other philosophers, so the value of philosophy itself is a matter of its relation not to a subject matter but to the rest of the conversation of humankind.

The differing emphasis we neo-Hegelians place on history is paralleled by the differing values we place on metaphilosophical discussion of the sort offered in the present volume. Neo-Kantians are always trying to get away from metaphilosophy and, as they say, "get down to *doing* some philosophy." For us, on the other hand, discussing what philosophy has been and might be is as respectable a way of doing philosophy as, for example, discussing how to give referentially opaque contexts their proper place in a semantic theory.

Both discussions are part of the same conversation, because to understand why referential opacity matters one has to think about why the founders of analytic philosophy wanted what they wanted and took the stands they did – what the point of an extensionalist semantics was supposed to be. Whereas neo-Kantians think that introducing a student to the problems that opaque contexts pose for formal semantics is enough to give her a good start on doing some good philosophy, neo-Hegelians think that students who have never reflected on what a semantic theory might be good for are undesirably unconversable. These students are in danger of writing dissertations whose, half-life may be very short, and which will be ignored, or even mocked, by the next generation. Historical and metaphilosophical self-consciousness, we think, is the best precaution against barren scholasticism.

Maybe someday we shall witness the worldwide and permanent triumph of analytic over conversational, or of conversational over analytic philosophy. But I find it very hard to imagine either possibility being actualized. This is because I see the two philosophical views as dialectically intertwined, each living each other's death and dying each other's life. At the present time we live in a world in which to study philosophy is inevitably to take sides – explicitly or implicitly, by instinct or after reflection – on some or all of the metaphilosophical and substantive issues that divide the neo-Kantians from the neo-Hegelians. Only a soulless Pecksniff, having once became aware of these issues, will feel no urge to rally around one or the other banner.

On the other hand, the distinctions I have been drawing are simply parts of an attempt to hold my own time in thought. Maybe the world will change, not because one of the two sides of the present split has triumphed but because something new will come along that will count as "philosophy." Maybe this change will be as radical as the one that came to pass in the course of the seventeenth century. By 1700, nobody was much interested in reformulating the quarrels between the fourteenth-century Dominicans (the Aristotle fans) and their Franciscan opponents (the Augustine fans). There may come a day when the quarrel between Kant and Hegel, and perhaps even the one between Plato and Nietzsche, will strike the intellectuals as equally tedious, and nobody will wish to update either. Then the present volume will appear very quaint indeed. For the time being, however, it is likely to prove of considerable use.

Part III

From Antirepresentationalism to Political Liberalism

Introduction

Written in the 1980s, the essays in this section chart Rorty's early attempts to articulate the cultural and political consequences of his philosophical critiques of the previous decade. In his own words, "they enlarge on how various areas of the culture (particularly science and politics) look from a nonrepresentationalist perspective" (ORT, p. 12). The therapeutic role of philosophy he called attention to in *Philosophy and the Mirror of Nature* involves persuading people "to throw away the indispensable ladders" our culture has used in the past to make progress toward a democratic utopia but which now have outlived their usefulness. Although he soon disavowed the phrase, in a 1983 essay by the same title he labeled this attempt "to defend the institutions and practices of the rich North Atlantic democracies" without the buttresses of transcultural and ahistorical accounts of rationality and morality, "postmodernist bourgeois liberalism" (ORT, p. 198).[1] Absent such "skyhooks," as he once called them, to get us out of our cultural and historical particularity, moral justification of our institutions and practices must work from within that particularity, rather than transcend it – this is the sense in which Rorty's self-conscious ethnocentrism should be understood. Moral and political discourse, on this view, becomes a matter of appeals to the communities with which we identify via historical narratives instead of appeals to objective theory. If we see vocabularies as tools for coping with reality rather than representing it, we can make room in our conception of inquiry for the insight that "narratives as well as laws, redescriptions as well as predictions, serve a useful purpose in helping us deal with the problems of society" (CP, p. 198). While he has been praising and defending pragmatism for some time, it is not until this period that Rorty begins to identify with pragmatism himself.[2]

1 On Rorty's disavowal of this phrase, see p. 139, this volume.
2 While there is an appearance in the 1984 essay "Solidarity and Objectivity?" (p. 234, this volume), for the most part it is not until a decade after the publication of *Mirror* that his use of "we Deweyans" and "we pragmatists" becomes commonplace. (See for example, PSH, p. 124; TP, p. 211n.) Some of Rorty's most in-depth analyses of James and Dewey do not come until the mid–late 1990s. See, for example, pragmatism as romantic polytheism (chapter 27, this volume); "Religious Faith, Intellectual Responsibility, and Romance," in PSH, pp. 148–67; "Pragmatism as Anti-Authoritarianism" in John R. Shook and Joseph Margolis (eds.), *A Companion to Pragmatism* (Malden, MA: Blackwell, 2006), pp. 257–66; "Some Inconsistencies in James' Varieties" in Wayne

Although predated by a couple of years the three essays that follow it, "Philosophy as Science, as Metaphor, and as Politics" offers a clear overview of how Rorty's critique of traditional philosophy, his adoption of a Quinean-Davidsonian conception of language, and his embrace of a Romantic view of the creation of new metaphors via poetry, come together to form a picture of social change. Approaching the topic in his systematic, analytic mode, he delineates three ways that new beliefs can be accommodated to existing beliefs and thereby force a "reweaving of the community's fabric belief," his conception of foundationless, historicist, self-criticism of culture: perception, inference, and metaphor. What makes the latter more advantageous than the first two is that it expands the bounds of our language, and thus our sense of the realm of possibility, by making meaning open-ended.[3] This is the "the relevance of a theory of metaphor to the critique of foundationalism," which he brings out by combining Dewey and Davidson: understanding moral progress in terms of "making rather than finding, of poetic achievement [...] rather than as the gradual unveiling, through the use of 'reason', of 'principles', or 'rights', or 'values'" (pp. 208, 252 this volume; ORT, p. 189).[4] Even though this view seems to reduce "large-scale change of belief" to "large-scale change of the meanings of one's words," as Rorty suggests, it also means that every new metaphor is "a call to change one's language and one's life" (p. 214, this volume).

In "a Deweyan culture" that has given up on what Thomas Nagel called "an ambition of transcendence," intersubjective agreement supplants objectivity and transcendence, so there is no way out, so to speak (ORT, p. 12). As Rorty describes in "Solidarity or Objectivity?" in such a culture it is a matter of making sense of one's life through stories relating oneself to a particular community, rather than to some nonhuman reality, like God or Truth. Thus, objectivity can be replaced by intersubjective agreement and transcendence with imaginative novelty. Generally speaking, "Solidarity or Objectivity?" deals with novelty in the context of our connections to others and "Freud and Moral Reflection" covers novelty in the context of our relation to ourselves, what Rorty calls "private morality" or the "morality of character." Putting the issues in moral and political terms, rather than in epistemological or metaphilosophical terms, he tells us, makes clearer what is at stake: "not how to define words like 'truth' or 'rationality' or 'knowledge'

Proudfoot (ed.), *William James and a Science of Religion* (New York: Columbia University Press, 2004), pp. 86–97; and "Kant vs. Dewey: The Current Situation of Moral Philosophy" in PCP, pp. 184–202.

3   See p. 219, this volume. This point is meant to counter the fundamental assumption of analytic philosophy that philosophizing consists primarily in "clarification, in patiently making explicit what has remained implicit," rather than in generating new meanings through novel metaphors, p. 219, this volume. In an earlier, more analytic essay written in 1981, he puts it this way:

> We are the poetic species, the one which can change itself by changing its behavior – and especially its linguistic behavior, the words it uses [...] To say, with nominalism, that language is ubiquitous and to deny, with verificationism, that there are intuitions to which our language must conform, is just to assert that we need nothing more than confidence in our own poetic power. ("Contemporary Philosophy of Mind," *Synthese* 53, no. 2 [1982], p. 346)

4   Rorty touts the importance of philosophers seeing themselves as "*making* rather than *finding*" in his earliest essays. See, for example, "The Limits of Reductionism," in I. C. Lieb (ed.), *Experience, Existence, and the Good* (Carbondale: Southern Illinois University Press, 1961), p. 114.

or 'philosophy,' but about what self-image our society should have" (p. 233, this volume). If our sense of community has "no foundation except shared hope and the trust created by such sharing," then all we can do is "extend the reference of 'us' as far we can" (pp. 238, 229 this volume).

Rorty's most direct presentation of his stance comes in "The Priority of Democracy to Philosophy," which marks his most explicit engagement with the ideas and texts of contemporary political theory to date.[5] His overarching aim in this essay is to sever Enlightenment politics from its philosophical "backup" in ahistorical foundations. The stance that democracy in fact needs such backup is captured by Max Horkheimer and Theodor Adorno's view, as Rorty characterizes it, "that liberal institutions and culture either should not or cannot survive the collapse of the philosophical justification that the Enlightenment provided for them" (p. 241, this volume). Discussing the work of political theorists like John Rawls and Michael Sandel, as well as other "communitarians," in light of this stance, Rorty defends the idea that changing the vocabularies we use to more pragmatist ones will enable us to see moral progress as a history of "poetic achievement by 'radically situated' individuals and communities, rather than as the gradual unveiling, through the use of 'reason,' of 'principles' or 'rights' or 'values'" (p. 252, this volume). He also explains the "air of light-minded aestheticism" he adopts here and elsewhere as part of an effort to "make the world's inhabitants more pragmatic, more tolerant, more liberal, more receptive to the appeal of instrumental rationality" (p. 256, this volume). Putting the move from objectivity to solidarity in political context, he holds that viewing our democratic institutions as "experiments in cooperation" instead of "attempts to embody a universal and ahistorical order" will better help us achieve our political aims (p. 258, this volume).

In "Freud and Moral Reflection" Rorty reads Freud as having "opened up new possibilities for the aesthetic life" and "helped us become increasingly more ironic, playful, free, and inventive in our choice of self-descriptions" (p. 270, this volume). This "ability to take a nominalistic, ironic view of oneself" is fully embraced by Rorty, becoming the centerpiece of *Contingency, Irony, and Solidarity,* where "Private Irony and Liberal Hope" first appeared. However, this same playful irony, what he calls here "the aesthetic search for novel experiences and novel language," threatens to undermine the creation of solidarity advocated in "Solidarity or Objectivity?" and in *Contingency.* So it is here in his reflection on Freud that the need to insulate public morality, our obligations to other human beings, from private morality, our obligation to, in Nietzsche's words, become who you are, is first articulated (ORT, p. 13).[6] Freud thus takes on an unexpected significance in the development of Rorty's understanding of morality and moral reflection. For one, he is a prime example of the kind of thinker who succeeded in doing what Rorty believes philosophers should aim to do, which is to spark changes in our self-image. The larger effect of Freud's insight that the ego "is not even master in its own house" is to "decenter" notions of an inner essence, true self, or common human nature as the origin of moral responsibility. For Rorty, Freud "reinvents the morality of character." But he "does nothing for either liberal or radical politics,

---

5   For an attempt to read Rorty as writing a form of political theory, see Christopher J. Voparil, *Richard Rorty: Politics and Vision* (Lanham, MD: Rowman & Littlefield, 2006).

6   For a more in-depth treatment of Rorty's public–private split, see the General Introduction above, pp. 37–41.

except perhaps to supply new terms of opprobrium with which to stigmatize tyrants and torturers" (pp. 259, 272, 276, this volume).[7]

In "Private Irony and Liberal Hope" Rorty offers a fuller account of the figure of "ironist" and the process of "redescription" through which ironists generate new "final vocabularies" and thus revise their moral identities. Since there is nothing to appeal to outside of our self-descriptions and no way to get down to some "intrinsic nature" or "real essence" – those are assumptions characteristic of "metaphysicians" rather than ironists – this process is simply a matter of expanding our circle of acquaintance so we can encounter other vocabularies to play off our own.[8] Besides actually meeting other people, the easiest way to do this is through books, where we can get to know "strange people" and "strange communities" (p. 285, this volume). Casting literary critics as "moral advisers," Rorty carves out a role in moral reflection for literary criticism as cultural criticism. Because they put us in touch with human rather than nonhuman realities, the ability of literature, journalism, and ethnography to create "imaginative acquaintance with alternative final vocabularies" makes them more central to the public aims of democratic life than philosophy, theology, or science.

Because redescription has the potential to humiliate – most people want to be taken on their own terms, not told their most cherished beliefs are revisable descriptions – Rorty must reconcile irony with liberalism, particularly since he understands "liberals," following Judith Shklar, as people for whom "cruelty is the worst thing they do" (p. 280, this volume). He can only achieve this by creating a division between public and private: "For my private purposes, I may redescribe you and everybody else in terms which have nothing to do with my attitude toward your actual or possible suffering." But if I am a liberal, "the part of my vocabulary which is relevant to [my public] actions requires me to become aware of all the various ways in which other human beings whom I might act upon can be humiliated" (p. 293, this volume). In sum, we must be "in alternate moments, Nietzsche and J. S. Mill" (p. 288, this volume). That such partitioning is possible is the premise on which Rorty's accommodation of private irony and liberal hope hinges.

7   More specifically, "Freudo-Marxist analyses of 'authoritarianism' have offered no better suggestions about how to keep the thugs from taking over" (p. 276n29, this volume).
8   As he puts it in an earlier chapter, "the world does not provide us with any criteria of choice between alternative metaphors [...] we can only compare languages or metaphors with one another, not with something beyond language called 'fact,'" CIS, p. 20.

11

Philosophy as Science, as Metaphor, and as Politics

I Introduction

Three answers have been given, in our century, to the question of how we should conceive of our relation to the Western philosophical tradition, answers which are paralleled by three conceptions of the aim of philosophizing. They are the Husserlian (or 'scientistic') answer, the Heideggerian (or 'poetic') answer and the pragmatist (or 'political') answer. The first answer is the most familiar, and was common to Husserl and his positivist opponents. On this view, philosophy is modeled on science, and is relatively remote from both art and politics.

The Heideggerian and pragmatist answers are reactions to this familiar 'scientistic' answer. Heidegger turns away from the scientist to the poet. The philosophical thinker is the only figure who is on the same level as the poet. The achievements of the great thinkers have as little to do with either mathematical physics or statecraft as do those of the great poets. By contrast, pragmatists such as Dewey turn away from the theoretical scientists to the engineers and the social workers – the people who are trying to make people more comfortable and secure, and to use science and philosophy as tools for that purpose. The Heideggerian thinks that the philosophical tradition needs to be reappropriated by being seen as a series of poetic achievements: the work of Thinkers, people who "have no choice but to find words for what a being *is* in the history of its Being."[1] The pragmatist thinks that the tradition needs to be utilized, as one utilizes a bag of tools. Some of these tools, these 'conceptual instruments' – including some which continue to have undeserved prestige – will turn out no longer to have a use, and can just be tossed out. Others can be refurbished. Sometimes new tools may have to be invented on the spot. Whereas the Heideggerian sees Husserl's "faith in the possibility of philosophy as a

Richard M. Rorty, "Philosophy as Science, as Metaphor, and as Politics," pp.13–33 in Avner Cohen and Marcelo Dascal (eds.), *The Institution of Philosophy: A Discipline in Crisis?* Reprinted with permission of Open Court Publishing Company, a division of Carus Publishing Company, Peru, IL, from *The Institution of Philosophy: A Discipline in Crisis?* by Avner Cohen and Marcelo Dascal (eds.), © 1989 by Open Court Publishing Company.

1 …keine Wahl haben, die vielmehr zum Wort bringen müssen, was das Seiende je in der Geschichte seines Seins *ist*: Heidegger, *Nietzsche II* (Pfullingen: Neske, 1962), 37. Translated in Heidegger, *Nietzsche*, vol. IV, trans. F. A. Cappuzi (New York: Harper and Row, 1982), 7.

task, that is, in the possibility of universal knowledge"[2] as a scientistic, mathematizing, misunderstanding of the greatness of the tradition, the pragmatist thinks of it as sentimental nostalgia, an attempt to keep old slogans and strategies alive after they have outlived their practical utility.[3]

Husserl thought the suggestion that we drop the ideal of universal, ahistorical, foundational philosophical knowledge, a suggestion common to pragmatism and to Nietzsche, was the final stage of a disastrous "change which set in at the turn of the past century in the general evaluation of the sciences."[4] On his view, "the total world-view of modern men, in the second half of the nineteenth century, let itself be determined by the positive sciences and be blinded by the 'prosperity' they produced" and this in turn produced "an indifferent turning-away from the questions which are decisive for a genuine humanity."[5]

Husserl thought of traditional rationalism and of empiricist skepticism as two sides of the same 'objectivist' coin.[6] He tried to place both within the framework of his own transcendental phenomenology. Heidegger agreed with Husserl about the relative unimportance of the empiricist–rationalist distinction, and also about the dangers of a technologized, pragmatic, culture. But Heidegger thought of pragmatism and transcendental phenomenology as merely two further products of the 'objectivist' tradition. He tried to place both pragmatism's abjuration of 'spirit' and Husserl's attempt to reclaim it within his own account of 'Western metaphysics'. He agreed with Husserl that

> an autonomous philosopher with the will to liberate himself from all prejudices…must have the insight that all the things he takes for granted *are* prejudices, that all prejudices are obscurities arising out of a sedimentation of the tradition…and that this is true even of the great task and idea which is called 'philosophy'.[7]

But Heidegger thought that neither Husserl nor the pragmatists were radical enough in their criticism of their predecessors' self-understanding. He distrusted the pragmatist attempt to replace the Platonic-Cartesian idea of "universal knowledge" with the Baconian dream of maximal control over nature. But he also distrusted Husserl's attempt to see Galilean *techne* as 'founded' in something 'transcendental'. For Heidegger, projects of 'founding' culture – either upon concrete human needs or upon transcendental subjectivity – were simply further expressions of the 'prejudices' which needed to be overcome.

2   Husserl, *The Crisis of European Sciences and Transcendental Phenomenology*, trans. David Carr (Evanston: Northwestern University Press, 1970), 17.
3   My failure to discuss Marxism in what follows, and to use it, rather than American pragmatism, to represent the "political" conception of the activity of philosophizing, is due to the conviction that Marxism is an inconsistent mixture of the pragmatism of the 'Theses on Feuerbach' with the scientism common to Marxism and positivism. Kolakowski's history of Marxism shows, I think, how every attempt to make Marxism more pragmatic and less scientific has been firmly suppressed by the institutions which Marxism has created.
4   Ibid., 5.
5   Ibid., 6.
6   See ibid., 83, on Descartes and Hobbes.
7   Ibid., 72.

Although Heidegger's assessment of our century's dangers was closer to Husserl's, his actual philosophical doctrines were closer to Dewey's. Like Husserl, Heidegger thought that "the European crisis has its roots in a misguided rationalism."[8] But he thought that a demand for foundations was itself a symptom of this misguided rationalism. *Sein und Zeit* is filled with criticisms of the doctrines which Husserl shared with Descartes. The treatment in that book of 'objective scientific knowledge' as a secondary, derivative, form of Being-in-the-World, derivative from the use of tools, is of a piece with Dewey's Baconianism.[9] Heidegger's dissolution of philosophical pseudo-problems through letting social practice be taken as a primary and unquestioned datum, rather than an explanandum, exemplifies what Robert Brandom has called "the ontological primacy of the social."[10]

Another way in which Heidegger and pragmatism belong together is in their deep distrust of the visual metaphors which link Husserl to Plato and Descartes. Husserl and Carnap shared the traditional Platonic hope to ascend to a point of view from which the interconnections between everything could be seen. For both, the aim of philosophy is to develop a formal scheme within which every facet of culture can be placed. Both are philosophers of what Hilary Putnam has called "the God's-eye view". Heidegger's term for such attempts at a God-like grasp of the realm of possibility, attempts to have a pigeonhole ready for every actual event which might occur, is 'the mathematical'. He defines *ta mathemata* as "that 'about' things which we really already know."[11] The search for the mathematical, for a formal ahistorical scheme, was, in Heidegger's view, the hidden link between Husserlian phenomenology, Carnapian positivism, and the objectivist tradition.

Dewey's insistence on the subordination of theory to practice, and his claim that the task of philosophy is to break the crust of convention, expresses the same distrust of the contemplative ideal, and of attempts to have an a priori place prepared for everything that may happen. But Heidegger's and Dewey's conceptions of philosophy were nevertheless very different. Their common opposition to foundationalism and to visual metaphors took radically different forms. In what follows I want to discuss these differences under two headings: their different treatments of the relationship between the metaphorical and the literal, and their different attitudes towards the relation between philosophy and politics. By turning from Dewey to a philosopher whose work seems to me to be the best current statement of a pragmatist position – Donald Davidson – I hope to be able to bring out the relevance of a theory of metaphor to the critique of foundationalism. By focusing on Heidegger's assimilation of philosophy to poetry, I hope to

8   Ibid., 290.

9   As Hubert Dreyfus and John Haugeland make clear, Husserl's reaction to this portion of *Sein und Zeit* was marked by an assumption that the *zuhanden* was as much grist for the phenomenological mill as the *vorhanden*, and specifically that a *Zeug* was "something identical, something identifiable again and again", and so something which would exhibit a universal essence. See Dreyfus and Haugeland, 'Husserl and Heidegger: Philosophy's Last Stand' in Michael Murray, ed., *Heidegger and Modern Philosophy* (New Haven:Yale University Press, 1978), 222–238 (especially the quotation from a fragmentary manuscript of Husserl's labeled "das ist gegen Heidegger" at p. 233).

10   Robert Brandom, 'Heidegger's Categories in *Being and Time*', *The Monist*, vol. 66 (1983), 389.

11   Heidegger, *What is a Thing?*, trans. Barton and Deutsch (South Bend: Gateway, 1967), 74.

bring out the difference between what I have called the 'political' and the 'poetic' answers to the question of our relationship to the philosophical tradition.

II Metaphor as the Growing Point of Language

Let me open up the topic of metaphor by making a curt, dogmatic, claim: there are three ways in which a new belief can be added to our previous beliefs, thereby forcing us to reweave the fabric of our beliefs and desires – viz., perception, inference and metaphor. Perception changes our beliefs by intruding a new belief into the network of previous beliefs. For example, if I open a door and see a friend doing something shocking, I shall have to eliminate certain old beliefs about him, and rethink my desires in regard to him. Inference changes our beliefs by making us see that our previous beliefs commit us to a belief we had not previously held – thereby forcing us to decide whether to alter those previous beliefs, or instead to explore the consequences of the new one. For example, if I realize, through a complicated detective-story train of reasoning, that my present beliefs entail the conclusion that my friend is a murderer, I shall have to either find some way to revise those beliefs, or else rethink my friendship.

Both perception and inference leave our language, our way of dividing up the realm of possibility, unchanged. They alter the truth-values of sentences, but not our repertoire of sentences. To assume that perceptions and inference are the *only* ways in which beliefs ought to be changed is to adopt what Heidegger identified as the 'mathematical' attitude. It is to assume that the language we presently speak is, as it were, all the language there is, all the language we shall ever need. Such a conception of language accords with the idea that the point of philosophy is what Husserl took it to be: to map out all possible logical space, to make explicit our implicit grasp of the realm of possibility. It supports the claim, common to Husserlian phenomenology and to analytic philosophy, that philosophizing consists in clarification, in patiently making explicit what has remained implicit.

By contrast, to think of metaphor as a third source of beliefs, and thus a third motive for reweaving our networks of beliefs and desires, is to think of language, logical space, and the realm of possibility, as open-ended. It is to abandon the idea that the aim of thought is the attainment of a God's-eye view. The philosophical tradition downgraded metaphor because recognizing metaphor as a third source of truth would have endangered the conception of philosophy as a process culminating in vision, *theoria*, contemplation of what is *vorhanden*. Such visual metaphors contrast with the auditory metaphors which Heidegger preferred (e.g., *Ruf des Gewissens, Stimme des Seins*). The latter are better metaphors for metaphor, because they suggest that cognition is not always recognition, that the acquisition of truth is not always a matter of fitting data into a pre-established scheme. A metaphor is, so to speak, a voice from outside logical space, rather than an empirical filling-up of a portion of that space, or a logical-philosophical clarification of the structure of that space. It is a call to change one's language and one's life, rather than a proposal about how to systematize them.

Such a view of metaphor requires that we follow Davidson in rejecting the claim that "a metaphor has, in addition to its literal sense or meaning, another sense or meaning".[12] Davidson's point is that it is misleading to interpret the expression 'the metaphorical use of language' as implying that lots of 'metaphorical meanings', in addition to lots of 'literal

12   Donald Davidson, *Inquiries into Truth and Interpretation* (Oxford: Clarendon Press, 1984), 246.

meanings', are already *vorhanden* in our language. On such a view, metaphor cannot expand logical space, for to learn the language is already to have learned all the possibilities for metaphor as well as all the possibilities for fact. A language is not changed by the invention of metaphor, since metaphorical speech is not invention but simply utilization of tools already at hand. By contrast, Davidson's view is that there is a strict distinction between meaning (the property which one attributes to words by noting standard infer-ential connections between the sentences in which they are used and other sentences) and use, and that "metaphor belongs exclusively to the domain of use".[13]

Davidson says that "most metaphors are false" but it would be better to say that most metaphors take the form of sentences which seem, *prima facie*, obviously false. Later on, however, these same sentences may come to be thought of as literally true. To take a trivial case, mentioned by Davidson, "Once upon a time...rivers and bottles did not, as they do now, literally have mouths".[14] To take a more important case, the first time some-one said 'Love is the only law' or 'The earth moves around the sun' the general response would have been 'You must be speaking metaphorically'. But, a hundred or a thousand years later, these sentences become candidates for literal truth. Our beliefs were, in the interval, rewoven to make room for these truths – a process which was indistinguishable from the process of changing the meanings of the words used in these sentences in such a way as to make the sentences literally true.

Notice that the claim I have just made – that large-scale change of belief is indistin-guishable from large-scale change of the meanings of one's words – follows from the definition of 'meaning' which I inserted parenthetically above. This definition of mean-ing encapsulates the Quine–Davidson approach to philosophy of language. This approach makes meanings neither Platonic essences nor Husserlian noemata but rather patterns of habitual use – what Sellars calls 'linguistic roles'. It thereby makes the Carnapian quest for 'analysis' of meanings seem a misleadingly 'formal' and 'transcendental' way of describ-ing the project of charting the behavior of a group of language-users. *Mutatis mutandis*, it does the same for the Husserlian project of 'grounding' culture through an inspection of noemata. More generally, it undermines any scientistic philosophical project, any project which depends upon the ahistorical version of what Davidson calls 'the dualism of scheme and content'. This version is the claim that philosophy can make explicit a scheme, a permanent neutral matrix of possibilities, which lies in the background of all our inquiries and practices.

I have argued elsewhere that Davidson's attack on this distinction is the best current expression of the pragmatist attempt to break with the philosophical tradition.[15] Here I want to present this attack as paralleling Heidegger's attack on the tradition's attempt to 'mathematize' the world (in the specifically Heideggerian sense of 'mathematical' mentioned above.) To think of metaphorical sentences as the forerunners of new uses of language, uses which may eclipse and erase old uses, is to think of metaphor as on a par

---

13   Ibid., 247. See also p. 259: "No theory of metaphorical meaning or metaphorical truth can help explain how metaphor works. Metaphor works on the same familiar linguistic tracks that the plainest sentences do ... What distinguishes metaphor is not meaning but use – in this it is like assertion, hinting, lying, promising and criticizing."

14   Ibid., 252.

15   See 'Pragmatism, Davidson and Truth' in *Essays on "Inquiries into Meaning and Truth"*, ed. Ernest LePore (Oxford: Blackwell's, 1986) and 'The Contingency of Language' (*London Review of Books*, vol. 8, no. 7, April 17, 1986).

with perception and inference, rather than thinking of it as having a merely 'heuristic' or 'ornamental' function.[16] More specifically, it is to think of truth as something which is *not* already within us. Rather, it is something which may only become available to us thanks to an idiosyncratic genius. Such a conception of truth legitimizes auditory metaphors: a voice from far off, a *Ruf des Gewissens*, a word spoken out of the darkness.

Another way of putting this point is to say, with Davidson, that "the irrational" is essential to intellectual progress. In a paper on Freud, Davidson notes that "mental causes which are not reasons" – that is, beliefs and desires which play a role in determining our behavior but which do not fit into the scheme of beliefs and desires which we would claim as ours – are needed not only to explain "deviant" behavior (as Freudian psychoanalytic theory employs them) but also to "explain our salutary efforts, and occasional successes, at self-criticism and self-improvement".[17]

Davidson's insistence in that paper on the importance of "mental causality that transcends reason" is focused on self-criticism and self-improvement in individual human beings, but I think his point is even more striking and plausible for the self-criticism of cultures. The "irrational" intrusions of beliefs which "make no sense" (i.e., cannot be justified by exhibiting their coherence with the rest of what we believe) are just those events which intellectual historians look back upon as 'conceptual revolutions'. Or, more precisely, they are the events which spark conceptual revolutions – seemingly crazy suggestions by people who were without honor in their countries, suggestions which strike *us* as luminous truths, truths which must always have been latent in 'human reason'. These events are the words spoken by the people Heidegger calls "Thinkers". From a point of view common to Heidegger and Davidson, the philosophical tradition is a long sequence of attempts to exhibit intellectual history as exhibiting a 'hidden rationality', as achieved by *die List der Vernunft*, where 'Vernunft' names something that has been there all the time, rather than simply some recently literalized metaphors.

Heidegger is concerned to deny that there is a topic of ahistorical inquiry called 'human reason' or 'the structure of rationality' or 'the nature of language' which has been the object of philosophical inquiry in all ages. Even in the '20s, before the 'Kehre', Heidegger was contradicting Husserl's criticism of historicism[18] by saying such things as

---

16   But this is not to say that it has a 'cognitive' function, if this means 'telling' us something, answering a previously formulated question. Its contribution to cognition is rather to give us a sentence which we are tempted to try to 'literalize' by changing the truth-values of, so to speak, various surrounding sentences. Davidson says about attempts to give 'cognitive content' to metaphors:

> But in fact there is no limit to what a metaphor calls to our attention, and much of what we are caused to notice is not propositional in character. When we try to say what a metaphor "means", we soon realize that there is no end to what we want to mention. (*Inquiries*, p. 263)

He goes on to analogize metaphors to pictures and to say that "words are the wrong currency to try to exchange for a picture". The attempt to think of metaphors as telling us something is the attempt to think of pictures or metaphors as being interchangeable with a set of sentences, instead of as providing (as do surprising perceptual data) a challenge to (a) redistribute truth-values among familiar sentences, and (b) invent further unfamiliar sentences.

17   Davidson, 'Paradoxes of Irrationality', in Richard Wollheim and James Hopkins, *Philosophical Essays on Freud* (Cambridge: Cambridge University Press, 1982), 305.

18   In, e.g., *Philosophie als Strenge Wissenschaft*.

> Construction in philosophy is necessarily destruction, that is to say, a de-constructing (Abbau) of traditional concepts carried out in a historical recursion to the tradition... Because destruction belongs to construction, philosophical cognition is essentially at the same time, in a certain sense, historical cognition.[19]

In the '40s he was to conclude that in *Sein und Zeit* he had not yet been historicist enough to accomplish this destruction. Referring to that early book he says "This destruction, like 'phenomenology' and all hermeneutical-transcendental questions, has not yet been thought in terms of the history of Being."[20] Heidegger identified 'human reason', 'rationality', and 'sound common sense', as these terms are used by philosophers, with the unselfconscious, *uneigentlich*, unquestioning, use of an inherited language. Philosophy is not simply the utilization of that tradition – not simply the distribution of truth-values over a range of sentences which are already "present" in the language – because "all essential philosophical questioning is necessarily untimely ... Philosophy is essentially untimely because it is one of those few things that can never find an immediate echo in the present."[21]

We may identify what finds no echo in the present with the sort of metaphor which is prima facie a pointless falsehood, but which nevertheless turns out to be what Heidegger calls "a word of Being", one in which "the call of Being" is heard. Consider, in the light of this identification, two pregnant sentences in which Heidegger describes "the task of philosophy":

> ...the ultimate business of philosophy is to preserve the *force of the most elemental words* in which Dasein expresses itself, and to keep the common understanding from leveling them off to that unintelligibility which functions in the end as a source of pseudo-problems.[22]

> It is the authentic function of philosophy to challenge historical being-there (Dasein) and hence, in the last analysis, Being (Sein) pure and simple.[23]

---

19   Heidegger, *The Basic Problems of Phenomenology,* trans. Hofstadter (Bloomington: Indiana University Press, 1982), 23. The original is at *Grunde probleme der Phänomenologie* (Frankfurt: Klostermann, 1975), 31.

20   Aber diese Destruktion ist wie die 'Phänomenologie' und alles hermeneutisch-transzendentale Fragen noch nicht seinsgeschichtlich gedacht: Heidegger, *Nietzsche* II, p. 415. I am grateful to Herbert Dreyfus for calling my attention to this passage. The English translation is from Heidegger, *The End of Philosophy,* ed. and trans. Joan Stambaugh (New York: Harper and Row, 1973), 15.

21   Die Philosophie ist wesenhaft unzeitgemäss, weil sie zu jenen wenigen Dingen gehört, deren Schicksal es bleibt, nie einen unmittelbaren Widerklang in ihrem jeweiligen Heute finden zu können und auch nie finden zu dürfen: Heidegger, *Einführung in die Metaphysik* (Tübingen: Niemeyer, 1953), 6. The English translation is at *Introduction to Metaphysics,* trans. Manheim (New Haven: Yale University Press, 1959), 8.

22   ...ist es am Ende das Geschäft der Philosophie, die *Kraft der elementarsten Worte*, in denen sich das Dasein ausspricht, davor zu bewahren, dass sie durch den gemeinen Verstand zur Unverständlichkeit nivelliert werden, die ihrerseits als Quelle fuer Scheinproblem fungiert. Heidegger, *Sein und Zeit* (Tübingen: Niemeyer, 1979), 220. English translation at *Being and Time,* trans. John Macquarrie and Edward Robinson (New York: Harper and Row, 1962), 262.

23   Erschwerung des geschichtlichen Daseins und damit im Grunde des Seins schlechthin ist vielmehr der echte Leistungsinn der Philosophie: Heidegger, *Einführung in die Metaphysik,* p. 9 (*Introduction to Metaphysics,* p. 11).

These sentences express what I am calling Heidegger's 'poetic' answer to the question of our relation to the tradition. On his account the aim of philosophical thought is to free us from the language we presently use by reminding us that this language is not that of 'human reason' but is the creation of the thinkers of our historical past. These thinkers are the poets of Being, the transcribers of "Being's poem – man".[24] To remind us of these thinkers, and to permit us to feel the force of their metaphors in the days before these had been leveled down into literal truths, before these novel uses of words were changed into familiar meanings of words, is the *only* aim which philosophy can have at the present time – not to facilitate but only to make more difficult, not to reweave our fabric of belief and desires but only to remind us of its historical contingency. Heidegger thinks that our time cannot profit from redistributing truth-values among the sentences currently in our repertoire. But he holds out little hope of a new prophetic age, one in which new words will be spoken, words which will enlarge this repertoire in unexpected ways. The most he will say is that such hopes will not be fulfilled without the preparatory work of restoring force to "the most elemental words" in which Dasein has expressed itself in the past. Our relation to the tradition must be a rehearing of what can no longer be heard, rather than a speaking of what has not yet been spoken.

III Poetry and Politics

To see the difference between Heidegger's 'poetic' view of our relation to the tradition and the 'political' view which I wish to attribute to American pragmatism, consider the distinction between 'pseudo-problems' and 'real' problems which Heidegger shares with Carnap. On the pragmatist view, as on Carnap's, a pseudo-problem is one which there is no point in discussing because, as William James put it, it turns upon a difference which "*makes* no difference". It is a "merely verbal problem" – that is, one whose resolution would leave the rest of our beliefs unchanged. This is close to Heidegger's own meaning, as is shown by the fact that some of his examples of pseudo-problems ("other minds", "the external world") are the same as Carnap's.

But there is a crucial difference. Whereas Carnap and the pragmatists think of traditional philosophy as pseudo-science, Heidegger thinks of it as hackneyed poetry – poetry so banal as to be unconscious self-parody. That is, he thinks of the pseudo-problems of the philosophical tradition as pointless reenactments of cliché situations. His objection to them is not that, unlike the real (technologically-oriented) problems solved by scientists, considering them will do us no practical good. Rather, it is that they debase a genre – the genre called 'philosophy'. He is complaining that this genre, which should be the one in which everything is made more difficult, has become an easy game, one which any fool can play. He despises the suggestion, found in scientistic philosophers like Husserl and Carnap, that philosophers might cooperate in the way that engineers do, that they should divide up the work that needs to be done into bite-sized chunks and assign one to each member of a team for 'linguistic analysis' or 'phenomenological description'.

The pragmatist would grant Heidegger's point that the great thinkers are the most idiosyncratic. They are the people like Hegel or Wittgenstein whose metaphors come out of nowhere, lightning bolts which blaze new trails. But whereas Heidegger thinks

---

24   From Heidegger's prose-poem *Aus der Erfahrung des Denkens*. Translated in Heidegger, *Poetry, Language, Thought,* trans. Hofstader (New York: Harper and Row, 1971), 4: "We are too late for the gods and too early for Being. Being's poem, just begun, is man."

that the task of exploring these newly suggested paths of thought is banausic, something which can be left to hacks, the pragmatist thinks that such exploration is the pay-off from the philosopher's work. He thinks of the thinker as serving the community, and of his thinking as futile unless it is followed up by a reweaving of the community's web of belief. That reweaving will assimilate, by gradually literalizing, the new metaphors which the thinker has provided. The proper honor to pay to new, vibrantly alive, metaphors, is to help them become dead metaphors as quickly as possible, to rapidly reduce them to the status of tools of social progress. The glory of the philosopher's thought is not that it initially makes everything more difficult (though that is, of course, true), but that in the end it makes things easier for everybody.

Because the pragmatist rejects scienticism just as Heidegger does, he or she rejects the scientistic idea that some new metaphor, some new philosophical idea, might reveal the permanent neutral matrix of inquiry, a matrix which now simply needs to be filled in by systematic teamwork. The reweaving of the community's fabric of belief is not to be done systematically; it is not a research program, not a matter of filling in what Heidegger calls a *Grundriss*.[25] It is a matter of scratching where it itches, and only where it itches. But whereas Heidegger thinks of this scratching, this liberating of culture from obsolete vocabularies through the work of weaving new metaphors into our communal web of beliefs and desires, as a process of banalization, the pragmatist thinks of it as the only suitable tribute to render the great philosopher. Without this utilization of his work, the great philosopher would have no social role to play, no political function. The pragmatist and Heidegger can agree that the poet and the thinker (in Heidegger's special 'elitist' senses of these terms) are the unacknowledged legislators of the social world. But whereas Heidegger thinks of the social world as existing for the sake of the poet and the thinker, the pragmatist thinks of it the other way round. For Dewey as for Hegel, the point of individual human greatness is its contribution to social freedom, where this is conceived of in the terms we inherit from the French Revolution.

So the crucial difference between the Heideggerian and the pragmatist attitude towards the philosophical tradition stems from a difference in attitude towards recent political history. The basic motive of pragmatism, like that of Hegelianism, was, I have argued elsewhere, a continuation of the Romantic reaction to the Enlightenment's sanc-tification of natural science.[26] Once scientistic rhetoric (which persists in both Hegel and Dewey, and obscures their more basic Romanticism) is cleared away, both Hegelianism and pragmatism can be seen as attempts to clear the ground for the kind of society which the French Revolution hoped to build: one in which every human potentiality is given free rein. In the terms I have been using in this paper, this aspiration amounts to the hope that every new metaphor will have its chance for self-sacrifice, a chance to become a dead metaphor by having been literalized into the language. More specifically, it is the hope that what Dewey calls "the crust of convention" will be as superficial as

25   See Heidegger, 'Die Zeit des Weltbildes' in *Vorträge und Aufsätze,* p. 71.
26   This claim may, in the light of Dewey's obsessive 'scientistic' rhetoric, seem paradoxical. I have tried to defend it in 'Nineteenth Century Idealism and Twentieth Century Textualism' (in my *Consequences of Pragmatism* (Minneapolis: University of Minnesota Press, 1982)), in 'Pragmatism Without Method' (in *Sidney Hook: Philosopher of Science and Freedom,* ed. Paul Kurtz (Buffalo: Prometheus Books, 1983), and in 'Reply to Sleeper and Edel', *Transactions of the C. S. Peirce Society,* vol. 21 (1985).

possible, that the social glue which holds society together – the language in which we state our shared beliefs and hopes – will be as flexible as possible.

One can only have such a hope if one thinks that, despite the fears of Husserl, Julien Benda, and contemporary communitarian critics of political liberalism, a democratic society can get along without the sort of reassurance provided by the thought that it has 'adequate philosophical foundations' or that it is 'grounded' in 'human reason'. On this view, the most appropriate foundation for a liberal democracy is a conviction by its citizens that things will go better for everybody if every new metaphor is given a hearing, if no belief or desire is held so sacred that a metaphor which endangers it is automatically rejected. Such a conviction amounts to the rejection of the claim that we, the democratic societies of the West, know what we want in advance – that we have more than a tentative and revisable *Grundriss* for our social projects. One task of the intellectuals in these societies will be to help their fellow-citizens live with the thought that we do not yet have an adequate language, and to wean them from the idea that there is something out there to be 'adequate' to. This amounts to suggesting that we try to eschew scientistic pronunciamentos which take for granted that we now have a secure grasp on the nature of the society, or of the good. It means admitting that the terms in which we state our communal convictions and hopes are doomed to obsolescence, that we shall *always* need new metaphors, new logical spaces, new jargons, that there will never be a final resting-place for thought, nor a social philosophy which is a *strenge Wissenschaft*.

It will be apparent that, in formulating the pragmatist view in this way, I am trying to turn such Heideggerian notions as 'clearing', 'opening', 'authenticity' and 'historical being-there' to un-Heideggerian purposes. I want to yoke them to political movements which Heidegger himself distrusted. For him, the political life of both the liberal democracies and the totalitarian states was of a piece with that 'technological frenzy' which seemed to him the essence of the modern age. The difference between the two did not really matter. By contrast, I want to suggest that we see the democracy-versus-totalitarianism issue as as basic as an intellectual issue can get. We need to eschew the idea, common to Heidegger and Adorno as well as to many contemporary *Marxisant* writers, that there is a phenomenon called 'modernity' which encompasses both bourgeois democracy and totalitarianism, and that one can achieve a philosophical grasp of this phenomenon in which the distinction between these two forms of social life is *aufgehoben*.

One way of putting this point is that although Heidegger was only accidentally a Nazi,[27] Dewey was essentially a social democrat. His thought has no point when

27   I would grant that Heidegger was, from early on, suspicious of democracy and of the 'disenchanted' world which Weber described. His thought was, indeed, essentially anti-democratic. But lots of Germans who were dubious about democracy and modernity did not become Nazis. Heidegger did because he was both more of a ruthless opportunist and more of a political ignoramus than most of the German intellectuals who shared his doubts. Although Heidegger's philosophy seems to me not to have specifically *totalitarian* implications, it does take for granted that attempts to feed the hungry, shorten the working day, etc., just do not have much to do with philosophy. For Heidegger, Christianity is merely a certain decadent form of Platonic metaphysics; the change from pagan to Christian moral consciousness goes unnoticed. The 'social gospel' side of Christianity which meant most to Tillich (a social democratic thinker who was nevertheless able to appropriate a lot of Heideggerian ideas and jargon) meant nothing to Heidegger.

detached from social democratic politics.[28] His pragmatism is an attempt to help achieve the greatest happiness of the greatest number by facilitating the replacement of language, customs, and institutions which impede that happiness. Heidegger dismissed this attempt as one which we can no longer take seriously. He thinks that Nietzsche helped us see that

> Metaphysics is history's open space, wherein it becomes a destining that the suprasensory world, the Ideas, God, the moral law, the authority of reason, progress, the happiness of the greatest number, culture, civilization, suffer the loss of their constructive force and become void.[29]

But for Dewey, "progress, the happiness of the greatest number, culture, civilization" do not belong on the same list as "the suprasensory world, the Ideas, God, the moral law, the authority of reason". The latter are dead metaphors which pragmatists can no longer find uses for. The former still have a point. The pragmatist does not claim to have an argument against the latter items and for the former items. He is not scientistic enough to think that there is some neutral philosophical standpoint which would supply premises for such an argument. He simply takes his stand within the democratic community and asks what an understanding of the thinkers of the past and of the present can do for such a community.

Heidegger thinks that a non-reductive, non-anachronistic, hearing of the words of these thinkers might put us in a position to appreciate where we now are (where, as Heidegger would say, Being now is). The pragmatist agrees, but reads them differently. He hears them as the young Hegel did – as urging us in the direction of greater human freedom, rather than in the direction of technological frenzy, of an age in which "human creativity finally passes over into business enterprise."[30] He agrees with both Husserl and Heidegger (and with Horkheimer and Adorno) that the age of scientific technology *may* turn out to be the age in which openness and freedom are rationalized out of existence. But his reply is that it *might* turn out to be the age in which the democratic community becomes the master, rather than the servant, of scientific rationality.

IV The Present Situation

In what precedes I have sketched what I take to be the central metaphilosophical disagreements of recent times. On my account, there are two basic lines of division: one

28   For an account of Dewey as a contributor to social democratic thought, see James T. Kloppenberg, *Uncertain Victory: Social Democracy and Progressivism in European and American Thought, 1870–1920* (New York: Oxford University Press, 1986). For some acute comments on the relation between my own version of pragmatism and political liberalism, see Christopher Norris, *Contest of Faculties: Philosophy and Theory after Deconstruction* (London: Methuen, 1985), chapter 6 ('Philosophy as a Kind of Narrative: Rorty on Post-modern Liberal Culture').

29   Die Metaphysik ist der Geschichtsraum, worin zum Geschick wird, dass die uebersinnliche Welt, die Ideen, Gott, das Sittengesetz, die Vernunftautorität, der Fortschritt, das Glück der Meisten, die Kultur, die Zivilisation ihre bauende Kraft einbüssen und nichtig werden: Heidegger, *Holzwege* (Frankfurt: Klostermann, 1972), 204, trans. W. Lovitt at Heidegger, *The Question Concerning Technology and Other Essays* (New York: Harper and Row, 1977), 65.

30   Das Schöpferische … geht zuletzt in das Geschäft über: *Holzwege*, p. 203 (*The Question Concerning Technology…*, p. 64).

between the scientism common to Husserl and positivism, and the other between two reactions to this scientism. The first reaction – Heidegger's – is dictated by a tacit and unarguable rejection of the project of the French Revolution, and of the idea that everything, including philosophy, is an instrument for the achievement of the greatest happiness of the greatest number. The second – Dewey's – is dictated by an equally tacit and unarguable acceptance of that project and that idea.

By way of a conclusion, I shall try to bring these distinctions to bear on the contemporary situation of the philosophical profession, of philosophy as an institution. One can look at this situation from the inside, and concentrate on the relations, within the profession, of competing philosophical schools. Or one can look at it from the outside, at the relations between the profession and the rest of culture.

Taking the inside view first, it is clear that there are really two institutions rather than one. Analytic philosophy has pretty well closed itself off from contact with non-analytic philosophy, and lives in its own world. The scientistic approach to philosophy which Husserl shared with Carnap lives on, forming a tacit presupposition of the work of analytic philosophers. Even though analytic philosophy now describes itself as post-positivistic, the idea that philosophy 'analyzes' or 'describes' some ahistorical formal 'structures' – an idea common to Husserl, Russell, Carnap, and Ryle – persists. However, there is little explicit metaphilosophical defense or development of this claim. Analytic philosophers are not much interested in either defining or defending the presuppositions of their work. Indeed, the gap between 'analytic' and 'non-analytic' philosophy nowadays coincides pretty closely with the division between philosophers who are not interested in historico-metaphilosophical reflections on their own activity and philosophers who are.

This difference in interests parallels a difference in reading habits, a difference in philosophical canons. If the preeminent figures in one's canon include Berkeley, Hume, Mill, and Frege, one will probably not be much interested in metaphilosophy. If they include Hegel, Nietzsche, and Heidegger, one probably will – not metaphilosophy in the form of methodology, the form it took in Husserl and in Russell, but rather in the form of an historical narrative which places the works of the philosophers within the historical development of the culture.

More analytic philosophers simply take for granted that such figures as Hume and Frege have isolated central, deep, problems – problems which are definatory of the discipline. They see no more need to construct or study historical narratives than students of physics do to study the history of physics. But some less complacent members of this school (e.g., Cora Diamond, Hilary Putnam, Thomas Nagel, Stanley Cavell) have a more ambivalent and nuanced relation to the analytic canon, and a less distant relation to historical narrative. Nagel, for example, suggests that the familiar textbook 'problems of philosophy' – the problems of which he himself proceeds to treat – are characteristic of 'the childhood of the intellect'. But he thinks that "a culture that tries to skip it [this stage of childhood] will never grow up."[31] He cautions against "deflationary metaphilosophical theories like positivism and pragmatism, which offer to raise us above the old battles."[32] On Nagel's view "Philosophy cannot

---

31   Thomas Nagel, *The View from Nowhere* (New York: Oxford University Press, 1985), 12.
32   Ibid., 11.

take refuge in reduced ambitions. It is after eternal and nonlocal truth, even though we know that is not what we are going to get."[33]

On the 'non-analytic' side of the divide, by contrast, the realization that we are not going to get this sort of truth is a reason for dropping old ambitions. For the tacit presupposition which unites non-analytic philosophers – those philosophers who reject metaphilosophical scientism – is that Nagel is wrong when he says that

> ...philosophy is not like a particular language. Its sources are preverbal and often precultural, and one of its most difficult tasks is to express unformed but intuitively felt problems in language without losing them.[34]

The mark of intellectual immaturity is, on this alternative account, precisely an ahistorical account of philosophy such as Nagel's, an account whose grip has only been broken in the last two hundred years. On the alternative account, philosophy is very much like a 'particular language' and the idea that a particular philosophical canon has isolated problems which are 'often precultural' is just the latest version of the empiricist 'Myth of the Given'. So these philosophers try to place the analysts' canon, and their list of problems, in history, rather than seeing both as in touch with something ahistorical, something natural to the species. The reason why Hegel, Nietzsche, and Heidegger loom so large in the alternative canon is that these philosophers specialize in narratives which 'place' rival canons.

There is little common ground between these two sets of metaphilosophical presuppositions, and therefore little possibility of debate between their proponents. The result is that the philosophical profession is divided into two institutionalized traditions which have little contact. Analytic philosophy, in so far as it takes notice of its rival, views it as an aestheticized and historicized form of idealism.[35] The 'continental' tradition, by contrast, views the 'analytic' tradition as escaping from history into a dogmatic and outworn realism, but it too takes little notice of the opposition.

Because neither side has much use for the notion that philosophy has a distinctive method, neither is about to offer large metaphilosophical self-descriptions of the sort in which Russell and Husserl indulged. Yet the crucial difference between them is, I think, still caught by the formula which I have used to catch the difference between Husserl on the one hand and Heidegger and Dewey on the other: they differ on the question of whether philosophy has a prelinguistic subject-matter, and thus on the question of whether there is an ahistorical reality to which a given philosophical vocabulary may or may not be adequate. The analytic tradition regards metaphor as a distraction from that reality, whereas the non-analytic tradition regards metaphor as the way of escaping from the illusion that there is such a reality. My hunch is that these traditions will persist side-by-side indefinitely. I cannot see any possibility of compromise, and I suspect that the most likely scenario is an

---

33   Ibid., 10.
34   Ibid., 11.
35   Nagel, for example, sees those who adopt alternative canons as being less closely in touch with reality than those who adopt his own – as 'idealist', in the sense of believing that "what there is and how things are cannot go beyond what we could in principle think about." (Ibid., 9) They suffer from "an insufficiently robust sense of reality and of its independence of any particular form of human understanding." (Ibid., 5) Nagel's attitude toward pragmatism parallels the attitude which Heidegger adopts toward what he calls "humanism" in the 'Letter on Humanism'.

increasing indifference of each school to the existence of the other. In time it may seem merely a quaint historical accident that both institutions bear the same name.[36]

What, then, of the place of the philosophical profession in the culture as a whole? For philosophers who think of themselves as quasi-scientists, this is not an important question. Analytic philosophy has little influence on other academic disciplines, and little interest either for practitioners of those disciplines or for the intellectuals. But analytic philosophers are not distressed by this fact. It is natural, given their scientistic metaphilosophy, that analytic philosophers are content to solve philosophical problems without worrying about the source of those problems or the consequences of their solution.[37]

By contrast, non-analytic philosophers typically dislike the thought that philosophy is (or is only) an academic discipline, merely one more *Wissenschaft*. They would like their work to be continuous either with literature on the one hand or with politics on the other, or both. Insofar as they succeed in making their work continuous with literature, they cease to belong to a separate institution: they are simply writers who happen to be familiar with a certain literary tradition (a tradition that starts with Plato and runs up through Hegel to the present). Thus there is little point in drawing institutional lines between the study of Sartre's treatises, of his critical essays, and of his stories. There is equally little point in worrying whether Nietzsche counts as a figure in the history of German literature (as he used to, before Heidegger helped him to a place in the philosophical canon) or in the history of philosophy. Anybody interested in Derrida's treatment of Socrates in *La Carte Postale* is likely also to be interested in Valery's treatment of him in *Eupalinos* and Nietzsche's in *The Birth of Tragedy*, and is unlikely to know or care that only one among these three great writers earned his bread as a philosophy professor.

When it comes to attempts to make non-analytic philosophy continuous with politics, however, things become more complex and problematic. For non-analytic philosophy is, with some exceptions, dominated by a Heideggerian vision of the modern world rather than a Deweyan one, and by despair over the condition of the world rather than by social hope. Because the typical member of this tradition is obsessed with the idea of 'radical criticism', when he or she turns to politics it is rarely in a reformist, pragmatic, spirit, but rather in a mood either of deep pessimism or of revolutionary fury. Except for a few

36   Occasionally a university sets up an 'alternative' philosophy department, bowing to the fact that two noncommunicating disciplines are currently going by the same name. This usually creates trouble, because the word 'philosophy' is still an honorific, and both departments resent its use by the other. Eventually some genius will resolve this entirely verbal issue by hitting upon just the right names for the two sorts of philosophy departments, names which will permit peaceful coexistence of the sort which now obtains between classics departments and departments of modern literature. (It is sometimes forgotten that classicists once objected furiously to the creation of departments of the latter sort. On their view, putting recent novels on a syllabus for a degree was a degradation of the university.)
37   There are exceptions. Analytic philosophers who specialize in 'applied ethics' have sometimes claimed that there are special skills associated with analytic philosophy which are useful in resolving policy dilemmas (on such matters as abortion, job discrimination, disarmament, and the like). But it is very hard to isolate any skills employed by philosophy professors who take up such issues which were not routinely employed by people (philosophers like J. S. Mill and non-philosophers like Macaulay) who took up similar issues in the last century, or are not being routinely employed by non-philosophers who write on such topics today. The notion of 'analytic skills' is, I think, a relic of the earlier idea of a special 'method of philosophical analysis'. Analytic philosophers have often written very well indeed on current policy dilemmas, but it is pointless to view their work as the product of a distinctive professional ability.

writers such as Habermas, 'continental' philosophers see no relation between social democratic politics and philosophizing.[38] So the only sort of politics with which this tradition is continuous is not the actual political discourse of the surviving democratic nations, but a kind of pseudo-politics reminiscent of Marxist study-groups of the thirties – a sort of continual self-correction of theory, with no conceivable relation to practice.[39]

As Deweyan social democrats, philosophers can be politically useful in the same way as can poets, playwrights, economists, and engineers. Members of these various professions can serve reformist social democratic politics by providing piecemeal nudges and cautions in respect to particular projects at particular times. But this sort of retail political utility is not the wholesale sort which Marxists, post-Marxist radicals, and neo-conservatives would like philosophers to have. They see political theory and philosophy as foundational because they see it as penetrating to a reality behind contemporary appearances. By contrast, the Deweyan sees the relevant 'reality' – human suffering and oppression – as already having been made clearly visible in the course of the last two centuries' attempt to realize the ideals of the French Revolution. The Deweyan is ruefully willing to admit that there are always going to be new varieties of suffering and oppression to be exposed (e.g. those endured by women as a class). He sees philosophy's role in exposing them as continuous with that of literature and of the social sciences. But he thinks contemporary democratic societies are *already* organized around the need for continual exposure of suffering and injustice, and that no 'radical critique' is required, but just attention to detail. So he thinks of the philosopher not as exposing the false or corrupt foundations of this society but as playing off the good and the bad features of this society against each other.

To my mind, the persistence on the left of this notion of 'radical critique' is an unfortunate residue of the scientistic conception of philosophy. Neither the idea of penetrating to a reality behind the appearances, nor that of theoretical foundations for politics, coheres with the conception of language and inquiry which, I have been arguing, is common to Heidegger and to Dewey. For both ideas presuppose that someday we shall penetrate to the true, natural, ahistorical matrix of all possible language and knowledge. Marx, for all his insistence on the priority of praxis, clung to both ideas, and they became dominant within Marxism after Lenin and Stalin turned Marxism into a state religion. But there is no reason why either should be adopted by those who are not obliged to practice this religion.

The moral I wish to draw from the story I have been telling is that we should carry through on the rejection of metaphilosophical scientism. That is, we should let the debate between those who see contemporary democratic societies as hopeless, and those who see them as our only hope, be conducted in terms of the actual problems now being faced by those societies. If I am right in thinking that the difference between Heidegger's and Dewey's ways of rejecting scientism is political rather than methodological or

---

38   Habermas is (despite what are, to my mind, unfortunate residues of scientism in his thought) the contemporary philosopher who most resembles Dewey – not only in doctrine but in his attitude toward his society, and in the role which he has played in the day-to-day, nitty-gritty, political debates of his time. Like Dewey, Habermas's thought is dominated by the question 'What sort of philosophical vocabulary and approach would serve human freedom best?' and by the conviction that the modern industrialized technological world is not hopeless, but, on the contrary, capable of continual self-improvement.

39   This is particularly evident in the U.S. and Britain, where there is often thought to be some natural affinity between neo-Heideggerian philosophizing and leftist politics.

metaphysical, then it would be well for us to debate political topics explicitly, rather than using Aesopian philosophical language.

If we did, then I think that we would realize how little theoretical reflection is likely to help us with our current problems. For once we have criticized all the self-deceptive sophistry, and exposed all the 'false consciousness', the result of our efforts is to find ourselves just where our grandfathers suspected we were: in the midst of a struggle for power between those who currently possess it (in our day: the oilmen of Texas or Quatar or Mexico, the *nomenklatura* of Moscow or Bucharest, the generals of Indonesia or Chile) and those who are starving or terrorized because they lack it. Neither twentieth-century Marxism, nor analytic philosophy, nor post-Nietzschean 'continental' philosophy has done anything to clarify this struggle. We have not developed any conceptual instruments with which to operate politically that are superior to those available at the turn of the century to Dewey or Weber.

The vocabulary of social democratic politics – the vocabulary which Dewey and Weber helped cobble together – probably does not require further sophistication by philosophers (though economists and sociologist and historians have done some useful up-dating). There are no facts about economic oppression or class struggle, or modern technology, which that vocabulary cannot describe and a more 'radical' metaphoric can. The horrors peculiar to the end of our century – imminent nuclear holocaust, the permanent drug-riddled black underclass in the U.S., the impossibility of feeding countries like Haiti and Chad except by massive charity which the rich nations are too selfish to provide, the unbreakable grip of the rich or the military on the governments of most of the Third World, the unbreakable grip of the KGB on the Russian people and of the Soviet army on a third of Europe – are no better describable with the help of more recent philosophical vocabulary than with the vocabulary used by our grandfathers. Nobody has come up with any proposal for ending any of these horrors which draws on new conceptual resources. Our political imagination has not been enlarged by the philosophy of our century. This is not because of the irrelevance or cowardice or irresponsibility of philosophy professors, but because of the sheer recalcitrance of the situation into which the human race has stumbled.

Dewey was lucky. His generation may have been the last which could feel confident of a future in which the race would work out its destiny without needing the religious and scientistic myths which had comforted it in the past – a future in which human freedom was entrusted to as yet undreamt-of metaphors, vocabularies still unborn. As the century has darkened, we find it less and less possible to imagine getting out of our present trap and into such a future. But Dewey was also right. If we ever have the courage to drop the scientist model of philosophy without falling back into a desire for holiness (as Heidegger did), then, no matter how dark the time, we shall no longer turn to the philosophers for rescue as our ancestors turned to the priests. We shall turn instead to the poets and the engineers, the people who produce startling new projects for achieving the greatest happiness of the greatest number.[40]

---

40   This paper is a revised version of one prepared for a conference at the University of Vienna on the occasion of the 50th anniversary of the publication of Husserl's *Krisis*. The earlier version appeared, in German translation, in Michael Benedikt and Rudol Berger, eds., *Die Krise der Phänomenologie und die Pragmatik des Wissenschaftsfortschritts* (Vienna: Verlag der Österreichischen Staatsdruckerei, 1986).

12

Solidarity or Objectivity?

There are two principal ways in which reflective human beings try, by placing their lives in a larger context, to give sense to those lives. The first is by telling the story of their contribution to a community. This community may be the actual historical one in which they live, or another actual one, distant in time or place, or a quite imaginary one, consisting perhaps of a dozen heroes and heroines selected from history or fiction or both. The second way is to describe themselves as standing in immediate relation to a non-human reality. This relation is immediate in the sense that it does not derive from a relation between such a reality and their tribe, or their nation, or their imagined band of comrades. I shall say that stories of the former kind exemplify the desire for solidarity, and that stories of the latter kind exemplify the desire for objectivity. Insofar as a person is seeking solidarity, he or she does not ask about the relation between the practices of the chosen community and something outside that community. Insofar as he seeks objectivity, he distances himself from the actual persons around him not by thinking of himself as a member of some other real or imaginary group, but rather by attaching himself to something which can be described without reference to any particular human beings.

The tradition in Western culture which centers around the notion of the search for Truth, a tradition which runs from the Greek philosophers through the Enlightenment, is the clearest example of the attempt to find a sense in one's existence by turning away from solidarity to objectivity. The idea of Truth as something to be pursued for its own sake, not because it will be good for oneself, or for one's real or imaginary community, is the central theme of this tradition. It was perhaps the growing awareness by the Greeks of the sheer diversity of human communities which stimulated the emergence of this ideal. A fear of parochialism, of being confined within the horizons of the group into which one happens to be born, a need to see it with the eyes of a stranger, helps produce the skeptical and ironic tone characteristic of Euripides and Socrates. Herodutus' willingness to take the barbarians seriously enough to describe their customs in detail may have been a necessary prelude to Plato's claim that the way to transcend skepticism is to

Richard M. Rorty, "Solidarity or Objectivity," *Nanzen Review of American Studies*, vol. 6 (1984): 1–19, © 1984 by Nanzen Review of American Studies: A Journal of Center for American Studies, Nanzen University, Nagoya. Reprinted with permission.

envisage a common goal of humanity – a goal set by human nature rather than by Greek culture. The combination of Socratic alienation and Platonic hope gives rise to the idea of the intellectual as someone who is in touch with the nature of things, not by way of the opinions of his community, but in a more immediate way.

Plato developed the idea of such an intellectual by means of distinctions between knowledge and opinion, and between appearance and reality. Such distinctions conspire to produce the idea that rational inquiry should make visible a realm to which non-intellectuals have little access, and of whose very existence they may be doubtful. In the Enlightenment, this notion became concrete in the adoption of the Newtonian physical scientist as a model of the intellectual. To most thinkers of the 18th century, it seemed clear that the access to Nature which physical science had provided should now be followed by the establishment of social, political and economic institutions which were in accordance with Nature. Ever since, liberal social thought has centered around social reform as made possible by objective knowledge of what human beings are like – not knowledge of what Greeks or Frenchmen or Chinese are like, but of humanity as such. We are the heirs of this objectivist tradition, which centers round the assumption that we must step outside our community long enough to examine it in the light of something which transcends it, namely, that which it has in common with every other actual and possible human community. This tradition dreams of an ultimate community which will have transcended the distinction between the natural and the social, which will exhibit a solidarity which is not parochial because it is the expression of an ahistorical human nature. Much of the rhetoric of contemporary intellectual life takes for granted that the goal of scientific inquiry into man is to understand "underlying structures," or "culturally invariant factors" or "biologically determined patterns."

Those who wish to ground solidarity in objectivity – call them "realists" – have to construe truth as correspondence to reality. So they must construct a metaphysics which has room for a special relation between beliefs and objects which will differentiate true from false beliefs. They also must argue that there are procedures of justification of belief which are natural and not merely local. So they must construct an epistemology which has room for a kind of justification which is not merely social but natural, springing from human nature itself, and made possible by a link between that part of nature and the rest of nature. On their view, the various procedures which are thought of as providing rational justification by one or another culture may or may not really *be* rational. For to be truly rational, procedures of justification *must* lead to the truth, to correspondence to reality, to the intrinsic nature of things.

By contrast, those who wish to reduce objectivity to solidarity – call them "pragmatists" – do not require either a metaphysics or an epistemology. They view truth as, in William James' phrase, what it is good for *us* to believe. So they do not need an account of a relation between beliefs and objects called "correspondence," nor an account of human cognitive abilities which ensures that our species is capable of entering into that relation. They see the gap between truth and justification not as something to be bridged by isolating a natural and trans-cultural sort of rationality which can be used to criticize certain cultures and praise others, but simply as the gap between the actual good and the possible better. From a pragmatist point of view, to say that what is rational for us now to believe may not be *true*, is simply to say that somebody may come up with a better idea. It is to say that there is always room for improved belief, since new evidence, or new hypotheses, or a whole new vocabulary, may come along.[1] For pragmatists, the desire for objectivity is not the desire to escape the limitations of one's community, but simply the desire for as much intersubjective agreement as possible, the desire to extend the reference of "us" as far as we can. Insofar as pragmatists make a distinction between knowledge and opinion, it is simply the distinction between topics on which such agreement is relatively easy to get and topics on which it is relatively hard to get.

"Relativism" is the traditional epithet applied to pragmatism by realists. Three different views are commonly referred to by this name. The first is the view that every belief is as good as every other. The second is the view that "true" is an equivocal term, having as many meanings as there are procedures of justification. The third is the view that there is nothing to be said about either truth or rationality apart from descriptions of the familiar procedures of justification which a given society – *ours* – uses in one or another area of inquiry. The pragmatist holds the ethnocentric third view. But he does not hold the self-refuting first view, nor the eccentric second view. He thinks that his views are better than the realists, but he does not think that his views correspond to the nature of things. He thinks that the very flexibility of the word "true" – the fact that it is merely an expression of commendation – insures its univocity. The term "true," on his account, means the same in all cultures, just as equally flexible terms like "here," "there," "good," "bad," "you" and "me" mean the same in all cultures. But the identity of meaning is, of course, compatible with diversity of reference, and with diversity of procedures for assigning the terms. So he feels free to use the term "true" as a general term of commendation in the same way as his realist opponent does – and in particular to use it to commend his own view.

However, it is not clear why "relativist" should be thought an appropriate term for the ethnocentric third view, the one which the pragmatist *does* hold. For the pragmatist is not holding a positive theory which says that something is relative to something else. He is, instead, making the purely *negative* point that we should drop the traditional distinction between knowledge and opinion, construed as the distinction between truth as correspondence to reality and truth as a commendatory term for well-justified beliefs.

1   This attitude towards truth, in which the consensus of a community rather than a relation to a non-human reality is taken as central, is characteristic not only of the American pragmatic tradition, but of Popper and of Habermas. It should be noted, however, that it is independent of Popper's insistence on replacing "confirmation" with "falsifiability" as the crucial idea in philosophy of science. That insistence has been resisted by most American philosophers of science as largely factitious. This resistance, combined with the fact that most of the views in philosophy of science and social philosophy which in Britain are viewed as distinctively Popperian were, in America, already familiar from Dewey, accounts for the fact that Popper has never loomed as large in the United States as in England. Habermas's own criticisms of Popper parallel those made by Deweyan holists of positivism. Habermas himself, however, has neglected the analogies between his own thought and Dewey's and has concentrated on his relation to Peirce. It is important to see, however, that the pragmatist notion of truth common to James and Dewey is not dependent on the Peirce-Habermas notion of an "ideal end of inquiry" nor of an "ideally free speech community." For criticism of these notions, which in my view are insufficiently ethnocentric, see my *Consequences of Pragmatism* (Minneapolis, 1982). p. xiv, "Pragmatism, Davidson and Truth" in *Essays in Honor of Donald Davidson*, ed. Ernest LePore (Minneapolis, 1984), and "Habermas and Lyotard on Post-Modernity," *Praxis International* (1984): 32–44 [reprinted in EHO].

The reason that the realist calls this negative claim "relativistic" is that he cannot believe that anybody would seriously deny that truth has an intrinsic nature. So when the pragmatist says that there is nothing to be said about truth save that each of us will commend as true those beliefs which he or she finds good to believe, the realist is inclined to interpret this as one more positive theory about the nature of truth: a theory according to which truth is simply the contemporary opinion of a chosen individual or group. Such a theory would, of course, be self-refuting. But the pragmatist does not have a theory of truth, much less a relativistic one. As a partisan of solidarity, his account of the value of cooperative human inquiry has only an ethical base, not an epistemological or metaphysical one. Not having *any* epistemology, *a fortiori* he does not have a relativistic one.

The question of whether truth or rationality has an intrinsic nature, or whether we ought to have a positive theory about either topic, is just the question of whether our self-description ought to be constructed around a relation to human nature or around a relation to a particular collection of human beings, whether we should desire objectivity or solidarity. It is hard to see how one could choose between these alternatives by looking more deeply into the nature of knowledge, or of man, or of nature. Indeed, the proposal that this issue might be so settled begs the question in favour of the realist, for it presupposes that knowledge, man, and nature *have* real essences which are relevant to the problem at hand. For the pragmatist, by contrast, "knowledge" is, like "truth," simply a compliment paid to the beliefs which we think so well justified that, for the moment, further justification is not needed. An inquiry into the nature of knowledge can, on his view, only be a socio-historical account of how various people have tried to reach agreement on what to believe.

This view which I am calling "pragmatism" is almost, but not quite, the same as what Hilary Putnam, in his recent *Reason, Truth and History*, calls "the internalist conception of philosophy."[2] Putnam defines such a conception as one which gives up the attempt at a God's-eye of things, the attempt at contact with the non-human which I have been calling "the desire for objectivity." Unfortunately, he accompanies his defense of the anti-realist views I am recommending with a polemic against a lot of the other people who hold these views – e.g., Kuhn, Feyerabend, Foucault, and myself. We are criticized as "relativists." Putnam presents "internalism" as a happy *via media* between realism and relativism. He speaks of "the plethora of relativistic doctrines being marketed today"[3] and in particular of "the French philosophers" as holding "some fancy mixture of cultural relativism and 'structuralism'."[4] But when it comes to criticizing these doctrines all that Putnam finds to attack is the so-called "incommensurability thesis": viz., "terms used in another culture cannot be equated in meaning or reference with any terms or expressions *we* possess."[5] He sensibly agrees with Donald Davidson in remarking that this thesis is self-refuting. Criticism of this thesis, however, is destructive of, at most, some incautious passages in some early writings by Feyerabend. Once this thesis is brushed aside, it is hard to see how Putnam himself differs from most of those he criticizes.

2   Hilary Putnam, *Reason, Truth and History* (Cambridge, 1981), pp. 49–50. A French translation of this book will be published by Editions Minuit.
3   Ibid., p. 119.
4   Ibid., p. x.
5   Ibid., p. 114.

Putnam accepts the Davidsonian point that, as he puts it, "the whole justification of an interpretative scheme … is that it renders the behavior of others at least minimally reasonable by *our* lights."[6] It would seem natural to go on from this to say that we cannot get outside the range of those lights, that we cannot stand on neutral ground illuminated only by the natural light of reason. But Putnam draws back from this conclusion. He does so because he construes the claim that we cannot do so as the claim that the range of our thought is restricted by what he calls "institutionalized norms," publically available criteria for settling all arguments, including philosophical arguments. He rightly says that there are no such criteria, arguing that the suggestion that there are is as self-refuting as the "incommensurability thesis." He is, I think, entirely right in saying that the notion that philosophy is or should become such an application of explicit criteria contradicts the very idea of philosophy.[7] One can gloss Putnam's point by saying that "philosophy" is precisely what a culture becomes capable of when it ceases to define itself in terms of explicit rules, and becomes sufficiently leisured and civilized to rely on inarticulate know-how, to substitute *phronesis* for codification, and conversation with foreigners for conquest of them.

But to say that we cannot refer every question to explicit criteria institutionalized by our society does not speak to the point which the people whom Putnam calls "relativists" are making. One reason these people are pragmatists is precisely that they share Putnam's distrust of the positivistic idea that rationality is a matter of applying criteria.

Such a distrust is common, for example, to Kuhn, Mary Hesse, Wittgenstein, Michael Polanyi and Michael Oakeshott. Only someone who did think of rationality in this way would dream of suggesting that "true" means something different in different societies. For only such a person could imagine that there was anything to pick out to which one might make "true" relative. Only if one shares the logical positivists' idea that we all carry around things called "rules of language" which regulate what we say when, will one suggest that there is no way to break out of one's culture.

In the most original and powerful section of his book, Putnam argues that the notion that "rationality … is defined by the local cultural norms" is merely the demonic counterpart of positivism. It is, as he says, "a scientistic theory inspired by anthropology as positivism was a scientistic theory inspired by the exact sciences." By "scientism" Putnam means the notion that rationality consists in the application of criteria.[8] Suppose we drop this notion, and accept Putnam's own Quinean picture of inquiry as the continual reweaving of a web of beliefs rather than as the application of criteria to cases. Then the notion of "local cultural norms" will lose its offensively parochial overtones. For now to say that we must work by our own lights, that we must be ethnocentric, is merely to say that beliefs suggested by another culture must be tested by trying to weave them together with beliefs we already have. It is a consequence of this holistic view of knowledge, a view *shared* by Putnam and those he criticizes as "relativists," that alternative cultures are not to be thought of on the model of alternative geometries. Alternative geometries are irreconcilable because they have axiomatic structures, and contradictory axioms. They are *designed* to be irreconcilable. Cultures are not so designed, and do not have axiomatic

---

6   Ibid., p. 119. See Davidson's "On the Very Idea of a Conceptual Scheme" (*Proceedings of the American Philosophical Association*, 1974), a classic statement of the view that we are necessarily ethnocentric.

7   See Putnam, p. 113.

8   Ibid., p. 126.

structures. To say that they have "institutionalized norms" is only to say, with Foucault, that knowledge is never separable from power – that one is likely to suffer if one does not hold certain beliefs at certain times and places. But such institutional backups for beliefs take the form of bureaucrats and policemen, not of "rules of language" and "criteria of rationality." To think otherwise is the Cartesian fallacy of seeing axioms where there are only shared habits, of viewing statements which summarize such practices as if they reported constraints enforcing such practices. Part of the force of Quine's and Davidson's attack on the distinction between the conceptual and the empirical is that the distinction between different cultures does not differ in kind from the distinction between different theories held by members of a single culture. The Tasmanian aborigines and the British colonists had trouble communicating, but this trouble was different only in extent from the difficulties in communication experienced by Gladstone and Disraeli. The trouble in all such cases is just the difficulty of explaining why other people disagree with us, of reweaving our beliefs so as to fit the fact of disagreement together with the other beliefs we hold. The same Quinean arguments which dispose of the positivists' distinction between analytic and synthetic truth dispose of the anthropologists' distinction between the inter-cultural and the intra-cultural.

On this holistic account of cultural norms, however, we do not need the notion of a universal trans-cultural rationality which Putnam invokes against those whom he calls "relativists." Just before the end of his book, Putnam says that once we drop the notion of a God's-eye point of view we realize that:

> We can only hope to produce a more rational *conception* of rationality or a better *conception* of morality if we operate from *within* our tradition (with its echoes of the Greek agora, of Newton, and so on, in the case of rationality, and with its echoes of scripture, of the philosophers, of the democratic revolutions, and so on, in the case of the philosophers, of the democratic revolutions, and so on, in the case of morality). We are invited to engage in a truly human dialogue...[9]

With this I entirely agree, and so, I take it, would Kuhn, Hesse, and most of the other so-called "relativists" – perhaps even Foucault. But Putnam then goes on to pose a further question:

> Does this dialogue have an ideal terminus? Is there a *true* conception of rationality, an ideal morality, even if all we ever have are our *conceptions* of these?

I do not see the point of this question. Putnam suggests that a negative answer – the view that "there is only the dialogue" – is just another form of self-refuting relativism. But, once again, I do not see how a claim that something does not exist can be construed as a claim that something is relative to something else. In the final sentence of his book, Putnam says that "The very fact that we speak of our different conceptions as different conceptions of *rationality* posits a *Grenzbegriff*, a limit-concept of ideal truth." But what is such a posit supposed to do, except to say that from God's point of view the human race is heading in the right direction? Surely Putnam's "internalism" should forbid him to say anything like that. To say that *we* think we're heading in the right direction is just

9   Ibid., p. 216.

to say, with Kuhn, that we can, by hindsight, tell the story of the past as a story of progress. To say that we still have a long way to go, that our present views should not be cast in bronze, is too platitudinous to require support by positing limit-concepts. So it is hard to see what difference is made by the difference between saying "there is only the dialogue" and saying "there is also that to which the dialogue converges."

I would suggest that Putnam here, at the end of the day, slides back into the scientism he rightly condemns in others. For the root of scientism, defined as the view that rationality is a matter of applying criteria, is the desire for objectivity, the hope that what Putnam calls "human flourishing" has a trans-historical nature. I think that Feyerabend is right in suggesting that until we discard the metaphor of inquiry, and human activity generally, as converging rather than proliferating, as becoming more unified rather than more diverse, we shall never be free of the motives which once led us to posit gods. Positing *Grenzbegriffe* seems merely a way of telling ourselves that a non-existent God would, if he did exist, be pleased with us. If we could ever be moved solely by the desire for solidarity, setting aside the desire for objectivity altogether, then we should think of human progress as making it possible for human beings to do more interesting things and be more interesting people, not as heading towards a place which has somehow been prepared for humanity in advance. Our self-image would employ images of making rather than finding, the images used by the Romantics to praise poets rather than the images used by the Greeks to praise mathematicians. Feyerabend seems to me right in trying to develop such a self-image for us, but his project seems misdescribed, by himself as well as by his critics, as "relativism."[10]

Those who follow Feyerabend in this direction are often thought of as necessarily enemies of the Enlightenment, as joining in the chorus which claims that the traditional self-descriptions of the Western democracies are bankrupt, that they somehow have been shown to be "inadequate" or "self-deceptive." Part of the instinctive resistance to attempts by Marxists, Sartreans, Oakeshottians, Gadamerians and Foucauldians to reduce objectivity to solidarity is the fear that our traditional liberal habits and hopes will not survive the reduction. Such feelings are evident, for example, in Habermas' criticism of Gadamer's position as relativistic and potentially repressive, in the suspicion that Heidegger's attacks on realism are somehow linked to his Nazism, in the hunch that Marxist attempts to interpret values as class interests are usually just apologies for Leninist takeovers, and in the suggestion that Oakeshott's skepticism about rationalism in politics is merely an apology for the *status quo*.

I think that putting the issue in such moral and political terms rather than in epistemological or metaphilosophical terms, makes clearer what is at stake. For now the question is not about how to define words like "truth" or "rationality" or "knowledge" or "philosophy," but about what self-image our society should have of itself. The ritual

---

10 See, e.g., Paul Feyerabend, SCIENCE IN A FREE SOCIETY (London, 1978), p. 9. where Feyerabend identifies his own view with "relativism (in the old and simple sense of Protagoras)." This identification follows his claim that "'Objectively' there is not much to choose between anti-semitism and humanitarianism." I think Feyerabend would have served himself better by saying that the scare-quoted word "objectively" should simply be set aside, together with the traditional philosophical distinctions between scheme and content which buttress the subjective-objective distinction, than by saying that we may keep the word and use it to say the sort of thing Protagoras said. What Feyerabend is really against is the correspondence theory of truth, not the idea that some views are true and others false.

invocation of the "need to avoid relativism" is most comprehensible as an expression of the need to preserve certain habits of contemporary European life. These are the habits nurtured by the Enlightenment, and justified by it in terms of an appeal of Reason, conceived as a trans-cultural human ability to correspond to reality, a faculty whose possession and use is demonstrated by obedience to explicit criteria. So the real question about relativism is whether these same habits of intellectual, social, and political life can be justified by a conception of rationality as criterionless muddling through, and by a pragmatist conception of truth.

I think that the answer to this question is that the pragmatist cannot justify these habits without circularity, but then neither can the realist. The pragmatists' justification of toleration, free inquiry, and the quest for undistorted communication can only take the form of a comparison between societies which exemplify these habits and those which do not, leading up to the suggestion that nobody who has experienced both would prefer the latter. It is exemplified by Winston Churchill's defense of democracy as the worst form of government imaginable, except for all the others which have been tried so far. Such justification is not by reference to a criterion, but by reference to various detailed practical advantages. It is circular only in that the terms of praise used to describe liberal societies will be drawn from the vocabulary of the liberal societies themselves. Such praise has to be in *some* vocabulary, after all, and the terms of praise current in primitive or theocratic or totalitarian societies will not produce the desired result. So the pragmatist admits that he has no ahistorical standpoint from which to endorse the habits of modern democracies he wishes to praise. These consequences are just what partisans of solidarity expect. But among partisans of objectivity they give rise, once again, to fears of the dilemma formed by ethnocentrism on the one hand and relativism on the other. Either we attach a special privilege to our own community, or we pretend an impossible tolerance for every other group.

I have been arguing that we pragmatists should grasp the ethnocentric horn of his dilemma. We should say that we must, in practice, privilege our own group, even though there can be no non-circular justification for doing so. We must insist that the fact that nothing is immune from criticism does not mean that we have a duty to justify everything. We Western liberal intellectuals should accept the fact that we have to start from where we are, and that this means that there are lots of views which we simply cannot take seriously. To use Neurath's familiar analogy, we can *understand* the revolutionary's suggestion that a sailable boat can't be made out of the planks which make up ours, and that we must simply abandon ship. But we cannot take his suggestion seriously. We cannot take it as a rule for action, so it is not a live option. For some people, to be sure, the option *is* live. These are the people who have always hoped to become a New Being, who have hoped to be converted rather than persuaded. But we – the liberal Rawlsian searchers for consensus, the heirs of Socrates, the people who wish to link their days dialectically each to each – cannot do so. Our community – the community of the liberal intellectuals of the secular modern West – wants to be able to give a *post factum* account of any change of view. We want to be able, so to speak, to justify ourselves to our earlier selves. This preference is not built into us by human nature. It is just the way we live now.[11]

---

11   This quest for consensus is opposed to the sort of quest for authenticity which wishes to free itself from the opinion of our community. See, for example, Vincent Descombes' account of

This lonely provincialism, this admission that we are just the historical moment that we are, not the representatives of something ahistorical, is what makes traditional Kantian liberals like Rawls draw back from pragmatism.[12] "Relativism," by contrast, is merely a red herring. The realist is, once again, projecting his own habits of thought upon the pragmatist when he charges him with relativism. For the realist thinks that the whole point of philosophical thought is to detach oneself from any particular community and look down at it from a more universal standpoint. When he hears the pragmatist repudiating the desire for such a standpoint he cannot quite believe it. He thinks that everyone, deep down inside, *must* want such detachment. So he attributes to the pragmatist a perverse form of his own attempted detachment, and sees him as an ironic, sneering aesthete who refuses to take the choice between communities seriously, a mere "relativist." But the pragmatist, dominated by the desire for solidarity, can only be criticized for taking his own community *too* seriously. He can only be criticized for ethnocentrism, not for relativism. To be ethnocentric is to divide the human race into the people to whom one must justify one's beliefs and the others. The first group – one's *ethnos* – comprises those who share enough of one's beliefs to make fruitful conversation possible. In this sense, everybody is ethnocentric when engaged in actual debate, no matter how much realist rhetoric about objectivity he produces in his study.[13]

Deleuze in *Modern French Philosophy* (Cambridge, 1980). p. 153: "Even if philosophy is essentially demystificatory, philosophers often fail to produce authentic critiques: they defend order, authority, institutions, 'decency,' everything in which the ordinary person believes." On the pragmatist and ethnocentric view I am suggesting, all that critique can or should do is to play off elements in "what the ordinary person believes" against other elements. To attempt to do more than this, as Delcuze does, is to fantasize rather than to converse.

12   In A THEORY OF JUSTICE Rawls tried to retain the authority of Kantian "practical reason" by imagining a social contract devised by choosers behind a "veil of ignorance" – using the "rational self-interest" of such choosers as a touchstone for the ahistorical validity of certain social institutions. This attempt has led to an important body of writing in Anglo-American social philosophy, covering the past decade and culminating in Michael Sandel's LIBERALISM AND THE LIMITS OF JUSTICE (Cambridge, 1982). Sandel argues that Rawls' picture of the "choice behind the veil" is incoherent. In the meantime, Rawls himself has adopted a meta-ethical view which is less insistent upon ahistorical validity. See his "Kantian Constructivism in Moral Theory," *Journal of Philosophy* 1977. Concurrently T. M. Scanlon has urged that the essence of the "contractualist" account of moral motivation is better understood as the desire to justify one's action than in terms of "rational self-interest." (See Scanlon, "Contractualism & Utilitarianism," in *Utilitarianism and Beyond*, A. Sem and B. Williams, eds., Cambridge, 1982.) Scanlon's emendation of Rawls leads in the same direction as Rawls' later work, since Scanlon's notion of "justification to others on grounds they could not reasonably reject," chimes with the view that what counts for social philosophy is what can be justified to particular historical communities, not to "humanity in general." On my view, the frequent remark that Rawls' rational choosers look much like 20th-century American liberals is perfectly just, but not a criticism of Rawls. I defend this view in "Postmodernist Bourgeois Liberalism," *Journal of Philosophy* 80, no. 10(1983): 583–9 [reprinted in ORT].

13   In an important paper called "The Truth in Relativism" (included in his *Moral Luck* (Cambridge, 1981)), Bernard Williams makes a similar point in terms of a distinction between "genuine confrontation" and "notional confrontation." The latter is the sort of confrontation which occurs, asymmetrically, between us and primitive tribesmen. The belief-system of such people does not present, as Williams puts it, a real option for us, for we cannot imagine going over

What is disturbing about the pragmatist's picture is not that it is relativistic but that it takes away two sorts of metaphysical comfort to which our intellectual tradition has become accustomed. One is the thought that membership in our biological species carries with it certain "rights," a notion which does not seem to make sense unless the biological similarities entail the possession of such a common mechanism, something which links our species to a non-human reality and thus gives the species moral dignity. This picture of rights as biologically transmitted is so basic to the political discourse of the Western democracies that we are troubled by any suggestion that "human nature" is not a useful moral concept. The second comfort is provided by the thought that our community cannot wholly die. The picture of a common human nature oriented towards correspondence to reality as it is in itself comforts us with the thought that even if our civilization is destroyed, even if all memory of our political or intellectual or artistic community is erased, the race is fated to recapture the virtues and the insights and the achievements which were the glory of that community. The notion of human nature as an inner structure which leads all members of the species to converge to the same point, to recognize the same theories, virtues, and works of art as worthy of honor, assures us that even if the Persians had won, the arts and sciences of the Greeks would sooner or later have appeared elsewhere. It assures us that even if the Orwellian bureaucrats of terror rule for a thousand years the achievements of the Western democracies will someday be duplicated by our remote descendents. It assures us that "man will prevail," that something reasonably like *our* world-view, *our* virtues, *our* art, will bob up again whenever human beings are left alone to cultivate their inner natures. The comfort of the realist picture is the comfort of saying not simply that there is a place prepared for our race in our advance, but also that we now know quite a bit about what that place looks like. The inevitable ethnocentrism to which we are all condemned is thus as much a part of the realist's comfortable view as of the pragmatists' uncomfortable one.

The pragmatist gives up the first sort of comfort because he thinks that to say that certain people have certain rights is merely to say that we should treat them in certain ways. It is not to give a *reason* for treating them in those ways. As to the second sort of comfort, he suspects that the hope that something resembling *us* will inherit the earth is impossible to eradicate, as impossible as eradicating the hope of surviving our individual deaths through some satisfying transfiguration. But he does not want to turn this hope into a theory of the nature of man. He wants solidarity to be our *only* comfort, and to be seen not to require metaphysical support.

My suggestion that the desire for objectivity is in part a disguised form of the fear of the death of our community echoes Nietzsche's charge that the philosophical tradition

---

to their view without "self-deception or paranoia." These are the people whose beliefs on certain topics overlap so little with ours that their inability to agree with us raises no doubt in our own mind about the correctness of our own beliefs. Williams' uses of "real option" and "notional confrontation" seem to me very enlightening, but I think that he turns them to purposes they will not serve. Williams wants to defend ethical relativism, defined as the claim that when ethical confrontations are merely notional "questions or appraisal do not genuinely arise." (p. 142). This seems to me an awkward result to which Williams is forced by his attempt to find something true in relativism, an attempt which is a corollary of his attempt to be realistic about physics. (See his *Descartes: The Project of Pure Enquiry* (London, 1977). On my view, there is no truth in relativism, but there is this much truth in ethnocentrism: we cannot justify our beliefs (in either physics or ethics) to everybody, but only to those whose beliefs overlap ours to some appropriate extent.

which stems from Plato is an attempt to avoid facing up to contingency, to escape from time and chance. Nietzsche thought that realism was to be condemned not only by arguments from its theoretical incoherence, the sort of argument we find in Putnam and Davidson, but also on practical, pragmatic, grounds. As he said:

> Ein wesentlicher Nachteil, welchen das Aufhören metaphysischer Ansichten mit sich bringt, leigt darin, dass das Individuum zu strong seine kurze Lebenszeit ins Auge fasst und keine stärkeren Antriebe empfängt, an dauerhaften, für Jahrhunderte angelegten Institutionen zu bauen.[14]

Nietzsche thought that the test of human character was the ability to live with the thought that there was no convergence. He wanted us to be able to think of truth as

> Ein bewegliches Heer von Metaphern, Metonymien, Anthropomorphismen, kurz eine Summe von menschlichen Relationen, die, poetisch and rhetorisch gesteigert, übertragen, geschmückt wurden und die nach langem Gebrauch einem Volke fest, kanonisch und verbindlich dünken.[15]

Nietzsche hoped that eventually there might be human beings who could and did think of truth in this way, but who still liked themselves, who saw themselves as *good* people for whom solidarity was *enough*.

I think that pragmatism's attack on the various structure–content distinctions which buttress the realist's notion of objectivity can best be seen as an attempt to let us think of truth in this Nietzschean way, as entirely a matter of solidarity. That is why I think we need to say, despite Putnam, that "there is only the dialogue," only *us.* and to throw out the last residues of the notion of "trans-cultural rationality." But this should not lead us to repudiate, as Nietzsche sometimes did, the elements in our movable host which embody the ideas of Socratic conversation, Christian fellowship, and Enlightenment science. Nietzsche ran together his diagnosis of philosophical realism as an expression of fear and resentment with his own resentful idiosyncratic idealizations of silence, solitude, and violence. Post-Nietzschean thinkers like Adorno and Heidegger and Foucault have run together Nietzsche's criticisms of the metaphysical tradition on the one hand with his criticisms of bourgeois civility, of Christian love, and of the nineteenth century's hope that science would make the world a better place to live, on the other. I do not think that there is any interesting connection between these two sets of criticisms. Pragmatism seems to me, as I have said, a philosophy of solidarity rather than of despair. From this point of view, Socrates' turn away from the gods, Christianity's turn from an Omnipotent Creator to the man who suffered on the Cross, and the Baconian turn from science as contemplation of eternal truth to science as instrument of social progress, can

14   Friederich Nietzsche, *Werke,* ed. Schlechta, I, p. 463. "An essential disadvantage which the cessation of the metaphysical outlook brings with it lies in the fact that the attention of the individual is too firmly fixed on his own brief span of life and receives no stronger impulse to work at the construction of enduring institutions intended to last for centuries" (Friedrich Nietzsche, *Human, All Too Human,* trans. R. J. Hollingdale. New York: Cambridge University Press, 1996), #22.

15   Ibid., III, p. 314. "a mobile army of metaphors, metonyms, and anthromorphisms – in short a sum of human relations, which have been enhanced, transposed, and embellished poetically and rhetorically and which after long use seem firm, canonical, and obligatory to a people" (Friedrich Nietzsche, "On Truth and Lie in an Extra-Moral Sense," in *The Portable Nietzsche,* ed. and trans. Walter Kaufmann. New York: Viking Penguin, 1982, pp.46–7.)

be seen as so many preparations for the act of social faith which is suggested by a Nietzschean view of truth.[16]

The best argument we partisans of solidarity have against the realistic partisans of objectivity is Nietzsche's argument that the traditional Western metaphysico-epistemological way of firming up our habits simply isn't working anymore. It isn't doing its job. It has become as transparent a device as the postulation of deities who turn out, by a happy coincidence, to have chosen *us* as their people. So the pragmatist suggestion that we substitute a "merely" ethical foundation for our sense of community – or, better, that we think of our sense of community as having no foundation except shared hope and the trust created by such sharing – is put forward on practical grounds. It is *not* put forward as a corollary of a metaphysical claim that the objects in the world contain no intrinsically action-guiding properties, nor of an epistemological claim that we lack a faculty of moral sense, nor of a semantical claim that truth is reducible to justification. It is a suggestion about how we might think of ourselves in order to avoid the kind of resentful belatedness – characteristic of the bad side of Nietzsche – which now characterizes much of high culture. This resentment arises from the realization, which I referred to at the beginning of this lecture, that the Enlightenment's search for objectivity has gone sour. The rhetoric of scientific objectivity, pressed too hard and taken too seriously, has led us to people like B. F. Skinner on the one hand and people like Althusser on the other – two equally pointless fantasies, both produced by the attempt to be "scientific" about our moral and political lives. Reaction against scientism led to attacks on natural science as a sort of false god. But there is nothing wrong with science, there is only something wrong with the attempt to divinize it, the attempt characteristic of realistic philosophy. This reaction has also led to attacks on liberal social thought of the type common to Mill and Dewey and Rawls as a mere ideological superstructure, one which obscures the realities of our situation and represses attempts to change that situation. But there is nothing wrong with liberal democracy, nor with the philosophers who have tried to enlarge its scope. There is only something wrong with the attempt to see their efforts as failures to achieve something which they were not trying to achieve – a demonstration of the "objective" superiority of our way of life over all other alternatives. There is, in short, nothing wrong with the hopes of the Enlightenment, the hopes which created the Western democracies. The value of the ideals of the Enlightenment is, for us pragmatists, just the value of some of the institutions and practises which they have created. In this lecture I have been trying to distinguish these institutions and practices from the philosophical justifications for them provided by partisans of objectivity, and to suggest an alternative justification.

16   See Hans Blumenberg, *Die Legitimat Der Neuzeit* (Frankfurt, 1974), for a story about the history of European thought which, unlike the stories told by Nietzsche and Heidegger, sees the Enlightenment as a definitive step forward. For Blumenberg, the development of "self-assertion," the kind of attitude characteristic of Bacon's description of the nature and purpose of scientific inquiry, needs to be distinguished from "self-foundation," the Cartesian project of grounding such inquiry upon ahistorical criteria of rationality. Blumenberg remarks, pregnantly, that the "historicist" criticism of the Enlightenment, criticism which began with the Romantics turning back towards the Middle Ages, undermines *Selbstbegründung* but not *Selbstbehauptung*: "Aus der Not der Selbstbehauptung ist die Souveränitat der Selbstbegründung geworden, die sich dem Risiko der Entdeckungen des Historismus aussetzt, in denen Antange auf Abhängigkeiten redu xicrt werden sollten." (Band I, "Säkulatisierung und Sclbstbehauptung," p. 216.)

13

The Priority of Democracy to Philosophy

Thomas Jefferson set the tone for American liberal politics when he said "it does me no injury for my neighbor to say that there are twenty Gods or no God."[1] His example helped make respectable the idea that politics can be separated from beliefs about matters of ultimate importance – that shared beliefs among citizens on such matters are not essential to a democratic society. Like many other figures of the Enlightenment, Jefferson assumed that a moral faculty common to the typical theist and the typical atheist suffices for civic virtue.

Many Enlightenment intellectuals were willing to go further and say that since religious beliefs turn out to be inessential for political cohesion, they should simply be discarded as mumbo jumbo – perhaps to be replaced (as in twentieth-century totalitarian Marxist states) with some sort of explicitly secular political faith that will form the moral consciousness of the citizen. Jefferson again set the tone when he refused to go that far. He thought it enough to privatize religion, to view it as irrelevant to social order but relevant to, and possibly essential for, individual perfection. Citizens of a Jeffersonian democracy can be as religious or irreligious as they please as long as they are not "fanatical." That is, they must abandon or modify opinions on matters of ultimate importance, the opinions that may hitherto have given sense and point to their lives, if these opinions entail public actions that cannot be justified to most of their fellow citizens.

This Jeffersonian compromise concerning the relation of spiritual perfection to public policy has two sides. Its absolutist side says that every human being, without the benefit of special revelation, has all the beliefs necessary for civic virtue. These beliefs spring from a universal human faculty, conscience – possession of which constitutes the specifically human essence of each human being. This is the faculty that gives the individual human dignity and rights. But there is also a pragmatic side. This side says that when the individual finds in her conscience beliefs that are relevant to public policy but

Richard M. Rorty, "The Priority of Democracy to Philosophy," pp. 257–82 in Merrill D. Peterson and Robert C. Vaughn, *The Virginia Statute for Religious Freedom* (Cambridge, 1988), © 1988 by Cambridge University Press. Reprinted with the permission of Cambridge University Press.

1   Thomas Jefferson, *Notes on the State of Virginia*, Query XVII, in *The Writings of Thomas Jefferson*, ed. A. A. Lipscomb and A. E. Bergh (Washington, D. C., 1905), 2: 217.

incapable of defense on the basis of beliefs common to her fellow citizens, she must sacrifice her conscience on the altar of public expediency.

The tension between these two sides can be eliminated by a philosophical theory that identifies justifiability to humanity at large with truth. The Enlightenment idea of "reason" embodies such a theory: the theory that there is a relation between the ahistorical essence of the human soul and moral truth that ensures that free and open discussion will produce "one right answer" to moral as well as to scientific questions.[2] Such a theory guarantees that a moral belief that cannot be justified to the mass of mankind is "irrational," and thus is not really a product of our moral faculty at all. Rather, it is a "prejudice," a belief that comes from some other part of the soul than "reason." It does not share in the sanctity of conscience, for it is the product of a sort of pseudoconscience – something whose loss is no sacrifice, but a purgation.

In our century, this rationalist justification of the Enlightenment compromise has been discredited. Contemporary intellectuals have given up the Enlightenment assumption that religion, myth, and tradition can be opposed to something ahistorical, something common to all human beings qua human. Anthropologists and historians of science have blurred the distinction between innate rationality and the products of acculturation. Philosophers such as Heidegger and Gadamer have given us ways of seeing human beings as historical all the way through. Other philosophers, such as Quine and Davidson, have blurred the distinction between permanent truths of reason and temporary truths of fact. Psychoanalysis has blurred the distinction between conscience and the emotions of love, hate, and fear, and thus the distinction between morality and prudence. The result is to erase the picture of the self common to Greek metaphysics, Christian theology, and Enlightenment rationalism: the picture of an ahistorical nature center, the locus of human dignity, surrounded by an adventitious and inessential periphery.

The effect of erasing this picture is to break the link between truth and justifiability. This, in turn, breaks down the bridge between the two sides of the Enlightenment compromise. The effect is to polarize liberal social theory. If we stay on the absolutist side, we shall talk about inalienable "human rights" and about "one right answer" to moral and political dilemmas without trying to back up such talk with a theory of human nature. We shall abandon metaphysical accounts of what a right is while nevertheless insisting that everywhere, in all times and cultures, members of our species have had the same rights. But if we swing to the pragmatist side, and consider talk of "rights" an attempt to enjoy the benefits of metaphysics without assuming the appropriate responsibilities, we shall still need something to distinguish the sort of individual conscience we respect from the sort we condemn as "fanatical." This can only be something relatively local and ethnocentric – the tradition of a particular community, the consensus of a particular culture. According to this view, what counts as rational or as fanatical is relative to the group to which we think it necessary to justify ourselves – to the body of shared belief that determines the reference of the word "we." The Kantian identification with a

---

2   Jefferson included a statement of this familiar Scriptural claim (roughly in the form in which it had been restated by Milton in *Areopagitica*) in the preamble to the Virginia Statute for Religious Freedom: "truth is great and will prevail if left to herself, … she is the proper and sufficient antagonist to error, and has nothing to fear from the conflict, unless by human interposition disarmed of her natural weapons, free argument and debate, errors ceasing to be dangerous when it is permitted freely to contradict them" (ibid., 2: 302).

central transcultural and ahistorical self is thus replaced by a quasi-Hegelian identification with our own community, thought of as a historical product. For pragmatist social theory, the question of whether justifiability to the community with which we identify entails truth is simply irrelevant.

Ronald Dworkin and others who take the notion of ahistorical human "rights" seriously serve as examples of the first, absolutist, pole. John Dewey and, as I shall shortly be arguing, John Rawls serve as examples of the second pole. But there is a third type of social theory – often dubbed "communitarianism" – which is less easy to place. Roughly speaking, the writers tagged with this label are those who reject both the individualistic rationalism of the Enlightenment and the idea of "rights," but, unlike the pragmatists, see this rejection as throwing doubt on the institutions and culture of the surviving democratic states. Such theorists include Robert Bellah, Alasdair MacIntyre, Michael Sandel, Charles Taylor, the early Roberto Unger, and many others. These writers share some measure of agreement with a view found in an extreme form, both in Heidegger and in Horkheimer and Adorno's *Dialectic of Enlightenment*. This is the view that liberal institutions and culture either should not or cannot survive the collapse of the philosophical justification that the Enlightenment provided for them.

There are three strands in communitarianism that need to be disentangled. First, there is the empirical prediction that no society that sets aside the idea of ahistorical moral truth in the insouciant way that Dewey recommended can survive. Horkheimer and Adorno, for example, suspect that you cannot have a moral community in a disenchanted world because toleration leads to pragmatism, and it is not clear how we can prevent "blindly pragmatized thought" from losing "its transcending quality and its relation to truth."[3] They think that pragmatism was the inevitable outcome of Enlightenment rationalism and that pragmatism is not a strong enough philosophy to make moral community possible.[4] Second, there is the moral judgment that the sort of human being who is produced by liberal institutions and culture is undesirable. MacIntyre, for example, thinks that our culture – a culture he says is dominated by "the Rich Aesthete, the Manager, and the Therapist" – is a *reductio ad absurdum* both of the philosophical views that helped create it and of those now invoked in its defense. Third, there is the claim that political institutions "presuppose" a doctrine about the nature of human beings and that such a doctrine must, unlike Enlightenment rationalism, make clear the essentially historical character of the self. So we find writers like Taylor and Sandel saying that

3 Max Horkheimer and Theodor W. Adorno, *Dialectic of Enlightenment* (New York: Seabury Press, 1972), p. xiii.
4 "For the Enlightenment, whatever does not conform to the rule of computation and utility is suspect. So long as it can develop undisturbed by any outward repression, there is no holding it. In the process, it treats its own ideas of human rights exactly as it does the older universals … Enlightenment is totalitarian" (ibid., p. 6). This line of thought recurs repeatedly in communitarian accounts of the present state of the liberal democracies; see, for example, Robert Bellah, Richard Madsen, William Sullivan, Ann Swidler, and Steven Tipton, *Habits of the Heart: Individualism and Commitment in American Life* (Berkeley: University of California Press, 1985): "There is a widespread feeling that the promise of the modern era is slipping away from us. A movement of enlightenment and liberation that was to have freed us from superstition and tyranny has led in the twentieth century to a world in which ideological fanaticism and political oppression have reached extremes unknown in previous history" (p. 277).

we need a theory of the self that incorporates Hegel's and Heidegger's sense of the self's historicity.

The first claim is a straightforward empirical, sociological-historical one about the sort of glue that is required to hold a community together. The second is a straightforward moral judgment that the advantages of contemporary liberal democracy are outweighed by the disadvantages, by the ignoble and sordid character of the culture and the individual human beings that it produces. The third claim, however, is the most puzzling and complex. I shall concentrate on this third, most puzzling, claim, although toward the end I shall return briefly to the first two.

To evaluate this third claim, we need to ask two questions. The first is whether there is any sense in which liberal democracy "needs" philosophical justification at all. Those who share Dewey's pragmatism will say that although it may need philosophical articulation, it does not need philosophical backup. On this view, the philosopher of liberal democracy may wish to develop a theory of the human self that comports with the institutions he or she admires. But such a philosopher is not thereby justifying these institutions by reference to more fundamental premises, but the reverse: He or she is putting politics first and tailoring a philosophy to suit. Communitarians, by contrast, often speak as though political institutions were no better than their philosophical foundations.

The second question is one that we can ask even if we put the opposition between justification and articulation to one side. It is the question of whether a conception of the self that, as Taylor says, makes "the community constitutive of the individual"[5] does in fact comport better with liberal democracy than does the Enlightenment conception of the self. Taylor summarizes the latter as "an ideal of disengagement" that defines a "typically modern notion" of human dignity: "the ability to act on one's own, without outside interference or subordination to outside authority." On Taylor's view, as on Heidegger's, these Enlightenment notions are closely linked with characteristically modern ideas of "efficacy, power, unperturbability."[6] They are also closely linked with the contemporary form of the doctrine of the sacredness of the individual conscience – Dworkin's claim that appeals to rights "trump" all other appeals. Taylor, like Heidegger, would like to substitute a less individualistic conception of what it is to be properly human – one that makes less of autonomy and more of interdependence.

I can preview what is to come by saying that I shall answer "no" to the first question about the communitarians' third claim and "yes" to the second. I shall be arguing that Rawls, following up on Dewey, shows us how liberal democracy can get along without philosophical presuppositions. He has thus shown us how we can disregard the third communitarian claim. But I shall also argue that communitarians like Taylor are right in saying that a conception of the self that makes the community constitutive of the self does comport well with liberal democracy. That is, if we *want* to flesh out our self-image as citizens of such a democracy with a philosophical view of the self, Taylor gives us pretty much the right view. But this sort of philosophical fleshing-out does not have the importance that writers like Horkheimer and Adorno, or Heidegger, have attributed to it.

Without further preface, I turn now to Rawls. I shall begin by pointing out that both in *A Theory of Justice* and subsequently, he has linked his own position to the Jeffersonian

5   Charles Taylor, *Philosophy and the Human Sciences*, vol. 2 of *Philosophical Papers* (Cambridge: Cambridge University Press, 1985), p. 8.
6   Ibid., p. 5.

ideal of religious toleration. In an article called "Justice as Fairness: Political not Metaphysical," he says that he is "going to apply the principle of toleration to philosophy itself," and goes on to say:

> The essential point is this: as a practical political matter no general moral conception can provide the basis for a public conception of justice in a modern democratic society. The social and historical conditions of such a society have their origins in the Wars of Religion following the Reformation and the development of the principle of toleration, and in the growth of constitutional government and the institutions of large market economies. These conditions profoundly affect the requirements of a workable conception of political justice: such a conception must allow for a diversity of doctrines and the plurality of conflicting, and indeed incommensurable conceptions of the good affirmed by the members of existing democratic societies.[7]

We can think of Rawls as saying that just as the principle of religious toleration and the social thought of the Enlightenment proposed to bracket many standard theological topics when deliberating about public policy and constructing political institutions, so we need to bracket many standard topics of philosophical inquiry. For purposes of social theory, we can put aside such topics as an ahistorical human nature, the nature of self-hood, the motive of moral behavior, and the meaning of human life. We treat these as irrelevant to politics as Jefferson thought questions about the Trinity and about transubstantiation.

Insofar as he adopts this stance, Rawls disarms many of the criticisms that, in the wake of Horkheimer and Adorno, have been directed at American liberalism. Rawls can agree that Jefferson and his circle shared a lot of dubious philosophical views, views that we might now wish to reject. He can even agree with Horkheimer and Adorno, as Dewey would have, that these views contained the seeds of their own destruction. But he thinks that the remedy may be not to formulate better philosophical views on the same topics, but (for purposes of political theory) benignly to neglect these topics. As he says:

> since justice as fairness is intended as a political conception of justice for a democratic society, it tries to draw solely upon basic intuitive ideas that are embedded in the political institutions of a democratic society and the public traditions of their interpretation. Justice as fairness is a political conception in part because it starts from within a certain political tradition. We hope that this political conception of justice may be at least supported by what we may call "overlapping consensus," that is, by a consensus that includes all the

---

7   John Rawls, "Justice as Fairness: Political not Metaphysical," *Philosophy and Public Affairs* 14 (1985): 225. Religious toleration is a constantly recurring theme in Rawls's writing. Early in *A Theory of Justice* (Cambridge, Mass.: Harvard University Press, 1971), when giving examples of the sort of common opinions that a theory of justice must take into account and systematize, he cites our conviction that religious intolerance is unjust (p. 19). His example of the fact that "a well-ordered society tends to eliminate or at least to control men's inclinations to injustice" is that "warring and intolerant sects are much less likely to exist" (p. 247). Another relevant passage (which I shall discuss below) is his diagnosis of Ignatius Loyola's attempt to make the love of God the "dominant good": "Although to subordinate all our aims to one end does not strictly speaking violate the principles of rational choice ... it still strikes us as irrational, or more likely as mad" (pp. 553–4).

opposing philosophical and religious doctrines likely to persist and gain adherents in a more or less just constitutional democratic society.[8]

Rawls thinks that "philosophy as the search for truth about an independent meta-physical and moral order cannot ... provide a workable and shared basis for a political conception of justice in a democratic society."[9] So he suggests that we confine ourselves to collecting, "such settled convictions as the belief in religious toleration and the rejection of slavery" and then "try to organize the basic intuitive ideas and principles implicit in these convictions into a coherent conception of justice."[10]

This attitude is thoroughly historicist and antiuniversalist.[11] Rawls can wholeheartedly agree with Hegel and Dewey against Kant and can say that the Enlightenment attempt to free oneself from tradition and history, to appeal to "Nature" or "Reason," was self-deceptive.[12] He can see such an appeal as a misguided attempt to make philosophy

8   Rawls, "Justice as Fairness," pp. 225–6. The suggestion that there are many philosophical views that will *not* survive in such conditions is analogous to the Enlightenment suggestion that the adoption of democratic institutions will cause "superstitious" forms of religious belief gradually to die off.

9   Ibid., p. 230.

10   Ibid.

11   For Rawls's historicism see, for example, *Theory of Justice*, p. 547. There, Rawls says that the people in the original position are assumed to know "the general facts about society," including the fact that "institutions are not fixed but change over time, altered by natural circumstances and the activities and conflicts of social groups." He uses this point to rule out, as original choosers of principles of justice, those "in a feudal or a caste system," those who are unaware of events such as the French Revolution. This is one of many passages that make clear (at least read in the light of Rawls's later work) that a great deal of knowledge that came late to the mind of Europe is present to the minds of those behind the veil of ignorance. Or, to put it another way, such passages make clear that those original choosers behind the veil exemplify a certain modern type of human being, not an ahistorical human nature. See also p. 548, where Rawls says, "Of course in working out what the requisite principles [of justice] are, we must rely upon current knowledge as recognized by common sense and the existing scientific consensus. We have to concede that as established beliefs change, it is possible that the principles of justice which it seems rational to choose may likewise change."

12   See Bellah et al., *Habits of the Heart*, p. 141, for a recent restatement of this "counter-Enlightenment" line of thought. For the authors' view of the problems created by persistence in Enlightenment rhetoric and by the prevalence of the conception of human dignity that Taylor identifies as "distinctively modern," see p. 21: "For most of us, it is easier to think about [how] to get what we want than to know exactly what we should want. Thus Brian, Joe, Margaret and Wayne [some of the Americans interviewed by the authors] are each in his or her own way confused about how to define for themselves such things as the nature of success, the meaning of freedom, and the requirements of justice. Those difficulties are in an important way created by the limitations in the common tradition of moral discourse they – and we – share." Compare p. 290: "the language of individualism, the primary American language of self-understanding, limits the way in which people think."

To my mind, the authors of *Habits of the Heart* undermine their own conclusions in the passages where they point to actual moral progress being made in recent American history, notably in their discussion of the civil-rights movement. There, they say that Martin Luther King, Jr., made the struggle for freedom "a practice of commitment within a vision of America as a community of memory" and that the response King elicited "came from the reawakened recognition by many

do what theology failed to do. Rawls's effort to, in his words, "stay on the surface, philosophically speaking" can be seen as taking Jefferson's avoidance of theology one step further.

On the Deweyan view I am attributing to Rawls, no such discipline as "philosophical anthropology" is required as a preface to politics, but only history and sociology. Further, it is misleading to think of his view as Dworkin does: as "rights-based" as opposed to "goal-based." For the notion of "basis" is not in point. It is not that we know, on antecedent philosophical grounds, that it is of the essence of human beings to have rights, and then proceed to ask how a society might preserve and protect these rights. On the question of priority, as on the question of the relativity of justice to historical situations, Rawls is closer to Walzer than to Dworkin.[13] Since Rawls does not believe that for purposes of political theory, we need think of ourselves as having an essence that precedes and antedates history, he would not agree with Sandel that for these purposes, we need have an account of "the nature of the moral subject," which is "in some sense necessary, non-contingent and prior to any particular experience."[14] Some of our ancestors may have required such an account, just as others of our ancestors required such an account, of their relation to their putative Creator. But *we* – we heirs of the Enlightenment for whom justice has become the first virtue – need neither. As citizens and as social theorists, we can be as indifferent to philosophical disagreements about the nature of the self as Jefferson was to theological differences about the nature of God.

This last point suggests a way of sharpening up my claim that Rawls's advocacy of philosophical toleration is a plausible extension of Jefferson's advocacy of religious toleration. Both "religion" and "philosophy" are vague umbrella terms, and both are subject to persuasive redefinition. When these terms are broadly enough defined, everybody, even atheists, will be said to have a religious faith (in the Tillichian sense of a "symbol of ultimate concern"). Everybody, even those who shun metaphysics and epistemology, will be said to have "philosophical presuppositions."[15] But for purposes of interpreting

---

Americans that their own sense of self was rooted in companionship with others who, though not necessarily like themselves, nevertheless shared with them a common history and whose appeals to justice and solidarity made powerful claims on our loyalty" (p. 252). These descriptions of King's achievement seem exactly right, but they can be read as evidence that the rhetoric of the Enlightenment offers at least as many opportunities as it does obstacles for the renewal of a sense of community. The civil-rights movement combined, without much strain, the language of Christian fellowship and the "language of individualism," about which Bellah and his colleagues are dubious.

13   See Michael Walzer, *Spheres of Justice* (New York: Basic, 1983), pp. 312 ff.

14   Michael Sandel, *Liberalism and the Limits of Justice* (Cambridge: Cambridge University Press, 1982), p. 49.

15   In a recent, as yet unpublished, paper, Sandel has urged that Rawls's claim that "philosophy in the classical sense as the search for truth about a prior and independent moral order cannot provide the shared basis for a political conception of justice" presupposes the controversial metaphysical claim that there is no such order. This seems to me like saying that Jefferson was presupposing the controversial theological claim that God is not interested in the name by which he is called by human beings. Both charges are accurate, but not really to the point. Both Jefferson and Rawls would have to reply, "I have no arguments for my dubious theological-metaphysical claim, because I do not know how to discuss such issues, and do not want to. My interest is in helping to preserve and create political institutions that will foster public indifference to such issues, while

Jefferson and Rawls, we must use narrower definitions. Let "religion" mean, for Jefferson's purposes, disputes about the nature and the true name of God – and even about his existence.[16] Let "philosophy" mean, for Rawls's purposes, disputes about the nature of human beings and even about whether there is such a thing as "human nature."[17] Using these definitions, we can say that Rawls wants views about man's nature and purpose to be detached from politics. As he says, he wants his conception of justice to "avoid … claims about the essential nature and identity of persons."[18] So presumably, he wants questions about the point of human existence, or the meaning of human life, to be reserved for private life. A liberal democracy will not only exempt opinions on such matters from legal coercion, but also aim at disengaging discussions of such questions from discussions of social policy. Yet it will use force against the individual conscience, just insofar as conscience leads individuals to act so as to threaten democratic institutions. Unlike Jefferson's, Rawls's argument against fanaticism is not that it threatens truth about the characteristics of an antecedent metaphysical and moral order by threatening free discussion, but *simply* that it threatens freedom, and thus threatens justice. Truth about the existence or nature of that order drops out.

The definition of "philosophy" I have just suggested is not as artificial and ad hoc as it may appear. Intellectual historians commonly treat "the nature of the human subject" as the topic that gradually replaced "God" as European culture secularized itself. This has been the central topic of metaphysics and epistemology from the seventeenth century to the present, and, for better or worse, metaphysics and epistemology have been taken to be the "core" of philosophy.[19] Insofar as one thinks that political conclusions require

---

putting no restrictions on private discussion of them." This reply, of course, begs the "deeper" question that Sandel wants to raise, for the question of whether we *should* determine what issues to discuss on political or on "theoretical" (for example, theological or philosophical) grounds remains unanswered. (At the end of this paper, I briefly discuss the need for philosophers to escape from the requirement to answer questions phrased in vocabularies they wish to replace, and in more detail in "Beyond Realism and Anti-Realism," in *Wo steht die sprachanalytische Philosophie heute?*, ed. Richard Heinrich and Ludwig Nagl (Vienna: Oldenbourg, 1986, pp. 103–15).

16   Jefferson agreed with Luther that philosophers had muddied the clear waters of the gospels. See Jefferson's polemic against Plato's "foggy mind" and his claim that "the doctrines which flowed from the lips of Jesus himself are within the comprehension of a child; but thousands of volumes have not yet explained the Platonisms engrafted on them; and for this obvious reason, that nonsense can never be explained" (*Writings of Thomas Jefferson*, 14: 149).

17   I am here using the term "human nature" in the traditional philosophical sense in which Sartre denied that there was such a thing, rather than in the rather unusual one that Rawls gives it. Rawls distinguishes between a "conception of the person" and a "theory of human nature," where the former is a "moral ideal" and the latter is provided by, roughly, common sense plus the social sciences. To have a theory of human nature is to have "general facts that we take to be true, or true enough, given the state of public knowledge in our society," facts that "limit the feasibility of the ideals of person and society embedded in that framework" ("Kantian Constructivism in Moral Theory," *Journal of Philosophy* 77 [1980]: 534).

18   Rawls, "Justice as Fairness," p. 223.

19   In fact, it has been for the worse. A view that made politics more central to philosophy and subjectivity less would both permit more effective defenses of democracy than those that purport to supply it with "foundations" and permit liberals to meet Marxists on their own, political, ground. Dewey's explicit attempt to make the central philosophical question "What serves democracy?" rather than "What permits us to argue for democracy?" has been, unfortunately,

extrapolitical grounding – that is, insofar as one thinks Rawls's method of reflective equilibrium[20] is not good enough – one will want an account of the "authority" of those general principles.

If one feels a need for such legitimation, one will want either a religious or a philosophical preface to politics.[21] One will be likely to share Horkheimer and Adorno's fear that pragmatism is not strong enough to hold a free society together. But Rawls echoes Dewey in suggesting that insofar as justice becomes the first virtue of a society, the need for such legitimation may gradually cease to be felt. Such a society will become accustomed to the thought that social policy needs no more authority than successful accommodation among individuals, individuals who find themselves heir to the same historical traditions and faced with the same problems. It will be a society that encourages the "end of ideology," that takes reflective equilibrium as the only method needed in discussing social policy. When such a society deliberates, when it collects the principles and intuitions to be brought into equilibrium, it will tend to discard those drawn from philosophical accounts of the self or of rationality. For such a society will view such accounts not as the foundations of political institutions, but as, at worst, philosophical mumbo jumbo, or, at best, relevant to private searches for perfection, but not to social policy.[22]

---

neglected. I try to make this point in "Philosophy as Science, as Metaphor, and as Politics," in *The Institution of Philosophy*, ed. Avner Cohen and Marcello Dascal (La Salle, IL: Open Court Press, 1989).

20   That is, give-and-take between intuitions about the desirability of particular consequences of particular actions and intuitions about general principles, with neither having the determining voice.

21   One will also, as I did on first reading Rawls, take him to be attempting to supply such legitimation by an appeal to the rationality of the choosers in the original position (the position of those who, behind a veil of ignorance that hides them from their life chances and their conceptions of the good, select from among alternative principles of justice) served simply "to make vivid … the restrictions that it seems reasonable to impose on arguments for principles of justice and therefore on those principles themselves" (*Theory of Justice*, p. 18).

But this warning went unheeded by myself and others, in part because of an ambiguity between "reasonable" as defined by ahistorical criteria and as meaning something like "in accord with the moral sentiments characteristic of the heirs of the Enlightenment." Rawls's later work has, as I have said, helped us come down on the historicist side of this ambiguity; see, for example, "Kantian Constructivism":"the original position is not an axiomatic (or deductive) basis from which principles most fitting to the conception of the person most likely to be held, at least implicitly, in a democratic society" (p. 572). It is tempting to suggest that one could eliminate all reference to the original position from *A Theory of Justice* without loss, but this is as daring a suggestion as that one might rewrite (as many have wished to do) Kant's *Critique of Pure Reason* without reference to the thing-in-itself. T. M. Scanlon has suggested that we can, at least, safely eliminate reference, in the description of the choosers in the original position, to an appeal to self-interest in describing the motives of those choosers ("Contractualism and Utilitarianism," in *Utilitarianism and Beyond*, ed. Bernard Williams and Amartya Sen [Cambridge: Cambridge University Press, 1982]). Since justifiability is, more evidently than self-interest, relative to historical circumstance, Scanlon's proposal seems to be more faithful to Rawls's overall philosophical program than Rawls's own formulation.

22   In particular, there will be no principles or intuitions concerning the universal features of human psychology relevant to motivation. Sandel thinks that since assumptions about motivation are part of the description of the original position, "what issues at one end in a theory of justice must

In order to spell out the contrast between Rawls's attempt to "stay on the surface, philosophically speaking" and the traditional attempt to dig down to "philosophical foundations of democracy," I shall turn briefly to Sandel's *Liberalism and the Limits of Justice*. This clear and forceful book provides very elegant and cogent arguments against the attempt to use a certain conception of the self, a certain metaphysical view of what human beings are like, to legitimize liberal politics. Sandel attributes this attempt to Rawls. Many people, including myself, initially took Rawls's *Theory of Justice* to be such an attempt. We read it as a continuation of the Enlightenment attempt to ground our moral intuitions on a conception of human nature (and, more specifically, as a neo-Kantian attempt to ground them on the notion of "rationality"). However, Rawls's writings subsequent to *A Theory of Justice* have helped us realize that we were misinterpreting his book, that we had overemphasized the Kantian and underemphasized the Hegelian and Deweyan elements. These writings make more explicit than did his book Rawls's metaphilosophical doctrine that "what justifies a conception of justice is not its being true to an order antecedent to and given to us, but its congruence with our deeper understanding of ourselves and our aspirations, and our realization that, *given our history and the traditions embedded in our public life,* it is the most reasonable doctrine *for us.*"[23]

When reread in the light of such passages, *A Theory of Justice* no longer seems committed to a philosophical account of the human self, but only to a historico-sociological description of the way we live now.

Sandel sees Rawls as offering us "deontology with a Humean face" – that is, a Kantian universalistic approach to social thought without the handicap of Kant's idealistic metaphysics. He thinks that this will not work, that a social theory of the sort that Rawls wants requires us to postulate the sort of self that Descartes and Kant invented to replace God – one that can be distinguished from the Kantian "empirical self" as having various "contingent desires, wants and ends," rather than being a mere concatenation of beliefs and desires. Since such a concatenation – what Sandel calls a "radically situated subject"[24] – is all that Hume offers us, Sandel thinks that Rawls's project is doomed.[25] On Sandel's account, Rawls's doctrine that "justice is the first virtue of social institutions" requires

---

issue at the other in a theory of the person, or more precisely, a theory of the moral subject" (*Liberalism and the Limits of Justice*, p. 47). I would argue that if we follow Scanlon's lead (note 17) in dropping reference to self-interest in our description of the original choosers and replacing this with reference to their desire to justify their choices to their fellows, then the only "theory of the person" we get is a sociological description of the inhabitants of contemporary liberal democracies.

23   Rawls, "Kantian Constructivism," p. 519. Italics added.

24   Sandel, *Liberalism and the Limits of Justice*, p. 21. I have argued for the advantages of thinking of the self as just such a concatenation; see "Postmodernist Bourgeois Liberalism," *Journal of Philosophy* 80 (1983): 583–9 and "Freud and Moral Reflection," in *The Pragmatists' Freud*, ed. Joseph E. Smith and William Kerrigan (Baltimore: Johns Hopkins University Press, 1986). When Sandel cites Robert Nozick and Daniel Bell as suggesting that Rawls "ends by dissolving the self in order to preserve it" (*Liberalism and the Limits of Justice*, p. 95), I should rejoin that it may be helpful to dissolve the metaphysical self in order to preserve the political one. Less obliquely stated: It may be helpful, for purposes of systematizing our intuitions about the priority of liberty, to treat the self as having no center, no essence, but *merely* as a concatenation of beliefs and desires.

25   "Deontology with a Humean face either fails as deontology or recreates in the original position the disembodied subject it resolves to avoid" (ibid., p. 14).

backup from the metaphysical claim that "teleology to the contrary, what is most essential to our personhood is not the ends we choose but our capacity to choose them. And this capacity is located in a self which must be prior to the ends it chooses."[26]

But reading *A Theory of Justice* as political rather than metaphysical, one can see that when Rawls says that "the self is prior to the ends which are affirmed by it,"[27] he need not mean that there is an entity called "the self" that is something distinct from the web of beliefs and desires that that self "has." When he says that "we should not attempt to give form to our life by first looking to the good independently defined,"[28] he is not basing this "should" on a claim about the nature of the self. "Should" is not to be glossed by "because of the intrinsic nature of morality"[29] or "because a capacity for choice is the essence of personhood," but by something like "because *we* – we modern inheritors of the traditions of religious tolerance and constitutional government – put liberty ahead of perfection."

This willingness to invoke what *we* do raises, as I have said, the specters of ethnocentrism and of relativism. Because Sandel is convinced that Rawls shares Kant's fear of these specters, he is convinced that Rawls is looking for an "'Archimedean point' from which to assess the basic structure of society" – a "standpoint neither compromised by its implication in the world nor dissociated and so disqualified by detachment."[30] It is just this idea that a standpoint can be "compromised by its implication in the world" that Rawls rejects in his recent writings. Philosophically inclined communitarians like Sandel are unable to envisage a middle ground between relativism and a "theory of the moral subject" – a theory that is not about, for example, religious tolerance and large market economies, but about human beings as such, viewed ahistorically. Rawls is trying to stake out just such a middle ground.[31] When he speaks of an "Archimedean point," he

26 Ibid., p. 19.

27 Rawls, *Theory of Justice*, p. 560.

28 Ibid.

29 It is important to note that Rawls explicitly distances himself from the idea that he is analyzing the very idea of morality and from conceptual analysis as the method of social theory (ibid., p. 130). Some of his critics have suggested that Rawls is practicing "reductive logical analysis" of the sort characteristic of "analytic philosophy"; see, for example, William M. Sullivan, *Reconstructing Public Philosophy* (Berkeley: University of California Press, 1982), pp. 94ff. Sullivan says that "this ideal of reductive logical analysis lends legitimacy to the notion that moral philosophy is summed up in the task of discovering, through the analysis of moral rules, both primitive elements and governing principles that must apply to any rational moral system, *rational* here meaning 'logically coherent'" (p. 96). He goes on to grant that "Nozik and Rawls are more sensitive to the importance of history and social experience in human life than were the classic liberal thinkers" (p. 97). But this concession is too slight and is misleading. Rawls's willingness to adopt "reflective equilibrium" rather than "conceptual analysis" as a methodological watchword sets him apart from the epistemologically oriented moral philosophy that was dominant prior to the appearance of *A Theory of Justice*. Rawls represents a reaction against the Kantian idea of "morality" as having an ahistorical essence, the same sort of reaction found in Hegel and in Dewey.

30 Sandel, *Liberalism and the Limits of Justice*, p. 17.

31 "… liberty of conscience and freedom of thought should not be founded on philosophical or ethical skepticism, nor on indifference to religious and moral interests. The principles of justice define an appropriate path between dogmatism and intolerance on the one side, and a reductionism which regards religion and morality as mere preferences on the other" (Rawls, *Theory of Justice*,

does not mean a point outside history, but simply the kind of settled social habits that allow much latitude for further choices. He says, for example,

> The upshot of these considerations is that justice as fairness is not at the mercy, so to speak, of existing wants and interests. It sets up an Archimedean point for assessing the social system without invoking a priori considerations. The long range aim of society is settled in its main lines irrespective of the particular desires and needs of its present members.... There is no place for the question whether men's desires to play the role of superior of inferior might not be so great that autocratic institutions should be accepted, or whether men's perception of the religious practices of others might not be so upsetting that liberty of conscience should not be allowed.[32]

To say that there is no place for the questions that Nietzsche or Loyola would raise is not to say that the views of either are unintelligible (in the sense of "logically incoherent" or "conceptually confused"). Nor is it to say that they are based on an incorrect theory of the self. Nor is it *just* to say that our preferences conflict with theirs.[33] It is to say that the conflict between these men and us is so great that "preferences" is the wrong word. It is appropriate to speak of gustatory or sexual preferences, for these do not

---

p. 243). I take it that Rawls is identifying "philosophical or ethical skepticism" with the idea that everything is just a matter of "preference," even religion, philosophy, and morals. So we should distinguish his suggestion that we "extend the principle of toleration to philosophy itself" from the suggestion that we dismiss philosophy as epiphenomenal. That is the sort of suggestion that is backed up by reductionist accounts of philosophical doctrines as "preferences" or "wish fulfillments" or "expressions of emotion" (see Rawls's criticism of Freudian reductionism in ibid., pp. 539ff.). Neither psychology nor logic nor any other theoretical discipline can supply non-question-begging reasons why philosophy should be set aside, any more than philosophy can supply such reasons why theology should be set aside. But this is compatible with saying that the general course of historical experience may lead us to neglect theological topics and bring us to the point at which, like Jefferson, we find a theological vocabulary "meaningless" (or, more precisely, useless). I am suggesting that the course of historical experience since Jefferson's time has led us to a point at which we find much of the vocabulary of modern philosophy no longer useful.

32   Ibid., pp. 261–2.

33   The contrast between "mere preference" and something less "arbitrary," something more closely related to the very nature of man or of reason, is invoked by many writers who think of "human rights" as requiring a philosophical foundation of the traditional sort. Thus my colleague David Little, commenting on my "Solidarity or Objectivity?" (*Post-Analytic Philosophy*, ed. John Rajchman and Cornel West [New York: Columbia University Press, 1985]), says "Rorty appears to permit criticism and pressure against those societies [the ones we do not like] *if we happen to want to* criticize and pressure them in pursuit of some interest or belief we may (at the time) have, and for whatever ethnocentric reasons we may happen to hold those interests or beliefs" ("Natural Rights and Human Rights: The International Imperative," in *Natural Rights and Natural Law: The Legacy of George Mason*, ed. Robert P. Davidow [Fairfax, Va.: George Mason University Press, 1986], pp. 67–122; italics in original). I would rejoin that Little's use of "happen to want to" presupposes a dubious distinction between necessary, built-in, universal convictions (convictions that it would be "irrational" to reject) and accidental, culturally determined convictions. It also presupposes the existence of such faculties as reason, will, and emotion, all of which the pragmatist tradition in American philosophy and the so-called existentialist tradition in European philosophy try to undercut. Dewey's *Human Nature and Conduct* and Heidegger's *Being and Time* both offer a moral psychology that avoids oppositions between "preference" and "reason."

matter to anybody but yourself and your immediate circle. But it is misleading to speak of a "preference" for liberal democracy.

Rather, we heirs of the Enlightenment think of enemies of liberal democracy like Nietzsche or Loyola as, to use Rawls's word, "mad." We do so because there is no way to see them as fellow citizens of our constitutional democracy, people whose life plans might, given ingenuity and good will, be fitted in with those of other citizens. They are not crazy because they have mistaken the ahistorical nature of human beings. They are crazy because the limits of sanity are set by what *we* can take seriously. This, in turn, is determined by our upbringing, our historical situation.[34]

If this short way of dealing with Nietzsche and Loyola seems shockingly ethnocentric, it is because the philosophical tradition has accustomed us to the idea that anybody who is willing to listen to reason – to hear out all the arguments – can be brought around to the truth. This view, which Kierkegaard called "Socratism" and contrasted with the claim that our point of departure may be simply a historical event, is intertwined with the idea that the human self has a center (a divine spark, or a truth-tracking faculty called "reason") and that argumentation will, given time and patience, penetrate to this center. For Rawls's purposes, we do not need this picture. We are free to see the self as centerless, as a historical contingency all the way through. Rawls neither needs nor wants to defend the priority of the right to the good as Kant defended it, by invoking a theory of the self that makes it more than an "empirical self," more than a "radically situated subject." He presumably thinks of Kant as, although largely right about the nature of justice, largely wrong about the nature and function of philosophy.

More specifically, he can reject Sandel's Kantian claim that there is a "distance between subject and situation which is necessary to any measure of detachment, is essential to the ineliminably *possessive* aspect of any coherent conception of the self."[35] Sandel defines this aspect by saying, "I can never fully be constituted by my attributes ... there must always be some attributes I *have* rather than am." On the interpretation of Rawls I am offering, we do not need a categorical distinction between the self and its situation. We can dismiss the distinction between an attribute of the self and a constituent of the self, between the self's accidents and its essence, as "merely" metaphysical.[36] If we are inclined to philosophize, we shall want the vocabulary offered by Dewey, Heidegger, Davidson,

---

34 "Aristotle remarks that it is a peculiarity of men that they possess a sense of the just and the unjust and that their sharing a common understanding of justice makes a polis. Analogously one might say, in view of our discussion, that a common understanding of justice as fairness makes a constitutional democracy" (Rawls, *Theory of Justice*, p. 243). In the interpretation of Rawls I am offering, it is unrealistic to expect Aristotle to have developed a conception of justice as fairness, since he simply lacked the kind of historical experience that we have accumulated since his day. More generally, it is pointless to assume (with, for example, Leo Strauss) that the Greeks had already canvassed the alternatives available for social life and institutions. When we discuss justice, we cannot agree to bracket our knowledge of recent history.

35 Sandel, *Liberalism and the Limits of Justice*, p. 20.

36 We can dismiss other distinctions that Sandel draws in the same way. Examples are the distinction between a voluntarist and a cognitive account of the original position (ibid., p. 121), that between "the identity of the subject" as the "product" rather than the "premise" of its agency (ibid., p. 152), and that between the question "Who am I?" and its rival as "the paradigmatic moral question" "What shall I choose?" (ibid., p. 153). These distinctions are all to be analyzed away as products of the "Kantian dualisms" that Rawls praises Hegel and Dewey for having overcome.

and Derrida, with its built-in cautions against metaphysics, rather than that offered by Descartes, Hume, and Kant.[37] For if we use the former vocabulary, we shall be able to see moral progress as a history of making rather than finding, of poetic achievement by "radically situated" individuals and communities, rather than as the gradual unveiling, through the use of "reason," of "principles" or "rights" or "values."

Sandel's claim that "the concept of a subject given prior to and independent of its objects offers a foundation for the moral law that ... powerfully completes the deonto-logical vision" is true enough. But to suggest such a powerful completion to Rawls is to offer him a poisoned gift. It is like offering Jefferson an argument for religious tolerance based on exegesis of the Christian Scriptures.[38] Rejecting the assumption that the moral law needs a "foundation" is just what distinguishes Rawls from Jefferson. It is just this that permits him to be a Deweyan naturalist who needs neither the distinction between will and intellect nor the distinction between the self's constituents and its attributes. He does not *want* a "complete deontological vision," one that would explain *why* we should give justice priority over our conception of the good. He is filling out the consequences of the claim that it is prior, not its presuppositions.[39] Rawls is not interested in conditions for the identity of the self, but only in conditions for citizenship in a liberal society.

Suppose one grants that Rawls is not attempting a transcendental deduction of American liberalism or supplying philosophical foundations for democratic institutions, but simply trying to systematize the principles and intuitions typical of American liber-als. Still, it may seem that the important questions raised by the critics of liberalism have been begged. Consider the claim that we liberals can simply dismiss Nietzsche and Loyola as crazy. One imagines these two rejoining that they are quite aware that their

---

37   For some similarities between Dewey and Heidegger with respect to anti-Cartesianism, see my "Overcoming the Tradition," in Richard Rorty, *Consequences of Pragmatism* (Minneapolis: University of Minnesota Press, 1982). For similarities between Davidson and Derrida, see Samuel Wheeler, "In-determinancy of French Translation," in *Essays on 'Inquiries into truth and interpretation,'* ed. Ernest LePore (Oxford: Basil Blackwell, 1986).

38   David Levin has pointed out to me that Jefferson was not above borrowing such arguments. I take this to show that Jefferson, like Kant, found himself in an untenable halfway position between theology and Deweyan social experimentalism.

39   Sandel takes "the primacy of the subject" to be not only a way of filling out the deonto-logical picture, but also a necessary condition of its correctness: "If the claim for the primacy of justice is to succeed, if the right is to be prior to the good in the interlocking moral and founda-tional senses we have distinguished, then some version of the claim for the primacy of the subject must succeed as well" (*Liberalism and the Limits of Justice*, p. 7). Sandel quotes Rawls as saying that "the essential unity of the self is already provided by the conception of the right" and takes this passage as evidence that Rawls holds a doctrine of the "priority of the self" (ibid., p. 21). But consider the context of this sentence. Rawls says: "The principles of justice and their realization in social forms define the bounds within which our deliberations take place. The essential unity of the self is already provided by the conception of right. Moreover, in a well-ordered society this unity is the same for all; everyone's conception of the good as given by his rational plan is a sub-plan of the larger comprehensive plan that regulates the community as a social union of social unions" (*Theory of Justice*, p. 563). The "essential unity of the self," which is in question here, is simply the system of moral sentiments, habits, and internalized traditions that is typical of the politically aware citizen of a constitutional democracy. This self is, once again, a historical product. It has nothing to do with the nonempirical self, which Kant had to postulate in the interests of Enlightenment universalism.

views unfit them for citizenship in a constitutional democracy and that the typical inhabitant of such a democracy would regard them as crazy. But they take these facts as further counts against constitutional democracy. They think that the kind of person created by such a democracy is not what a human being should be.

In finding a dialectical stance to adopt toward Nietzsche or Loyola, we liberal democrats are faced with a dilemma. To refuse to argue about what human beings should be like seems to show a contempt for the spirit of accommodation and tolerance, which is essential to democracy. But it is not clear how to argue for the claim that human beings ought to be liberals rather than fanatics without being driven back on a theory of human nature, on philosophy. I think that we must grasp the first horn. We have to insist that not every argument need to be met in the terms in which it is presented. Accommodation and tolerance must stop short of a willingness to work within any vocabulary that one's interlocutor wishes to use, to take seriously any topic that he puts forward for discussion. To take this view is of a piece with dropping the idea that a single moral vocabulary and a single set of moral beliefs are appropriate for every human community everywhere, and to grant that historical developments may lead us to simply *drop* questions and the vocabulary in which those questions are posed.

Just as Jefferson refused to let the Christian Scriptures set the terms in which to discuss alternative political institutions, so we either must refuse to answer the question "What sort of human being are you hoping to produce?" or, at least, must not let our answer to this question dictate our answer to the question "Is justice primary?"[40] It is no more evident that democratic institutions are to be measured by the sort of person they create than that they are to be measured against divine commands. It is not evident that they are to be measured by anything more specific than the moral intuitions of the particular historical community that has created those institutions. The idea that moral and political controversies should always be "brought back to first principles" is reasonable if it means merely that we should seek common ground in the hope of attaining agreement. But it is misleading if it is taken as the claim that there is a natural order of premises from which moral and political conclusions are to be inferred – not to mention the claim that some particular interlocutor (for example, Nietzsche or Loyola) has already discerned that order. The liberal response to the communitarians' second claim must be, therefore, that even if the typical character types of liberal democracies *are* bland, calculating, petty, and unheroic, the prevalence of such people may be a reasonable price to pay for political freedom.

The spirit of accommodation and tolerance certainly suggests that we should seek common ground with Nietzsche and Loyola, but there is no predicting where, or whether, such common ground will be found. The philosophical tradition has assumed that there are certain topics (for example, "What is God's will?" "What is man?" "What rights are intrinsic to the species?") on which everyone has, or should have, views and that these topics are prior in the order of justification to those at issue in political deliberation. This assumption goes along with the assumption that human beings have a natural center that philosophical inquiry can locate and illuminate. By contrast, the view that human beings are centerless networks of beliefs and desires and that their vocabularies and opinions are

---

40   This is the kernel of truth in Dworkin's claim that Rawls rejects "goal-based" social theory, but this point should not lead us to think that he is thereby driven back on a "rights-based" theory.

determined by historical circumstance allows for the possibility that there may not be enough overlap between two such networks to make possible agreement about political topics, or even profitable discussion of such topics.[41] We do not conclude that Nietzsche and Loyola are crazy because they hold unusual views on certain "fundamental" topics; rather, we conclude this only after extensive attempts at an exchange of political views have made us realize that we are not going to get anywhere.[42]

One can sum up this way of grasping the first horn of the dilemma I sketched earlier by saying that Rawls puts democratic politics first, and philosophy second. He retains the Socratic commitment to free exchange of views without the Platonic commitment to the possibility of universal agreement – a possibility underwritten by epistemological doctrines like Plato's Theory of Recollection[43] or Kant's theory of the relation between pure and empirical concepts. He disengages the question of whether we ought to be tolerant and Socratic from the question of whether this strategy will lead to truth. He is content that it should lead to whatever inter-subjective reflective equilibrium may be obtainable, given the contingent make-up of the subjects in question. Truth, viewed in the Platonic way, as the grasp of what Rawls calls "an order antecedent to and given to us," is simply not relevant to democratic politics. So philosophy, as the explanation of the relation between such an order and human nature, is not relevant either. When the two come into conflict, democracy takes precedence over philosophy.

This conclusion may seem liable to an obvious objection. It may seem that I have been rejecting a concern with philosophical theories about the nature of men and women on the basis of just such a theory. But notice that although I have frequently said that Rawls *can be content* with a notion of the human self as a centerless web of historically conditioned beliefs and desires, I have not suggested that he *needs* such a theory. Such a theory does not offer liberal social theory a *basis*. If one *wants* a model of the human self, then this picture of a centerless web will fill the need. But for purposes of liberal social theory, one can do without such a model. One can get along with common sense and social science, areas of discourse in which the term "the self" rarely occurs.

41   But one should not press this point so far as to raise the specter of "untranslatable languages." As Donald Davidson has remarked, we would not recognize other organisms as actual or potential language users – or, therefore, as persons – unless there were enough overlap in belief and desire to make translation possible. The point is merely that efficient and frequent communication is only a necessary, not a sufficient, condition of agreement.

42   Further, such a conclusion is *restricted* to politics. It does not cast doubt on the ability of these men to follow the rules of logic or their ability to do many other things skillfully and well. It is thus not equivalent to the traditional philosophical charge of "irrationality." That charge presupposes that inability to "see" certain truths is evidence of the lack of an organ that is essential for human functioning generally.

43   In Kierkegaard's *Philosophical Fragments*, to which I have referred earlier, we find the Platonic Theory of Recollection treated as the archetypal justification of "Socratism" and thus as the symbol of all forms (especially Hegel's) of what Bernard Williams has recently called "the rationalist theory of rationality" – the idea that one is rational only if one can appeal to universally accepted criteria, criteria whose truth and applicability all human beings can find "in their heart." This is the philosophical core of the Scriptural idea that "truth is great, and will prevail," when that idea is dissociated from the Pauline idea of "a New Being" (in the way that Kierkegaard refused to dissociate it).

If, however, one has a taste for philosophy – if one's vocation, one's private pursuit of perfection, entails constructing models of such entities as "the self," "knowledge," "language," "nature," "God," or "history," and then tinkering with them until they mesh with one another – one *will* want a picture of the self. Since my own vocation is of this sort, and the moral identity around which I wish to build such models is that of a citizen of a liberal democratic state, I commend the picture of the self as a centerless and contingent web to those with similar tastes and similar identities. But I would not commend it to those with a similar vocation but dissimilar moral identities – identities built, for example, around the love of God, Nietzschean self-overcoming, the accurate representation of reality as it is in itself, the quest for "one right answer" to moral questions, or the natural superiority of a given character type. Such persons need a more complex and interesting, less simple-minded model of the self – one that meshes in complex ways with complex models of such things as "nature" or "history." Nevertheless, such persons may, for pragmatic rather than moral reasons, be loyal citizens of a liberal democratic society. They may despise most of their fellow citizens, but be prepared to grant that the prevalence of such despicable character types is a lesser evil than the loss of political freedom. They may be ruefully grateful that their private senses of moral identity and the models of the human self that they develop to articulate this sense – the ways in which they deal with their aloneness – are not the concern of such a state. Rawls and Dewey have shown how the liberal state can ignore the difference between the moral identities of Glaucon and of Thrasymachus, just as it ignores the difference between the religious identities of a Catholic archbishop and a Mormon prophet.

There is, however, a flavor of paradox in this attitude toward theories of the self. One might be inclined to say that I have evaded one sort of self-referential paradox only by falling into another sort. For I am presupposing that one is at liberty to rig up a model of the self to suit one-self, to tailor it to one's politics, one's religion, or one's private sense of the meaning of one's life. This, in turn, presupposes that there is no "objective truth" about what the human self is *really* like. That, in turn, seems a claim that could be justified only on the basis of a metaphysico-epistemological view of the traditional sort. For surely if anything is the province of such a view, it is the question of what there is and is not a "fact of the matter" about. So my argument must ultimately come back to philosophical first principles.

Here I can only say that if there were a discoverable fact of the matter about what there is a fact of the matter about, then it would doubtless be metaphysics and epistemology that would discover that meta-fact. But I think that the very idea of a "fact of the matter" is one we would be better off without. Philosophers like Davidson and Derrida have, I think, given us good reason to think that the *physis–nomos, in se–ad nos,* and objective–subjective distinctions were steps on a ladder that we can now safely throw away. The question of whether the reasons such philosophers have given for this claim are themselves metaphysico–epistemological reasons, and if not, what sort of reasons they are, strikes me as pointless and sterile. Once again, I fall back on the holist's strategy of insisting that reflective equilibrium is all we need try for – that there is no natural order of justification of beliefs, no predestined outline for argument to trace. Getting rid of the idea of such an outline seems to me one of the many benefits of a conception of the self as a centerless web. Another benefit is that questions about whom we need justify ourselves to – questions about who counts as a fanatic and who deserves an answer – can be treated as just further matters to be sorted out in the course of attaining reflective equilibrium.

I can, however, make one point to offset the air of light-minded aestheticism I am adopting toward traditional philosophical questions. This is that there is a moral purpose behind this light-mindedness. The encouragement of light-mindedness about traditional philosophical topics serves the same purposes as does the encouragement of light-mindedness about traditional theological topics. Like the rise of large market economies, the increase in literacy, the proliferation of artistic genres, and the insouciant pluralism of contemporary culture, such philosophical super-ficiality and light-mindedness helps along the disenchantment of the world. It helps make the world's inhabitants more pragmatic, more tolerant, more liberal, more receptive to the appeal of instrumental rationality.

If one's moral identity consists in being a citizen of a liberal polity, then to encourage light-mindedness will serve one's moral purposes. Moral commitment, after all, does not require taking seriously all the matters that are, for moral reasons, taken seriously by one's fellow citizens. It may require just the opposite. It may require trying to josh them out of the habit of taking those topics so seriously. There may be serious reasons for so joshing them. More generally, we should not assume that the aesthetic is always the enemy of the moral. I should argue that in the recent history of liberal societies, the willingness to view matters aesthetically – to be content to indulge in what Schiller called "play" and to discard what Nietzsche called "the spirit of seriousness" – has been an important vehicle of moral progress.

I have now said everything I have to say about the third of the communitarian claims that I distinguished at the outset: the claim that the social theory of the liberal state rests on false philosophical presuppositions. I hope I have given reasons for thinking that insofar as the communitarian is a critic of liberalism, he should drop this claim and should instead develop either of the first two claims: the empirical claim that democratic institutions cannot be combined with the sense of common purpose that predemocratic societies enjoyed, or the moral judgment that the products of the liberal state are too high a price to pay for the elimination of the evils that preceded it. If communitarian critics of liberalism stuck to these two claims, they would avoid the sort of terminal wistfulness with which their books typically end. Heidegger, for example, tells us that "we are too late for the gods, and too early for Being." Unger ends *Knowledge and Politics* with an appeal to a *Deus absconditus*. MacIntyre ends *After Virtue* by saying that we "are awaiting not for a Godot, but for another – doubtless very different – St. Benedict."[44] Sandel ends his book by saying that liberalism "forgets the possibility that when politics goes well, we can know a good in common that we cannot know alone," but he does not suggest a candidate for this common good.

Instead of thus suggesting that philosophical reflection, or a return to religion, might enable us to re-enchant the world, I think that communitarians should stick to the question of whether disenchantment has, on balance, done us more harm than good, or created more dangers than it has evaded. For Dewey, communal and public disenchantment is the price we pay for individual and private spiritual liberation, the kind of liberation that Emerson thought characteristically American. Dewey was as well aware as Weber that there is a price to be paid, but he thought it well worth paying. He assumed that no good achieved by earlier societies would be worth recapturing if the price were a

---

44   See Jeffrey Stout's discussion of the manifold ambiguities of this conclusion in "Virtue Among the Ruins: An Essay on MacIntyre," *Neue Zeitschrift für Systematische Theologie und Religionsphilosophie* 26 (1984): 256–73, especially, 269.

diminution in our ability to leave people alone, to let them try out their private visions of perfection in peace. He admired the American habit of giving democracy priority over philosophy by asking, about any vision of the meaning of life, "Would not acting out this vision interfere with the ability of others to work out their own salvation?" Giving priority to that question is no more "natural" than giving priority to, say, MacIntyre's question "What sorts of human beings emerge in the culture of liberalism?" or Sandel's question "Can a community of those who put justice first ever be more than a community of strangers?" The question of which of these questions is prior to which others is, necessarily, begged by *everybody*. Nobody is being any more arbitrary than anybody else. But that is to say that nobody is being arbitrary at all. Everybody is just insisting that the beliefs and desires they hold most dear should come first in the order of discussion. That is not arbitrariness, but sincerity.

The danger of re-enchanting the world, from a Deweyan point of view, is that it might interfere with the development of what Rawls calls "a social union of social unions,"[45] some of which may be (and in Emerson's view, should be) very small indeed. For it is hard to be both enchanted with one version of the world and tolerant of all the others. I have not tried to argue the question of whether Dewey was right in this judgment of relative danger and promise. I have merely argued that such a judgment neither presupposes nor supports a theory of the self. Nor have I tried to deal with Horkheimer and Adorno's prediction that the "dissolvent rationality" of the Englightenment will eventually cause the liberal democracies to come unstuck.

The only thing I have to say about this prediction is that the collapse of the liberal democracies would not, in itself, provide much evidence for the claim that human

45   This is Rawls's description of "a well-ordered society (corresponding to justice as fairness)" (*Theory of Justice*, p. 527). Sandel finds these passages metaphorical and complains that "intersubjective and individualistic images appear in uneasy, sometimes unfelicitous combination, as if to betray the incompatible commitments contending within" (*Liberalism and the Limits of Justice*, pp. 150ff.). He concludes that "the moral vocabulary of community in the strong sense cannot in all cases be captured by a conception that [as Rawls has said his is] 'in its theoretical basis is individualistic.'" I am claiming that these commitments will look incompatible only if one attempts to define their philosophical presuppositions (which Rawls himself may occasionally have done too much of), and that this is a good reason for not making such attempts. Compare the Enlightenment view that attempts to sharpen up the theological presuppositions of social commitments had done more harm than good and that if theology cannot simply be discarded, it should at least be left as fuzzy (or, one might say, "liberal") as possible. Oakeshott has a point when he insists on the value of theoretical muddle for the health of the state.

Elsewhere Rawls has claimed that "there is no reason why a well-ordered society should encourage primarily individualistic values if this means ways of life that lead individuals to pursue their own way and to have no concern for the interest of others" ("Fairness to Goodness," *Philosophical Review* 84 [1975]: 550). Sandel's discussion of this passage says that it "suggests a deeper sense in which Rawls' conception is individualistic," but his argument that this suggestion is correct is, once again, the claim that "the Rawlsian self is not only a subject of possession, but an antecedently individuated subject" (*Liberalism and the Limits of Justice*, p. 61 ff.). This is just the claim I have been arguing against by arguing that there is no such thing as "the Rawlsian self" and that Rawls "takes for granted that every individual consists of one and only one system of desires" (ibid., p. 62), but it is hard to find evidence for this claim in the texts. At worst, Rawls simplifies his presentation by imagining each of his citizens as having only one such set, but this simplifying assumption does not seem central to his view.

societies cannot survive without widely shared opinions on matters of ultimate importance – shared conceptions of our place in the universe and our mission on earth. Perhaps they cannot survive under such conditions, but the eventual collapse of the democracies would not, in itself, show that this was the case – any more than it would show that human societies require kings or an established religion, or that political community cannot exist outside of small city-states.

Both Jefferson and Dewey described America as an "experiment." If the experiment fails, our descendants may learn something important. But they will not learn a philosophical truth, any more than they will learn a religious one. They will simply get some hints about what to watch out for when setting up their next experiment. Even if nothing else survives from the age of the democratic revolutions, perhaps our descendants will remember that social institutions *can* be viewed as experiments in cooperation rather than as attempts to embody a universal and ahistorical order. It is hard to believe that this memory would not be worth having.

Acknowledgment

I am grateful to David Levin, Michael Sandel, J. B. Schneewind, and A. J. Thomas Jefferson, for comment on earlier drafts of this paper.

14

Freud and Moral Reflection

The Mechanical Mind: Hume and Freud

Freud thought of himself as part of the same "decentering" movement of thought to which Copernicus and Darwin belonged. In a famous passage, he says that psychoanalysis "seeks to prove to the ego that it is not even master in its own house, but must content itself with scanty information of what is going on unconsciously in its mind." He compares this with the realization that "our earth was not the centre of the universe but only a tiny fragment of a cosmic system of scarcely imaginable vastness" and with the discovery, by Darwin, of our "ineradicable animal nature".[1]

Copernicus, Darwin, and Freud do have something important in common, but Freud does not give us a clear idea of what that is. It is not evident that successive decenterings add up to a history of humiliation; Copernicus and Darwin might claim that by making God and the angels less plausible, they have left human beings on top of the heap. The suggestion that we have discovered, humiliatingly, that humanity is less important than we had thought is not perspicuous. For it is not clear what "importance" can mean in this context. Further, the claim that psychoanalysis has shown that the ego is not master in its own house is unhelpful, for the relevant sense of "mastery" is unclear. Does our sense of our importance, or our capacity for self-control, really depend on the belief that we are transparent to ourselves? Why should the discovery of the unconscious add humiliation to the discovery of the passions?

I think one gets a better idea of the similarity Freud was trying to describe by contrasting a world of natural kinds with a world of machines – a world of Aristotelian substances with a world of homogenous particles combining and disassociating according to universal laws. Think of the claim that "man is a natural kind" not as saying that

Richard M. Rorty, "Freud and Moral Reflection," pp.1–27 in Joseph H. Smith and William Kerrigan (eds.), *Pragmatism's Freud: The Moral Disposition of Psychoanalysis* (Baltimore: Johns Hopkins University Press, 1986), © 1986 by The Forum on Psychiatry and the Humanities, Washington School of Psychiatry. Reprinted by permission.

1 The Standard Edition of the Complete Psychological Works of Sigmund Freud, trans. James Strachey (London: Hogarth Press, 1966), 16: 284–5. Future references will be to this edition (abbreviated S.E.) and will be inserted in the text.

human beings are at the center of something, but that they *have* a center, in a way that a machine does not. A substance that exemplifies an Aristotelian natural kind divides into a central essence – one that provides a built-in purpose – and a set of peripheral accidents. But an artifact's formal and final causes may be distinct; the same machine, for example, may be used for many different purposes. A machine's purpose is not built in.[2] If humanity is a natural kind, then perhaps we can find our center and so learn how to live well. But if we are machines, then it is up to us to invent a use for ourselves.

What was decisive about the Copernican Revolution was not that it moved the human being from the center of the universe, but that it began, in Dyksterhuis's phrase, the "mechanization of the world picture."[3] Copernicus and Newton between them made it hard to think of the universe as an edifying spectacle. When an infinite universe of pointless corpuscles replaced a closed world, it became hard to imagine what it would be like to look down upon the Creation and find it good.[4] The universe began

2   There can be such a thing as a "purer" Aristotelian substance – one that realizes its essence better because it is less subject to irrelevant accidental changes. (Indeed, Aristotle arranges substances in a hierarchy according to their degree of materiality, their degree of susceptibility to such changes – a hierarchy with "pure actuality" at the top.) But there is no such thing as a purified machine, though there may be another machine that accomplishes the same purpose more efficiently. Machines have no centers to which one can strip them down; stripped-down versions of machines are different machines, machines for doing or producing different things, not more perfect versions of the same machine.

3   The Copernican model of the heavens could not have been accepted without also accepting the corpuscularian mechanics of Galileo and Descartes (see Kuhn, *The Copernican Revolution*, on this point). That mechanics was the entering wedge for a Newtonian paradigm of scientific explanation – one that predicted events on the basis of a universal homogenous microstructure, rather than revealing the different natures of the various natural kinds. The reason why "the new philosophy" cast all in doubt was not that people felt belittled when the sun took the place of the earth but that it had become hard to see what, given Newtonian space, could be meant by the universe having a center. As it became harder to know what a God's-eye view would be like, it became harder to believe in God. As it became harder to think of the common-sense way of breaking up the world into "natural" kinds as more than a practical convenience, it became harder to make sense of the Aristotelian essence–accident distinction. So the very idea of the "nature" of something as setting the standards that things of that sort ought to fulfill began to blur.

4   In particular, it became difficult to see what the point of *man* could be – difficult to preserve anything like Aristotle's "functional" concept of man. See MacIntyre, *After Virtue*:

Moral arguments within the classical, Aristotelian tradition – whether in its Greek or its medieval versions – involve at least one central functional concept, the concept of *man* understood as having an essential nature and an essential purpose or function. ... Aristotle takes it as a starting-point for ethical inquiry that the relationship of "man" to "living well" is analogous to that of "harpist" to "playing the harp well." ... But the use of "man" as a functional concept is far older than Aristotle and it does not initially derive from Aristotle's metaphysical biology. It is rooted in the forms of a social life in which the theorists of the classical tradition give expression. For according to that tradition, to be a man is to fill a set of roles, each of which has its own point and purpose: a member of a family, a citizen, soldier, philosopher, servant of God. It is only when man is thought of as an individual prior to and apart from all roles that "man" ceases to be a functional concept. (56)

I take up MacIntyre's suggestion that we need to recapture such a concept in the final section of this essay.

to look like a rather simple, boring machine, rambling off beyond the horizon, rather than like a bounded and well-composed tableau. So the idea of a center no longer seemed applicable. Analogously, the result of Darwin's and Mendel's mechanization of biology was to set aside an edifying hierarchy of natural kinds. Viewing the various species of plants and animals as the temporary results of interactions between fortuitous environmental pressures and random mutations made the world of living creatures as pointless as Newtonian mechanics had made cosmology. Mechanization meant that the world in which human beings lived no longer taught them anything about how they should live.

In trying to see how Freud fits into this story of decentering-as-mechanization, one should begin by noting that Freud was not the first to suggest that, having mechanized everything else, we mechanize the mind as well. Hume had already treated ideas and impressions not as properties of a substratal self but as mental atoms whose arrangement *was* the self. This arrangement was determined by laws of association, analogues of the law of gravitation. Hume thought of himself as the Newton of the mind, and the mechanical mind he envisaged was – viewed from above, so to speak – just as morally pointless as Newton's corpuscularian universe.

Hume, however, suggested that the mechanization of neither nature nor the mind mattered for purposes of finding a self-image. With a sort of protopragmatist insouciance, he thought that talk about the atoms of Democritus, Newton's shining lights, and his own "impressions and ideas" offered, at most, a handy way of describing things and people for purposes of predicting and controlling them. For moral purposes, for purposes of seeing life as having a point, such talk might be irrelevant. Like Blake, Hume was prepared to say that the view from above – the view of the Baconian predictor and controller – was irrelevant to our sense of centeredness. His pragmatical reconciliation of freedom and determinism, like his reconciliation of armchair skepticism with theoretical curiosity and practical benevolence, is an invitation to take the mechanization of the mind lightly – as no more than an intriguing intellectual exercise, the sort of thing that a young person might do in order to become famous.

It is tempting to respond to Freud in the same way that Hume responded to his own mechanizing efforts: to say that for purposes of moral reflection a knowledge of Freudian unconscious motivation is as irrelevant as a knowledge of Humean associations or of neurophysiology. But this response is unconvincing. Unlike Hume, Freud *did* change our self-image. Finding out about our unconscious motives is not just an intriguing exercise, but more like a moral obligation. What difference between Hume's and Freud's ways of extending mechanization to the mind accounts for Freud's relevance to our moral consciousness?

If one views Freud's dictum that the ego is not master in its own house as saying merely that we often act in ways that could not have been predicted on the basis of our introspectible beliefs and desires, Freud will be merely reiterating a commonplace of Greek thought. If one views it as the claim that the mind can, for purposes of prediction and control, be treated as a set of associative mechanisms, a realm in which there are no accidents, Freud will be saying little that Hume had not said. So one must find another interpretation. One gets a clue, I think, from the fact that the phrase "not even master in its own house" is to the point only if some other person is behaving as if he or she were in charge. The phrase is an appropriate response to the incursion of an unwanted guest – for example, to the onset of schizophrenia. But it is not an appropriate reaction, for example, to an explanation of the dependence of our mood on our endocrine system. For glands are not, so to speak, quasi people with whom to struggle. Nor are neurons, which is why the possible identity of the mind with the brain is of no moral interest. Physiological discoveries can tell us how to predict and control ourselves – including how to predict and control our beliefs and desires – without threatening or changing our self-image. For such discoveries do not suggest that we are being shouldered aside by somebody else.

Psychological mechanisms will seem more decentering than physiological mechanisms only if one is of a naturally metaphysical turn of mind, insistent on pressing the questions, "But what am I *really?* What is my *true* self? What is *essential* to me?" Descartes and Kant had this sort of mind and so, in our day, do reductionist metaphysicians such as B. F. Skinner and antireductionist champions of "subjectivity" and "phenomenology" such as Thomas Nagel and Richard Wollheim. But the mechanization of nature made protopragmatists of most people, allowing them to shrug off questions of essence. They became accustomed to speaking one sort of language for Baconian purposes of prediction and control and another for purposes of moral reflection. They saw no need to raise the question of which language represented the world or the self as it is "in itself."[5] Yet Freudian discoveries are troubling even for pragmatists. Unlike the atoms of Democritus or Hume, the Freudian unconscious does not look like something that we might usefully, to achieve certain of our purposes, describe ourselves as. It looks like somebody who is stepping into our shoes, somebody who has different purposes than we do. It looks like a person using us rather than a thing we can use.

This clue – the fact that psychological mechanisms look most disturbing and decentering when they stop looking like mechanisms and start looking like persons – has been followed up by Donald Davidson. In a remarkable essay called "Paradoxes of Irrationality," Davidson notes that philosophers have always been upset by Freud's insistence on "partitioning" the self. They have tended to reject Freud's threatening picture of quasi selves lurking beneath the threshold of consciousness as an unnecessarily vivid way of describing the incoherence and confusion that may afflict a single self. They hope thereby to remain faithful to the common-sense assumption that a single human body typically contains a single self. Davidson defends Freudian partitioning by pointing out that there is no reason to say "You unconsciously believe that *p*" rather than "There is something within you which causes you to act as if you believed that *p*," unless one is prepared to

---

round out the characterization of the unconscious quasi self who "believes that *p*" by ascribing a host of other beliefs (mostly true, and mostly consistent with *p*) to that quasi self. One can only attribute a belief to something if one simultaneously attributes lots of other mostly true and mostly consistent beliefs. Beliefs and desires, unlike Humean ideas and impressions, come in packages.[6]

Davidson puts these holistic considerations to work as follows. He identifies (not explicitly, but, if my reading of him is right, tacitly) being a person with being a coherent and plausible set of beliefs and desires. Then he points out that the force of saying that a human being sometimes behaves irrationally is that he or she sometimes exhibits behavior that cannot be explained by reference to a single such set. Finally, he concludes that the point of "partitioning" the self between a consciousness and an unconscious is that the latter can be viewed as an alternative set, inconsistent with the familiar set that we identify with conciousness, yet sufficiently coherent internally to count as a person. This strategy leaves open the possibility that the same human body can play host to two or more persons. These persons enter into causal relations with each other, as well as with the body whose movements are brought about by the beliefs and desires of one or the other of them. But they do not, normally, have conversational relations. That is, one's unconscious beliefs are not *reasons* for a change in one's conscious beliefs, but they may *cause* changes in the latter beliefs, just as may portions of one's body (e.g., the retina, the fingertips, the pituitary gland, the gonads).

To see the force of Davidson's suggestion is to appreciate the crucial difference between Hume and Freud. This is that Hume's mental atoms included only subpropositional components of beliefs – mostly names of perceptible and introspectible qualia. The mechanization of the self that Hume suggested, and that associationist psychology developed, amounted to little more than a transposition into mentalistic terminology of a rather crude physiology of perception and memory. By contrast, Freud populated inner space not with analogues of Boylean corpuscles but with analogues of persons – internally coherent clusters of belief and desire. Each of these quasi persons is, in the Freudian picture, a part of a single unified *causal* network, but not of a single person (since the criterion for individuation of a person is a certain minimal coherence among its beliefs and desires). Knowledge of all these persons is necessary to predict and control a human being's behavior (and in particular his or her "irrational" behavior), but only one of these persons will be available (at any given time) to introspection.

The Rational Unconscious as Conversational Partner

If one accepts this Davidsonian explanation of Freud's basic strategy, then one has taken a long step toward seeing why psychoanalysis can aptly be described as a decentering. For now one can see Freudian mechanisms as having, so to speak, a human interest that no physiological or Humean mechanism could have. One can see why it is hard to dismiss the Freudian unconscious as just one more useful, if paradoxical, redescription of

6   Even if, as Hume thought, there is a possible universe consisting only of one sense-impression, we cannot make sense of the idea of a universe consisting only of the belief that, for example, Caesar crossed the Rubicon. Further, there is no such thing as an incoherent arrangement of Humean mental atoms. But there is such a thing as a set of beliefs and desires so incoherent that we cannot attribute them to a single self.

the world that science has invented for purposes of saving the phenomena – the sort of redescription that can be ignored by everyday, practical purposes (as, for example, one ignores heliocentrism). The suggestion that some unknown persons are causing us (or, to stress the alienation produced by this suggestion, causing our bodies) to do things we would rather not do is decentering in a way that an account of heavenly bodies (or of the descent of man) is not. One will be thrown off base by this suggestion even if one has no interest in Aristotelian, metaphysical questions about one's "essence" or one's "true self." One can be entirely pragmatical in one's approach to life and still feel that something needs to be *done* in response to such a suggestion.

To take Freud's suggestion seriously is to wish to become acquainted with these unfamiliar persons, if only as a first step toward killing them off. This wish will take the place, for a pragmatical Freudian, of the religious and metaphysical desire to find one's "true center." It initiates a task that can plausibly be described as a moral obligation – the task whose goal is summed up in the phrase "where id was, there shall ego be." This goal does not require the Aristotelian notion that one's ego is more "natural" or more truly "oneself" than one's id. But adopting this goal does restore a point to the imperative "Know thyself," an imperative that one might have thought inapplicable to the self-as-machine.

On Freud's account of self-knowledge, what we are morally obligated to know about ourselves is not our essence, not a common human nature that is somehow the source and locus of moral responsibility. Far from being of what we share with the other members of our species, self-knowledge is precisely of what divides us from them: our accidental idiosyncrasies, the "irrational" components in ourselves, the ones that split us up into incompatible sets of beliefs and desires. The study of "the nature of the mind," construed as the study either of Humean association of ideas or of Freudian metapsychology, is as pointless, for purposes of moral reflection, as the study of the laws of celestial motion. What *is* of interest is the study of the idiosyncratic raw material whose processing Humean and Freudian mechanisms are postulated to predict, and of the idiosyncratic products of this processing. For only study of these concrete details will let us enter into conversational relations with our unconscious and, at the ideal limit of such conversation, let us break down the partitions.

The view of Freud that I am proposing will seem plausible only if one makes a clear distinction between two senses of "the unconscious": (1) a sense in which it stands for one or more well-articulated systems of beliefs and desires, systems that are just as complex, sophisticated, and internally consistent as the normal adult's conscious beliefs and desires; and (2) a sense in which it stands for a seething mass of inarticulate instinctual energies, a "reservoir of libido" to which consistency is irrelevant. In the second sense, the unconscious is just another name for "the passions," the lower part of the soul, the bad, false self. Had this been the only sense Freud gave to the term, his work would have left our strategies of character-development, and our self-image, largely unchanged. What is novel in Freud's view of the unconscious is his claim that our unconscious selves are not dumb, sullen, lurching brutes, but rather the intellectual peers of our conscious selves, possible conversational partners for those selves. As Rieff puts it, "Freud democratized genius by giving everyone a creative unconscious" (1961, 36).[7]

---

7   See also Trilling, *Beyond Culture* (79): "[Freud] showed us that poetry is indigenous to the very constitution of the mind; he saw the mind as being, in the greater part of its tendency, exactly a poetry-making faculty." Bersani makes the same point when he says, "Psychoanalytic theory has

This suggestion that one or more clever, articulate, inventive persons are at work behind the scene – cooking up our jokes, inventing our metaphors, plotting our dreams, arranging our slips, and censoring our memories – is what grips the imagination of the lay reader of Freud. As Freud himself said, if psychoanalysis had stuck to the neuroses, it would never have attracted the attention of the intellectuals.[8] It was the application of psychoanalytical notions to normal life that first suggested that Freud's ideas might call for a revision in our self-image. For this application breaks the connection between the Platonic reason-passion distinction and the conscious-unconscious distinction. It substitutes a picture of sophisticated transactions between two or more "intellects" for the traditional picture of one "intellect" struggling with a mob of "irrational" brutes.

The Platonic tradition had thought of articulate beliefs – or, more generally, propositional attitudes – as the preserve of the higher part of the soul. It thought of the lower parts as "bodily," as animallike, and in particular as prelinguistic. But a witty unconscious is necessarily a linguistic unconscious. Further, if "rational" means "capable of weaving complex, internally consistent, networks of belief" rather than "capable of contemplating reality as it is," then a witty unconscious is also a *rational* unconscious – one that can no more tolerate inconsistency than can consciousness.[9] So we need to distinguish the unconscious as "the deepest strata of our minds, made up of instinctual impulses," strata that know "nothing that is negative, and no negation," in which "contradictories coincide" (*S.E.* 14:296), from the unconscious as the sensitive, whacky, backstage partner who feeds us our best lines. The latter is somebody who has a well-worked-out, internally consistent view of the world – though one that may be hopelessly wrong on certain crucial points. One needs to distinguish Freud's banal claim that "our intellect is a feeble and dependent thing, a plaything and tool of our instincts and affects" (*S.E.* 14:301) – which is just a replay of Hume's claim that "reason is, and ought to be, the slave of the passions"[10] – from his interesting and novel claim that the conscious-unconscious distinction cuts across the human-animal and reason-instinct distinctions.

---

made the notion of fantasy so richly programmatic that we should no longer be able to take for granted the distinction between art and life, or to feel that the word 'creative' has any analytic value at all" (1977, 138).

8   "The importance of psycho-analysis for psychiatry would never have drawn the attention of the intellectual world to it or won it a place in *The History of our Times*. This result was brought about by the relation of psycho-analysis to normal, not to pathological, mental life" (Freud, *S.E.* 19:205; see also 18:240). Even if analytic psychiatry should some day be abandoned in favor of chemical and microsurgical forms of treatment, the connections that Freud drew between such emotions as sexual yearning and hostility on the one hand, and between dreams and parapraxes on the other, would remain part of the common sense of our culture.

9   See Davidson, "Paradoxes of Irrationality," especially his discussion of "the paradox of rationality" (303).

10   *Any* associationist psychology will make *that* claim. For it is a corollary of the claim that reason is not a faculty of contemplating essence but only a faculty of inferring beliefs from other beliefs. Since the initial premises of such inferences must then be supplied by something other than reason, and if the only faculty relevantly opposed to faculty that can be opposed to "reason" is "passion," then Hume's claim follows trivially. But it would, of course, be more consistent with the mechanistic vocabulary of associationist psychology to drop talk of faculties and, in particular, to drop the terms "reason" and "passion." Once the mind becomes a machine instead of a quasi person, it no longer has faculties, much less higher and lower ones. Hume is interlacing the old vocabulary of faculties with the results of new associationism for the sake of shock value.

If one concentrates on the latter claim, then one can see Freud as suggesting that, on those occasions when we are tempted to complain that two souls dwell, alas, in our breast, we think of the two as one more-or-less sane and one more-or-less crazy human soul, rather than as one human soul and one bestial soul. On the latter, Platonic model, self-knowledge will be a matter of self-purification − of identifying our true, human, self and expelling, curbing, or ignoring the animal self. On the former model, self-knowledge will be a matter of getting acquainted with one or more crazy quasi people, listening to their crazy accounts of how things are, seeing why they hold the crazy views they do, and learning something from them. It will be a matter of self-enrichment. To say "Where id was, there will ego be" will not mean "Whereas once I was driven by instinct, I shall become autonomous, motivated solely by reason." Rather, it will mean something like: "Once I could not figure out why I was acting so oddly, and hence wondered if I were, somehow, under the control of a devil or a beast. But now I shall be able to see my actions as rational, as making sense, though perhaps based on mistaken premises. I may even discover that those premises were not mistaken, that my unconscious knew better than I did."[11]

The advantage of this way of thinking of the passions is that it enables one to take a similar view of conscience. For just as this view humanizes what the Platonic tradition took to be the urges of an animal, so it humanizes what that tradition thought of as divine inspiration. It makes conscience, like passion, one more set of human beliefs and desires − another story about how the world is, another Weltanschauung. Most

---

11   This way of stating the aim of psychoanalytic treatment may seem to make everything sound too sweetly reasonable. It suggests that the analyst serves as a sort of moderator at a symposium: he or she introduces, for example, a consciousness which thinks that Mother is a long-suffering object of pity to an unconscious, which thinks of her as a voracious seductress, letting the two hash out the pros and cons. It is of course true that the facts of resistance forbid the analyst to think in conversational terms. He or she must instead think in terms of Freud's various topographico-hydraulic models of libidinal flow, hoping to find in these models suggestions about how to overcome resistance, what meaning to assign to novel symptoms, and so forth.

But it is also true that the patient has no choice but to think in conversational terms. (This is why self-analysis will usually not work, why treatment can often do what reflection cannot.) For purposes of the patient's conscious attempt to reshape his or her character, he or she cannot use a self-description in terms of cathexes, libidinal flow, and the like; topographic-hydraulic models cannot form part of one's self-image, any more than can a description of one's endocrine system. When the patient thinks about competing descriptions of his or her mother, the patient has to think dialectically, to grant that there is much to be said on both sides. To think, as opposed to react to a new stimulus, simply *is* to compare and contrast candidates for admission into one's set of beliefs and desires. So, while the analyst is busy thinking causally, in terms of the patient's reactions to stimuli (and in particular the stimuli that occur while the patient is on the couch), the patient has to think of his or her unconscious as, at least potentially, a conversational partner.

These two ways of thinking seem to me alternative tools, useful for different purposes, rather than contradictory claims. I do not think (despite the arguments of, for example, Paul Ricoeur and Roy Schafer) that there is a tension in Freud's thought between "energetics" and "hermeneutics." Rather, the two seem to me to be as compatible as, for example, microstructural and macrostructural descriptions of the same object (e.g., Eddington's table). But to defend my eirenic attitude properly I should offer an account of "resistance" that chimes with Davidson's interpretation of the unconscious, and I have not yet figured out how to do this. (I am grateful to George Thomas, Seymour Rabinowitz, and Cecil Cullender for pointing out this difficulty to me.)

important, it makes it *just* another story – not one that (in the case of the passions) is automatically suspect nor one that (in the case of conscience) is automatically privileged. It treats, so to speak, the three different stories told by the id, the superego, and the ego as alternative extrapolations from common experience – in particular, experience of childhood events. Each story is an attempt to make these events coherent with later events, but the stimuli provided by such events are (usually) so diverse and confusing that no *single* consistent set of beliefs and desires is able to make them all hang together.

To view these three (or more) stories as on a par, as alternative explanations of a confusing situation, is part of what Rieff calls "Freud's egalitarian revision of the traditional idea of an hierarchical human nature" (1966, 56). To adopt a self-image that incorporates this egalitarian revision is to think that there is no single right answer to the question "What *did* happen to me in the past?" It is also to think that there is no such answer to the question "What sort of person am I now?" It is to recognize that the choice of a vocabulary in which to describe either one's childhood or one's character cannot be made by inspecting some collection of "neutral facts" (e.g., a complete videotape of one's life history). It is to give up the urge to purification, to achieve a stripped-down version of the self, and to develop what Rieff calls "tolerance of ambiguities ... the key to what Freud considered the most difficult of all personal accomplishments: a genuinely stable character in an unstable time" (1966, 57). On the view I am offering, Freud gave us a new technique for achieving a genuinely stable character: the technique of lending a sympathetic ear to our own tendencies to instability, by treating them as alternative ways of making sense of the past, ways that have as good a claim on our attention as do the familiar beliefs and desires that are available to introspection. His mechanistic view of the self gave us a vocabulary that lets us describe all the various parts of the soul, conscious and unconscious alike, in homogenous terms: as equally plausible candidates for "the true self."

But to say that all the parts of the soul are equally plausible candidates is to discredit both the idea of a "true self" and the idea of "the true story about how things are." It is to view the enlightened, liberated self – the self that has finally succeeded in shaping itself – as a self that has given up the need to "see things steadily and see them whole," to penetrate beyond shifting appearances to a constant reality. Maturity will, according to this view, consist rather in an ability to seek out new redescriptions of one's own past – an ability to take a nominalistic, ironic, view of oneself. By turning the Platonic parts of the soul into conversational partners for one another, Freud did for the variety of interpretations of each person's past what the Baconian approach to science and philosophy did for the variety of descriptions of the universe as a whole. He let us see alternative narratives and alternative vocabularies as instruments for change, rather than as candidates for a correct depiction of how things are in themselves.

Much of what I have been saying is summarized in Freud's remark, "If one considers chance to be unworthy of determining our fate, it is simply a relapse into the pious view of the Universe which Leonardo himself was on the way to overcoming when he wrote that the sun does not move" (*S.E.* 11:137).[12] This recommendation that we see chance

---

12 It is interesting that in the passage cited Freud is referring back to a passage (*S.E.* 11:76) where he credits Leonardo not only with anticipating Copernicus but with having "divined the

as "not unworthy of determining our fate" has as a corollary that we see ourselves as having the beliefs and emotions we do, including our (putatively) "specifically moral" beliefs and emotions, because of some very particular, idiosyncratic things that have happened in the history of the race, and to ourselves in the course of growing up. Such a recognition produces the ability to be Baconian about oneself. It lets one see oneself as a Rube Goldberg machine that requires much tinkering, rather than as a substance with a precious essence to be discovered and cherished. It produces what Whitehead called "the virtues which Odysseus shares with the foxes" – rather than, for example, those which Achilles shares with the lions, or those which Plato and Aristotle hoped to share with the gods.

From this Baconian angle, the point of psychoanalysis is the same as that of reflection on the sort of character one would like to have, once one ceases to take a single vocabulary for granted and begins the attempt to revise and enlarge the very vocabulary in which one is at present reflecting. The point of both exercises is to find new self-descriptions whose adoption will enable one to alter one's behavior. Finding out the views of one's unconscious about one's past is a way of getting some additional suggestions about how to describe (and change) oneself in the future. As a way of getting such suggestions, psychoanalysis differs from reading history, novels, or treatises on moral philosophy only in being more painful, in being more likely to produce radical change, and in requiring a partner.

Purification and Self-Enlargement

Because morality is associated both with human solidarity and with tragedy, my claim that attention to personal idiosyncrasy "remoralizes" a mechanistic self may seem paradoxical. One might protest, in the spirit of Kant, that the whole point of morality is self-forgetfulness, not making an exception of oneself, seeing oneself as counting for no more than any other human being, being motivated by what is common to all humanity. To emphasize idiosyncrasy is to emphasize the comic variety of human life rather than the tragedies that morality hopes to avert.

The appearance of paradox results from the fact that "morality" can mean either the attempt to be just in one's treatment of others or the search for perfection in oneself. The former is public morality, codifiable in statutes and maxims. The latter is private morality, the development of character. Like Freud, I am concerned only with the latter. Morality as the search for justice swings free of religion, science, metaphysics, and psychology. It is the relatively simple and obvious side of morality – the part that nowadays, in the wake of Freud, is often referred to as "culture" or "repression." This is the side of morality that instructs us to tell the truth, avoid violence, eschew sex with near relations, keep our promises, and abide by the Golden Rule.

The story of progress in public morality is largely irrelevant to the story of the mechanization of the world view.[13] Galileo, Darwin, and Freud did little to help or hinder such progress. They have nothing to say in answer either to the Athenian question "Does

---

history of the stratification and fossilization in the Arno valley," a suggestion that Leonardo anticipated Darwin as well.

13   The Enlightenment attempt to connect the two by seeing both feudalism and Aristotelian science as instances of "prejudice and superstition" was a self-deceptive neo-Aristotelian attempt

justice pay?" or to the Californian question "How much repression need I endure?" Freud, in particular, has no contribution to make to social theory. His domain is the portion of morality that cannot be identified with "culture"; it is the private life, the search for a character, the attempt of individuals to be reconciled with themselves (and, in the case of some exceptional individuals, to make their lives works of art).[14]

Such an attempt can take one of two antithetical forms: a search for purity or a search for self-enlargement. The ascetic life commended by Plato and criticized by Nietzsche is the paradigm of the former. The "aesthetic" life criticized by Kierkegaard is the paradigm of the latter. The desire to purify oneself is the desire to slim down, to peel away everything that is accidental, to will one thing, to intensify, to become a simpler and more transparent being. The desire to enlarge oneself is the desire to embrace more and more possibilities, to be constantly learning, to give oneself over entirely to curiosity, to end by having envisaged all the possibilities of the past and of the future. It was the goal shared by, for example, de Sade, Byron, and Hegel.[15] On the view I am presenting, Freud is an apostle of this aesthetic life, the life of unending curiosity, the life that seeks to extend its own bound rather than to find its center.

For those who decline the options offered by de Sade and Byron (sexual experimentation, political engagement), the principal technique of self-enlargement will be Hegel's: the enrichment of language. One will see the history of both the race and oneself as the development of richer, fuller ways of formulating one's desires and hopes, and thus making those desires and hopes themselves – and thereby oneself – richer and fuller. I shall call such a development the "acquisition of new vocabularies of moral reflection." By "a vocabulary of moral reflection" I mean a set of terms in which one compares oneself to other human beings. Such vocabularies contain terms like *magnanimous, a true Christian, decent, cowardly, God-fearing, hypocritical, self-deceptive, epicene, self-destructive, cold, an antique Roman, a saint, a Julien Sorel, a Becky Sharpe, a red-blooded American, a shy gazelle, a hyena, depressive, a Bloomsbury type, a man of respect, a grande dame.* Such terms are possible answers to the question "What is he or she like?" and thus possible answers to the question "What am *I* like?" By summing up patterns of behavior, they are tools for criticizing the character of others and for creating one's own. They are the terms one uses when one tries to resolve moral dilemmas by asking "What sort of person would I be if I did this?"

---

to preserve the idea of man as an animal whose essence is rationality, while simultaneously identifying rationality with certain newly created institutions.

14   Here I am agreeing with Rieff against, for example, Fromm and Marcuse: "Psychoanalysis is the doctrine of the private man defending himself against public encroachment. He cultivates the private life and its pleasures, and if he does take part in public affairs it is for consciously private motives" (Rieff 1961, 278). Rieff seems to me right in saying that Freud had little to say about how and whether society might be made "less repressive": "Like those who worked for shorter hours but nevertheless feared what men might do with their leisure, Freud would have welcomed more constructive releases from our stale moralities, but did not propose to substitute a new one. Our private ethics were his scientific problem: he had no new public ethics to suggest, no grand design for the puzzle of our common life" (1966, 38).

15   See Hans Blumenberg's discussion of "theoretical curiosity," and especially his contrast between the medieval criticism of curiosity and Bacon's praise of it, in *The Legitimacy of the Modern Age.*

This question is, of course, not the only question one asks when reflecting about what to do. One also asks, for example, "How would I justify myself to so-and-so?" and "Would this action violate the general rule that …?" But answers to these questions will reflect the vocabulary of moral reflection at one's disposal. That vocabulary helps one decide to which sort of people to justify oneself. It puts some flesh on abstract rules like the categorical imperative and "Maximize human happiness!" It is distinctions between such vocabularies, rather than between general principles, that differentiate the moralities of communities, historical epochs, and epochs in the life of the curious intellectual. The availability of a richer vocabulary of moral deliberation is what one chiefly has in mind when one says that we are, morally speaking, more sensitive and sophisticated than our ancestors or than our younger selves.

Much could be said about how the addition of specifically psychoanalytic concepts to religious and philosophical concepts (and to the invocation of historical and literary archetypes) has influenced contemporary patterns of moral deliberation.[16] My theme, however, is different. I want to focus on the way in which Freud, by helping us see ourselves as centerless, as random assemblages of contingent and idiosyncratic needs rather than as more or less adequate exemplifications of a common human essence, opened up new possibilities for the aesthetic life. He helped us become increasingly ironic, playful, free, and inventive in our choice of self-descriptions. This has been an important factor in our ability to slough off the idea that we have a true self, one shared with all other humans, and the related notion that the demands of this true self – the specifically moral demands – take precedence over all others. It has helped us think of moral reflection and sophistication as a matter of self-creation rather than self-knowledge. Freud made the paradigm of self-knowledge the discovery of the fortuitous materials out of which we must construct ourselves rather than the discovery of the principles to which we must conform. He thus made the desire for purification seem more self-deceptive, and the quest for self-enlargement more promising.

By contrast, the history of modern philosophy has centered on attempts to preserve an enclave of nonmechanism, and thus to keep alive the notion of a "true self" and the plausibility of a morality of self-purification. Descartes was willing to follow Galileo in dissolving all the Aristotelian natural kinds into so many vortices of corpuscles, with one exception. He wanted the mind to remain exempt from this dissolution. The mind and its faculties (notably intellect, conceived of as immediate, nondiscursive grasp of truth) were to remain as Platonism and Christianity had conceived of them. This enclave of nonmechanism that Descartes claimed to have descried became the preserve of a subject called "metaphysics."[17] Kant recognized the ad hoc and factitious character of this Cartesian attempt to keep the world safe for nonmechanism, and so he developed a different, more drastic, strategy to achieve the same end. He was willing to put mind and matter on a par, and to follow Hume in dissolving what he called "the empirical self" into predictable associations of mental atoms. But he distinguished that self from the true

16   See, for example, Adam Morton, "Freudian Commonsense." I think that Morton asks just the right questions, although I have doubts about the character-personality distinction that he draws.

17   Consider Leibniz's novel and influential use of the terms *physics* and *metaphysics* to name the study of mechanism and of nonmechanism, respectively – to distinguish between the area in which Newton was right and the area in which Aristotle and the scholastics had been right.

self, the moral self, the part of the self that was an agent of rather than a subject of scientific inquiry.

This still smaller and more mysterious enclave of nonmechanism became the preserve of a subject called "moral philosophy." Kant tried to make morality a nonempirical matter, something that would never again have anything to fear from religion, science, or the arts, nor have anything to learn from them.[18] For, Kant explained, the reason why the New Science had described a world with no moral lesson, a world without a moral point, was that it described a world of appearance. By contrast, the true world was a world that was, so to speak, nothing but point: nothing but a moral imperative, nothing but a call to moral purity.

One result of Kant's initiative was to impoverish the vocabulary of moral philosophy and to turn the enrichment of our vocabulary of moral reflection over to novelists, poets, and dramatists.[19] The nineteenth-century novel, in particular, filled a vacuum left by the retreat of one-half of moral philosophy into idealist metaphysics and the advance of the other half into politics.[20] Another result was what Alasdair MacIntyre calls the invention of "the individual" – a moral self who existed "prior to and apart from all roles,"[21] who was independent of any social or historical context. To say that the moral self exists apart from all roles means that it will remain the same no matter what situation it finds itself in, no matter what language it uses to create its self-image, no matter what its vocabulary of moral deliberation may be. That, in turn, means that the moral self has no need to work out a sensitive and sophisticated vocabulary as an instrument to create its character. For the only character that matters is the one it already has. Once it began to seem (as it

18   As J. B. Schneewind has pointed out to me, this remark is accurate only for Kant's early thinking on morality. Later in his life the purity and isolation claimed for morality in the *Grundlagen* became compromised in various ways. It was, however, the early writings on morality that became associated with Kant's name, and that his successors were concerned to criticize.

19   See Murdoch, *The Sovereignty of Good* (58): "It is a shortcoming of much contemporary moral philosophy that it eschews discussion of the separate virtues, preferring to proceed directly to some sovereign concept such as sincerity, or authenticity, or freedom, thereby imposing, it seems to me, an unexamined and empty idea of unity, and impoverishing our moral language in an important area." Murdoch's claim that "the most essential and fundamental aspect of our culture is the study of literature, since this is an education in how to picture and understand human situations" (34) would have meant something different two hundred years ago. For then the term *literature* covered Hume's *Enquiries* and his *History* as well as novels, plays, and poems. Our modern contrast between literature and moral philosophy is one result of the development that Murdoch describes:

Philosophy ... has been busy dismantling the old substantial picture of the "self," and ethics has not proved itself able to rethink this concept for moral purposes.... Moral philosophy, and indeed morals, are thus undefended against an irresponsible and undirected self-assertion which goes easily hand-in-hand with some brand of pseudo-scientific determinism. An unexamined-sense of the strength of the machine is combined with an illusion of leaping out of it. The younger Sartre, and many British moral philosophers, represent this last dry distilment of Kant's views of the world. (47–48)

20   The latter phenomenon is exemplified by, for example, Bentham and Marx – philosophers who have been responsible for much good in the public sphere but who are useless as advisers on the development of moral character.

21   See the passage from MacIntyre quoted in note 3.

did to Kant) that we had always known a priori all there was to know about the "morally relevant" portion of human beings, the Hegelian urge to enrich our vocabulary of moral reflection began to seem (as it did to Kierkegaard) a merely "aesthetic" demand, something that might amuse a leisured elite but which had no relevance to our moral responsibilities.[22]

This account of modern philosophy can be summarized by saying that when modern science made it hard to think of man as a natural kind, philosophy responded by inventing an unnatural kind. It was perhaps predictable that the sequence of descriptions of this self that begins with Descartes should end with Sartre: the self as a blank space in the middle of a machine – an *être-pour-soi*, a "hole in being." By contrast, Freud stands with Hegel against Kant, in an attitude of Nietzschean exuberance rather than Sartrean embarrassment. He offers us a way to reinvent the search for enlargement, and thereby reinvents the morality of character. I can summarize my account of how he does this in five points:

1. Whereas everybody from Plato to Kant had identified our central self, our conscience, the standard-setting, authoritative part of us, with universal truths, general principles, and a common human nature, Freud made conscience just one more, not particularly central, part of a larger, homogenous machine. He identified the sense of duty with the internalization of a host of idiosyncratic, accidental episodes. On his account our sense of moral obligation is not a matter of general ideas contemplated by the intellect, but rather of traces of encounters between particular people and our bodily organs. He saw the voice of conscience not as the voice of the part of the soul that deals with generalities as opposed to the part that deals with particulars, but rather as the (usually distorted) memory of certain very particular events.

2. This identification did not take the form of a reductive claim that morality was "nothing but …" delayed responses to forgotten stimuli. Since Freud was willing to view *every* part of life, every human activity, in the same terms, there was no contrast to be drawn between the "merely" mechanical and reactive character of moral experience and the free and spontaneous character of something else (e.g., science, art, philosophy or psychoanalytic theory).

3. Nor did this identification of conscience with memory of idiosyncratic events take the form of the claim that talk about such events was a ("scientific") substitute for moral deliberation. Freud did not suggest that we would see ourselves more clearly, or choose more wisely, by restricting our vocabulary of moral reflection to psychoanalytic terms. On the contrary, Freud dropped the Platonic metaphor of "seeing ourselves more clearly" in favor of the Baconian idea of theory as a tool for bringing about desirable change.[23] He was far from thinking that psychoanalytic theory was the *only* tool needed for self-enlargement.

22   For a contemporary account of the contrast between the Kantian and the Hegelian attitudes, see Alan Donagan, *A Theory of Morality* (chap. 1, especially p. 10), on "Hegel's doctrine of the emptiness of the moral point of view."
23   Rieff makes this contrast between Platonic and Baconian attitudes, saying that the latter, the "second theory of theory," views theory as "arming us with the weapons for transforming reality instead of forcing us to conform to it. … Psychoanalytic theory belongs to the second tradition"

4. This Baconian attitude was the culmination of the mechanizing movement that had begun in the seventeenth century. That movement had replaced the attempt to contemplate the essences of natural kinds with the attempt to tinker with the machines that compose the world. But not until Freud did we get a usable way of thinking of *ourselves* as machines to be tinkered with, a self-image that enabled us to weave terms describing psychic mechanisms into our strategies of character-formation.

5. The increased ability of the syncretic, ironic, nominalist intellectual to move back and forth between, for example, religious, moral, scientific, literary, philosophical, and psychoanalytical vocabularies without asking the question "And which of these shows us how things *really* are?" – the intellectual's ability to treat vocabularies as tools rather than mirrors – is Freud's major legacy. He broke some of the last chains that bind us to the Greek idea that we, or the world, have a nature that, once discovered, will tell us what we should do with ourselves. He made it far more difficult than it was before to ask the question "Which is my true self?" or "What is human nature?" By letting us see that even in the enclave which philosophy had fenced off, there was nothing to be found save traces of accidental encounters, he left us able to tolerate the ambiguities that the religious and philosophical traditions had hoped to eliminate.

"The Rich Aesthete, the Manager, and the Therapist"

My account of Freud as a Baconian has taken for granted that the move from Aristotelian to Baconian views of the nature of knowledge, like that from an ethics of purity to one of self-enrichment, was desirable. My enthusiasm for the mechanization and decentering of the world is dictated by my assumption that the ironic, playful intellectual is a desirable character-type, and that Freud's importance lies in his contribution to the formation of such a character. These assumptions are challenged by those who see the mechanization of nature as a prelude to barbarism. Such critics emphasize, as I have, the link between a pragmatic, tinkering approach to nature and the self, and the aesthetic search for novel experiences and novel language. But they condemn both.

The most thoroughly thought-out, if most abstract, account of the relation between technology and aestheticism is offered by Heidegger.[24] But the more concrete criticisms of modern ways of thinking offered by Alasdair MacIntyre in *After Virtue* are more immediately relevant to the topics I have been discussing. MacIntyre would agree, more or less, with my description of the connections between Baconian ways of thought and Nietzschean values. But he takes the fact that the paradigmatic character-types of modernity are "the Rich Aesthete, the Manager, and the Therapist" (MacIntyre 1981, 29) to

---

(1966, 55–56). This view of Freud's aim is central to my account of his achievement, and I am much indebted to Rieff's work.

24 See Heidegger's essays "The Question Concerning Technology" and "The Age of the World View" in *The Question concerning Technology and Other Essays*. I suggest a Deweyan response to Heidegger's view of technology at the end of "Heidegger Wider die Pragmatisten" (Rorty 1984) – a response that is in harmony with that offered by Blumenberg. MacIntyre would join me in repudiating Heidegger's attack on technology but would retain Heidegger's account of the shift in moral consciousness that followed upon the abandonment of an Aristotelian world view.

show that these ways of thought, and these values, are undesirable. In MacIntyre's view, the abandonment of an Aristotelian "functional concept of man" leads to "emotivism" – "the obliteration of any genuine distinction between manipulative and non-manipulative social relations" (22).

MacIntyre is, I think, right in saying that contemporary moral discourse is a confusing and inconsistent blend of notions that make sense only in an Aristotelian view of the world (e.g., "reason," "human nature," "natural rights") with mechanistic, anti-Aristotelian notions that implicitly repudiate such a view. But whereas MacIntyre thinks we need to bring back Aristotelian ways of thinking to make our moral discourse coherent, I think we should do the opposite and make the discourse coherent by discarding the last vestiges of those ways of thinking.[25] I would welcome a culture dominated by "the Rich Aesthete, the Manager, and the Therapist" so long as *everybody* who wants to gets to be an aesthete (and, if not rich, as comfortably off as most – as rich as the Managers can manage, guided by Rawls's Difference Principle).

Further, I think that we can live with the Freudian thought that everything everybody does to everyone else (even those they love blindly and helplessly) can be described, for therapeutic or other purposes, as manipulation. The postulation of unintrospectible systems of beliefs and desires ensures that there will be a coherent and informative narrative to be told in those terms, one that will interpret all personal and social relations, even the tenderest and most sacred, in terms of "making use of" others. Once those extra persons who explain akrasia and other forms of irrationality are taken into account, there are, so to speak, too many selves for "selflessness" to seem a useful notion. But the increased ability to explain, given by Freud's postulation of additional persons, hardly prevents us from drawing the common-sense distinction between manipulating people (i.e., consciously, and deceptively, employing them as instruments for one's own purposes) and not manipulating them. The availability of a description for explanatory purposes does not entail its use in moral reflection, any more than it precludes it.

MacIntyre construes "emotivism" as the only option left, once one abandons the Aristotelian idea of man, because he retains a pre-Freudian[26] division of human faculties. In terms of this division, "desire" or "will" or "passion" represents the only alternative to "reason" (construed as a faculty of seeing things as they are in themselves). But dividing people up this way begs the question against other ways of describing them – for example, Freud's way. Freud (at least according to the Davidsonian interpretation I have developed here) drops the whole idea of "faculties," and substitutes the notion of a plurality of sets of beliefs and desires. MacIntyre's definition of "emotivism" ("the doctrine that all evaluative judgments and more specifically all moral judgments are *nothing but* expressions of preference, expressions of attitude or feeling" [11]) makes sense only if there is

---

25   It is tempting to say that I would accept MacIntyre's claim that the only real choice is between Aristotle and Nietzsche, and then side with Nietzsche. But the choice is too dramatic and too simple. By the time MacIntyre gets rid of the nonsense in Aristotle (e.g., what he calls the "metaphysical biology"), Aristotle does not look much like himself. By the time I would finish discarding the bits of Nietzsche I do not want (e.g., his lapses into metaphysical biology, his distrust of Hegel, his *ressentiment*, etc.) he would not look much like Nietzsche. The opposition between these two ideal types is useful only if one does not press it too hard.

26   Or, more generally, premechanist (and thus pre-Humean; see note 9 on Hume and faculty psychology).

something else such judgments might have been – for example, expressions of a correct "rational" grasp of the nature of the human being.

Moral psychology, like moral discourse, is at present an incoherent blend of Aristotelian and mechanist ways of speaking. I would urge that if we eradicate the former, "emotivism" will no longer be an intelligible position. More generally, if we take Freud to heart, we shall not have to choose between an Aristotelian "functional" concept of humanity, one that will provide moral guidance, and Sartrean "dreadful freedom." For the Sartrean conception of the self as pure freedom will be seen as merely the last gasp of the Aristotelian tradition – a self-erasing expression of the Cartesian determination to find *something* nonmechanical at the center of the machine, if only a "hole in being."[27] We shall not need a picture of "the human self" in order to have morality – neither of a nonmechanical enclave nor of a meaningless void where such an enclave ought to have been.

It seems a point in my favor that MacIntyre does not answer the question of whether it is "rationally justifiable [*pace* Sartre] to conceive of each human life as a unity" (MacIntyre 1981, 189) by saying (with Aristotle) "yes, because the function of man is...." Rather, he offers us "a concept of a self whose unity resides in the unity of a narrative which links birth to life to death as narrative beginning to middle to end" (191).[28] MacIntyre tacitly drops the Aristotelian demand that the themes of each such narrative be roughly the same for each member of a given species, and that they stay roughly constant throughout the history of the species. He seems content to urge that in order for us to exhibit the virtue of "integrity or constancy" we must see our lives in such narrative terms. To attempt that virtue is just what I have been calling "the search for perfection," and I agree that this search requires the construction of such narratives. But if we do drop the Aristotelian demand, contenting ourselves with narratives tailored ad hoc to the contingencies of individual lives, then we may welcome a Baconian culture dominated by "the Rich Aesthete, the Manager, and the Therapist" – not necessarily as the final goal of human progress, but at least as a considerable improvement on cultures dominated by, for example, the Warrior or the Priest.

On my account of Freud, his work enables us to construct richer and more plausible narratives of this ad hoc sort – more plausible because they will cover *all* the actions one performs in the course of one's life, even the silly, cruel, and self-destructive actions.

---

27 Metaphysicians like Sartre would, to paraphrase Nietzsche, rather have a metaphysics of nothingness than no metaphysics. This was a trap around which Heidegger circled in his early work but eventually walked away from, leaving Sartre to take the plunge.

28 There seems to be a tension in MacIntyre's book between the early chapters, in which it is suggested that unless we can identify a telos common to all members of our species we are driven to the "emotivist" view that "all moral judgments are *nothing but* expressions of preference" (11), and chapters 14–15. In the latter chapters, which MacIntyre thinks of as a rehabilitation of Aristotelianism (see 239), nothing is done to defeat the suggestion that all moral judgments are nothing but choices among competing narratives, a suggestion that is compatible with the three paradigmatically Aristotelian doctrines that MacIntyre lists on pp. 183–86 of his book. By dropping what he calls "Aristotle's metaphysical biology" (183), MacIntyre also drops the attempt to evaluate "the claims to objectivity and authority" of "the lost morality of the past" (21). For unless a knowledge of the function of the human species takes us beyond MacIntyre's Socratic claim that "the good life for man is the life spent in seeking for the good life for man" (204), the idea of one narrative being more "objective and authoritative" than another, as opposed to being more detailed and inclusive, goes by the board.

More generally, Freud helped us see that the attempt to put together such a narrative – one that minimizes neither the contingency nor the decisive importance of the input into the machine that each of us is – must take the place of an attempt to find the function common to all such machines. If one takes Freud's advice, one finds psychological narratives without heroes or heroines. For neither Sartrean freedom, nor the will, nor the instincts, nor an internalization of a culture, nor anything else will play the role of "the true self." Instead, one tells the story of the whole machine *as* machine, without choosing a particular set of springs and wheels as protagonist. Such a story can help us, if anything can, stop the pendulum from swinging between Aristotelian attempts to discover our essence and Sartrean attempts at self-creation *de novo*.

This suggestion that our stories about ourselves must be stories of centerless mechanisms – of the determined processing of contingent input – will seem to strip us of human dignity only if we think we need *reasons* to live romantically, or to treat others decently, or to be treated decently ourselves. Questions like "Why should I hope?" or "Why should I not use others as means?" or "Why should my torturers not use me as a means?" are questions that can *only* be answered by philosophical metanarratives that tell us about a nonmechanical world and a nonmechanical self – about a world and a self that have centers, centers that are sources of authority. Such questions are tailored to fit such answers. So if we renounce such answers, such metanarratives, and fall back on narratives about the actual and possible lives of individuals, we shall have to renounce the needs that metaphysics and moral philosophy attempted to satisfy. We shall have to confine ourselves to questions like, "If I do this rather than that now, what story will I tell myself later?" We shall have to abjure questions like, "Is there something deep inside my torturer – his rationality – to which I can appeal?"

The philosophical tradition suggests that there is, indeed, something of this sort. It tends to take for granted that our dignity depends on the existence of something that can be opposed to "arbitrary will." This thing, usually called "reason," is needed to give "authority" to the first premises of our practical syllogisms. Such a view of human dignity is precisely what Freud called "the pious view of the Universe." He thought that the traditional oppositions between reason, will, and emotion – the oppositions in terms of which MacIntyre constructs his history of ethics – should be discarded in favor of distinctions between various regions of a homogenous mechanism, regions that embody a plurality of persons (that is, of incompatible systems of belief and desire). So the only version of human dignity that Freud lets us preserve is the one MacIntyre himself offers: the ability of each of us to tailor a coherent self-image for ourselves and then use it to tinker with our behavior. This ability replaces the traditional philosophical project of finding a coherent self-image that will fit the entire species to which we belong.

Given this revisionary account of human dignity, what becomes of human solidarity? In my view, Freud does nothing for either liberal or radical politics, except perhaps to supply new terms of opprobrium with which to stigmatize tyrants and torturers.[29] On

---

29   But diagnoses of the Freudian mechanisms that produce suitable candidates for the KGB and the Gestapo, of the sort made popular by Adorno and others who talk about "authoritarian personalities," add little to the familiar pre-Freudian suggestion that we might have fewer bully boys to cope with if people had more education, leisure, and money. The Adorno-Horkheimer suggestion that the rise of Nazism within a highly developed and cultivated nation shows that this familiar liberal solution is inadequate seems to me unconvincing. At any rate, it seems safe to say

the contrary, he diminishes our ability to take seriously much of the traditional jargon of both liberalism and radicalism – notions such as "human rights" and "autonomy" and slogans such as "man will prevail" and "trust the instincts of the masses." For these notions and slogans are bound up with Aristotelian attempts to find a center for the self.

On the other hand, Freud does nothing to diminish a sense of human solidarity that, rather than encompassing the entire species, restricts itself to such particular communal movements as modern science, bourgeois liberalism, or the European novel. If we avoid describing these movements in terms of metaphysical notions like "the search for truth," or "the realization of human freedom," or "the attainment of self-consciousness," histories of them will nevertheless remain available as larger narratives within which to place the narratives of our individual lives. Freud banishes philosophical metanarratives,[30] but he has nothing against ordinary historical narratives. Such narratives tell, for example, how we got from Galileo to Gell-Man, or from institutions that defended merchants against feudal overlords to institutions that defend labor against capital, or from *Don Quixote* to *Pale Fire*.[31]

Letting us see the narratives of our own lives as episodes within such larger historical narratives is, I think, as much as the intellectuals are able to do in aid of morality.[32] The attempt of religion and metaphysics to do more – to supply a backup for moral intuitions by providing them with ahistorical "authority" – will always be self-defeating. For (given the present rate of social change) another century's worth of history will always make the last century's attempt to be ahistorical look ridiculous. The only result of such attempts is to keep the pendulum swinging between moral dogmatism and moral skepticism.[33] What metaphysics could not do, psychology, even very "deep" psychology, is not going to do either; we pick up Freud by the wrong handle if we try to find an account of "moral motivation" that is more than a reference to the historical contingencies that shaped the process of acculturation in our region and epoch.

Historical narratives about social and intellectual movements are the best tools to use in tinkering with ourselves, for such narratives suggest vocabularies of moral deliberation in which to spin coherent narratives about our individual lives. By contrast, the vocabulary Freud himself used in much of his writing – an individualist, Stoic vocabulary, charged with ironic resignation – does little for the latter purpose. It has too much in common with the vocabulary of the self-erasing narratives of Rameau's nephew, Dostoevsky's "Underground Man," and Sartre's Roquentin: stories about machines chewing themselves to pieces. By contrast, narratives that help one identify oneself with communal movements engender a sense of being a machine geared into a larger machine.

---

that Freudo-Marxist analyses of "authoritarianism" have offered no better suggestions about how to keep the thugs from taking over.

30   I borrow the term *metanarrative* from Jean-Francois Lyotard's *The Postmodern Condition*. For further discussion of how the narrative of bourgeois liberalism can be separated from metanarratives, see Rorty, "Postmodernist Bourgeois Liberalism."

31   See Milan Kundera, "The Novel and Europe." Kundera ends his essay by asking, "But if the idea of progress arouses my suspicion, what are the values to which I feel attached?" and responds, "My answer is as sincere as it is ridiculous: I am attached to nothing apart from the European novel, that unrecognized inheritance that comes to us from Cervantes."

32   I defend this historicist, ethnocentric point at some length in "Solidarity or Objectivity?" and again in "Le Cosmopolitanisme sans Emancipation."

33   For a discussion of the causes and effects of such pendulum swings, see Annette Baier, "Doing without Moral Theory?"

This is a sense worth having. For it helps reconcile an existentialist sense of contingency and mortality with a Romantic sense of grandeur. It helps us realize that the best way of tinkering with ourselves is to tinker with something else — a mechanist way of saying that only he who loses his soul will save it.

Acknowledgment

This paper is a revised version of the Edith Weigert Lecture, sponsored by the Forum on Psychiatry and the Humanities, Washington School of Psychiatry, October 19, 1984.

In deciding what revisions to make, I profited greatly from the seminar with members of the Forum on Psychiatry and the Humanities, held the day after the lecture, as well as from comments on my original version, which I received from Irvin Ehrenpreis, Alexander Nehamas, and J. B. Schneewind.

References

Baier, Annette. "Doing without Moral Theory?" In Baier, *Postures of the Mind: Essays on Mind and Morals.* Minneapolis: University of Minnesota Press, 1985.

Bersani, Leo. *Baudelaire and Freud.* Berkeley and Los Angeles: University of California Press, 1977.

Blumenberg, Hans. *The Legitimacy of the Modern Age.* Cambridge, Mass: MIT Press, 1983.

Davidson, Donald. "Paradoxes of Irrationality." In *Philosophical Essays on Freud*, edited by Richard Wollheim and James Hopkins. Cambridge: Cambridge University Press, 1982.

Donagan, Alan. *A Theory of Morality*, Chicago: University of Chicago Press, 1977.

Freud, Sigmund. *The Standard Edition of the Complete Psychological Works of Sigmund Freud.* Edited and translated by James Strachey. 24 Vols. London: Hogarth, 1953–74:
   Leonardo da Vinci and a Memory of His Childhood (1910), vol. 11.
   "Thoughts for the Times on War and Death" (1915), vol. 14.
   Introductory Lectures on Psycho-Analysis (1916), vol. 16.
   "Two Encyclopaedia Articles" (1923), vol. 18.
   "A Short Account of Psycho-Analysis" (1924), vol. 19.

Heidegger, Martin. *The Question concerning Technology and Other Essays.* Translated by William Lovitt. New York: Harper & Row, 1977.

Kuhn, Thomas S. *The Copernican Revolution.* Cambridge, Mass. Havard University Press, 1957.

Kundera, Milan. "The Novel and Europe." *New York Review of Books*, July 19, 1984, pp. 15 ff.

Lyotard, Jean-Francois. *The Postmodern Condition.* Minneapolis: University of Minnesota Press, 1984.

MacIntyre, Alasdair. *After Virtue.* Notre Dame, Ind.: University of Notre Dame Press, 1981.

Morton, Adam. "Freudian Commonsense." In *Philosophical Essays on Freud*, edited by Richard Wollheim and James Hopkins. Cambridge: Cambridge University Press, 1982.

Murdoch, Iris. *The Sovereignty of Good.* New York: Schocken Books, 1971.

Rieff, Philip. *Freud: The Mind of the Moralist.* New York: Harper & Row, 1961.

Rieff, Philip. *Triumph of the Therapeutic.* New York: Harper & Row, 1966.

Rorty, Richard. "Postmodernist Bourgeois Liberalism." *Journal of Philosophy* 80 (1983): 583–89.

Rorty, Richard. "Heidegger Wider die Pragmatisten." *Neue Hefte für Philosophie* 23 (1984): 1–22.

Rorty, Richard. "Le Cosmopolitanisme sans Emancipation: En Réponse a Jean-Francois Lyotard." *Critique* 41 (1985): 569–80, 584.

Rorty, Richard. "Solidarity or Objectivity?" In *Post-Analytic Philosophy*, edited by John Rajchman and Cornel West. New York: Columbia University Press, 1985.

Trilling, Lionel. *Beyond Culture.* New York: Harcourt, Brace, 1965.

15

Private Irony and Liberal Hope

All human beings carry about a set of words which they employ to justify their actions, their beliefs, and their lives. These are the words in which we formulate praise of our friends and contempt for our enemies, our long-term projects, our deepest self-doubts and our highest hopes. They are the words in which we tell, sometimes prospectively and sometimes retrospectively, the story of our lives. I shall call these words a person's "final vocabulary."

It is "final" in the sense that if doubt is cast on the worth of these words, their user has no noncircular argumentative recourse. Those words are as far as he can go with language; beyond them there is only helpless passivity or a resort to force. A small part of a final vocabulary is made up of thin, flexible, and ubiquitous terms such as "true," "good," "right," and "beautiful." The larger part contains thicker, more rigid, and more parochial terms, for example, "Christ," "England," "professional standards," "decency," "kindness," "the Revolution," "the Church," "progressive," "rigorous," "creative." The more parochial terms do most of the work.

I shall define an "ironist" as someone who fulfills three conditions: (1) She has radical and continuing doubts about the final vocabulary she currently uses, because she has been impressed by other vocabularies, vocabularies taken as final by people or books she has encountered; (2) she realizes that argument phrased in her present vocabulary can neither underwrite nor dissolve these doubts; (3) insofar as she philosophizes about her situation, she does not think that her vocabulary is closer to reality than others, that it is in touch with a power not herself. Ironists who are inclined to philosophize see the choice between vocabularies as made neither within a neutral and universal metavocabulary nor by an attempt to fight one's way past appearances to the real, but simply by playing the new off against the old.

I call people of this sort "ironists" because their realization that anything can be made to look good or bad by being redescribed, and their renunciation of the attempt to formulate criteria of choice between final vocabularies, puts them in the position which Sartre called "meta-stable": never quite able to take themselves seriously because always aware that the

"Private Irony and Liberal Hope," pp. 73–95, in Richard M. Rorty, *Contingency, Irony, and Solidarity* (New York, 1989), © 1989 by Cambridge University Press. Reprinted with the permission of Cambridge University Press.

terms in which they describe themselves are subject to change, always aware of the contingency and fragility of their final vocabularies, and thus of their selves. Such people take naturally to the line of thought developed in the first two chapters of this book. If they are also liberals – people for whom (to use Judith Shklar's definition) "cruelty is the worst thing they do" – they will take naturally to the views offered in the third chapter.

The opposite of irony is common sense. For that is the watchword of those who unself-consciously describe everything important in terms of the final vocabulary to which they and those around them are habituated. To be commonsensical is to take for granted that statements formulated in that final vocabulary suffice to describe and judge the beliefs, actions and lives of those who employ alternative final vocabularies. People who pride themselves on common sense will find the line of thought developed in Part I distasteful.

When common sense is challenged, its adherents respond at first by generalizing and making explicit the rules of the language game they are accustomed to play (as some of the Greek Sophists did, and as Aristotle did in his ethical writings). But if no platitude formulated in the old vocabulary suffices to meet an argumentative challenge, the need to reply produces a willingness to go beyond platitudes. At that point, conversation may go Socratic. The question "What is x?" is now asked in such a way that it cannot be answered simply by producing paradigm cases of x-hood. So one may demand a definition, an essence.

To make such Socratic demands is not yet, of course, to become an ironist in the sense in which I am using this term. It is only to become a "metaphysician," in a sense of that term which I am adapting from Heidegger. In this sense, the metaphysician is someone who takes the question "What is the intrinsic nature of (e.g., justice, science, knowledge, Being, faith, morality, philosophy)?" at face value. He assumes that the presence of a term in his own final vocabulary ensures that it refers to something which *has* a real essence. The metaphysician is still attached to common sense, in that he does not question the platitudes which encapsulate the use of a given final vocabulary, and in particular the platitude which says there is a single permanent reality to be found behind the many temporary appearances. He does not redescribe but, rather, analyzes old descriptions with the help of other old descriptions.

The ironist, by contrast, is a nominalist and a historicist. She thinks nothing has an intrinsic nature, a real essence. So she thinks that the occurrence of a term like "just" or "scientific" or "rational" in the final vocabulary of the day is no reason to think that Socratic inquiry into the essence of justice or science or rationality will take one much beyond the language games of one's time. The ironist spends her time worrying about the possibility that she has been initiated into the wrong tribe, taught to play the wrong language game. She worries that the process of socialization which turned her into a human being by giving her a language may have given her the wrong language, and so turned her into the wrong kind of human being. But she cannot give a criterion of wrongness. So, the more she is driven to articulate her situation in philosophical terms, the more she reminds herself of her rootlessness by constantly using terms like "Weltanschauung," "perspective," "dialectic," "conceptual framework," "historical epoch," "language game," "redescription," "vocabulary," and "irony."

The metaphysician responds to that sort of talk by calling it "relativistic" and insisting that what matters is not what language is being used but what is *true*. Metaphysicians think that human beings by nature desire to know. They think this because the vocabulary they have inherited, their common sense, provides them with a picture of knowledge as a relation between human beings and "reality," and the idea that we have a need and a duty to enter into this relation. It also tells us that "reality," if properly asked, will help us determine what our final vocabulary should be. So metaphysicians believe that there are, out there in the world, real essences which it is our duty to discover and which are disposed to assist in their own discovery. They do not believe that anything can be made to look good or bad by being redescribed – or, if they do, they deplore this fact and cling to the idea that reality will help us resist such seductions.

By contrast, ironists do not see the search for a final vocabulary as (even in part) a way of getting something distinct from this vocabulary right. They do not take the point of discursive thought to be *knowing,* in any sense that can be explicated by notions like "reality," "real essence," "objective point of view," and "the correspondence of language of reality." They do not think its point is to find a vocabulary which accurately represents something, a transparent medium. For the ironists, "final vocabulary" does not mean "the one which puts all doubts to rest" or "the one which satisfies our criteria of ultimacy, or adequacy, or optimality." They do not think of reflection as being governed by criteria. Criteria, on their view, are never more than the platitudes which contextually define the terms of a final vocabulary currently in use. Ironists agree with Davidson about our inability to step outside our language in order to compare it with something else, and with Heidegger about the contingency and historicity of that language.

This difference leads to a difference in their attitude toward books. Metaphysicians see libraries as divided according to disciplines, corresponding to different objects of knowledge. Ironists see them as divided according to traditions, each member of which partially adopts and partially modifies the vocabulary of the writers whom he has read. Ironists take the writings of all the people with poetic gifts, all the original minds who had a talent for redescription – Pythagoras, Plato, Milton, Newton, Goethe, Kant, Kierkegaard, Baudelaire, Darwin, Freud – as grist to be put through the same dialectical mill. The metaphysicians, by contrast, want to start by getting straight about which of these people were poets, which philosophers, and which scientists. They think it essential to get the genres right – to order texts by reference to a previously determined grid, a grid which, whatever else it does, will at least make a clear distinction between knowledge claims and other claims upon our attention. The ironist, by contrast, would like to avoid cooking the books she reads by using *any* such grid (although, with ironic resignation, she realizes that she can hardly help doing so).

For a metaphysician, "philosophy," as defined by reference to the canonical Plato–Kant sequence, is an attempt to know about certain things – quite general and important things. For the ironist, "philosophy," so defined, is the attempt to apply and develop a particular antecedently chosen final vocabulary – one which revolves around the appearance-reality distinction. The issue between them is, once again, about the contingency of our language – about whether what the common sense of our own culture shares with Plato and Kant is a tip-off to the way the world is, or whether it is just the characteristic mark of the discourse of people inhabiting a certain chunk of space-time. The metaphysician assumes that our tradition can raise no problems which it cannot solve – that the vocabulary which the ironist fears may be merely "Greek" or "Western" or "bourgeois" is an instrument which will enable us to get at something universal. The metaphysician agrees with the Platonic Theory of Recollection, in the form in which this theory was restated by Kierkegaard, namely, that we have the truth within us, that we have built-in criteria which enable us to recognize the right final vocabulary when we hear it. The cash value of this theory is that our contemporary final vocabularies are close enough to the right one to let us converge upon it – to formulate premises from which the right conclusions will be reached. The metaphysician thinks that although we may not have all the answers, we have already got criteria for the right answers. So he thinks "right" does not merely mean "suitable for those who speak as we do" but has a stronger sense – the sense of "grasping real essence."

For the ironist, searches for a final vocabulary are not destined to converge. For her, sentences like "All men by nature desire to know" or "Truth is independent of the human mind" are simply platitudes used to inculcate the local final vocabulary, the common sense of the West. She is an ironist just insofar as her own final vocabulary does not contain such notions. Her description of what she is doing when she looks for a better final vocabulary than the one she is currently using is dominated by metaphors of making rather than finding, of diversification and novelty rather than convergence to the antecedently present. She thinks of final vocabularies as poetic achievements rather than as fruits of diligent inquiry according to antecedently formulated criteria.

Because metaphysicians believe that we already possess a lot of the "right" final vocabulary and merely need to think through its implications, they think of philosophical inquiry as a matter of spotting the relations between the various platitudes which provide contextual definitions of the terms of this vocabulary. So they think of refining or clarifying the use of terms as a matter of weaving these platitudes (or, as they would prefer to say, these intuitions) into a perspicuous system. This has two consequences. First, they tend to concentrate on the thinner, more flexible, more ubiquitous items in this vocabulary – words like "true," "good," "person," and "object." For the thinner the term, the more platitudes will employ it. Second, they take the paradigm of philosophical inquiry to be logical argument – that is spotting the inferential relationships between propositions rather than comparing and contrasting vocabularies.

The typical strategy of the metaphysician is to spot an apparent contradiction between two platitudes, two intuitively plausible propositions, and then propose a distinction which will resolve the contradiction. Metaphysicians then go on to embed this distinction within a network of associated distinctions – a philosophical theory – which will take some of the strain off the initial distinction. This sort of theory construction is the same method used by judges to decide hard cases, and by theologians to interpret hard texts. That activity is the metaphysician's paradigm of rationality. He sees philosophical theories as converging – a series of discoveries about the nature of such things as truth and personhood, which get closer and closer to the way they really are, and carry the culture as a whole closer to an accurate representation of reality.

The ironist, however, views the sequence of such theories – such interlocked patterns of novel distinctions – as gradual, tacit substitutions of a new vocabulary for an old one. She calls "platitudes" what the metaphysician calls "intuitions." She is inclined to say that when we surrender an old platitude (e.g., "The number of biological species is fixed" or "Human beings differ from animals because they have sparks of the divine with them" or "Blacks have no rights which whites are bound to respect"), we have made a change rather than discovered a fact. The ironist, observing the sequence of "great philosophers" and the interaction between their thought and its social setting, sees a series of changes in the linguistic and other practices of the Europeans. Whereas the metaphysician sees the modern Europeans as particularly good at discovering how things really are, the ironist sees them as particularly rapid in changing their self-image, in re-creating themselves.

The metaphysician thinks that there is an overriding intellectual duty to present arguments for one's controversial views – arguments which will start from relatively uncontroversial premises. The ironist thinks that such arguments – logical arguments – are all very well in their way, and useful as expository devices, but in the end not much more than ways of getting people to change their practices without admitting they have done so. The ironist's preferred form of argument is dialectical in the sense that she takes the unit of persuasion to be a vocabulary rather than a proposition. Her method is redescription rather than inference. Ironists specialize in redescribing ranges of objects or events in partially neologistic jargon, in the hope of inciting people to adopt and extend that jargon. An ironist hopes that by the time she has finished using old words in new senses, not to mention introducing brand-new words, people will no longer ask questions phrased in the old words. So the ironist thinks of logic as ancillary to dialectic, whereas the metaphysician thinks of dialectic as a species of rhetoric, which in turn is a shoddy substitute for logic.

I have defined "dialectic" as the attempt to play off vocabularies against one another, rather than merely to infer propositions from one another, and thus as the partial substitution of redescription for inference. I used Hegel's word because I think of Hegel's *Phenomenology* both as the beginning of the end of the Plato–Kant tradition and as a paradigm of the ironist's ability to exploit the possibilities of massive redescription. In this view, Hegel's so-called dialectical method is not an argumentative procedure or a way of unifying subject and object, but simply a literary skill – skill at producing surprising gestalt switches by making smooth, rapid transitions from one terminology to another.

Instead of keeping the old platitudes and making distinctions to help them cohere, Hegel constantly changed the vocabulary in which the old platitudes had been stated; instead of constructing philosophical theories and arguing for them, he avoided argument by constantly shifting vocabularies, thereby changing the subject. In practice, though not in theory, he dropped the idea of getting at the truth in favor of the idea of making things new. His criticism of his predecessors was not that their propositions were false but that their languages were obsolete. By inventing this sort of criticism, the younger Hegel broke away from the Plato–Kant sequence and began a tradition of ironist philosophy which is continued in Nietzsche, Heidegger, and Derrida. These are the philosophers who define their achievement by their relation to their predecessors rather than by their relation to the truth.

A more up-to-date word for what I have been calling "dialectic" would be "literary criticism." In Hegel's time it was still possible to think of plays, poems, and novels as making vivid something already known, of literature as ancillary to cognition, beauty to truth. The older Hegel thought of "philosophy" as a discipline which, because cognitive in a way that art was not, took precedence over art. Indeed, he thought that this discipline, now that it had attained maturity in the form of his own Absolute Idealism, could and would make art as obsolete as it made religion. But, ironically and dialectically enough, what Hegel actually did, by founding an ironist tradition within philosophy, was help decognitivize, de-metaphysize philosophy. He helped turn it into a literary genre.[1] The young Hegel's practice undermined the possibility of the sort of convergence to

---

1 From this point of view, both analytic philosophy and phenomenology were throwbacks to a pre-Hegelian, more or less Kantian, way of thinking – attempts to preserve what I am calling

truth about which the older Hegel theorized. The great commentators on the older Hegel are writers like Heine and Kierkegaard, people who treated Hegel the way we now treat Blake, Freud, D. H. Lawrence, or Orwell.

We ironists treat these people not as anonymous channels for truth but as abbreviations for a certain final vocabulary and for the sorts of beliefs and desires typical of its users. The older Hegel became a name for such a vocabulary, and Kierkegaard and Nietzsche have become names for others. If we are told that the actual lives such men lived had little to do with the books and the terminology which attracted our attention to them, we brush this aside. We treat the names of such people as the names of the heroes of their own books. We do not bother to distinguish Swift from *saeva indignatio,* Hegel from Geist, Nietzsche from Zarathustra, Marcel Proust from Marcel the narrator, or Trilling from The Liberal Imagination. We do not care whether these writers managed to live up to their own self-images.[2] What we want to know is whether to adopt those images – to re-create ourselves, in whole or in part, in these people's image. We go about answering this question by experimenting with the vocabularies which these people concocted. We redescribe ourselves, our situation, our past, in those terms and compare the results with alternative redescriptions which use the vocabularies of alternative figures. We ironists hope, by this continual redescription, to make the best selves for ourselves that we can.

Such comparison, such playing off of figures against each other, is the principal activity now covered by the term "literary criticism." Influential critics, the sort of critics who propose new canons – people like Arnold, Pater, Leavis, Eliot, Edmund Wilson, Lionel Trilling, Frank Kermode, Harold Bloom – are not in the business of explaining the real meaning of books, nor of evaluating something called their "literary merit." Rather, they spend their time placing books in the context of other books, figures in the context of other figures. This placing is done in the same way as we place a new friend or enemy in the context of old friends and enemies. In the course of doing so, we revise our opinions of both the old and the new. Simultaneously, we revise our own moral identity by revising our own final vocabulary. Literary criticism does for ironists what the search for universal moral principles is supposed to do for metaphysicians.

For us ironists, nothing can serve as a criticism of a final vocabulary save another such vocabulary; there is no answer to a redescription save a re-re-redescription. Since there is nothing beyond vocabularies which serves as a criterion of choice between them, criticism is a matter of looking on this picture and on that, not of comparing both pictures with the original. Nothing can serve as a criticism of a person save another person, or of a culture save an alternative culture – for persons and cultures are, for us, incarnated vocabularies. So our doubts about our own characters or our own culture can be resolved or assuaged only by enlarging our acquaintance. The easiest way of doing that is to read books, and so ironists

---

"metaphysics" by making it the study of the "conditions of possibility" of a medium (consciousness, language).

2 See Alexander Nehamas, *Nietzsche: Life as Literature,* p. 234, where Nehamas says that he is not concerned with "the miserable little man who wrote [Nietzsche's books]." Rather he is concerned (p. 8) with Nietzsche's "effort to create an artwork of himself, a literary character who is also a philosopher [which is also] his effort to offer a positive view without falling back into the dogmatic tradition." In the view I am suggesting, Nietzsche may have been the first philosopher to do consciously what Hegel had done unconsciously.

spend more of their time placing books than in placing real live people. Ironists are afraid that they will get stuck in the vocabulary in which they were brought up if they only know the people in their own neighborhood, so they try to get acquainted with strange people (Alcibiades, Julien Sorel), strange families (the Karamazovs, the Casaubons), and strange communities (the Teutonic Knights, the Nuer, the mandarins of the Sung).

Ironists read literary critics, and take them as moral advisers, simply because such critics have an exceptionally large range of acquaintance. They are moral advisers not because they have special access to moral truth but because they have been around. They have read more books and are thus in a better position not to get trapped in the vocabulary of any single book. In particular, ironists hope that critics will help them perform the sort of dialectical feat which Hegel was so good at. That is, they hope critics will help them continue to admire books which are prima facie antithetical by performing some sort of synthesis. We would like to be able to admire both Blake and Arnold, both Nietzsche and Mill, both Marx and Baudelaire, both Trotsky and Eliot, both Nabokov and Orwell. So we hope some critic will show how these men's books can be put together to form a beautiful mosaic. We hope that critics can resdescribe these people in ways which will enlarge the canon, and will give us a set of classical texts as rich and diverse as possible. This task of enlarging the canon takes the place, for the ironist, of the attempt by moral philosophers to bring commonly accepted moral intuitions about particular cases into equilibrium with commonly accepted general moral principles.[3]

It is a familiar fact that the term "literary criticism" has been stretched further and further in the course of our century. It originally meant comparison and evaluation of plays, poems, and novels – with perhaps an occasional glance at the visual arts. Then it got extended to cover past criticism (for example, Dryden's, Shelley's, Arnold's, and Eliot's prose, as well as their verse). Then, quite quickly, it got extended to the books which had supplied past critics with their critical vocabulary and were supplying present critics with theirs. This meant extending it to theology, philosophy, social theory, reformist political programs, and revolutionary manifestos. In short, it meant extending it to every book likely to provide candidates for a person's final vocabulary.

Once the range of literary criticism is stretched that far there is, of course, less and less point in calling it *literary* criticism. But for accidental historical reasons, having to do with the way in which intellectuals got jobs in universities by pretending to pursue academic specialties, the name has stuck. So instead of changing the term "literary criticism" to something like "culture criticism," we have instead stretched the word "literature" to cover whatever the literary critics criticize. A literary critic in what T. J. Clarke has called the "Trotskyite-Eliotic" culture of New York in the '30s and '40s was expected to have read *The Revolution Betrayed* and *The Interpretation of Dreams*, as well as *The Wasteland, Man's Hope*, and *An American Tragedy*. In the present Orwellian-Bloomian

3   I am here borrowing Rawls's notion of "reflective equilibrium." One might say that literary criticism tries to produce such equilibrium between the proper names of writers rather than between propositions. One of the easiest ways to express the difference between "analytic" and "Continental" philosophy is to say that the former sort trades in propositions and the latter in proper names. When Continental philosophy made its appearance in Anglo-American literature departments, in the guise of "literary theory," this was not the discovery of a new method or approach but simply the addition of further names (the names of philosophers) to the range of those among which equilibrium was sought.

culture she is expected to have read *The Gulag Archipelago, Philosophical Investigations*, and *The Order of Things* as well as *Lolita* and *The Book of Laughter and Forgetting*. The word "literature" now covers just about every sort of book which might conceivably have moral relevance – might conceivably alter one's sense of what is possible and important. The application of this term has nothing to do with the presence of "literary qualities" in a book. Rather than detecting and expounding such qualities, the critic is now expected to facilitate moral reflection by suggesting revisions in the canon of moral exemplars and advisers, and suggesting ways in which the tensions within this canon may be eased – or, where necessary, sharpened.

The rise of literary criticism to preeminence within the high culture of the democracies – its gradual and only semiconscious assumption of the cultural role once claimed (successively) by religion, science, and philosophy – has paralleled the rise in the proportion of ironists to metaphysicians among the intellectuals. This has widened the gap between the intellectuals and the public. For metaphysics is woven into the public rhetoric of modern liberal societies. So is the distinction between the moral and the "merely" aesthetic – a distinction which is often used to relegate "literature" to a subordinate position within culture and to suggest that novels and poems are irrelevant to moral reflection. Roughly speaking, the rhetoric of these societies takes for granted most of the oppositions which I claimed (at the beginning of Chapter 3) have become impediments to the culture of liberalism.

This situation has led to accusations of "irresponsibility" against ironist intellectuals. Some of these accusations come from know-nothings – people who have not read the books against which they warn others, and are just instinctively defending their own traditional roles. The know-nothings include religious fundamentalists, scientists who are offended at the suggestion that being "scientific" is not the highest intellectual virtue, and philosophers for whom it is an article of faith that rationality requires the deployment of general moral principles of the sort put forward by Mill and Kant. But the same accusations are made by writers who know what they are talking about, and whose views are entitled to respect. As I have already suggested, the most important of these writers is Habermas, who has mounted a sustained, detailed, carefully argued polemic against critics of the Enlightenment (e.g., Adorno, Foucault) who seem to turn their back on the social hopes of liberal societies. In Habermas's view, Hegel (and Marx) took the wrong tack in sticking to a philosophy of "subjectivity" – of self-reflection – rather than attempting to develop a philosophy of intersubjective communication.

As I said in Chapter 3, I want to defend ironism, and the habit of taking literary criticism as the presiding intellectual discipline, against polemics such as Habermas's. My defense turns on making a firm distinction between the private and the public. Whereas Habermas sees the line of ironist thinking which runs from Hegel through Foucault and Derrida as destructive of social hope, I see this line of thought as largely irrelevant to public life and to political questions. Ironist theorists like Hegel, Nietzsche, Derrida, and Foucault seem to me invaluable in our attempt to form a private self-image, but pretty much useless when it comes to politics. Habermas assumes that the task of philosophy is to supply some social glue which will replace religious belief, and to see Enlightenment talk of "universality" and "rationality" as the best candidate for this glue. So he sees this kind of criticism of the Enlightenment, and of the idea of rationality, as dissolving the bonds between members of liberal societies. He thinks of the contextualism and perspectivalism for which I praised Nietzsche, in previous chapters, as irresponsible subjectivism.

Habermas shares with the Marxists, and with many of those whom he criticizes, the assumption that the real meaning of a philosophical view consists in its political implications, and that the ultimate frame of reference within which to judge a philosophical, as opposed to a merely "literary," writer, is a political one. For the tradition within which Habermas is working, it is as obvious that political philosophy is central to philosophy as, for the analytic tradition, that philosophy of language is central. But, as I said in Chapter 3, it would be better to avoid thinking of philosophy as a "discipline" with "core problems" or with a social function. It would also be better to avoid the idea that philosophical reflection has a natural starting point – that one of its subareas is, in some natural order of justification, prior to the others. For, in the ironist view I have been offering, there is no such thing as a "natural'" order of justification for beliefs or desires. Nor is there much occasion to use the distinctions between logic and rhetoric, or between philosophy and literature, or between rational and nonrational methods of changing other people's minds.[4] If there is no center to the self, then there are only different ways of weaving new candidates for belief and desire into antecedently existing webs of belief and desire. The only important political distinction in the area is that between the use of force and the use of persuasion.

Habermas, and other metaphysicians who are suspicious of a merely "literary" conception of philosophy, think that liberal political freedoms require some consensus about what is universally human. We ironists who are also liberals think that such freedoms require no consensus on any topic more basic than their own desirability. From our angle, all that matters for liberal politics is the widely shared conviction that, as I said in Chapter 3, we shall call "true" or "good" whatever is the outcome of free discussion – that if we take care of political freedom, truth and goodness will take care of themselves.

"Free discussion" here does not mean "free from ideology," but simply the sort which goes on when the press, the judiciary, the elections, and the universities are free, social mobility is frequent and rapid, literacy is universal, higher education is common, and peace and wealth have made possible the leisure necessary to listen to lots of different people and think about what they say. I share with Habermas the Peircelike claim that the only general account to be given of our criteria for truth is one which refers to "undistorted communication,"[5] but I do not think there is much to be said about what counts as "undistorted" except "the sort you get when you have democratic political institutions and the conditions for making these institutions function."[6]

---

4   Where these webs of belief and desire are pretty much the same for large numbers of people, it does become useful to speak of an "appeal to reason" or to "logic," for this simply means an appeal to a widely shared common ground by reminding people of propositions which form part of this ground. More generally, all the traditional metaphysical distinctions can be given a respectable ironist sense by sociologizing them – treating them as distinctions between contingently existing sets of practices, or strategies employed within such practices, rather than between natural kinds.

5   This is not to say that "true" can be defined as "what will be believed at the end of inquiry." For criticism of this Peircian doctrine, see Michael Williams, "Coherence, Justification and Truth," *Review of Metaphysics* 34 (1980): 243–272, and section 2 of my "Pragmatism, Davidson and Truth," in Ernest Lepore, ed. *Truth and Interpretation: Perspectives on the Philosophy of Donald Davidson*, pp. 333–355.

6   In contrast, Habermas and those who agree with him that *Ideologiekritik* is central to philosophy think that there is quite a lot to say. The question turns on whether one thinks that one can give an interesting sense to the word "ideology" – make it mean more than "bad idea."

The social glue holding together the ideal liberal society described in the previous chapter consists in little more than a consensus that the point of social organization is to let everybody have a chance at self-creation to the best of his or her abilities, and that that goal requires, besides peace and wealth, the standard "bourgeois freedoms." This conviction would not be based on a view about universally shared human ends, human rights, the nature of rationality, the Good for Man, nor anything else. It would be a conviction based on nothing more profound than the historical facts which suggest that without the protection of something like the institutions of bourgeois liberal society, people will be less able to work out their private salvations, create their private self-images, reweave their webs of belief and desire in the light of whatever new people and books they happen to encounter. In such an ideal society, discussion of public affairs will revolve around (1) how to balance the needs for peace, wealth, and freedom when conditions require that one of these goals be sacrificed to one of the others and (2) how to equalize opportunities for self-creation and then leave people alone to use, or neglect, their opportunities.

The suggestion that this is all the social glue liberal societies need is subject to two main objections. The first is that as a practical matter, this glue is just not thick enough – that the (predominantly) metaphysical rhetoric of public life in the democracies is essential to the continuation of free institutions. The second is that it is psychologically impossible to be a liberal ironist – to be someone for whom "cruelty is the worst thing we do," and to have no metaphysical beliefs about what all human beings have in common.

The first objection is a prediction about what would happen if ironism replaced metaphysics in our public rhetoric. The second is a suggestion that the public-private split I am advocating will not work: that no one can divide herself up into a private self-creator and a public liberal, that the same person cannot be, in alternate moments, Nietzsche and J. S. Mill.

I want to dismiss the first of these objections fairly quickly, in order to concentrate on the second. The former amounts to the prediction that the prevalence of ironist notions among the public at large, the general adoption of antimetaphysical, antiessentialist views about the nature of morality and rationality and human beings, would weaken and dissolve liberal societies. It is possible that this prediction is correct, but there is at least one excellent reason for thinking it false. This is the analogy with the decline of religious faith. That decline, and specifically the decline of people's ability to take the idea of post-mortem rewards seriously, has not weakened liberal societies, and indeed has strengthened them. Lots of people in the eighteenth and nineteenth centuries predicted the opposite. They thought that hope of heaven was required to supply moral fiber and social glue – that there was little point, for example, in having an atheist swear to tell the truth in a court of law. As it turned out, however, willingness to endure suffering for the sake of future reward was transferable from individual rewards to social ones, from one's hopes for paradise to one's hopes for one's grandchildren.[7]

The reason liberalism has been strengthened by this switch is that whereas belief in an immortal soul kept being buffeted by scientific discoveries and by philosophers' attempts to keep pace with natural science, it is not clear that any shift in scientific or philosophical opinion could hurt the sort of social hope which characterizes modern liberal

---

7   Hans Blumenberg takes this transfer as central to the development of modern thought and society, and he makes a good case.

societies – the hope that life will eventually be freer, less cruel, more leisured, richer in goods and experiences, not just for our descendants but for everybody's descendants. If you tell someone whose life is given meaning by this hope that philosophers are waxing ironic over real essence, the objectivity of truth, and the existence of an ahistorical human nature, you are unlikely to arouse much interest, much less do any damage. The idea that liberal societies are bound together by philosophical beliefs seems to me ludicrous. What binds societies together are common vocabularies and common hopes. The vocabularies are, typically, parasitic on the hopes – in the sense that the principal function of the vocabularies is to tell stories about future outcomes which compensate for present sacrifices.

Modern, literate, secular societies depend on the existence of reasonably concrete, optimistic, and plausible *political* scenarios, as opposed to scenarios about redemption beyond the grave. To retain social hope, members of such a society need to be able to tell themselves a story about how things might get better, and to see no insuperable obstacles to this story's coming true. If social hope has become harder lately, this is not because the clerks have been committing treason but because, since the end of World War II, the course of events has made it harder to tell a convincing story of this sort. The cynical and impregnable Soviet Empire, the continuing shortsightedness and greed of the surviving democracies, and the exploding, starving populations of the Southern Hemisphere make the problems our parents faced in the 1930s – Fascism and unemployment – look almost manageable. People who try to update and rewrite the standard social democratic scenario about human equality, the scenario which their grandparents wrote around the turn of the century, are not having much success. The problems which metaphysically inclined social thinkers believe to be caused by our failure to find the right sort of theoretical glue – a philosophy which can command wide assent in an individualistic and pluralistic society – are, I think, caused by a set of historical contingencies. These contingencies are making it easy to see the last few hundred years of European and American history – centuries of increasing public hope and private ironism – as an island in time, surrounded by misery, tyranny, and chaos. As Orwell put it, "The democratic vistas seem to end in barbed wire."

I shall come back to this point about the loss of social hope when I discuss Orwell in Chapter 8. For the moment, I am simply trying to disentangle the public question "Is absence of metaphysics politically dangerous?" from the private question "Is ironism compatible with a sense of human solidarity?" To do so, it may help to distinguish the way nominalism and historicism look at present, in a liberal culture whose public rhetoric – the rhetoric in which the young are socialized – is still metaphysical, from the way they might look in a future whose public rhetoric is borrowed from nominalists and historicists. We tend to assume that nominalism and historicism are the exclusive property of intellectuals, of high culture, and that the masses cannot be so blasé about their own final vocabularies. But remember that once upon a time atheism, too, was the exclusive property of intellectuals.

In the ideal liberal society, the intellectuals would still be ironists, although the non-intellectuals would not. The latter would, however, be commonsensically nominalist and historicist. So they would see themselves as contingent through and through, without feeling any particular doubts about the contingencies they happened to be. They would not be bookish, nor would they look to literary critics as moral advisers. But they would be commonsensical nonmetaphysicians, in the way in which more and more people in the rich democracies have been commonsensical nontheists. They would feel no more need to answer the questions "*Why* are you a liberal? Why do you *care* about the humiliation of strangers?" than the average sixteenth-century Christian felt to answer the question "Why are you a Christian?" or than most people nowadays feel to answer the question "Are you saved?"[8] Such a person would not need a justification for her sense of human solidarity, for she was not raised to play the language game in which one asks and gets justifications for that sort of belief. Her culture is one in which doubts about the public rhetoric of the culture are met not by Socratic requests for definitions and principles, but by Deweyan requests for concrete alternatives and programs. Such a culture could, as far as I can see, be every bit as self-critical and every bit as devoted to human equality as our own familiar, and still metaphysical, liberal culture – if not more so.

But even if I am right in thinking that a liberal culture whose public rhetoric is nominalist and historicist is both possible and desirable, I cannot go on to claim that there could or ought to be a culture whose public rhetoric is *ironist*. I cannot imagine a culture which socialized its youth in such a way as to make them continually dubious about their own process of socialization. Irony seems inherently a private matter. On my definition, an ironist cannot get along without the contrast between the final vocabulary she inherited and the one she is trying to create for herself. Irony is, if not intrinsically resentful, at least reactive. Ironists have to have something to have doubts about, something from which to be alienated.

This brings me to the second of the two objections I listed above, and thus to the idea that there is something about being an ironist which unsuits one for being a liberal, and that a simple split between private and public concerns is not enough to overcome the tension.

One can make this claim plausible by saying that there is at least a prima facie tension between the idea that social organization aims at human equality and the idea that human beings are simply incarnated vocabularies. The idea that we all have an overriding obligation to diminish cruelty, to make human beings equal in respect to their liability to suffering, seems to take for granted that there is something within human beings which deserves respect and protection quite independently of the language they speak. It suggests that a nonlinguistic ability, the ability to feel pain, is what is important, and that differences in vocabulary are much less important.

Metaphysics – in the sense of a search for theories which will get at real essence – tries to make sense of the claim that human beings are something more than centerless webs of beliefs and desires. The reason many people think such a claim essential to liberalism is that if men and women were, indeed, nothing more than sentential attitudes – nothing more than the presence or absence of dispositions toward the use of sentences phrased in some historically conditioned vocabulary – then not only human nature, but human *solidarity,* would begin to seem an eccentric and dubious idea. For solidarity with all possible vocabularies seems impossible. Metaphysicians tell us that unless there is some sort of common ur-vocabulary, we have no "reason" not to be cruel to those whose final vocabularies are very unlike ours. A universalistic ethics seems incompatible with ironism, simply because it is hard to imagine stating such an ethic without some doctrine about the nature of man. Such an appeal to real essence is the antithesis of ironism.

8   Nietzsche said, with a sneer, "Democracy is Christianity made natural" (*Will to Power*, no. 215). Take away the sneer, and he was quite right.

So the fact that greater openness, more room for self-creation, is the standard demand made by ironists on their societies is balanced by the fact that this demand seems to be merely for the freedom to speak a kind of ironic theoretical metalanguage which makes no sense to the man in the street. One can easily imagine an ironist badly wanting more freedom, more open space, for the Baudelaires and the Nabokovs, while not giving a thought to the sort of thing Orwell wanted: for example, getting more fresh air down into the coal mines, or getting the Party off the backs of the proles. This sense that the connection between ironism and liberalism is very loose, and that between metaphysics and liberalism pretty tight, is what makes people distrust ironism in philosophy and aestheticism in literature as "elitist."

This is why writers like Nabokov, who claim to despise "topical trash" and to aim at "aesthetic bliss," look morally dubious and perhaps politically dangerous. Ironist philosophers like Nietzsche and Heidegger often look the same, even if we forget about their use by the Nazis. By contrast, even when we are mindful of the use made of Marxism by gangs of thugs calling themselves "Marxist governments," the use made of Christianity by the Inquisition, and the use Gradgrind made of utilitarianism, we cannot mention Marxism, Christianity, or utilitarianism without respect. For there was a time when each served human liberty. It is not obvious that ironism ever has.

The ironist is the typical modern intellectual, and the only societies which give her the freedom to articulate her alienation are liberal ones. So it is tempting to infer that ironists are naturally antiliberal. Lots of people, from Julien Benda to C. P. Snow, have taken a connection between ironism and antiliberalism to be almost self-evident. Nowadays many people take for granted that a taste for "deconstruction" – one of the ironists' current catchwords – is a good sign of lack of moral responsibility. They assume that the mark of the morally trustworthy intellectual is a kind of straightforward, unselfconscious, transparent prose – precisely the kind of prose no self-creating ironist wants to write.

Although some of these inferences may be fallacious and some of these assumptions ungrounded, nevertheless there is something right about the suspicion which ironism arouses. Ironism, as I have defined it, results from awareness of the power of redescription. But most people do not want to be redescribed. They want to be taken on their own terms – taken seriously just as they are and just as they talk. The ironist tells them that the language they speak is up for grabs by her and her kind. There is something potentially very cruel about that claim. For the best way to cause people long-lasting pain is to humiliate them by making the things that seemed most important to them look futile, obsolete, and powerless.[9] Consider what happens when a child's precious possessions – the little things around which he weaves fantasies that make him a little different from all other children – are redescribed as "trash," and thrown away. Or consider what happens when these possessions are made to look ridiculous alongside the possessions of another, richer, child. Something like that presumably happens to a primitive culture when it is conquered by a more advanced one. The same sort of thing sometimes happens to nonintellectuals in the presence of intellectuals. All these are milder forms of what happened to Winston Smith when he was arrested: They broke his

---

9   See Judith Shklar's discussion of humiliation on p. 37 of her *Ordinary Vices* (Cambridge, Mass.: Harvard University Press, 1984) and Ellen Scarry's discussion of the use of humiliation by torturers in chap. 1 of *The Body in Pain*.

paperweight and punched Julia in the belly, thus initiating the process of making him describe himself in O'Brien's terms rather than his own. The redescribing ironist, by threatening one's final vocabulary, and thus one's ability to make sense of oneself in one's own terms rather than hers, suggests that one's self and one's world are futile, obsolete, *powerless*. Redescription often humiliates.

But notice that redescription and possible humiliation are no more closely connected with ironism than with metaphysics. The metaphysician also redescribes, even though he does it in the name of reason rather than in the name of the imagination. Redescription is a generic trait of the intellectual, not a specific mark of the ironist. So why do ironists arouse *special* resentment? We get a clue to an answer from the fact that the metaphysician typically backs up his redescription with argument — or, as the ironist redescribes the process, disguises his redescription under the cover of argument. But this in itself does not solve the problem, for argument, like redescription, is neutral between liberalism and antiliberalism. Presumably the relevant difference is that to offer an argument in support of one's redescription amounts to telling the audience that they are being *educated,* rather than simply reprogrammed — that the Truth was already in them and merely needed to be drawn out into the light. Redescription which presents itself as uncovering the interlocutor's true self, or the real nature of a common public world which the speaker and the interlocutor share, suggests that the person being redescribed is being empowered, not having his power diminished. This suggestion is enhanced if it is combined with the suggestion that his previous, false, self-description was imposed upon him by the world, the flesh, the devil, his teachers, or his repressive society. The convert to Christianity or Marxism is made to feel that being redescribed amounts to an uncovering of his true self or his real interests. He comes to believe that his acceptance of that redescription seals an alliance with a power mightier than any of those which have oppressed him in the past.

The metaphysician, in short, thinks that there is a connection between redescription and power, and that the right redescription can make us free. The ironist offers no similar assurance. She has to say that our chances of freedom depend on historical contingencies which are only occasionally influenced by our self-redescriptions. She knows of no power of the same size as the one with which the metaphysician claims acquaintance. When she claims that her redescription is better, she cannot give the term "better" the reassuring weight the metaphysician gives it when he explicates it as "in better correspondence with reality."

So I conclude that what the ironist is being blamed for is not an inclination to humiliate but an inability to empower. There is no reason the ironist cannot be a liberal, but she cannot be a "progressive" and "dynamic" liberal in the sense in which liberal metaphysicians sometimes claim to be. For she cannot offer the same sort of social hope as metaphysicians offer. She cannot claim that adopting her redescription of yourself or your situation makes you better able to conquer the forces which are marshaled against you. On her account, that ability is a matter of weapons and luck, not a matter of having truth on your side, or having detected the "movement of history."

There are, then, two differences between the liberal ironist and the liberal metaphysician. The first concerns their sense of what redescription can do for liberalism; the second, their sense of the connection between public hope and private irony. The first difference is that the ironist thinks that the *only* redescriptions which serve liberal purposes are those which answer the question "What humiliates?" whereas the metaphysician also wants to answer the question "Why should I avoid humiliating?" The liberal metaphysician wants our *wish to be kind* to be bolstered by an argument, one which entails a self-redescription which will highlight a common human essence, an essence which is something more than our shared ability to suffer humiliation. The liberal ironist just wants our *chances of being kind,* of avoiding the humiliation of others, to be expanded by redescription. She thinks that recognition of a common susceptibility to humiliation is the *only* social bond that is needed. Whereas the metaphysician takes the morally relevant feature of the other human beings to be their relation to a larger shared power – rationality, God, truth, or history, for example – the ironist takes the morally relevant definition of a person, a moral subject, to be "something that can be humiliated." Her sense of human solidarity is based on a sense of a common danger, not on a common possession or a shared power.

What, then, of the point I made earlier: that people want to be described in their own terms? As I have already suggested, the liberal ironist meets this point by saying that we need to distinguish between redescription for private and for public purposes. For my private purposes, I may redescribe you and everybody else in terms which have nothing to do with my attitude toward your actual or possible suffering. My private purposes, and the part of my final vocabulary which is not relevant to my public actions, are none of your business. But as I am a liberal, the part of my final vocabulary which is relevant to such actions requires me to become aware of all the various ways in which other human beings whom I might act upon can be humiliated. So the liberal ironist needs as much imaginative acquaintance with alternative final vocabularies as possible, not just for her own edification, but in order to understand the actual and possible humiliation of the people who use these alternative final vocabularies.

The liberal metaphysician, by contrast, wants a final vocabulary with an internal and organic structure, one which is not split down the middle by a public–private distinction, not just a patchwork. He thinks that acknowledging that everybody wants to be taken on their own terms commits us to finding a least common denominator of those terms, a single description which will suffice for both public and private purposes, for self-definition and for one's relations with others. He prays, with Socrates, that the inner and the outer man will be as one – that irony will no longer be necessary. He is prone to believe, with Plato, that the parts of the soul and of the state correspond, and that distinguishing the essential from the accidental in the soul will help us distinguish justice from injustice in the state. Such metaphors express the liberal metaphysician's belief that the metaphysical public rhetoric of liberalism must remain central to the final vocabulary of the individual liberal, because it is the portion which expressed what she shares with the rest of humanity – the portion that makes solidarity possible.[10]

But that distinction between a central, shared, obligatory portion and a peripheral, idiosyncratic, optional portion of one's final vocabulary is just the distinction which the

10   Habermas, for example, attempts to save something of Enlightenment rationalism through a "discourse theory of truth" which will show that the "moral point of view" is a "universal" and "does not express merely the moral intuitions of the average, male, middle-class member of a modern Western society" (Peter Dews, ed., *Autonomy and Solidarity: Interviews with Jürgen Habermas* [London: Verso, 1986]). For the ironist, the fact that nobody had ever had such intuitions before the rise of modern Western societies is quite irrelevant to the question of whether she should share them.

ironist refuses to draw. She thinks that what unites her with the rest of the species is not a common language but *just* susceptibility to pain and in particular to that special sort of pain which the brutes do not share with the humans – humiliation. On her conception, human solidarity is not a matter of sharing a common truth or a common goal but of sharing a common selfish hope, the hope that one's world – the little things around which one has woven into one's final vocabulary – will not be destroyed. For public purposes, it does not matter if everybody's final vocabulary is different, as long as there is enough overlap so that everybody has some words with which to express the desirability of entering into other people's fantasies as well as into one's own. But those overlapping words – words like "kindness" or "decency" or "dignity" – do not form a vocabulary which all human beings can reach by reflection on their natures. Such reflection will not produce anything except a heightened awareness of the possibility of suffering. It will not produce a *reason to care* about suffering. What matters for the liberal ironist is not finding such a reason but making sure that she *notices* suffering when it occurs. Her hope is that she will not be limited by her own final vocabulary when faced with the possibility of humiliating someone with a quite different final vocabulary.

For the liberal ironist, skill at imaginative identification does the work which the liberal metaphysician would like to have done by a specifically moral motivation – rationality, or the love of God, or the love of truth. The ironist does not see her ability to envisage, and desire to prevent, the actual and possible humiliation of others – despite differences of sex, race, tribe, and final vocabulary – as more real or central or "essentially human" than any other part of herself. Indeed, she regards it as an ability and a desire which, like the ability to formulate differential equations, arose rather late in the history of humanity and is still a rather local phenomenon. It is associated primarily with Europe and America in the last three hundred years. It is not associated with any power larger than that embodied in a concrete historical situation, for example, the power of the rich European and American democracies to disseminate their customs to other parts of the world, a power which was enlarged by certain past contingencies and has been diminished by certain more recent contingencies.

Whereas the liberal metaphysician thinks that the good liberal knows certain crucial propositions to be true, the liberal ironist thinks the good liberal has a certain kind of know-how. Whereas he thinks of the high culture of liberalism as centering around theory, she thinks of it as centering around literature (in the older and narrower sense of that term – plays, poems, and, especially, novels). He thinks that the task of the intellectual is to preserve and defend liberalism by backing it up with some true propositions about large subjects, but she thinks that this task is to increase our skill at recognizing and describing the different sorts of little things around which individuals or communities center their fantasies and their lives. The ironist takes the words which are fundamental to metaphysics, and in particular to the public rhetoric of the liberal democracies, as just another text, just another set of little human things. Her ability to understand what it is like to make one's life center around these words is not distinct from her ability to grasp what it is like to make one's life center around the love of Christ or of Big Brother. Her liberalism does not consist in her devotion to those particular words but in her ability to grasp the function of many different sets of words.

These distinctions help explain why ironist philosophy has not done, and will not do, much for freedom and equality. But they also explain why "literature" (in the older and narrower sense), as well as ethnography and journalism, is doing a lot. As I said earlier, pain is nonlinguistic: It is what we human beings have that ties us to the nonlanguage-using beasts. So victims of cruelty, people who are suffering, do not have much in the way of a language. That is why there is no such things as the "voice of the oppressed" or the "language of the victims." The language the victims once used is not working any-more, and they are suffering too much to put new words together. So the job of putting their situation into language is going to have to be done for them by somebody else. The liberal novelist, poet, or journalist is good at that. The liberal theorist usually is not.

The suspicion that ironism in philosophy has not helped liberalism is quite right, but that is not because ironist philosophy is inherently cruel. It is because liberals have come to expect philosophy to do a certain job – namely, answering questions like "Why not be cruel?" and "Why be kind?" – and they feel that any philosophy which refuses this assignment must be heartless. But that expectation is a result of a metaphysical upbring-ing. If we could get rid of the expectation, liberals would not ask ironist philosophy to do a job which it cannot do, and which it defines itself as unable to do.

The metaphysician's association of theory with social hope and of literature with pri-vate perfection is, in an ironist liberal culture, reversed. Within a liberal metaphysical cul-ture the disciplines which were charged with penetrating behind the many private appearances to the one general common reality – theology, science, philosophy – were the ones which were expected to bind human beings together, and thus to help eliminate cruelty. Within an ironist culture, by contrast, it is the disciplines which specialize in thick description of the private and idiosyncratic which are assigned this job. In particular, nov-els and ethnographies which sensitize one to the pain of those who do not speak our language must do the job which demonstrations of a common human nature were sup-posed to do. Solidarity has to be constructed out of little pieces, rather than found already waiting, in the form of an ur-language which all of us recognize when we hear it.

Conversely, within our increasingly ironist culture, philosophy has become more important for the pursuit of private perfection rather than for any social task. In the next two chapters, I shall claim that ironist philosophers are private philosophers – philoso-phers concerned to intensify the irony of the nominalist and the historicist. Their work is illsuited to public purposes, of no use to liberals qua liberals. In Chapters 7 and 8, I shall offer examples of the way in which novelists can do something which is socially useful – help us attend to the springs of cruelty in ourselves, as well as to the fact of its occurrence in areas where we had not noticed it.

Part IV

Pragmatism, Literature, and Democracy

Introduction

During the 1990s, social and political concerns come to the forefront of Rorty's work in an unprecedented way. If his work in the previous decade makes a theoretical case for why liberal democracy not only can survive a poeticized, postmetaphysical culture but can flourish, in the essays collected in this section he puts these notions into practice, outlining the political value of the humanities and humanistic sensibilities within a pragmatist literary culture. While these ideas had been percolating for a decade or two and are the result of dynamics within Rorty's internal intellectual development, the events of 1989 imbued these concerns with a heightened sense of immediacy, given the lacuna created in the collective imaginary of the Left by the apparent demise of the utopian vision that originated in Marx. Rorty's work of this period cannot be disassociated from his growing concerns about the irrelevancy of what he variously termed the postmodern, Foucauldian, or Cultural Left to concrete political reform. In typical fashion, Rorty assimilates the world-transforming events of 1989 to his larger philosophical critique, stating in 1991,

> I would hope that we have reached a time at which we can finally get rid of the conviction common to Plato and Marx that there *must* be large theoretical ways of finding out how to end injustice, as opposed to small experimental ways.

While Rorty's explicit attempt "to banalize the entire vocabulary of leftist political deliberation" struck many as a de-radicalization of the Left's emancipatory potential, he makes a case on pragmatic grounds of greater efficiency and efficacy that his "piecemeal reformism" would yield greater results than the postmodern Left's overtheoretical radical rhetoric when it comes to alleviating social injustices.[1]

What stands out in these essays is Rorty's explicit effort to establish the political value of narratives and stories over philosophy and theory. The brief piece "The Humanistic Intellectual" outlines 11 theses that broadly characterize his emergent view of the kind of wide-ranging, politically engaged, humanistic intellectual, like himself, by now well-established in his position as University Professor of Humanities at the University of Virginia, who actively engages in such efforts. In "Philosophers, Novelists, and Intercultural

---

1   See "The End of Leninism, Havel, and Social Hope" (TP, pp. 228–9).

Comparisons," Rorty defends the novel, following Franco–Czech novelist and critic Milan Kundera, as a genre "roughly synonymous" with a "democratic utopia" – "an imaginary future society in which nobody dreams of thinking that God, or the Truth, or the Nature of Things, is on their side" (p. 314, this volume). Reading Dickens as "a sort of anti-Heidegger" – a feat only Rorty could pull off – he suggests that the relevance of the novel for moral reflection resides in the way particular characters can function as the basis of a moral vocabulary that, rather than leading us to get entangled in questions about human nature or the meaning of life and seek "one right answer," prompt us to notice the details about other human beings and work toward the achievement of tolerance and "comfortable togetherness." The creation of linguistic novelty remains the primary means by which a culture can change itself and "break out of a tradition into a previously imagined future."[2]

Rorty expands his view of the role of the humanities in moral and political deliberation in "De Man and the American Cultural Left," emphasizing the importance of books that make us "more aware of the suffering caused by American institutions" (p. 328, this volume). However, he takes care to distinguish this sense of the politicization of the humanities from that advocated by members of the "Cultural Left" – intellectuals influenced by the likes of de Man, Derrida, and Foucault. Despite sharing their critiques of traditional philosophy – their "antiessentialism" and "antilogocentrism" – Rorty takes issues with their assumption that "accepting such doctrines is *necessary* for overcoming social and economic repression" (p. 326, this volume). For one thing, Rorty simply does not think that affirming "the end of Logocentrism" or "the death of God" calls for a change in our "self-image." This is a key point: Rorty does not believe that one's philosophical and political views are woven that tightly; accepting "pluralist and pragmatic antiessentialism" means that such connections are always contingent and one among many possibilities. For another, inflated claims about the power of the species of "critical-linguistic analysis" common to Derrida and de Man seem to Rorty to "set up an altar to Literature [...] on the spot where we once worshiped the radiant, effulgent Logos." In the end, what Rorty's pragmatism amounts to is "lots of cultural oppositions but no privileged central discipline or practice." Nothing about the radical philosophical critiques of the Cultural Left – or his own, for that matter – suggest any better alternative to "consensual, reformist politics of the sort Dewey favored" (p. 324, this volume). The discontent with the Cultural Left expressed here would continue to grow.[3]

The essays "Feminism and Pragmatism" and "Human Rights, Rationality, and Sentimentality" put forth one of the more conspicuous motifs in Rorty's later work: the idea of achieving moral progress through the creation of more inclusive communities. More generally, they offer some of the more developed statements of Rorty's political theory. His vision, ultimately, is of a "global democratic utopia" – that is, "a planet on which all members of the species are concerned about the fates of all other members" (TP, p. 12). If we can get people to view the commonalities they share as

2   For more on the role of literary characters in moral reflection, see REDEMPTION FROM EGOTISM (chapter 23, this volume); and the chapters on Orwell and Nabokov in *Contingency, Irony, and Solidarity* (CIS). See also "The Inspirational Value of Great Works of Literature" in *Achieving Our Country* (AOC).

3   See the essays of AOC, especially, "The Eclipse of the Reformist Left" and "A Cultural Left."

more salient than the differences that divide them, then the reach of the category "people like us" can be extended to include as many as possible. Because this approach puts our ability to sympathize with different and distant others at the center of moral progress, novels, narratives, and "sad, sentimental stories" are more useful than universal moral obligations uncovered through the workings of Reason.

"Feminism and Pragmatism" gives a good account of the link between linguistic novelty and the creation of such inclusive communities.[4] Called a "paradigm-breaking transformation" that takes his pragmatism "in a new direction," this essay offers some of Rorty's most sophisticated thinking about politics, in particular about the politics of marginalized groups.[5] Rorty underscores the importance of alternative descriptions of previously unrecognized forms of injustice and suffering, not only so that they are noticed, but because of the need "to expand the logical space necessary for adequate moral deliberation" around these injustices so that they can be seen as such. Drawing on feminist thinkers like Catherine MacKinnon, Marilyn Frye, Adrienne Rich, and others, he also offers insightful discussion of the importance of oppressed and marginalized groups achieving "semantic authority" over themselves, which often requires a measure of exclusivity or separatism for a time so that a new moral identity can be created (p. 347, this volume). Philosophy's function, Rorty holds here, is "to clear the road for prophets and poets, to make intellectual life a bit simpler and safer for those who have visions of new communities" (p. 340, this volume). Explaining the utility of this approach in the context of human rights, in "Human Rights, Rationality, and Sentimentality" Rorty elaborates on the larger endeavor of "sentimental education" that is necessary to achieve this global democratic utopia. The context of his essay is the ethnic cleansing in the former Yugoslavia that was at the center of human rights struggles at the time. Borrowing Annette Baier's Humean notion of a "progress of sentiments" as an alternative to Kantian moral obligation, here too Rorty defends the value of novels like *Uncle Tom's Cabin* for cultivating the kind of moral development that would help bring about a "cosmopolitan utopia."

A principal endeavor of Rorty's in the 1990s is supplying an alternative story that mobilizes "what remains of our pride in being Americans" in the hope of altering the self-images of the academic Left. In "Looking Backwards from the Year 2096" Rorty constructs such a story. Originally titled "Fraternity Reigns," the piece offers a fictional

---

4   See also his "Feminism, Ideology, and Deconstruction: A Pragmatist View," *Hypatia* 8 (2), Spring 1993: 96–103. For critical responses to Rorty's argument about the benefits of pragmatism for feminism see: Carol Bacchi, "'Pragmatism' Be Damned: Richard Rorty's Death Wish for Feminism," *Hecate* 18 (1992): 97–105; Susan Bordo, "The Cultural Overseer and the Tragic Hero: Comedic and Feminist Perspectives on the Hubris of Philosophy," *Soundings* 65 (1982): 181–205; Nancy Fraser, "From Irony to Prophecy to Politics: A Response to Richard Rorty," *Michigan Quarterly Review* 30 (1991): 259–66; J. M. Fritzman, "Thinking with Fraser about Rorty, Feminism, and Pragmatism," *Praxis International* 13 (1993): 113–25; Dorothy Leland, "Rorty on the Moral Concern of Philosophy: A Critique from a Feminist Point of View," *Praxis International* 8 (1988): 273–83; Sabina Lovibond, "Feminism and Pragmatism: A Reply to Richard Rorty," *New Left Review* 193 (May/June 1992): 56–74; and Catherine Wilson, "How Did Dinosaurs Die Out? How Did Poets Survive?" *Radical Philosophy* 62 (Autumn 1992): 20–3.
5   Fraser, "From Irony to Prophecy to Politics," p. 262; J. M. Fritzman, "Thinking with Fraser about Rorty, Feminism, and Pragmatism," p. 116. Fraser believes that "the effort to think about feminism has had a major impact on the structure of Rorty's thought."

account of major events of the twenty-first century, highlighting the Second Great Depression, the loss of democracy for three decades following an economic collapse during the Dark Years, and the advent of the Democratic Vistas Party. Throughout it is citizens' "fragile sense of American fraternity" and social hope that keeps the country and its ideals intact.

A much fuller case for the indispensability of national pride as "a necessary condition for self-improvement" from within is presented in "American National Pride," the lead essay of *Achieving Our Country*. Countering familiar assumptions amongst liberal political theorists about detached and isolated rational individuals, Rorty advances the view that democratic deliberation requires an emotional engagement – "feelings of intense shame or of glowing pride" – if it is to be productive. Drawing not only on Dewey but on Walt Whitman and James Baldwin, from whom he borrows the phrase that gives the book its title, Rorty evinces a conception of connected criticism defined by a "quasi-communitarian rhetoric" where citizens are agents rather than spectators. Whitman's notion of the United States as "themselves the greatest poem" projects a vision of "a finite, human, historical project" rather than something "eternal and nonhuman" (p. 378, this volume). What Rorty affirms in the case of Baldwin is his "continued unwillingness to forgive with a continuing identification with the country that brought over his ancestors in chains" (p. 376, this volume). This is the cornerstone of Rorty's political theory: a shared sense of national identity is an absolutely essential component of citizenship. At the same time, Rorty's vision of "a new culture" is defined by a "romance of endless diversity – a "poetic agon, in which jarring dialectical discords would be resolved in previously unheard harmonies" (p. 382, this volume).

The essay "Redemption from Egotism"[6] contains Rorty's most developed and substantive discussion of the literary culture alluded to throughout his work as an alternative to a philosophical culture "dominated by the quest for redemptive knowledge about how things really are" (p. 402, this volume).[7] The difference between these cultures for Rorty is expressed in the contrast between philosophy's "dream of completeness" and the "desire for openness" that characterizes a literary culture in which we "remain open to the possibility that the next book you read, or the next person you meet, will change your life" (p. 392, this volume). It is the difference between seeking "redemption from ignorance" and "seeking redemption from egotism," where egotism is defined as being "satisfaction that the vocabulary one uses when deciding how to act is all right just as it is, and that there is no need to figure out what vocabularies others are using" (p. 395, this volume). As he has argued elsewhere, because novels put us in touch with other people, giving us a window into how people quite unlike us think of themselves, on this view they can make us more tolerant of "strange, and initially repellent, sorts of people," prompting us to consider important Millean questions about how to balance their needs with ours. Here he engages Martha Nussbaum's influential work on the intersection between literature and moral philosophy, highlighting precisely where his account differs

6   This 2001 essay was previously published in Spanish and German, but appears here for the first time in English. For a brief time, an English draft of this essay was available on Rorty's Stanford webpage.

7   As he puts it here, he sees the rise of the novel as "something that may help initiate a new form of cultural life by helping us create a self-image for human beings as different as the one Aristotle proposed as his cosmology is from our own" (p. 404, this volume).

from hers.[8] But what Rorty also emphasizes in this essay, in ways that recall Dewey's pronouncement that "Growth is the only moral end," is the novel's role in "enlarging ourselves."[9] In an interesting choice of phrase, Rorty offers Henry James and Marcel Proust as exemplars of "spiritual growth," understood as "any attempt to transform oneself into a better sort of person by changing one's sense of what matters most" (p. 404, this volume). Counterbalancing the weight put on sympathy, solidarity, and commonality in so much of his other work, his primary concern in this essay is on the importance of achieving "greater individuality and greater self-reliance."

8   See Martha Nussbaum, *Love's Knowledge: Essays on Philosophy and Literature* (New York: Oxford University Press, 1990) and *Poetic Justice: The Literary Imagination and Public Life* (Boston: Beacon Press, 1995). On these same issues, see also Alexander Nehamas, "What Should We Expect from Reading? (There are Only Aesthetic Values)," *Salmagundi* 111 (Summer 1996): 27–58; and Rorty's response in the same issue, "Duties to the Self and Duties to Others: Comments on Paper by Alexander Nehamas," pp. 59–67. For an attempt to interject William James into these debates, see Christopher J. Voparil, "Jonquils and Wild Orchids: James and Rorty on the Politics of Aesthetic Experience," *Journal of Speculative Philosophy* 23, no. 2 (2009): 100–9.

9   Rorty cites this line from Dewey's *Reconstruction in Philosophy* in "Truth without Correspondence to Reality" (p. 418, this volume).

16

The Humanistic Intellectual:
Eleven Theses

1.   We should not try to define "the humanities" by asking what the humanities departments share which distinguishes them from the rest of the university. The interesting dividing line is, instead, one that cuts across departments and disciplinary matrices. It divides people busy conforming to well-understood criteria for making contributions to knowledge from people trying to expand their own moral imaginations. These latter people read books in order to enlarge their sense of what is possible and important – either for themselves as individuals or for their society. Call these people the "humanistic intellectuals." One often finds more such people in the anthropology department than in the classics department, and sometimes more in the law school than in the philosophy department.

2.   If one asks what good these people do, what social function they perform, neither "teaching" nor "research" is a very good answer. Their idea of teaching – or at least of the sort of teaching they hope to do – is not exactly the communication of knowledge, but more like stirring the kids up. When they apply for a leave or a grant, they may have to fill out forms about the aims and methods of their so-called research projects, but all they really want to do is read a lot more books in the hope of becoming a different sort of person.

3.   So the real social function of the humanistic intellectuals is to instill doubts in the students about the students' own self-images, and about the society to which they belong. These people are the teachers who help insure that the moral consciousness of each new generation is slightly different from that of the previous generation.

4.   But when it comes to the rhetoric of public support for higher education, we do not talk much about this social function. We cannot tell boards of trustees, government commissions, and the like, that our function is to stir things up, to make our society feel guilty, to keep it off balance. We cannot say that the taxpayers employ us to make sure that their children will think differently than they do. Somewhere deep down, everybody – even the average taxpayer – knows that that is one of the things colleges and universities are for. But nobody can afford to make this fully explicit and public.

5.   We humanistic intellectuals find ourselves in a position analogous to that of the "social-gospel" or "liberation theology" clergy, the priests and ministers who think of themselves as working to build the kingdom of God on earth. Their opponents describe their activity as leftist political action. The clergy, they say, are being paid to relay God's word, but are instead meddling in politics. We are accused of being paid to contribute to and communicate knowledge, while instead "politicizing the humanities." Yet we cannot take the idea of unpoliticized humanities any more seriously than our opposite numbers in the clergy can take seriously the idea of a depoliticized church.

6.   We are still expected to make the ritual noises to which the trustees and the funding agencies are accustomed – noises about "objective criteria of excellence," "fundamental moral and spiritual values," "the enduring questions posed by the human condition," and so on, just as the liberal clergy is supposed to mumble their way through creeds written in an earlier and simpler age. But those of us who have been impressed by the anti-Platonic, anti-essentialist, historicizing, naturalizing writers of the last few centuries (people like Hegel, Darwin, Freud, Weber, Dewey, and Foucault) must either become cynical or else put our own tortured private constructions on these ritual phrases.

7.   This tension between public rhetoric and private sense of mission leaves the academy in general, and the humanistic intellectuals in particular, vulnerable to heresy-hunters. Ambitious politicians like William Bennett – or cynical journalists like the young William Buckley (author of *God and Man at Yale*) or Charles Sykes (author of *Profscam*) – can always point out gaps between official rhetoric and actual practice. Usually, however, such heresy-hunts peter out quickly in the face of faculty solidarity. The professors of physics and law, people whom nobody wants to mess with, can be relied upon to rally around fellow AAUP members who teach anthropology or French, even if they neither know nor care what the latter do.

8.   In the current flap about the humanities, however, the heresy-hunters have a more vulnerable target than usual. This target is what Allan Bloom calls "the Nietzscheanized left." This left is an anomaly in America. In the past the American left has asked our country to be true to its ideals, to go still further along the path of expanding human freedom which our forefathers mapped: the path which led us from the abolition of slavery through women's suffrage, the Wagner Act, and the Civil Rights Movement, to contemporary feminism and gay liberation. But the Nietzscheanized left tells the country it is rotten to the core – that it is a racist, sexist, imperialist society, one which can't be trusted an inch, one whose every utterance must be ruthlessly deconstructed.

9.   Another reason this left is a vulnerable target is that it is extraordinarily self-obsessed and ingrown, as well as absurdly over-philosophized. It takes seriously Paul de Man's weird suggestion that "one can approach the problems of ideology and by extension the problems of politics only on the basis of critical-linguistic analysis." It seems to accept Hillis Miller's fantastic claim that "the millenium [of universal peace and justice among men] would come if all men and women became good readers in de Man's sense." When asked for a utopian sketch of our country's future, the new leftists reply along the lines of one of Foucault's most fatuous remarks. When asked why he never sketched a utopia, Foucault said, "I think that to imagine another system is to extend our participation in the present system." De Man, and Foucault were (and Miller is) a lot better than these unfortunate remarks would suggest, but some of their followers are a

lot worse. This over-philosophized and self-obsessed left is the mirror image of the over-philosophized and self-obsessed Straussians on the right. The contempt of both groups for contemporary American society is so great that both have rendered themselves impotent when it comes to national, state, or local politics. This means that they get to spend *all* their energy on academic politics.

10.   The two groups are currently staging a sham battle about how to construct reading lists. The Straussians say that the criterion for what books to assign is intrinsic excellence, and the Nietzscheanized left says that it is fairness – e.g., fairness to females, blacks, and Third Worlders. They are both wrong. Reading lists should be constructed so as to preserve a delicate balance between two needs. The first is the need of the students to have common reference points with people in previous generations and in other social classes – so that grandparents and grandchildren, people who went to the University of Wisconsin at Whitewater and people who went to Stanford, will have read a lot of the same books. The second is the need of the teachers to be able to teach the books which have moved them, excited them, changed their lives – rather than having to teach a syllabus handed down by a committee.

11.   Philosophers of education, well-intended committees, and governmental agencies have attempted to understand, define, and manage the humanities. The point, however, is to keep the humanities changing fast enough so that they remain indefinable and unmanageable. All we need to keep them changing that fast is good old-fashioned academic freedom. Given freedom to shrug off the heresy-hunters and their cries of "politicization!," as well as freedom for each new batch of assistant professors to despise and repudiate the departmental Old Guard to whom they owe their jobs, the humanities will continue to be in good shape. If you don't like the ideological weather in the local English department these days, wait a generation. Watch what happens to the Nietzscheanized left when it tries to replace itself, along about the year 2010. I'm willing to bet that the brightest new Ph.D.'s in English that year will be people who never want to hear the terms "binary opposition" or "hegemonic discourse" again as long as they live.

17

Heidegger, Kundera,
and Dickens

Suppose that the nations which make up what we call "the West" vanish tomorrow, wiped out by thermonuclear bombs. Suppose that only Eastern Asia and sub-Saharan Africa remain inhabitable, and that in these regions the reaction to the catastrophe is a ruthless campaign of de-Westernization – a fairly successful attempt to obliterate the memory of the last three hundred years. But imagine also that, in the midst of this de-Westernizing campaign, a few people, mostly in the universities, squirrel away as many souvenirs of the West – books, magazines, small artifacts, reproductions of works of art, movie films, videotapes, and so on – as they can conceal.

Now imagine that, around the year 2500, memory of the catastrophe fades, the sealed-off cellars are uncovered, and artists and scholars begin to tell stories about the West. There will be many different stories, with many different morals. One such story might center on increasing technological mastery, another on the development of artistic forms, another on changes in sociopolitical institutions, and another on the lifting of sexual taboos. There would be dozens of other guiding threads which story-tellers might seize upon. The relative interest and usefulness of each will depend upon the particular needs of the various African and Asian societies within which they are disseminated.

If, however, there are *philosophers* among the people who write such stories, we can imagine controversies arising about what was "paradigmatically" Western, about the *essence* of the West. We can imagine attempts to tie all these stories together, and to reduce them to one – the one true account of the West, pointing out the one true moral of its career. We think of *philosophers* as prone to make such attempts because we tend to identify an area of a culture as "philosophy" when we note an attempt to substitute theory for narrative, a tendency toward essentialism. Essentialism has been fruitful in many areas – most notably in helping us to see elegant mathematical relationships behind complex structures. But we have gradually become suspicious of essentialism as applied

Richard M. Rorty, "Philosophers, Novelists, and Intercultural Comparisons: Heidegger, Kundera, and Dickens," pp. 3–20 in Eliot Deutsch (ed.), *Culture and Modernity: East–West Philosophic Perspectives* (Honolulu: University of Hawaii Press, 1991), © 1991 by Eliot Deutsch. Reprinted by kind permission of Eliot Deutsch.

to human affairs, in areas such as history, sociology, and anthropology. The attempt to find laws of history or essences of cultures – to substitute theory for narrative as an aid to understanding ourselves, others, and the options which we present to one another – has been notoriously unfruitful. Writings as diverse as Karl Popper's on Hegel and Marx, Charles Taylor's on positivistic social science, and Alasdair MacIntyre's or Michael Oakeshott's on the importance of traditions have helped us realize this unfruitfulness.

Despite growing recognition that the essentialistic habits of thought which pay off in the natural sciences do not assist moral and political reflection, we Western philosophers still show a distressing tendency to essentialism when we offer intercultural comparisons. This comes out most clearly in our recent willingness to talk about "the West" not as an ongoing, suspenseful adventure in which we are participating but rather as a structure which we can step back from, inspect at a distance. This willingness is partly the cause, and partly the effect, of the profound influence of Nietzsche and Heidegger on contemporary Western intellectual life. It reflects the sociopolitical pessimism which has afflicted European and American intellectuals ever since we gave up on socialism without becoming any fonder of capitalism – ever since Marx ceased to present an alternative to Nietzsche and Heidegger. This pessimism, which often calls itself "postmodernism," is a rueful sense that the hopes for greater freedom and equality which mark the recent history of the West were somehow deeply self-deceptive. Postmodernist attempts to encapsulate and sum up the West have made it increasingly tempting to contrast the West as a whole with the rest of the world as a whole. Such attempts make it easy to start using "the East" or "non-Western modes of thought" as the names of a mysterious redemptive force, as something which may still offer hope.

In this essay, I shall be protesting against this recent tendency to encapsulate the West, to treat it as a finished-off object which we are now in a position to subject to structural analysis. In particular, I want to protest against the tendency to take Heidegger's account of the West for granted. There is, it seems to me, a growing willingness to read Heidegger as the West's final message to the world. This message consists largely of the claim that the West has, to use one of Heidegger's favorite phrases, "exhausted its possibilities." Heidegger was one of the great synoptic imaginations of our century, but his extraordinary gifts make his message sound more plausible than I think it is. We need to remember that the scope of Heidegger's imagination, great as it was, was largely restricted to philosophy and lyric poetry, to the writings of those to whom he awarded the title of "Thinker" or of "Poet." Heidegger thought that the essence of a historical epoch could be discovered by reading the works of the characteristic philosopher of that epoch and identifying his "Understanding of Being." He thought that the history of the West could best be understood by finding a dialectical progression connecting the works of successive great philosophical thinkers. Philosophers by trade are especially susceptible to the persuasive power of Heidegger's account of the West's history and prospects. But I think that this susceptibility is a professional deformation which we should struggle to overcome.

As a way of counteracting Heidegger and, more generally, the kind of post-Heideggerian thinking which refuses to see the West as a continuing adventure, I want to put forward Dickens as a sort of anti-Heidegger. I can sum up my sense of the respective importance of Dickens and Heidegger by saying that, if my imaginary Asians and Africans were, for some reason, unable to preserve the works of both men, I should much prefer that they preserve Dickens'. For Dickens could help them grasp a complex of attitudes that was important to the West, and perhaps unique to the West, in a way that neither Heidegger nor any other philosopher could. The example of Dickens could help them think of the novel, and particularly the novel of moral protest, rather than of the philosophical treatise, as the genre in which the West excelled. Focusing on this genre would help them to see not technology, but rather the hope of freedom and equality as the West's most important legacy. From the point of view I shall be adopting, the interaction of West and East is better exemplified by the playing of Beethoven's Ninth Symphony in Tienanmen Square than by the steel mills of Korea or the influence of Japanese prints on Van Gogh.[1]

To lay out this point of view, I shall do three things in the remainder of this essay. First, I shall offer an account of Heidegger as one more example of what Nietzsche called "the ascetic priest." Second, I shall summarize and gloss Milan Kundera's account of the novel as the vehicle of a revolt against the ontotheological treatise, of an anticlerical reaction against the cultural dominance of the ascetic priests. Third, I shall use Dickens to illustrate Kundera's suggestion that the novel is the characteristic genre of democracy, the genre most closely associated with the struggle for freedom and equality.

Heidegger's later work was an attempt to provide the one right answer to the question asked by my imaginary African and Asian philosophers of the future. Heidegger would advise these philosophers to start thinking about the West by thinking about what killed it – technology – and to work backward from there. With a bit of luck, they could then recreate the story which Heidegger himself told, the story he called "the history of Being." For Heidegger, the West begins with the pre-Socratics, with what he calls the separation between the "what" and the "that." This separation between what a thing is in itself and the relations which it has to other things engenders distinctions between essence and accident, reality and appearance, objective and subjective, rational and irrational, scientific and unscientific, and the like – all the dualisms which mark off epochs in the history of an increasing lust for power, an increased inability to let beings be. This is the history which Heidegger summarizes in Nietzsche's phrase *die Wüste wächst*, the wasteland spreads.[2]

As Heidegger tells this story, it culminates in what he calls the "age of the world-picture," the age in which everything is Enframed, seen as providing an occasion either for manipulation or for aesthetic delectation. It is an age of giantism, of aesthetico-technological frenzy. It is the age in which people build 100-megaton bombs, slash down rain forests, try to create art more thoroughly postmodern than last year's, and bring hundreds of philosophers together to compare their respective world pictures. Heidegger sees all these activities as aspects of a single phenomenon: the age of the world picture is the age in which human beings become entirely forgetful of Being, entirely oblivious to the possibility that anything can stand outside a means-end relationship.

Seeing matters in this way is an instance of what Habermas describes as Heidegger's characteristic "abstraction by essentialization." In 1935 Heidegger saw Stalin's Russia and Roosevelt's America as "metaphysically speaking, the same." In 1945 he saw the

---

1   The students were reported to have played a recording of this symphony as the troops were being held up by masses of people jamming the highways leading into the square. The same point about the impact of the West could be made by reference to the student speakers' repeated invocations of Thoreau and of Martin Luther King.

2   See Martin Heidegger, *What Is Called Thinking*, trans. by J. Glenn Gray (New York: Harper and Row, 1968), pp. 29 ff. (*Was Heisst Denken?* [Tübingen: Niemeyer, 1954], pp. 11 ff.).

Holocaust and the expulsion of ethnic Germans from Eastern Europe as two instances of the same phenomenon. As Habermas puts it, "under the leveling gaze of the philosopher of Being even the extermination of the Jews seems merely an event equivalent to many others."[3] Heidegger specializes in rising above the need to calculate relative quantities of human happiness, in taking a larger view. For him successful and unsuccessful adventures – Ghandi's success and Dubček's failure, for example – are just surface perturbations, distractions from essence by accidents, hindrances to an understanding of what is *really* going on.

Heidegger's refusal to take much interest in the Holocaust typifies the urge to look beneath or behind the narrative of the West for the *essence* of the West, the urge which separates the philosophers from the novelists. Someone dominated by this urge will tell a story only as part of the process of clearing away appearance in order to reveal reality. Narrative is, for Heidegger, always a second-rate genre – a tempting but dangerous one. At the beginning of *Sein und Zeit*, Heidegger warned against the temptation to confuse ontology with the attempt to tell a story that relates beings to other beings, *mython tina diegeisthai*.[4] At the end of his career he takes back his earlier suggestion that what he called "the task of thinking" might be accomplished by *Seinsgeschichte*, by telling a story about how metaphysics and the West exhausted their possibilities. Now he realizes that he must cease to tell stories about metaphysics, must leave metaphysics to itself, if he is ever to undertake this task.[5]

Despite this suspicion of epic and preference for lyric, the ability to spin a dramatic tale was Heidegger's greatest gift. What is most memorable and original in his writings, it seems to me, is the new dialectical pattern he finds in the sequence of canonical Western philosophical texts. His clue to this pattern was, I think, Nietzsche's construal of the ascetic priests' attempts at wisdom, contemplation, and imperturbability as furtive and resentful expressions of those priests' will to power.

Heidegger, however, tried to out-Nietzsche Nietzsche by reading Nietzsche himself as the last of the metaphysicians. He hoped thereby to free himself from the resentment which, despite himself, Nietzsche displayed so conspicuously. Heidegger thought that if he could free himself from this resentment, and from the urge to dominate, he could free himself from the West and so, as he said, quoting Hölderlin, "sing a new song." He thought that he could become free of the will to power as a result of having seen through its last disguise. He thought that by leaving metaphysics to itself, turning from *Seinsgeschichte* to *Denken*, from *Sein* to *Ereignis*, he could accomplish the transition from epic to lyric, turn from the West to something Wholly Other than the West.

But on my reading, Heidegger was simply one more ascetic priest and his attempt to encapsulate the West, to sum it up and distance himself from it, was one more power play. Heidegger was intensely aware of the danger that he was making such a play. But to be intensely aware of the danger is not necessarily to escape it. On my reading, Heidegger is still doing the same sort of thing that Plato tried to do when he created a supersensible world from which to look down on Athens, or Augustine when he imagined a City

3   J. Habermas, "Work and Weltanschauung: The Heidegger Controversy from a German Perspective," *Critical Inquiry* 15 (Winter 1989): p. 453.
4   Heidegger, *Sein und Zeit*, 10th ed. (Tübingen: Niemeyer, 1963), p. 6.
5   See Heidegger, *On Time and Being*, trans. by Joan Stambaugh (New York: Harper and Row, 1972), pp. 24, 41 (*Zur Sache des Denkens* [Tübingen: Niemeyer, 1969], pp. 25, 44).

of God from which to look down on the Dark Ages. He is opting out of the struggles of his fellow humans by making his mind its own place, his own story the only story that counts, making himself the redeemer of his time precisely by his abstention from action. All that Heidegger manages to do is to historicize the Platonic divided line. He tips it over on its side. The Heideggerian counterpart of Plato's world of appearance seen from above is the West seen from beyond metaphysics. Whereas Plato looks down, Heidegger looks back. But both are hoping to distance themselves from, cleanse themselves of, what they are looking at.

This hope leads both men to the thought that there must be some purificatory askesis which can render them fit for intercourse with something Wholly Other – for impregnation by the Form of the Good, for example, or for Openness to Being. This thought is obviously an important part of the Western tradition, and it has obvious analogues (and perhaps sources) in the East. That is why Heidegger is the twentieth-century Western thinker most frequently "put into dialogue" with Eastern philosophy.[6] Such Heideggerian themes as the need to put aside the relations between beings and beings, to escape from busy-ness, to become receptive to the splendor of the simple, are easy to find in the East.

But there are other elements in Western thought, the elements which Heidegger despised, which are much harder to put into dialogue with anything in the East. In particular, as I shall be saying in more detail shortly, there is the novel – a Rabelaisian response to the ascetic priests. So, insofar as we philosophers become content either with a dialogue between Plato and the East or with one between Heidegger and the East, we may be taking the easy way out of the problems of intercultural comparison. Insofar as we concentrate on philosophy, we may find ourselves concentrating on a certain specific human type which can be counted upon to appear in *any* culture – the ascetic priest, the person who wants to set himself apart from his fellow humans by making contact with what he calls his "true self" or "Being" or "Brahman" or "Nothingness."

All of us philosophers have at least a bit of the ascetic priest in us. We all hanker after essence and share a taste for theory as opposed to narrative. If we did not, we should probably have gone into some other line of work. So we have to be careful not to let this taste seduce us into the presumption that, when it comes to other cultures, only our counterparts, those with tastes similar to our own, are reliable sources of information. We should stay alert to the possibility that comparative philosophy not only is not a royal road to intercultural comparison, but may even be a distraction from such comparison. For it may turn out that we are really comparing nothing more than the adaptations of a single transcultural character type to different environments.

Those who embody this character type are always trying to wash the language of their respective tribes off their tongues. The ascetic priest finds this language *vicious*, in Sartre's sense. His ambition is to get above, or past, or out of, what can be said in language. His

---

6　See, for example, Graham Parkes, ed., *Heidegger and Asian Thought* (Honolulu: University of Hawaii Press, 1987). As what I say below makes clear, I have doubts about Parkes' claim (p. 2) that "Heidegger's claim to be the first Western thinker to have overcome the tradition should be taken more seriously if his thought can be brought to resonate deeply with ideas that arose in totally foreign cultural milieux, couched in more or less alien languages, over two millennia ago." This resonance can also be taken as a sign of regression rather than of transcendence – as a way of returning to the womb rather than a way of overcoming.

goal is always the ineffable. Insofar as he is forced to use language, he wants a language which either gives a purer sense to the words of the tribe or, better yet, a language entirely disengaged from the business of the tribe, irrelevant to the mere pursuit of pleasure and avoidance of pain. Only such a person can share Nietzsche's and Heidegger's contempt for the people whom Nietzsche called "the last men." Only he can see the point of Heidegger's disdainful remark that the greatest disaster – the spread of the wasteland, *die Verwüstung der Erde*, understood as the forgetfulness of Being – may "easily go hand in hand with a guaranteed living standard for all men, and with a uniform state of happiness for all men."[7] Ascetic priests have no patience with people who think that mere happiness or mere decrease of suffering might compensate for *Seinvergessenheit*, for an inability to be in touch with something Wholly Other.

My description of the ascetic priest is deliberately pejorative and gendered. I am sketching a portrait of a phallocentric obsessive, someone whose attitude toward women typically resembles Socrates' attitude when he was asked whether there are Forms of hair and mud. Such a person shares Nietzsche's endlessly repeated desire for, above all else, cleanliness. He also shares Heidegger's endlessly repeated desire for simplicity. He has the same attitude toward sexual as to economic commerce: he finds it *messy*. So he is inclined both to keep women in their traditional subordinate place, out of sight and out of mind, and to favor a caste system which ranks the manly warriors, who bathe frequently, above the smelly traders in the bazaar. But the warrior is, of course, outranked by the priest – who bathes even more frequently and is still manlier. The priest is manlier because what is important is not the fleshly phallus but the immaterial one – the one which penetrates through the veil of appearances and makes contact with true reality, reaches the light at the end of the tunnel in a way that the warrior never can.

It is easy, with the help of people like Rabelais, Nietzsche, Freud, and Derrida, to make such seekers after ineffability and immateriality sound obnoxious. But to do them justice, we should remind ourselves that ascetic priests are very *useful* people. It is unlikely that there would have been much high culture in either West or East if there had not been a lot of ascetic priests in each place. For the result of trying to find a language different from the tribe's is to enrich the language of later generations of the tribe. The more ascetic priests a society can afford to support, the more surplus value is available to provide these priests with the leisure to fantasize, the richer and more diverse the language and projects of that society are likely to become. The spin-offs from private projects of purification turn out to have enormous social utility. Ascetic priests are often not much fun to be around, and usually are useless if what you are interested in is happiness, but they have been the traditional vehicles of linguistic novelty, the means by which a culture is able to have a future interestingly different from its past. They have

---

7   See Heidegger, *What Is Called Thinking?* p. 30 (*Was Heisst Denken?* p. 11). Heidegger goes on to say that Nietzsche's words *die Wüste wächst* "come from another realm than the appraisals of our age" (*ays einem anderen Ort als die gaengigen Beurteilungen unserer Zeit*). For another passage which brushes aside happiness as beneath the Thinker's consideration, see *The Question Concerning Technology*, trans. by W. Lovitt (New York: Harper and Row, 1977), p. 65 (*Holzwege* [Frankfurt: Klustermann, 1972], p. 204): "Metaphysics is history's open space wherein it becomes a destining that the suprasensory world, the Ideas, God, the moral law, the authority of reason, progress, the happiness of the greatest number, culture, civilization, suffer the loss of their constructive force and become void."

enabled cultures to change themselves, to break out of tradition into a previously unimagined future.

My purpose in this essay, however, is not to arrive at a final, just evaluation either of Heidegger in particular or of ascetic priests in general. Instead, it is to develop an antithesis between the ascetic taste for theory, simplicity, structure, abstraction, and essence and the novelist's taste for narrative, detail, diversity, and accident. From now on, I shall be preaching a sermon on the following text from Kundera's *The Art of the Novel:*

> The novel's wisdom is different from that of philosophy. The novel is born not of the theoretical spirit but of the spirit of humor. One of Europe's major failures is that it never understood the most European of the arts – the novel; neither its spirit, nor its great knowledge and discoveries, or the autonomy of its history. The art inspired by God's laughter does not by nature serve ideological certitudes, it contradicts them. Like Penelope, it undoes each night the tapestry that the theologians, philosophers and learned men have woven the day before.
>
> …I do not feel qualified to debate those who blame Voltaire for the gulag. But I do feel qualified to say: The eighteenth century is not only the century of Rousseau, of Voltaire, of Holbach; it is also (perhaps above all!) the age of Fielding, Sterne, Goethe, Laclos.[8]

The first moral I draw from this passage is that we should stay on the lookout, when we survey other cultures, for the rise of new genres – genres which arise in reaction to, and as an alternative to, the attempt to *theorize* about human affairs. We are likely to get more interesting, and more practically useful, East–West comparisons if we supplement dialogues between our respective theoretical traditions with dialogues between our respective traditions of antitheory. In particular, it would help us Western philosophers get our bearings in the East if we could identify some Eastern cultural traditions which made fun of Eastern philosophy. The kind of fun I have in mind is not the in-house kind which we philosophers make of one another (for example, the kind of fun which Plato makes of Protagoras, Hume of natural theology, Kierkegaard of Hegel, or Derrida of Heidegger). It is rather that made by people who either could not follow a philosophical argument if they tried, or by people who have no wish to try. We need to be on the look-out not just for Japanese Heideggers, Indian Platos, and Chinese Humes, but for Chinese Sternes and Indonesian Rabelaises. I am too ignorant to know whether there *are* any people of the latter sort, but I hope and trust that there are. Somewhere in the East there *must* have been people who enjoyed unweaving the tapestries which the saints and sages had woven.

The need to unweave these tapestries can be thought of as the revenge of the vulgar upon the priests' indifference to the greatest happiness of the greatest number. This indifference is illustrated by the way in which Horkheimer and Adorno look for a dialectic of Enlightenment which will permit them to weave *Candide* into the same patter as Auschwitz, the way in which they allow contemplation of that pattern to convince them that Enlightenment hopes were vain. It is also illustrated by the way in which Heidegger blurs the distinction between automobile factories and death camps. We philosophers not only want to see dialectical patterns invisible to the vulgar, we want these patterns to be clues to the outcomes of world-historical dramas. For all our ascetism, we want to see

8   Kundera, *The Art of the Novel*, trans. by Linda Asher (New York: Grove Press, 1986), p. 160.

ourselves, and people like ourselves, as engaged in something more than merely private projects. We want to relate our private obsessions, our private fantasies of purity, novelty, and autonomy, to something larger than ourselves, something with causal power, something hidden and underlying which secretly determines the course of human affairs.[9]

From Kundera's point of view, the philosopher's essentialistic approach to human affairs, his attempt to substitute contemplation, dialectic, and destiny for adventure, narrative, and change, is a disingenuous way of saying: what matters for me takes precedence over what matters for you, entitles me to ignore what matters to you, because I am in touch with something – reality – with which you are not. The novelist's rejoinder to this is: it is comical to believe that one human being is more in touch with something nonhuman than another human being. It is comical to use one's quest for the ineffable Other as an excuse for ignoring other people's quite different quests. It is comical to think that *anyone* could transcend the quest for happiness, to think that any theory could be more than a means to happiness, that there is something called Truth which transcends pleasure and pain. The novelist sees us as Voltaire saw Leibniz, as Swift saw the scientists of Laputa, and as Orwell saw Marxist theoreticians – as comic figures. What is comic about us is that we make ourselves unable to see things which everybody else can see – things like decreased suffering and increased happiness – by convincing ourselves that these things are "mere appearance."

The novelist's substitute for the appearance-reality distinction is a display of diversity of points of view, a plurality of descriptions of the same events. What the novelist finds especially comic is the attempt to privilege one of these descriptions, to take it as an excuse for ignoring all the others. What he or she finds most heroic is not the ability sternly to reject all descriptions save one, but rather the ability to move back and forth between them. I take this to be the point Kundera is making when he says:

> It is precisely in losing the certainty of truth and the unanimous agreement of others that man becomes an individual. The novel is the imaginary paradise of individuals. It is the territory where no one possesses the truth, neither Anna nor Karenin, but where everyone has the right to be understood, both Anna and Karenin.[10]

Kundera is here making the term "the novel" roughly synonymous with "the democratic utopia" – with an imaginary future society in which nobody dreams of thinking that God, or the Truth, or the Nature of Things, is on her or his side. In such a utopia nobody would dream of thinking that there is something more real than pleasure or pain, or that there is a duty laid upon us which transcends the search for happiness. A democratic utopia would be a community in which tolerance and curiosity, rather than truth-seeking, are the chief intellectual virtues. It would be one in which there is nothing remotely approximating a state religion or a state philosophy. In such a community, all that is left of philosophy is the maxim of Mill's *On Liberty*, or of a Rabelaisian carnival: everybody can do what they want if they don't hurt anybody else while doing it. As Kundera says, "The world of one single Truth and the relative ambiguous world of the novel are molded of entirely different substances."

---

9   I discuss this urge, with reference to Heidegger, on pp. 107 f. and 119 f. of my *Contingency, Irony and Solidarity* (Cambridge: Cambridge University Press, 1989).

10   Kundera, *The Art of the Novel*, p. 159.

One can, if one likes, see Kundera and Heidegger as trying to overcome a common enemy: the tradition of Western metaphysics, the tradition which hints at the One True Description that exhibits the underlying pattern behind apparent diversity. But there is a big difference between what the two men propose as an alternative to this tradition. For Heidegger the opposite of metaphysics is Openness to Being, something most easily achieved in a pretechnological peasant community with unchanging customs. Heidegger's utopia is pastoral, a sparsely populated valley in the mountains, a valley in which life is given shape by its relationship to the primordial Fourfold – earth, sky, man, and gods. Kundera's utopia is carnivalesque, Dickensian, a crowd of eccentrics rejoicing in each other's idiosyncracies, curious for novelty rather nostalgic for primordiality. The bigger, more varied, and more boisterous the crowd the better. For Heidegger, the way to overcome the urge to domination is to take a step back and to see the West and its history of power plays from afar, as the sage sees the Wheel of Life from afar. For Kundera the way to overcome the urge to domination is to realize that everybody has and always will have this urge, but to insist that nobody is more or less justified in having it than anybody else. Nobody stands for the truth, or for Being, or for Thinking. Nobody stands for *anything* Other or Higher. We all just stand for ourselves, equal inhabitants of a paradise of individuals in which everybody has the right to be understood but nobody has the right to rule.

Kundera summarizes his attitude toward the ascetic priest when he says:

> Man desires a world where good and evil can be clearly distinguished, for he has an innate and irrepressible desire to judge before he understands. Religions and ideologies are founded on this desire. … They require that somebody be right: either Anna Karenina is the victim of a narrow-minded tyrant, or Karenin is the victim of an immoral woman; either K. is an innocent man crushed by an unjust Court, or the Court represents divine justice and K. is guilty.

> This "either-or" encapsulates an inability to tolerate the essential relativity of things human, an inability to look squarely at the absence of the Supreme Judge.[11]

Kundera, in a brief allusion to Heidegger, politely interprets his term "forgetfulness of Being" as forgetfulness of this essential relativity.[12] But Heidegger never, even in his early "pragmatist" phase,[13] believed in essential relativity in Kundera's sense of the term. Heidegger's genre is the lyric, not the novel; his hero is Hölderlin, not Rabelais or Cervantes. For Heidegger the other human beings exist for the sake of the Thinker and the Poet. Where there is a Thinker or a Poet, there human life is justified, for there something Wholly Other touches and is touched. Where there is not, the wasteland spreads.

---

11   Ibid., p. 7.

12   Ibid., p. 5. Here, at the beginning of his book, Kundera thinks of Husserl's *Lebenswelt* and Heidegger's *In-der-West-Sein* as standing over against "the one-sided nature of the European sciences, which reduced the world to a mere object of technical and mathematical investigation," and casually assimilates both to his own notion of "the essential relativity of human affairs." But this assimilation is overly polite, and misleading. Husserl and Heidegger were insistent on getting down to the basic, underlying structure of the *Lebenswelt*, or of *In-der-Welt-Sein*. For Kundera, we make up this structure as we go along.

13   See Mark Okrent, *Heidegger's Pragmatism* (Ithaca: Cornell University Press, 1988), for an account of Heidegger's career that distinguishes the pragmatism, the emphasis on *Vorwurf* and *Bezuglichkeit*, in *Sein und Zeit* from the post-*Kehre* quietism.

Whereas for Heidegger there are certain moments in certain lives which both redeem history and permit history to be encapsulated, for Kundera the thing to do with history is to keep it going, to throw oneself into it. But this throwing oneself into history is not the sort which is recommended by the ideological revolutionary. It is not a matter of replacing Tradition with Reason or Error with Truth. Kundera thinks that if we want to know what went wrong with the expectations of the Enlightenment we should read Flaubert rather than Horkheimer and Adorno. He says:

> Flaubert discovered stupidity. I daresay that is the greatest discovery of a century so proud of its scientific thought. Of course, even before Flaubert, people knew stupidity existed, but they understood it somewhat differently: it was considered a simple absence of knowledge, a defect correctable by education. Flaubert's vision of stupidity is this: Stupidity does not give way to science, technology, modernity, progress; on the contrary, it progresses right along with progress![14]

I take Kundera to be saying that the Enlightenment was wrong in hoping for an age without stupidity. The thing to hope for is, instead, an age in which the prevalent varieties of stupidity will cause less unnecessary pain than is caused in our age by our varieties of stupidity. To every age its own glory and its own stupidity. The job of the novelist is to keep us up to date on both. Because there is no Supreme Judge and no One Right Description, because there is no escape to a Wholly Other, this is the most important possible job. But it is a job which can only be undertaken with a whole heart by someone who is untroubled by dreams of an ahistorical framework within which human history is enacted, a universal human nature by reference to which history can be explained, or a far-off divine event toward which history moves. To appreciate the essential relativity of human affairs, in Kundera's sense, is to give up the last traces of the ascetic priest's attempt to escape from time and change, the last traces of the attempt to see us as actors in a drama already written before we came on the scene. Heidegger thought that he could escape from metaphysics, from the idea of a Single Truth, by historicizing Being and Truth. He thought that he could escape Platonic escapism by telling a story about the *Ereignis* which was the West, rather than about *Sein*. But from Kundera's point of view Heidegger's attempt was just one more attempt to escape from time and chance, though this time an escape into historicity rather than into eternity. For Kundera, eternity and historicity are equally comic, equally essentialist, notions.

The difference between Kundera's and Heidegger's reaction to the Western metaphysical tradition comes out best in their attitude toward closure. It is as important for Kundera to see the Western adventure as open-ended – to envisage forever new sorts of novels, recording strange new joys and ingenious new stupidities – as it is for Heidegger to insist that the West has exhausted its possibilities. This comes out in Kundera's insistence that the novel does not have a *nature*, but *only* a history, that the novel is a "sequence of discoveries."[15] There is no Platonic Form for the novel as a genre to live up to, no essential structure which some novels exhibit better than others, any more than there exists such a Form or such a structure for human beings. The novel can no more exhaust its possibilities than human beings can exhaust their hope for happiness. As Kundera says,

14   Ibid., p. 162.
15   Ibid., p. 14.

"The only context for grasping the novel's worth is the history of the European novel. The novelist need answer to no one but Cervantes."[16]

The same point emerges when Kundera insists that the history of the novel and of Europe cannot be judged by the actual political future of Europe – or by the actual fate, whatever it may be, of the West. In particular, the West blowing itself up with its own bombs should not be read as a judgment on the novel, or on Europe – nor should the coming of an endless totalitarian night. To do so would be like judging a human life by reference to some ludicrous accident which ends it violently, or like judging Western technology by reference to Auschwitz. As Kundera says:

> Once upon a time I too thought that the future was the only competent judge of our works and actions. Later on I understood that chasing after the future is the worst conformism of all, a craven flattery of the mighty. For the future is always mightier than the present. It will pass judgment upon us, of course. But without any competence.

Kundera continues:

> But if the future is not a value for me, then to what am I attached? To God? Country? The people? The individual?

> My answer is as ridiculous as it is sincere. I am attached to nothing but the depreciated legacy of Cervantes.[17]

Kundera's phrase "paradise of individuals" has an obvious application to Dickens, because the most celebrated and memorable feature of his novels is the unsubsumable, uncategorizable idiosyncracy of the characters. Dickens' characters resist being subsumed under moral typologies, being described as exhibiting these virtues and those vices. Instead, the names of Dickens' characters *take the place* of moral principles and of lists of virtues and vices. They do so by permitting us to describe each other as "a Skimpole," "a Mr. Pickwick," "a Gradgrind," "a Mrs. Jellaby," "a Florence Dombey." In a moral world based on what Kundera calls "the wisdom of the novel" moral comparisons and judgments would be made with the help of proper names rather than general terms or general principles. A society which took its moral vocabulary from novels rather than from ontotheological or ontico-moral treatises would not ask itself questions about human nature, the point of human existence, or the meaning of human life. Rather, it would ask itself what we can do so as to get along with each other, how we can arrange things so as to be comfortable with one another, how institutions can be changed so that everyone's right to be understood has a better chance of being gratified.

To those who share Nietzsche's sense that the "last men" give off a bad smell, it will be ludicrous to suggest that *comfort* is the goal of human social organization and moral reflection. But this suggestion would not have seemed ludicrous to Dickens. That is why Dickens has been anathematized by Marxists and other ascetic priests as a "bourgeois reformer." The term "bourgeois" is the Marxist equivalent of Nietzsche's term "last man" – it stands for everything which the ascetic priest wants to wash off. For Marxism, like Platonism and Heideggerianism, wants more for human beings than comfort. It wants transformation,

16   Ibid., p. 144.
17   Ibid., p. 20.

transformation according to a single universal plan; Marxists are continually envisaging what they call "new socialist man." Dickens did not want anybody to be transformed, except in one respect: he wanted everyone to notice and understand the people he or she passed on the street. He wanted people not to make each other uncomfortable by apply-ing moral labels, but to recognize that all their fellow humans – Dombey and Mrs. Dombey, Anna and Karenin, K. and the Lord Chancellor – had a right to be understood.

Despite having no higher goal than comfortableness of human association, Dickens did an enormous amount for equality and freedom. The last line of Swift's self-written epitaph – "Imitate him if you dare: he served human liberty"[18] – would do for Dickens' tablet as well. But Dickens performed his services to human liberty not with the help of the "savage indignation" which Swift rightly ascribed to himself but with something more bourgeois – sentimental tears and what Orwell called "generous anger." Dickens strikes us as a more bourgeois writer than the man who described the Yahoos because he is more comfortable with, and hopeful for, human beings. One indication of this comfortableness is the fact on which Orwell remarked in the following passage:

> In *Oliver Twist, Hard Times, Bleak House, Little Dorrit*, Dickens attacked English institutions with a ferocity that has never since been approached. Yet he managed to do it without mak-ing himself hated, and, more than this, the very people he attacked have swallowed him so completely that he has become a national institution himself.[19]

The important point is that Dickens did not make himself hated. I take it that this was partly because he did not attack anything as abstract as "humanity as such," or the age or the society in which he lived, but rather concrete cases of particular people ignoring the suffering of other particular people. He was thus able to speak as "one of us" – as the voice of one who happened to notice something to which the rest of us could be counted upon to react with similar indignation as soon as we notice it.[20]

---

18   Yeats' translation of Swift's "… *imitare si poteris, strenuum pro virili libertatis vindicem*."
19   George Orwell, *Collected Essays, Journalism and Letters*, vol. 1 (Harmondsworth: Penguin, 1968), pp. 414–415. In his illuminating *The Politics of Literary Reputation: The Making and Claiming of 'St. George' Orwell* (Oxford: Oxford University Press, 1989), John Rodden has noted both that Orwell in this essay "directly identified himself with Dickens" (p. 181) and that the identification worked, in the sense that "What Orwell wrote of Dickens [in the last sentence of the passage I have quoted] soon applied to himself" (p. 22). One facet of the identification was the patriotism common to the two men – a sense of identification with England and its history which trumped any theory about the place of England in universal history. From the theorist's point of view, patriotism is invariably suspicious, as is any loyalty to a mere sector of space-time. But for people like Orwell, Dickens, and Kundera, the only substitute for patriotism is attachment to some other spatiotemporal sector, to the history of something which is not a country – e.g., the history of the European novel, "the depreciated legacy of Cervantes."
20   Orwell, in *Collected Essays*, vol. 1, p. 460, says that "Even the millionaire suffers from a vague sense of guilt, like a dog eating a stolen leg of mutton. Nearly everyone, regardless of what his conduct may be, responds emotionally to the idea of human brotherhood. Dickens voiced a code which was and on the whole still is believed in, even by people who violate it. It is difficult oth-erwise to explain why he could be both read by working people (a thing that has happened to no other novelist of his stature) and buried in Westminister Abbey." If one had asked Dickens whether he had thought that ideal and that code inherent in human nature, or rather an historically

Dickens was, as Orwell says, "a good-tempered antinomian," a phrase which would apply equally to Rabelais, Montaigne, or Cervantes, but hardly to Luther or Voltaire or Marx. So I take "generous anger" to mean something like "anger which is without malignity because it assumes that the evil has merely to be noticed to be remedied." This was the kind of anger later found in Harriet Beecher Stowe and Martin Luther King, but not the kind of anger found in the ascetic priests. For the latter believe that social change is not a matter of mutual adjustment but of re-creation – that to make things better we must create a new kind of human being, one who is aware of reality rather than appearance. Their anger is *ungenerous* in the sense that it is aimed not at a lack of understanding of particular people by other particular people but rather at an ontological deficit common either to people in general or, at least, to all those of the present age. The generosity of Dickens', Stowe's, and King's anger comes out in their assumption that people merely need to turn their eyes toward those who are getting hurt and notice the *details* of the pain being suffered, rather than need to have their entire cognitive apparatus restructured.

As an empirical claim, this assumption is often falsified. As a moral attitude, it marks the difference between people who tell stories and people who construct theories about that which lies beyond our present imagination, because beyond our present language. I think that when Orwell identified a capacity for generous anger as the mark of "a free intelligence," he was adumbrating the same sort of opposition between the theorist and the novelist which I am trying to develop in this essay. Earlier I said that theorists like Heidegger saw narrative as always a second-best, a propaedeutic, to a grasp of something deeper than the visible detail, the true meaning behind the familiar and commonplace one. Novelists like Orwell and Dickens are inclined to see theory as always a second-best, never more than a reminder for a particular purpose, the purpose of telling a story better. I suggest that the history of social change in the modern West shows that the latter conception of the relation between narrative and theory is the more fruitful.

To say that it is more fruitful is just to say that, when you weigh the good and the bad that the social novelists have done against the good and the bad that the social theorists have done, you find yourself wishing that there had been more novels and fewer theories. You wish that the leaders of successful revolutions had read fewer books which gave them general ideas and more books which gave them an ability to identify imaginatively with those whom they were to rule. When you read books like Kolakowski's history of Marxism, you understand why the Party theoretician, the man responsible for the "correct ideological line," has always been, apart from the maximum leader himself, the most feared and hated member of the Central Committee. This may remind you that Guzman, the leader of the quasi-Maoist Sendero Luminoso movement in Peru, wrote his dissertation on Kant. It may also remind you that Heidegger's response to the imprisonment of his Social Democratic colleagues in 1933 came down to "Don't bother me with petty details."

The important thing about novelists as compared with theorists is that they are good at details. This is another reason why Dickens is a useful paradigm of the novel. To quote Orwell again, "The outstanding, unmistakable mark of Dickens' writing is the *unnecessary detail*"; "He is all fragments, all details – rotten architecture, but wonderful gargoyles – and never better than when he is building up some character who will

---

contingent development, he would presumably have replied that he neither knew nor cared. That is the kind of question which "the wisdom of the novel" rejects as without interest or point.

later on be forced to act inconsistently."[21] If we make Dickens paradigmatic of the West, as I hope my fantasized Africans and Asians would, then we shall see what was most instructive about the recent history of the West in its increased ability to tolerate diversity. Viewed another way, this is an increased ability to treat apparent inconsistency not as something to be rejected as unreal or as evil, but as a mark of the inadequacy of our current vocabularies of explanation and adjudication.[22] This change in our treatment of apparent inconsistency is correlated with an increasing ability to be comfortable with a variety of different sorts of people, and therefore with an increasing ability to leave people alone to follow their own lights. This willingness is reflected in the rise of pluralistic bourgeois democracies, societies in which politics becomes a matter of sentimental calls for alleviation of suffering rather than of moral calls to greatness.

It may seem strange to attribute this sort of willingness to the recent West – a culture often said, with excellent reason, to be racist, sexist, and imperialist. But it is of course also a culture which is very *worried* about being racist, sexist, and imperialist, as well as about being Euro-centric, parochial, and intellectually intolerant. It is a culture which has become very conscious of its capacity for murderous intolerance and thereby perhaps more wary of intolerance, more sensitive to the desirability of diversity, than any other of which we have record. I have been suggesting that we Westerners owe this consciousness and this sensitivity more to our novelists than to our philosophers or to our poets.

When tolerance and comfortable togetherness become the watchwords of a society, one should no longer hope for world-historical greatness. If such greatness – radical difference from the past, a dazzlingly unimaginable future – is what one wants, ascetic priests like Plato, Heidegger, and Suslov will fill the bill. But if it is not, novelists like Cervantes, Dickens, and Kundera may suffice.[23] Because philosophy as a genre is closely associated with the quest for such greatness – with the attempt to focus all one's thoughts into a single narrow beam and send them out beyond the bounds of all that has been previously thought – it is among the *philosophers* of the West that contemporary Western self-hatred is most prevalent. It must be tempting for Africans and Asians – the principal victims of Western imperialism and racism – to see this self-hatred as about what the West deserves. But I would suggest that we take this self-hatred as just one more symptom of the old familiar quest for purity which runs through the annals of the ascetic priesthood in both East and West. If we set these annals to one side, we may have a better chance of finding something distinctive in the West which the East can use, and conversely.

21   These two quotes are from Orwell, *Collected Essays*, vol. 1, pp. 450 and 454, respectively.
22   I have argued elsewhere ("Freud and Moral Deliberation," in *The Pragmatist's Freud*, ed. Smith and Kerrigan (Johns Hopkins University Press, 1986)) that the increased popularity of Freudian explanations of untoward actions is an example of this changed attitude toward apparent inconsistency.
23   Byron is a good example of someone who saw the rising stock of tolerance and comfortableness as endangering the possibility of greatness. As my colleague Jerome McGann has pointed out to me, he took out this exasperation on, among other people, Cervantes: "Cervantes smiled Spain's chivalry away;/A single laugh demolished the right arm/Of his own country; – seldom since that day/Has Spain had heroes" (*Don Juan*, XIII, 11). I have not said much about the poetry–novel contrast (as opposed to the philosophy–novel contrast) in this essay, but I would suggest that there is as much difference between Byron and Dickens as between either and Heidegger. That is why literature-vs.-philosophy is too coarse-grained a contrast to be useful. Mill and Dickens, or Farrell and Dewey, are closer to each other than Dickens is to Proust, or Byron to Hölderlin.

18

De Man and the American Cultural Left

Paul de Man was one of the most beloved and influential teachers of recent times. He was the person primarily responsible for the movement which we now call "deconstruction." The special twist which de Man put on certain Heideggerian and Derridean themes has been the single most influential contribution to what is sometimes called, by its enemies, "the politicization of the humanities" in American universities. De Man's interpretations of these men's work laid the foundation for the attempt, widespread among American academics in recent years, to reinvigorate leftist social criticism by deploying new philosophico-literary weapons. This attempt is central to the activities of what Henry Gates has called "the American Cultural Left," defined by him as "a Rainbow Coalition" of deconstructionists, feminists, people working in gay and ethnic studies, and so on.

Members of the Cultural Left typically believe that we have recently acquired a radically new understanding of the nature of language and of literature. They think that this shift is comparable in importance to the shift from Aristotelian to Galilean mechanics, and that it has similarly important moral and political consequences. For the Cultural Left, "reading" – in the special sense which de Man gave to that term – has become a watchword in the same way that "scientific method" was a watchword in the 1920s and 1930s. In that period, everyone from H.G. Wells to John Dewey was telling us that life and politics would become better if only we could adopt the attitude and the habits of the natural scientist. We are now being told the same sort of thing about the attitude and habits of the literary critic. For example, J. Hillis Miller, one of de Man's closest friends and followers, has said that "the millenium [of universal peace and justice among men] would come if all men and women became good readers in de Man's sense."[1]

To see how Miller could be led to say such a thing, consider the following passages from de Man. In his 1967 essay "Criticism and Crisis" de Man says:

> the statement about language, that sign and meaning can never coincide, is what is precisely taken for granted in the kind of language called literary. Literature, unlike everyday language,

"De Man and the American Cultural Left," pp.129–39 in Richard M Rorty, *Essays on Heidegger and Others: Philosophical Papers*, vol. 2 (New York, 1991), © 1991 by Cambridge University Press. Reprinted with the permission of Cambridge University Press.

1   J. Hillis Miller, *The Ethics of Reading* (New York: Columbia University Press, 1987), p. 58.

begins on the far side of this knowledge; it is the only form of language free from the fallacy of unmediated expression.[2]

Slightly later in the same essay, de Man identifies freedom from the fallacy of unmediated expression with the discovery "of desire as a fundamental pattern of being that discards any possibility of satisfaction." The consciousness that results from this discovery, de Man continues,

> consists of the presence of a nothingness. Poetic language names this void with ever-renewed understanding and … it never tires of naming it again. This persistent naming is what we call literature.[3]

To see the point of these passages, one needs to see what de Man means by "the fallacy of unmediated expression," the fallacy of thinking that "sign and meaning can coincide." Committing this fallacy is roughly the same thing as being what Derrida calls "logocentric." Logocentrists believe that language sometimes accurately represents something nonlinguistic, that sometimes sign and meaning coincide, in the sense that the sign perfectly represents something else – its meaning. The meaning, in turn, is a thought in somebody's mind which itself may perfectly represent something nonmental. For logocentrists, language is at its best when it is perfectly transparent to reality – "identical with its object," as Aristotle and Hegel put it.

Those who do not commit the fallacy of unmediated expression discard these metaphors of transparency and identity and accept Saussure's claim that language is a "play of differences." They believe that signs have meaning by virtue of their relations to other signs – relations of similarity and dissimilarity, rather than by their coincidence with something mental. They further believe that all thought is in language, so that thoughts too have meaning only by virtue of their relations to other thoughts. For antilogocentrists, therefore, truth is not a matter of transparency to, or correspondence with, reality, but rather a matter of relating thoughts or signs to one another.

Antilogocentrism is a special case of antiessentialism, of the radical holism common to Wittgenstein, Quine, Dewey, Davidson, and Derrida. Logocentrism is simply essentialism as applied to sentences and beliefs. Once one drops the essentialist idea that things have both intrinsic and relational properties – properties which they have "in themselves" and properties which they have merely in relation to, e.g., human desires and interests – then a Saussurian notion of language and a Davidsonian antirepresentationalist account of knowledge follow naturally. To claim that language is a play of differences, with Saussure, is just to say, with Wittgenstein, that the meaning of a word is its use in the language, and to add with Quine that the unit of empirical significance is the whole of science. One can generalize Quine's and Wittgenstein's points by saying that the significance of a sentence, like that of a belief or a desire, is its place in a web of other sentences, or beliefs or desires. To say this is to emphasize the context-sensitivity of signs and of thoughts – to treat them not as quasi-things but as nodes in a web of relations. But that is simply to describe them as antiessentialists wish *everything* – tables, quarks, people, social institutions – to be described.

2   Paul de Man, *Blindness and Insight,* 2nd ed. (Minneapolis: University of Minnesota Press, 1983), p. 17.
3   Ibid., p. 18.

De Man puts his own special twist on Derridean polemic against logocentrism and on antiessentialist redescriptions when he says, in an essay on Derrida's interpretation of Rousseau, that "Rousseau escapes from the logocentric fallacy precisely to the extent that his language is *literary*."[4] De Man thinks that literature has *always* been antiessentialist. For him, culture has always been divided into two uses of language: the literary use of language in which language reveals its true, relational nature, on the one hand, and commonsensical, scientific, and philosophical uses of language on the other. The latter uses of language *conceal* this nature.

This startling claim that literature has always been making a philosophical point connects with de Man's claim that literature has always offered us a way of living which "discards any possibility of satisfaction."[5] For de Man, the fact that language is a play of relations is just one more example of the more general fact that desire is, in its inmost nature, unsatisfiable. That is why he says that the attempt to "do away with literature" is the attempt to avoid facing "the nothingness of human things."[6] Here de Man echoes Sartre's claim that "man is a futile passion" – futile because he is the being who has no essence but who nevertheless insists on attributing an essence to himself. De Man shares Sartre's sense of human life as a perpetual oscillation. At one pole of this oscillation is the desire to attain a God's-eye view, to incarnate the very logos of reality, internalize the intrinsic nature of things. At the other pole is the thought that this attempt is impossible because there is no such logos and no such nature. What is original with de Man is the claim that the sense of the "nothingness of human things," of the impossibility of realizing the central human desire – has always been evident in what he calls "literary language." For de Man, literature has always hinted at what Nietzsche, Heidegger, Sartre, and Derrida have now made philosophically explicit; that instead of thinking of ourselves, logocentrically, as *knowers*, we must now think of ourselves as confronting a void – an abyss which cannot be known but can only, in de Man's words, be "named with ever-renewed understanding." Instead of thinking of ourselves as living according to the constraints set by the nature of physical reality and the dictates of moral imperatives, we must think of ourselves as "[unable] to escape from a condition that is felt to be unbearable." It is, de Man says, the "distinctive character of literature" to make this inability manifest.[7]

The sort of pluralist and pragmatic antiessentialism which I take over from Dewey agrees with all of de Man's antilogocentric, Derridean premises, but denies that they entail his existentialist, Sartrean conclusions. We pragmatists do not see the end of logocentrism or the death of God as requiring us to adopt a new self-image. For us, no argumentative roads lead from antiessentialist philosophy to the choice of such an image. Nor do any argumentative roads lead from this kind of philosophy to any particular brand of politics. The absence of an intrinsic human nature, and thus of built-in moral obligations, seems to us pragmatists compatible with any and every decision about what sort of life to lead, or what sort of politics to pursue. The repudiation of the traditional logocentric image of the human being as Knower does not seem to us to entail that we face an abyss, but merely that we face a range of choices.

4 Ibid., p. 138.
5 Ibid., p. 17.
6 Ibid., p. 18.
7 Ibid., p. 162.

Sartre's point that we have a tendency to repudiate and evade this freedom of choice is perfectly just, but there is no reason to think that when we recognize this tendency we have thereby discovered the nature of what it is to be human. On a pragmatist view, antiessentialists like Sartre and de Man should not turn essentialist at the last moment by claiming to have discovered such a nature. Sartre should not have said "Man's essence is to have no essence," but should have confined himself to saying "Human beings no more have an essence than anything else does." De Man should not have assimilated the Saussurian-Derridean antiessentialist account of how signs function to the claim that desire "as such" is intrinsically unsatisfiable, that this unsatisfiability is the *essence* of desire. Some desires are satisfiable and some are not. The *logocentrists'* desires may not be satisfiable, but other people have other desires which are satisfiable: for example, the desire for individual self-creation and the desire for social justice.

Like Heidegger and Derrida, de Man treats the end of essentialism and logocentrism as an event of world-historical significance. We pragmatists treat it as merely the latest stage in a gradual and continuous shift in human beings' sense of their relation to the rest of the universe – a change which led from worshiping Gods to worshiping sages to worshiping empirical scientific inquirers. With luck, this process will end by leaving us unable to *worship* anything. But the resulting inability to love one thing with all one's heart, soul, and mind, will not entail the inability to rejoice in a lot of different things. It will not necessarily produce a condition we find unbearable, nor a void, nor an abyss. So we pragmatists see no reason to set up an altar to Literature – to the Dark God whose voice is in the literariness of language – on the spot where we once worshiped the radiant, effulgent Logos. Pragmatists would prefer to have no high altars, and instead just have lots of picture galleries, book displays, movies, concerts, ethnographic museums, museums of science and technology, and so on – lots of cultural options but no privileged central discipline or practice.

One reason we pragmatists have this preference is that we see the sort of cultural pluralism which rejects metaphors of centrality and depth as chiming with democratic politics – with the spirit of tolerance which has made constitutional democracies possible. We see this tolerance as saying that public policy and public institutions must be neutral on questions of what is central to human life, questions about the goal or point of human existence. Contemporary democratic societies are built around the assumption that we have to develop institutions which are suitable for people who have wildly different ideas on such topics – for example, worshipers of God, of science, of literature, and of nothing in particular.

Although we antiessentialists obviously cannot deduce the truth of antiessentialism from its suitability for democratic societies, much less claim that it is a necessary foundation for such societies, we do regard this suitability as a point in its favor. The American Cultural Left, however, influenced by Foucault as well as de Man, sees the contemporary democratic states, including our own, as either imperialist powers or disciplinary societies or both. They do not regard harmony between Dewey's antiessentialism and American institutions as a recommendation, for they do not think much of those institutions. They see philosophical views which suggest consensual, reformist politics of the sort Dewey favored as "complicit" with the "discourses of power" which are the invisible regulators of life in the bourgeois democracies. Just as the Marxists of the 1930s thought of Dewey as "the philosopher of American imperialism," so the contemporary Cultural Left views us pragmatists as at best socially irresponsible and at worst apologists for a repressive ideology.[8]

The contemporary American Cultural Left would like to recapture the drive and direction which the left of the 1930s thought that it had gotten from Marxism. Like that older left, our Cultural Left wants its own special talents and competences – the sorts of talents which suit one for philosophy, history, or literary criticism, and the sort of competences which one acquires through advanced study in such disciplines – to be directly applicable to political purposes. As Lentricchia puts it, leftists whose only political outlets are sit-ins, picketing, and the like "are being crushed by feelings of guilt and occupational alienation."[9]

For professors of literature who want a way of making their specialized skill and knowledge politically relevant, of getting leftist politics into their classrooms and their books, the writings of the later de Man are a godsend. Just as Sartre became disgusted by the apolitical tone of what he had written in the 1930s and 1940s, and proclaimed in 1960 that "existentialism is only an enclave within Marxism," so de Man, as he grew older and more influential, became sensitive to criticism of his work as merely a new aestheticism. In an essay published in 1982 he claimed that

> more than any other mode of inquiry, including economics, the linguistics of literariness is a powerful and indispensable tool in the unmasking of ideological aberrations, as well as a determining factor in accounting for their occurrence. Those who reproach literary theory for being oblivious to social and historical (that is to say ideological) reality are merely stating their fear at having their own ideological mystifications exposed by the tool they are trying to discredit.[10]

In an interview given the year before his death, de Man went a step further, claiming that the sort of close reading which he attempted and taught was *indispensable* to political thought. Then he said

> I have always maintained that one could approach the problems of ideology and by extension the problems of politics *only* [italics added] on the basis of critical-linguistic analysis.[11]

These two passages have set the theme for much of the writing of the American Cultural Left. This left has come to take for granted that what Lentricchia calls its sense of "occupational alienation" can in fact be overcome. It can be overcome because the

---

8   Frank Lentricchia, in his *Criticism and Social Change* (Chicago: University of Chicago Press, 1983) explains why leftist teachers of literature need to relate their academic work to their politics, and criticizes pragmatism as inadequate for their purposes. The criticisms of pragmatism which Lentricchia makes are typical of the American Cultural Left. Lentricchia sees my own work, e.g., as tending toward a "divorce of culture from political power" (p. 19), a claim echoed by Jonathan Culler, who says that the "complacency" of my pragmatism "seems altogether appropriate to the age of Reagan" (*Framing the Sign* [Norman, Okla.: University of Oklahoma Press, 1988], p. 55). (In later sections of his book however (particularly pp. 38–52), Lentricchia offers criticisms of de Man which parallel my own.)

9   Ibid., p. 7.

10   De Man, *The Resistance to Theory* (Minneapolis: University of Minnesota Press, 1986), p. 11.

11   Ibid., p. 121.

sort of thing one learns in graduate study in the humanities, and in particular in the study of literature, is precisely what is needed to enable one to "approach the problems of politics."

From a pragmatist point of view, there is a grain of truth in this claim, but only a grain. It is true that the study of literature sensitizes one to the way in which any phenomenon may be described in a lot of different ways. So readers of literature become aware of rhetoric, of the fact that what seems true will depend upon the interplay between the language used and an audience's expectations. Literary study helps one realize that today's literal and objective truth is just the corpse of yesterday's metaphor. Those who study and teach the history of literature are in a good position to see how the vocabularies of moral and political deliberation can be changed by the literary imagination, the way in which poets have occasionally functioned as unacknowledged legislators. In the course of their teaching, they can occasionally see deep changes taking place in the students' image of themselves or of their society. Witnessing such changes makes it easy for teachers of literature to take seriously Stephen Dedalus's desire "to forge in the smithy of my soul the uncreated conscience of my race." It also lets them understand that Lincoln was not just making a bad joke when he told Harriet Beecher Stowe that she had brought about the Civil War. Again, their role in promulgating and enforcing a literary canon makes it easy for them to see that such a canon can function as a repressive force – how decisions about which books to assign can make it harder for students to think about what is wrong with their previous socialization, and thus to think about what is wrong with their society.

Having granted all these points, however, we pragmatists still want to insist that what de Man says in the passages I have cited is absurd. It is just not the case that one has to have a Saussurian-Wittgensteinian-Derridean understanding of the nature of language in order to think clearly and usefully about politics. One does not have to be an antiessentialist in philosophy in order to be politically imaginative or politically useful. Philosophy is not *that* important for politics, nor is literature. Lots of people who accept theocentric or Kantian logocentric accounts of moral obligation unconsciously and uncritically – starting with Kant himself – have done very well at political thinking. They have been invaluable to social reform and progress. The same can be said of lots of essentialists – for example, all those people who still think that either natural or social science can change our self-image for the better by telling us what we really, essentially, intrinsically, are.

Even though we pragmatists commend our antiessentialism and antilogocentrism on the ground of its harmony with the practices and aims of a democratic society, we do not want to claim that accepting and applying such doctrines is *necessary* for overcoming social and economic repression. After all, a lot of such repression is so blatant and obvious that it does not take any great analytic skills or any great philosophical self-consciousness to see what is going on. It does not, for example, take any "critical-linguistic analysis" to notice that millions of children in American ghettos grew up without hope while the U.S. government was preoccupied with making the rich richer – with assuring a greedy and selfish middle class that it was the salt of the earth. Even economists, plumbers, insurance salesmen, and biochemists – people who have never read a text closely, much less deconstructed it – can recognize that the immiseration of much of Latin America is partially due to the deals struck between local plutocracies and North American banks and governments.

We pragmatists view the "critique of ideology" as an occasionally useful tactical weapon in social struggles, but as one among many others. We see no evidence to confirm de Man's claim that those familiar with "the linguistics of literariness" are likely to be more useful than, say, statisticians or muckraking journalists. Suggesting that this sort of linguistics is somehow central or essential to political thought seems to us like suggesting that, say, antisubmarine mines are central or essential to modern warfare. Only an admiral who had spent too long in the bureau that lets contracts for new kinds of mines would make the latter claim. Only a professor of literature suffering from a really extreme case of "occupational alienation" would make the sort of claims which de Man makes. Only someone who takes both literature and philosophy far too seriously would say, as Hillis Miller does, that

> Language promises, but what it promises is itself. This promise it can never keep. It is this fact of language, a necessity beyond the control of any user of language, which makes things happen as they do happen in the material world of history.[12]

Language can be described, and has been usefully described by de Man and Derrida, as making promises it cannot keep. This description is genuinely enlightening when one is thinking about the attempts of essentialist intellectuals to penetrate through appearance to reality, to find the area where the *ultimate* levers of power are concealed, the vocabulary which finally puts *everything* in the right perspective. But history is not a conspiracy of essentialist intellectuals, nor are such intellectuals the principal instruments of social injustice. Lots of different things, ranging from the assignment of textbooks through the greed of legislators and the obsessions of dictators to the outbreak of epidemics, "make things happen as they do happen in the material world of history." To take Derrida's and de Man's useful and original antiessentialist redescription of language as the key to morality and politics is one more example of turning essentialist at the last minute.

This sort of simplistic and self-deceptive hypostatization of language or of literature is, however, a natural result of loving, or hating, one thing with all one's heart and soul and mind. It is a natural result of trying to bring everything together – one's most private emotional needs and one's public responsibilities, one's secret self-image and one's shame at the leisure and wealth that permit one to devote oneself to the cultivation of that self-image. So the worship of some such hypostatization is the characteristic temptation of the intellectuals. The intellectuals are people whose talents suit them for the task of redescription – the task of finding new metaphors, words in which to formulate new beliefs and desires. They are the people who are not content with the vocabulary into which they were socialized, and who are able to invent a new one. They are self-creators, in the sense that they can escape from the moral and political vocabulary into which they were socialized and become new people by reshaping their self-image. But just insofar as they retain a sense of the needs of other human beings, they feel alienated from these others – all those who do not speak the new language which the intellectual has invented in the course of reinventing herself. They also feel guilty insofar as they cannot relate their own projection of self-invention to the needs of those less capable of redescription and reinvention.

One way to get out from under this sense of guilt and alienation is illustrated by Nietzsche's occasional attempts to proclaim himself superhuman, and therefore entitled to neglect the needs of mere humans. Another, much more common way, illustrated by other passages in Nietzsche, is to hypostatize the central term of one's newly created vocabulary, to treat this term ("Reason,""the movement of History,""Language") as the One True Name of God. For this strategy helps one see oneself as a prophet, or perhaps even a redeemer. It helps one see one's own inner transfiguration as auguring the transformation of the human world, and in particular of the social arrangements which have left the needs of others unsatisfied.

Marxists are notorious for adopting this latter alternative, and Aron was right to call Marxism "the opium of the intellectuals." But from my antiessentialist angle, the hallucinatory effects of Marxism, and of the post-Marxist combination of de Man and Foucault currently being smoked by the American Cultural Left, are just special cases of the hallucinatory effects of all essentialist thought. Once this hallucinatory quality was best illustrated by science worship – by the people who told us that the millennium would come when we took a scientific approach to value-choice and conflict-resolution. Nowadays it is best illustrated by literature-worship – by the people who say the sorts of absurd things which I have quoted.

Still, saying absurd things is perfectly compatible with being a force for good. The Cultural Left has come in for a lot of flak lately – particularly from people who write for *The New Criterion* and the *National Review* and who are more interested in bashing liberals than in social justice. I hope that what I am saying about the Cultural Left will not be confused with what these people are saying. They go on about how the literature departments of American colleges and universities are being taken over by unscrupulous intellectual charlatans whose political goals outweigh their intellectual responsibilities. From my point of view, any leftist political movement – any movement which tries to call our attention to what the strong are currently doing to the weak – is a lot better than no left. Dialectical materialism was a pretty incoherent and silly philosophical system, and it eventually fell into the hands of mad tyrants. But it got quite a bit of good done while it lasted. Now that Marxism no longer looks plausible even in Paris, leftists who feel the need for a powerful philosophical backup are resorting to de Man and Foucault. But they are still doing a lot more good than most of their critics are doing.

Irving Howe has remarked, with some justice, that this Cultural Left is interested in taking over, not the government, but the English Department. But we should remember that in the 1920s and 1930s lots of Deweyan pragmatists were more interested in taking over the sociology and political science departments than in taking over the government. They had considerable success in doing so, and so students in social science courses were assigned books which made them more aware of the suffering caused by American institutions. The success of de Manians in taking over literature departments will have a similar effect. For the curricular emphases which they initiate will, in the course of a generation or so, trickle down into the high schools, and the conventional wisdom inculcated into young Americans will be changed.

Let me offer a couple of examples of such changes. Henry Gates, Deborah McDowell, and other specialists in Afro-American literature have helped rescue from oblivion Zora Neale Hurston's novel *Their Eyes Were Watching God*. People who got Ph.D. degrees in English during the 1980s are as likely to have read this novel as those who got their Ph.D.'s in the 1950s were to have read *The Diary of Anne Frank*, or as those who got their Ph.D.'s in the 1920s were to have read *The Mill on the Floss*. When I was in high school, I was assigned *The Mill on the Floss*. My fifteen-year-old daughter is currently being assigned *The Diary of Anne Frank*, I think it quite likely that any grandaughter I may have will, while in high school, be assigned *Their Eyes Were Watching God*. If she is, she will be a lot better informed about American history, rural poverty, and being black than I was at her age, and will be a more useful citizen in consequence.

Another example: while attending a rally of the Cultural Left at Duke University I heard Eve Klossofsky Sedgwick describe the prohibiting of gay high school teachers from counseling gay high school students about their gayness as "child abuse." My first reaction was that this was merely the sort of hyperbolic metaphor suitable for pep rallies, not to be taken literally. But by the time Sedgwick had finished her lecture I had literalized her metaphor. The examples she gave convinced me that this prohibition was, in fact, child abuse. While wondering what might undo the prohibition (which before hearing Sedgwick had struck me as as commonsensical as, when in high school, I had found antisodomy statutes) it occurred to me that gays might someday organize celebrations in the schools of one of the big events in American gay history – the Stonewall Riots. Maybe, in the early twenty-first century, it will be as commonplace for high schools to commemorate Stonewall as it is for them to celebrate Martin Luther King's birthday. (If this suggestion seems implausible, think how implausible the idea of celebrating King's birthday would have seemed to J. Edgar Hoover at the time of Selma.)

If either of the speculations I have offered come true, it will be because people like Gates and Sedgwick have patiently, over many years, plugged away despite the mockery and hostility of many of their professional colleagues. It is true that such struggles are not much like throwing cobblestones from barricades, or like risking the Gulag for publishing poems in *samizdat*. Still, unless some of today's academics are willing to struggle against such mockery and hostility, the education of the next generation of Americans will suffer a great deal. So will the moral tone of American public life. In exchange for the hope of such goods, one can afford to suppress a good deal of exasperation at de Man's hypostatizations.

If the sort of thing that Gates and Sedgwick are doing is to count as the politicization of the humanities, then we shall have to count what Locke and Hobbes did as the politicization of philosophy, what the founders of American sociology did as the politicization of social science, and what Shelley and the younger Wordsworth did as the politicization of literature. One point on which the Cultural Left is absolutely right to insist is that the social sciences and the humanities will, unless they become completely moribund, always be politicized, one way or another. There is no way to keep these disciplines alive if they become separated from the process of moral and political deliberation.

The only sense in which we want *un*politicized scholarship is that we do not want unpolitical scholars, or scholars of unpopular political persuasions, to be interfered with by those whose political views dominate their departments or their universities. But that is a matter of academic freedom and collegial good manners, not a matter of keeping the academy separate from political struggle. Threats to freedom and civility are, obviously, as frequent from the left as from the right. Doubtless American literature departments will, as the cultural leftists age from a band of Young Turks into an entrenched Old Guard, see many instances of injustice to junior faculty who have no taste for leftist politics, or who are dismissive of the political vocabulary of their elders. There are already indications that leftist political correctness is becoming a criterion for faculty hiring. But, with luck, these injustices will be no worse than those which contemporary academic leftists endured from exponents of "traditional humanistic values" in the course of their own rise to power.

19

Feminism and Pragmatism

When two women ascended to the Supreme Court of Minnesota, Catharine MacKinnon asked: "Will they use the tools of law as women, for all women?" She continued as follows:

> I think that the real feminist issue is not whether biological males or biological females hold positions of power, although it is utterly essential that women be there. And I am not saying that viewpoints have genitals. My issue is what our identifications are, what our loyalties are, who our community is, to whom we are accountable. If it seems as if this is not very concrete. I think it is because we have no idea what women as women would have to say. I'm evoking for women a role that we have yet to make, in the name of a voice that, unsilenced, might say something that has never been heard.[1]

Urging judges to "use the tools of law as women, for all women" alarms universalist philosophers. These are the philosophers who think that moral theory should come up with principles which mention no group smaller than "persons" or "human beings" or "rational agents." Such philosophers would be happier if MacKinnon talked less about accountability to women *as* women and more about an ideal Minnesota, or an ideal America, one in which all human beings would be treated impartially. Universalists would prefer to think of feminism as Mary Wollstonecraft and Olympe de Gouges did, as a matter of rights which are already recognizable and describable, although not yet granted. This describability, they feel, makes MacKinnon's hope for a voice saying something never heard before unnecessary, overly dramatic, hyperbolic.

Universalist philosophers assume, with Kant, that all the logical space necessary for moral deliberation is now available – that all important truths about right and wrong can not only be stated, but be made plausible, in language already to hand. I take MacKinnon to be siding with historicists like Hegel and Dewey, and to be saying that

Presented as The Tanner Lecture on Human Values at the University of Michigan, December 7, 1990. Richard M. Rorty, "Feminism and Pragmatism," *Michigan Quarterly Review*, vol. 30 (2), Spring 1991: 231–58. © 1991 by Richard Rorty. Reprinted with permission from the Estate of Richard Rorty.

1   MacKinnon, "On Exceptionality" in her *Feminism Unmodified: Discourses on Life and Law* (Cambridge, Mass.: Harvard University Press, 1987), p. 77.

moral progress depends upon expanding this space. She illustrates the need for such expansion when she notes that present sex-discrimination law assumes that women "have to meet either the male standard for males or the male standard for females. ... For purposes of sex discrimination law, to be a woman means either to be like a man or to be like a lady."[2] In my terms, MacKinnon is saying that unless women fit into the logical space prepared for them by current linguistic and other practices, the law does not know how to deal with them. MacKinnon cites the example of a judicial decision that permitted women to be excluded from employment as prison guards, because they are so susceptible to rape. The court, she continues, "took the viewpoint of the reasonable rapist on women's employment opportunities."[3] "The conditions that create women's rapeability as the definition of womanhood were not even seen as susceptible to change."[4]

MacKinnon thinks that such assumptions of unchangeability will only be overcome once we can hear "what women as women would have to say." I take her point to be that assumptions become visible *as* assumptions only if we can make the contradictories of those assumptions sound plausible. So injustices may not be perceived as injustices, even by those who suffer them, until somebody invents a previously unplayed role. Only if somebody has a dream, and a voice to describe that dream, does what looked like nature begin to look like culture, what looked like fate begin to look like a moral abomination. For until then only the language of the oppressor is available, and most oppressors have had the wit to teach the oppressed a language in which the oppressed will sound crazy – *even to themselves* – if they describe themselves *as* oppressed.[5]

MacKinnon's point that logical space may need to be expanded before justice can be envisaged, much less done, can be restated in terms of John Rawls's claim that moral theorizing is a matter of attaining reflective equilibrium between general principles and particular intuitions – particular reactions of revulsion, horror, satisfaction, or delight to real or imagined situations or actions. MacKinnon sees moral and legal principles,

2   *Ibid.*, p. 71. See also Carolyn Whitbeck's point that "the category, lesbian, both in the minds of its male inventors and as used in male-dominated culture is that of a physiological female who is in other respects a stereotypical male." See "Love, Knowledge and Transformation" in *Hypatia Reborn*, ed. Azizah Y. al-Hibri and Margaret A. Simons (Bloomington: Indiana University Press, 1990), p. 220. Compare Marilyn Frye's reference to "that other fine and enduring patriarchal institution, Sex Equality" in *The Politics of Reality* (Trumansburg, NY: The Crossing Press, 1983), p. 108.
3   *Ibid.*, p. 38.
4   *Ibid.*, p. 73.
5   At p. 33, Frye remarks that "For subordination to be permanent and cost effective, it is necessary to create conditions such that the subordinated group acquiesces to some extent in the subordination." Ideally, these will be conditions such that a member of the subordinate group who does not acquiesce will sound crazy. Frye suggests at p. 112 that a person's sounding crazy is a good indicator that you are oppressing that person. See also MacKinnon, *op. cit.*, p. 105: "Especially when you are part of a subordinated group, your own definition of your injuries is powerfully shaped by your assessment of whether you could get anyone to do anything about it, including anything official." E.g., a non-crazy claim to have been raped is one acceptable to those (usually males) in a position to offer support or reprisal. Only where there is a socially-accepted remedy can there have been a real (rather than crazily imagined) injury.

particularly those phrased in terms of equal rights, as impotent to change those reactions.[6] So she sees feminists as needing to alter the data of moral theory rather than needing to formulate principles which fit pre-existent data better. Feminists are trying to get people to feel indifference or satisfaction where they once recoiled, and revulsion and rage where they once felt indifference or resignation.

One way to change instinctive emotional reactions is to provide new language which will facilitate new reactions. By "new language" I mean not just new words but also creative misuses of language – familiar words used in ways which initially sound crazy. Something traditionally regarded as a moral abomination can become an object of general satisfaction, or conversely, as a result of the increased popularity of an alternative description of what is happening. Such popularity extends logical space by making descriptions of situations which used to seem crazy seem sane. Once, for example, it would have sounded crazy to describe homosexual sodomy as a touching expression of devotion, or to describe a woman manipulating the elements of the Eucharist as a figuration of the relation of the Virgin to her Son. But such descriptions are now acquiring popularity. At most times, it sounds crazy to describe the degradation and extirpation of helpless minorities as a purification of the moral and spiritual life of Europe. But at certain periods and places – under the Inquisition, during the Wars of Religion, under the Nazis – it did not.

Universalistic moral philosophers think that the notion of "violation of human rights" provides sufficient conceptual resources to explain why some traditional occasions of revulsion really are moral abominations and others only appear to be. They think of moral progress as an increasing ability to see the reality behind the illusions created by superstition, prejudice, and unreflective custom. The typical universalist is a moral realist, someone who thinks that true moral judgments are *made* true by something out there in the world. Universalists typically take this truth-maker to be the intrinsic features of human beings *qua* human. They think you can sort out the real from the illusory abominations by figuring out which those intrinsic features are, and that all that is required to figure this out is hard, clear, thought.

Historicists, by contrast, think that it "intrinsic" means "ahistorical, untouched by historical change," then the only intrinsic features of human beings are those they share with the brutes – for example, the ability to suffer and inflict pain. Every other feature is up for grabs. Historicists say, with Susan Hurley, that "the existence of certain shared practices, any of which might not have existed, is all that our having determinate reasons ... to do anything rests on."[7] So they think that we are not yet in a position to know what human beings are, since we do not yet know what practices human beings may start sharing.[8]

6   When Olympe de Gouges appealed in the name of women to The Declaration of the Rights of Men and Citizens, even the most revolution-minded of her male contemporaries thought she was crazy. When Canadian feminists argued, in the 1920s, that the word "persons" in an act specifying the conditions for being a Senator covered women as well as men, the Supreme Court of Canada decided that the word should not be so construed, because it never had been. (The Judicial Committee of the Privy Council, be it said, later ruled in the feminists' favor.)

7   I am quoting here from Samuel Scheffler's quotation from Hurley in his review of her *Natural Reasons* (Oxford: Oxford University Press, 1989) in the *London Review of Books*. I have not yet been able to locate the page from which Scheffler is quoting.

8   In a recent article on Rawls ("Reason and Feeling in Thinking about Justice," *Ethics* 99, p. 248), Susan Moller Okin points out that thinking in Rawls's original position is not a matter of thinking like a "disembodied nobody" but rather of thinking like lots of different people in turn – thinking

Univeralists talk as if any rational agent, at any epoch, could somehow have envisaged all the possible morally relevant differences, all the possible moral identities, brought into existence by such shared practices. But for MacKinnon, as for Hegel and Dewey, we know, at most, only those possibilities which history has actualized so far. MacKinnon's central point, as I read her, is that "a woman" is not yet the name of a way of being human – not yet the name of a moral identity, but, at most, the name of a disability.[9]

Taking seriously the idea of as yet unrealized possibilities, and of as yet unrecognized moral abominations resulting from failure to envisage those possibilities, requires one to take seriously the suggestion that we do not presently have the logical space necessary for adequate moral deliberation. Only if such suggestions are taken seriously can passages like the one I quoted from MacKinnon be read as prophecy rather than empty hyperbole. But this means revising our conception of moral progress. We have to stop talking about the need to go from distorted to undistorted perception of moral reality, and instead talk about the need to modify our practices so as to take account of new descriptions of what has been going on.

Here is where pragmatist philosophy might be useful to feminist politics. For pragmatism redescribes both intellectual and moral progress by substituting metaphors of evolutionary development for metaphors of progressively less distorted perception. By dropping a representationalist account of knowledge, we pragmatists drop the appearance-reality distinction in favor of a distinction between beliefs which serve some purposes and beliefs which serve other purposes – for example, the purposes of one group and those of another group. We drop the notion of beliefs being made true by reality, as well as the distinction between intrinsic and accidental features of things. So we drop questions about (in Nelson Goodman's phrase) The Way the World Is. We thereby drop the ideas of The Nature of Humanity and of The Moral Law, considered as objects which inquiry is trying to represent accurately, or as objects which make true moral judgments true. So we have to give up the comforting belief that competing groups will always be able to reason together on the basis of plausible and neutral premises.

From a pragmatist angle, neither Christianity nor the Enlightenment nor contemporary feminism are cases of cognitive clarity overcoming cognitive distortion. They are, instead, examples of evolutionary struggle – struggle which is Mendelian rather than Darwinian in character, in that it is guided by no immanent teleology. The history of human social practices is continuous with the history of biological evolution, the only difference being that what Richard Dawkins and Daniel Dennett call "memes" gradually take over the role of Mendel's genes. Memes are things like turns of speech, terms of aesthetic or moral praise, political slogans, proverbs, musical phrases, stereotypical icons, and the like. Memes compete with one another for the available cultural space as

---

from the point of view of "every 'concrete other' whom one might turn out to be." Hurley (*Natural Reasons,* p. 381) makes the same point. The historicity of justice – a historicity which Rawls has acknowledged in his papers of the 1980s – amounts to the fact that history keeps producing new sorts of "concrete others" whom one might turn out to be.

9   See the theme of "woman as partial man" in Whitbeck's "Theories of Sex Difference" in *Women and Values,* ed. Marilyn Pearsall (Belmont, CA: Wadsworth, 1986), pp. 34–50. This theme is developed in fascinating detail in Thomas Laqueur, *Making Sex; Body and Gender from the Greeks to Freud* (Cambridge, Mass.: Harvard University Press, 1990).

genes compete for the available *Lebensraum*.[10] Different batches of both genes and memes are carried by different human social groups, and so the triumph of one such group amounts to the triumph of those genes or memes. But no gene or meme is closer to the purpose of evolution or to the nature of humanity than any other – for evolution has no purpose and humanity no nature. So the moral world does not divide into the intrinsically decent and the intrinsically abominable, but rather into the goods of different groups and different epochs. As Dewey put it, "The worse or evil is a rejected good. In deliberation and before choice no evil presents itself as evil. Until it is rejected, it is a competing good. After rejection, it figures not as a lesser good, but as the bad of that situation."[11] On a Deweyan view, the replacement of one species by another in a given ecological niche, or the enslavement of one human tribe or race by another, or of the human females by the human males, is not an intrinsic evil. The latter is a rejected good, rejected on the basis of the greater good which feminism is presently making imaginable. The claim that this good is greater is like the claim that mammals are preferable to reptiles, or Aryans to Jews; it is an ethnocentric claim made from the point of view of a given cluster of genes or memes. There is no larger entity which stands behind that cluster and makes its claim true (or makes some contradictory claim true).

Pragmatists like myself think that this Deweyan account of moral truth and moral progress comports better with the prophetic tone in contemporary feminism than do universalism and realism. Prophecy, as we see it, is all that non-violent political movements can fall back on when argument fails. Argument for the rights of the oppressed *will* fail just insofar as the only language in which to state relevant premises is one in which the relevant emancipatory premises sound crazy. We pragmatists see universalism and realism as committed to the idea of a reality-tracking faculty called "reason" and an unchanging moral reality to be tracked, and thus unable to make sense of the claim that

---

10   Michael Cross and Mary Beth Averill, in their "Evolution and Patriarchal Myths" (In *Discovering Reality,* ed. Sandra Harding and Merrill B. Hintikka) suggest that the term "struggle" is a specifically masculist way of describing evolution and ask, "Why not see nature as bounteous, rather than parsimonlous, and admit that opportunity and cooperation are more likely to abet novelty, innovation and creation than are struggle and competition?" (p. 85). The question gives me pause, and I have no clear answer to it. All I have is the hunch that, with memes as with genes, tolerant pluralism will sooner or later, in the absence of interstellar travel, have to come to terms with shortage of space for self-expression.

There is a more general point involved here, the one raised by Jo-Ann Pilardi's claim that Hegel, Freud and others "were burdened with a notion of identity which defines it as oppositional, one which was derived from the psychosocial development of male children." See "On the War Path and Beyond" in *Hypatia Reborn* (cited above, p. 12.) Just such a notion of identity is central to my claims in this paper – and particularly to the claims about the possible benefits of feminist separatism in the paper's later pages. So I am employing what many feminist writers would consider specifically male assumptions. All I can say in reply is that the notion of identity as oppositional seems to me hard to eliminate from such books as Frye's – and especially from her discussion of feminist anger. Anger and opposition seem to me the root of most moral prophecy, and it is the prophetic aspect of feminism that I am emphasizing in this paper.

11   *Human Nature and Conduct* (*Middle Works,* vol. 14), p. 193. See also "Outlines of a Critical Theory of Ethics" (*Early Works,* vol. 3, p. 379): "Goodness is not remoteness from badness. In one sense, goodness is based upon badness; that is, good action is always based upon action good once, but bad if persisted in under changing circumstances."

a new voice is needed. So we commend ourselves to feminists on the ground that we can fit that claim into our view of moral progress with relative case.

We see it as unfortunate that many feminists intermingle pragmatist and realist rhetoric. For example, MacKinnon at one point defines feminism as the belief "that women are human beings in truth but not in social reality."[12] The phrase "in truth" here can only mean "in a reality which is distinct from social reality," one which is as it is whether or not women ever succeed in saying what has never been heard. Such invocations of an ahistoricist realism leave it unclear whether MacKinnon sees women as appealing from a bad social practice to something which transcends social practice, appealing from appearance to reality, or instead sees them as doing the same sort of thing as the early Christians, the early socialists, the Albigensians, and the Nazis did: trying to actualize hitherto undreamt-of possibilities by putting new linguistic and other practices into play, and erecting new social constructs.[13]

Some contemporary feminist philosophers are sympathetic to the latter alternative, because they explicitly reject universalism and realism. They do so because they see both as symptoms of what Derrida has called "phallogocentrism" – what MacKinnon calls "the epistemological stance ... of which male dominance is the politics."[14] Other such philosophers, however, warn against accepting the criticisms of universalism and realism common to Nietzsche, Heidegger and Derrida – against finding an ally in what is sometimes called "postmodernism." Sabina Lovibond, for example, cautions against throwing Enlightenment universalism and realism overboard. "How can any one ask me to say goodbye to 'emancipatory metanarratives'", she asks, "when my own emancipation is still such a patchy, hit-or-miss affair?"[15] Lovibond's universalism comes out when she says

12 MacKinnon, p. 126.

13 Suppose we define a moral abomination, with Jeffrey Stout, as something which goes against our sense of "the seams of our moral universe," one which crosses the lines between, as he puts it, "the categories of our cosmology and our social structure" (Stout, *Ethics After Babel* [Boston: Beacon Press, p. 159]). Then the choice between a realist and pragmatist rhetoric is the choice between saying that moral progress gradually aligns these seams with the *real* seams, and saying that it is a matter of simultaneously reweaving and enlarging a fabric which is not intended to be congruent with an antecedent reality. Giving an example of such a seam, Stout says (p. 153). "The sharper the line between masculine and feminine roles and the greater the importance of that line in determining matters such as the division of labor and the rules of inheritance, the more likely it is that sodomy will be abominated." Later he says (p. 158). "The question is not whether homosexuality is intrinsically abominable but rather what, all things considered, we should do with the relevant categories of our cosmology and social structure." As with the abominableness of homosexual sodomy, so, we pragmatists think, with the abominableness of the absence or presence of patriarchy. In all such cases, up to and including the abominableness of torturing people for the sheer pleasure of watching them writhe, pragmatists think that the question is not about intrinsic properties but about what we should do with the relevant categories – a question which boils down to what descriptions we should use of what is going on.

14 MacKinnon, p. 50.

15 "Feminism and Postmodernism," *New Left Review*, Winter 1989, p. 12. For a somewhat more tempered account of the relation of postmodernism to feminism see Kate Soper, "Feminism, Humanism and Postmodernism," *Radical Philosophy* 55 (Summer 1990), pp. 11–17. In their "Social Criticism Without Philosophy: An Encounter Between Feminism and Postmodernism" (in *Universal Abandon?*, ed. Andrew Ross (Minneapolis: University of Minnesota Press, 1988), Nancy Fraser and Linda Nicholson argue that "a robust postmodern-feminist paradigm of social criticism without

that "It would be arbitrary to work for sexual equality unless one believed that human society was disfigured by inequality *as such*." Her realism comes out in her claim that feminism has a "background commitment … to the elimination of (self-interested) cognitive distortion."[16]

I share Lovibond's doubts about the apocalyptic tone, and the rhetoric of unmasking, prevalent among people who believe that we are living in a "postmodern" period.[17] But, on all the crucial philosophical issues, I am on the side of Lovibond's postmodernist opponents.[18] I hope that feminists will continue to consider the possibility of dropping realism and universalism, dropping the notion that the subordination of women is *intrinsically* abominable, dropping the claim that there is something called "right" or "justice" or "humanity" which has always been on their side, making their claims true. I agree with those whom Lovibond paraphrases as saying "the Enlightenment rhetoric of 'emancipation', 'autonomy' and the like is complicit in a fantasy of escape from the embodied condition."[19] In particular, it is complicit in the fantasy of escape from an historical

---

philosophy is possible" (p. 100). I of course agree, but I am less sure about the need for, and utility of, "social-theoretical analysis of large-scale inequalities" (p. 90) than are Fraser and Nicholson.

This is because I am less sure than Fraser about the possibility that "the basic institutional framework of [our] society could be unjust" (Fraser, "Solidarity or Singularity?" in *Reading Rorty*, ed. Alan Malachowski [Oxford: Blackwell, 1990], p. 318), and hence about "the utility of a theory that could specify links among apparently discrete social problems via the basic institutional structure" (p. 319). I suspect my differences with Fraser are concrete and political rather than abstract and philosophical. She sees, and I do not see, attractive alternatives (more or less Marxist in shape) to such institutions as private ownership of the means of production and constitutional democracy, attractive alternatives to the traditional social-democratic project of constructing an egalitarian welfare state within the context of these two basic institutions. I am not sure whether our differences are due to Fraser's anti-foundationalist theory hope (see note 17 below) or to my own lack of imagination.

16   *Ibid.*, p. 28. See Lovibond's reference at p. 12 to "remaking society along rational, egalitarian lines." The idea that egalitarianism is more rational than elitism, rational in a sense which provides reasons for action *not* based on contingent shared practices, is central to the thinking of most liberals who are also moral realists.

17   A rhetoric of "unmasking hegemony" presupposes the reality-appearance distinction which opponents of phallogocentrism claim to have set aside. Many self-consciously "postmodern" writers seems to me trying to have it both ways – to view masks as going all the way down while still making invidious comparisons between other people's masks and the way things will look when all the masks have been stripped off. These postmodernists continue to indulge the had habits characteristic of those Marxists who insist that morality is a matter of class interest, and then add that everybody has a moral obligation to identify with the interests of a particular class. Just as "ideology" came to mean little more than "other people's ideas," so "product of hegemonic discourse" has come to mean little more than "product of other people's way of talking." I agree with Stanley Fish that much of what goes under the heading of "post-modernism" exemplifies internally inconsistent "anti-foundationalist theory hope." See Fish, *Doing What Comes Naturally: Change, Rhetoric and the Practice of Theory in Literary and Legal Studies* (Durham: Duke University Press. 1989), pp. 346, 437–8.

18   I am not fond of the term "postmodernism" and was a bit startled (as presumably was MacIntyre) to find Lovibond saying that Lyotard, MacIntyre and I are "among the most forceful exponents of the arguments and values which constitute postmodernism within academic philosophy." (p. 5). Still, I recognize the similarities between our positions which lead Lovibond to group the three of us together. Some of these similarities are outlined by Fraser and Nicholson at pp. 85ff, of the article cited in note 15.

19   *Ibid.*, p. 12.

situation into an ahistoricist empyrean – one in which moral theory can be pursued, like Euclidean geometry, within an unalterable, unextendable, logical space. Although practical politics will doubtless often require feminists to speak with the universalist vulgar, I think that they might profit from thinking with the pragmatists.

One of the best things about contemporary feminism, it seems to me, is its ability to eschew such Enlightenment fantasies of escape. My favorite passages in MacKinnon are ones in which she says things like "we are not attempting to be objective about it, we're attempting to represent the point of view of women."[20] Feminists are much less inclined than Marxists were to fall back on a comfortable doctrine of immanent teleology. There is a lot of feminist writing which can be read as saying: we are *not* appealing from phallist appearance to non-phallist reality. We are *not* saying that the voice in which women will some day speak will be better at representing reality than present-day masculist discourse. We are not attempting the impossible task of developing a non-hegemonic discourse, one in which truth is no longer connected with power. We are not trying to do away with social constructs in order to find something that is not a social construct. We are just trying to help women out of the traps men have constructed for them, help them get the power they do not presently have, and help them create a moral identity as women.

I have argued in the past that Deweyan pragmatism, when linguistified along the lines suggested by Putnam and Davidson, gives you all that is politically useful in the Nietzsche–Heidegger–Derrida–Foucault tradition. Pragmatism, I claim, offers all the dialectical advantages of postmodernism while avoiding the self-contradictory postmodernist rhetoric of unmasking. I admit that insofar as feminists adopt a Deweyan rhetoric of the sort I have just described, they commit themselves to a lot of apparent paradoxes, and incur the usual charges of relativism, irrationalism and power-worship.[21] But these disadvantages are, I think, outweighed by the advantages. By describing themselves in Deweyan terms, feminists would free themselves from Lovibond's demand for a general theory of oppression – a way of seeing oppression on the basis of race, class, sexual preference, and gender as so many instances of a general failure to treat equals equally.[22] They would thereby avoid the embarrassments of the universalist claim that the term "human being" – or even the term "woman" – names an unchanging essence, an

---

20   MacKinnon, p. 86. See also pp. 50, 54, for the "postmodernist" suggestion that the quest for objectivity is a specifically masculist one.

21   We pragmatists are often told that we reduce moral disagreement to a mere struggle for power by denying the existence of reason, or human nature, conceived as something which provides a neutral court of appeal. We often rejoin that the need for such a court, the need for something ahistorical which will ratify one's claims, is itself a symptom of power-worship – of the conviction that unless something large and powerful is on one's side, one shouldn't bother trying.

22   Developing this point would take too long. Were more time and space available, I should argue that trying to integrate feminism into a general theory of oppression – a frequent reaction to the charge that feminists are oblivious to racial and economic injustice – is like trying to integrate Galilean physics into a general theory of scientific error. The latter attempt is as familiar as it is fruitless. The conviction that there is an interesting general theory about human beings or their oppression seems to me like the conviction that there is an interesting general theory about truth and our failure to achieve it. For the same reasons that transcendental terms like "true" and "good" are not susceptible of definition, neither error nor oppression has a single neck which a single critical slash might sever.

ahistorical natural kind with a permanent set of intrinsic features. Further, they would no longer need to raise what seem to me unanswerable questions about the accuracy of their representations of "woman's experience." They would instead see themselves as *creating* such an experience by creating a language, a tradition, and an identity.

In the remainder of this paper I want to develop this distinction between expression and creation in more detail. But first I want to insert a cautionary remark about the relative insignificance of philosophical movements as compared to social-political movements. Yoking feminism with pragmatism is like yoking Christianity with Platonism, or socialism with dialectical materialism. In each case, something big and important, a vast social hope, is being yoked with something comparatively small and unimportant, a set of answers to philosophical questions – questions which arise only for people who find philosophical topics intriguing rather than silly. Universalists – of both the bourgeois liberal and the Marxist sort – often claim that such questions are in fact urgent, for political movements *need* philosophical foundations. But we pragmatists cannot say this. We are not in the foundations business. *All* we can do is to offer feminists a few pieces of special-purpose ammunition – for example, some additional replies to charges that their aims are unnatural, their demands irrational, or their claims hyperbolic.

So much for an overview of my reasons for trying to bring feminism and pragmatism together. I want now to enlarge on my claim that a pragmatist feminist will see herself as helping to create women rather than attempting to describe them more accurately. I shall do so by taking up two objections which might be made to what I have been saying. The first is the familiar charge that pragmatism is inherently conservative, biased in favor of the status quo.[23] The second objection arises from the fact that if you say that

---

Maria Lugones is an example of a feminist theorist who sees a need for a general philosophical theory of oppression and liberation. She says, for example, that "the ontological or metaphysical possibility of liberation remains to be argued, explained, uncovered" ("Structure/Antistructure and Agency under Oppression", *Journal of Philosophy* 87 [October 1990], p. 502). I should prefer to stick to merely empirical possibilities of liberation. Although I entirely agree with Lugones about the need to "give up the unified self" (p. 503), I do not see this as a matter of ontology, but merely as a way of putting the familiar point that the same human being can contain different coherent sets of belief and desire – different roles, different personalities, etc. – correlated with the different groups to which he or she belongs or whose power he or she must acknowledge. A more important disagreement between us, perhaps, concerns the desirability of harmonizing one's various roles, self-images, etc., in a single unifying story about oneself. Such unification – the sort of thing which I describe below as overcoming splits – seems to me desirable. Lugones, on the other hand, urges the desirability of "experiencing oneself in the limen" (p. 506).

23 For a good example of this charge, see Jonathan Culler, *Framing the Sign: Criticism and its Institutions* (Oklahoma City: University of Oklahoma Press, 1988), p. 55: "… the humanities must make their way between, on the one hand, a traditional, foundationalist conception of their task and, on the other, the so-called 'new pragmatism' to which some critics of foundationalism have retreated. If philosophy is not a foundationalist discipline, argues Richard Rorty, then it is simply engaged in a conversation; it tells stories, which succeed simply by their success. Since there is no standard or reference point outside the system of one's beliefs to appeal to, critical arguments and theoretical reflections can have no purchase on these beliefs or the practices informed by them. Ironically, then, the claim that philosophers and theoreticians tell stories, which originates as a critique of ideology … becomes a way of protecting a dominant ideology and its professionally successful practitioners from the scrutiny of argument, by deeming that critique can have no leverage against ordinary beliefs, and that theoretical arguments have no consequences. This pragmatism, whose complacency seems altogether appropriate

women need to be created rather than simply freed, you seem to be saying that in some sense women do not now fully exist. But then there seems no basis for saying that men have done women wrong, since you cannot wrong the non-existent.

Hilary Putnam, the most important contemporary philosopher to call himself a pragmatist, has said that "a statement is true of a situation just in case it would be correct to use the words of which the statement consists in that way in describing the situation." Putting the matter this way immediately suggests the question: correct by whose standards? Putnam's position that "truth and rational acceptability are interdependent notions"[24] makes it hard to see how we might ever appeal from the oppressive conventions of our community to something non-conventional, and thus hard to see how we could ever engage in anything like "radical critique." So it may seem that we pragmatists, in our frenzied efforts to undercut epistemological skepticism by doing away with what Davidson calls "the scheme–content distinction," have also undercut political radicalism.

---

to the Age of Reagan, subsists only by a theoretical argument of the kind it in principle opposes, as an ahistorical 'preformism': what one does must be based on one's beliefs, but since there are no foundations outside the system of one's beliefs, the only thing that could logically make one change a belief is something one already believes."

Culler is right in saying that we pragmatists hold the latter view, but wrong in suggesting that we think that *logical* changes in belief are the only respectable ones. What I have called "creative misuses" of language are *causes* to change one's belief, even if not *reasons* to change them. See the discussion of Davidson on metaphor in various papers in my *Objectivity, Relativism and Truth* (Cambridge: Cambridge University Press, 1991) for more on this cause-reason distinction, and for the claim that most moral and intellectual progress is achieved by non-"logical" changes in belief. Culler is one of the people I had in mind in note 17 above – the people who want to hang on to the primacy of logic (and thus of "theoretical reflection" and "critique") while abandoning logocentrism. I do not think this can be done.

Culler's charge can be found in many other authors, e.g., Joseph Singer, "Should Lawyers Care About Philosophy?," *Duke Law Journal* 1989, p. 1752: "… Rorty … has marginalized the enterprise of philosophy, thereby depriving pragmatism of any critical bite." On my view, pragmatism bites other philosophies, but not social problems as such – and so is as useful to fascists like Mussolini and conservatives like Oakeshott as it is to liberals like Dewey. Singer thinks that I have "identified reason with the status quo" and defined "truth as coextensive with the prevailing values in a society" (p. 1763). These claims are, I think, the result of the same inference as Culler draws in the passage quoted above. Both Singer and Culler want philosophy to be capable of setting goals, and not to be confined to the merely ancillary role I describe in note 26 below.

24 See Putnam's *Representation and Reality* (Cambridge, Mass.: Massachusetts Institute of Technology Press, 1988), pp. 114–15, for the passages cited. See also Robert Brandom's formulation of "phenomenalism about truth" as the view that "being true is to be understood as being *properly* taken-true (believed)." Brandom says that what is of most interest about the classical pragmatist stories (Peirce, James) is "the dual commitment to a normative account of claiming or believing [Bain's and Peirce's account of belief as a rule for action] that does not lean on a supposedly explanatory antecedent notion of truth, and the suggestion that truth can then be understood phenomenonalistically, in terms of features of these independently characterized takings-true." See Brandom, "Pragmatism, Phenomenalism, Truth Talk," *Midwest Studies in Philosophy* XII (1988), p. 80. Brandom (as well as Davidson and I) would agree with Putnam that "truth does not transcend use" but I think all three of us might be puzzled by Putnam's further claim that "whether an epistemic situation is any good or not depends on whether many different statements are true." This seems to me like saying that whether a person is wealthy or not depends on how much money she has.

Pragmatists should reply to this charge by saying that they cannot make sense of an appeal from our community's practices to anything except the practice of a real or imagined alternative community. So when prophetic feminists say that it is not enough to make the practices of our community coherent, that the very *language* of our community must be subjected to radical critique, pragmatists add that such critique can only take the form of imagining a community whose linguistic and other practices are different from our own. Once one grants MacKinnon's point that one can only get so far with an appeal to make present beliefs more coherent by treating women on a par with men, once one sees the need for something more than an appeal to rational acceptability by the standards of the existing community, then such an act of imagination is the only recourse.

This means that one will praise movements of liberation not for the accuracy of their diagnoses but for the imagination and courage of their proposals. The difference between pragmatism and positions such as Marxism, which retain the rhetoric of scientism and realism, can be thought of as the difference between radicalism and utopianism. Radicals think that there is a basic mistake being made, a mistake deep down at the roots. They think that deep thinking is required to get down to this deep level, and that only there, when all the superstructural appearances have been undercut, can things be seen as they really are. Utopians, however, do not think in terms of mistakes or of depth. They abandon the contrast between superficial appearance and deep reality in favor of the contrast between a painful present and a possibly less painful, dimly-seen, future. Pragmatists cannot be radicals, in this sense, but they can be utopians. They do not see philosophy as providing instruments for radical surgery, or microscopes which make precise diagnosis possible.[25] Philosophy's function is rather to clear the road for prophets and poets, to make intellectual life a bit simpler and safer for those who have visions of new communities.[26]

25   Joseph Singer, in the article cited in note 23, praises Elizabeth Spelman for "using the tools of philosophy to promote justice," and suggests that one such use is to show that "the categories and forms of discourse we use ... have important consequences in channeling our attention in particular directions." Surely it is no disrespect to Spelman's achievement, nor to philosophy, to insist that it takes no special tools, no special philosophical expertise, to make and develop this latter point? The use of notions like "powerful methods" and "precise analytical instruments" in the rhetories of analytic philosophy and of Marxism constitutes, to my mind, misleading advertising. An unfortunate result of such mystification is that whenever a philosophy professor like Spelman or me does something useful, it is assumed that we were doing something distinctively philosophical, something philosophers are specially trained to do. If we then fail to go on to do something else which needs to be done, we will usually be charged with using an obsolete and inadequate set of philosophical tools.

26   See Dewey's "From Absolutism to Experimentalism" in *Later Works of John Dewey*, vol. 5 (Carbondale: Southern Illinois University Press, 1984), p. 160: "Meantime a chief task of those who call themselves philosophers is to help get rid of the useless lumber that blocks our highways of thought, and strive to make straight and open the paths that lead to the future." There is a lot of this road-clearing rhetoric in Dewey, rhetoric which is continuous with Locke's description of himself as an under-laborer to those who seemed to him the prophetic spirits of his time – corpuscularian scientists like Newton and Boyle. Both metaphors suggest that the philosophers' job is to drag outdated philosophy out of the way of those who are displaying unusual courage and imagination.

Singer, in the article cited in note 23, says that "Dewey, unlike Rorty, saw the problems of philosophy as inseparable from the problems of collective life," and that "by separating philosophy from justice, Rorty's vision reinforces existing power relations ..." (p. 1759). It is true that

So far I have taken MacKinnon as my example of a feminist with such a vision. But of course she is only one of many. Another is Marilyn Frye, who says, in her powerful book *The Politics of Reality*, that "there probably is really no distinction, in the end, between imagination and courage." For, she continues, it takes courage to overcome "a mortal dread of being outside the field of vision of the arrogant eye." This is the eye of a person who prides himself on spotting the rational unacceptability of what is being said – that is, its incoherence with the rest of the beliefs of those who currently control life-chances and logical space. So feminists must, Frye goes on to say, "dare to rely on ourselves to make meaning and we have to imagine ourselves capable of … weaving the web of meaning which will hold us in some kind of intelligibility."[27] Such courage is indistinguishable from the imagination it takes to hear oneself as the spokesperson of a merely possible community, rather than as a lonely, and perhaps crazed, outcast from an actual one.

MacKinnon and many other feminists use "liberalism" as a name for an inability to have this sort of courage and imagination. "In the liberal mind," MacKinnon says, "the worse and more systematic one's mistreatment is, the more it seems justified. Liberalism … never sees power as power, yet can see as significant only that which power does."[28] The phenomenon she is pointing to certainly exists, but "liberalism" seems to me the wrong name for it. So, of course, does "pragmatism". I think the main reason – apart from some reflexes left over from early Marxist conditioning – why pejorative uses of the terms "liberal" and "pragmatist" are still common among political radicals is that if you say, with Putnam, that "truth does not transcend use," you may easily be taken as referring to actual, present use. Again, if you deny that truth is a matter of correspondence to reality, you may easily be taken as holding that a true belief is one that coheres with what most people currently believe. If you think that emancipatory moral or social thought requires penetrating to a presently unglimpsed reality beneath the current appearances, and find pragmatists telling you that there is no such reality, you may easily conclude that a pragmatist cannot help the cause of emancipation.

When, however, we remember that John Dewey – a paradigmatic liberal as well as a paradigmatic pragmatist – spent a great deal of time celebrating the sort of courage and imagination Frye describes, we may be willing to grant that the relation between pragmatism and emancipation is more complex. Dewey said remarkably little about the situation of women, but one of the few things he did say is worth quoting:

> Women have as yet made little contribution to philosophy, but when women who are not mere students of other persons' philosophy set out to write it, we cannot conceive that it will be the same in viewpoint or tenor as that composed from the standpoint of the different masculine experience of things. Institutions, customs of life, breed certain systematized predilections and aversions. The wise man reads historic philosophies to detect in them intellectual formulations of men's habitual purposes and cultivated wants, not to gain insight into the ultimate nature of things or information about the make-up of reality. As

---

Dewey often speaks as if social problems and philosophical problems were interlocked, but I should argue that all these passages can best be interpreted in the road-clearing sense I have just suggested. Dewey never, I think, saw pragmatism in the way in which Marxists saw dialectical materialism – as a philosophical key which unlocks the secrets of history or of society.

27   This and the previous quote are from Frye, p. 80.
28   MacKinnon, p. 221. Cp. 137.

far as what is loosely called reality figures in philosophies, we may be sure that it signifies those selected aspects of the world which are chosen because they lend themselves to the support of men's judgment of the worth-while life, and hence are most highly prized. In philosophy, "reality" is a term of value or choice.[29]

Suppose we think, as feminists often do, of "men's habitual purposes and cultivated wants" as "the habitual purposes and cultivated wants of the males, the half of the species which long ago enslaved the other half." This permits us to read Dewey as saying: if you find yourself a slave, do not accept your masters' descriptions of the real; do not work within the boundaries of their moral universe; instead, try to invent a reality of your own by selecting aspects of the world which lend themselves to the support of *your* judgment of the worth-while life."[30]

Dewey's doctrine of the means – end continuum might have led him to add: do not expect to know what sort of life is worth-while right off the bat, for that is one of the things you will constantly change your mind about in the process of selecting a reality. You can neither pick your goals on the basis of a clear and explicit claim about the nature of moral reality, nor derive such a claim from clear and explicit goals. There is no method or procedure to be followed except courageous and imaginative experimentation. Dewey would, I think, have been quick to see the point of Frye's description of her own writing as "a sort of flirtation with meaninglessness – dancing about a region of cognitive gaps and negative semantic spaces, kept aloft only by the rhythm and momentum of my own motion, trying to plumb abysses which are generally agreed not to exist."[31] For meaninglessness is exactly what you have to flirt with when you are in between social, and in particular linguistic, practices – unwilling to take part in an old one but not yet having succeeded in creating a new one.

The import of Dewey's pragmatism for movements such as feminism can be seen if we paraphrase Dewey as follows: do not charge a current social practice or a currently spoken language with being unfaithful to reality, with getting things wrong. Do not criticize it as a result of ideology or prejudice, where these are tacitly contrasted with your own employment of a truth-tracking faculty called "reason" or a neutral method called "disinterested observation." Do not even criticize it as "unjust" if "unjust" is supposed to mean more than "sometimes incoherent even on its own terms." Instead of appealing from the transitory current appearances to the permanent reality, appeal to a still only dimly imagined future practice. Drop the appeal to neutral criteria, and the claim that something large like Nature or Reason or History or the Moral Law is on the

---

29   "Philosophy and Democracy," *The Middle Works of John Dewey*, v. 11, p. 145.

30   To use an analogy suggested by Charlotte Perkins Gilman's poem "Similar Cases," it is as if one said to the creatures which were eventually to become the mammals: "Do not try to imitate the ways in which those larger and more powerful fish cope with their environment. Rather, find ways of doing things which will help you find a new environment." ("Similar Cases" is perhaps most easily available at pp. 363–4 of Ann Lane, *To Herland and Beyond: The Life and Works of Charlotte Perkins Gilman* [New York: Pantheon, 1990]. The point of the poem is that if it were true that, as feminists were often told, "you can't change your nature" we should have had neither biological nor cultural evolution.)

31   *The Politics of Reality*, p. 154.

side of the oppressed. Instead, just make invidious comparisons between the actual present and a possible, if inchoate, future.[32]

So much for the relations between pragmatism and political radicalism. I have been arguing that the two are compatible and mutually supporting. This is because pragmatism allows for the possibility of expanding logical space, and thereby for an appeal to courage and imagination rather than to putatively neutral criteria. What pragmatism loses when it gives up the claim to have right or reality on its side it gains in ability to acknowledge the presence of what Frye calls "abysses which are generally agreed not to exist." These are situations which give the universalist and the realist trouble – ones in

---

32   As I suggested earlier, it is easy to bring together Dewey's claim that, in philosophy, "real" is as evaluative a term as "good" with "postmodernist" views – for example, those found in Chris Weedon's book *Feminist Practice and Poststructuralist Theory*. Pretty much the only difference between Weedon's criticism of the philosophical tradition and Dewey's is one which also separates contemporary pragmatists like Putnam and Davidson from Dewey – the use of "language" instead of Dewey's word "experience" as the name of what it is important for the oppressed to reshape. Weedon, like Putnam and Davidson and unlike Dewey, is what Wilfrid Sellars called a "psychological nominalist" – someone who believes that all awareness is a linguistic affair. At p. 32 she says "Like Althusserian Marxism, feminist poststructuralism makes the primary assumption that it is language which enables us to think, speak and give meaning to the world around us. Meaning and consciousness do not exist outside language." The difference with Dewey has few consequences, however, since Dewey would have heartily agreed with Weedon (p. 131) that one should not view language "as a transparent tool for expressing facts" but as "the material in which particular, often conflicting versions of facts are constructed."

The only real advantage to psychological nominalism for feminists, perhaps, is that it replaces hard-to-discuss (I am tempted to say "metaphysical") questions about whether women have a different *experience* than men, or Africans a different experience than Europeans, or about whether the experience of upper-class African women is more like that of lower-class European men than that of upper-class European women, with easier-to-discuss (more evidently empirical) questions about what *language* these various groups of people use to justify their actions, exhibit their deepest hopes and fears, etc. Answers to the latter questions are jumping-off places for practical suggestions about different languages which they might use, or might have used. I share MacKinnon's skepticism about the idea that "viewpoints have genitals" and Sandra Harding's skepticism about the utility of notions like "woman's morality," "woman's experience," and "woman's standpoint." See Harding's "The Curious Coincidence of Feminine and African Moralities: Challenges for Feminist Theory," in *Women and Moral Theory*, ed. Eva Kittay and Diana Meyers (Totowa, NJ: Rowman and Littlefield, 1987), pp. 296–315.

Although most of the doctrines (e.g., essentialism, Cartesian individualism, moral universalism) which Weedon attributes to "liberal humanism" are doctrines Dewey (a notorious liberal humanist) also targeted, Weedon does not seem able to eschew a longing for what Mary Hawkesworth calls "a successor science which can refute once and for all the distortions of androcentrism." See Hawkesworth, "Knowers, Knowing, Known: Feminist Theory and the Claims of Truth" in *Feminist Theory in Practice and Process*, ed. Micheline R. Malson, et al. (Chicago: University of Chicago Press, 1989), p. 331. But once you put aside universalism, you should neither hope for knock-down refutations nor talk about "distortion." Hawkesworth goes on to criticize Harding for saying that "Feminist analytical categories *should* be unstable at this moment in history" (Harding, "The Instability of the Analytical Categories of Feminist Theory," in the same collection, at p. 19). But prophecy and unstable categories go together, and Harding's claim chimes with many of the passages I have been quoting from Frye. Harding's further claim that "we [feminists] should learn how to regard the instabilities themselves as valuable resources" is one that Dewey would have cheered.

which plenty of assent-commanding descriptions are available, but such that none of these descriptions do what is needed.

I turn now to the paradox I noted earlier: the suggestion that women are only now coming into existence, rather than having been deprived of the ability to express what was deep within them all the time. I take MacKinnon's evocation of a "role that women have yet to make" as a way of suggesting that women are only now beginning to put together a moral identity *as* women. To find one's moral identity in being an X means being able to do the following sort of thing: make your Xness salient in your justification of important uncoerced choices, make your Xness an important part of the story you tell yourself when you need to recover your self-confidence, make your relations with other X's central to your claim to be a responsible person. These are all things men have usually been able to do by reminding themselves that they are, come what may, *men*. They are things which men have made it hard for women to do by reminding themselves that they are women. As Frye puts it, men have assigned themselves the status of "full persons" – people who enjoy what she calls "unqualified participation in the radical 'superiority' of the species,"[33] and withheld this status from women. The result of men constantly, fervently and publicly thanking God that they are *not* women has been to make it hard for women to thank God that they are. For a woman to say that she finds her moral identity in being a woman would have sounded, until relatively recently, as weird as for a slave to say that he or she finds his or her moral identity in being a slave.

Most feminists might agree that it was only with the beginnings of the feminist movement that it began to become possible for women to find their moral identities in being women.[34] But most feminists are probably still realist and universalist enough to insist that there is a difference between the claim that one cannot find one's moral identity in being an X and the claim that an X is not yet a full-fledged person, a person to whom injustice has been done by forbidding her to find her moral identity in her X-hood. For the great advantage of realism and universalism over pragmatism is that it permits one to say that women were everything they are now, and *therefore* were entitled to everything they are now trying to get – even when they did not know, and might even have explicitly denied, that they were entitled to it.

For us pragmatists, however, it is not so easy to say that. For we see personhood as a matter of degree, not as an all-or-nothing affair, something evenly distributed around the species. We see it as something that slaves typically have less of than their masters. This is not because there are such things as "natural slaves" but because of the masters' control over the language spoken by the slaves – their ability to make the slave think of his or her pain as fated and even somehow deserved, something to be borne rather than resisted. We cannot countenance the notion of a deep reality which reposes unrecognized beneath the superficial appearances. So we have to take seriously the idea, made familiar by such writers as Charles Taylor, that interpretation goes all the way down: that what a human being is, for moral purposes, is largely a matter of how he or she describes himself or herself. We have to take seriously the idea that what you experience yourself to be is largely a function of what it makes sense to describe yourself as in the languages you are able to use. We have to say that the Deltas and Epsilons of Huxley's *Brave New*

---

33   Frye, pp. 48–49.
34   I am too ignorant about the history of feminism – about how long and how continuous the feminist tradition has been – to speculate about when things began to change.

World, and the proles of Orwell's *Nineteen Eighty-Four,* were persons only in the sense in which fertilized human ova or human infants are persons – in the sense, namely, that they are capable of being made into persons. So we pragmatists have to identify most of the wrongness of past male oppression with its suppression of past potentiality, rather than in its injustice to past actuality.

In order to say that women are only now in the process of achieving a moral identity as women, I do not need to deny that some women have, in every epoch, had doubts about, and offered alternatives to, the standard, androcentric, descriptions of women. All I need to deny is that women have been able to *forget* the latter descriptions – the ones which make them seem incapable of being full persons. I am denying that women in previous epochs have been able to avoid being torn, split, between the men's description of them and whatever alternative descriptions they have given to themselves. As an example of the sort of thing I have in mind – of the need to name, and thus to begin to bridge, what Frye calls "abysses generally agreed not to exist" – consider Adrienne Rich's description of her situation when young. She was, she says, "split between the girl who wrote poems, who defined herself as writing poems, and the girl who was to define herself by her relationships with men."[35] I want to interpret Rich's individual situation as an allegory of the more general situation in which women found themselves before feminism achieved lift-off – of their inability to stop defining themselves in terms of their relationships with men. To envisage this inability, consider how Rich's situation differed from that of a young man in a similar situation.

Since Byron and Goethe men have thought of writing poems as one of the best ways to create an autonomous self, to avoid having to define oneself in the terms used by one's parents, teachers, employers and rulers. Since 1820 or thereabouts, a young man has had the option of defining himself as a poet, of finding his moral identity in writing verse. But, Rich tells us, this is not easy for a young woman.

What is the difficulty? It is not that there is any dearth of true descriptions which Rich might have applied to herself. There were no well-formed – that is, generally intelligible – questions to which Rich could not have given true, well-formed answers. But nevertheless there was, she tells us, a split. The various true descriptions which she applied did not fit together into a whole. But, she is implicitly suggesting, a young male poet's descriptions would have fitted together easily. Rich was, in her youth, unable to attain the kind of coherence, the kind of integrity, which we think of as characteristic of full persons. For persons who are capable of the full glory of humanity are capable of seeing themselves steadily and whole. Rather than feel that splits are tearing them apart, they can see tensions between their alternative self-descriptions as, at worst, necessary elements in a harmonious variety-in-unity.

Rich's account of herself as split rings true for, as she shows in her essay on Emily Dickinson and elsewhere, the language-games men have arranged that young women should play force them to treat the men in their lives (or, the absence of men in their lives) as the independent variable and everything else – even their poems – as dependent variables. So insofar as Rich could not tie her poems in with her relationships with men, she had a problem. She was split. She could not be, so to speak, a full-time poet, because a language she could not forget did not let one be both a full-time poet and a full-time female. By

35   Rich, *On Lies, Secrets, and Silence: Selected Prose 1966–1978* (New York and London: Norton, 1979), p. 40.

contrast, since Byron, the language has let one be a full-time poet and a full-time hero (just as, since Socrates, it has been possible to be a full-time intellectual and a full-time hero).

What might solve Rich's problem? Well, perhaps nowadays it is a little easier for a young woman to define herself by and in her poems than when Rich was young – simply because she may have read books by Rich, Frye and others. But only a little easier. What would make it *really* easy? Only, I would suggest, the sort of circumstance which made it easy for a young man in the generation after Byron to make his poetic activity the independent variable in the story he told himself about himself. In the previous generation there had been what now looks to us like a band of brothers – Hölderlin and Keats, Byron and Goethe, Shelley and Chamisso. Bliss was it in that dawn to be alive, and to be a young male with poetic gifts was to be able to describe oneself in heroic terms, terms which one could not have used earlier without sounding crazy. That band of brothers founded an invisible club, a very good club, one which is still giving new members a warm welcome.[36] So young male poets do not face abysses when they attempt self-definition. But, as Rich points out, Emily Dickinson was not allowed into that club.[37] So, to make things *really* easy for future Dickinsons and Riches, there would have to be a good, well-established club which they could join.

Here, I take it, is where feminist separatism comes in. Rich asks that

> we understand lesbian/feminism in the deepest, most radical sense: as that love for ourselves and other women, that commitment to the freedom of all of us, which transcends the cat-egory of "sexual preference" and the issue of civil rights, to become a politics of *asking women's questions*, demanding a world in which the integrity of all women – not a chosen few – shall be honored and validated in every aspect of culture.[38]

Someone who tries to fit what Rich is saying into a map drawn on a universalist and realist grid will have trouble locating any space separate from that covered by "the cate-gory of 'sexual preference' " or by "the issue of civil rights." For justice, on this universalist view, is a matter of our providing each other with equal advantages. Nothing, in this vision, *could* transcend civil rights and the realization of those rights by institutional change. So, for example, lesbian separatism is likely to be seen simply as an arrangement by which those with a certain sexual preference can escape stigma until such time as the laws have been extended to protect lesbians' rights and the mores have caught up with the laws.

Frye offers a contrasting view of the function of separatism when she writes:

> *Re* the new being and meaning which are being created now by lesbian-feminists, we *do* have semantic authority, and, collectively, can and do define with effect. I think it is only by

---

36 The continued attractions of this club in our own cynical century are evidenced by the fact that, even as Bernard Shaw was having Candida make fun of Marchbanks, Joyce had Stephen Dedalus write that he would "forge in the smithy of my soul the uncreated conscience of my race." Joyce was not making fun of Stephen, and even Shaw admitted that Candida "does not know the secret in the poet's heart."

37 "What might, in a male writer – a Thoreau, let us say, or a Christopher Smart or William Blake – seem a legitimate strangeness, a unique intention, has been in one of our two major poets [Dickinson] devalued into a kind of naivete, girlish ignorance, feminine lack of professionalism, just as the poet herself has been made into a sentimental object. ('Most of us are half in love with this dead girl,' confesses Archibald MacLeish. Dickinson was fifty-five when she died.)" (Rich, p. 167).

38 Rich, p. 17.

maintaining our boundaries through controlling concrete access to us that we can enforce on those who are not-us our definitions of ourselves, hence force on them *the fact of our existence* and thence open up the *possibility* of our having semantic authority with them.[39]

I take Frye's point to be, in part, that individuals – even individuals of great courage and imagination – cannot achieve semantic authority, *even semantic authority over themselves*, on their own. To get such authority you have to hear your own statements as part of a shared practice. Otherwise you yourself will never know whether they are more than ravings, never know whether you are a heroine or a maniac. People in search of such authority need to band together and form clubs, exclusive clubs. For if you want to work out a story about who you are – put together a moral identity – which decreases the importance of your relationships to one set of people and increases the importance of your relationships to another set, the physical absence of the first set of people may be just what you need. So feminist separatism may indeed, as Rich says, have little to do with sexual preference or with civil rights, and a lot to do with making things easier for women of the future to define themselves in terms not presently available. These would be terms which made it easy for "women as women" to have what Dewey calls "habitual purposes and cultivated wants" – purposes and wants which, as Rich says, only a chosen few women presently have.

To sum up: I am suggesting that we see the contemporary feminist movement as playing the same role in intellectual and moral progress as was played by, for example, Plato's Academy, the early Christians meeting in the catacombs, the invisible Copernican colleges of the seventeenth century, groups of workingmen gathering to discuss Tom Paine's pamphlets, and lots of other clubs which were formed to try out new ways of speaking, and to gather the moral strength to go out and change the world. For groups build their moral strength by achieving increasing semantic authority over their members, thereby increasing the ability of those members to find their moral identities in their membership of such groups.

When a group forms itself in conscious opposition to those who control the life-chances of its members, and succeeds in achieving semantic authority over its members, the result may be its ruthless suppression – the sort of thing that happened to the Albigensians and which Margaret Atwood has imagined happening to the feminists. But it may also happen that, as the generations succeed one another, the masters, those in control, gradually find their conceptions of the possibilities open to human beings changing. For example, they may gradually begin to think of the options open to their own children as including membership in the group in question. The new language spoken by the separatist group may gradually get woven into the language taught in the schools.

Insofar as this sort of thing happens, eyes become less arrogant and the members of the group cease to be treated as wayward children, or as a bit crazy (the ways in which Emily Dickinson was treated). Instead, they gradually achieve what Frye calls "full personhood" in the eyes of everybody, having first achieved it only in the eyes of fellow-members of their own club. They begin to be treated as full-fledged human beings, rather than being seen, like children or the insane, as degenerate cases – as beings entitled to love and protection, but not to participation in deliberation on serious matters. For to be a full-fledged person in a given society is a matter of double

39 Frye, p. 106n.

negation: it is *not* to think of oneself as belonging to a group which powerful people in that society thank God they do *not* belong to.

In our society, straight white males of my generation – even earnestly egalitarian straight white males – cannot easily stop themselves from feeling guilty relief that they were not born women or gay or black, any more than they can stop themselves from being glad that they were not born mentally retarded or schizophrenic. This is in part because of a calculation of the obvious socio-economic disadvantages of being so born, but not entirely. It is also the sort of instinctive and ineffable horror which noble children used to feel at the thought of having been born to non-noble parents, even very rich non-noble parents.[40]

At some future point in the development of our society, guilty relief over not having been born a woman may not cross the minds of males, any more than the question "noble or base-born?" now crosses their minds.[41] That would be the point at which both males and females had *forgotten* the traditional androcentric language, just as we have all forgotten about the discussion between base and noble ancestry. But if this future comes to pass, we pragmatists think, it will not be because the females have been revealed to possess something – namely, full human dignity – which everybody, even they themselves, once mistakenly thought they lacked. It will be because the linguistic and other practices of the common culture have come to incorporate some of the practices characteristic of imaginative and courageous outcasts.

The new language which, with luck, will get woven into the language taught to children will not, however, be the language which the outcasts spoke in the old days, before the formation of separatist groups. For that was infected by the language of the masters. It will be, instead, a language gradually put together in separatist groups in the course of a long series of flirtations with meaninglessness. Had there been no stage of separation, there would have been no subsequent stage of assimilation. No prior antithesis, no new synthesis. No carefully nurtured pride in membership in a group which might not have attained self-consciousness were it not for its oppression, no expansion of the range of possible moral identities, and so no evolution of the species. This is what Hegel called the cunning of reason, and what Dewey thought of as the irony of evolution.

Someone who takes the passage I quoted from Dewey seriously will not think of oppressed groups as learning to *recognize* their own full personhood and then gradually, by stripping away veils of prejudice, leading their oppressors to confront reality. For they will not see full personhood as an intrinsic attribute of the oppressed, any more than they see human beings having a central and inviolable core surrounded by culturally-conditioned

---

40   This is the sort of ineffable horror which creates a sense of moral abomination (at, e.g., intercaste marriage), and thus furnishes the intuitions which one tries to bring into reflective equilibrium with one's principles. To view moral abominableness as capable of being produced or erased by changing the language taught to the young is the first step toward a non-universalist conception of moral progress.

41   To realize how far away such a future is, consider Eve Kosofsky Sedgwick's point that we shall only do justice to gays when we become as indifferent to whether our children turn out gay or straight as we are to whether they become doctors or lawyers. Surely she is right, and yet how many parents at the present time can even imagine such indifference? For the reasons suggested by Stout (see note 13 above), I suspect that neither sexism nor homophobia can vanish while the other persists.

beliefs and desires – a core for which neither biology nor history can account. To be a pragmatist rather than a realist in one's description of the acquisition of full personhood requires thinking of its acquisition by blacks, gays and women in the same terms as we think of its acquisition by Galilean scientists and Romantic poets. We say that the latter groups invented new moral identities for themselves by getting semantic authority over themselves. As time went by, they succeeded in having the language they had developed become part of the language everybody spoke. Similarly, we have to think of gays, blacks and women inventing themselves rather than discovering themselves, and thus of the larger society as coming to terms with something new.

This means taking Frye's phrase "new *being*" literally, and saying that there were very few female full persons around before feminism got started, in the same sense in which there were very few full-fledged Galilean scientists before the seventeenth century. It was of course *true* in earlier times that women should not have been oppressed, just as it was *true* before Newton said so that gravitational attraction accounted for the movements of the planets.[42] But, despite what Scripture says, truth will not necessarily prevail. "Truth" is not the name of a power which eventually wins through, it is just the nominalization of an approbative adjective. So just as a pragmatist in the philosophy of science cannot use the truth of Galileo's views as an explanation either of his success at prediction or of his gradually increasing fame,[43] so a pragmatist in moral philosophy cannot use the rightness of the feminist cause as an explanation either of its attraction for contemporary women or of its possible future triumph. For such explanations require the notion of a truth-tracking faculty, one which latches on to antecedently existing truth-makers. Truth is ahistorical, but that is not because truths are made true by ahistorical entities.

Frye's term "new being" may seem even more unnecessarily hyperbolic than MacKinnon's "new voice," but we pragmatists can take it at face value and realists cannot. As I read Frye, the point is that before feminism began to gather women together into a kind of club, there were female eccentrics like Wollstonecraft and de Gouges, but these were not women who existed *as* women, in MacKinnon's sense of "as." They were eccentric because they failed to fit into roles which men had contrived for them to fill, and because there were as yet no other roles. For roles require a community – a web of social expectations and habits which define the role in question. The community may be small, but, like a club as opposed to a convocation, or a

---

42 Pragmatists need not deny that true sentences are always true (as I have, unhappily, suggested in the past that they might – notably in my *"Waren die Gesetze Newtons schon vor Newton wahr?" Jahrbuch des Wissenschaftskollegs zu Berlin*, 1987). Stout (*Ethics After Babel*, chapter 11) rightly rebukes me for these suggestions, and says that pragmatists should agree with everybody else that "Slavery is absolutely wrong" has always been true – even in periods when this sentence would have sounded crazy to everybody concerned, even the slaves (who hoped that their fellow-tribespeople would return in force and enslave their present masters). All that pragmatists need is the claim that this sentence is not *made* true by something other than the beliefs which we would use to support it – and, in particular, not by something like The Nature of Human Beings.

43 I have criticized realists' claims to explain predictive success by truth in Part I of my forthcoming *Objectivity, Relativism and Truth* (Cambridge: Cambridge University Press, 1991). A related point – that the success of a true theory needs just as much historico-sociological explanation as the success of a false one – is made by Barry Barnes and other members of the so-called "Edinburgh school" of sociology of science.

new species as opposed to a few atypical mutant members of an old species, it only exists insofar as it is self-sustaining and self-reproducing.[44]

To sum up for the last time: prophetic feminists like MacKinnon and Frye foresee a new being not only for women but for society. They foresee a society in which the male–female distinction is no longer of much interest. Feminists who are also pragmatists will not see the formation of such a society as the removal of social constructs and the restoration of the way things were always meant to be. They will see it as the production of a better set of social constructs than the ones presently available, and thus as the creation of a new and better sort of human being.

---

44   It may seem that the view I am offering is the one which Frye rejects under the name of "the institutional theory of personhood" – the theory that, as she puts it, "'person' denotes a social and institutional role and that one may be allowed or forbidden to adopt that role" (p. 49). She says that this view "must be attractive to the phallist, who would fancy the power to create persons." But I do not want to say that men have the power to make full persons out of women by an act of grace, in the way in which sovereigns have the power to make nobles out of commoners. On the contrary, I would insist that men could not do this if they tried, for they are as much caught as are women in the linguistic practices which make it hard for women to be full persons. The utopia I foresee, in which these practices are simply forgotten, is not one which could be attained by an act of condescension on the part of men, any more than an absolute monarch could produce an egalitarian utopia by simultaneously ennobling all her subjects.

20

Human Rights, Rationality, and Sentimentality

In a report from Bosnia some months ago,[1] David Rieff said "To the Serbs, the Muslims are no longer human. ... Muslim prisoners, lying on the ground in rows, awaiting interrogation, were driven over by a Serb guard in a small delivery van." This theme of dehumanization recurs when Rieff says:

> A Muslim man in Bosansi Petrovac ... [was] forced to bite off the penis of a fellow-Muslim. ... If you say that a man is not human, but the man looks like you and the only way to identify this devil is to make him drop his trousers – Muslim men are circumcised and Serb men are not – it is probably only a short step, psychologically, to cutting off his prick. ... There has never been a campaign of ethnic cleansing from which sexual sadism has gone missing.

The moral to be drawn from Rieff's stories is that Serbian murderers and rapists do not think of themselves as violating human rights. For they are not doing these things to fellow human beings, but to *Muslims*. They are not being inhuman, but rather are discriminating between the true humans and the pseudohumans. They are making the same sort of distinction as the Crusaders made between humans and infidel dogs, and the Black Muslims make between humans and blue-eyed devils. The founder of my university was able both to own slaves and to think it self-evident that all men were endowed by their creator with certain inalienable rights. He had convinced himself that the consciousness of Blacks, like that of animals, "participate[s] more of sensation than reflection."[2] Like the Serbs, Mr. Jefferson did not think of himself as violating *human* rights.

Richard M. Rorty, "Human Rights, Rationality, and Sentimentality," pp. 112–34 in Stephen Shute and Susan Hurley (eds.), *On Human Rights: The Oxford Amnesty Lectures*. © 1993 by Basic Books. Reprinted by permission of Basic Books, a member of Perseus Book Group.

1 "Letter from Bosnia," *New Yorker*, November 23, 1992, 82–95.
2 "Their griefs are transient. Those numberless afflictions, which render it doubtful whether heaven has given life to us in mercy or in wrath, are less felt, and sooner forgotten with them. In general, their existence appears to participate more of sensation than reflection. To this must be ascribed their disposition to sleep when abstracted from their diversions, and unemployed in

The Serbs take themselves to be acting in the interests of true humanity by purifying the world of pseudohumanity. In this respect, their self-image resembles that of moral philosophers who hope to cleanse the world of prejudice and superstition. This cleansing will permit us to rise above our animality by becoming, for the first time, wholly rational and thus wholly human. The Serbs, the moralists, Jefferson, and the Black Muslims all use the term "men" to mean "people like us." They think the line between humans and animals is not simply the line between featherless bipeds and all others. They think the line divides some featherless bipeds from others: There are animals walking about in humanoid form. We and those like us are paradigm cases of humanity, but those too different from us in behavior or custom are, at best, borderline cases. As Clifford Geertz puts it, "Men's most importunate claims to humanity are cast in the accents of group pride."[3]

We in the safe, rich, democracies feel about the Serbian torturers and rapists as they feel about their Muslim victims: They are more like animals than like us. But we are not doing anything to help the Muslim women who are being gang raped or the Muslim men who are being castrated, any more than we did anything in the thirties when the Nazis were amusing themselves by torturing Jews. Here in the safe countries we find ourselves saying things like "That's how things have always been in the Balkans," suggesting that, unlike us, those people are used to being raped and castrated. The contempt we always feel for losers – Jews in the thirties, Muslims now – combines with our disgust at the winners' behavior to produce the semiconscious attitude: "a plague on both your houses." We think of the Serbs or the Nazis as animals, because ravenous beasts of prey are animals. We think of the Muslims or the Jews being herded into concentration camps as animals, because cattle are animals. Neither sort of animal is very much like us, and there seems no point in human beings getting involved in quarrels between animals.

The human–animal distinction, however, is only one of the three main ways in which we paradigmatic humans distinguish ourselves from borderline cases. A second is by invoking the distinction between adults and children. Ignorant and superstitious people, we say, are like children; they will attain true humanity only if raised up by proper education. If they seem incapable of absorbing such education, that shows they are not really the same kind of being as we educable people are. Blacks, the whites in the United States and in South Africa used to say, are like children. That is why it is appropriate to address Black males, of whatever age, as "boy." Women, men used to say, are permanently childlike; it is therefore appropriate to spend no money on their education, and to refuse them access to power.

When it comes to women, however, there are simpler ways of excluding them from true humanity: for example, using "man" as a synonym of "human being." As feminists have pointed out, such usages reinforce the average male's thankfulness that he was not born a woman, as well as his fear of the ultimate degradation: feminization. The extent of the latter fear is evidenced by the particular sort of sexual sadism Rieff describes. His point that such sadism is never absent from attempts to purify the species or cleanse the

---

labor. An animal whose body is at rest, and who does not reflect must be disposed to sleep of course." Thomas Jefferson, "Notes on Virginia," *Writings*, ed. Lipscomb and Bergh (Washington, D.C.: 1905), 1: 194.

3   Geertz, "Thick Description" in his *The Interpretation of Culture* (New York: Basic Books, 1973), 22.

territory confirms Catharine MacKinnon's claim that, for most men, being a woman does not count as a way of being human. Being a nonmale is the third main way of being nonhuman. There are several ways of being nonmale. One is to be born without a penis; another is to have one's penis cut or bitten off; a third is to have been penetrated by a penis. Many men who have been raped are convinced that their manhood, and thus their humanity, has been taken away. Like racists who discover they have Jewish or Black ancestry, they may commit suicide out of sheer shame, shame at no longer being the kind of featherless biped that counts as human.

Philosophers have tried to clear this mess up by spelling out what all and only the featherless bipeds have in common, thereby explaining what is essential to being human. Plato argued that there is a big difference between us and the animals, a difference worthy of respect and cultivation. He thought that human beings have a special added ingredient which puts them in a different ontological category than the brutes. Respect for this ingredient provides a reason for people to be nice to each other. Anti-Platonists like Nietzsche reply that attempts to get people to stop murdering, raping, and castrating each other are, in the long run, doomed to fail – for the real truth about human nature is that we are a uniquely nasty and dangerous kind of animal. When contemporary admirers of Plato claim that all featherless bipeds – even the stupid and childlike, even the women, even the sodomized – have the same inalienable rights, admirers of Nietzsche reply that the the very idea of "inalienable human rights" is, like the idea of a special added ingredient, a laughably feeble attempt by the weaker members of the species to fend off the stronger.

As I see it, one important intellectual advance made in our century is the steady decline in interest in the quarrel between Plato and Nietzsche. There is a growing willingness to neglect the question "What is our nature?" and to substitute the question "What can we make of ourselves?" We are much less inclined than our ancestors were to take "theories of human nature" seriously, much less inclined to take ontology or history as a guide to life. We have come to see that the only lesson of either history or anthropology is our extraordinary malleability. We are coming to think of ourselves as the flexible, protean, self-shaping, animal rather than as the rational animal or the cruel animal.

One of the shapes we have recently assumed is that of a human rights culture. I borrow the term "human rights culture" from the Argentinian jurist and philosopher Eduardo Rabossi. In an article called "Human Rights Naturalized," Rabossi argues that philosophers should think of this culture as a new, welcome fact of the post-Holocaust world. They should stop trying to get behind or beneath this fact, stop trying to detect and defend its so-called "philosophical presuppositions." On Rabossi's view, philosophers like Alan Gewirth are wrong to argue that human rights cannot depend on historical facts. "My basic point," Rabossi says, is that "the world has changed, that the human rights phenomenon renders human rights foundationalism outmoded and irrelevant."[4]

---

4 Rabossi also says that he does not wish to question "the idea of a rational foundation of morality." I am not sure why he does not. Rabossi may perhaps mean that in the past – for example, at the time of Kant – this idea still made a kind of sense, but it makes sense no longer. That, at any rate, is my own view. Kant wrote in a period when the only alternative to religion seemed to be something like science. In such a period, inventing a pseudoscience called "the system of transcendental philosophy" – setting the stage for the show-stopping climax in which one pulls moral obligation out of a transcendental hat – might plausibly seem the only way of saving morality from the hedonists on one side and the priests on the other.

Rabossi's claim that human rights foundationalism is *outmoded* seems to me both true and important; it will be my principal topic in this lecture. I shall be enlarging on, and defending, Rabossi's claim that the question whether human beings really have the rights enumerated in the Helsinki Declaration is not worth raising. In particular, I shall be defending the claim that nothing relevant to moral choice separates human beings from animals except historically contingent facts of the world, cultural facts.

This claim is sometimes called "cultural relativism" by those who indignantly reject it. One reason they reject it is that such relativism seems to them incompatible with the fact that our human rights culture, the culture with which we in this democracy identify ourselves, is morally superior to other cultures. I quite agree that ours is morally superior, but I do not think this superiority counts in favor of the existence of a universal human nature. It would only do so if we assumed that a moral claim is ill-founded if not backed up by knowledge of a distinctively human attribute. But it is not clear why "respect for human dignity" – our sense that the differences between Serb and Muslim, Christian and infidel, gay and straight, male and female should not matter – must presuppose the existence of any such attribute.

Traditionally, the name of the shared human attribute which supposedly "grounds" morality is "rationality." Cultural relativism is associated with irrationalism because it denies the existence of morally relevant transcultural facts. To agree with Rabossi one must, indeed, be irrationalist in that sense. But one need not be irrationalist in the sense of ceasing to make one's web of belief as coherent, and as perspicuously structured, as possible. Philosophers like myself, who think of rationality as simply the attempt at such coherence, agree with Rabossi that foundationalist projects are outmoded. We see our task as a matter of making our own culture – the human rights culture – more self-conscious and more powerful, rather than of demonstrating its superiority to other cultures by an appeal to something transcultural.

We think that the most philosophy can hope to do is summarize our culturally influenced intuitions about the right thing to do in various situations. The summary is effected by formulating a generalization from which these intuitions can be deduced, with the help of noncontroversial lemmas. That generalization is not supposed to ground our intuitions, but rather to summarize them. John Rawls's "Difference Principle" and the U.S. Supreme Court's construction, in recent decades, of a constitutional "right to privacy" are examples of this kind of summary. We see the formulation of such summarizing generalizations as increasing the predictability, and thus the power and efficiency, of our institutions, thereby heightening the sense of shared moral identity which brings us together in a moral community.

Foundationalist philosophers, such as Plato, Aquinas, and Kant, have hoped to provide independent support for such summarizing generalizations. They would like to infer these generalizations from further premises, premises capable of being known to be true independently of the truth of the moral intuitions which have been summarized. Such premises are supposed to justify our intuitions, by providing premises from which the content of those intuitions can be deduced. I shall lump all such premises together under the label "claims to knowledge about the nature of human beings." In this broad sense, claims to know that our moral intuitions are recollections of the Form of the Good, or that we are the disobedient children of a loving God, or that human beings differ from other kinds of animals by having dignity rather than mere value, are all claims about human nature. So are such counterclaims as that human beings are merely vehicles for selfish genes, or merely eruptions of the will to power.

To claim such knowledge is to claim to know something which, though not itself a moral intuition, can *correct* moral intuitions. It is essential to this idea of moral knowledge that a whole community might come to know that most of their most salient intuitions about the right thing to do were wrong. But now suppose we ask: *Is* there this sort of knowledge? What kind of question is that? On the traditional view, it is a philosophical question, belonging to a branch of epistemology known as "metaethics." But on the pragmatist view which I favor, it is a question of efficiency, of how best to grab hold of history – how best to bring about the utopia sketched by the Enlightenment. If the activities of those who attempt to achieve this sort of knowledge seem of little use in actualizing this utopia, that is a reason to think there is no such knowledge. If it seems that most of the work of changing moral intuitions is being done by manipulating our feelings rather than increasing our knowledge, that will be a reason to think that there is no knowledge of the sort which philosophers like Plato, Aquinas, and Kant hoped to acquire.

This pragmatist argument against the Platonist has the same form as an argument for cutting off payment to the priests who are performing purportedly war-winning sacrifices – an argument which says that all the real work of winning the war seems to be getting done by the generals and admirals, not to mention the foot soldiers. The argument does not say: Since there seem to be no gods, there is probably no need to support the priests. It says instead: Since there is apparently no need to support the priests, there probably are no gods. We pragmatists argue from the fact that the emergence of the human rights culture seems to owe nothing to increased moral knowledge, and everything to hearing sad and sentimental stories, to the conclusion that there is probably no knowledge of the sort Plato envisaged. We go on to argue: Since no useful work seems to be done by insisting on a purportedly ahistorical human nature, there probably is no such nature, or at least nothing in that nature that is relevant to our moral choices.

In short, my doubts about the effectiveness of appeals to moral knowledge are doubts about causal efficacy, not about epistemic status. My doubts have nothing to do with any of the theoretical questions discussed under the heading of "metaethics," questions about the relation between facts and values, or between reason and passion, or between the cognitive and the noncognitive, or between descriptive statements and action-guiding statements. Nor do they have anything to do with questions about realism and antirealism. The difference between the moral realist and the moral antirealist seems to pragmatists to be a difference which makes no practical difference. Further, such metaethical questions presuppose the Platonic distinction between inquiry which aims at efficient problem-solving and inquiry which aims at a goal called "truth for its own sake." That distinction collapses if one follows Dewey in thinking of all inquiry – in physics as well as in ethics – as practical problem-solving, or if one follows Peirce in seeing every belief as action-guiding.[5]

---

5   The present state of metaethical discussion is admirably summarized in Stephen Darwall, Allan Gibbard, and Peter Railton, "Toward *Fin de Siècle* Ethics: Some Trends," *The Philosophical Review* 101 (1992): 115–89. This comprehensive and judicious article takes for granted that there is a

Even after the priests have been pensioned off, however, the memories of certain priests may still be cherished by the community – especially the memories of their prophecies. We remain profoundly grateful to philosophers like Plato and Kant, not because they discovered truths but because they prophesied cosmopolitan utopias – utopias most of whose details they may have got wrong, but utopias we might never have struggled to reach had we not heard their prophecies. As long as our ability to know, and in particular to discuss the question "What is man?" seemed the most important thing about us human beings, people like Plato and Kant accompanied utopian prophecies with claims to know something deep and important – something about the parts of the soul, or the transcendental status of the common moral consciousness. But this ability, and those questions, have, in the course of the last two hundred years, come to seem much less important. Rabossi summarizes this cultural sea change in his claim that human rights foundationalism is outmoded. In the remainder of this lecture, I shall take up the questions: *Why* has knowledge become much less important to our self-image than it was two hundred years ago? Why does the attempt to found culture on nature, and moral obligation on knowledge of transcultural universals, seem so much less important to us than it seemed in the Enlightenment? Why is there so little resonance, and so little point, in asking whether human beings in fact have the rights listed in the Helsinki Declaration? Why, in short, has moral philosophy become such an inconspicuous part of our culture?

A simple answer is that between Kant's time and ours Darwin argued most of the intellectuals out of the view that human beings contain a special added ingredient. He convinced most of us that we were exceptionally talented animals, animals clever enough to take charge of our own future evolution. I think this answer is right as far as it goes,

---

problem about "vindicating the objectivity of morality" (127), that there is an interesting question as to whether morals is "cognitive" or "non-cognitive," that we need to figure out whether we have a "cognitive capacity" to detect moral properties (148), and that these matters can be dealt with ahistorically.

When these authors consider historicist writers such as Alasdair MacIntyre and Bernard Williams, they conclude that they are "[meta]*théoriciens malgré eux*" who share the authors' own "desire to understand morality, its preconditions and its prospects" (183). They make little effort to come to terms with suggestions that there may be no ahistorical entity called "morality" to be understood. The final paragraph of the paper does suggest that it might be helpful if moral philosophers knew more anthropology, or psychology, or history. But the penultimate paragraph makes clear that, with or without such assists, "contemporary metaethics moves ahead, and positions gain in complexity and sophistication."

It is instructive, I think, to compare this article with Annette Baier's "Some Thoughts On How We Moral Philosophers Live Now," *The Monist* 67 (1984): 490. Baier suggests that moral philosophers should "at least occasionally, like Socrates, consider why the rest of society should not merely tolerate but subsidize our activity." She goes on to ask, "Is the large proportional increase of professional philosophers and moral philosophers a good thing, morally speaking? Even if it scarcely amounts to a plague of gadflies, it may amount to a nuisance of owls." The kind of metaphilosophical and historical self-consciousness and self-doubt displayed by Baier seems to me badly needed, but it is conspicuously absent in *Philosophy in Review* (the centennial issue of *The Philosophical Review* in which "Toward *Fin de Siècle* Ethics" appears). The contributors to this issue are convinced that the increasing sophistication of a philosophical subdiscipline is enough to demonstrate its social utility, and are entirely unimpressed by murmurs of "decadent scholasticism."

but it leads to a further question: Why did Darwin succeed, relatively speaking, so very easily? Why did he not cause the creative philosophical ferment caused by Galileo and Newton?

The revival by the New Science of the seventeenth century of a Democritean-Lucretian corpuscularian picture of nature scared Kant into inventing transcendental philosophy, inventing a brand-new kind of knowledge, which could demote the corpuscularian world picture to the status of "appearance." Kant's example encouraged the idea that the philosopher, as an expert on the nature and limits of knowledge, can serve as supreme cultural arbiter.[6] By the time of Darwin, however, this idea was already beginning to seem quaint. The historicism which dominated the intellectual world of the early nineteenth century had created an antiessentialist mood. So when Darwin came along, he fitted into the evolutionary niche which Herder and Hegel had begun to colonize. Intellectuals who populate this niche look to the future rather than to eternity. They prefer new ideas about how change can be effected to stable criteria for determining the desirability of change. They are the ones who think both Plato and Nietzsche outmoded.

The best explanation of both Darwin's relatively easy triumph, and our own increasing willingness to substitute hope for knowledge, is that the nineteenth and twentieth centuries saw, among the Europeans and Americans, an extraordinary increase in wealth, literacy, and leisure. This increase made possible an unprecedented acceleration in the rate of moral progress. Such events as the French Revolution and the ending of the trans-Atlantic slave trade prompted nineteenth-century intellectuals in the rich democracies to say: It is enough for us to know that we live in an age in which human beings can make things much better for ourselves.[7] We do not need to dig behind this historical fact to nonhistorical facts about what we really are.

In the two centuries since the French Revolution, we have learned that human beings are far more malleable than Plato or Kant had dreamed. The more we are impressed by this malleability, the less interested we become in questions about our ahistorical nature. The more we see a chance to recreate ourselves, the more we read Darwin not as offering one more theory about what we really are but as providing reasons why we need not ask what we really are. Nowadays, to say that we are clever animals is not to say something

6   Fichte's *Vocation of Man* is a useful reminder of the need that was felt, circa 1800, for a cognitive discipline called philosophy that would rescue utopian hope from natural science. It is hard to think of an analogous book written in reaction to Darwin. Those who couldn't stand what Darwin was saying tended to go straight back past the Enlightenment to traditional religious faith. The unsubtle, unphilosophical opposition, in nineteenth-century Britain and France, between science and faith suggests that most intellectuals had become unable to believe that philosophy might produce some sort of superknowledge, knowledge that might trump the results of physical and biological inquiry.

7   Some contemporary intellectuals, especially in France and Germany, take it as obvious that the Holocaust made it clear that the hopes for human freedom which arose in the nineteenth century are obsolete – that at the end of the twentieth century we postmodernists know that the Enlightenment project is doomed. But even these intellectuals, in their less preachy and sententious moments, do their best to further that project. So they should, for nobody has come up with a better one. It does not diminish the memory of the Holocaust to say that our response to it should not be a claim to have gained a new understanding of human nature or of human history, but rather a willingness to pick ourselves up and try again.

philosophical and pessimistic but something political and hopeful, namely: If we can work together, we can make ourselves into whatever we are clever and courageous enough to imagine ourselves becoming. This sets aside Kant's question "What is Man?" and substitutes the question "What sort of world can we prepare for our great-grandchildren?"

The question "What is Man?" in the sense of "What is the deep ahistorical nature of human beings?" owed its popularity to the standard answer to that question: We are the *rational* animal, the one which can know as well as merely feel. The residual popularity of this answer accounts for the residual popularity of Kant's astonishing claim that sentimentality has nothing to do with morality, that there is something distinctively and transculturally human called "the sense of moral obligation" which has nothing to do with love, friendship, trust, or social solidarity. As long as we believe *that*, people like Rabossi are going to have a tough time convincing us that human rights foundationalism is an outmoded project.

To overcome this idea of a *sui generis* sense of moral obligation, it would help to stop answering the question "What makes us different from the other animals?" by saying "We can know, and they can merely feel." We should substitute "We can feel *for each other* to a much greater extent than they can." This substitution would let us disentangle Christ's suggestion that love matters more than knowledge from the neo-Platonic suggestion that knowledge of the truth will make us free. For as long as we think that there is an ahistorical power which makes for righteousness – a power called truth, or rationality – we shall not be able to put foundationalism behind us.

The best, and probably the only, argument for putting foundationalism behind us is the one I have already suggested: It would be more efficient to do so, because it would let us concentrate our energies on manipulating sentiments, on sentimental education. That sort of education sufficiently acquaints people of different kinds with one another so that they are less tempted to think of those different from themselves as only quasi-human. The goal of this manipulation of sentiment is to expand the reference of the terms "our kind of people" and "people like us."

All I can do to supplement this argument from increased efficiency is to offer a suggestion about how Plato managed to convince us that knowledge of universal truths mattered as much as he thought it did. Plato thought that the philosopher's task was to answer questions like "Why should I be moral? Why is it rational to be moral? Why is it in my interest to be moral? Why is it in the interest of human beings as such to be moral?" He thought this because he believed the best way to deal with people like Thrasymachus and Callicles was to demonstrate to them that they had an interest of which they were unaware, an interest in being rational, in acquiring self-knowledge. Plato thereby saddled us with a distinction between the true and the false self. That distinction was, by the time of Kant, transmuted into a distinction between categorical, rigid, moral obligation and flexible, empirically determinable, self-interest. Contemporary moral philosophy is still lumbered with this opposition between self-interest and morality, an opposition which makes it hard to realize that my pride in being a part of the human rights culture is no more external to my self than my desire for financial success.

It would have been better if Plato had decided, as Aristotle was to decide, that there was nothing much to be done with people like Thrasymachus and Callicles, and that the problem was how to avoid having children who would be like Thrasymachus and Callicles. By insisting that he could re-educate people who had matured without acquiring appropriate moral sentiments by invoking a higher power than sentiment, the power of reason, Plato got moral philosophy off on the wrong foot. He led moral philosophers to concentrate on the rather rare figure of the psychopath, the person who has no concern for any human being other than himself. Moral philosophy has systematically neglected the much more common case: the person whose treatment of a rather narrow range of featherless bipeds is morally impeccable, but who remains indifferent to the suffering of those outside this range, the ones he or she thinks of as pseudohumans.[8]

Plato set things up so that moral philosophers think they have failed unless they convince the rational egotist that he should not be an egotist – convince him by telling him about his true, unfortunately neglected, self. But the rational egotist is not the problem. The problem is the gallant and honorable Serb who sees Muslims as circumcised dogs. It is the brave soldier and good comrade who loves and is loved by his mates, but who thinks of women as dangerous, malevolent whores and bitches.

Plato thought that the way to get people to be nicer to each other was to point out what they all had in common – rationality. But it does little good to point out, to the people I have just described, that many Muslims and women are good at mathematics or engineering or jurisprudence. Resentful young Nazi toughs were quite aware that many Jews were clever and learned, but this only added to the pleasure they took in beating them up. Nor does it do much good to get such people to read Kant, and agree that one should not treat rational agents simply as means. For everything turns on who counts as a fellow human being, as a rational agent in the only relevant sense – the sense in which rational agency is synonomous with membership in *our* moral community.

For most white people, until very recently, most Black people did not so count. For most Christians, up until the seventeenth century or so, most heathen did not so count. For the Nazis, Jews did not so count. For most males in countries in which the average annual income is under four thousand dollars, most females still do not so count. Whenever tribal and national rivalries become important, members of rival tribes and nations will not so count. Kant's account of the respect due to rational agents tells you that you should extend the respect you feel for people like yourself to all featherless bipeds. This is an excellent suggestion, a good formula for secularizing the Christian doctrine of the brotherhood of man. But it has never been backed up by an argument based on neutral premises, and it never will be. Outside the circle of post-Enlightenment European culture, the circle of relatively safe and secure people who have been manipulating each others' sentiments for two hundred years, most people are simply unable to understand why membership in a biological species is supposed to suffice for membership in a moral community. This is not because they are insufficiently rational. It is, typically, because they live in a world in which it would be just too risky – indeed, would often be insanely dangerous – to let one's sense of moral community stretch beyond one's family, clan, or tribe.

---

8   Nietzsche was right to remind us that "these same men who, amongst themselves, are so strictly constrained by custom, worship, ritual gratitude and by mutual surveillance and jealousy, who are so resourceful in consideration, tenderness, loyalty, pride and friendship, when once they step outside their circle become little better than uncaged beasts of prey." *The Genealogy of Morals*, trans. Golffing (Garden City, N.Y.: Doubleday, 1956), 174.

To get whites to be nicer to Blacks, males to females, Serbs to Muslims, or straights to gays, to help our species link up into what Rabossi calls a "planetary community" dominated by a culture of human rights, it is of no use whatever to say, with Kant: Notice that what you have in common, your humanity, is more important than these trivial differences. For the people we are trying to convince will rejoin that they notice nothing of the sort. Such people are *morally* offended by the suggestion that they should treat someone who is not kin as if he were a brother, or a nigger as if he were white, or a queer as if he were normal, or an infidel as if she were a believer. They are offended by the suggestion that they treat people whom they do not think of as human as if they were human. When utilitarians tell them that all pleasures and pains felt by members of our biological species are equally relevant to moral deliberation, or when Kantians tell them that the ability to engage in such deliberation is sufficient for membership in the moral community, they are incredulous. They rejoin that these philosophers seem oblivious to blatantly obvious moral distinctions, distinctions any decent person will draw.

This rejoinder is not just a rhetorical device, nor is it in any way irrational. It is heartfelt. The identity of these people, the people whom we should like to convince to join our Eurocentric human rights culture, is bound up with their sense of who they are *not*. Most people – especially people relatively untouched by the European Enlightenment – simply do not think of themselves as, first and foremost, a human being. Instead, they think of themselves as being a certain *good* sort of human being – a sort defined by explicit opposition to a particularly bad sort. It is crucial for their sense of who they are that they are *not* an infidel, *not* a queer, *not* a woman, *not* an untouchable. Just insofar as they are impoverished, and as their lives are perpetually at risk, they have little else than pride in not being what they are not to sustain their self-respect. Starting with the days when the term "human being" was synonomous with "member of our tribe," we have always thought of human beings in terms of paradigm members of the species. We have contrasted *us*, the *real* humans, with rudimentary, or perverted, or deformed examples of humanity.

We Eurocentric intellectuals like to suggest that we, the paradigm humans, have overcome this primitive parochialism by using that paradigmatic human faculty, reason. So we say that failure to concur with us is due to "prejudice." Our use of these terms in this way may make us nod in agreement when Colin McGinn tells us, in the introduction to his recent book,[9] that learning to tell right from wrong is not as hard as learning French. The only obstacles to agreeing with his moral views, McGinn explains, are "prejudice, vested interest and laziness."

One can see what McGinn means: If, like many of us, you teach students who have been brought up in the shadow of the Holocaust, brought up believing that prejudice against racial or religious groups is a terrible thing, it is not very hard to convert them to standard liberal views about abortion, gay rights, and the like. You may even get them to stop eating animals. All you have to do is convince them that all the arguments on the other side appeal to "morally irrelevant" considerations. You do this by manipulating their sentiments in such a way that they imagine themselves in the shoes of the despised and oppressed. Such students are already so nice that they are eager to define their identity in nonexclusionary terms. The only people they have trouble being nice to are the ones they consider irrational – the religious fundamentalist, the smirking rapist, or the swaggering skinhead.

---

9   Colin McGinn, *Moral Literacy: or, How to Do the Right Thing* (London: Duckworth, 1992), 16.

Producing generations of nice, tolerant, well-off, secure, other-respecting students of this sort in all parts of the world is just what is needed – indeed *all* that is needed – to achieve an Enlightenment utopia. The more youngsters like this we can raise, the stronger and more global our human rights culture will become. But it is not a good idea to encourage these students to label "irrational" the intolerant people they have trouble tolerating. For that Platonic-Kantian epithet suggests that, with only a little more effort, the good and rational part of these other people's souls could have triumphed over the bad and irrational part. It suggests that we good people know something these bad people do not know, and that it is probably their own silly fault that they do not know it. All they have to do, after all, is to think a little harder, be a little more self-conscious, a little more rational.

But the bad people's beliefs are not more or less "irrational" than the belief that race, religion, gender, and sexual preference are all morally irrelevant – that these are all trumped by membership in the biological species. As used by moral philosophers like McGinn, the term "irrational behavior" means no more than "behavior of which we disapprove so strongly that our spade is turned when asked *why* we disapprove of it." It would be better to teach our students that these bad people are no less rational, no less clearheaded, no more prejudiced, than we good people who respect otherness. The bad people's problem is that they were not so lucky in the circumstances of their upbringing as we were. Instead of treating as irrational all those people out there who are trying to find and kill Salman Rushdie, we should treat them as deprived.

Foundationalists think of these people as deprived of truth, of moral knowledge. But it would be better – more specific, more suggestive of possible remedies – to think of them as deprived of two more concrete things: security and sympathy. By "security" I mean conditions of life sufficiently risk-free as to make one's difference from others inessential to one's self-respect, one's sense of worth. These conditions have been enjoyed by Americans and Europeans – the people who dreamed up the human rights culture – much more than they have been enjoyed by anyone else. By "sympathy" I mean the sort of reaction that the Athenians had more of after seeing Aeschylus' *The Persians* than before, the sort that white Americans had more of after reading *Uncle Tom's Cabin* than before, the sort that we have more of after watching TV programs about the genocide in Bosnia. Security and sympathy go together, for the same reasons that peace and economic productivity go together. The tougher things are, the more you have to be afraid of, the more dangerous your situation, the less you can afford the time or effort to think about what things might be like for people with whom you do not immediately identify. Sentimental education only works on people who can relax long enough to listen.

If Rabossi and I are right in thinking human rights foundationalism outmoded, then Hume is a better advisor than Kant about how we intellectuals can hasten the coming of the Enlightenment utopia for which both men yearned. Among contemporary philosophers, the best advisor seems to me to be Annette Baier. Baier describes Hume as "the woman's moral philosopher" because Hume held that "corrected (sometimes rule-corrected) sympathy, not law-discerning reason, is the fundamental moral capacity".[10] Baier would like us to get rid of both the Platonic idea that we have a true self, and the Kantian idea that it is rational to be moral. In aid of this project, she suggests that we think

10   Baier, "Hume, the Women's Moral Theorist?," in Eva Kittay and Diana Meyers, eds., *Women and Moral Theory* (Totowa, N.J.: Rowman and Littlefield, 1987), 40.

of "trust" rather than "obligation" as the fundamental moral notion. This substitution would mean thinking of the spread of the human rights culture not as a matter of our becoming more aware of the requirements of the moral law, but rather as what Baier calls "a progress of sentiments."[11] This progress consists in an increasing ability to see the similarities between ourselves and people very unlike us as outweighing the differences. It is the result of what I have been calling "sentimental education." The relevant similarities are not a matter of sharing a deep true self which instantiates true humanity, but are such little, superficial, similarities as cherishing our parents and our children – similarities that do not interestingly distinguish us from many nonhuman animals.

To accept Baier's suggestions, however, we should have to overcome our sense that sentiment is too weak a force, and that something stronger is required. This idea that reason is "stronger" than sentiment, that only an insistence on the unconditionality of moral obligation has the power to change human beings for the better, is very persistent. I think that this persistence is due mainly to a semiconscious realization that, if we hand our hopes for moral progress over to sentiment, we are in effect handing them over to *condescension*. For we shall be relying on those who have the power to change things – people like the rich New England abolitionists, or rich bleeding hearts like Robert Owen and Friedrich Engels – rather than on something that has power over *them*. We shall have to accept the fact that the fate of the women of Bosnia depends on whether TV journalists manage to do for them what Harriet Beecher Stowe did for black slaves, whether these journalists can make us, the audience back in the safe countries, feel that these women are more like us, more like real human beings, than we had realized.

To rely on the suggestions of sentiment rather than on the commands of reason is to think of powerful people gradually ceasing to oppress others, or ceasing to countenance the oppression of others, out of mere niceness, rather than out of obedience to the moral law. But it is revolting to think that our only hope for a decent society consists in softening the self-satisfied hearts of a leisure class. We want moral progress to burst up from below, rather than waiting patiently upon condescension from the top. The residual popularity of Kantian ideas of "unconditional moral obligation" – obligation imposed by deep ahistorical noncontingent forces – seems to me almost entirely due to our abhorrence for the idea that the people on top hold the future in their hands, that everything depends on them, that there is nothing more powerful to which we can appeal against them.

Like everyone else, I too should prefer a bottom-up way of achieving utopia, a quick reversal of fortune which will make the last first. But I do not think this is how utopia will in fact come into being. Nor do I think that our preference for this way lends any support to the idea that the Enlightenment project lies in the depths of every human soul. So why does this preference make us resist the thought that sentimentality may be the best weapon we have? I think Nietzsche gave the right answer to this question: We resist out of resentment. We *resent* the idea that we shall have to wait for the strong to

---

11   Baier's book on Hume is entitled *A Progress of Sentiments: Reflections on Hume's Treatise* (Cambridge, Mass.: Harvard University Press, 1991). Baier's view of the inadequacy of most attempts by contemporary moral philosophers to break with Kant comes out most clearly when she characterizes Allan Gibbard (in his book *Wise Choices, Apt Feelings*) as focusing "on the feelings that a patriarchal religion has bequeathed to us," and says that "Hume would judge Gibbard to be, as a moral philosopher, basically a divine disguised as a fellow expressivist" (312).

turn their piggy little eyes to the suffering of the weak. We desperately hope that there is something stronger and more powerful that will *hurt* the strong if they do *not* – if not a vengeful God, then a vengeful aroused proletariat, or, at least, a vengeful superego, or, at the very least, the offended majesty of Kant's tribunal of pure practical reason. The desperate hope for a noncontingent and powerful ally is, according to Nietzsche, the common core of Platonism, of religious insistence on divine omnipotence, and of Kantian moral philosophy.[12]

Nietzsche was, I think, right on the button when he offered this diagnosis. What Santayana called "supernaturalism," the confusion of ideals and power, is all that lies behind the Kantian claim that it is not only nicer, but more rational, to include strangers within our moral community than to exclude them from it. If we agree with Nietzsche and Santayana on this point, however, we do not thereby acquire any reason to turn our backs on the Enlightenment project, as Nietzsche did. Nor do we acquire any reason to be sardonically pessimistic about the chances of this project, in the manner of admirers of Nietzsche like Santayana, Ortega, Heidegger, Strauss, and Foucault.

For even though Nietzsche was absolutely right to see Kant's insistence on unconditionality as an expression of resentment, he was absolutely wrong to treat Christianity, and the age of the democratic revolutions, as signs of human degeneration. He and Kant, alas, shared something with each other which neither shared with Harriet Beecher Stowe – something which Iris Murdoch has called "dryness" and which Jacques Derrida has called "phallogocentrism." The common element in the thought of both men was a desire for purity. This sort of purity consists in being not only autonomous, in command of oneself, but also in having the kind of self-conscious self-sufficiency which Sartre describes as the perfect synthesis of the in-itself and the for-itself. This synthesis could only be attained, Sartre pointed out, if one could rid oneself of everything sticky, slimy, wet, sentimental, and womanish.

Although this desire for virile purity links Plato to Kant, the desire to bring as many different kinds of people as possible into a cosmopolis links Kant to Stowe. Kant is, in the history of moral thinking, a transitional stage between the hopeless attempt to convict Thrasymachus of irrationality and the hopeful attempt to see every new featherless biped who comes along as one of us. Kant's mistake was to think that the only way to have a modest, damped-down, non-fanatical version of Christian brotherhood after letting go of the Christian faith was to revive the themes of pre-Christian philosophical thought. He wanted to make knowledge of a core self do what can be done only by the continual refreshment and re-creation of the self, through interaction with selves as unlike itself as possible.

Kant performed the sort of awkward balancing act required in transitional periods. His project mediated between a dying rationalist tradition and a vision of a new, democratic world, the world of what Rabossi calls "the human rights phenomenon." With the advent of this phenomenon, Kant's balancing act has become outmoded and irrelevant. We are now in a good position to put aside the last vestiges of the ideas that human beings are distinguished by the capacity to know rather than by the capacities for friendship and inter-marriage, distinguished by rigorous rationality rather than by flexible sentimentality. If we do so, we shall have dropped the idea that assured knowledge of a

---

12 Nietzsche's diagnosis is reinforced by Elizabeth Anscombe's famous argument that atheists are not entitled to the term "moral obligation."

PRAGMATISM, LITERATURE, AND DEMOCRACY

truth about what we have in common is a prerequisite for moral education, as well as the idea of a specifically moral motivation. If we do all these things, we shall see Kant's *Foundations of the Metaphysics of Morals* as a placeholder for *Uncle Tom's Cabin* – a concession to the expectations of an intellectual epoch in which the quest for quasi-scientific knowledge seemed the only possible response to religious exclusionism.[13]

Unfortunately, many philosophers, especially in the English-speaking world, are still trying to hold on to the Platonic insistence that the principal duty of human beings is to *know*. That insistence was the lifeline to which Kant and Hegel thought we had to cling.[14] Just as German philosophers in the period between Kant and Hegel saw themselves as saving "reason" from Hume, many English-speaking philosophers now see themselves saving reason from Derrida. But with the wisdom of hindsight, and with Baier's help, we have learned to read Hume not as a dangerously frivolous iconoclast but as the wettest, most flexible, least phallogocentric thinker of the Enlightenment. Someday, I suspect, our descendants may wish that Derrida's contemporaries had been able to read him not as a frivolous iconoclast, but rather as a sentimental educator, another of "the women's moral philosophers."[15]

If one follows Baier's advice one will not see it as the moral educator's task to answer the rational egotist's question "Why should I be moral?" but rather to answer the much

---

13 See Jane Tompkins, *Sensational Designs: The Cultural Work of American Fiction, 1790–1860* (New York: Oxford University Press, 1985), for a treatment of the sentimental novel that chimes with the point I am trying to make here. In her chapter on Stowe, Tompkins says that she is asking the reader "to set aside some familiar categories for evaluating fiction – stylistic intricacy, psychological subtlety, epistemological complexity – and to see the sentimental novel not as an artifice of eternity answerable to certain formal criteria and to certain psychological and philosophical concerns, but as a political enterprise, halfway between sermon and social theory, that both codifies and attempts to mold the values of its time" (126).

The contrast that Tompkins draws between authors like Stowe and "male authors such as Thoreau, Whitman and Melville, who are celebrated as models of intellectual daring and honesty" (124), parallels the contrast I tried to draw between public utility and private perfection in my *Contingency, Irony and Solidarity* (Cambridge, England: Cambridge University Press, 1989). I see *Uncle Tom's Cabin* and *Moby Dick* as equally brilliant achievements, achievements that we should not attempt to rank hierarchically, because they serve such different purposes. Arguing about which is the better novel is like arguing about which is the superior philosophical treatise: Mill's *On Liberty* or Kierkegaard's *Philosophical Fragments*.

14 Technically, of course, Kant denied knowledge in order to make room for moral faith. But what is transcendental moral philosophy if not the assurance that the noncognitive imperative delivered via the common moral consciousness shows the existence of a "fact of reason" – a fact about what it is to be a human being, a rational agent, a being that is something more than a bundle of spatio-temporal determinations? Kant was never able to explain how transcendental knowledge could be knowledge, but he was never able to give up the attempt to claim such knowledge.

On the German project of defending reason against Hume, see Fred Beiser, *The Fate of Reason: German Philosophy From Kant to Fichte* (Cambridge, Mass.: Harvard University Press, 1987).

15 I have discussed the relation between Derrida and feminism in "Feminism, Ideology and Deconstruction: A Pragmatist View," *Hypatia* 8.2 (Spring 1993): 96–103, and also in my reply to Alexander Nehamas in *Lire Rorty* (Paris: Éclat, 1992). Richard Bernstein is, I think, basically right in reading Derrida as a moralist, even though Thomas McCarthy is also right in saying that "deconstruction" is of no political use.

more frequently posed question "Why should I care about a stranger, a person who is no kin to me, a person whose habits I find disgusting?" The traditional answer to the latter question is "Because kinship and custom are morally irrelevant, irrelevant to the obligations imposed by the recognition of membership in the same species." This has never been very convincing, since it begs the question at issue: whether mere species membership is, in fact, a sufficient surrogate for closer kinship. Furthermore, that answer leaves one wide open to Nietzsche's discomfiting rejoinder: *That* universalistic notion, Nietzsche will sneer, would only have crossed the mind of a slave – or, perhaps, the mind of an intellectual, a priest whose self-esteem and livelihood both depend on getting the rest of us to accept a sacred, unarguable, unchallengeable paradox.

A better sort of answer is the sort of long, sad, sentimental story which begins "Because this is what it is like to be in her situation – to be far from home, among strangers," or "Because she might become your daughter-in-law," or "Because her mother would grieve for her." Such stories, repeated and varied over the centuries, have induced us, the rich, safe, powerful, people, to tolerate, and even to cherish, powerless people – people whose appearance or habits or beliefs at first seemed an insult to our own moral identity, our sense of the limits of permissible human variation.

To people who, like Plato and Kant, believe in a philosophically ascertainable truth about what it is to be a human being, the good work remains incomplete as long as we have not answered the question "Yes, but am I under a *moral obligation* to her?" To people like Hume and Baier, it is a mark of intellectual immaturity to raise that question. But we shall go on asking that question as long as we agree with Plato that it is our ability to know that makes us human.

Plato wrote quite a long time ago, in a time when we intellectuals had to pretend to be successors to the priests, had to pretend to know something rather esoteric. Hume did his best to josh us out of that pretense. Baier, who seems to me both the most original and the most useful of contemporary moral philosophers, is still trying to josh us out of it. I think Baier may eventually succeed, for she has the history of the last two hundred years of moral progress on her side. These two centuries are most easily understood not as a period of deepening understanding of the nature of rationality or of morality, but rather as one in which there occurred an astonishingly rapid progress of sentiments, in which it has become much easier for us to be moved to action by sad and sentimental stories.

This progress has brought us to a moment in human history in which it is plausible for Rabossi to say that the human rights phenomenon is a "fact of the world." This phenomenon may be just a blip. But it may mark the beginning of a time in which gang rape brings forth as strong a response when it happens to women as when it happens to men, or when it happens to foreigners as when it happens to people like us.

21

Looking Backwards
From the Year 2096

Our long, hesitant, painful recovery, over the last five decades, from the breakdown of democratic institutions during the Dark Years (2014–2044) has changed our political vocabulary, as well as our sense of the relation between the moral order and the economic order. Just as 20th-century Americans had trouble imagining how their pre-Civil War ancestors could have stomached slavery, so we at the end of the 21st century have trouble imagining how our great-grandparents could have legally permitted a C.E.O. to get 20 times more than her lowest-paid employees. We cannot understand how Americans a hundred years ago could have tolerated the horrific contrast between a childhood spent in the suburbs and one spent in the ghettos. Such inequalities seem to us evident moral abominations, but the vast majority of our ancestors took them to be regrettable necessities.

As long as their political discourse was dominated by the notion of "rights" – whether "individual" or "civil" – it was hard for Americans to think of the results of unequal distribution of wealth and income as immoral. Such rights talk, common among late-20th-century liberals, gave conservative opponents of redistributionist policies a tremendous advantage: "the right to a job" (or "to a decent wage") had none of the resonance of "the right to sit in the front of the bus" or "the right to vote" or even "the right to equal pay for equal work." Rights in the liberal tradition were, after all, powers and privileges to be wrested from the state, not from the economy.

Of course socialists had, since the mid-19th century, urged that the economy and the state be merged to guarantee economic rights. But it had become clear by the middle of the 20th century that such merging was disastrous. The history of the pre-1989 "socialist" countries – bloody dictatorships that paid only lip service to the fraternity for which the socialist revolutionaries had yearned – made it plausible for conservatives to argue that extending the notion of rights to the economic order would be a step down the road to serfdom. By the end of the 20th century, even left-leaning American intellectuals agreed that "socialism, no wave of the future, now looks (at best) like a

Richard M. Rorty, "Fraternity Reigns," *The New York Times Magazine*, 28, September 29, 1996: 155–8. © 1996 by Richard Rorty. Reprinted with permission from the Estate of Richard Rorty.

temporary historical stage through which various nations passed before reaching the great transition to capitalist democracy."[1]

The realization by those on the left that a viable economy required free markets did not stop them from insisting that capitalism would be compatible with American ideals of human brotherhood only if the state were able to redistribute wealth. Yet this view was still being criticized as "un-American" and "socialist" at the beginning of the present century, even as, under the pressures of a globalized world economy, the gap between most Americans' incomes and those of the lucky one-third at the top widened. Looking back, we think how easy it would have been for our great-grandfathers to have forestalled the social collapse that resulted from these economic pressures. They could have insisted that all classes had to confront the new global economy together. In the name of our common citizenship, they could have asked everybody, not just the bottom two-thirds, to tighten their belts and make do with less. They might have brought the country together by bringing back its old pride in fraternal ideals.

But as it happened, decades of despair and horror were required to impress Americans with lessons that now seem blindingly obvious.

The apparent incompatibility of capitalism and democracy is, of course, an old theme in American political and intellectual life. It began to be sounded more than two centuries ago. Historians divide our history into the 100 years before the coming of industrial capitalism and the more than 200 years since. During the first period, the open frontier made it possible for Americans to live in ways that became impossible for their descendants. If you were white in 19th-century America, you always had a second chance: something was always opening up out West.

So the first fault line in American politics was not between the rich and the poor. Instead, it was between those who saw chattel slavery as incompatible with American fraternity and those who did not. (Abolitionist posters showed a kneeling slave asking, "Am I not a man, and a brother?") But only 40 years after the Civil War, reformers were already saying that the problem of chattel slavery had been replaced by that of wage slavery.

The urgency of that problem dominates Herbert Croly's progressivist manifesto of 1909, "The Promise of American Life." Croly argued that the Constitution, and a tradition of tolerant individualism, had kept America hopeful and filled with what he called "genuine good-fellowship" during its first hundred years. But beginning with the first wave of industrialization in the 1870's and 1880's, things began to change. Wage slavery – a life of misery and toil, without a sense of participation in the national life, and without any trace of the frontiersman's proud independence – became the fate of more and more Americans. Alexis de Tocqueville had rejoiced that an opulent merchant and his shoemaker, when they met on the streets of Philadelphia in 1840, would exchange political opinions. "These two citizens," he wrote, "are concerned with affairs of state, and they

---

1   From the article "Socialism," by the labor historian Sean Wilentz, in the first edition of "A Companion to American Thought," eds. Richard Fox and James Kloppenberg (London and New York: Blackwell, 1995). That edition appeared exactly 100 years before the current one, which contains the article "Fraternity" excerpted here. Whereas the first edition contained no essay on fraternity, the latest edition has neither an essay on socialism nor one on rights. (For the full text of "Fraternity," see pp. 247–298 of "A Companion to American Thought," seventh edition, eds. Cynthia Rodriguez, S. J., and Youzheng Patel (London and New York: Blackwell, 2095).

do not part without shaking hands." Croly feared that this kind of unforced fraternity was becoming impossible.

From Croly to John Kenneth Galbraith and Arthur Schlesinger in the 1960's, reformers urged that we needed some form of redistribution to bring back Tocquevillian comity. They battled with conservatives who claimed that redistributive measures would kill economic prosperity. The reformers insisted that what Theodore Roosevelt had called "the money power" and Dwight Eisenhower "the military–industrial complex" was the true enemy of American ideals. The conservatives rejoined that the only enemy of democracy was the state and that the economy must be shielded from do-gooders.

This debate simmered through the first two decades following the Second World War. During that relatively halcyon period, most Americans could get fairly secure, fairly well-paying jobs and could count on their children having a better life than theirs. White America seemed to be making slow but steady progress toward a classless society. Only the growth of the increasingly miserable black underclass reminded white Americans that the promise of American life was still far from being fulfilled.

The sense that this promise was still alive was made possible, in part, by what the first edition of the "Companion" called the "rights revolution." Most of the moral progress that took place in the second half of the 20th century was brought about by the Supreme Court's invocation of constitutional rights, in such decisions as Brown v. Board of Education (1954) and Romer v. Evans (1996), the first Supreme Court decision favorable to homosexuals. But this progress was confined almost entirely to improvements in the situation of groups identified by race, ethnicity or sexuality. The situation of women and of homosexuals changed radically in this period. Indeed, it is now clear that those changes, which spread from America around the world, were the most lasting and significant moral achievements of the 20th century.

But though such groups could use the rhetoric of rights to good effect, the trade unions, the unemployed and those employed at the ludicrously low minimum wage ($174 an hour, in 2095 dollars, compared with the present minimum of $400) could not. Perhaps no difference between present-day American political discourse and that of 100 years ago is greater than our assumption that the first duty of the state is to prevent gross economic and social inequality, as opposed to our ancestors' assumption that the government's only moral duty was to insure equal protection of the laws laws that, in their majestic impartiality, allowed the rich and the poor to receive the same hospital bills.

The Supreme Court, invoking this idea of equal protection, began the great moral revival we know as the Civil Rights Movement. The Brown decision initiated both an explosion of violence and an upsurge of fraternal feeling. Some white Americans burned crosses and black churches. Many more had their eyes opened to the humiliations being inflicted on their fellow citizens: if they did not join civil rights marches, they at least felt relieved of guilt when the Court threw out miscegenation laws and when Congress began to protect black voting rights. For a decade or so there was an uplifting sense of moral improvement. For the first time, white and black Americans started to think of each other as fellow citizens.

By the beginning of the 1980's, however, this sense of fraternity was only a faint memory. A burst of selfishness had produced tax revolts in the 70's, stopping in its tracks the fairly steady progress toward a full-fledged welfare state that had been under way since the New Deal. The focus of racial hate was transferred from the rural South to the big cities, where a criminal culture of unemployed (and, in the second generation, virtually unemployable) black youths grew up – a culture of near constant violence, made possible by the then-famous American "right to bear arms." All the old racial prejudices were revived by white suburbanites' claims that their tax money was being used to coddle criminals. Politicians gained votes by promising to spend what little money could be squeezed from their constituents on prisons rather than on day care.

Tensions between the comfortable middle-class suburbs and the rest of the country grew steadily in the closing decades of the 20th century, as the gap between the educated and well paid and the uneducated and ill paid steadily widened. Class division came into existence between those who made "professional" salaries and those whose hourly wage kept sinking toward the minimum. But the politicians pretended to be unaware of this steady breakdown of fraternity.

Our nation's leaders, in the last decade of the old century and the first of the new, seemed never to have thought that it might be dangerous to make automatic weapons freely and cheaply available to desperate men and women – people without hope – living next to the centers of transportation and communication. Those weapons burst into the streets in 2014, in the revolution that, leaving the cities in ruins and dislocating American economic life, plunged the country into the Second Great Depression.

The insurgency in the ghettos, coming at a time when all but the wealthiest Americans felt desperately insecure, led to the collapse of trust in government. The collapse of the economy produced a war of all against all, as gasoline and food became harder and harder to buy, and as even the suburbanites began to brandish guns at their neighbors. As the generals never stopped saying throughout the Dark Years, only the military saved the country from utter chaos.

Here, in the late 21st century, as talk of fraternity and unselfishness has replaced talk of rights, American political discourse has come to be dominated by quotations from Scripture and literature, rather than from political theorists or social scientists. Fraternity, like friendship, was not a concept that either philosophers or lawyers knew how to handle. They could formulate principles of justice, equality and liberty, and invoke these principles when weighing hard moral or legal issues. But how to formulate a "principle of fraternity"? Fraternity is an inclination of the heart, one that produces a sense of shame at having much when others have little. It is not the sort of thing that anybody can have a theory about or that people can be argued into having.

Perhaps the most vivid description of the American concept of fraternity is found in a passage from John Steinbeck's 1939 novel, "The Grapes of Wrath." Steinbeck describes a desperately impoverished family, dispossessed tenant farmers from Oklahoma, camped out at the edge of Highway 66, sharing their food with an even more desperate migrant family. Steinbeck writes: " 'I have a little food' plus 'I have none.' If from this problem the sum is 'We have a little food,' the movement has direction." As long as people in trouble can sacrifice to help people who are in still worse trouble, Steinbeck insisted, there is fraternity, and therefore social hope.

The movement Steinbeck had in mind was the revolutionary socialism that he, like many other leftists of the 1930's, thought would be required to bring the First Great Depression to an end. "The quality of owning," he wrote, "freezes you forever into the 'I,' and cuts you off forever from the 'we.' " Late-20th-century liberals no longer believed in getting rid of private ownership, but they agreed that the promise of American life could be redeemed only as long as Americans were willing to sacrifice for the sake of fellow Americans – only as long as they could see the government not as stealing their tax money but as needing it to prevent unnecessary suffering.

The Democratic Vistas Party, the coalition of trade unions and churches that toppled the military dictatorship in 2044, has retained control of Congress by successfully convincing the voters that its opponents constitute "the parties of selfishness." The traditional use of "brother" and "sister" in union locals and religious congregations is the principal reason why "fraternity" (or, among purists, "siblinghood") is now the name of our most cherished ideal.

In the first two centuries of American history Jefferson's use of rights had set the tone for political discourse, but now political argument is not about who has the right to what but about what can best prevent the re-emergence of hereditary castes – either racial or economic. The old union slogan "An injury to one is an injury to all" is now the catch phrase of American politics. "Solidarity Forever" and "This Land Is Your Land" are sung at least as often as "The Star-Spangled Banner."

Until the last 50 years, moral instruction in America had inculcated personal responsibility, and most sermons had focused on individual salvation. Today morality is thought of neither as a matter of applying the moral law nor as the acquisition of virtues but as fellow feeling, the ability to sympathize with the plight of others.

In the churches, the "social gospel" theology of the early 20th century has been rediscovered. Walter Rauschenbusch's "Prayer against the servants of Mammon" ("Behold the servants of Mammon, who defy thee and drain their fellow-men for gain … who have made us ashamed of our dear country by their defilements and have turned our holy freedom into a hollow name … ") is familiar to most churchgoers. In the schools, students learn about our country's history from social novels describing our past failures to hang together when we needed to, the novels of Steinbeck, Upton Sinclair, Theodore Dreiser, Richard Wright and, of course, Russell Banks's samizdat novel, "Trampling the Vineyards" (2021).

Historians unite in calling the 20th the "American" century. Certainly it was in the 20th century that the United States was richest, most powerful, most influential and most self-confident. Our ancestors 100 years ago still thought of the country as destined to police, inform and inspire the world. Compared with the Americans of 100 years ago, we are citizens of an isolationist, unambitious, middle-grade nation.

Our products are only now becoming competitive again in international markets, and Democratic Vistas politicians continue to urge that our consistently low productivity is a small price to pay for union control of the workplace and worker ownership of the majority of firms. We continue to lag behind the European Community, which was able to withstand the pressures of a globalized labor market by having a full-fledged welfare state already in place, and which (except for Austria and Great Britain) was able to resist the temptation to impoverish the most vulnerable in order to keep its suburbanites affluent. Spared the equivalent of our own Dark Years, Europe still, despite all that China can do, holds the position we lost in 2014: it still dominates both the world's economy and its culture.

For two centuries Americans believed that they were as far ahead of Europe, in both virtue and promise, as Europe was ahead of the rest of the world. But American exceptionalism did not survive the Dark Years: we no longer think of ourselves as singled out by divine favor. We are now, once again, a constitutional democracy, but we have proved as vulnerable as Germany, Russia and India to dictatorial takeovers. We have a sense of fragility, of susceptibility to the vicissitudes of time and chance, which Walt Whitman and John Dewey may never have known.

Perhaps no American writer will ever again begin a book, as Croly did, by saying, "The faith of Americans in their own country is religious, if not in its intensity, at any rate in its almost absolute and universal authority." But our chastened mood, our lately learned humility, may have made us better able to realize that everything depends on keeping our fragile sense of American fraternity intact.

22

American National Pride:
Whitman and Dewey

National pride is to countries what self-respect is to individuals: a necessary condition for self-improvement. Too much national pride can produce bellicosity and imperialism, just as excessive self-respect can produce arrogance. But just as too little self-respect makes it difficult for a person to display moral courage, so insufficient national pride makes energetic and effective debate about national policy unlikely. Emotional involvement with one's country – feelings of intense shame or of glowing pride aroused by various parts of its history, and by various present-day national policies – is necessary if political deliberation is to be imaginative and productive. Such deliberation will probably not occur unless pride outweighs shame.

The need for this sort of involvement remains even for those who, like myself, hope that the United States of America will someday yield up sovereignty to what Tennyson called "the Parliament of Man, the Federation of the World." For such a federation will never come into existence unless the governments of the individual nation-states cooperate in setting it up, and unless the citizens of those nation-states take a certain amount of pride (even rueful and hesitant pride) in their governments' efforts to do so.

Those who hope to persuade a nation to exert itself need to remind their country of what it can take pride in as well as what it should be ashamed of. They must tell inspiring stories about episodes and figures in the nation's past – episodes and figures to which the country should remain true. Nations rely on artists and intellectuals to create images of, and to tell stories about, the national past. Competition for political leadership is in part a competition between differing stories about a nation's self-identity, and between differing symbols of its greatness.

In America, at the end of the twentieth century, few inspiring images and stories are being proffered. The only version of national pride encouraged by American popular culture is a simpleminded militaristic chauvinism. But such chauvinism is overshadowed by a widespread sense that national pride is no longer appropriate. In both popular and elite culture, most descriptions of what America will be like in the twenty-first century are written in tones either of self-mockery or of self-disgust.

Consider two recent novels: Neal Stephenson's *Snow Crash*, a bestseller, and Leslie Marmon Silko's *Almanac of the Dead*, a critical triumph which was not as widely read. Both are powerful novels. Readers of either may well think it absurd for Americans to continue to take pride in their country.

Snow Crash tells of a twenty-first-century America in which the needs of the entrepreneurs have won out over hopes of a free and egalitarian society. The country has been divided into small franchised enclaves, within each of which a single corporation – IBM, the Mafia, GenTech – holds the rights of high and low justice. The U.S. government has gone into business for itself and is one more corporate entity, running its own little enclaves. But the government is not even first among equals. There is no overall political entity, much less any sense of citizenship, that binds the eastern and western states together, or that links even the various districts of the big cities.

In *Snow Crash*, the relation of the United States to the rest of the world is symbolized by Stephenson's most frightening creation – what he calls the "Raft." This is an enormous agglomeration of floating hulks, drifting endlessly round and round the Pacific Rim, inhabited by millions of Asians who hope to jump ship and swim to North America. The Raft is a sort of vast international slum ruled by cruel and anarchic criminal gangs; it is quite different from the orderly franchises run by profitable business enterprises, respecting each others' boundaries and rights, in what used to be the United States of America. Pride in being an American citizen has been replaced by relief at being safer and better-fed than those on the Raft. Lincoln and Martin Luther King are no more present to the imagination of Stephenson's Americans than were Cromwell or Churchill to the imagination of the British whom Orwell described in his book 1984.

Snow Crash capitalizes on the widespread belief that giant corporations, and a shadowy behind-the-scenes government acting as an agent for the corporations, now make all the important decisions. This belief finds expression in popular thrillers like Richard Condon's *Manchurian Candidate* and *Winter Kills*, as well as in more ambitious works like Thomas Pynchon's *Vineland* and Norman Mailer's *Harlot's Ghost*. The view that the visible government is just a false front is a plausible extrapolation from the fact that we are living in a Second Gilded Age: even Mark Twain might have been startled by the shamelessness with which our politicians now sell themselves.[1]

Novels like Stephenson's, Condon's, and Pynchon's are novels not of social protest but rather of rueful acquiescence in the end of American hopes. Silko's *Almanac of the Dead* also assumes that democratic government has become a farce, but her novel is dominated by self-disgust rather than self-mockery. Its focus is on the relation of European-Americans to Native Americans and to the descendants of the slaves brought

---

1   One particularly good example of such purchase is the Senate's vote for an ad hoc change in the law so as to hinder the Teamsters Union from organizing the Federal Express Company. See the debate on this matter initiated by Senator Edward Kennedy's speech (*Congressional Record,* October 1, 1996, pp. S12097ff.), especially Senator Paul Simon's remarks: "I think we have to honestly ask ourselves, why is Federal Express being given preferential treatment in this body now? I think the honest answer is Federal Express has been very generous in their campaign contributions" (p. S12106). After the Senate had voted in the company's favor, a spokesman for Federal Express was quoted as saying, "We played political hardball, and we won."

from Africa. Silko's novel ends with a vision in which the descendants of the European conquerors and immigrants are forced back to Europe, thereby fulfilling Native American prophecies that the whites would be a temporary disaster, a plague that would last no more than five hundred years. Silko portrays the American government collapsing amid riots and food shortages, as the descendants of the Maya and the Aztecs stream into California, Arizona, and Texas.

One does not need to know whether Silko has read Foucault or Heidegger to see her novel as offering a vision of recent history similar to the one which readers of those two philosophers often acquire. In this vision, the two-hundred-year history of the United States – indeed, the history of the European and American peoples since the Enlightenment – has been pervaded by hypocrisy and self-deception. Readers of Foucault often come away believing that no shackles have been broken in the past two hundred years: the harsh old chains have merely been replaced with slightly more comfortable ones. Heidegger describes America's success in blanketing the world with modern technology as the spread of a wasteland. Those who find Foucault and Heidegger convincing often view the United States of America as Silko does: as something we must hope will be replaced, as soon as possible, by something utterly different.

Such people find pride in American citizenship impossible, and vigorous participation in electoral politics pointless. They associate American patriotism with an endorsement of atrocities: the importation of African slaves, the slaughter of Native Americans, the rape of ancient forests, and the Vietnam War. Many of them think of national pride as appropriate only for chauvinists: for the sort of American who rejoices that America can still orchestrate something like the Gulf War, can still bring deadly force to bear whenever and wherever it chooses. When young intellectuals watch John Wayne war movies after reading Heidegger, Foucault, Stephenson, or Silko, they often become convinced that they live in a violent, inhuman, corrupt country. They begin to think of themselves as a saving remnant – as the happy few who have the insight to see through nationalist rhetoric to the ghastly reality of contemporary America. But this insight does not move them to formulate a legislative program, to join a political movement, or to share in a national hope.

The contrast between national hope and national self-mockery and self-disgust becomes vivid when one compares novels like *Snow Crash* and *Almanac of the Dead* with socialist novels of the first half of the century – books like *The Jungle, An American Tragedy*, and *The Grapes of Wrath*. The latter were written in the belief that the tone of the Gettysburg Address was absolutely right, but that our country would have to transform itself in order to fulfill Lincoln's hopes. Transformation would be needed because the rise of industrial capitalism had made the individualist rhetoric of America's first century obsolete.

The authors of these novels thought that this rhetoric should be replaced by one in which America is destined to become the first cooperative commonwealth, the first classless society. This America would be one in which income and wealth are equitably distributed, and in which the government ensures equality of opportunity as well as individual liberty. This new, quasi-communitarian rhetoric was at the heart of the Progressive Movement and the New Deal. It set the tone for the American Left during the first six decades of the twentieth century. Walt Whitman and John Dewey, as we shall see, did a great deal to shape this rhetoric.

The difference between early twentieth-century leftist intellectuals and the majority of their contemporary counterparts is the difference between agents and spectators.

In the early decades of this century, when an intellectual stepped back from his or her country's history and looked at it through skeptical eyes, the chances were that he or she was about to propose a new political initiative. Henry Adams was, of course, the great exception – the great abstainer from politics. But William James thought that Adams' diagnosis of the First Gilded Age as a symptom of irreversible moral and political decline was merely perverse. James's pragmatist theory of truth was in part a reaction against the sort of detached spectatorship which Adams affected.

For James, disgust with American hypocrisy and self-deception was pointless unless accompanied by an effort to give America reason to be proud of itself in the future. The kind of proto-Heideggerian cultural pessimism which Adams cultivated seemed, to James, decadent and cowardly. "Democracy," James wrote, "is a kind of religion, and we are bound not to admit its failure. Faiths and utopias are the noblest exercise of human reason, and no one with a spark of reason in him will sit down fatalistically before the croaker's picture."[2]

In 1909, at the beginning of his book *The Promise of American Life*, Herbert Croly echoed James:

> The faith of Americans in their own country is religious, if not in its intensity, at any rate in its almost absolute and universal authority ... As children we hear it asserted or implied in the conversation of our elders. Every new stage of our educational training provides some additional testimony on its behalf ... We may distrust and dislike much that is done in the name of our country by our fellow-country-men; but our country itself, its demo-cratic system, and its prosperous future are above suspicion.[3]

If anybody attributed this sort of civic religion to Americans today, it would be assumed that he was speaking only of the chauvinists – of the Americans who think of John Wayne rather than of Abraham Lincoln as our representative man, and of America as invincible rather than as kind. Novels like Silko's, Stephenson's, Mailer's, and Pynchon's are our equivalent of Adams' resigned pessimism.

It rarely occurs to present-day American leftists to quote either Lincoln or Whitman. It is no longer the case that, in Croly's words, "every new stage of our educational train-ing provides some additional testimony" on behalf of Americans' faith in their country. On the contrary, a contemporary American student may well emerge from college less convinced that her country has a future than when she entered. She may also be less inclined to think that political initiatives can create such a future. The spirit of detached spectatorship, and the inability to think of American citizenship as an opportunity for action, may already have entered such a student's soul.

In this first lecture I shall try to describe the role of Whitman and Dewey in creating the image of America which was ubiquitous on the American Left prior to the Vietnam War. I say "image" rather than "myth" or "ideology" because I do not think that there is a nonmythological, nonideological way of telling a country's story. Calling a story "mythi-cal" or "ideological" would be meaningful only if such stories could be contrasted with an "objective" story. But though objectivity is a useful goal when one is trying to calculate

---

2   William James, "The Social Value of the College-Bred," in James, *Essays, Comments, and Reviews* (Cambridge, Mass.: Harvard University Press, 1987), p. 109.

3   Herbert Croly, *The Promise of American Life* (New York: Capricorn Books, 1964; orig. pub. 1909), p. 1.

means to ends by predicting the consequences of action, it is of little relevance when one is trying to decide what sort of person or nation to be. Nobody knows what it would be like to try to be objective when attempting to decide what one's country really is, what its history really means, any more than when answering the question of who one really is oneself, what one's individual past really adds up to. We raise questions about our individual or national identity as part of the process of deciding what we will do next, what we will try to become.

As an example of such a process of decision, consider James Baldwin's book *The Fire Next Time*. Early in that book Baldwin says, "This is the crime of which I accuse my country and my countrymen, and for which neither I nor time nor history will ever forgive them, that they have destroyed and are destroying hundreds of thousands of lives and do not know it and do not want to know it."[4] This lack of forgiveness can easily take the form it does in the theology of the Nation of Islam – with whose prophet, Elijah Muhammad, Baldwin describes an encounter. The Black Muslims say that white people started out as homunculi created by a diabolical scientist. This hypothesis seems to them the best explanation for the inhuman cruelty of the slave auctions and the lynchings.

Those who accept Elijah Muhammad's story use it to convey the wholehearted, gut-wrenching disgust for white America which is manifest in Silko's novel. But as Baldwin's narrative of self-creation unfolds, we watch him combining a continued unwillingness to forgive with a continuing identification with the country that brought over his ancestors in chains. "I am not," he writes, "a ward of America; I am one of the first Americans to arrive on these shores."[5]

In another passage Baldwin says, "In short, we, the black and the white, deeply need each other here if we are really to become a nation – if we are really, that is, to achieve our identity, our maturity, as men and women."[6] He ends his book with a sentence which has been quoted over and over again: "If we – and now I mean the relatively conscious whites and the relatively conscious blacks, who must, like lovers, insist on, or create, the consciousness of the others – do not falter in our duty now, we may be able, handful that we are, to end the racial nightmare, and achieve our country, and change the history of the world." The difference between Elijah Muhammad's decision about how to think of America and the one reached by Baldwin is the difference between deciding to be a spectator and to leave the fate of the United States to the operation of nonhuman forces, and deciding to be an agent.

I do not think there is any point in arguing that Elijah Muhammad made the right decision and Baldwin the wrong one, or vice versa. Neither forgave, but one turned away from the project of achieving the country and the other did not. Both decisions are intelligible. Either can be made plausible. But there are no neutral, objective criteria which dictate one rather than the other.

For the same reasons that I think there is no point in asking whether Baldwin made the right decision, I think there is no point in asking whether Lincoln or Whitman or Dewey got America right. Stories about what a nation has been and should try to be are not attempts at accurate representation, but rather attempts to forge a moral identity. The argument between Left and Right about which episodes in our history we

4   James Baldwin, *The Fire Next Time* (New York: Dell, 1988; orig. pub. 1963), p. 5.
5   Ibid., p. 98.
6   Ibid., p. 97.

Americans should pride ourselves on will never be a contest between a true and a false account of our country's history and its identity. It is better described as an argument about which hopes to allow ourselves and which to forgo.

As long as our country has a politically active Right and a politically active Left, this argument will continue. It is at the heart of the nation's political life, but the Left is responsible for keeping it going. For the Right never thinks that anything much needs to be changed: it thinks the country is basically in good shape, and may well have been in better shape in the past. It sees the Left's struggle for social justice as mere troublemaking, as utopian foolishness. The Left, by definition, is the party of hope. It insists that our nation remains unachieved. As the historian Nelson Lichtenstein has said, "All of America's great reform movements, from the crusade against slavery to the labor upsurge in the 1930's, defined themselves as champions of a moral and patriotic nationalism, which they counterposed to the parochial and selfish elites which stood athwart their vision of a virtuous society."[7]

Insofar as a Left becomes spectatorial and retrospective, it ceases to be a Left. I shall be claiming in these lectures that the American Left, once the old alliance between the intellectuals and the unions broke down in the course of the Sixties, began to sink into an attitude like Henry Adams'. Leftists in the academy have permitted cultural politics to supplant real politics, and have collaborated with the Right in making cultural issues central to public debate. They are spending energy which should be directed at proposing new laws on discussing topics as remote from the country's needs as were Adams' musings on the Virgin and the Dynamo. The academic Left has no projects to propose to America, no vision of a country to be achieved by building a consensus on the need for specific reforms. Its members no longer feel the force of James's and Croly's rhetoric. The American civic religion seems to them narrow-minded and obsolete nationalism.

Whitman and Dewey were among the prophets of this civic religion. They offered a new account of what America was, in the hope of mobilizing Americans as political agents. The most striking feature of their redescription of our country is its thoroughgoing secularism.[8] In the past, most of the stories that have incited nations to projects of self-improvement have been stories about their obligations to one or more gods. For much of European and American history, nations have asked themselves how they appear in the eyes of the Christian God. American exceptionalism has usually been a belief in special divine favor, as in the writings of Joseph Smith and Billy Graham. By contrast, Elijah Muhammad and Leslie Marmon Silko are examples of inverted exceptionalism: in their visions, white America will be the object of special divine wrath.

---

7 Nelson Lichtenstein, *The Most Dangerous Man in Detroit: Walter Reuther and the Fate of American Labor* (New York: Basic Books, 1994), p. 383.

8 I use "secularism" in the sense of "anticlericalism" rather than of "atheism." Dewey's dislike of "aggressive atheism" is made clear in *A Common Faith*. I have argued elsewhere that Dewey, like James, wanted pragmatism to be compatible with religious belief – but only with a privatized religious belief, not with the sort of religious belief that produces churches, especially churches which take political positions. See Rorty, "Religious Faith, Intellectual Responsibility, and Romance," in Ruth-Anna Putnam, ed., *The Cambridge Companion to William James* (Cambridge: Cambridge University Press, 1997); idem, "Pragmatism as Romantic Polytheism," in Morris Dickstein, ed., *The New Pragmatism* (Durham, N.C.: Duke University Press, 1998); idem, "Religion as Conversation-Stopper," *Common Knowledge* 3 (Spring 1994): 1–6. This last is a reply to Stephen Carter's argument that religious voices should be heard in the public square.

Dewey and Whitman wanted Americans to continue to think of themselves as exceptional, but both wanted to drop any reference to divine favor or wrath. They hoped to separate the fraternity and loving kindness urged by the Christian scriptures from the ideas of supernatural parentage, immortality, providence, and – most important – sin. They wanted Americans to take pride in what America might, all by itself and by its own lights, make of itself, rather than in America's obedience to any authority – even the authority of God. Thus Whitman wrote:

> And I call to mankind, Be not curious about God, For I who am curious about each am not curious about God.[9]

Whitman thought there was no need to be curious about God because there is no standard, not even a divine one, against which the decisions of a free people can be measured. Americans, he hoped, would spend the energy that past human societies had spent on discovering God's desires on discovering one another's desires. Americans will be curious about every other American, but not about anything which claims authority over America.

Kenneth Rexroth claims that Whitman invented the idea of "the realization of the American Dream as an apocalypse, an eschatological event which would give the life of man its ultimate significance." He goes on to say:

> Other religions have been founded on the promise of the Community of Love, the Abode of Peace, the Kingdom of God. Whitman identified with his own nation-state. We excuse such ideas only when they began 3,000 years ago in the Levantine desert. In our own time we suspect them of dangerous malevolence. Yet Whitman's vision exposes and explodes all the frauds that pass for the American Way of Life. It is the last and greatest vision of the American potential.[10]

Everything Rexroth says in this passage seems to me correct, except for the phrase "last and greatest." Whitman had successful imitators in his attempt to tie up the history of our nation-state with the meaning of human life. Perhaps because I am a philosophy professor, and have a special interest in philosophical restatements of moral ideals, I think that John Dewey was the most successful and most useful of these imitators.

Whitman explicitly said that he would "use the words America and democracy as convertible terms."[11] Dewey was less explicit, but when he uses "truly democratic" as a supreme honorific, he is obviously envisaging an achieved America. Both Dewey and Whitman viewed the United States as an opportunity to see ultimate significance in a finite, human, historical project, rather than in something eternal and nonhuman. They both hoped that America would be the place where a religion of love would finally replace a religion of fear. They dreamed that Americans would break the traditional link between the religious impulse, the impulse to stand in awe of something greater than oneself, and the infantile need for security, the childish hope of escaping from time and

9   *Leaves of Grass,* p. 85. All references to both *Leaves of Grass* and *Democratic Vistas* are to Walt Whitman, *Complete Poetry and Selected Prose* (New York: Library of America, 1982).

10   Kenneth Rexroth, "Walt Whitman," *Saturday Review* 3 (September 1966), reprinted in Graham Clarke, ed., *Walt Whitman: Critical Assessments,* vol. 3 (New York: Routledge, 1994), p. 241.

11   Whitman, *Democratic Vistas,* p. 930.

chance. They wanted to preserve the former and discard the latter. They wanted to put hope for a casteless and classless America in the place traditionally occupied by knowledge of the will of God. They wanted that utopian America to replace God as the unconditional object of desire. They wanted the struggle for social justice to be the country's animating principle, the nation's soul.

"Democracy," Dewey said, "is neither a form of government nor a social expediency, but a metaphysic of the relation of man and his experience in nature."[12] For both Whitman and Dewey, the terms "America" and "democracy" are shorthand for a new conception of what it is to be human – a conception which has no room for obedience to a nonhuman authority, and in which nothing save freely achieved consensus among human beings has any authority at all. Steven Rockefeller is right to say that "[Dewey's] goal was to integrate fully the religious life with the American democratic life."[13] But the sort of integration Dewey hoped for is not a matter of blending the worship of an eternal Being with hope for the temporal realization, in America, of this Being's will. It is a matter of forgetting about eternity. More generally, it is a matter of replacing shared knowledge of what is already real with social hope for what might become real. The word "democracy," Whitman said, "is a great word, whose history ... remains unwritten, because that history has yet to be enacted."[14]

Forgetting about eternity, and replacing knowledge of the antecedently real with hope for the contingent future, is not easy. But both tasks have been a good deal easier since Hegel. Hegel was the first philosopher to take time and finitude as seriously as any Hobbesian materialist, while at the same time taking the religious impulse as seriously as any Hebrew prophet or Christian saint. Spinoza had attempted such a synthesis by identifying God with Nature, but Spinoza still thought it desirable to see things under the aspect of eternity. Hegel rejoined that any view of human history under that aspect would be too thin and abstract to be of any religious use. He suggested that the meaning of human life is a function of how human history turns out, rather than of the relation of that history to something ahistorical. This suggestion made it easier for two of Hegel's readers, Dewey and Whitman, to claim that the way to think about the significance of

12   John Dewey, "Maeterlinck's Philosophy of Life," in *The Middle Works of John Dewey*, vol. 6 (Carbondale: Southern Illinois University Press, 1978), p. 135. Dewey says that Emerson, Whitman, and Maeterlinck are the only three to have grasped this fact about democracy. Dewey's term "metaphysic" is a bit unfortunate. He might have expressed his meaning better by saying that, Nietzsche to the contrary, democracy is the principal means by which a more evolved form of humanity will come into existence.

  Kenneth Burke once wrote (*A Grammar of Motives*, p. 504) that "characters possess *degrees of being* in proportion to the variety of perspectives from which they can with justice be perceived. Thus we could say that plants have 'less being' than animals, because each higher order admits and requires a new dimension of terms not literally relevant to the lower orders." Democratic humanity, Dewey and Burke might have agreed, has "more being" than predemocratic humanity. The citizens of a democratic, Whitmanesque society are able to create new, hitherto unimagined roles and goals for themselves. So a greater variety of perspectives, and of descriptive terms, becomes available to them, and can with justice be used to account for them.

13   Steven Rockefeller, *John Dewey: Religious Faith and Democratic Humanism* (New York: Columbia University Press, 1991), p. 4.

14   Whitman, *Democratic Vistas*, p. 960.

the human adventure is to look forward rather than upward: to contrast a possible human future with the human past and present.

Marx, unfortunately, has been the most influential of the left-wing Hegelians. But Marx mistakenly thought that Hegel's dialectic could be used for predictive as well as inspirational purposes. That is why Marxists have produced the form of historicism which Karl Popper rightly criticized as impoverished. But there is another form of Hegelian historicism which survives Popper's criticisms intact. In this form, historicism is simply the temporalization of what Plato, and even Kant, try to eternalize. It is the temporalization of ultimate significance, and of awe.

Dewey's philosophy is a systematic attempt to temporalize everything, to leave nothing fixed. This means abandoning the attempt to find a theoretical frame of reference within which to evaluate proposals for the human future. Dewey's romantic hope was that future events would make every proposed frame obsolete. What he dreaded was stasis: a time in which everybody would take for granted that the purpose of history had been accomplished, an age of spectators rather than agents, a country in which arguments between Right and Left would no longer be heard.

Dewey read a lot of Hegel when he was young. He used Hegel to purge himself first of Kant, and later of orthodox Christianity. Whitman read only a little, but what he read was enough to make him exclaim with delight. "Only Hegel," Whitman wrote in his notebooks, "is fit for America – is large enough and free enough."[15] "I rate [Hegel]," he goes on to say, "as Humanity's chiefest teacher and the choicest loved physician of my mind and soul."[16]

Hegel's philosophy of history legitimized and underwrote Whitman's hope to substitute his own nation-state for the Kingdom of God. For Hegel told a story about history as the growth of freedom, the gradual dawning of the idea that human beings are on their own, because there is nothing more to God than his march through the world – nothing more to the divine than the history of the human adventure. In a famous passage, Hegel pointed across the Atlantic to a place where as yet unimagined wonders might be worked: "America is the country of the future ... the land of desire for all those who are weary of the historical arsenal of old Europe."[17]

Whitman probably never encountered this passage, but he knew in his bones that Hegel *should* have written that sentence. It was obvious to him that Hegel had written a prelude to the American saga. Hegel's works, Whitman said, might "not inappropriately be this day collected and bound up under the conspicuous title: *Speculations for the use of North America, and Democracy there.*"[18] This is because Hegel thinks God remains

---

15   Whitman, *Notebooks and Unpublished Prose Manuscripts,* in Whitman, *Collected Writings,* vol. 6, ed. Edward F. Grier (New York: New York University Press, 1984), p. 2011. See pp. 2007–2008 for helpful editorial notes and references to secondary material which discusses the extent of Whitman's reading in Hegel, and the nature of Hegel's influence on him. He seems to have read only as much Hegel as was translated by Frederic Hedge in his 1847 book, *German Prose Writers* – mainly the Introduction to the *Lectures on the Philosophy of History* – as well as an intelligent five-page summary of Hegel's system by Joseph Gostick.

16   Whitman, *Notebooks and Unpublished Prose Manuscripts,* p. 2012.

17   Hegel, *Lectures on the Philosophy of World-History: Introduction – Reason in History,* trans. H. B. Nisbet (Cambridge: Cambridge University Press, 1975), pp. 170–171.

18   "Carlyle from American Points of View," in Whitman, *Prose Works* (Philadelphia: David McKay, 1900), p. 171.

incomplete until he enters time – until, in Christian terminology, he becomes incarnate and suffers on the Cross. Hegel uses the doctrine of Incarnation to turn Greek metaphysics on its head, and to argue that without God the Son, God the Father would remain a mere potentiality, a mere Idea. Without time and suffering, God is, in Hegel's terms, a "mere abstraction." Hegel verges on saying something Whitman actually did say: "The whole theory of the special and supernatural and all that was twined with it or educed out of it departs as a dream ... It is not consistent with the reality of the soul to admit that there is anything in the universe more divine than men and women."[19]

Whitman, like most American thinkers of the nineteenth century, believed that the Golgotha of the Spirit was in the past, and that the American Declaration of Independence had been an Easter dawn. Because the United States is the first country founded in the hope of a new kind of human fraternity, it would be the place where the promise of the ages would first be realized. Americans would form the vanguard of human history, because, as Whitman says, "the Americans of all nations at any time upon the earth have probably the fullest poetical nature. The United States themselves are essentially the greatest poem."[20] They are also the fulfillment of the human past. "The blossoms we wear in our hats," Whitman wrote, "are the growth of two thousand years."[21]

Whitman thought that we Americans have the most poetical nature because we are the first thoroughgoing experiment in national self-creation: the first nation-state with nobody but itself to please – not even God. We are the greatest poem because we put ourselves in the place of God: our essence is our existence, and our existence is in the future. Other nations thought of themselves as hymns to the glory of God. We redefine God as our future selves.

Neither Dewey nor Whitman, however, was committed to the view that things would *inevitably* go well for America, that the American experiment in self-creation would succeed. The price of temporalization is contingency. Because they rejected any idea of Divine Providence and any idea of immanent teleology, Dewey and Whitman had to grant the possibility that the vanguard of humanity may lose its way, and perhaps lead our species over a cliff. As Whitman put it, "The United States are destined either to surmount the gorgeous history of feudalism, or else prove the most tremendous failure of time."[22] Whereas Marx and Spencer claimed to know what was bound to happen, Whitman and Dewey denied such knowledge in order to make room for pure, joyous hope.

The trouble with Europe, Whitman and Dewey thought, was that it tried too hard for knowledge: it tried to find an answer to the question of what human beings should be like. It hoped to get authoritative guidance for human conduct. One of the first Europeans to suggest abandoning this hope was Wilhelm von Humboldt, a founder of ethnography and a philosopher who greatly influenced Hegel. In a passage which Mill used as the epigraph for his *On Liberty*, von Humboldt wrote that the point of social organization is to make evident "the absolute and essential importance of human development in its richest diversity." Whitman picked up this particular ball from Mill and cited *On Liberty* in the first paragraph of his *Democratic Vistas*. There Whitman says that Mill demands "two main constituents, or sub-strata, for a truly

19   Whitman, *Leaves of Grass,* p. 16.
20   Ibid., p. 5.
21   Ibid., p. 71.
22   Whitman, *Democratic Vistas,* p. 930.

grand nationality – lst, a large variety of character – and 2d, full play for human nature to expand itself in numberless and even conflicting directions."[23]

Mill and Humboldt's "richest diversity" and Whitman's "full play" are ways of saying that no past human achievement, not Plato's or even Christ's, can tell us about the ultimate significance of human life. No such achievement can give us a template on which to model our future. The future will widen endlessly. Experiments with new forms of individual and social life will interact and reinforce one another. Individual life will become unthinkably diverse and social life unthinkably free. The moral we should draw from the European past, and in particular from Christianity, is not instruction about the authority under which we should live, but suggestions about how to make ourselves wonderfully different from anything that has been.

This romance of endless diversity should not, however, be confused with what nowadays is sometimes called "multiculturalism." The latter term suggests a morality of live-and-let-live, a politics of side-by-side development in which members of distinct cultures preserve and protect their own culture against the incursions of other cultures. Whitman, like Hegel, had no interest in preservation or protection. He wanted competition and argument between alternative forms of human life – a poetic agon, in which jarring dialectical discords would be resolved in previously unheard harmonies. The Hegelian idea of "progressive evolution," which was the nineteenth century's great contribution to political and social thought, is that everybody gets played off against everybody else. This should occur nonviolently if possible, but violently if necessary, as was in fact necessary in America in 1861. The Hegelian hope is that the result of such struggles will be a new culture, better than any of those of which it is the synthesis.[24] This new culture will be better because it will contain more variety in unity – it will be a tapestry in which more strands have been woven together. But this tapestry, too, will eventually have to be torn to shreds in order that a larger one may be woven, in order that the past may not obstruct the future.

There is, I think, little difference in doctrine between Dewey and Whitman. But there is an obvious difference in emphasis: the difference between talking mostly about love and talking mostly about citizenship. Whitman's image of democracy was of lovers embracing. Dewey's was of a town meeting. Dewey dwelt on the need to create what the Israeli philosopher Avishai Margalit has called a *decent* society, defined as one in which *institutions* do not humiliate. Whitman's hopes were centered on the creation of what Margalit calls, by contrast, a *civilized* society, defined as one in which *individuals* do not humiliate each other – in which tolerance for other people's fantasies and choices is instinctive and habitual.[25] Dewey's principal target was institutionalized selfishness, whereas Whitman's was the socially acceptable sadism which is a consequence of sexual repression, and of the inability to love.

Dewey disliked and distrusted Franklin D. Roosevelt, but many of his ideas came into their own in the New Deal. Whitman's hopes, on the other hand, began to be realized

---

23   Ibid., p. 929.

24   Whitman hoped that the Era of Reconstruction would be the birth of such a new culture. See David S. Reynolds, *Walt Whitman's America: A Cultural Biography* (New York: Random House, 1995), ch. 14.

25   See Avishai Margalit, *The Decent Society* (Cambridge, Mass.: Harvard University Press, 1996), p. 1.

only in the youth culture of the 1960s. Whitman would have been delighted by rock-and-roll, drugs, and the kind of casual, friendly copulation which is insouciant about the homosexual–heterosexual distinction. The historiography of the Sixties has come to be dominated by New Left politics, but we need to remember that lots of young people in the Sixties viewed Tom Hayden with the same suspicion as they viewed Lyndon Johnson. Their principal concern was cultural rather than political change.[26] Dewey might have approved of the rock-and-roll culture in a guarded and deliberate way, but Whitman would have thrown himself into it wholeheartedly.[27]

Dewey would not have expressed his desire to exalt and encourage his country by saying, as Whitman did, that he "who would be the greatest poet" must "attract his own land body and soul to himself and hang on its neck with incomparable love and plunge his seminal muscle into its merits and demerits."[28] But Dewey might have written other bits of *Leaves of Grass* – for example, "I speak the password primeval... I give the sign of democracy;/By God! I will accept nothing which all cannot have their counterpart of on the same terms."[29] One can also imagine him writing:

> Logic and sermons never convince,
> The damp of night drives deeper into my soul.

> Only what proves itself to every man and woman is so,
> Only what nobody denies is so.[30]

These passages in Whitman can be read as presaging the doctrine that made pragmatism both original and infamous: its refusal to believe in the existence of Truth, in the sense of something not made by human hands, something which has authority over human beings. The closest Hegel got to this pragmatist doctrine was his dictum that philosophy is its own time held in thought.

Despite this historicism, Hegel could never bring himself to assert the primacy of the practical over the theoretical – what Hilary Putnam, defining the essence of pragmatism, has called the primacy of the agent point of view. Dewey, like Marx in the Eleventh Thesis on Feuerbach, took the primacy of the practical all the way. His pragmatism is an answer to the question "What can philosophy do for the United States?" rather than to the question "How can the United States be philosophically justified?" He abandoned the question "Why should one prefer democracy to feudalism, and self-creation to obedience to authority?" in favor of the question "Given the preferences we Americans share, given the adventure on which we are embarked, what should we say about truth, knowledge, reason, virtue, human nature, and all the other traditional philosophical topics?" America will, Dewey hoped, be the first nation-state to have the courage to renounce hope of justification from on high – from a source which is immovable and

26   I am indebted to Mark Edmundson for this point about the somewhat unbalanced historiography of the Sixties.

27   For an account of the importance of rock-and-roll to the Sixties, see the chapter "Zappa and Havel" in Paul Berman's *A Tale of Two Utopias: The Political Journey of the Generation of 1968* (New York: Norton, 1996).

28   Whitman, *Leaves of Grass,* p. 23.

29   Ibid., p. 50.

30   Ibid., p. 56.

eternal. Such a country will treat both its philosophy and its poetry as modes of self-expression, rather than ask its philosophers to provide it with reassurance.

The culminating achievement of Dewey's philosophy was to treat evaluative terms such as "true" and "right" not as signifying a relation to some antecedently existing thing – such as God's Will, or Moral Law, or the Intrinsic Nature of Objective Reality – but as expressions of satisfaction at having found a solution to a problem: a problem which may someday seem obsolete, and a satisfaction which may someday seem misplaced. The effect of this treatment is to change our account of progress. Instead of seeing progress as a matter of getting closer to something specifiable in advance, we see it as a matter of solving more problems. Progress is, as Thomas Kuhn suggested, measured by the extent to which we have made ourselves better than we were in the past rather than by our increased proximity to a goal.

Late in his life, Dewey tried to "state briefly the democratic faith in the formal terms of a philosophical proposition." The proposition was that democracy is the only form of moral and social faith which does not "rest upon the idea that experience must be subjected at some point or other to some form of external control: to some 'authority' alleged to exist outside the processes of experience."[31] This formulation echoes Whitman's exclamation, "How long it takes to make this American world see that it is, in itself, the final authority and reliance!"[32] Antiauthoritarianism is the motive behind Dewey's opposition to Platonic and theocentric metaphysics, and behind his more original and far more controversial opposition to the correspondence theory of truth: the idea that truth is a matter of accurate representation of an antecedently existing reality. For Dewey, the idea that there was a reality "out there" with an intrinsic nature to be respected and corresponded to was not a manifestation of sound common sense. It was a relic of Platonic otherworldliness.

Repudiating the correspondence theory of truth was Dewey's way of restating, in philosophical terms, Whitman's claim that America does not need to place itself within a frame of reference. Great Romantic poems, such as "Song of Myself" or the United States of America, are supposed to break through previous frames of reference, not be intelligible within them. To say that the United States themselves are essentially the greatest poem is to say that America will create the taste by which it will be judged. It is to envisage our nation-state as both self-creating poet and self-created poem.

So much for my interpretation of Whitman's and Dewey's attempts thoroughly to secularize America – to see America as the paradigmatic democracy, and thus as the country which would pride itself as one in which governments and social institutions exist only for the purpose of making a new sort of individual possible, one who will take nothing as authoritative save free consensus between as diverse a variety of citizens as can possibly be produced. Such a country cannot contain castes or classes, because the kind of self-respect which is needed for free participation in democratic deliberation is incompatible with such social divisions.

For Whitman and Dewey, a classless and casteless society – the sort of society which American leftists have spent the twentieth century trying to construct – is neither more natural nor more rational than the cruel societies of feudal Europe or

31   "Creative Democracy – The Task before Us," in *Later Works of John Dewey,* vol. 14 (Carbondale: Southern Illinois University Press, 1988), p. 229.
32   Whitman, *Democratic Vistas,* p. 956.

of eighteenth-century Virginia. All that can be said in its defense is that it would produce less unnecessary suffering than any other, and that it is the best means to a certain end: the creation of a greater diversity of individuals – larger, fuller, more imaginative and daring individuals. To those who want a demonstration that less suffering and greater diversity should be the overriding aims of political endeavor, Dewey and Whitman have nothing to say. They know of no more certain premises from which such a belief might be deduced.

This conception of the purpose of social organization is a specifically leftist one. The Left, the party of hope, sees our country's moral identity as still to be achieved, rather than as needing to be preserved. The Right thinks that our country already has a moral identity, and hopes to keep that identity intact. It fears economic and political change, and therefore easily becomes the pawn of the rich and powerful – the people whose selfish interests are served by forestalling such change.

I do not think that subsequent American leftists have made any advance on Dewey's understanding of the relation between the individual and society. Dewey was as convinced as Foucault that the subject is a social construction, that discursive practices go all the way down to the bottom of our minds and hearts. But he insisted that the only point of society is to construct subjects capable of ever more novel, ever richer, forms of human happiness. The vocabulary in which Dewey suggested we discuss our social problems and our political initiatives was part of his attempt to develop a discursive practice suitable for that project of social construction.

To take pride in collaborating in this project is not to endorse what Baldwin called the

> collection of myths to which white Americans cling: that their ancestors were all freedom-loving heroes, that they were born in the greatest country the world has ever seen, or that Americans are invincible in battle and wise in peace, that Americans have always dealt honorably with Mexicans and Indians and all other neighbors or inferiors, that American men are the world's most direct and virile, that American women are pure.[33]

The sort of pride Whitman and Dewey urged Americans to feel is compatible with remembering that we expanded our boundaries by massacring the tribes which blocked our way, that we broke the word we had pledged in the Treaty of Guadalupe Hidalgo, and that we caused the death of a million Vietnamese out of sheer macho arrogance.

But, one might protest, is there then *nothing* incompatible with American national pride? I think the Dewey–Whitman answer is that there are many things that should chasten and temper such pride, but that nothing a nation has done should make it impossible for a constitutional democracy to regain self-respect. To say that certain acts *do* make this impossible is to abandon the secular, antiauthoritarian vocabulary of shared social hope in favor of the vocabulary which Whitman and Dewey abhorred: a vocabulary built around the notion of sin.

People who take this latter notion seriously find Dewey and Whitman childlike, naive, and dangerous. They see both as lacking a sense of the tragic, of the abyss. For such people, it is a fundamental moral fact that the commission of certain acts – acts which can be specified without regard for historical changes or cultural differences – is

33 Baldwin, *The Fire Next Time,* p. 101.

incompatible with further self-respect. But Dewey has a different conception of the fundamental moral fact. For him what makes us moral beings is that, for each of us, there are some acts we believe we ought to die rather than commit. Which acts these are will differ from epoch to epoch, and from person to person, but to be a moral agent is to be unable to imagine living with oneself after committing these acts.

But now suppose that one has in fact done one of the things one could not have imagined doing, and finds that one is still alive. At that point, one's choices are suicide, a life of bottomless self-disgust, and an attempt to live so as never to do such a thing again. Dewey recommends the third choice. He thinks you should remain an agent, rather than either committing suicide or becoming a horrified spectator of your own past. He regards self-loathing as a luxury which agents – either individuals or nations – cannot afford. He was quite aware of the possibility, and indeed the likelihood, of tragedy.[34] But he utterly repudiated the idea of sin as an explanation of tragedy.

People who take the notion of sin seriously – admirers of Saint Augustine such as Reinhold Niebuhr and Jean Bethke Elshtain – are appalled by this line of thought.[35] They view it as merely the light-minded, Californian view that one should treat any crime one happens to commit as a useful learning experience. But Andrew Delbanco gets Dewey exactly right when he says that for him "evil was the failure of imagination to reach beyond itself, the human failure to open oneself to a spirit that both chastises one for confidence in one's own righteousness and promises the enduring comfort of reciprocal love. There is a sense in which all of Dewey's thought was an extended commentary on Emerson's remark 'the only sin is limitation.'" Delbanco goes on to say, correctly, that this understanding of evil was basic to the Progressive Movement in American politics, and to its confidence in education and social reform. He is also correct when he concludes that "such a view of the human imagination as restless within established forms had no room for the idea of a fixed standard by which deviance from the truth could be measured and denounced."[36]

Delbanco has his doubts about whether we can afford to abandon the idea of such a standard. Leo Strauss, Harvey Mansfield, and many others have no such doubts. They see belief in such a standard as essential to individual and social decency. But what these critics see as Dewey's naiveté and light-mindedness I see as his intellectual courage – the courage to abandon the idea that it is possible to attain, in either science or morals, what Hilary Putnam calls a "God's-eye view." Dewey abandoned the idea that one can say how things really are, as opposed to how they might best be described in order to meet some particular human need. In this respect he is in agreement with Nietzsche, and with such critics of "the metaphysics of presence" as Derrida and Heidegger. For all these

---

34 See the title essay in Sidney Hook, *Pragmatism and the Tragic Sense of Life* (New York: Basic Books, 1974).

35 For an account of Niebuhr's criticisms of Dewey, see Daniel F. Rice, *Reinhold Niebuhr and John Dewey: An American Odyssey* (Albany: SUNY Press, 1993). For a recent admiring treatment of Niebuhr (and of Henry Adams), see John Patrick Diggins, *The Promise of Pragmatism* (Chicago: University of Chicago Press, 1994). For Elshtain's restatement of Augustine, see her *Augustine and the Limits of Politics* (Notre Dame: Notre Dame University Press, 1995); for Delbanco's, see his book *The Death of Satan: How Americans Have Lost the Sense of Evil* (New York: Farrar, Straus and Giroux, 1995).

36 Delbanco, *The Death of Satan,* pp. 175–176.

philosophers, objectivity is a matter of intersubjective consensus among human beings, not of accurate representation of something nonhuman. Insofar as human beings do not share the same needs, they may disagree about what is objectively the case. But the resolution of such disagreement cannot be an appeal to the way reality, apart from any human need, really is. The resolution can only be political: one must use democratic institutions and procedures to conciliate these various needs, and thereby widen the range of consensus about how things are.

Those who find this line of philosophical thought horrifying do not agree with Dewey and Foucault that the subject is a social construction, and that discursive practices go all the way down. They think that moral idealism depends on moral universalism – on an appeal to universally shared demands, built into human nature, or to the nature of social practice. I have argued against this claim in the past, and I shall not use these lectures to do so again. Instead, I shall end by returning to the contrast between agents and spectators with which I began.

I said earlier that we now have, among many American students and teachers, a spectatorial, disgusted, mocking Left rather than a Left which dreams of achieving our country. This is not the only Left we have, but it is the most prominent and vocal one. Members of this Left find America unforgivable, as Baldwin did, and also unachievable, as he did not. This leads them to step back from their country and, as they say, "theorize" it. It leads them to do what Henry Adams did: to give cultural politics preference over real politics, and to mock the very idea that democratic institutions might once again be made to serve social justice. It leads them to prefer knowledge to hope.

I see this preference as a turn away from secularism and pragmatism – as an attempt to do precisely what Dewey and Whitman thought should not be done: namely, to see the American adventure within a fixed frame of reference, a frame supplied by theory. Paradoxically, the leftists who are most concerned not to "totalize," and who insist that everything be seen as the play of discursive differences rather than in the old metaphysics-of-presence way, are also the most eager to theorize, to become spectators rather than agents.[37] But that is helping yourself with one hand to what you push away with the other. The further you get from Greek metaphysics, Dewey urged, the less anxious you should be to find a frame within which to fit an ongoing historical process.

This retreat from secularism and pragmatism to theory has accompanied a revival of ineffability. We are told over and over again that Lacan has shown human desire to be inherently unsatisfiable, that Derrida has shown meaning to be undecidable, that Lyotard has shown commensuration between oppressed and oppressors to be impossible, and that events such as the Holocaust or the massacre of the original Americans are unrepresentable. Hopelessness has become fashionable on the Left – principled, theorized, philosophical hopelessness. The Whitmanesque hope which lifted the hearts of the American Left before the 1960s is now thought to have been a symptom of a naive "humanism."

I see this preference for knowledge over hope as repeating the move made by leftist intellectuals who, earlier in the century, got their Hegelianism from Marx rather than Dewey. Marx thought we should be scientific rather than merely utopian – that we should interpret the historical events of our day within a larger theory. Dewey did not. He thought one had to view these events as the protocols of social experiments whose outcomes are unpredictable.

37 *Spectare* is the Latin translation of the Greek verb *theorein*. Both words mean "to look at."

The Foucauldian Left represents an unfortunate regression to the Marxist obsession with scientific rigor. This Left still wants to put historical events in a theoretical context. It exaggerates the importance of philosophy for politics, and wastes its energy on sophisticated theoretical analyses of the significance of current events. But Foucauldian theoretical sophistication is even more useless to leftist politics than was Engels' dialectical materialism. Engels at least had an eschatology. Foucauldians do not even have that. Because they regard liberal reformist initiatives as symptoms of a discredited liberal "humanism," they have little interest in designing new social experiments.

This distrust of humanism, with its retreat from practice to theory, is the sort of failure of nerve which leads people to abandon secularism for a belief in sin, and in Delbanco's "fixed standard by which deviance from the truth can be measured and denounced." It leads them to look for a frame of reference outside the process of experimentation and decision that is an individual or a national life. Grand theories – eschatologies like Hegel's or Marx's, inverted eschatologies like Heidegger's, and rationalizations of hopelessness like Foucault's and Lacan's – satisfy the urges that theology used to satisfy. These are urges which Dewey hoped Americans might cease to feel. Dewey wanted Americans to share a civic religion that substituted utopian striving for claims to theological knowledge.

In the remaining lectures I shall be contrasting the Deweyan, pragmatic, participatory Left as it existed prior to the Vietnam War and the spectatorial Left which has taken its place. One consequence of that disastrous war was a generation of Americans who suspected that our country was unachievable – that that war not only could never be forgiven, but had shown us to be a nation conceived in sin, and irredeemable. This suspicion lingers. As long as it does, and as long as the American Left remains incapable of national pride, our country will have only a cultural Left, not a political one.

23

Redemption from Egotism: James and Proust as Spiritual Exercises

1. Bloomian Autonomy and the Avoidance of Cant

Harold Bloom is America's wisest, most learned, and most helpful student of literature. He has recently published a book called *How to Read and Why*. In it he says that "The ultimate answer to the question 'Why read?' is that only deep, constant reading fully establishes and augments an autonomous self".[1]

By "reading" Bloom means "reading novels, plays, short stories and poems." The dozens of books that he tells us how to read in his new book do not include any philosophical works. It is an implicit premise of his work that imaginative, rather than argumentative, literature is the most efficient way to achieve autonomy. The philosophers and religious writers he discusses in his other books are people like Emerson and Joseph Smith, the founder of Mormonism – writers who make as little use of argument as do Pindar or Nabokov. By using "reading" to mean reading books which do not argue, Bloom is falling in with the practice of what I have been calling, in these lectures, "the literary culture."

Much of Bloom's advice about how to read concerns the need to avoid what he calls "ideology." When he uses this term, he is thinking primarily of attempts to use Heideggerian-Derridean critiques of metaphysics, or Marxist-Foucauldian critiques of capitalism or of "power," to tell you what to look for when reading imaginative literature. He believes – rightly, in my opinion – that the dominance in US departments of literature first of "theory" and then of "cultural studies" has made it more difficult for students to read well. For such attempts to give politics or philosophy hegemony over literature diminish the redemptive power of works of the imagination.

Bloom's criticism of transitory and local academic fashions is not terribly important in itself. But it underlines his conviction that it is imaginative novelty, rather than argumentation, that does most for the autonomy of the entranced reader. Bloom need not deny that works of political economy such as Marx's, or of philosophy such as Derrida's, can offer such novelty, nor that exposure to such novelties can transform a reader's life. But

1   Harold Bloom, *How to Read and Why* (New York: Touchstone, 2000), p. 195.

the kind of autonomy he is thinking of is primarily the sort that liberates one from one's own previous ways of thinking about the lives and fortunes of individual human beings.

It is by causing us to rethink our judgments of particular people that imaginative literature does most to help us break with our own pasts. The resulting liberation may, of course, lead one to try to change the political or economic or religious or philosophical status quo. Such an attempt may begin a lifetime of effort to break through the received ideas that serve to justify present-day institutions. But it also may result merely in one's becoming a more sensitive, more knowledgeable, wiser person. The latter is the sort of change that comes over Lambert Strether (the hero of James's novel *The Ambassadors*). This sort of change — increase of sympathy rather than change of ideas — contrasts with the sort of change that comes over Tom Joad (the hero of Steinbeck's *The Grapes of Wrath*), and also with the sort described in novels that focus on loss or acquisition of religious faith.

Bloom's thesis about how to attain this sort of autonomy chimes with my claim that the replacement of religion and philosophy by literature is a change for the better. We are both saying that the best way to achieve Heideggerian authenticity — the best way, as Nietzsche said, to "become who you are" — is not to ask "what is the truth?" but rather to ask "what sorts of people are there in the world, and how do they fare?"

Answers to this question are provided by novels like Steinbeck's, Zola's and Stowe's — novels that tell you about the wretchedly poor. They are also provided by novels like James' and Proust's that tell you about rich people expanding their horizons. Reading either sort of novel may help the reader to transcend the parents, teachers, customs, and institutions that have blinkered her imagination, and thereby permit her to achieve greater individuality and greater self-reliance.

Bloom regards ideology — in the sense of a set of general ideas which provide a context in which the reader places every book she reads — as an enemy of autonomy. Insofar as he is suspicious of treatises by theologians and philosophers it is because he fears they may give rise to bad reading habits. His ideal reader hopes that the next book she reads will recontextualize all the books she has previously read — that she will encounter an authorial imagination so strong as to sweep her off her feet, transport her into a world she has never known existed. In this new world, all the authors and characters with whom she has previously been acquainted will look different — as Milton looks different when one encounters him in Blake, Hegel when one encounters him in Marx, or Hamlet when one encounters him in Eliot. The reader's real-life friends, relations and neighbors will also look different, as will their motives and choices.

Elsewhere I have said that what Heidegger called authenticity and what Bloom calls autonomy are pretty much the same thing.[2] The attempt to achieve either is epitomized in the maxim that Bloom quotes from Dr. Johnson "Clear your mind of cant." "Cant," in this sense, means something like "what people usually say without thinking, the standard thing to say, what one normally says." In Heideggerian terms it is what "das Man" says.

Cant can be anything from the untutored common sense (the so-called "folk wisdom") of a peasant village, through the unthinking reiteration of quotations from sacred scripture, to the equally unthinking reiteration of the best-known sentences in the works of Heidegger or of Bloom himself. What makes cant cant is not its content but its easy accessibility and intelligibility — its ready-made character. Cant is what imaginative attempts at redescription become when they lose their freshness, and thus their ability to make us suspicious of received ideas. Every piece of cant was once a poetic achievement — a fresh

---

2   PHILOSOPHY AS A TRANSITIONAL GENRE (chapter 30, this volume).

and novel way of thinking about things. Every poetic achievement runs the danger of being turned into cant. Such a transformation is almost inevitable for argumentative works that have become staples of the educational process. It is less easily achieved, fortunately, in the case of non-argumentative works, and particular works of fiction.

To sum up what I have been saying: all writing that is not merely a matter of conveying information offers, explicitly or implicitly, a context in which to put many propositions we have previously believed, many of the people we have known, many parts of our own life-stories, and many of the books we have previously read. Poems, novels, and works of literary criticism such as Johnson's and Eliot's and Bloom's do this, just as do systems of philosophy, or compendia of folk-wisdom. But the former sort of writing is less easily turned into cant. This is because it hints rather than proclaims, suggests rather than argues, and offers implicit rather than explicit advice. The more poetic and the less argumentative a piece of writing is, the less easy it is to make it bear an unambiguous interpretation, and so the less easy to turn into "what we would normally say." Clarity and rigor are virtues in argumentative writing, but they are not relevant to plays or poems.

If there were such a thing as redemptive truth, the sort of truth that philosophy has traditionally hoped to offer, it would redeem by virtue of its explicit content, not because of its non-cognitive relation to a particular audience. Grasping the content of what one hears or reads is a matter of fitting what is said into a coherent set of inferential relationships to other utterances. Clarity and rigor are measures of ease of fit. So redemptive truth, if it existed, would be recognized as such because it would produce maximal clarity and maximal coherence.

By contrast, making the acquaintance of Dostoevsky or Iago, Emma Bovary or Marcel Proust, Milton's Satan or St. Luke's Christ, may well change one's behavior toward oneself or toward others, and perhaps even toward things in general. But the change is not a matter of everything falling nicely into place, fitting together beautifully. It is instead a matter of finding oneself transported, moved to a place from which a different prospect is available.

The contrast between imaginative and argumentative writing is parallel to the one that Kierkegaard draws between "what is said" and "how it is said." What is said is content – that is to say, the result of placing the utterance within a familiar inferential pattern. How it is said is a matter of the effect produced on a particular reader at a particular moment by the utterance. Kierkegaard drew this distinction between the how and the what in terms of the difference between "truth as subjectivity" and "objective" truth. But the term "subjective truth" is an oxymoron that produces more confusion than enlightenment. A better way to capture the distinction Kierkegaard wanted to draw is to invoke the difference between causes and reasons.[3]

A turn of phrase in a conversation or a novel or a poem – a new way of putting things, a novel metaphor or simile – can make all the difference to the way we look at a whole range of phenomena. So can an encounter with a new and strange person, in real life or in a novel or a play. But we are usually at a loss when asked to spell out what new proposition we came to believe as a result of exposure to the phrase or the person. The difference to the way we think is not a matter of adding a new belief to our repertoire. Kierkegaard's paradigm case of what he called "truth as subjectivity" was the Christian's relation to Christ – a relation that cannot be reduced to belief in the articles

3   Søren Kierkegaard, *Concluding Unscientific Postscript*, trans. David F. Swenson and Walter Lowrie (Princeton, NJ: Princeton University Press).

of a creed. Our relation to Iago or Dostoevsky, to our parents, or to our first love, is equally irreducible. These people cause us to act differently without necessarily having given us reasons for doing so.

The distinction between causes and reasons ties in with the difference between Bloom's desire for openness and the philosopher's desire for completeness. Bloom quotes Rabbi Tarphon as saying "It is not necessary for you to complete the work, but neither are you free to desist from it." He glosses this as "If it were necessary for any among us to complete the work, then we might break off in despair, because the work can never be completed".[4]

The work in question is that of enlarging oneself. That requires being ready to be bowled over by tomorrow's experiences – to remain open to the possibility that the next book you read, or the next person you meet, will change your life. Increased rationality – increased coherence of belief and desire – cannot close itself off from this possibility of disruption without falling victim to cant. You are such a victim insofar as you believe that you already possess criteria for judging the value of any books or people you may encounter – criteria that will provide you with good and sufficient reasons for tucking each of them into some familiar pigeonhole. To avoid such victimization, you must give up one of the dreams of philosophy – the dream of completeness, of the imperturbability attributed by the wise, of the mastery supposedly possessed by those who have, once and for all, achieved completion by achieving enlightenment.

There is, Bloom could easily grant, no such thing as complete autonomy – a mind entirely free of cant, entirely its own. (Though perhaps Shakespeare came close.) But there does not have to be such a thing. For Bloom's point, like Rabbi Tarphon's, is that it is the journey that matters. The fantasy of a resting-place prepared for us at the end of the journey is one that we should see as both impossible and undesirable, even though such fantasies are perhaps inevitable. When literature replaces religion and philosophy, it becomes clear that nobody and no thing could have prepared such a place. Instead, each generation of imaginative writers offers new suggestions about what such a place might look like, only to have this suggestion mocked by the next generation. This mockery will begin to be heard as soon as the earlier suggestion has begun to sound like cant.

2. The Novel

I want now to narrow my focus from imaginative literature in general to the novel – the genre that Henry James rightly called "the most independent, the most elastic, most prodigious of literary forms."[5] The novel is the best illustration of Bloom's claim about the results of constant and intense reading. It played the central role in the moral education of young intellectuals in the West during the century that has just ended.

Given the immense influence that the novel has come to have in recent times, it is hard for us to remember that such writers as Milton and Spinoza, Dr. Johnson and Hume, Burke and Kant, were familiar with only a few, rather primitive, examples of this genre. The burgeoning of the novel in the nineteenth and twentieth centuries has altered the map of the Western intellectual world. It has done so in ways that the philosophers and literary critics of the seventeenth and eighteenth century could never have foreseen.

---

4   *How to Read and Why.* p. 280.
5   *The Ambassadors,* Everyman edition, p. 19.

The emergence of the novel has contributed to a growing conviction among the intellectuals that when we think about the effects of our actions on other human beings we can simply ignore a lot of questions that our ancestors traditionally thought relevant. These include Euthyphro's question about whether our actions are pleasing to the gods, Plato's question about whether they are dictated by a clear vision of the Good, and Kant's question about whether their maxims can be universalized. Instead, a decision about what to do should be determined by as rich and full a knowledge of other people as possible – in particular, knowledge of their own descriptions of their actions and of themselves. Our actions can be justified only when we are able to see how these actions look from the points of view of all those affected by them.

Most novels tell us how other erring mortals think of themselves, how they contrive to put the actions that appall us in a good light, how they give meaning to their miserable or tragic or banal lives. Seen in this light, what novels do for us is to let us know how people quite unlike ourselves think of themselves, how they contrive to put actions that appall us in a good light, how they give their lives meaning. The problem of how to live our own lives then becomes a problem of how to balance our needs against theirs, and their self-descriptions against ours. To have a more educated, developed and sophisticated moral outlook is to be able to grasp more of these needs, and to understand more of these self-descriptions.

I have said previously that religion, in its unphilosophized form, resembles the novel in that it attempts to put us in relations to persons which are not mediated by questions of truth. The relation between a pious but uneducated Athenian of the fifth century and one of the Olympian deities, like that between an illiterate Christian and Christ, is an attempt to find redemption by getting in touch with a special, very powerful, immortal, sort of person. As Nietzsche said in *The Birth of Tragedy*, that sort of search for redemption becomes tinted with questions of truth only when Socrates, "with his belief in the explicability of the nature of things," suggests that "the mechanism of making concepts, judgments and inferences [is to be] prized above all other human activities".[6] The search becomes philosophical only after people like Socrates and Euripides have taken a skeptical stance toward the gods, a stance that Homer, and perhaps even Aeschylus, would have been incapable of adopting.

The big difference, however, between religious worship and novel-reading is that immortals are the object of adoration or self-abnegating love or fearful obedience, rather than people in whose shoes we are trying to put ourselves. As soon as we begin to want to understand the gods, or to make Christianity or Buddhism reasonable, religion begins to fade away and be replaced by philosophy. That is why Martin Luther described such attempts at reasonableness as diabolical temptations, and why Kierkegaard described them as occasions of sin. Novels rarely offer us god-like heroes and heroines, to whom our reaction resembles that of religious believers toward deities. (Though some, of course, do – Superman comic books and the fantasies of Ayn Rand, for example.)

Obviously, the novel is not the only literary genre which helps us achieve such sophistication. Homer's epics, Herodotus's travelogues, Thucydides's history, Theophrastus's characterology, and Plutarch's biographies did this sort of work in the ancient world, supplemented by such primitive fictions as those of Petronius and Apuleius. In our own time, ethnography, historiography, and journalism continue to broaden our sense of the possibilities open to human lives. But the novel is the genre which gives us most help in grasping the variety of human life and the contingency of our own moral vocabulary.

6   Friedrich Nietzsche, *The Birth of Tragedy* Section 15.

Novels are the principal means which help us imagine what it is like to be a cradle Catholic losing his faith, a redneck fundamentalist taking Jesus into her heart, a victim of Pinochet coping with the disappearance of her children, a kamikaze pilot of the Second World War living with the fact of Japan's defeat, a bomber pilot who dropped fire-bombs on Tokyo coping with the moral price of America's victory, or an idealistic politician coping with the pressures that multinational corporations bring to bear on the political process.

Novel-reading often increases tolerance for strange, and initially repellent, sorts of people. But the motto of the novel is not "to understand all is to forgive all." Rather, it is "Before you decide that an action was unforgivable, make sure that you know how it looked to the agent." You may well conclude that it was indeed unforgivable, but the knowledge of why it was done may help you avoid committing actions that you yourself will later find unforgivable. That is why reading a great many novels is the process by which young intellectuals of our time hope to become wise. This hope is the same that drove young intellectuals of the seventeenth and eighteenth centuries to read a great many religious and philosophical treatises.

These earlier readers were enmeshed in what Heidegger called the "onto-theological tradition." They sought truth as something distinct from either human or divine persons. By contrast, reading novels is a way of getting in touch with persons, just as reading Hesiod and the Old Testament were, for their original readers, ways of getting in touch with persons. To say that the way to get in better touch with the truth is to get in touch with an increased variety of persons is a natural consequence of the view that the propositions we are entitled to call true are those that we think can be justified to all those whose opinion matters.

The latter view, best represented by Habermas's theory of communicative reason, is a humanistic view of truth that breaks sharply with the onto-theological tradition. If one both takes this view of truth and is unable to believe in the existence of non-human persons, then the search for objective truth becomes an attempt to find intersubjective agreement among the children of one's own time rather than correspondence to non-human, ahistorical, reality. Once this transformation in one's conception of truth occurs, the next question is: To what sorts of people do we have to justify our beliefs and actions? This, in turn, raises the question: What sort of people are there, and which ones matter? That last question is the one that novels help us answer.

Philosophers and theologians who are dubious about the idea that novels are impor-tant for moral education think that one can answer the sort of question I have just raised by saying, for example, "all children of God matter" or "all rational agents matter" or "all those affected by our actions matter." But questions always arise about whether infidels count as children of God, or the densely ignorant and stupid as rational agents, or whether we are justified in being paternalistic toward those who do not grasp their own best interests. An increasing sense of the vacuity of general formulae for deciding hard cases leads us away from philosophy and toward literary forms that tell us more about what these recalcitrant sort of people look like to themselves.

I can sum up much of what I have been saying as follows: people read religious scrip-tures and philosophical treatises to escape from ignorance of how non-human things are, but they read novels to escape from egotism. "Egotism," in the sense in which I am using the term, does not mean "selfishness." It means something more like "self-satisfaction." It is a willingness to assume that one already has all the knowledge necessary for deliberation, all the understanding of the consequences of a contemplated action that could be needed. It is the idea that one is now fully informed, and thus in the best possible position to make correct choices.

Egotists who are inclined to philosophize hope to short-circuit the need to find out what is on the mind of other people. They would like to go straight to the way things are (to the will of God, or the moral law, or the nature of human beings) without passing through other people's self-descriptions. Religion and philosophy have often served as shields for fanaticism and intolerance because they suggest that this sort of short-circuiting has actually been accomplished. Novel-readers, by contrast, are seeking redemption from insensitivity rather than from impiety or irrationality. They may not know or care whether there is a way things really are, but they worry about whether they are sufficiently aware of the needs of others. Viewed from this angle, the hegemony of the novel can be viewed as an attempt to carry through on Christ's suggestion that love is the only law.

To be egotistic in the relevant sense is to be satisfied that the vocabulary one uses when deciding how to act is all right just as it is, and that there is no need to figure out what vocabularies others are using which justify them, in their own eyes, from doing things one regards as wrong. Euthyphro was egoistic, and so was Mr. Gradgrind. Euthyphro thought he had religious justification for his egoism, and Mr. Gradgrind philosophical justification. Socrates reminded Euthyphro that the gods differ among themselves about what is morally important. Dickens reminded his Gradgrind-minded readers that there are other ways of describing the results of their actions than the one provided by the vocabulary of utilitarianism.

The relevant difference between Socrates and Dickens is that Socrates, with his taste for what Nietzsche called "the mechanism of making concepts, judgments and inferences," was hoping for certainty: for the ability to make unquestionably correct decisions once he had found the right definition of the term "pious." Dickens, on the other hand, was interested neither in defining terms nor in correct inferences, but rather in making us aware of forms of suffering that we might have overlooked. The contrast I have been drawing between seeking redemption from ignorance and seeking redemption from egotism runs parallel to the distinction between seeking greater self-confidence and seeking greater awareness of what hurts other people.

This contrast also runs parallel to the distinctions between *knowing that* and *knowing how*, and between the skills of the axiomatizing mathematician and those of the artisan. The person who hopes to render more confident moral judgments as a result of the study of religious or philosophical treatises is usually hoping to find a principle that will permit of application to concrete cases, for an algorithm that will resolve moral dilemmas. But the person who hopes for greater sensitivity just wants to develop the know-how that will let him make the best of what is always likely to be a pretty bad job – a situation in which people are likely to get hurt, no matter what decision is taken.

3. James and Proust as Paradigms of the Novel

I shall take up this contrast between principles and sensitivity again below, when I discuss Martha Nussbaum's attempt to treat Henry James's novels as contributions to moral philosophy. But first I want to narrow my focus still more, and to turn from generalizations about the novel as a genre to some remarks about two novelists, James and Marcel Proust. The works of these two men typically play a special role in the lives of their admirers.

For a large number of people in the world today, their sense of who they are is bound up with their memories of certain novels they read when they were young. When they reflect on their idea of a perfect human life, they remember the worlds into which those novels introduced them, and the people who inhabited those worlds. When they try to recall what experiences have made the most difference to the ways in which they deal with other human beings, they remember the effects of the first reading of those novels. In the West, Proust is probably the novelist most frequently cited by people of this sort. In anglophone countries, James is mentioned with comparable frequency.

Literary tradition and influence are of course largely national affairs. Most of the novels which made a big difference to their readers were written in those readers' native languages, and dealt with local conditions – particularly the familial and social problems which troubled them in our youth, and the cultural changes which were going on while they were growing up. But certain novelists have become objects of adoration by cults whose membership is not restricted to nations or regions. Members of these cults are bound to one another, despite differences in ethnicity and nationality, in somewhat the same way that Christians from Japan and from Denmark, or Muslims from Morocco and Indonesia, are bound to one another. When they are thrown together in foreign parts, they rejoice to find a fellow-worshipper, someone who cherishes the same images and the same texts that they do themselves. Proust and James are novelists around whom such cults have grown up.

For cultists like myself, remembering our first reading of these authors is central to the story we tell about our own growing up. They helped make us the people we are, and our gratitude remains intense. Insofar as we consider any books sacred, their novels count as such. So we find it irritating and misleading to find them brought under the category of "the aesthetic," as opposed to "the moral" or "the spiritual." We can of course acknowledge that there are beautiful passages in these novels, and that they are triumphs of literary craftsmanship. But these facts are no more essential to our relation to these books than the prose of the King James Version is to the Christian's relation to Christ, or the architecture of Nara and Kyoto is to the religious life of the Japanese Buddhist.

James and Proust do a lot for the plausibility of Bloom's suggestion that the spiritual education of the young might better be entrusted to imaginative literature than to religious tradition or to the study of moral philosophy. For anybody who has been caught up in the work of either man is likely to be exceptionally sensitive to the dangers of egotism. Such people are more aware than most of how easy it is to describe other people in ways tailored to our own needs rather than to theirs. Readers of James and Proust are not only more aware to the needs of others, but are also more likely to aspire to the sort of experience which is vaguely and roughly called "a higher state of consciousness." The moments of understanding and revelation which occur more and more frequently as novels like *The Ambassadors* and *The Guermantes Way* reach their climaxes are the analogue, in these readers' lives, of the life-changing events that Henry James' brother William described in his book *The Varieties of Religious Experience*.

This analogy with religious experience helps differentiate James and Proust from such novelists as Dickens and Balzac. All four have been made into cult figures, but the Dickensians form a different sort of cult from the Proustians. Both are made of people who love to revisit their favorite characters and scenes from the novels, to allude to their favorite passages, and to discuss the relative merits and demerits of the various characters.

But most Dickensians would not say that Dickens had changed their lives, as opposed to enriching their lives. Dickens (like Trollope and Wodehouse) confirms our intuitions, whereas Proust unsettles them.

Proust and James are often thought of as educating us in the way that Socrates and Shakespeare educated us. For they do not just give us vivid portraits of previously unfamiliar people, they also force us to experience vivid doubts about ourselves. Such doubts may of course arise in reading any novel, as when we encounter a character in whom we recognize some of our own most unpleasant traits. But the sorts of doubts aroused by reading James and Proust go deeper than that. Their books raise the same kinds of doubts as books like *The Pilgrim's Progress* raise for Christians. These are doubts about whether there is any health in us, whether our egotism may not go much deeper than we have realized.

Just as those who have had what they describe as religious experiences are rarely able to spell out what new truths they learned by having them, so worshippers of Proust and James are usually baffled when asked what truths they picked up from these men's novels that they might otherwise have missed. It is the experience of reading the novel that makes one into a rather different sort of person, not the utility of a belief one might have acquired by various other means, even if one had never picked up that particular book. Just as Christians will say that their relationship to Jesus is not exactly to the author of the Sermon on the Mount, but rather to someone with whom they live on terms of intimacy, so many readers of James and Proust will insist that what matters is their relation to the novels themselves, or perhaps to the novelist himself, rather than to any set of beliefs for which the novels might be cited as justification.

John Bayley, in his introduction to James's *The Wings of the Dove*, says that James's

> later mode of artistic inquiry is a way of overcoming loneliness, of extending an almost tactile intimacy to the potential reader through the mode of words … Consciousness seems shared between author, characters and reader, and the participation of the last has its own special rewards and fascinations, which can arise out of bafflement itself. Intimacy is never a matter of being told what to think. It is like the secret converse of lovers, whose understanding is not dependent on a single authority.[7]

The sense of having engaged in such secret converse with James or with Proust is what binds members of their cults together.

Just as religious readers find themselves caught up in something larger than themselves, something that occasionally resembles orgasmic ecstasy, so readers of James and Proust find themselves caught up in the sort of suddenly shared enlargement of the imagination and suddenly shared intensity of appreciation of the passing moment that occurs when two lovers find their loves reciprocated. Proust and James offer their readers redemption, but not redemptive truth, just as his or her love redeems the lover, but does not add to his or her knowledge.

4. Martha Nussbaum on James

Many recent writers have done their best to say why James and Proust have the power they do – why they have become paradigms of novel-writing in the way that Galileo and Newton became paradigms of scientific explanation, or Locke and Kant paradigms of philosophical reflection. One of the most influential of these writers is Martha Nussbaum,

7   Henry James, *The Wings of the Dove*, ed. John Bayley (New York: Penguin, 1986), p. 8.

whose reading of James in her pathbreaking and liberating book *Love's Knowledge* began a widespread discussion of the relation between moral philosophy and literature.[8]

Nussbaum tries to bring James together with Aristotle, and specfically with Aristotle's moral philosophy. Her work is part of a trend that has emerged in recent decades within anglophone philosophy: a turn away from Kant, and more generally away from the idea that morality is a matter of applying general principles. Philosophers have grown tired of the pendulum swing between Kant's categorical imperative and the greatest-happiness principle of Mill and Bentham. They have begun to adopt a pox-on-both-your-houses attitude, and to look around for a way of philosophizing about right and wrong that is not an attempt to establish universal moral truths. So Aristotle's anti-Platonic insistence that moral virtue cannot be reduced to the application of such truths has come back into vogue.

Nussbaum treats the Aristotelian approach to moral philosophy as helping us make sense of the change in patterns of moral education that has taken place since the days when Kant and Mill wrote – a change that I have been emphasizing in these lectures, and which Nussbaum was one of the first philosophers to take seriously. This change has made the reading of fiction central to the attempt of young intellectuals to find themselves. As Nussbaum points out, Aristotle's way of thinking about moral education softens the dichotomy between literature and philosophy created by Plato's and Kant's preferences for explicit definition and for deductive moral reasoning.

Nussbaum defines "perception" as "the ability to discern, acutely and responsively, the salient features of one's particular situation" (p. 37). She goes on to say:

> It is very clear, in both Aristotle and James, that one point of the emphasis on perception is to show the ethical crudeness of moralities based exclusively on general rules, and to demand for ethics a much finer responsiveness to the concrete – including features that have not been seen before and could not therefore have been housed in any antecedently built system of rules.

Nussbaum insists, however, that perception by itself will not do. Perceptiveness can be displayed simply by acting well, whereas moral knowledge – an answer to the question "How should a human being live?" is a matter of matter of discovering and stating truths. Inarticulate skill is not enough. Although many readers of Aristotle have interpreted his claim that ethical virtue is a matter of *phronesis* rather than *episteme* as saying that the discovery of truths is irrelevant to the acquisition of moral virtue, Nussbaum does not read him in this way. For she thinks of moral philosophy as aiming at a "true and accurate depiction of various elements of life" (p. 6).

On her view poetry and philosophy are both truth-seeking activities, and the truths they find help us answer some of the same questions. She says that the Greeks viewed "dramatic poetry and what we now call philosophical inquiry in ethics" as "ways of pursuing a single and general question, namely, how human beings should live" (p. 15). Nussbaum attempts to reconcile this roughly "cognitivist" approach to moral philosophy, and this very un-Nietzschean approach to Greek dramatic poetry, with the claim that Proust and James would be right to deny that any morally relevant truths communicated by literature could "in principle be adequately stated without literature and grasped in that form by a mature mind" (p. 7).

---

8   Mastha Nussbaum, *Love's Knowledge: Essays on Philosophy and Literature* (New York: Oxford University Press, 1990).

She argues that "for an interesting family of [views about the nature of the relevant portions of human life] a literary narrative of a certain sort is the only type of text that can state them fully and fittingly, without contradiction" (p. 7). Nussbaum puts the same point in other words when she says that "only the style of a certain sort of narrative artist can adequately state certain important truths about the world, embodying them in its shape and setting up in the reader the activities that are appropriate for grasping them" (p. 6).

Unlike Nussbaum, I do not find the notion of "stating truths about the world" a felicitous way of describing what James and Proust do for members of their cults. Nor do I think that it would happily describe what St. Teresa of Avila and Thomas à Kempis do for those who read these authors over and over again. Nevertheless, I heartily agree with Nussbaum that "there are valuable aspects of human moral experience that are not tapped by traditional books of moral philosophy" (p. 143). She and I agree that "a philosophical book would have a hard time mounting a direct argument" for the claim that "infidelity and failure of response are more or less inevitable features even of the best examples of loving" (pp. 139–140). But when she asks us to see the novel and the philosophical treatise as such, and Henry James and Aristotle in particular, as collaborating in a common task – namely specifying "the good life for a human being" – I think that she understates both the difference between our intellectual world and Aristotle's, and the superiority of ours over his.

Aristotle tells us that the hope for an explicit decision procedure for resolving moral dilemmas, a hope which he attributes to Plato, is vain. That critique of Plato seems to me a sensible way of debunking a misguided attempt to transform moral deliberation into something more like mathematical demonstration. But the Aristotle who tells us that there is a natural kind called "human being" and a good appropriate to that natural kind, is too much of a Platonic essentialist for my pragmatist taste. Though able to give up the idea of a moral episteme, Aristotle was not able to give up the idea that human beings share a common nature, and that philosophy can list truths about what that nature consists of – not just truths of the sort that we relegate to physiology, but truths of the sort that provide moral counsel. Many commentators have asked whether Aristotle managed to find a satisfactory middle ground between Plato and the poets. Nussbaum seems sure that he did so, but I remain unconvinced.

As I see it, James is good at showing us what it is like to notice things about other people – their needs, their fears, their self-descriptions, their descriptions of other people – which we are usually too egotistic to take account of. This seems to me what he had in mind when, in a sentence Nussbaum quotes from the Preface to *The Golden Bowl*, James says that reading the novel is "the very record and mirror of the general adventure of one's intelligence" (p. 143). But I do not find it helpful to describe this noticing sort of intelligence as part of the process of discovering the good life for human beings. That seems like treating the skill of the tea-taster – the person who is aware of subtle differences between the tea made from leaves produced in different climates and seasons – as part of the process of discovering the good taste for tea.

We would usually say that the tea-taster's ability at noticing is an example of "knowing how" rather than of knowing that certain propositions are true and some false. We can of course convert the former into the latter by saying that she knows many truths – for example, "These tea leaves come from half way down the hill in Gopal Mukerji's tea garden" – that the rest of us do not. But to know many such facts is not to have a theory about the nature of tea, nor about how to arrange teas in an hierarchical order. Similarly, to notice far more things about individual human beings than most people do is not to be able to contribute to an understanding of what it is to be a human being, nor to be able to say what sort of life is best for human beings as such.

My point is not simply that "knowing how to live well" is a better description of what we get both from Aristotle's *Nichomachean Ethics* and from James's *The Golden Bowl* than "knowing what the good life for a human being is." It is that neither phrase is of much use. Both are too general – on a level with "knowing tea." Only if one believes in the possibility of redemptive truth – the sort of thing which, on my account, philosophy hoped to provide but religion and literature do not – will one feel comfortable with either. Nussbaum is more inclined to such belief than I am. Her writings on literature and philosophy seem to me torn between loyalty to the idea that there is a subject of study called "ethics," defined as "the search for a specification of the good life for a human being" and the suspicion, drawn from her reading of novels, that there is, at most, the ability to become what James called "finely aware and richly responsible."

Just as the most efficient way for a young Greek to figure out how to hit the Aristotelian mean between paired excesses was to hang around with the sort of leisure-class, politically active, males whom Aristotle admired, so the efficient way for a contemporary youth to become finely aware and richly responsible is to read a lot of novels – not just Proust and James but all those lesser novels that help us grasp the needs and self-descriptions of our fellow inhabitants of a certain time and place. But the know-how acquired by these two processes does not have much to do with specifying the good life for a human being, as opposed to helping somebody who has to deal with these particular sorts of people from thoughtlessly doing unnecessary damage.

Aristotle – half demi-Platonic metaphysician and half taxonomic biologist – found "the good life for a human being" a suitable description of his topic in *Nichomachean Ethics*. We heirs of Herder and Hegel, who see the Greeks as one culture among others, are also heirs of Darwin, who see our species not as endowed with a truth-tracking faculty called "reason" but rather as endowed with language, and thus with the ability to engage in social cooperation. These two inheritances conspire to make many of us more dubious than is Nussbaum about the attempt to revive Aristotle's vocabulary, and to treat Aristotle as more than a competent expositor of the common sense of his peers.

To recur to a point I made earlier, whereas Nussbaum thinks of herself as paying James a compliment by describing him as contributing to moral philosophy, I find this description not exactly derogatory, but certainly malapropos. I would reserve that compliment for people like Kant, Mill, or Rawls. Rawls, as I read him, made a contribution to moral philosophy by formulating what he calls the "Difference Principle" – a principle that nicely sums up many of the moral intuitions shared by contemporary social democrats, just as Kant's categorical imperative nicely summed up many of those shared by eighteenth-century friends of the French Revolution. It makes sense to say that Rawls, by putting forward the Difference Principle, offers us a truth – one we recognize in the same way that we recognize all other truths, by seeing that it coheres nicely with most of our previous beliefs.[9]

By contrast, I see Henry James as writing for a much smaller audience than Rawls. His audience – the kind of people who are likely to become members of the Jacobite cult – are not in search of knowledge, but rather are trying (or find themselves tempted by James into trying) for a kind of moral virtuosity. This moral virtuosity is the secular

---

9   See John Rawls, *A Theory of Justice* (Cambridge, MA: Harvard University Press, 1971).

analogue of the kind of religious virtuosity facilitated by reading *The Imitation of Christ*. To try to squeeze James into the same box as Aristotle and Rawls seems to me like trying to squeeze Thomas à Kempis into the same box as Aquinas and Bishop Butler. The similarities seem to me much less important than the differences.

To bring Aristotle and James together ignores the fact that James's main contribution to his reader's lives is a sense of the possibility of a new level of consciousness – what Nabokov called "a sense of another world where beauty, kindness, generosity … are the norm." The lives of the Jacobites are not enriched in the way that acquiring new true beliefs enriches, but in the way that a glimpse of a new form of life does. To follow the changes in the ways in which Maggie Verver, Charlotte Stant, Prince Amerigo and Fanny Assingham think of and treat one another as *The Golden Bowl* goes along is gradually to enter a world as different from the one we usually inhabit as the third level of Plato's divided line is from the second, or as different as the lives of the mystics are from those of the ordinary religious believer.

Like Plato, however, Nussbaum wants to assimilate all such ascent to a better grasp on what is really there. That is why she thinks it important to note that James is in no danger of "relativism" because he is "committed to the real" (p. 163), and why she proposes an analogy between the "moral knowledge" James gives us and greater sensory acuity (and therefore greater objectivity).[10] I resist this assimilation because I think it preserves a notion of redemptive truth that is appropriate to philosophy but not for pre-philosophical religion or post-philosophical novels.

I turn now to Nussbaum's claim, cited earlier, that some truths cannot be expressed except in narrative form. In my view this is as tempting, but as misguided, as the claim that metaphors should be read as having unparaphrasable meanings. I agree with Davidson's criticism of this latter claim, and with his alternative view that, though metaphors may change people's lives, they do not do so by communicating meanings. I would say that narratives may change people's lives, but they do not do so by communicating truths. Metaphors, Davidson argues, are causes but not reasons. So, I should argue, are narratives.

Reading Rawls or Kant or Mill gives you a reason for doing something – a moral principle from which you can try to deduce the need to act in a certain way. Reading James or Proust gives you practice in doing something that may lead you to act in a certain way. The urge to attribute meanings to metaphors and truth-candidacy to narratives seems to me to originate in the rationalist, Platonic, conviction that the only thing that should be allowed to change our lives is learning how that something really is. No meaning means no intentional content, which in turn means no possibility of correspondence to reality. As a result of such inferences, rationalists conclude that the power of metaphor must consist in making truth-candidates available that cannot be made available by other means. To say that novels do not offer truth would be, for rationalists, to say that novels should be viewed with the same suspicion as that with which Plato viewed the poets. So rationalists who think that they should not be so viewed have to find a way of construing them as purveying truth.

Nussbaum, to be sure, resists the suggestion that she is a rationalist in the narrow sense in which Plato, but not Aristotle, deserves this pejorative epithet. She broadens the notion of rationality until it becomes coextensive with practically every mental activity except blindly and stubbornly resisting suggestions about alternative ways to describe

10   *Love's Knowledge*, pp. 163–4.

what is going on. The trouble with flattening out the concept of "reason" in this way, however, is that the pursuit of truth gets flattened out into any and every attempt to render one's beliefs and desires coherent with one another, or at least with every such attempt that is accompanied by conversability, by a willingness to hear the other side.[11]

The distinction between "knowing that" and "knowing how" is blurred by this flattening process. I want to keep that distinction sharp because I want to emphasize the distinction between a philosophical culture – one dominated by the quest for redemptive knowledge about how things really are – and a literary culture. Whereas Nussbaum wants to emphasize the similarities between Aristotle and James, I want to emphasize the differences.

One way of highlighting these differences is to remark that the area of culture we call "moral philosophy" would never have existed had people not started agreeing with Socrates that reflective equilibrium is not good enough – if he had not insisted that the universal is prior to the particular, and that we therefore need universal rules and fixed definitions. So when Nussbaum says that Aristotle and James are moral philosophers who hold that the particular is prior to the universal she seems to me to be stretching the use of the term "moral philosophy" too far. For in this stretched sense any conversation about what to do – including the sort of conversations that Cephalus, Pericles, Lysis, and Phaedrus might have had with each other before they ever met Socrates – counts as moral philosophizing.

A further reason why my cultural politics, and therefore my account of the relation between philosophy and the novel, differ from Nussbaum's is that I do not share her view that "…this is a rich and wonderful time in moral theory." She says that "One cannot find for generations, since the time of John Stuart Mill, if not earlier – an era in which there has been so much excellent, adventurous, and varied work on the central ethical and political questions of human life" (p. 159). I would argue that most of the work on these questions that is being done today is not done in philosophy departments, and that the relevant work done in those departments in the days of Dewey was on a par with that done in the days of Rawls.

As I see it, moral and political principles of the sort put forward by Kant, Mill, and Rawls summarize the intuitions that have been developed in the course of a certain stretch of historical experience. Moral philosophy of the principle-formulating sort, the sort that is often done these days in philosophy departments, is parasitic on the larger moral and political experience of the species. This is the sort of experience that is gained from living through such events as the Wars of Religion, the French Revolution, the rise of industrial capitalism, the Holocaust, the American Civil Rights Movement of the middle of the twentieth century, the end of the colonial empires, and the successive waves of feminist activism.

The intuitions which are generated by reflection on such events, and therefore the principles that summarize these intuitions, can, to be sure, be viewed in a representation-alist way, as glimpses of an enduring moral reality. Seeing them this way, as Nussbaum does, leads one to view historical change as telling us more about what human beings were always like, and what their moral duties always were, rather than as telling us how human beings have changed in the course of time. Seeing them in the way Nussbaum prefers leads one to view historical change as leading to a grasp of the eternal truth of propositions rather than simply to a decrease in social and individual egotism, and to increased flexibility and sympathy in the making of moral decisions.

11   See ibid., chapters 2.

But if, as I do, one sees these changes not as cognitive gains but as enlargements of the imagination, one will think of moral theory of the sort Nussbaum admires as a matter of playing catch-up. Whereas Nussbaum shares what Nietzsche called Socrates's "theoretical optimism," and so views the philosophy professors of the day whom she most admires as forming an avant-garde, I follow Hegel in thinking that when moral philosophy paints its gray on gray, that is a sign that a certain set of moral intuitions have become familiar and banal.

This difference between us leads Nussbaum to say that novelists such as James are under an obligation "to render reality, precisely and faithfully" and to add that "in this task they are very much assisted by general principles, and by the habits and attachments that are their internalizations" (p. 155). By contrast, I think "rendering reality" the wrong compliment to pay to James (although admittedly, it is one he was inclined to pay to himself). Whenever a novelist creates a character with a set of self-descriptions and a moral outlook that we had never before imagined, we can of course say, if we like, that an aspect of reality has been captured that had not previously been so well rendered. But it is the novelty of the character and the utility of our acquaintance with her that justifies our praise, rather than the fidelity of representation. We did not know that aspect was there to be represented before we met Dimitri Karamazov or Hyacinth Robinson, nor that a moral dilemma could be regarded as Fanny Assingham does before we overheard her talking about it with her husband.

Analogously, we are on the lookout for scientific theories or political proposals that combine novelty and utility. If we then praise them for getting something (physical nature, the relation between the states and its citizens) right, it is not because we are can compare the theory or proposal with the thing gotten right and see that they match. In short, the intertwined compliments of "successful truth-seeking," "cognitive achievement" and "faithful represenation of reality" seem to me the vestiges of an outdated philosophical tradition, whereas to Nussbaum they seem the obvious and natural way to appreciate a novelist's achievement. So Nussbaum's claim that "habits and attachments" are internalizations of general principles seems to me, once again, to put the cart before the horse. I see the habits and attachments as doing the work, and the principles as attempts by theorists to find a handy way of summarizing those habits and attachments.

Nussbaum's cognitivist approach to morality leads naturally to the thought that "knowing that" (knowledge of general principles) leads to the sort of superior moral know-how that James and his characters exhibit. My insistence on keeping the distinction sharp between these two ways of knowing leads me to think of the formulation of principles as of only pedagogic importance, and of moral theory as a way of packaging the past for the use of the future rather than as a way of getting closer to the way things really are. So I cannot see the force of Nussbaum's claim that James safeguards himself against "relativism" by being "thoroughly committed to the real" (p. 163). "Relativism" seems to me a bugbear fabricated in order to frighten people into thinking that principles are more than handy summaries of intuitions.

Where Nussbaum sees moral philosophers as trying to attain reflective equilibrium between rules and perceptions, I would say that, like novelists, they help us to attain equilibrium between familiar perceptions which we have inherited from upbringing and tradition (the ones conveniently summarized by principles) and new intuitions that historical events and new acquaintances (real or fictional) have recently caused us to have. So whereas Nussbaum favors what she calls "the very simple Aristotelian idea that ethics is the search for a specification of the good life for a human being" (p. 139), I find "the good life for a human being," like "the accurate representation of moral reality," an empty, useless notion. The idea of "the good life for a human being" is Aristotle's rather weak and awkward substitute for Plato's "Idea of the Good." Both notions presuppose the Socratic idea that moral progress is a result of self-knowledge.

Moral philosophy can be stretched to include novels like James's only by deploying a "realist" view, claiming that anything that contributes to moral progress does so by helping us more faithfully to describe something already dimly seen. All the reasons that have led philosophers to turn away from this view of progress, and to switch from a Platonic rhetoric of discovery to a Nietzschean rhetoric of creation, work against this view. But, of course, either rhetoric can save the phenomena. So my disagreement with Nussbaum should not be seen, at least from my side, as a quarrel about what was or was not always already there to be discovered. It is, like the debates about "realism" presently going on within in philosophy of science and epistemology, simply a quarrel about whether to emphasize continuities or discontinuities between diverse human activities.

I want to see the rise of the novel in the last two centuries as something new under the sun, something that may help initiate a new form of cultural life by helping to create a self-image for human beings as different from the one Aristotle proposed as his cosmology is from our own. That is why Nussbaum's attempt to describe James' novels as contributions to moral philosophy strikes me as analogous to a grand old firm – one whose wares are no longer much in demand – buying up a younger and more flourishing enterprise, and then sticking its own corporate logo on that firm's more saleable products.

5. Novel-Reading as a Spiritual Exercise

At various points in this lecture I have offered an analogy between the use by Christian believers of authors such as St. Bonaventure, Thomas à Kempis, St. Ignatius Loyola, and John Bunyan and secularists' use of Proust and James. I shall close by developing this analogy a little further.

The term "spiritual development" is usually used only in reference to the attempt to get in touch with the divine. But it is occasionally used in a broader sense, one in which it covers any attempt to transform oneself into a better sort of person by changing one's sense of what matters most. In this broader sense of the term, I would urge that the novels of Proust and James help us achieve spiritual growth, and thereby help many of us do what devotional reading helped our ancestors to do.

Using the term "spiritual" in this sense has the advantage of avoiding both "aesthetic" and "moral" when explaining why Proust and James seem so important to so many. As I said earlier, the question of whether these men's novels are 'beautiful" does not strike members of their cults as having much point. But to say that the novels are morally rather than, or as well as, aesthetically important seems to leave something out. What it leaves out, I have suggested, is the sense of exaltation that readers of these novels share with religious people who come away from reading devotional literature with a sense of having visited a better world.

This sense of exaltation is not the same thing as being bowled over by the sheer rhetorical or poetic power of one's favorite passages. Such passages play the role that their favorite passages in sacred scripture play for the religious. They become mantras, and reciting them brings very present help in time of trouble. Thus secular Russian intellectuals, en route to the Gulag, exchanged quotations from Pushkin and Byron, or sang Mozart arias, in order to remind themselves that cold and hunger and wretchedness were not all there was to human life. The religious intellectuals at the other end of the same freight car were fulfilling the same need by reciting their favorite psalms.

The sense of exaltation I am trying to describe is, instead, a result of reading books as wholes, of following plots through to the end, rather than with being rendered momentarily delirious by a startling poetic figure, a perfectly crafted couplet, or a splendidly balanced antithesis. It may result from following the career of a figure such as Lambert Strether or Isabel Archer, in the same way that one might followe the career of Christian in *A Pilgrim's Progress*, or the attempts at ever greater purity of heart described by Loyola. Following such careers lifts up the heart by letting the reader hope that she herself might eventually overcome the immaturity, the confusion, and the incoherence of her days.

For the religious intellectual, this hope is for union with God, with something sublime, mysterious, unconditioned, belonging to another world. For the intellectual who finds James and Proust exalting, it is the hope that she will be able someday to see her life in this world as a work of art – that she will someday be able to look back and bring everything together into some sort of pattern – her loves and her rivalries, her fantasies and her defeats, herself in youth and in old age. It is the hope that all the people and events that have been important to her can be brought together into a coherent story of maturation. It is the hope for rounded completion and self-recognition, and is more like a longing for shapeliness than like the ambition of transcendence.

The principal character whose career is followed by the reader of *Remembrance of Things Past* is Marcel the narrator. He is the person whom all of Proust's readers take to be identical with the novelist, and with whose hopes and guilts and hesitations they themselves identify. So when the narrator, in the last volume, realizes that he is now in a position to write his novel, it is their triumph as well as his. They share both his confidence and his exaltation. By writing a novel about a man who keeps hoping to write the novel that the reader is reading, and who finally succeeds, Proust brings about the same sense of intimacy that Bayley describes as experienced by readers of James. By his success, Proust gives the idea that one's life can be a work of art – an idea familiar from Pater, Wilde, and Nietzsche – substance and plausibility of a sort it could not have acquired otherwise.

Those who find Proust's novel pointless or offensive are likely to call Proust an egotist. But to cultists like myself he is the person who did the most to help us understand the dangers of self-centeredness. He did so precisely by paying more careful attention to himself, and to everybody he met, than most of us can manage. By portraying dozens and dozens of self-centered people, and himself as the most self-centered of all, he helped his readers understand what they needed to watch out for, what they needed to be afraid of, as well as what they might hope for. He used self-centeredness against itself, and thus accomplished the sort of creative self-overcoming that Nietzsche praised.

Not even members of the Proust cult think that this would be a better world if we all passed our lives in the way that Proust passed his. But because we do not think that there is such a thing as "the good life for man," we do not think that this universalizability test is relevant. We do not think that everybody should live their life in the way in which Socrates, or Christ, or Nietzsche lived theirs either. We want as many different creative self-overcomings as we can get, for the more such examples we have before us the more useful advice we can pick up about how such a thing is possible.

But we do not think that creative self-overcoming is the only sort of life that it befits a human being to lead. Human happiness would certainly be greatly increased if that sort of life became an option for more people than it is now, but that does not mean that everybody should try it. Members of the Proust cult do not think everybody can profit from attempting to do so, any more than the Catholic Church thinks that everyone can profit from attempting to become a saint.

The big difference between the Proustians and the Catholics, and more generally between the religious and the literary cultures, is that devotional reading emphasizes purification rather than enlargement, getting rid of distractions rather than incorporating them in a larger unity. Novel-reading, on the other hand, aims at encompassing multitudes rather than eliminating superfluities. One reason Proust's novel is exemplary is that it is long and complex enough to take in most of what was important in the author's life.

Although not everybody should try to overcome themselves, everybody can and should hope to end their lives with some sense of what it meant, how it hung together, what form it took. This is easy to do if one's life was nothing but remorseless grinding dawn-to-dusk toil, or if it was lived within the confines of a backwoods village, or of a narrow and unquestioned faith. Yet these are just the sorts of lives that people who use novels as aids to spiritual development think of as in danger of "meaninglessness." (Think here of the novel-reading heroines of *Madame Bovary* and of Sinclair Lewis' *Main Street*.) The epithet is used because such people think a that a life has meaning just insofar as the person living it is able to find some unity in, impose some form on, as great a variety of persons and things and events as possible.

It is often claimed that the special sort of pleasure we get from beautiful objects comes from their ability to combine unity and variety, so it may seem that taking this combination as an aim for a human life is possible only for aesthetes – leisured, spoiled, morally irresponsible flaneurs. But the hope for this sort of combination is not incompatible with moral strenuousness, nor even with moral entrepreneurship. To say that everybody can and should try to look back on their life and find form and meaning in it is not yet to say anything about the extent of one's responsibilities to others. James and Proust do not, as far as I can see, offer much advice on how to balance those responsibilities with responsibilities to oneself. Still, one will be safer in the hands of people who admired their novels than in the hands of readers who found those novels pointless.

Part V

Philosophy as Cultural Politics

Introduction

That Rorty would appeal to "cultural politics" in his final volume of essays may seem odd, given his polemic against the displacement of "real" politics by cultural politics in *Achieving Our Country* (AOC).[1] Yet the trajectory of Rorty's thought had been moving away from appeals to objective, nonhuman categories and toward the historically constituted human realm for quite some time. What distinguishes pragmatism from traditional philosophy for Rorty is that it is not afraid to offer "cultural-political arguments" for particular linguistic practices rather than "metaphysical or epistemological arguments." The difference is that in the realm of cultural politics arguments are of the "non-criteria-governed sort" since there is nothing to appeal to outside of our cultural particularity that will yield universally accepted criteria (PCP, pp. 156, 21). Seen in this light, cultural politics is another name for the "conversation of mankind" invoked in the final section of *Philosophy and the Mirror of Nature* (PMN) nearly three decades earlier. Once the traditional assumptions that privilege philosophy have been abandoned, we can see that "All areas of culture are parts of the same endeavor to make life better" (PSH, p. xxv). Although he does not refer to "cultural politics" as such in these essays, we follow Rorty's lead in adopting that label as a description of what he was up to in his later work.[2] As he characterizes it in the preface to his final volume of philosophical papers, *Philosophy as Cultural Politics* (PCP), to "intervene in cultural politics" is to promote moral progress or "cultural change" by contributing to "humanity's ongoing conversation about what to do with itself" through suggesting "novelties" that alter the course of this conversation (PCP, pp. ix–x).[3]

---

1   See p. 377, this volume and AOC, passim.

2   For Rorty's most extended discussion of cultural politics, see "Cultural Politics and the Question of the Existence of God" in *Philosophy as Cultural Politics* (PCP), which appears to be his first use of the phrase in this new sense, although the phrase does appear in REDEMPTION FROM EGOTISM (p. 402, this volume). His only explicit discussion of cultural politics in the current volume is a paragraph in ANALYTIC AND CONVERSATIONAL PHILOSOPHY (p. 198, this volume).

3   As examples of such novelties, he includes: proposals for new roles that men and women might play, sketches of an ideal community, and suggestions about how to reconcile seemingly conflicting outlooks. He continues, "Dewey hoped that philosophy professors would see such intervention as their principal assignment" (PCP, pp. ix–x).

Although he has not yet adopted this nomenclature, the richest account of what phi-losophy as cultural politics entails comes in a series of lectures called "Hope in Place of Knowledge" given in Vienna and Paris in 1993.[4] In broad terms, this conception of phi-losophy is authorized by a series of shifts that, taken together, redirect the resources of philosophy toward what amounts to a project of changing the culture that Rorty calls "Emersonian self-creation on a communal scale" (p. 421, this volume). Hope replaces knowledge, appeals to the future replace appeals to an independent reality, stories replace rational arguments, a sense of self-reliance replaces the attempt to ground the past in the eternal, and an ability to sympathize or identify with the suffering of others replaces universal moral obligation. In *Philosophy and Social Hope* (PSH), Rorty refers to this vision as "my own version [of] pragmatism," conceding from the outset that this version "makes no pretense of being faithful to the thoughts of either James or Dewey," and instead offers his own "sometimes idiosyncratic, restatements of Jamesian and Deweyan themes" (PSH, p. xiii).[5]

That said, "Truth without Correspondence to Reality" offers some of Rorty's most overt and wide-ranging use of the pragmatist tradition. Engaging not only James and Dewey but Emerson, Whitman, and more recent pragmatist thinkers, like Cornel West, he interprets both pragmatism and America itself as "expressions of a hopeful, melioris-tic, experimental frame of mind" (p. 416, this volume). In the spirit of Emerson and Dewey, he underscores the importance of "making philosophy an instrument of change rather than of conservation, thereby making it American rather than European" (p. 419, this volume). "Ethics without Principles" is an extended marshaling of Rorty's Deweyanism against familiar staples of Kantian moral philosophy, like the distinction between morality and prudence, and the notion of unconditional moral obligation, in favor of a Humean conception of morality as a matter of cultivating sentiments to make us more sensitive and responsive to a larger group of other humans.[6] Pragmatism, he asserts, can be thought of as "an attempt to alter our self-image" (p. 425, this volume). The hope, as he puts it, is to "minimize one difference at a time" by invoking "a thou-sand little commonalities" rather than "specify one great big one, their common human-ity" (pp. 431–2, this volume).

In "Justice as a Larger Loyalty," one of Rorty's most significant forays into political theory, he develops the notion of moral development put forth in "Ethics without Principles" – "re-marking human selves so as to enlarge the variety of relationships which constitute those selves" (p. 429, this volume) – into a full-fledged conception of justice. Here too Kantianism is the foil. Rortyan loyalty juxtaposes a community of trust,

---

4   The three lectures are "Truth Without Correspondence to Reality," "A World without Substances or Essences," and "Ethics Without Principles." Although they appeared in German and French in 1994 and 1995, respectively, they do not appear in English until the publication of *Philosophy and Social Hope* (PSH) in 1999. The versions of the first and third lectures that appear in this volume each have been edited down by a few pages to make it possible to reprint them both.

5   Rorty makes a similar concession in "Dewey Between Hegel and Darwin," having been suf-ficiently battered on this front already: "So I shall describe what Dewey might have said, and in my view should have said, rather than what he did say. I shall construct a hypothetical Dewey who was a pragmatist without being a radical empiricist, and a naturalist without being a panpsychist" (TP, p. 292).

6   See also his "Kant vs. Dewey: The Current Situation of Moral Philosophy" in PCP.

an historicist moral identity, felt sentiments, a strong contextualism, and an appeal to sympathy to Kantian justice's universal obligation, transcendental self, abstract principles, context-free validity, and appeal to reason. If we can expand the scope of "one of us" to include not just the human species but "all living creatures on our home planet," then a sense of loyalty to that group offers the most compelling basis for moving us to remedy injustices suffered by any being in that group. In articulating this view, Rorty addresses recent work by Michael Walzer, John Rawls, and Jurgen Habermas on this topic. From the outset, what Rorty contributes to these debates is an explicit focus on the need to situate our discussions of justice within the context of relations between the "rich democracies" of the West and the rest of the developing world, particularly in light of globalization. Although Rorty in the end defends the institutions and practices that are the fruits of (contingent) moral progress in the West over the last few centuries, he stresses that it matters how they are defended. If those in the West attempt to build "a community of trust" with non-Westerners by offering an "instructive story" about its achievements, rather than claiming "transcultural moral validity" for its views because of a better use of their reason or a better realization of some universal human capacity, we can make more progress toward a "global moral community." The Enlightenment rationalist justification for this goal has impeded its realization.

"Pragmatism as Romantic Polytheism" is an eclectic, wide-ranging essay that probes the romantic roots of pragmatism. A decade and a half earlier, Rorty had asserted that the contribution of Nietzsche and James to establishing a post-Philosophical literary culture was to "replace romanticism with pragmatism" (p. 131, this volume). This essay provides the background for that claim, offering Rorty's most sustained treatment of Nietzsche's relation to pragmatism, as well as some of his more in-depth discussions of James.[7] To his familiar story of literature and poetry replacing philosophy and religion as a source of ideals, he adds a new twist: the metaphor of polytheism as a stand-in for pluralism – "the idea that there are diverse, conflicting, but equally valuable forms of human life." This pluralism is the chief virtue of the secular "polytheism" Rorty offers as a redescription of pragmatism. "You are a polytheist," he tells us, in a definition that covers not only Nietzsche and James but John Stuart Mill and Isaiah Berlin, "if you think that there is no actual or possible object of knowledge that would permit you to commensurate and rank all human needs" (p. 446, this volume). Understood in this way, polytheism provides the basis for an "ethics of love" – "a Christianity that is merely ethical" – that comports with a postmetaphysical conception of democracy that Rorty associates with Dewey. Becoming polytheistic means replacing "both monotheism and the kind of metaphysics or science that purports to tell you what the world is *really* like" with democratic politics (p. 447, this volume). Rorty calls this the "anti-authoritarian motif" of pragmatism: "the idea that anything could have authority over the members of a democratic community save the free, collective, decisions of that community" (p. 452, this volume).[8] This essay sketches a "pragmatist philosophy of religion" that embodies this motif.

---

7   On James, see also "Religious Faith, Intellectual Responsibility, and Romance" in PSH; "Pragmatism and Romanticism" in PCP; and "Some Inconsistencies in James' Varieties" in Wayne Proudfoot (ed.), *William James and a Science of Religion* (New York: Columbia University Press, 2004), pp. 86–97.

8   For more on this issue, see Rorty, "Pragmatism as Anti-Authoritarianism" in John R. Shook and Joseph Margolis (eds.), *A Companion to Pragmatism* (Malden, MA: Blackwell Publishing, 2006), pp. 257–66.

Rorty takes a similar stance in "Religion in the Public Square," a follow-up and revision of his earlier essay, "Religion as a Conversation-Stopper."[9] While Rorty softens his previous claim that religion should be kept out of the public square, calling his earlier stance "hasty and insufficiently thoughtful," he keeps his repudiation of religion as "*mere* appeal to authority" in public discourse (p. 461, this volume). Likening this appeal to the recourse to "unarguable first principles" in philosophy, he draws a distinction between explaining the reasons behind a political belief grounded in religious conviction and citing scriptural or divine authority to put one's views beyond the reach of democratic debate. As he explains in the earlier piece,

> the epistemology suitable for such a democracy is one in which the only test of a political proposal is its ability to gain assent from people who retain radically diverse ideas about the point and meaning of human life, about the path to private perfection.

Reinforcing this egalitarian epistemology, he holds that moral decisions in a liberal democracy "are best made by public discussion in which voices claiming to be God's, or reason's, or science's, are put on a par with everybody else's" (PSH, pp. 172–3).[10] The insight that informs his emendated position is that the greatest threat to this kind of public discussion is not individuals of faith or even "congregations of religious believers ministered to be pastors," but "ecclesiastical organizations" that claim to offer "authoritative guidance to believers" rather than "pastoral care." In the end, for Rorty it is "mostly religion above the parish level that does the damage" (p. 456, this volume).

Even as late as the 2000 essay "Is 'Cultural Recognition' a Useful Concept for Leftist Politics?" Rorty's professed skepticism about the political value of "cultural studies" makes his own embrace of the notion of philosophy as cultural politics shortly thereafter seem rather unlikely, especially since this skepticism is at least in part directed toward the American academic Left's overestimation of the utility of philosophy. As representatives of this Left Rorty cites Judith Butler and Nancy Fraser[11] – in particular, their views of the importance of recognizing cultural differences – and what he calls "the academic arms of the new social movements": departments of Women's Studies, African-American Studies, and Gay Studies. He retraces some familiar ground from *Achieving Our Country*, contrasting the more recent cultural Left with an older Left less distrustful of reform and more attuned to economic issues, and underscoring the difference between "asking not to be singled out for ill-treatment and asking for attention to, and respect for, one's

---

9   See "Religion as a Conversation-Stopper" (PSH, pp. 168–74), a review of Stephen L. Carter, *The Culture of Disbelief: How American Law and Politics Trivialize Religious Devotion* (New York: Basic Books, 1993).

10   In "Cultural Politics and the Question of the Existence of God," he puts it this way, drawing on Robert Brandom: "the appeal to God, like the appeal to 'the law' is always superfluous, since, as long as there is disagreement about what the purported authority says, the idea of 'authority' is out of place" (PCP, p. 9).

11   For Nancy Fraser's response to this essay, see her "Why Overcoming Prejudice is Not Enough: A Rejoinder to Richard Rorty," *Critical Horizons* 1 (2000): 21–7, reprinted in Nancy Fraser and Kevin Olson, *Adding Insult to Injury: Debating Redistribution, Recognition, and Representation* (London: Verso, 2008), pp. 82–8.

distinctive features" as a response to the existence of prejudice (p. 467, this volume). He gets shots in against the belief that "spotting latent incoherence in ideas, identities, and institutions, in the Derridean manner" is as useful to remedying injustice and alleviating suffering as "training in battered women's shelters, AIDS support groups, or Head Start programs for black kids in ghettoes" (p. 469, this volume). Consistent with positions taken in previous essays, he emphasizes the need to highlight commonalities and what we share with those unlike us, rather than recognize differences. The new wrinkle that emerges in this essay is his framing the recognition of group differences in an Emersonian spirit as a threat to what he calls "self-creating independence" – the power to develop new self-images by redescribing ourselves. Challenging the prevailing invocation of Hegel by advocates of the politics of recognition, he notes the difference between recognizing the dignity of individuals as individuals, as opposed to as members of a particular community. The goal of combining "the encouragement of the greatest possible human diversity" with the contingent commonality that results from "transitory comings-together of individuals" he affirms here is a hallmark of his liberalism between Mill and Dewey.

Following a fitting tribute to fellow pragmatist traveler Richard Bernstein, "Philosophy as a Transitional Genre" offers what Rorty calls "just one more retelling of my tediously familiar up-from-representationalism story."[12] In brief, it is "the old Nietzschean story about how 'Truth' took the place of 'God' in a secular culture, and why we should get rid of this God-surrogate in order to become more self-reliant" (p. 474, this volume). Reducing his narrative of the intellectual development of the West to its simplest terms, he casts philosophy as a transitional genre in the progression from religion to literature as the source of redemption in the culture.[13] With the advent of a literary culture, as we have seen, for Rorty our relations – "non-cognitive relations," importantly – to other humans come to the forefront. Our "increased self-reliance," he believes, obviates the need to trump the complexity and incommensurability of diverse forms of human existence by justifying our own beliefs as a function of a non-human reality or the way things really are. On this view, modern science is seen as "an edifying example of tolerant conversability" and "a model of rational cooperation" within which political discourse can proceed, rather than a source of redemptive truth (p. 486, this volume). When it comes to such cooperation though, we must still draw a line between public and private, so that the individual's quest for autonomy and authenticity need not be subsumed under the shared vocabularies that make political deliberation possible. Rorty's goal, in the end, is to achieve the Good Global Society, yet in a way that abandons the need to enforce universal agreement about the best form of human life within it. For in this vision there is no "standard against which the products of the imagination can be measured other than their social utility, as this utility is judged by a maximally free, leisured and tolerant global

---

12   The version of this essay included here contains two sections that do not appear in the version collected in PCP: the opening preamble on Bernstein and the final section, "The 'Decadence' of a Literary Culture." An earlier draft of this essay from 2000 bore the title, "The Decline of Redemptive Truth and the Rise of a Literary Culture."

13   For a thoughtful attempt to read pragmatism more generally in this spirit, see Colin Koopman, *Pragmatism as Transition: Historicity and Hope in James, Dewey, and Rorty* (New York: Columbia University Press, 2009).

community." The idea is to "cooperate on communal projects" without having to reconcile differences (p. 488, this volume). If Rorty appears to look forward to philosophy's disappearance in this essay, it is only in the sense that he believes we "need to get beyond representationalism, and thus into an intellectual world in which human beings are responsible only to each other" (p. 474, this volume).

24

Truth without
Correspondence to Reality

Pragmatism is often said to be a distinctively American philosophy. Sometimes this is said in tones of contempt, as it was by Bertrand Russell. Russell meant that pragmatism is a shallow philosophy, suitable for an immature country. Sometimes, however, it is said in praise, by people who suggest that it would be un-American, and thus immoral, not to be a pragmatist – for to oppose pragmatism is to oppose the democratic way of life.

Although I think that Russell's contempt for both pragmatism and America was unjustified, I also think that this sort of praise of pragmatism is misguided. Philosophy and politics are not that tightly linked. There will always be room for a lot of philosophical disagreement between people who share the same politics, and for diametrically opposed political views among philosophers of the same school. In particular, there is no reason why a fascist could not be a pragmatist, in the sense of agreeing with pretty much everything Dewey said about the nature of truth, knowledge, rationality and morality. Nietzsche would have agreed with Dewey against Plato and Kant on all these specifically philosophical topics. Had they debated, the *only* substantial disagreement between Nietzsche and Dewey would have been about the value of egalitarian ideas, ideas of human brotherhood and sisterhood, and thus about the value of democracy.

It is unfortunate, I think, that many people hope for a tighter link between philosophy and politics than there is or can be. In particular, people on the left keep hoping for a philosophical view which cannot be used by the political right, one which will lend itself only to good causes.[1] But there never will be such a view; any philosophical view

Richard M. Rorty, "Truth without Correspondence to Reality," excerpts from pp. 23–46 in *Philosophy and Social Hope* (New York: Penguin, 1999), © 1999 by Richard Rorty. Produced by permission of Penguin Books Ltd.

1 Otto Neurath is reputed to have said that 'no one can use logical empiricism to ground a totalitarian argument', and certainly the members of the Vienna Circle, like many contemporary writers, saw Heidegger's philosophy and Hitler's politics as bound up with each other. But one should remember that no one can use logical empiricism, or pragmatism, to ground an *antitotalitarian* argument. No argumentative roads from epistemological or semantic premises will take one

is a tool which can be used by many different hands. Just as you cannot learn much about the value of Heidegger's views on truth and rationality from the fact that he was a Nazi, so you cannot learn much about the value of Dewey's (quite similar) views on the same subjects from the fact that he was a lifelong fighter for good, leftist political causes, nor from the fact that he shared Walt Whitman's sense that 'the United States are themselves the greatest poem'. Your opinion of pragmatism can, and should, be independent of your opinion of either democracy or America.

For all that, Dewey was not entirely wrong when he called pragmatism 'the philosophy of democracy'. What he had in mind is that both pragmatism and America are expressions of a hopeful, melioristic, experimental frame of mind. I think the most one can do by way of linking up pragmatism with America is to say that both the country and its most distinguished philosopher suggest that we can, in politics, substitute *hope* for the sort of knowledge which philosophers have usually tried to attain. America has always been a future-oriented country, a country which delights in the fact that it invented itself in the relatively recent past.

In what follows, I shall be arguing that it helps understand the pragmatists to think of them as saying that the distinction between the past and the future can substitute for all the old philosophical distinctions – the ones which Derrideans call 'the binary oppositions of Western metaphysics'. The most important of these oppositions is that between reality and appearance. Others include the distinctions between the unconditioned and the conditioned, the absolute and the relative, and the properly moral as opposed to the merely prudent.

As I shall be using the term 'pragmatism', the paradigmatic pragmatists are John Dewey and Donald Davidson. But I shall be talking mostly about Dewey, and will bring in Davidson only occasionally (to help out in the clinches, so to speak). It is customary to distinguish the 'classical pragmatists' – Peirce, James and Dewey – from such living 'neopragmatists' as Quine, Goodman, Putnam and Davidson. The break between the two is the so-called 'linguistic turn'. This was the turn philosophers took when, dropping the topic of experience and picking up that of language, they began taking their cue from Frege rather than from Locke. In the US, this turn was taken only in the 1940s and 1950s, and it was as a result of this turn that James and Dewey ceased to be read in American philosophical departments.

When people try to associate Americanism and pragmatism, it is usually only the classical pragmatists whom they have in mind. The so-called neopragmatists do not concern themselves much with moral and social philosophy, nor do they see themselves as representing anything distinctively American. As a student of Carnap, Quine was taught that philosophy should stay close to logic, and keep its distance from politics, literature and history. Quine's students, Goodman and Davidson, take this Carnapian view for granted. Of the neopragmatists I have listed, only Putnam has, in his later writings, stepped beyond the limits Carnap set.

Of the three classical pragmatists, only James and Dewey deliberately and self-consciously related their philosophical doctrines to the country of which they were prominent citizens. Peirce thought of himself as part of an international community of

---

to political conclusions, any more than to conclusions about the relative value of literary works. But it is nevertheless obvious why those who favour a pragmatist account of the nature of human knowledge tend to admire Whitman and Jefferson more than they do Baudelaire or Hitler.

inquirers, working on technical and specialized problems which had little to do with historical developments or national cultures.[2] When he referred to political issues and social trends, it was in the same left-handed way in which Quine refers to them – as topics which have little to do with philosophy.

James and Dewey, however, took America seriously; both reflected on the world-historical significance of their country. Both were influenced by Emerson's evolutionary sense of history, and in particular by his seminal essay on 'The American Scholar'. This essay rejoices in the difference between the Old World and the New, and Oliver Wendell Holmes called it 'our national Declaration of Intellectual Independence'. Both men threw themselves into political movements – especially anti-imperialist movements – designed to keep America true to itself, to keep it from falling back into bad old European ways. Both used the word 'democracy' – and the quasi-synonymous word 'America' – as Whitman had: as names of something sacred. In an essay of 1911, Dewey wrote:

> Emerson, Walt Whitman and Maeterlinck are thus far, perhaps, the only men who have been habitually, and, as it were, instinctively aware that democracy is neither a form of government nor a social expediency, but a metaphysic of the relation of man and his experience in nature ...[3]

As Cornel West has made clear,[4] one needs to have read some Emerson in order to understand the source of the 'instinctive awareness' which James and Dewey shared. West says that Emerson

> associates a mythic self with the very content and character of America. His individualism pertains not simply to discrete individuals but, more important, to a normative and exhortative conception of the individual *as* America. His ideological projection of the first new nation is in terms of a mythic self ... a heroic American Scholar, one who has appropriated God-like power and might and has acquired the confidence to use this power and might for 'the conversion of the world'.[5]

At bottom, however, Emerson, like his disciple Nietzsche, was not a philosopher of democracy but of private self-creation, of what he called 'the infinitude of the private man'. Godlike power was never far from Emerson's mind. His America was not so much a community of fellow citizens as a clearing in which Godlike heroes could act out self-written dramas.

---

2   Peirce had little use for Emerson, but in his later period, when he was developing a 'metaphysics of evolutionary love', he confessed that though he was 'not conscious of having contracted any of that virus' of 'Concord transcendentalism', it was probable that 'some benignant form of the disease was implanted in my soul unawares' (C. S. Peirce, *Collected Papers*, Hartshorne and Weiss, eds. (Cambridge, Mass.: Harvard University Press, 1936), vol.VI, section 102).

3   John Dewey, 'Maeterlinck's Philosophy of Life' in *The Middle Works of John Dewey* (Carbondale, Ill.: Southern Illinois University Press, 1978), vol.VI.

4   See West's *The American Evasion of Philosophy: A Genealogy of Pragmatism* (Madison: University of Wisconsin Press, 1989), ch. 1. West explains his title, which refers to Emerson's having set aside the Cartesian problematic which had dominated European philosophy, at p. 36.

5   West, pp. 12–13.

In contrast, Whitman's tone, like James's and Dewey's, is more secular and more communal than Emerson's. So perhaps the best way to grasp the attitude towards America which James and Dewey took for granted, and shared with the audiences who heard their lectures, is to reread Whitman's *Democratic Vistas*, written in 1867. That book opens by saying:

> As the greatest lessons of Nature through the universe are perhaps the lessons of variety and freedom, the same present the greatest lessons also in New World politics and progress...
>
> America, filling the present with greatest deeds and problems, cheerfully accepting the past, including feudalism (as indeed, the present is but the legitimate birth of the past, including feudalism) counts, as I reckon, for her justification and success, (for who, as yet, dare claim success?) almost entirely on the future ... For our New World I consider far less important for what it has done, or what it is, than for results to come.[6]

In this essay I shall focus on Whitman's phrase 'counts ... for her justification and success ... almost entirely upon the future'. As I see it, the link between Whitmanesque Americanism and pragmatist philosophy – both classical and 'neo-' – is a willingness to refer all questions of ultimate justification to the future, to the substance of things hoped for. If there is anything distinctive about pragmatism it is that it substitutes the notion of a better human future for the notions of 'reality', 'reason' and 'nature'. One may say of pragmatism what Novalis said of Romanticism, that it is 'the apotheosis of the future'.

As I read Dewey, what he somewhat awkwardly called 'a new metaphysic of man's relation to nature', was a generalization of the moral of Darwinian biology. The only justification of a mutation, biological or cultural, is its contribution to the existence of a more complex and interesting species somewhere in the future. Justification is always justification from the point of view of the survivors, the victors; there is no point of view more exalted than theirs to assume. This is the truth in the ideas that might makes right and that justice is the interest of the stronger. But these ideas are misleading when they are construed metaphysically, as an assertion that the present status quo, or the victorious side in some current war, stand in some privileged relation to the way things really are. So 'metaphysic' was an unfortunate word to use in describing this generalized Darwinism which is democracy. For that word is associated with an attempt to replace appearance by reality.

Pragmatists – both classical and 'neo-' – do not believe that there is a way things really are. So they want to replace the appearance–reality distinction by that between descriptions of the world and of ourselves which are less useful and those which are more useful. When the question 'useful for what?' is pressed, they have nothing to say except 'useful to create a better future'. When they are asked, 'Better by what criterion?', they have no detailed answer, any more than the first mammals could specify in what respects they were better than the dying dinosaurs. Pragmatists can only say something as vague as: Better in the sense of containing more of what we consider good and less of what we consider bad. When asked, 'And what exactly do you consider good?', pragmatists can only say, with Whitman, 'variety and freedom', or, with Dewey, 'growth'. 'Growth itself,' Dewey said, 'is the only moral end.[7]

[...]

6   Walt Whitman, *Complete Poetry and Selected Prose* (New York: The Library of America, 1982), p. 929.

7   John Dewey, *Reconstruction in Philosophy, The Middle Works of John Dewey*, vol. XII, p. 181.

Dewey argues that so far the thrust of philosophy has been conservative; it has typically been on the side of the leisure class, favouring stability over change. Philosophy has been an attempt to lend the past the prestige of the eternal. 'The leading theme of the classic philosophy of Europe,' he says, has been to make metaphysics 'a substitute for custom as the source and guarantor of higher moral and social values'.[8] Dewey wanted to shift attention from the eternal to the future, and to do so by making philosophy an instrument of change rather than of conservation, thereby making it American rather than European. He hoped to do so by denying – as Heidegger was to deny later on – that philosophy is a form of knowledge. This means denying that there is or could be an extra-cultural foundation for custom, and acknowledging openly that, 'In philosophy, "reality" is a term of value or choice.'[9] He wanted to get rid of what he called 'the notion, which has ruled philosophy ever since the time of the Greeks, that the office of knowledge is to uncover the antecedently real, rather than, as is the case with our practical judgments, to gain the kind of understanding which is necessary to deal with problems as they arise'.[10] In saying that democracy is a 'metaphysic of the relation of man and his experience in nature', he is saying that the institutions of a truly nonfeudal society would produce, and be produced by, a nondualistic way of thinking about reality and knowledge. This way of thinking would, for the first time, put the intellectuals at the service of the productive class rather than the leisure class. Pragmatism would, for the first time, treat theory as an aid to practice, rather than seeing practice as a degradation of theory.

[...]

So far I have been trying to give an overview of Dewey's place in the intellectual scheme of things by saying something about his relation to Emerson, Whitman, Kant, Hegel and Marx. Now I want to become a bit more technical, and to offer an interpretation of the most famous pragmatist doctrine – the pragmatist theory of truth. I want to show how this doctrine fits into a more general programme: that of replacing Greek and Kantian dualisms between permanent structure and transitory content with the distinction between the past and the future. I shall try to show how the things which James and Dewey said about truth were a way of replacing the task of justifying past custom and tradition by reference to unchanging structure with the task of replacing an unsatisfactory present with a more satisfactory future, thus replacing certainty with hope. This replacement would, they thought, amount to Americanizing philosophy. For they agreed with Whitman that America is the country which counts for its 'reason and justification' upon the future, and *only* upon the future.

Truth is what is supposed to distinguish knowledge from well-grounded opinion – from justified belief.[11] But if the true is, as James said, 'the name of whatever proves itself to be good in the way of belief, and good, too, for definite, assignable, reasons',[12] then it is not clear in what respects a true belief is supposed to differ from one which is merely

8 Dewey, *Reconstruction in Philosophy*, p. 89.
9 Dewey, 'Philosophy and Democracy', *The Middle Works of John Dewey*, vol. XI, p. 45.
10 Dewey, *The Quest for Certainty*, p. 14.
11 For present purposes I can neglect the so-called 'fourth condition of knowledge' proposed by Edmund Gettier – that a belief be brought about in appropriate ways, in addition to being held, justified and true.
12 William James, *Pragmatism* (Cambridge, Mass.: Harvard University Press, 1978), p. 43.

justified. So pragmatists are often said to confuse truth, which is absolute and eternal, with justification, which is transitory because relative to an audience.

Pragmatists have responded to this criticism in two principal ways. Some, like Peirce, James and Putnam, have said that we can retain an absolute sense of 'true' by identifying it with 'justification in the ideal situation' – the situation which Peirce called 'the end of inquiry'. Others, like Dewey (and, I have argued, Davidson),have suggested that there is little to be said about truth, and that philosophers should explicitly and self-consciously *confine* themselves to justification, to what Dewey called 'warranted assertibility'.

I prefer the latter strategy. Despite the efforts of Putnam and Habermas to clarify the notion of 'ideal epistemic situation', that notion seems to me no more useful than that of 'correspondence to reality', or any of the other notions which philosophers have used to provide an interesting gloss on the word 'true'. Furthermore, I think that any 'absoluteness' which is supposedly ensured by appeal to such notions is equally well ensured if, with Davidson, we insist that human belief cannot swing free of the nonhuman environment and that, as Davidson insists, most of our beliefs (most of *anybody's* beliefs) must be true.[13] For this insistence gives us everything we wanted to get from 'realism' without invoking the slogan that 'the real and the true are "independent of our beliefs"' – a slogan which, Davidson rightly says, it is futile either to accept or to reject.[14]

Davidson's claim that a truth theory for a natural language is nothing more or less than an empirical explanation of the causal relations which hold between features of the environment and the holding true of sentences, seems to me all the guarantee we need that we are, always and everywhere, 'in touch with the world'. If we have such a guarantee, then we have all the insurance we need against 'relativism' and 'arbitrariness'. For Davidson tells us that we can never be more arbitrary than the world lets us be. So even if there is no Way the World Is, even if there is no such thing as 'the intrinsic nature of

13   See Davidson's 'A Coherence Theory of Truth and Knowledge' (in *Truth and Interpretation: Perspectives on the Philosophy of Donald Davidson* (Oxford: Blackwell, 1986)) for his argument for this claim. Despite Malpas's strictures (cited in the previous note), and Davidson's refusal to call himself a pragmatist on the ground that it is definatory of pragmatism to define truth as warranted assertibility, I still think it fruitful to see Davidson as carrying through on the classical pragmatists' project. One justification for describing him in these terms can be gleaned from Robert Brandom's 'Pragmatism, Phenomenalism, and Truth Talk' (*Midwest Studies in Philosophy*, vol. 12, pp. 75–94). There Brandom suggests that we think of the basic insight of the classical pragmatists as what he calls 'phenomenalism' about truth – defined as the denial 'that there is more to the phenomenon of truth than the proprieties of such takings [i.e., of holding true, treating as true, etc.]' (p. 77). If one substitutes 'than the sort of explanation of the proprieties of such takings provided by an empirical T-theory for a language', then Davidson too counts as 'phenomenalist' in the relevant sense.

14   See Davidson, 'Structure and Content', p. 305. I regret that Malpas resuscitates the term 'realism' to describe Davidson's (and Heidegger's) view at the conclusion of his book (pp. 276–7). As Malpas says, this is not the sense of the term 'used by Nagel, Putnam or Dummett'. I think it is needlessly confusing to invent a new sense to fit Davidson and Heidegger. I would prefer something like 'anti-scepticism' or 'anti-Cartesianism' to designate the inescapability of *in-der-Welt-sein* affirmed by both philosophers. For what is involved is not a positive thesis, but simply the abjuration of a particular picture which has held us captive – the picture I have called (in the introduction to my *Objectivity, Relativism and Truth*) 'representationalism', and which Michael Williams (whose work I discuss below) calls 'epistemological realism'.

reality', there are still causal pressures. These pressures will be described in different ways at different times and for different purposes, but they are pressures none the less.

The claim that 'pragmatism is unable to account for the absoluteness of truth' confuses two demands: the demand that we explain the relation between the world and our claims to have true beliefs and the specifically epistemological demand either for present certainty or for a path guaranteed to lead to certainty, if only in the infinitely distant future. The first demand is traditionally met by saying that our beliefs are made true by the world, and that they correspond to the way things are. Davidson denies both claims. He and Dewey agree that we should give up the idea that knowledge is an attempt to *represent* reality. Rather, we should view inquiry as a way of using reality. So the relation between our truth claims and the rest of the world is causal rather than representational. It causes us to hold beliefs, and we continue to hold the beliefs which prove to be reliable guides to getting what we want. Goodman is right to say that there is no one Way the World Is, and so no one way it is to be accurately represented. But there are lots of ways to act so as to realize human hopes of happiness. The attainment of such happiness is not something distinct from the attainment of justified belief; rather, the latter is a special case of the former.

Pragmatists realize that this way of thinking about knowledge and truth makes certainty unlikely. But they think that the quest for certainty – even as a long-term goal – is an attempt to escape from the world. So they interpret the usual hostile reactions to their treatment of truth as an expression of resentment, resentment at being deprived of something which earlier philosophers had mistakenly promised. Dewey urges that the quest for certainty be replaced with the demand for imagination – that philosophy should stop trying to provide reassurance and instead encourage what Emerson called 'self-reliance'. To encourage self-reliance, in this sense, is to encourage the willingness to turn one's back both on the past and on the attempt of 'the classical philosophy of Europe' to ground the past in the eternal. It is to attempt Emersonian self-creation on a communal scale. To say that one should replace knowledge by hope is to say much the same thing: that one should stop worrying about whether what one believes is well grounded and start worrying about whether one has been imaginative enough to think up interesting alternatives to one's present beliefs. As West says, 'For Emerson, the goal of activity is not simply domination, but also provocation; the telos of movement and flux is not solely mastery, but also stimulation.[15]

[...]

As I see the history of pragmatism, there are two great differences between the classical pragmatists and the neopragmatists. The first I have already mentioned: it is the difference between talking about 'experience', as James and Dewey did, and talking about 'language', as Quine and Davidson do. The second is the difference between assuming that there is something called 'the scientific method', whose employment increases the likelihood of one's beliefs being true, and tacitly abandoning this assumption. Peirce, in his essay on 'The Fixation of Belief', one of the founding documents of pragmatism, tried to describe what he called 'the method of science'.[16]

15 West, p. 26.
16 His description of this method in that essay of 1877 is foundationalist in spirit, and not easy to reconcile with the antifoundationalism of the 1868 essays 'Questions Concerning Certain Faculties Claimed for Man' and 'Some Consequences of Four Incapacities'.

Dewey and his students, notably Hook, insisted on the importance of this method. That insistence was the principal area of overlap between Deweyan pragmatism and the logical empiricism which briefly replaced it in American philosophy departments. But as American philosophy moved into its postpositivistic stage, less and less was heard about the scientific method, and about the distinction between science and nonscience.

[...]

As I see the present situation of pragmatism, postpositivistic analytic philosophy has made it clearer to us than it was to Peirce and Dewey that we should no longer try to follow up on the *Theaetetus* by trying to find something interesting to say about the connection between justification and truth. We should agree with William James on just the point on which he differed from Peirce and Dewey, namely that science and religion are *both* respectable paths for acquiring respectable beliefs, albeit beliefs which are good for quite different purposes. What we have learned, principally from Kuhn and from Davidson, is that there is nothing like Descartes' 'natural order of reasons' to be followed when we justify beliefs. There is no activity called 'knowing' which has a nature to be discovered, and at which natural scientists are particularly skilled. There is simply the process of justifying beliefs to audiences. None of these audiences is closer to nature, or a better representative of some ahistorical ideal of rationality, than any other. The idea of a subject of study called 'rationality' goes at the same time, and for the same reasons, as the idea of a subject of study called 'knowledge'.

A Dewey who had let himself be persuaded by James to give up on scientism and methodolatry could agree with Davidson that there is nothing to be said about truth of the sort epistemologists want said. Once one has said, with Peirce, that beliefs are rules of action rather than attempts to represent reality, and, with Davidson, that 'belief is in its nature veridical',[17] one can take the moral of naturalism to be that knowledge is not a natural kind needing study and description, rather than that we must provide a naturalized epistemology. Such a reformed Dewey could also have welcomed Davidson's point that truth is not an epistemic concept.[18] This point entails, among other things, that no interesting connection will ever be found between the concept of truth and the concept of justification.[19] The only connection between these two notions is that, for the same reason that most beliefs are true, most beliefs are justified.

---

17   In 'A Coherence Theory of Truth and Knowledge', p. 314.
18   See Davidson, 'Structure and Content', p. 298.
19   Had Dewey taken not only this point, but also Davidson's point that 'relativism about truth is perhaps always a symptom of infection by the epistemological virus', I think that he would have said fewer of the relativistic-sounding things for which he was constantly attacked by Lovejoy, Russell and others. Had he taken Williams' point, he would have realized that he could say most of what he wanted to say about what was wrong with traditional epistemological discussions of truth by talking about the context-dependent character of justification. Unlike Davidson, who takes a necessary condition of being a pragmatist to be precisely the infection by the virus in question, I take the only necessary condition to be the one Brandom offers: believing that there is nothing to said about truth which cannot be said on the basis of facts about, and explanations of, the proprieties of holding true. On such proprieties, see the closing pages of 'Structure and Content', in which Davidson expatiates on the role of norms and affects in belief-ascription, and thus in constructing T-theories.

For, a believer who is (unlike a child or a psychotic) a fully fledged member of her community will always be able to produce justification for most of her beliefs – justification which meets the demands of that community. There is, however, no reason to think that the beliefs she is best able to justify are those which are most likely to be true, nor that those she is least able to justify are those which are most likely to be false. The fact that most beliefs are justified is, like the fact that most beliefs are true, merely one more consequence of the holistic character of belief-ascription. That, in turn, is a consequence of the fact that beliefs which are expressed as meaningful sentences neces- sarily have lots of predictable inferential connections with lots of other meaningful sentences. We cannot, no matter how hard we try, continue to hold a belief which we have tried, and conspicuously failed, to weave together with our other beliefs into a justificatory web. No matter how much I want to believe an unjustifiable belief, I cannot will myself into doing so. The best I can do is distract my own attention from the ques- tion of why I hold certain beliefs. For most matters of common concern, however, my community will insist that I attend to this question. So such distraction is only feasible for private obsessions, such as my conviction that some day my lucky number will win the jackpot.

It may seem strange to say that there is no connection between justification and truth. This is because we are inclined to say that truth is the aim of inquiry. But I think we pragmatists must grasp the nettle and say that this claim is either empty or false. Inquiry and justification have lots of mutual aims, but they do not have an overarching aim called truth. Inquiry and justification are activities we language-users cannot help engaging in; we do not need a goal called 'truth' to help us do so, any more than our digestive organs need a goal called health to set them to work. Language-users can no more help justify- ing their beliefs and desires to one another than stomachs can help grinding up food- stuffs. The agenda for our digestive organs is set by the particular foodstuffs being processed, and the agenda for our justifying activity is provided by the diverse beliefs and desires we encounter in our fellow language-users. There would only be a 'higher' aim of inquiry called 'truth' if there were such a thing as *ultimate* justification – justification before God, or before the tribunal of reason, as opposed to any merely finite human audience.

But, given a Darwinian picture of the world, there can be no such tribunal. For such a tribunal would have to envisage all the alternatives to a given belief, and know every- thing that was relevant to criticism of every such alternative. Such a tribunal would have to have what Putnam calls a 'God's eye view' – a view which took in not only every feature of the world as described in a given set of terms, but that feature under every other possible description as well. For if it did not, there would remain the possibility that it was as fallible as the tribunal which sat in judgment on Galileo, a tribunal which we condemn for having required justification of new beliefs in old terms. If Darwin is right, we can no more make sense of the idea of such a tribunal than we can make sense of the idea that biological evolution has an aim. Biological evolution produces ever new species, and cultural evolution produces ever new audiences, but there is no such thing as the species which evolution has in view, nor any such thing as the 'aim of inquiry'.

To sum up, my reply to the claim that pragmatists confuse truth and justification is to turn this charge against those who make it. They are the ones who are confused, because they think of truth as something towards which we are moving, something we get closer to the more justification we have. By contrast, pragmatists think that there are a lot of detailed things to be said about justification to any given audience, but nothing to be said about justification in general. That is why there is nothing general to be said about the nature or limits of human knowledge, nor anything to be said about a connection between justification and truth. There is nothing to be said on the latter subject not because truth is atemporal and justification temporal, but because *the* only *point in contrasting the true with the merely justified is to contrast a possible future with the actual present.*

25

Ethics Without Principles

I have been suggesting that we think of pragmatism as an attempt to alter our self-image so as to make it consistent with the Darwinian claim that we differ from other animals simply in the complexity of our behaviour. To adopt this image of ourselves as exceptionally clever animals is to set aside the Greek way of distinguishing ourselves from the brutes. Plato and Aristotle suggested that the other animals lived in a world of sensory appearance, that their lives consisted of adjusting to the changes of these appearances, and that they were thus incapable of *knowing*, for knowledge consists in penetrating behind appearance to reality. Pragmatists, in contrast, treat inquiry – in both physics and ethics – as the search for adjustment, and in particular for that sort of adjustment to our fellow humans which we call 'the search for acceptable justification and eventual agreement'. I have argued that we should substitute this latter search for the traditional descriptions of the quest for truth.

In the previous chapter ["A World without Substances of Essences" (PSH)] I portrayed pragmatism as a generalized form of antiessentialism – as an attempt to break down the distinction between the intrinsic and the extrinsic features of things. By thinking of everything as relational through and through, pragmatists attempt to get rid of the contrast between reality and appearance. Pragmatists hope to make it impossible for the sceptic to raise the question, 'Is our knowledge of things adequate to the way things really are?' They substitute for this traditional question the *practical* question, 'Are our ways of describing things, of relating them to other things so as to make them fulfil our needs more adequately, as good as possible? Or can we do better? Can our future be made better than our present?'

In this chapter I turn to the distinction between morality and prudence. This distinction is traditionally drawn by opposing unconditional and categorical obligations to conditional and hypothetical ones. Pragmatists have doubts about the suggestion that anything is unconditional, because they doubt that anything is, or could be, nonrelational. So they need to reinterpret the distinctions between morality and prudence, morality and expediency, and morality and self-interest, in ways which dispense with the notion of unconditionality.

Richard M. Rorty, "Ethics without Principles," excerpts from pp. 72–90 in *Philosophy and Social Hope* (New York: Penguin, 1999), © 1999 by Richard Rorty. Reproduced by permission of Penguin Books Ltd.

Dewey suggested that we reconstruct the distinction between prudence and morality in terms of the distinction between routine and non-routine social relationships. He saw 'prudence' as a member of the same family of concepts as 'habit' and 'custom'. All three words describe familiar and relatively uncontroversial ways in which individuals and groups adjust to the stresses and strains of their non-human and human environments. It is obviously prudent both to keep an eye out for poisonous snakes in the grass and to trust strangers less than members of one's own family. 'Prudence', 'expediency' and 'efficiency' are all terms which describe such routine and uncontroversial adjustments to circumstance.

Morality and law, on the other hand, begin when controversy arises. We invent both when we can no longer just do what comes naturally, when routine is no longer good enough, or when habit and custom no longer suffice. These will no longer suffice when the individual's needs begin to clash with those of her family, or her family's with those of the neighbours, or when economic strain begins to split her community into warring classes, or when that community must come to terms with an alien community. On Dewey's account, the prudence–morality distinction is, like that between custom and law, a distinction of degree – the degree of need for conscious deliberation and explicit formulation of precepts – rather than a distinction of kind. For pragmatists like Dewey, there is no distinction of kind between what is useful and what is right. For, as Dewey said, 'Right is only an abstract name for the multitude of concrete demands in action which others impress upon us, and of which we are obliged, if we would live, to take some account.'[1] The utilitarians were right when they coalesced the moral and the useful, even though they were wrong in thinking that utility is simply a matter of getting pleasure and avoiding pain. Dewey agrees with Aristotle, against Bentham, that human happiness cannot be reduced to the accumulation of pleasures.

From Kant's point of view, however, Aristotle, Bentham and Dewey are equally blind to the true nature of morality. To identify moral obligation with the need to adjust one's behaviour to the needs of other human beings is, for Kantians, either vicious or simpleminded. Dewey seems to Kantians to have confused duty with self-interest, the intrinsic authority of the moral law with the banausic need to bargain with opponents whom one cannot overcome.

Dewey was well aware of this Kantian criticism. Here is one of the passages in which he attempted to answer it:

> Morals, it is said, imply the subordination of fact to ideal consideration, while the view presented [Dewey's own view] makes morals secondary to bare fact, which is equal to depriving them of dignity and jurisdiction … The criticism rests upon a false separation. It argues in effect that either ideal standards antecede customs and confer their moral quality upon them, or that in being subsequent to custom[s] and evolved from them, they are mere accidental by-products. But how does it stand with language? … Language grew out of unintelligent babblings, instinctive motions called gestures, and the pressure of circumstance. But nevertheless language once called into existence is language and operates as language.[2]

The point of Dewey's analogy between language and morality is that there was no decisive moment at which language stopped being a series of reactions to the stimuli

---

1   John Dewey, *Human Nature and Conduct, The Middle Works of John Dewey* (Carbondale, Ill.: Southern Illinois University Press, 1983), vol. XIV, p. 224.
2   Dewey, pp. 56–7.

provided by the behaviour of other humans and started to be an instrument for expressing beliefs. Similarly, there was no point at which practical reasoning stopped being prudential and became specifically moral, no point at which it stopped being merely useful and started being authoritative.

[…]

So much for the standard Deweyan criticism of the Kantian way of viewing the distinction between morality and prudence. I want now to turn to another distinction, that between reason and sentiment, thinking and feeling. Doing so will let me relate Dewey's views to those of Annette Baier. Baier, one of the leading feminist philosophers of the present day, takes David Hume as her model. She praises Hume as the 'woman's moral philosopher' because of his willingness to take sentiment, and indeed sentimentality, as central to the moral consciousness. She also praises him for 'de-intellectualizing and de-sanctifying the moral endeavor … presenting it as the human equivalent of various social controls in animal or insect populations'.[3] Though Baier rarely mentions Dewey, and Dewey rarely discusses Hume's moral philosophy at any length, these three militantly anti-Kantian philosophers are on the same side of most arguments. All three share the same distrust of the notion of 'moral obligation'. Dewey, Baier and Hume can all agree with Nietzsche that the pre-Socratic Greeks were free from the 'timidity', the fear of having to make hard choices, which led Plato to search for immutable moral truth. All three see the temporal circumstances of human life as difficult enough without sado-masochistically adding immutable, unconditional obligations.

Baier has proposed that we substitute the notion of 'appropriate trust' for that of 'obligation' as our central moral concept. She has said that

> there is no room for moral theory as something which is more philosophical and less committed than moral deliberation, and which is not simply an account of our customs and styles of justification, criticism, protest, revolt, conversion, and resolution.[4]

In words that echo some of Dewey's, Baier says that 'the villain is the rationalist, law-fixated tradition in moral philosophy',[5] a tradition which assumes that 'behind every moral intuition lies a universal rule'.[6] That tradition assumes that Hume's attempt to think of moral progress as a progress of sentiments fails to account for moral obligation. But, on Baier's view, as on Dewey's, there is nothing to account for moral obligation does not have a nature, or a source, different from tradition, habit and custom. Morality is simply a new and controversial custom. Our sense that prudence is unheroic and morality heroic is merely the recognition that testing out the relatively untried is more dangerous, more risky, than doing what comes naturally.

Baier and Dewey agree that the central flaw in much traditional moral philosophy has been the myth of the self as nonrelational, as capable of existing independently of any concern for others, as a cold psychopath needing to be constrained to take account of other people's needs. This is the picture of the self which philosophers since Plato have

3 Annette Baier, *Postures of the Mind* (Minneapolis: University of Minnesota Press, 1985), p. 147.
4 Baier, p. 232.
5 Baier, p. 236.
6 Baier, p. 208.

expressed in terms of the division between 'reason' and 'the passions' – a division which
Hume unfortunately perpetuated in his notorious inversion of Plato, his claim that
'reason is, and should be, the slave of the passions'. Ever since Plato, the West has construed the reason–passion distinction as paralleling the distinction between the universal
and the individual, as well as that between unselfish and selfish actions. The religious,
Platonic and Kantian traditions have thus saddled us with a distinction between the true
self and the false self, the self which hears the call of conscience and the self which is
merely 'self-interested'. The latter self is merely prudential, and not yet moral.

Baier and Dewey both argue that this notion of the self as cold, self-interested, calculating, psychopath should be set aside. If we really were such selves, the question 'Why
should I be moral?' would be forever unanswerable. Only when we masochistically picture ourselves as such selves do we feel the need to punish ourselves by quailing before
divine commands, or before Kant's tribunal of pure practical reason. But if we follow the
pragmatists' advice to see everything as constituted by its relations to everything else, it
is easy to detect the fallacy which Dewey described as 'transforming the (truistic) fact of
acting *as* a self into the fiction of acting always *for* self'.[7] We shall commit this fallacy, and
continue to think of the self as a psychopath in need of restraint, as long as we accept
what Dewey called the 'belief in the fixity and simplicity of the self'. Dewey associated
this belief with 'the theologians' ... dogma of the unity and ready-made completeness
of the soul'.[8] But he might equally well have associated it with the argument of Plato's
Phaedo, or with Kant's doctrine that the moral self is a nonempirical self.

If we put such notions of unity and readymade completeness to one side, we can say, with
Dewey, that 'selfhood (except insofar as it has encased itself in a shell of routine) is in process
of making, and that any self is capable of including within itself a number of inconsistent
selves, of unharmonized dispositions'.[9] This notion of multiple inconsistent selves is, as Donald
Davidson has shown, a good way of naturalizing and demystifying the Freudian notion of the
unconscious.[10] But the most important link between Freud and Dewey is the one which
Baier emphasizes: the role of the family, and in particular of maternal love, in creating non-
psychopaths, that is, human selves who find concern for others entirely natural. Baier says, in
words which Dewey might have written, that 'the secular equivalent of faith in God ... is
faith in the human community and its evolving procedures – in the prospects for many-
handed cognitive ambitions and moral hopes'.[11] But she sees that faith as rooted in the faith
most of us have in our parents and siblings. The trust which holds a family together is Baier's
model for the secular faith which may hold together modern, posttraditional societies.

Freud helped us to see that we get psychopaths – people whose self-conception
involves no relations to others – only when parental love, and the trust which such love
creates in the child, are absent. To see the point Baier wants us to appreciate, consider the
question: Do I have a moral obligation to my mother? My wife? My children? 'Morality'

7   Dewey, p. 95.
8   Dewey, p. 96.
9   Dewey, p. 96.
10   See Donald Davidson, 'Paradoxes of Irrationality' in *Philosophical Essays on Freud*, Richard
Wollheim and James Hopkins, eds. (Cambridge: Cambridge University Press, 1982). Davidson's
view of Freud is expanded and developed by Marcia Cavell in her *The Psychoanalytic Mind: From
Freud to Philosophy* (Cambridge, Mass.: Harvard University Press, 1993).
11   Baier, p. 293.

and 'obligation' here seem inapposite. For doing what one is obliged to do contrasts with doing what comes naturally, and for most people responding to the needs of family members is the most natural thing in the world. Such responses come naturally because most of us define ourselves, at least in part, by our relations to members of our family. Our needs and theirs largely overlap; we are not happy if they are not. We would not wish to be well fed while our children go hungry; that would be unnatural. Would it also be immoral? It is a bit strange to say so. One would only employ this term if one encountered a parent who was also a pathological egoist, a mother or father whose sense of self had nothing to do with her or his children – the sort of person envisaged by decision theory, someone whose identity is constituted by 'preference rankings' rather than by fellow feeling.

By contrast, I may feel a specifically *moral* obligation to deprive both my children and myself of a portion of the available food because there are starving people outside the door. The word 'moral' is appropriate here because the demand is less *natural* than the demand to feed my children. It is less closely connected with my sense of who I am. But the desire to feed the hungry stranger may of course *become* as tightly woven into my self-conception as the desire to feed my family. Moral development in the individual, and moral progress in the human species as a whole, is a matter of re-marking human selves so as to enlarge the variety of the relationships which constitute those selves. The ideal limit of this process of enlargement is the self envisaged by Christian and Buddhist accounts of sainthood – an ideal self to whom the hunger and suffering of *any* human being (and even, perhaps, that of any other animal) is intensely painful. The ideal of human brotherhood is seen by the pragmatist as the culmination of a process of adjustment which is also a process of recreating human beings.

[...]

From this point of view, moral progress is not a matter of an increase of rationality – a gradual diminution of the influence of prejudice and superstition, permitting us to see our moral duty more clearly. Nor is it what Dewey called an increase of intelligence, that is, increasing one's skill at inventing courses of action which simultaneously satisfy many conflicting demands. People can be very intelligent, in this sense, without having wide sympathies. It is neither irrational nor unintelligent to draw the limits of one's moral community at a national, or racial, or gender border. But it is undesirable – morally undesirable. So it is best to think of moral progress as a matter of increasing *sensitivity*, increasing responsiveness to the needs of a larger and larger variety of people and things. Just as the pragmatists see scientific progress not as the gradual attenuation of a veil of appearance which hides the intrinsic nature of reality from us, but as the increasing ability to respond to the concerns of ever larger groups of people – in particular, the people who carry out ever more acute observations and perform ever more refined experiments – so they see moral progress as a matter of being able to respond to the needs of ever more inclusive groups of people.

[...]

So far in this chapter I have been suggesting in rather general terms why the pragmatist wants to get rid of the notion of 'unconditional moral obligation'. In the hope of greater concreteness and vividness, I turn now to another example of unconditionality: the notion of unconditional human rights. Such rights are said to form the fixed boundaries of political and moral deliberation. In American jurisprudence, Ronald Dworkin tells us, rights 'trump' every consideration of social expediency and efficiency. In much political discussion, it is taken for granted that the rights which the US courts have interpreted the US Constitution to bestow, and those universal human rights enumerated in the Helsinki Declaration, are beyond discussion. They are the unmoved movers of much of contemporary politics.

From a pragmatist's point of view, the notion of 'inalienable human rights' is no better and no worse a slogan than that of 'obedience to the will of God'. Either slogan, when invoked as an unmoved mover, is simply a way of saying that our spade is turned – that we have exhausted our argumentative resources. Talk of the will of God or of the rights of man, like talk of 'the honour of the family' or of 'the fatherland in danger' are not suitable targets for philosophical analysis and criticism. It is fruitless to look behind them. None of these notions should be analyzed, for they are all ways of saying, 'Here I stand: I can do no other.' These are not reasons for action so much as announcements that one has thought the issue through and come to a decision.

Pragmatists think that the quarrel between rationalist metaphysicians and Nietzsche is without interest.[12] They grant to Nietzsche that reference to human rights is merely a convenient way of summarizing certain aspects of *our* real or proposed practices. Analogously, to say that the intrinsic nature of reality consists of atoms and the void is, for a pragmatist, a way of saying that *our* most successful scientific explanations interpret macrostructural change as a result of microstructural change. To say that God wills us to welcome the stranger within our gates is to say that hospitality is one of the virtues upon which *our* community most prides itself. To say that respect for human rights demanded our intervention to save the Jews from the Nazis, or the Bosnian Muslims from the Serbs, is to say that a failure to intervene would make *us* uncomfortable with ourselves, in the way in which knowledge that our neighbours are hungry while we have plenty on the table ourselves makes us unable to continue eating. To speak of human rights is to explain our actions by identifying ourselves with a community of like-minded persons – those who find it natural to act in a certain way.

Claims of the sort I have just made – claims which have the form 'To say such-and-such is to say so-and-so' – are often interpreted in terms of the reality–appearance distinction. So, metaphysically inclined thinkers, obsessed by the distinction between knowledge and opinion or between reason and passion, will interpret my claims as 'irrationalist' and 'emotivist'. But pragmatists do not intend these as claims about what is *really* going on – claims that what appeared to be a fact is actually a value, or what appeared to be a cognition is actually an emotion. Rather, these claims are practical recommendations on what to talk about, suggestions about the terms in which controversy on moral questions is best conducted. On the subject of atoms, the pragmatist thinks that we should not debate the issue of whether unobservable microstructure is a reality or just a convenient fiction. On the subject of human rights, the pragmatist thinks that we should not debate whether human rights have been there all the time, even when nobody recognized them, or are just the social construction of a civilization influenced by Christian doctrines of the brotherhood of man.

12   This is a point which I emphasize in my 'Human Rights, Rationality, and Sentimentality', included in *Of Human Rights: Oxford Amnesty Lectures, 1993* (New York: Basic Books, 1993) and reprinted in my *Truth and Progress* (Cambridge: Cambridge University Press, 1998). That paper offers a more extended version of the view of human rights which I am summarizing here.

Of course they are social constructions. So are atoms, and so is everything else. For, as I suggested in chapter 3, to be a social construction is simply to be the intentional object of a certain set of sentences – sentences used in some societies and not in others. All that it takes to be an object is to be talked about in a reasonably coherent way, but not everybody needs to talk in all ways – nor, therefore, about all objects. Once we give up the idea that the point of discourse is to represent reality accurately, we will have no interest in distinguishing social constructs from other things. We shall confine ourselves to debating the utility of alternative constructs.

To debate the utility of the set of social constructs we call 'human rights' is to debate the question of whether inclusivist societies are better than exclusivist ones. That is to debate the question of whether communities which encourage tolerance of harmless deviance should be preferred to those communities whose social cohesion depends on conformity, on keeping outsiders at a distance and on eliminating people who try to corrupt the youth. The best single mark of our progress toward a fully fledged human rights culture may be the extent to which we stop interfering with our children's marriage plans because of the national origin, religion, race, or wealth of the intended partner, or because the marriage will be homosexual rather than heterosexual.

Those who wish to supply rational, philosophical foundations for a human rights culture say that what human beings have in common outweighs such adventitious factors as race or religion. But they have trouble spelling out what this commonality consists of. It is not enough to say that we all share a common susceptibility to pain, for there is nothing distinctively human about pain. If pain were all that mattered, it would be as important to protect the rabbits from the foxes as to protect the Jews from the Nazis. If one accepts a naturalistic, Darwinian account of human origins, it is not helpful to say that we all have reason in common, for on this account to be rational is simply to be able to use language. But there are many languages, and most of them are exclusionist. The language of human rights is no more or less characteristic of our species than languages which insist on racial or religious purity.[13]

Pragmatists suggest that we simply give up the philosophical search for commonality. They think that moral progress might be accelerated if we focused instead on our ability to make the particular little things that divide us seem unimportant – not by comparing them with the one big thing that unites us but by comparing them with other little things. Pragmatists think of moral progress as more like sewing together a very large, elaborate, polychrome quilt, than like getting a clearer vision of something true and deep. As I remarked earlier, they like to replace traditional metaphors of depth or height with metaphors of breadth and extent. Convinced that there is no subtle human essence which philosophy might grasp, they do not try to replace superficiality with depth, nor to rise above the particular in order to grasp the universal. Rather, they hope to minimize one difference at a time – the difference between Christians and Muslims in a particular village in Bosnia, the difference between blacks and whites in a particular town in Alabama, the difference between gays and straights in a particular Catholic congregation in Quebec. The hope is to sew such groups together with a thousand little

---

13 Here again I agree with Habermas about the linguistic character of rationality. But I try to use this doctrine to show that we do not need to think in universalist terms. Habermas's universalism forbids him to adopt the view of human rights I am offering here.

stitches – to invoke a thousand little commonalities between their members, rather than specify one great big one, their common humanity.

This picture of moral progress makes us resist Kant's suggestion that morality is a matter of reason, and makes us sympathetic to Hume's suggestion that it is a matter of sentiment. If we were limited to these two candidates, we should side with Hume. But we would prefer to reject the choice, and to set aside faculty psychology once and for all. We recommend dropping the distinction between two separately functioning sources of beliefs and desires. Instead of working within the confines of this distinction, which constantly threatens us with the picture of a division between a true and real self and a false and apparent self, we once again resort to the distinction with which I began the first essay in this section: the distinction between the present and the future.

More specifically, we see both intellectual and moral progress not as a matter of getting closer to the True or the Good or the Right, but as an increase in imaginative power. We see imagination as the cutting edge of cultural evolution, the power which – given peace and prosperity – constantly operates so as to make the human future richer than the human past. Imagination is the source both of new scientific pictures of the physical universe and of new conceptions of possible communities. It is what Newton and Christ, Freud and Marx, had in common: the ability to redescribe the familiar in unfamiliar terms.

Such redescription was practised by the early Christians when they explained that the distinction between Jew and Greek was not as important as had been thought. It is being practised by contemporary feminists, whose descriptions of sexual behaviour and marital arrangements seem as strange to many men (and, for that matter, many women) as St Paul's indifference to traditional Judaic distinctions seemed to the scribes and the pharisees. It is what the Founding Fathers of my country attempted when they asked people to think of themselves not so much as Pennsylvanian Quakers or Catholic Marylanders but as citizens of a tolerant, pluralistic, federal republic. It is being attempted by those passionate advocates of European unity who hope that their grandchildren will think of themselves as European first and French or German second. But an equally good example of such redescription is Democritus' and Lucretius' suggestion that we try thinking of the world as rebounding atoms, and Copernicus' suggestion that we try thinking of the sun as at rest.

I hope that what I have been saying has helped make clear what I meant by urging that we substitute hope for knowledge. The difference between the Greek conception of human nature and the post-Darwinian, Deweyan conception is the difference between closure and openness – between the security of the unchanging and the Whitmanesque and Whiteheadian romance of unpredictable change. This element of romantic hope, this willingness to substitute imagination for certainty, and curiosity for pride, breaks down the Greek distinction between contemplation and action. Dewey saw that distinction as the great incubus from which intellectual life in the West needed to escape. His pragmatism was, as Hilary Putnam has said, an 'insistence on the supremacy of the agent point of view'. I have interpreted this supremacy as the priority of the need to create new ways of being human, and a new heaven and a new earth for these new humans to inhabit, over the desire for stability, security and order.

26

Justice as a Larger Loyalty

All of us would expect help if, pursued by the police, we asked our family to hide us. Most of us would extend such help even when we know our child or our parent to be guilty of a sordid crime. Many of us would be willing to perjure ourselves in order to supply such a child or parent with a false alibi. But if an innocent person is wrongly convicted as a result of our perjury, most of us will be torn by a conflict between loyalty and justice.

Such a conflict will be felt, however, only to the extent to which we can identify with the innocent person whom we have harmed. If the person is a neighbor, the conflict will probably be intense. If a stranger, especially one of a different race, class, or nation, it may be considerably weaker. There has to be *some* sense in which he or she is "one of us," before we start to be tormented by the question of whether or not we did the right thing when we committed perjury. So it may be equally appropriate to describe us as torn between conflicting loyalties – loyalty to our family and to a group large enough to include the victim of our perjury – rather than between loyalty and justice.

Our loyalty to such larger groups will, however, weaken, or even vanish altogether, when things get really tough. Then people whom we once thought of as like ourselves will be excluded. Sharing food with impoverished people down the street is natural and right in normal times, but perhaps not in a famine, when doing so amounts to disloyalty to one's family. The tougher things get, the more ties of loyalty to those near at hand tighten, and the more those to everyone else slacken.

Consider another example of expanding and contracting loyalties: our attitude toward other species. Most of us today are at least half-convinced that the vegetarians have a point, and that animals do have some sort of rights. But suppose that the cows, or the kangaroos, turn out to be carriers of a newly mutated virus, which, though harmless to them, is invariably fatal to humans. I suspect that we would then shrug off accusations of "speciesism" and participate in the necessary massacre. The idea of justice between species will suddenly become irrelevant, because things have gotten very tough indeed, and our loyalty to our own species must come first. Loyalty to a larger community – that of all living creatures on our home planet – would, under such circumstances, quickly fade away.

Richard M. Rorty, "Justice as a Larger Loyalty," pp. 9–22 in Ron Bontekoe and Marietta Stpaniants (eds.), *Justice and Democracy: Cross-Cultural Perspectives*, © 1997 by University of Hawaii Press. Reprinted with permission from the University of Hawaii Press.

As a final example, consider the tough situation created by the accelerating export of jobs from the First World to the Third. There is likely to be a continuing decline in the average real income of most American families. Much of this decline can plausibly be attributed to the fact that you can hire a factory worker in Thailand for a tenth of what you would have to pay a worker in Ohio. It has become the conventional wisdom of the rich that American and European labor is overpriced on the world market. When American business people are told that they are being disloyal to the United States by leaving whole cities in our Rust Belt without work or hope, they sometimes reply that they place justice over loyalty.[1] They argue that the needs of humanity as a whole take moral precedence over those of their fellow-citizens and override national loyalties. Justice requires that they act as citizens of the world.

Consider now the plausible hypothesis that democratic institutions and freedoms are viable only when supported by an economic affluence that is achievable regionally but impossible globally. If this hypothesis is correct, democracy and freedom in the First World will not be able to survive a thoroughgoing globalization of the labor market. So the rich democracies face a choice between perpetuating their own democratic institutions and traditions and dealing justly with the Third World. Doing justice to the Third World would require exporting capital and jobs until everything is leveled out – until an honest day's work, in a ditch or at a computer, earns no higher a wage in Cincinnati or Paris than in a small town in Botswana. But then, it can plausibly be argued, there will be no money to support free public libraries, competing newspapers and networks, widely available liberal arts education, and all the other institutions that are necessary to produce enlightened public opinion, and thus to keep governments more or less democratic.

What, on this hypothesis, is the right thing for the rich democracies to do? Be loyal to themselves and each other? Keep free societies going for a third of mankind at expense of the remaining two-thirds? Or sacrifice the blessings of political liberty for the sake of egalitarian economic justice?

These questions parallel those confronted by the parents of a large family after a nuclear holocaust. Do they share the food supply they have stored in the basement with their neighbors, even though the stores will then only last a day or two? Or do they fend those neighbors off with guns? Both moral dilemmas bring up the same question: Should we contract the circle for the sake of loyalty, or expand it for the sake of justice?

I have no idea of the right answer to these questions, neither about the right thing for these parents to do, nor about the right thing for the First World to do. I have posed them simply to bring a more abstract, and merely philosophical, question into focus. That question is: Should we describe such moral dilemmas as conflicts between loyalty and justice, or rather, as I have suggested, between loyalties to smaller groups and loyalties to larger groups?

This amounts to asking: Would it be a good idea to treat "justice" as the name for loyalty to a certain very large group, the name for our largest current loyalty, rather than

---

1   Donald Fites, the CEO of the Caterpillar tractor company, explained his company's policy of relocation abroad by saying that "as a human being, I think what is going on is positive. I don't think it is realistic for 250 million Americans to control so much of the world's GNP." Quoted in Edward Luttwak, *The Endangered American Dream* (New York: Simon & Schuster, 1993), p. 184.

the name of something distinct from loyalty? Could we replace the notion of "justice" with that of loyalty to that group – for example, one's fellow-citizens, or the human species, or all living things? Would anything be lost by this replacement?

Moral philosophers who remain loyal to Kant are likely to think that a *lot* would be lost. Kantians typically insist that justice springs from reason, and loyalty from sentiment. Only reason, they say, can impose universal and unconditional moral obligations, and our obligation to be just is of this sort. It is on another level from the sort of affectional relations that create loyalty. Jürgen Habermas is the most prominent contemporary philosopher to insist on this Kantian way of looking at things: the thinker least willing to blur either the line between reason and sentiment, or the line between universal validity and historical consensus. But contemporary philosophers who depart from Kant, either in the direction of Hume (like Annette Baier) or in the direction of Hegel (like Charles Taylor) or in that of Aristotle (like Alasdair MacIntyre), are not so sure.

Michael Walzer is at the other extreme from Habermas. He is wary of terms like "reason" and "universal moral obligation." The heart of his new book, *Thick and Thin*, is the claim that we should reject the intuition that Kant took as central: the intuition that "men and women everywhere begin with some common idea or principle or set of ideas and principles, which they then work up in many different ways." Walzer thinks that this picture of morality "starting thin" and "thickening with age" should be inverted. He says that, "Morality is thick from the beginning, culturally integrated, fully resonant, and it reveals itself thinly only on special occasions, when moral language is turned to special purposes."[2] Walzer's inversion suggests, though it does not entail, the neo-Humean picture of morality sketched by Annette Baier in her book *Moral Prejudices*. On Baier's account, morality starts out not as an obligation but as a relation of reciprocal trust among a closely knit group, such as a family or clan. To behave morally is to do what comes naturally in your dealings with your parents and children or your fellow clan-members. It amounts to respecting the trust they place in you. Obligation, as opposed to trust, enters the picture only when your loyalty to a smaller group conflicts with your loyalty to a larger group.[3]

When, for example, the families confederate into tribes, or the tribes into nations, you may feel obliged to do what does not come naturally: to leave your parents in the lurch by going off to fight in the wars, or to rule against your own village in your capacity as a federal administrator or judge. What Kant would describe as the resulting conflict between moral obligation and sentiment, or between reason and sentiment, is, on a non-Kantian account of the matter, a conflict between one set of loyalties and another set of loyalties. The idea of a *universal* moral obligation to respect human dignity gets replaced by the idea of loyalty to a very large group – the human species. The idea that moral obligation extends beyond that species to an even larger group becomes the idea of loyalty to all those who, like yourself, can experience pain – even the cows and the kangaroos – or perhaps even to all living things, even the trees.

This non-Kantian view of morality can be rephrased as the claim that one's moral identity is determined by the group or groups with which one identifies – the group

2 Michael Walzer, *Thick and Thin: Moral Argument at Home and Abroad* (Notre Dame: Notre Dame University Press, 1994), p. 4.
3 Baier's picture is quite close to that sketched by Wilfrid Sellars and Robert Brandom in their quasi-Hegelian accounts of moral progress as the expansion of the circle of beings who count as "us."

or groups to which one cannot be disloyal and still like oneself. Moral dilemmas are not, in this view, the result of a conflict between reason and sentiment but between alternative selves, alternative self-descriptions, alternative ways of giving a meaning to one's life. Non-Kantians do not think that we have a central, true self by virtue of our membership in the human species – a self that responds to the call of reason. They can, instead, agree with Daniel Dennett that a self is a center of narrative gravity. In non-traditional societies, most people have several such narratives at their disposal, and thus several different moral identities. It is this plurality of identities that accounts for the number and variety of moral dilemmas, moral philosophers, and psychological novels in such societies.

Walzer's contrast between thick and thin morality is, among other things, a contrast between the detailed and concrete stories you can tell about yourself as a member of a smaller group and the relatively abstract and sketchy story you can tell about yourself as a citizen of the world. You know more about your family than about your village, more about your village than about your nation, more about your nation than about humanity as a whole, more about being human than about simply being a living creature. You are in a better position to decide what differences between individuals are morally relevant when dealing with those whom you can describe thickly, and in a worse position when dealing with those whom you can only describe thinly. This is why, as groups get larger, law has to replace custom, and abstract principles have to replace *phronēsis*. So Kantians are wrong to see *phronēsis* as a thickening up of thin abstract principles. Plato and Kant were misled by the fact that abstract principles are designed to trump parochial loyalties into thinking that the principles are somehow prior to the loyalties – that the thin is somehow prior to the thick.

Walzer's thick–thin distinction can be aligned with Rawls' contrast between a shared *concept* of justice and various conflicting *conceptions* of justice. Rawls sets out that contrast as follows:

> the concept of justice, applied to an institution, means, say, that the institution makes no arbitrary distinctions between persons in assigning basic rights and duties, and that its rules establish a proper balance between competing claims. ... [A] conception includes, besides this, principles and criteria for deciding which distinctions are arbitrary and when a balance between competing claims is proper. People can agree on the meaning of justice and still be at odds, since they affirm different principles and standards for deciding these matters.[4]

Phrased in Rawls' terms, Walzer's point is that thick "fully resonant" *conceptions* of justice, complete with distinctions between the people who matter most and the people who matter less, come first. The thin concept, and its maxim "do not make arbitrary distinctions between moral subjects," is articulated only on special occasions. On those occasions, the thin concept can often be turned against any of the thick conceptions from which it emerged, in the form of critical questions about whether it may not be merely arbitrary to think that certain people matter more than others.

Neither Rawls nor Walzer think, however, that unpacking the thin concept of justice will, by itself, resolve such critical questions by supplying a criterion of arbitrariness. They do not think that we can do what Kant hoped to do – derive solutions to moral

4   John Rawls, *Political Liberalism* (New York: Columbia University Press, 1993), p. 14n.

dilemmas from the analysis of moral concepts. To put the point in the terminology I am suggesting: we cannot resolve conflicting loyalties by turning away from them all toward something categorically distinct from loyalty – the universal moral obligation to act justly. So we have to drop the Kantian idea that the moral law starts off pure but is always in danger of being contaminated by irrational feelings that introduce arbitrary discriminations among persons. We have to substitute the Hegelian-Marxist idea that the so-called moral law is, at best, a handy abbreviation for a concrete web of social practices. This means dropping Habermas' claim that his "discourse ethics" articulates a transcendental presupposition of the use of language, and accepting his critics' claim that it articulates only the customs of contemporary liberal societies.[5]

Now I want to raise the question of whether to describe the various moral dilemmas with which I began as conflicts between loyalty and justice, or rather as conflicting loyalties to particular groups, in a more concrete form. Consider the question of whether the demands for reform made on the rest of the world by Western liberal societies are made in the name of something not merely Western – something like morality, or humanity, or rationality – or are simply expressions of loyalty to local, Western, conceptions of justice. Habermas would say that they are the former. I would say that they are the latter, but are none the worse for that. I think it is better not to say that the liberal West is better informed about rationality and justice, and instead to say that, in making demands on nonliberal societies, it is simply being true to itself.

In a recent paper called "The Law of Peoples," Rawls discusses the question of whether the conception of justice he has developed in his books is something peculiarly Western and liberal or rather something universal. He would like to be able to claim universality. He says that it is important to avoid "historicism," and believes that he can do this if he can show that the conception of justice suited to a liberal society can be extended beyond such societies through formulating what he calls "the law of peoples."[6] He outlines, in that paper, an extension of the constructivist procedure proposed in his *A Theory of Justice* – an extension which, by continuing to separate the right from the good, lets us encompass liberal and non-liberal societies under the same law.

As Rawls develops this constructivist proposal, however, it emerges that this law applies only to *reasonable* peoples, in a quite specific sense of the term "reasonable." The conditions that nonliberal societies must honor in order to be "accepted by liberal societies as members in good standing of a society of peoples" include the following: "its

---

5 This sort of debate runs through a lot of contemporary philosophy. Compare, for example, Walzer's contrast between starting thin and starting thick with that between the Platonic-Chomskian notion that we start with meanings and descend to use, and the Wittgensteinian-Davidsonian notion that we start with use and then skim off meaning as needed for lexicographical or philosophical purposes.

6 Rawls, "The Law of Peoples" in *On Human Rights: The Oxford Amnesty Lectures, 1993*, Stephen Shute and Susan Hurley, eds. (New York: Basic Books, 1993), p. 44. I am not sure why Rawls thinks historicism is undesirable, and there are passages, both early and recent, in which he seems to throw in his lot with the historicists. (See the passage quoted in note 9 below from his recent "Reply to Habermas.") Some years ago I argued for the plausibility of an historicist interpretation of the metaphilosophy of Rawls' *A Theory of Justice* in my "The Priority of Democracy to Philosophy," reprinted in my *Objectivity, Relativism and Truth* (Cambridge: Cambridge University Press, 1991).

system of law must be guided by a common good conception of justice ... that takes impartially into account what it sees not unreasonably as the fundamental interests of all members of society."[7]

Rawls takes the fulfillment of that condition to rule out violation of basic human rights. These rights include "at least certain minimum rights to means of subsistence and security (the right to life), to liberty (freedom from slavery, serfdom, and forced occupations) and (personal) property, as well as to formal equality as expressed by the rules of natural justice (for example, that similar cases be treated similarly)."[8] When Rawls spells out what he means by saying that the admissible nonliberal societies must not have unreasonable philosophical or religious doctrines, he glosses "unreasonable" by saying that these societies must "admit a measure of liberty of conscience and freedom of thought, even if these freedoms are not in general equal for all members of society." Rawls' notion of what is reasonable, in short, confines membership of the society of peoples to societies whose institutions encompass most of the hard-won achievements of the West in the two centuries since the Enlightenment.

It seems to me that Rawls cannot both reject historicism and invoke this notion of reasonableness. For the effect of that invocation is to build most of the West's recent decisions about which distinctions between persons are arbitrary into the conception of justice that is implicit in the law of peoples. The differences between different *conceptions* of justice, remember, are differences between what features of people are seen as relevant to the adjudication of their competing claims. There is obviously enough wriggle room in phrases like "similar cases should be treated similarly" to allow for arguments that believers and infidels, men and women, blacks and whites, gays and straights should be treated as relevantly *dis*similar. So there is room to argue that discrimination on the basis of such differences is *not* arbitrary. If we are going to exclude from the society of peoples societies in which infidel homosexuals are not permitted to engage in certain occupations, those societies can quite reasonably say that we are, in excluding them, appealing not to something universal, but to very recent developments in Europe and America.

I agree with Habermas when he says, "What Rawls in fact prejudges with the concept of an 'overlapping consensus' is the distinction between modern and premodern forms of consciousness, between 'reasonable' and 'dogmatic' world interpretations." But I disagree with Habermas, as I think Walzer also would, when he goes on to say that Rawls

> can defend the primacy of the right over the good with the concept of an overlapping consensus only if it is true that postmetaphysical worldviews that have become reflexive under modern conditions are epistemically superior to dogmatically fixed, fundamentalistic worldviews – indeed, only if such a distinction can be made with absolute clarity.

Habermas' point is that Rawls needs an argument from transculturally valid premises for the superiority of the liberal West. Without such an argument, he says, "the disqualification of 'unreasonable' doctrines that cannot be brought into harmony with the proposed 'political' concept of justice is inadmissible."[9]

---

7 "The Law of Peoples," pp. 81, 61.

8 Ibid., p. 62.

9 All quotations in this paragraph are from Jürgen Habermas, *Justification and Application: Remarks on Discourse Ethics* (Cambridge: MIT Press, 1993), p. 95. Habermas is here commenting on Rawls'

Such passages make clear why Habermas and Walzer are at opposite poles. Walzer is taking for granted that there can be no such thing as a non-question-begging demonstration of the epistemic superiority of the Western idea of reasonableness. There is, for Walzer, no tribunal of transcultural reason before which to try the question of superiority. Walzer is presupposing what Habermas calls "a strong contextualism for which there is no single 'rationality'." On this conception, Habermas continues, "individual 'rationalities' are correlated with different cultures, worldviews, traditions, or forms of life. Each of them is viewed as internally interwoven with a particular understanding of the world."[10]

I think that Rawls' constructivist approach to the law of peoples can work if he adopts what Habermas calls a "strong contextualism." Doing so would mean giving up the attempt to escape historicism, as well as the attempt to supply a universalistic argument for the West's most recent views about which differences between persons are arbitrary. The strength of Walzer's *Thick and Thin* seems to me to be its explicitness about the need to do this. The weakness of Rawls' account of what he is doing lies in an ambiguity between two senses of universalism. When Rawls says that "a constructivist liberal doctrine is universal in its reach, once it is extended to … a law of peoples,"[11] he is not saying that it is universal in its validity. Universal reach is a notion that sits well with constructivism, but universal validity is not. It is the latter that Habermas requires. That is why Habermas thinks that we need really heavy philosophical weaponry, modeled on Kant's – why he insists that only transcendental presuppositions of any possible communicative practice will do the job.[12] To be faithful to his own constructivism, I think, Rawls has to agree with Walzer that this job does not need to be done.

Rawls and Habermas often invoke, and Walzer almost never invokes, the notion of "reason." In Habermas, this notion is always bound up with that of context-free validity. In Rawls, things are more complicated. Rawls distinguishes the reasonable from the rational, using the latter to mean simply the sort of means-end rationality that is employed in engineering, or in working out a Hobbesian *modus vivendi*. But he often invokes a third notion, that of "practical reason," as when he says that the authority of a constructivist liberal doctrine "rests on the principles and conceptions of practical reason."[13] Rawls' use of this Kantian term may make it sound as if he agreed with Kant and

---

use of "reasonable" in writings earlier than "The Law of Peoples," since the latter appeared subsequent to Habermas' book.

When I wrote the present paper, the exchange between Rawls and Habermas published in *The Journal of Philosophy* (vol. 92, no. 3, March 1995) had not yet appeared. This exchange rarely touches on the question of historicism versus universalism. But one passage in which this question emerges explicitly is to be found on p. 179 of Rawls' "Reply to Habermas": "Justice as fairness is substantive … in the sense that it springs from and belongs to the tradition of liberal thought and the larger community of political culture of democratic societies. It fails then to be properly formal and truly universal, and thus to be part of the quasi-transcendental presuppositions (as Habermas sometimes says) established by the theory of communicative action."

10   Loc. cit.

11   "The Law of Peoples," p. 46.

12   My own view is that we do not need, either in epistemology or in moral philosophy, the notion of universal validity. I argue for this in "Sind Aussagen Universelle Geltungsansprüche?" *Deutsche Zeitschrift für Philosophie*, (*Band* 42, 6/1994), pp. 975–88. Habermas and Apel find my view paradoxical and likely to produce performative self-contradiction.

13   "The Law of Peoples," p. 46.

Habermas that there is a universally distributed human faculty called practical reason (existing prior to, and working quite independently of, the recent history of the West), a faculty that tells us what counts as an arbitrary distinction between persons and what does not. Such a faculty would do the job Habermas thinks needs doing: detecting transcultural moral validity.

But this cannot, I think, be what Rawls intends. For he also says that his own constructivism differs from all philosophical views that appeal to a source of authority, and in which "the universality of the doctrine is the direct consequence of its source of authority." As examples of sources of authority, he cites "(human) reason, or an independent realm of moral values, or some other proposed basis of universal validity."[14] So I think we have to construe his phrase "the principles and conceptions of practical reason" as referring to *whatever* principles and conceptions are in fact arrived at in the course of creating a community.

Rawls emphasizes that creating a community is not the same thing as working out a *modus vivendi* – a task which requires only means–end rationality, not practical reason. A principle or conception belongs to practical reason, in Rawls' sense, if it emerged in the course of people starting thick and getting thin, thereby developing an overlapping consensus and setting up a more inclusive moral community. It would not so belong if it had emerged under the threat of force. Practical reason for Rawls is, so to speak, a matter of procedure rather than of substance – of how we agree on what to do rather than of what we agree on.

This definition of practical reason suggests that there may be only a verbal difference between Rawls' and Habermas' positions. For Habermas' own attempt to substitute "communicative reason" for "subject-centered reason" is itself a move toward substituting "how" for "what." The first sort of reason is a source of truth, truth somehow coeval with the human mind. The second sort of reason is not a source of anything, but simply the activity of justifying claims by offering arguments rather than threats. Like Rawls, Habermas focuses on the difference between persuasion and force, rather than, as Plato and Kant did, on the difference between two parts of the human person – the good rational part and the dubious passionate or sensual part. Both would like to de-emphasize the notion of the *authority* of reason – the idea of reason as a faculty which issues decrees – and substitute the notion of rationality as what is present whenever people communicate, whenever they try to justify their claims to one another, rather than threatening each other.

The similarities between Rawls and Habermas seem even greater in the light of Rawls' endorsement of Thomas Scanlon's answer to the "fundamental question why anyone should care about morality at all," namely that "we have a basic desire to be able to justify our actions to others on grounds that they could not reasonably reject – reasonably, that is, given the desire to find principles that others similarly motivated could not reasonably reject."[15] This suggests that the two philosophers might agree on the following claim: The only notion of rationality we need, at least in moral and social philosophy, is that of a situation in which people do not say "your own current interests dictate that you agree to our proposal," but rather "your own central beliefs, the ones which are central to your own moral identity, suggest that you should agree to our proposal."

14   Both quotations are from "The Law of Peoples," p. 45.
15   I quote here from Rawls' summary of Scanlon's view at *Political Liberalism*, p. 49n.

This notion of rationality can be delimited using Walzer's terminology by saying that rationality is found wherever people envisage the possibility of getting from different thicks to the same thin. To appeal to interests rather than beliefs is to urge a *modus vivendi*. Such an appeal is exemplified by the speech of the Athenian ambassadors to the unfortunate Melians, as reported by Thucydides. To appeal to your enduring beliefs as well as to your current interests is to suggest that what gives you your *present* moral identity – your thick and resonant complex of beliefs – may make it possible for you to develop a new, supplementary, moral identity.[16] It is to suggest that what makes you loyal to a smaller group may give you reason to cooperate in constructing a larger group, a group to which you may in time become equally loyal or perhaps even more loyal. The difference between the absence and the presence of rationality, on this account, is the difference between a threat and an offer – the offer of a new moral identity and thus a new and larger loyalty, a loyalty to a group formed by an unforced agreement between smaller groups.

In the hope of minimizing the contrast between Habermas and Rawls still further, and of rapprochement between both and Walzer, I want to suggest a way of thinking of rationality that might help to resolve the problem I posed earlier: the problem of whether justice and loyalty are different sorts of things, or whether the demands of justice are simply the demands of a larger loyalty. I said that question seemed to boil down to the question of whether justice and loyalty had different sources – reason and sentiment, respectively. If the latter distinction disappears, the former one will not seem particularly useful. But if by rationality we mean simply the sort of activity that Walzer thinks of as a thinning out process – the sort that, with luck, achieves the formulation and utilization of an overlapping consensus – then the idea that justice has a different source than loyalty no longer seems plausible.[17]

For, on this account of rationality, being rational and acquiring a larger loyalty are two descriptions of the same activity. This is because *any* unforced agreement between individuals and groups about what to do creates a form of community, and will, with luck, be the initial stage in expanding the circles of those whom each party to the agreement had previously taken to be "people like ourselves." The opposition between rational argument and fellow-feeling thus begins to dissolve. For fellow-feeling may, and often does, arise from the realization that the people whom one thought one might have to go to war with, use force on, are, in Rawls' sense, "reasonable." They are, it turns out, enough like us to see the point of compromising differences in order to live in peace, and of abiding by the agreement that has been hammered out. They are, to some degree at least, trustworthy.

From this point of view, Habermas' distinction between a strategic use of language and a genuinely communicative use of language begins to look like a difference between positions on a spectrum – a spectrum of degrees of trust. Baier's suggestion that we take trust rather than obligation to be our fundamental moral concept would thus produce

16   Walzer thinks it is a good idea for people to have lots of different moral identities. "[T]hick, divided selves are the characteristic products of, and in turn require, a thick, differentiated, and pluralistic society" (*Thick and Thin*, p. 101).

17   Note that in Rawls' semitechnical sense an overlapping consensus is not the result of discovering that various comprehensive views already share common doctrines, but rather something that might never have emerged had the proponents of these views not started trying to cooperate.

a blurring of the line between rhetorical manipulation and genuine validity-seeking argument – a line that I think Habermas draws too sharply. If we cease to think of reason as a source of authority, and think of it simply as the process of reaching agreement by persuasion, then the standard Platonic and Kantian dichotomy of reason and feeling begins to fade away. That dichotomy can be replaced by a continuum of degrees of overlap of beliefs and desires.[18] When people whose beliefs and desires do not overlap very much disagree, they tend to think of each other as crazy or, more politely, as irrational. When there is considerable overlap, on the other hand, they may agree to differ and regard each other as the sort of people one can live with – and eventually, perhaps, the sort one can be friends with, intermarry with, and so on.[19]

To advise people to be rational is, on the view I am offering, simply to suggest that somewhere among their shared beliefs and desires there may be enough resources to permit agreement on how to coexist without violence. To conclude that someone is irredeemably *irrational* is not to realize that she is not making proper use of her God-given faculties. It is rather to realize that she does not seem to share enough relevant beliefs and desires with us to make possible fruitful conversation about the issue in dispute. So, we reluctantly conclude, we have to give up on the attempt to get her to enlarge her moral identity, and settle for working out a *modus vivendi* – one which may involve the threat, or even the use, of force.

A stronger, more Kantian, notion of rationality would be invoked if one said that being rational guarantees a peaceful resolution of conflicts – that if people are willing to reason together long enough, what Habermas calls "the force of the better argument" will lead them to concur.[20] This stronger notion strikes me as pretty useless. I see no point in saying that it is more rational to prefer one's neighbors to one's family in the event of a nuclear holocaust, or more rational to prefer leveling off incomes around the world to preserving the institutions of liberal Western societies. To use the word "rational" to commend one's chosen solution to such dilemmas, or to use the term "yielding to the force of the better argument" to characterize one's way of making up one's mind, is to pay oneself an empty compliment.

More generally, the idea of "the better argument" makes sense only if one can identify a natural, transcultural relation of relevance, which connects propositions with one another so as to form something like Descartes' "natural order of reasons." Without such a natural order, one can only evaluate arguments by their efficacy in producing agreement among particular persons or groups. But the required notion of natural, intrinsic relevance – relevance dictated not by the needs of any given community but by human

---

18 Davidson has, I think, demonstrated that any two beings that use language to communicate with one another necessarily share an enormous number of beliefs and desires. He has thereby shown the incoherence of the idea that people can live in separate worlds created by differences in culture or status or fortune. There is always an immense overlap – an immense reserve army of common beliefs and desires to be drawn on at need. But this immense overlap does not, of course, prevent accusations of craziness or diabolical wickedness. For only a tiny amount of nonoverlap about certain particularly touchy subjects (the border between two territories, the name of the One True God) may lead to such accusations, and eventually to violence.

19 I owe this line of thought about how to reconcile Habermas and Baier to Mary Rorty.

20 This notion of "the better argument" is central to Habermas' and Apel's understanding of rationality. I criticize it in the article cited above in note 14.

reason as such – seems no more plausible or useful than that of a God whose Will can be appealed to in order to resolve conflicts between communities. It is, I think, merely a secularized version of that earlier notion.

Non-Western societies in the past were rightly skeptical of Western conquerors who explained that they were invading in obedience to divine commands. More recently, they have been skeptical of Westerners who suggest that they should adopt Western ways in order to become more rational. (This suggestion has been abbreviated by Ian Hacking as "Me rational, you Jane.") On the account of rationality I am recommending, both forms of skepticism are equally justified. But this is not to deny that these societies *should* adopt recent Western ways by, for example, abandoning slavery, practicing religious toleration, educating women, permitting mixed marriages, tolerating homosexuality and conscientious objection to war, and so on. As a loyal Westerner, I think they should indeed do all these things. I agree with Rawls about what it takes to count as reasonable, and about what kind of societies we Westerners should accept as members of a global moral community.

But I think that the rhetoric we Westerners use in trying to get everyone to be more like us would be improved if we were more frankly ethnocentric, and less professedly universalist. It would be better to say: Here is what we in the West look like as a result of ceasing to hold slaves, beginning to educate women, separating church and state, and so on. Here is what happened after we started treating certain distinctions between people as arbitrary rather than fraught with moral significance. If you would try treating them that way, you might like the results. Saying that sort of thing seems preferable to saying: Look at how much better we are at knowing what differences between persons are arbitrary and which not – how much more *rational* we are.

If we Westerners could get rid of the notion of universal moral obligations created by membership in the species, and substitute the idea of building a community of trust between ourselves and others, we might be in a better position to persuade non-Westerners of the advantages of joining in that community. We might be better able to construct the sort of global moral community that Rawls describes in "The Law of Peoples." In making this suggestion, I am urging, as I have on earlier occasions, that we need to peel apart Enlightenment liberalism from Enlightenment rationalism.

I think that discarding the residual rationalism that we inherit from the Enlightenment is advisable for many reasons. Some of these are theoretical and of interest only to philosophy professors, such as the apparent incompatibility of the correspondence theory of truth with a naturalistic account of the origin of human minds.[21] Others are more practical. One practical reason is that getting rid of rationalistic rhetoric would permit the West to approach the non-West in the role of someone with an instructive story to tell, rather than in the role of someone purporting to be making better use of a universal human capacity.

---

21   For a claim that such a theory of truth is essential to "the Western Rationalist Tradition," see John Searle, "Rationality and Realism: What Difference does it Make?" *Daedalus* (vol. 122, no. 4, Fall 1992), pp. 55–84. See also my reply to Searle in "Does Academic Freedom Have Philosophical Presuppositions?" *Academe* (vol. 80, no. 6, November/December 1994), pp. 52–63. I argue there that we should be better off without the notion of "getting something right," and that writers such as Dewey and Davidson have shown us how to keep the benefits of Western rationalism without the philosophical hangups caused by the attempt to explicate this notion.

Pragmatism as Romantic Polytheism

In 1911 a book appeared in Paris with the title *Un Romantisme Utilitaire: Étude sur le Mouvement Pragmatiste*. This was the first of three volumes on the subject by René Berthelot. Berthelot had been struck by the resemblances between the views of William James, John Dewey, Nietzsche, Bergson, Poincaré, and certain Catholic Modernists. He was the first to treat them as belonging to the same intellectual movement. A convinced Cartesian, Berthelot disliked and distrusted all these thinkers, but he wrote about them with acuity and verve. He traced the romantic roots of pragmatism back behind Emerson to Schelling and Hoelderlin, and the utilitarian roots to the influence of Darwin and Spencer.[1] But he thought that the difference between these two modes of thought was too great to permit synthesis. "In all its different forms," Berthelot said, "pragmatism reveals itself to be a romantic utilitarianism: that is its most obviously original feature and also its most private vice and its hidden weakness."[2]

Berthelot was probably the first to call Nietzsche "a German pragmatist," and the first to emphasize the resemblance between Nietzsche's perspectivism and the pragmatist theory of truth. This resemblance − frequently noted since, notably in a seminal chapter of Arthur Danto's book on Nietzsche − is most evident in the *The Gay Science*. There Nietzsche says "We do not even have any organ at all for *knowing*, for 'truth'; we 'know' … just as much as may be *useful* in the interest of the human herd."[3] This

Richard M. Rorty, "Pragmatism as Romantic Polytheism," pp. 21–36 in Morris Dickstein (ed.), *The Revival of Pragmatism: New Essays on Social Thought, Law, and Culture*, © 1998 by Duke University Press. Reprinted by kind permission of Morris Dickstein.

1 René Berthelot, *Un Romantisme Utilitaire: Étude sur le Mouvement Pragmatiste*, vol. 1 (Paris: F. Alcan, 1911), pp. 62–63. Berthelot also looked back behind Darwin and Spencer to Hume, whom he regarded as "la transition entre la psychologie utilitaire et intellectualiste d'Helvétius et la psychologie vitaliste de l'instinct que nous rencontrons chez les Ecossais." He views Lamarck as "la transition entre cette conception vitaliste de la biologie et ce qu'on peut appeler l'utilitarisme mécanique de Darwin" (vol. 1, p. 85).

2 Berthelot, *Romantisme Utilitaire*, vol. 1, p. 128.

3 Friedrich Nietzsche, *The Gay Science*, section 354: Wir haben eben gar kein Organ fuer das *Erkennen*, fuer die 'Wahrheit'; wir 'wissen' … gerade so viel, als im Interesse der Menschen-Herde, der Gattung, *nuetzlich* sein mag.

Darwinian view lies behind James' claim that "thinking is for the sake of behavior" and his identification of truth as "the good in the way of belief."

That identification amounts to accepting Nietzsche's claim that human beings should be viewed, for epistemological purposes, as what Nietzsche called "clever animals." Beliefs are to be judged solely by their utility in fulfilling these animals' varied needs. James and Nietzsche did for the word "true" what John Stuart Mill had done for the word "right." Just as Mill says that there is no ethical motive apart from the desire for the happiness of human beings, so James and Nietzsche say that there is no will to truth distinct from the will to happiness. All three philosophers think that the terms "true" and "right" gain their meaning from their use in evaluating the relative success of efforts to achieve happiness.

Nietzsche, to be sure, had no use for Mill, but this was a result of arrogant ignorance, which resulted in a failure to grasp the difference between Mill and Bentham. James, on the other hand, dedicated his first philosophical treatise to Mill's memory, and tried to cultivate not only the debunking, Benthamite strain in Mill's thought but also the romantic, Coleridgean strain. The latter led Mill to choose an epigraph from Wilhelm von Humboldt for *On Liberty*: "The grand, leading principle, towards which every argument unfolded in these pages directly converges, is the absolute and essential importance of human development in its richest diversity." As a romantic utilitarian, Mill wanted to avoid Benthamite reductionism, and to defend a secular culture against the familiar charge of blindness to higher things.

This led him, as M. H. Abrams has pointed out, to share Arnold's view that literature could take the place of dogma. Abrams quotes Alexander Bain as saying of Mill that "he seemed to look upon Poetry as a Religion, or rather as Religion and Philosophy in One." Abrams also quotes a letter of Mill's which says that "the new utilitarianism" – his own as opposed to Bentham's – holds "Poetry not only on a par with, but the necessary condition of, any true and comprehensive Philosophy." Abrams argues that Mill and Arnold, despite their differences, drew the same moral from the English Romantics: that poetry could and should take on "the tremendous responsibility of the functions once performed by the exploded dogmas of religion and religious philosophy."[4] The exploded dogmas included the claim that, whereas there can be many great poems, there can be only one true religion, because only one true God. Poetry cannot be a substitute for a monotheistic religion, but it can serve the purposes of a secular version of polytheism.

The substitution of poetry for religion as a source of ideals, a movement that began with the Romantics, seems to me usefully described as a return to polytheism. For if, with the utilitarians, you reject the idea that a nonhuman authority can rank human needs, and thus dictate moral choices to human beings, you will favor what Arnold called "Hellenism" over what he called "Hebraism." You will reject the idea, characteristic of the evangelical Christians whom Arnold thought of as "Hebraist," that it suffices to love God and keep his commandments. You will substitute what Arnold called the idea of "a human nature perfect on all its sides."[5] Different poets will perfect different sides of human nature, by projecting different ideals. A romantic utilitarian will probably drop the idea of diverse

4   M. H. Abrams, *The Mirror and the Lamp* (New York: Oxford University Press, 1953; quotes on pp. 334–35, 333 (quoting a letter to Lytton Bulwer), and 335 respectively.

5   Matthew Arnold, *Culture and Anarchy*, ed. Samuel Lipman (New Haven: Yale University Press, 1994), p. 37.

immortal persons, such as the Olympian deities, but she will retain the idea that there are diverse, conflicting, but equally valuable forms of human life.

A polytheism of this sort is recommended in a famous passage near the end of *The Varieties of Religious Experience* at which James says

> If an Emerson were forced to be a Wesley, or a Moody forced to be a Whitman, the total human consciousness of the divine would suffer. The divine can mean no single quality, it must mean a group of qualities, by being champions of which in alternation, different men may all find worthy missions. Each attitude being a syllable in human nature's total message, it takes the whole of us to spell the meaning out completely.[6]

James' loose use of the term "the divine" makes it pretty much equivalent to "the ideal." In this passage he is doing for theology what Mill had done for politics when he cited von Humboldt's claim that "human development in its richest diversity" is the aim of social institutions.

There is a passage in Nietzsche in praise of polytheism that complements the one I have just quoted from James. In section 143 of *The Gay Science* he argues that morality – in the wide sense of the need for acceptance of binding laws and customs – entails "hostility against the impulse to have an ideal of one's own." But, he says, the pre-Socratic Greeks provided an outlet for individuality by permitting human beings "to behold, in some distant overworld, a *plurality of norms*: one god was not considered a denial of another god, nor blasphemy against him." In this way, Nietzsche says, "the luxury of individuals was first permitted; it was here that one first honored the rights of individuals." For in pre-Socratic polytheism "the free-spiriting and many-spiriting of man attained its first preliminary form – the strength to create for ourselves our own new eyes."[7]

Here is a definition of "polytheism" that covers both Nietzsche and James. You are a polytheist if you think that there is no actual or possible object of knowledge that would permit you to commensurate and rank all human needs. Isaiah Berlin's well-known doctrine of incommensurable human values is, in my sense, a polytheistic manifesto. To be a polytheist in this sense you do not have to believe that there are nonhuman persons with power to intervene in human affairs. All you need do is to abandon the idea that we should try to find a way of making everything hang together, which will tell all human beings what to do with their lives, and tell all of them the same thing.

Polytheism, in the sense I have defined it, is pretty much coextensive with romantic utilitarianism. For once one sees no way of ranking human needs other than playing them off against one another, human happiness becomes all that matters. Mill's *On Liberty* provides all the ethical instruction you need – all the philosophical advice you are ever going to get about your responsibilities to other human beings. For human

---

6   William James, *Varieties of Religious Experience* (Cambridge: Harvard University Press, 1985), p. 384.

7   "Aber ueber sich and ausser sich, in einer fernen Ueberwelt, durfte man eine *Mehrzahl von Normen* sehen; der eine Gott war nicht die Leugnung oder Laesterung des anderen Gottes. ... Hier erlaubte man sich zuerst Individuen, hier ehrte man zuerst das Recht von Individuen. ... In Polytheismus lag die Freigeisterei und Vielgeisterei des Menschen vorgebildet; die Kraft, sich neue und eigne Augen zu schaffen" (Nietzsche, *The Gay Science*, sec. 143).

perfection becomes a private concern, and our responsibility to others becomes a matter of permitting them as much space to pursue these private concerns – to worship their own gods, so to speak – as is compatible with granting an equal amount of space to all. The tradition of religious toleration is extended to moral toleration.

This privatization of perfection permits James and Nietzsche to agree with Mill and Arnold that poetry should take over the role that religion has played in the formation of individual human lives. They also agree that nobody should take over the function of the clergy. For poets are to a secularized polytheism what the priests of a universal church are to monotheism. Once you become polytheistic, you will turn away not only from priests but from such priest-substitutes as metaphysicians and physicists – from anyone who purports to tell you how things *really* are, anyone who invokes the distinction between the true world and the apparent world that Nietzsche ridiculed in *Twilight of the Idols*. Both monotheism and the kind of metaphysics or science that purports to tell you what the world is *really* like are replaced with democratic politics. A free consensus about how much space for private perfection we can allow each other takes the place of the quest for "objective" values, the quest for a ranking of human needs that does not depend upon such consensus.

So far I have been playing along with Berthelot's emphasis on the similarities between Nietzsche and the American pragmatists. Now I want to turn to the two most obvious differences between them: their attitude toward democracy and their attitude toward religion. Nietzsche thought democracy was "Christianity for the people" – Christianity deprived of the nobility of spirit of which Christ himself, and perhaps a few of the more strenuous saints, had been capable. Dewey thought of democracy as Christianity cleansed of the hieratic, exclusionist elements. Nietzsche thought those who believed in a traditional monotheistic God were foolish weaklings. Dewey thought of them as so spell-bound by the work of one poet as to be unable to appreciate the work of other poets. Dewey thought that the sort of "aggressive atheism" on which Nietzsche prided himself is unnecessarily intolerant. It has, he said, "something in common with traditional supernaturalism."[8]

I want first to argue that Nietzsche's contempt for democracy was an adventitious extra, inessential to his overall philosophical outlook. Then I shall get down to my main task in this paper – defending Dewey's tolerance for religious belief against those who think that pragmatism and religion do not mix.

Nietzsche was a utilitarian only in the sense that he saw no goals for human beings to pursue other than human happiness. He had no interest in the greatest happiness of the greatest number, but only in that of a few exceptional human beings – those with the capacity to be *greatly* happy. Democracy seemed to him a way of trivializing human existence. By contrast, James and Dewey took for granted, as Mill had, the ideal of universal human fraternity. Echoing Mill, James wrote, "Take any demand, however slight, which any creature, however weak, may make. Ought it not, for its own sole sake, to be desired?"[9]

8   John Dewey, "A Common Faith," in *Later Works of John Dewey*, ed. Jo Ann Boydston (Carbondale: Southern Illinois University Press, 1986), vol. 9, p. 36.
9   William James, *The Will to Believe* (Cambridge: Harvard University Press, 1979), p. 149.

Romantic utilitarianism, pragmatism, and polytheism are compatible with both wholehearted enthusiasm and whole-hearted contempt for democracy. The frequent complaint that a philosopher who holds the pragmatic theory of truth cannot give you a reason not to be a fascist is perfectly justified. But neither can that person give you a reason to be a fascist. For once you become a polytheist in the sense I just defined, you have to give up on the idea that philosophy can help you choose among the various deities and the various forms of life offered. The choice between enthusiasm and contempt for democracy becomes more like a choice between Walt Whitman and Robinson Jeffers than between competing sets of philosophical arguments.

Those who find the pragmatist identification of truth with what is good to believe morally offensive often say that Nietzsche, rather than James and Dewey, drew the proper inference from the abandonment of the idea of an object of knowledge that tells one how to rank human needs. Those who think of pragmatism as a species of irrationalism, and of irrationalism as selling the pass to fascism, say that James and Dewey were blind to the antidemocratic consequences of their own ideas, and naive to think that one can be both a good pragmatist and a good democrat.

Such critics make the same mistake that Nietzsche made. They think that the idea of fraternity is inextricable from Platonism. Platonism, in this sense, is the idea that the will to truth is distinct from the will to happiness – or, to be a bit more precise, the claim that human beings are divided between a quest for a lower, animal form of happiness and a higher, God-like form of happiness. Nietzsche mistakenly thought that once (with Darwin's help) you had given up this idea, and had gotten used to the idea that you are just a clever animal, you could have no reason to wish for the happiness of all human beings. He was so impressed by the fact that Christianity would have seemed ludicrous to the Homeric heroes that he was unable, except at occasional fleeting moments, to think of Christianity as the work of strong poets. So Nietzsche assumed that once poetry had replaced religion as the source of ideals, there would be no place for either Christianity or democracy.

Nietzsche would have done better to ask himself whether the Christian emphasis on human fraternity – the idea that for Christians there is neither Jew nor Greek, and the related idea that love is the only law – might have been only accidentally, for contingent historical reasons, associated with Platonism. This ideal might have gotten along nicely without the logocentrism of the Gospel of John, and without Augustine's unfortunate suggestion that Plato had prefigured Christian truth. In a different, but possible, world, some early Christian might have anticipated James' remark about Emerson and Wesley by writing "If Caesar were forced to be Christ, the total human consciousness of the divine would suffer."

A Christianity that was merely ethical – the sort Jefferson and other Enlightenment thinkers commended and was later propounded by theologians of the social gospel – might have sloughed-off exclusionism by viewing Jesus as one incarnation of the divine among others. The celebration of an ethics of love would then have taken its place within the relatively tolerant polytheism of the Roman Empire, having disjoined the ideal of human brotherhood from the claim to represent the will of an omnipotent and monopolistic Heavenly Father (not to mention the idea that there is no salvation outside the Christian Church).

Had they preached such a merely moral and social gospel, the Christians would never have bothered to develop a natural theology. So thirteenth-century Christians would not have worried about whether the Scriptures could be reconciled with Aristotle. Seventeenth-century believers would not have worried about whether they could be reconciled with Newton, nor those in the nineteenth century about whether they could be reconciled with Darwin. These hypothetical Christians would have treated Scripture as useful for purposes for which Aristotle, Newton, and Darwin were useless, and as useless for purposes of prediction and control of the environment. As things stood, however, the Christian churches remained obsessed by the Platonic idea that both Truth and God are One. So it was natural, when physical science began to make some progress, that its practitioners should take over this rhetoric, and thereby stir up a war between science and theology, between Scientific Truth and Religious Faith.

I have imagined such a non-Platonic and nonexclusivist form of Christianity in order to emphasize that no chain of inference links the ideal of human fraternity to the ideal of escaping from a world of appearance inhabited by animals to a real world in which humans will become as gods. Nietzsche and contemporary critics who see Nietzsche and Dewey as holding similarly dangerous "irrationalist" doctrines have been tricked by Plato into believing that, unless there is such a real world, Thrasymachus, Callicles, and Hitler are unanswerable. But they are unanswerable only in the sense that, *pace* Habermas, there are no premises to which they must assent simply by virtue of being rational, language-using animals. *A fortiori*, there are no such premises that would lead them to agree that they should treat all other human beings as brothers and sisters. Christianity as a strong poem, one poem among many, can be as socially useful as Christianity backed up by the Platonist claim that God and Truth are interchangeable terms.

Although I do not think that there is an inferential path that leads from the antirepresentationalist view of truth and knowledge common to Nietzsche, James, and Dewey either to democracy or antidemocracy, I do think there is a plausible inference from democratic convictions to such a view. Your devotion to democracy is unlikely to be wholehearted if you believe, as monotheists typically do, that we can have knowledge of an "objective" ranking of human needs that can overrule the result of democratic consensus. But if your devotion is wholehearted, then you will welcome the utilitarian and pragmatist claim that we have no will to truth distinct from the will to happiness.

So much for the disagreement between Nietzsche and his American colleagues about the value of democracy. I turn now to the other big difference between Nietzsche on the one hand and James and Dewey on the other. Nietzsche thinks religious belief is intellectually disreputable; James and Dewey do not.

In order to defend James and Dewey's tolerance for theism against Nietzsche, I shall sketch a pragmatist philosophy of religion in five brief theses. Then I shall try to relate these theses to what James and Dewey actually said about belief in God.

First, it is an advantage of the antirepresentationalist view of belief that James took over from Bain and Peirce – the view that beliefs are habits of action – that it frees us from the responsibility to unify all our beliefs into a single worldview. If our beliefs are all parts of a single attempt to represent a single world, then they must all hang together fairly tightly. But if they are habits of action, then, because the purposes served by action may blamelessly vary, so may the habits we develop to serve those purposes.

Second, Nietzsche's attempt to "see science through the optic of art, and art through that of life," like Arnold's and Mill's substitution of poetry for religion, is an attempt to make more room for individuality than can be provided either by orthodox monotheism, or by the Enlightenment's attempt to put science in the place of religion as a source of Truth. So the attempt, by Tillich and others, to treat religious faith as "symbolic," and thereby to treat religion as poetic and poetry as religious, and neither as competing with science, is on the right track. But to make it convincing we need to drop the idea that some parts of culture fulfill our need to know the truth and others fulfill lesser aims. The pragmatists' romantic utilitarianism does drop this idea: if there is no will to truth apart from the will to happiness, there is no way to contrast the cognitive with the noncognitive, the serious with the nonserious.

Third, pragmatism does permit us to make another distinction, one that takes over some of the work previously done by the old distinction between the cognitive and the noncognitive. The new distinction is between projects of social cooperation and projects of individual self-development. Intersubjective agreement is required for the former projects, but not for the latter. Natural science is a paradigmatic project of social cooperation: the project of improving man's estate by taking account of every possible observation and experimental result in order to facilitate the making of predictions that will come true. Law is another such paradigm. Romantic art, by contrast, is a paradigmatic project of individual self-development. Religion, if it can be disconnected from both science and morals – from the attempt to predict the consequences of our actions and the attempt to rank human needs – may be another such paradigm.

Fourth, the idea that we should love Truth is largely responsible for the idea that religious belief is "intellectually irresponsible." But there is no such thing as the love of Truth. What has been called by that name is a mixture of the love of reaching intersubjective agreement, the love of gaining mastery over a recalcitrant set of data, the love of winning arguments, and the love of synthesizing little theories into big theories. It is never an objection to a religious belief that there is no evidence for it. The only possible objection to it can be that it intrudes an individual project into a social and cooperative project, and thereby offends against the teachings of *On Liberty*. Such intrusion is a betrayal of one's responsibilities to cooperate with other human beings, not of one's responsibility to Truth or to Reason.

Fifth, the attempt to love Truth, and to think of it as One, and as capable of commensurating and ranking human needs, is a secular version of the traditional religious hope that allegiance to something big, powerful, and nonhuman will persuade that powerful being to take your side in your struggle with other people. Nietzsche despised any such hope as a sign of weakness. Pragmatists who are also democrats have a different objection to such hope for allegiance with power. They see it as a betrayal of the ideal of human fraternity that democracy inherits from the Judeo-Christian religious tradition. That ideal finds its best expression in the doctrine, common to Mill and James, that every human need should be satisfied unless doing so causes too many other human needs to go unsatisfied. The pragmatist objection to religious fundamentalists is not that fundamentalists are *intellectually* irresponsible in disregarding the results of natural science. Rather it is that they are *morally* irresponsible in attempting to circumvent the process of achieving democratic consensus about how to maximize happiness. They sin not by ignoring Mill's inductive methods, but by ignoring his reflections on liberty.

I turn now to the question of how the view of religious belief epitomized in my five theses accords with the views of James and Dewey. It would not, I think, have been congenial to James. But I think it might have suited Dewey. So I shall argue that it is Dewey's rather unambitious and half-hearted *A Common Faith*, rather than James' brave and exuberant "Conclusion" to *Varieties of Religious Experience*, that coheres best with the romantic utilitarianism which both accepted.

James says, in that chapter of *Varieties*, that "the pivot round which the religious life revolves ... is the interest of the individual in his private personal destiny." By "repudiating the personal point of view," however, science gives us a picture of nature that "has no distinguishable ultimate tendency with which it is possible to feel a sympathy." The "driftings of the cosmic atoms" are "a kind of aimless weather, doing and undoing, achieving no proper history, and leaving no result."[10] On the view I have just outlined, he should have followed this up by saying "But we are free to describe the universe in many different ways. Describing it as the drifting of cosmic atoms is useful for the social project of working together to control our environment and improve man's estate. But that description leaves us entirely free to say, for example, that the Heavens proclaim the glory of God."

Sometimes James seems to take this line, as when, with obvious approval, he quotes James Henry Leuba as saying

> *God is not known, he is not understood, he is used* – sometimes as meat-purveyor, sometimes as moral support, sometimes as friend, sometime as an object of love. If he proves himself useful, the religious consciousness can ask no more than that. Does God really exist? How does he exist? What is he? are so many irrelevant questions. Not God, but life, more life, a larger, richer, more satisfying life, is, in the last analysis, the end of religion.

Unfortunately, however, almost immediately after quoting Leuba James says "we must next pass beyond the point of view of merely subjective utility and make inquiry into the intellectual content itself." He then goes on to argue that the material he has gathered together in *Varieties* provides empirical evidence for the hypothesis that "the conscious person is continuous with a wider self through which saving experiences come." He calls this "a positive content of religious experience which, it seems to me, is literally and objectively true as far as it goes."[11]

On the view I have been suggesting, this claim to literal and objective truth is unpragmatic, hollow, and superfluous. James should have rested content with the argument of "The Will to Believe." As I read that essay, it says that we have a right to believe what we like when we are, so to speak, on our own time.[12] But we abandon this right when we are engaged in, for example, a scientific or a political project. For when so engaged it is necessary to reconcile our beliefs, our habits of action, with those of others. On our own time, by contrast, our habits of action are nobody's business but our own. A romantic polytheist will rejoice in what Nietzsche called the "free-spiritedness and many-spiritedness" of individuals, and see the only constraint on this freedom and this diversity as the need not to injure others.

10   James, *Varieties of Religious Experience*, pp. 387–88.
11   *Ibid.*, pp. 399 and 405, respectively.
12   See my "Religious Faith, Intellectual Responsibility, and Romance," in *The Cambridge Companion to William James*, ed. Ruth Anna Putnam (Cambridge: Cambridge University Press, 1997).

James wobbled on the question of whether what he called "the religious hypothesis" was something to be adopted on "passional" or on "intellectual" grounds. This hypothesis says that "the best things are the more eternal things, the overlapping things, the things in the universe that throw the last stone, so to speak, and say the final word."[13] In "The Will to Believe" this is put forward as a hypothesis to which considerations of evidence are irrelevant, and must therefore be turned over to our emotions. But in the "Conclusion" to *Varieties of Religious Experience*, the hypothesis that "God's existence is the guarantee of an ideal order that shall be permanently preserved" is one for which he has accumulated evidence. There he also says that the least common denominator of religious beliefs is that "The solution [to the problem presented by a 'sense that there is something wrong about us as we naturally stand'] is that we are saved from the wrongness by making proper connection with the higher powers." Again, he says that "the conscious person is continuous with a wider self from which saving experiences come."[14]

James should not have made a distinction between issues to be decided by intellect and issues to be decided by emotion. If he had not, he might have wobbled less. What he should have done instead was to distinguish issues that you must resolve cooperatively with others and issues that you are entitled to resolve on your own. The first set of issues are about conciliating your habits of action with those of other human beings. The second set are about getting your own habits of action to cohere with each other sufficiently so that you acquire a stable, coherent, self-image. But such a self-image does not require monotheism, or the belief that Truth is One. It is compatible with the idea that you have many different needs, and that the beliefs that help you fill one set of needs are irrelevant to, and need not be made to cohere with, those that help you to fill another set.

Dewey avoided James' mistakes in this area. One reason he did so is that he was much less prone to a sense of guilt than was James. After he realized that his mother had made him unnecessarily miserable by burdening him with a belief in original sin, Dewey simply stopped thinking that, in James' words, "there is something wrong about us as we naturally stand." He no longer believed that we could be "saved from the wrongness by making proper connection with the higher powers." He thought that all that was wrong with us was that the Christian ideal of fraternity had not yet been achieved – society had not yet become pervasively democratic. That was not a problem to be solved by making proper connection with higher powers, but a problem of men to be solved by men.

Dewey's steadfast refusal to have any truck with the notion of original sin, and his suspicion of anything that smacked of such a notion is bound up with his lifelong distaste for the idea of authority – the idea that anything could have authority over the members of a democratic community save the free, collective, decisions of that community. This anti-authoritarian motif is perhaps clearest in his "Christianity and Democracy" – an early essay to which Alan Ryan has recently called our attention, saying that it is "a dazzling and dazzlingly brave piece of work."[15] Indeed it is. It must have seemed strange to the University of Michigan's Christian Students Association to be told, in 1892, that "God is essentially and only the self-revealing" and that "the revelation is complete only as men come to realize him."

13   James, *The Will to Believe*, p. 29.
14   James, *Varieties of Religious Experience*, pp. 407, 400, 405 respectively.
15   Alan Ryan, *John Dewey and the High Tide of American Liberalism* (New York: Norton, 1995), p. 102.

Dewey spelled out what he meant by going on to say, "Had Jesus Christ made an absolute, detailed and explicit statement upon all the facts of life, that statement would not have had meaning – it would not have been revelation – until men began to realize in their own action the truth that he declared – until they themselves began to *live* it."[16] This amounts to saying that even if a nonhuman authority tells you something, the only way to figure out whether what you have been told is true is to see whether it gets you the sort of life you want. The only way is to apply the utilitarian test for whether the suggestion made proves to be "good in the way of belief." Granted that hearing what such a being has to say may change your wants, you nevertheless test those new wants and that purported truth in the same way: by living them, trying them out in everyday life, seeing whether they make you and yours happier.

Suppose that a source you believe to be nonhuman tells you that all men are brothers, that the attempt to make yourself and those you cherish happier should be expanded into an attempt to make all human beings happy. For Dewey, the source of this suggestion is irrelevant. You might have heard it from a god or a guru, but you might just as well have found it carved out by the waves on a sandy beach. It has no validity unless it is treated as an hypothesis, tried out, and found successful. The good thing about Christianity, Dewey is saying, is that it has been found to work.

More specifically, what has been found to work is the idea of fraternity and equality as a basis for social organization. This worked not just as a Thrasymachian device for avoiding pain – what Rawls calls a "mere modus vivendi" – but as a source of the kind of spiritual transfiguration that Platonism and the Christian churches have told us would have to wait upon a future intersection of time with eternity. It makes possible precisely the sort of nobility of spirit that Nietzsche mistakenly thought could be had only by the exceptional few – those who were capable of being greatly happy.

"Democracy," Dewey says, "is neither a form of government nor a social expediency, but a metaphysic of the relation of man and his experience in nature."[17] The point of calling it a metaphysic is not, of course, that it is an accurate account of the fundamental relation of reality, but that if one shares Whitman's sense of glorious democratic vistas stretching on indefinitely into the future one has everything which Platonists hoped to get out of such an account. For Whitman offers what Tillich called "a symbol of ultimate concern," of something that can be loved with all one's heart and soul and mind.

Plato's mistake, in Dewey's view, was having identified the ultimate object of *eros* with something unique, atemporal, and nonhuman rather than with an indefinitely expansible pantheon of transitory temporal accomplishments, both natural and cultural. This mistake lent aid and comfort to monotheism. Dewey might well have agreed with Nietzsche that "Monotheism, this rigid consequence of the doctrine of one normal human type – the faith in one normal god beside whom there are only pseudo-gods – was perhaps the greatest danger that has yet confronted humanity."[18]

16 John Dewey, *Early Works of John Dewey* (Carbondale: Southern Illinois University Press, 1969), vol. 3, pp. 6–7.
17 Dewey, "Maeterlinck's Philosophy of Life," *The Middle Works of John Dewey*, vol. 6. Dewey says that Emerson, Whitman, and Maeterlinck are the only three to have grasped this fact about democracy.
18 Nietzsche, *The Gay Science*, section 143: "Der Monotheismus … diese starre Konsequenz der Lehre von einem Normalmenschen – also der Glaube an einen Normalgott, neben dem es nur noch falsche Luegengoetter gibt – war vielleicht die groesste Gefahr der bisherigen Menscheit."

When Christianity is treated as a merely social gospel, it acquires the advantage which Nietzsche attributes to polytheism: it makes the most important human achievement "creating for ourselves our own new eyes," and thereby "honors the rights of individuals." As Dewey put it, "Government, business, art, religion, all social institutions have … a purpose[:] … to set free the capacities of human individuals. … [T]he test of their value is the extent to which they educate every individual into the full stature of his possibility."[19] In a democratic society, everybody gets to worship his or her personal symbol of ultimate concern, unless worship of that symbol interferes with the pursuit of happiness by his or her fellow-citizens. Accepting that utilitarian constraint, the one Mill formulated in *On Liberty*, is the only obligation imposed by democratic citizenship, the only exception to democracy's commitment to honor the rights of individuals.

This means that nobody is under any constraint to seek Truth, nor to care, any more than Sherlock Holmes did, whether the earth revolves around the sun or conversely. Scientific theories become, as do theological and philosophical ones, optional tools for the facilitation of individual or social projects. Scientists thereby lose the position they inherited from the monotheistic priesthood, as the people who pay proper tribute to the authority of something "not ourselves."

"Not ourselves" is a term that tolls like a bell throughout the text of Arnold's *Literature and Dogma*, and this may be one of the reasons Dewey had a particular dislike for Arnold.[20] Once he got out from under his mother's Calvinism, Dewey distrusted nothing more than the suggestion that there was a nonhuman authority to which human beings owed respect. He praised democracy as the *only* form of "moral and social faith" that does *not* "rest upon the idea that experience must be subjected at some point or other to some form of external control: to some 'authority' alleged to exist outside the process of experience."[21]

This passage in an essay of 1939 echoes one written forty-seven years earlier. In "Christianity and Democracy" Dewey had said that "The one claim that Christianity makes is that God is truth; that as truth He is love and reveals Himself fully to man, keeping back nothing of Himself; that man is so one with the truth thus revealed that it is not so much revealed *to* him as *in* him; he is its incarnation."[22] For Dewey God is in no way Kierkegaard's Wholly Other. Nor is he One. Rather, he is all the varied sublimities human beings come to see through the eyes that they themselves create.

If atheism were identical with antimonotheism, then Dewey would have been as aggressive an atheist as has ever lived. The idea that God might have kept something back, that there might be something not ourselves that it was our duty to discover, was as distasteful to him as was the idea that God could tell us which of our needs took priority over others. He reserved his awe for the universe as a whole, "the community

---

19   Dewey, *Reconstruction in Philosophy*, in *Middle Works*, vol. 12, p. 186.
20   See Dewey, *A Common Faith*, in *Later Works*, vol. 9, p. 36, and also Dewey's early essay "Poetry and Philosophy." In the latter Dewey says that "the source of regret which inspires Arnold's lines is his consciousness of a twofold isolation of man – his isolation from nature, his isolation from his fellow-man" (*Early Works*, vol. 3, p. 115).
21   "Creative Democracy – The Task Before Us" (1939). The passage cited is in *Later Works*, vol. 14, p. 229. Dewey says that he is here "stating briefly the democratic faith in the formal terms of a philosophic position."
22   Dewey, *Early Works*, vol. 4, p. 5.

of causes and consequences in which we, together with those not born, are enmeshed." "The continuing life of this comprehensive community of beings," he said, "includes all the significant achievement of men in science and art and all the kindly offices of inter- course and communication."

Notice, in the passages I have just quoted, the phrase "together with those not born" and also the adjective "continuing." Dewey's distaste for the eternity and stability on which monotheism prides itself is so great that he can never refer to the universe as a whole without reminding us that the universe is still evolving – still experimenting, still fashioning new eyes with which to see itself.

Wordsworth's version of pantheism meant a great deal to Dewey, but Whitman's insistence on futurity meant more. Wordsworth's pantheism saves us from what Arnold called "Hebraism" by making it impossible to treat, as Dewey put it, "the drama of sin and redemption enacted within the isolated and lonely soul of man as the one thing of ultimate importance." But Whitman does something more. He tells us that nonhuman nature culminates in a community of free men, in their collaboration in building a soci- ety in which, as Dewey said, "poetry and religious feeling will be the unforced flowers of life."[23]

Dewey's principal symbol of what he called "the union of the ideal and the actual" was the United States of America treated as Whitman treated it: as a symbol of openness to the possibility of as yet undreamt of, ever more diverse, forms of human happiness. Much of what Dewey wrote consists of endless reiteration of Whitman's caution that "America ... counts, as I reckon, for her justification and success, (for who, as yet, dare claim success?) almost entirely on the future. ... For our New World I consider far less important for what it has done, or what it is, than for results to come."[24]

23 Dewey, *Reconstruction in Philosophy*, in *Middle Works*, vol. 12, p. 201.
24 Walt Whitman, *Democratic Vistas*, in *Complete Poetry and Selected Prose* (New York: Library of America, 1982), p. 929.

28

Religion in the Public Square: A Reconsideration

Some years ago I wrote a response to Stephen Carter's book, *The Culture of Disbelief* (1994). Carter had argued that it was unfair to religious believers to try to keep religious convictions out of the public square. I replied that such exclusion was part of a reasonable compromise between secular democratic governments and ecclesiastical organizations.

Various forms of this traditional compromise are familiar: In the U.S. the government offers toleration, and various special privileges, for almost anything that chooses to call itself a religion. In exchange, the churches are supposed not to use the pulpit, or church funds, to support political candidates and proposals – or at least not to do so in so blatant a way as to lose their tax exemptions. The terms of this compromise are open to continual renegotiation.

In my reply to Carter I urged that democratic societies should, in the manner of Jefferson, think of themselves as having exchanged toleration for an assurance that believers would leave their religion at home when discussing political questions in public. However, reading Nicholas Wolterstorff's writings on this subject, notably an essay called "Why We Should Reject What Liberalism Tells Us about Speaking and Acting for Religious Reasons" (1997a), has convinced me that my response to Carter was hasty and insufficiently thoughtful. I have been impressed by Wolterstorff's arguments, and also by some of Jeffrey Stout's criticisms (in a forthcoming book) of my response to Carter. So I shall offer a chastened, and more cautious, restatement of my anti-clerical views.

I want to start back-pedaling by making a distinction between congregations of religious believers ministered to by pastors and what I shall be calling "ecclesiastical organizations" – organizations that accredit pastors and claim to offer authoritative guidance to believers. Only the latter are the target of secularists like myself. Our anti-clericalism is aimed at the Catholic bishops, the Mormon General Authorities, the televangelists, and all the other religious professionals who devote themselves not to pastoral care but to promulgating orthodoxy and acquiring economic and political clout. We think that it is mostly religion above the parish level that does the damage. For ecclesiastical organizations

Richard M. Rorty, "Religion in the Public Square: A Reconsideration," *Journal of Religious Ethics*, vol. 31 (1), Spring 2003, © 2003 Journal of Religious Ethics, Inc. Reproduced by permission of Blackwell Publishing Ltd.

typically maintain their existence by deliberately creating ill-will toward people who belong to other such organizations, and toward people whose behavior they presume to call immoral. They thereby create unnecessary human misery.

Secularists of my sort hope that ecclesiastical organizations will eventually wither away. We share Dewey's feeling that militant atheism is as unattractive as militant religious proselytizing, but we want to distinguish between atheism and anti-clericalism. We recognize that the disappearance of ecclesiastical institutions would leave a gap in the lives of religious believers, for they will no longer have a sense of being part of a great and powerful worldly institution. But that gap will be filled, we like to think, by a increased sense of participation in the advance of humanity – theists and atheists together, shoulder to shoulder – toward the fulfillment of social ideals.

As social justice increases, we hope there will be less temptation for the poor to murder the rich, and consequently less need for religion as a device for diminishing social unrest, and less temptation to hope for pie in the sky. So the only role left for religious belief will be to help individuals find meaning in their lives, and to serve as a help to individuals in their times of trouble. Religion will, in this secularist utopia, be pruned back to the parish level.

The social ideals we secular humanists champion are often cast in religious terms. But we hope that they will eventually cease to be so stated. This is not because we think that there is something intrinsically wrong with religious language. Religious belief, according to the "ethics of belief" that I share with William James, is not irrational, or intrinsically wrong-headed. But, in the first place, putting political convictions in religious terms gives aid and comfort to ecclesiastical organizations, and thus to religious exclusivism, contempt for people who should be accorded the same respect as the rest of their fellow-citizens. In the second place, leftist politics – the sort whose sacred texts are *On Liberty* and *Utilitarianism* – is strengthened just insofar as belief in a providential deity who will provide pie in the sky is weakened.

So we secularists have come to think that the best society would be one in which political action conducted in the name of religious belief is treated as a ladder up which our ancestors climbed, but one that now should be thrown away. We grant that ecclesiastical organizations have sometimes been on the right side, but we think that the occasional Gustavo Guttierez or Martin Luther King does not compensate for the ubiquitous Joseph Ratzingers and Jerry Falwells. History suggests to us that such organizations will always, on balance, do more harm than good.

I turn now to Wolterstorff's essays on the relation between religion and contemporary liberalism. He has convinced me that he is right to insist that both law and custom should leave him free to say, in the public square, that his endorsement of redistributionist social legislation is a result of his belief that God, in such passages as Psalm 72, has commanded that the cause of the poor should be defended. For I can think of no law or custom that would hinder him from doing so that would not hinder me from citing passages in John Stuart Mill in justification of the same legislation.

The fact that Psalm 72 belongs to a set of Scriptures claimed by various ecclesiastical organizations which I regard as politically dangerous is not a good reason to hinder Wolterstorff from citing this Psalm, any more than the fact that many people regard Mill's utilitarianism as morally dangerous is a good reason to stop me citing *On Liberty*. Neither law nor custom should stop either of us from bringing our favorite texts with us into the public square.

Suppose, however, that someone says that his reason for opposing legislation that permits same-sex marriage, or that repeals the anti-sodomy laws, is his commitment to the belief that Scripture, and in particular, the familiar homophobic passages in Leviticus and in Paul, trump all the arguments in favor of such legislation. Here I cannot help feeling that, though the law should not forbid someone from citing such texts in support of a political position, custom *should* forbid it. Citing such passages should be deemed not just in bad taste, but as heartlessly cruel, as reckless persecution, as incitement to violence. Religious people who claim a right to express their homophobia in public because it is a result of their religious convictions should, I think, be ashamed of themselves, and should be made to feel ashamed. Such citation should count as hate speech, and be treated as such.

I agree with the ACLU that most hate speech laws are probably impossible to reconcile with the First Amendment. But the absence of such laws should not prevent us from responding to the claim that homosexual sodomy is an abomination with "How dare you make your religious convictions an excuse for inflicting this kind of suffering on your fellow-citizens!" People who quote Leviticus 18:22 with approval should be shunned and despised. Our attitude to them should be the same as that toward people who remark that, though of course Hitler was a bad thing, it cannot be denied that the Jews *did* kill Christ – or, to vary the example, people who urge that, although the lynch mobs went too far, it is a truly terrible thing for a white woman to have sex with a black man.

This response would come pretty close to doing what Carter and Wolterstorff think should not be done: excluding certain appeals to religious conviction from the public square. So it would be nice if I could appeal to a principle which differentiated between citing Psalm 72 in favor of government-financed health insurance and citing Leviticus 18:22 in opposition to changes in the law that would make life in the U.S. more bearable for gays and lesbians. But I do not have one. I wholeheartedly believe that religious people should trim their utterances to suit my utilitarian views, and that in citing Leviticus they are, whether they know it or not, finding a vent for their own sadistic impulses. But I do not know how to make either of these propositions plausible to them.

I do not think that it is helpful to say that the homophobes are being "irrational." The efforts of moral philosophers to show that sexual orientation is "morally irrelevant" seem to me to beg all the questions against their opponents. So I view the struggle between utilitarians and homophobic Christian fundamentalists as no more a struggle between reason and unreason than is the Catholic–Protestant struggle in Northern Ireland. There is nothing called "reason" that stands above such struggles. On the subject of the vacuity of epistemological foundationalism, Wolterstorff and I are as one. We agree that there is no particular ground for believing that all reasonable and rational people will eventually come to agree on Rawls' principles of justice, or on any "comprehensive philosophical or religious doctrine" (see Wolterstorff 1997a).

We also agree that Robert Audi is wrong in deducing from "the concept of a liberal democracy" that it is incumbent on the citizens of such a democracy to "have an epistemologically adequate and motivationally sufficient basis for their political discussion, decisions and actions that is independent of each and every religion present in society" (1997b, 147). Like Wolterstorff, I have doubts about the utility of the notions of "epistemological adequacy" and "motivational sufficiency." I am not sure that we have criteria for measuring either. But even if such criteria could be supplied, I doubt that there is at present a consensus that good citizenship requires us to have non-religious bases for our political views.

I should be delighted if there were such a consensus, because I should be delighted if the U.S. became a society which was self-consciously and openly utilitarian in its understanding of the purpose of legislation and public policy. If we secular humanists have our way, the liberal democracies will eventually mutate into societies whose most sacred texts were written by John Stuart Mill. But there is a long way to go before that ideal is reached.

The extent of my agreement with Wolterstorff on philosophical questions leads me to think that my deepest disagreement with him is on empirical matters. We disagree about how much harm is being done in our own day by ecclesiastical organizations. We have different attitudes toward the following proposition, one that he puts in the mouth of his liberal opponents: "It's just too dangerous to let religious people debate political issues outside their own confessional circles ... the only way to forestall religious wars is to get people to stop invoking God and to stop invoking canonical scriptures when arguing and determining politics" (1997a, 167). Wolterstorff says that he finds no cogency in the reasoning that leads to this conclusion.

He adds, however, "I think that if I had been living in the seventeenth century I would have found it cogent." Wolterstorff thinks that the twentieth century is very different in the relevant respects from the seventeenth and that "liberalism's myopic preoccupation with religious wars is outdated." I disagree, and not just because of what is happening in, for example, Northern Ireland and Uttar Pradesh. My main reason for disagreement is that I think it would be difficult to convince either European Jews or American homosexuals that the difference between the two centuries is all that great. Nowadays the problem within most of the countries in which Christianity is the majority religion is not the possibility of religious war, but the sort of everyday peacetime sadism that uses religion to excuse cruelty.

The Protestant and Catholic churches of Western Europe did not exactly make war on the Jews during the nineteenth and early twentieth century. But they did keep up a steady barrage of contempt, combined with support for politicians running on anti-Semitic platforms, and with silence concerning the sadistic pogroms-cum-gang-rapes which provided weekend amusement for the devoutly religious peasants of Central and Eastern Europe. After the Holocaust, these churches fell all over themselves expounding the difference between their own religiously based anti-Semitism and the Nazis' racially based anti-Semitism. But the Jews have had difficulty appreciating this distinction. They think, correctly in my opinion, that if the Christian clergy had, in the century or so before Hitler, simply ceased to mention the Jews in their sermons, the Holocaust could not have happened.

There is, after all, not much basis for anti-Semitism in the Christian Scriptures. Its prominent role in the history of Christianity is the contribution of Christian ecclesiastical organizations. Those organizations would not have been unfaithful to Scripture if they had abstained from incitement to contempt and to sadistic brutality against Jews, but they would have lacked a way of bolstering the bigoted exclusivism that was one of their chief sources of money and power.

The situation is the same, nowadays, for homosexuals in the United States, who find themselves confronting two main enemies: ministers of the Christian religion who cite Leviticus 18:22 and gay bashers. The former are, unfortunately, considered respectable members of the community. Indeed, they exert very considerable political influence, even at the national level. These ministers sometimes try to distinguish themselves from the gay-bashers by saying that even though sodomy is an abomination, Christians must be kind and merciful even to the most disgusting and shameless sinners. The gays and lesbians, however, persist in thinking that if the churches would stop quoting Leviticus and Paul on the subject of sodomy, would stop saying that tolerance for homosexuals is a mark of moral decline, and would stop using tax-exempt funds to campaign for repeal of pro-gay ordinances and statutes, there would be fewer gay-bashers around.

Many gays and lesbians who are themselves religious believers might well agree with Wolterstorff that the homophobes have the right to bring religious reasons into the public square in order to urge the passage of laws to ensure that homosexuals cannot get married, can be discriminated against in employment and housing, and can be arrested for having sex. But they find it strange that such a large proportion of the time, money and energy of the Christian churches in the U.S. is devoted to this purpose. They are struck by the fact that religious reasons are now pretty much the *only* reasons brought forward in favor of treating them with contempt. Except for the mindless gay-bashing thugs, their fellow-churchgoers are the *only* people who still think that sodomy is a big deal. So gays and lesbians might reasonably conclude that the reason Christian pulpits have become the principal source of homophobia is the same as the reason that they were the principal source of European anti-Semitism – namely, that encouraging exclusivist bigotry brings money and power to ecclesiastical organizations.

A hundred years ago Polish and Russian Jews suspected that the joyous enthusiasm of the Christians who gang-raped Jewish girls during the pogroms did not really have much to do with the refusal of the Jews to acknowledge the divinity of Christ, or with their role in bringing him to trial before Pilate. The presence of Jews in a village down the road was, it seemed to them, just a good excuse for the local Christians to get their rocks off. The Orthodox and Catholic clergy recognized that pogroms played this role, and they did not want to be party-poopers. They found that they could become popular with their congregations by tacitly suggesting that such parties were held, so to speak, under divine auspices. It strikes many American homosexuals that the relation between the Christian clergy and the gay-bashers is much the same. There is nothing like a sense of banding together against a group that one has heard described as an object of divine disapproval and of justified disgust to encourage and excuse sadistic violence.

As I see it, we in America presently have a standoff between a sizable body of opinion that treats gays and lesbians as contemptible and despicable and another body of opinion that treats those who quote Leviticus 18:22 as contemptible and despicable. The former say that the latter are offensive to religious sensibilities. The latter say that the former are merely hiding sadistic grins behind sanctimonious masks. They are two sides of a *Kulturkampf*. Philosophers such as John Rawls, Thomas Scanlon, and Robert Audi have attempted to draw up rules of engagement for the *Kulturkampf*. I agree with Jeffrey Stout that attempts to find rules that are neutral between the two sides are pretty hopeless. So is the attempt to say that one or another contribution to political discourse is illegitimate.

I am torn, however, between agreement with Wolterstorff's defense of his right to cite Psalm 72 and the feeling that religious believers should not justify their support of or opposition to legislation *simply* by saying "Scripture says" or "Rome has spoken; the matter is closed" or "My church teaches...." It is one thing to explain how a given political stance is bound up with one's religious belief, and another to think that it is enough, when defending a political view, simply to cite authority, scriptural or otherwise.

It is OK for Christian believers to have Christian reasons for supporting redistribution of wealth or opposing same-sex marriage, but I am not sure it counts as having such reasons if the person who finds such marriage inconceivable is unwilling or unable even to discuss, for example, the seeming tension between Leviticus 22:18 and I Corinthians 13. The believer's fellow citizens should not take her as offering a reason unless she can say a lot more than that a certain ecclesiastical institution holds a certain view, or that such an institution insists that a given Scriptural passage be taken seriously, and at face value.

I would not consider myself to be seriously discussing politics with my fellow-citizens if I *simply* quoted passages from Mill at them, as opposed to using those passages to help me articulate my views. I cannot think of myself as engaged in such discussion if my opponent *simply* quotes the Bible, or a papal encyclical, at me. So I think that Audi is not *entirely* wrong when he says that "the concept of a liberal democracy" forbids certain moves being made in the course of political discussion. What should be discouraged is *mere* appeal to authority.

Protestantism has often, and rightly, been thought to be more congenial to liberal democracy than Catholicism. This is because the idea of "the priesthood of all believers" encourages the believer to interpret Scripture, theology and devotional literature on his own, rather than simply waiting to be informed by church officials about what is required to be a member in good standing of a given denomination. The latter attitude does seem to be the sort of thing democratic societies have a right to discourage.

Obviously they cannot do so by passing laws that tell congregants not to take ecclesiastical institutions as seriously as Catholics are asked to take papal authority. But there is nothing wrong, I think, with insisting that candidates for office do what John F. Kennedy did: namely, to make very clear indeed that they have no intention of taking ecclesiastical authority seriously when exercising the functions of the office to which they aspire. Kennedy did not say that he would cease to take the Catholic faith seriously. Nobody would have asked him to, and nobody would have believed him if he had done so. But there is a difference between the faith and the institution, and it has been an important feature of American democracy that that difference has become more and more salient in our political life.

I see this increasing salience as part of a welcome trend toward thinking that religion should be pruned back to the parish level. We should continue to view with alarm every attempt by ecclesiastical authorities to tell individual parishes or individual believers how to conduct themselves, or to limit the freedom of congregations to agree among themselves on the form of worship to be conducted.

This amounts to saying that I see liberal Protestantism as the form of Christian religious life most congenial to a liberal democracy. When I read that Stanley Hauerwas thinks that Rauschenbusch and Niebuhr were complicit in "the exclusion from the politics of democracy of any religious convictions that are not 'humble,'" I am inclined to respond that these two theologians didn't want humble convictions, but rather humbler ecclesiastical institutions – institutions that were more concerned with social justice and less with sustaining their own authority and political clout. When I am told by Stout that opponents of humility such as Hauerwas, MacIntyre and Milbank are now favored over Rauschenbusch and Niebuhr by students in Protestant seminaries, I fear for the republic. This bad news leads me to return to the *Kulturkampf* with redoubled vigor.

As an atheist, I may seem to have no business taking sides in matters that divide Christians from one another. But as a citizen I have every right to do so. If I think liberal democratic institutions are in danger from tax-exempt ecclesiastical institutions, I shall do well to warn my fellow-citizens against their insidious influence, just as I do when they are endangered by greedy corporations. I have as much right to urge the social ostracism of homophobic preachers as they do to abuse gays and lesbians.

My response to Steven Carter's book was titled "Religion as a Conversation-Stopper." Stout rightly rejoined, on Carter's behalf, that it is false that religion is "essentially" a conversation-stopper, because it is not "essentially" anything. But, Stout continued, it is true that one variety of expressions of religious belief does indeed stop the conversation, as when somebody says, "Don't ask me for reasons. I don't have any. It is a matter of faith."

As Stout properly reminds us, this kind of reply is not confined to the religious. It is the one I should have to make if I were asked why I believe that the aim of political life should be the greatest happiness of the greatest number. So, instead of saying that religion was a conversation-stopper, I should have simply said that citizens of a democracy should try to put off invoking conversation-stoppers as long as possible. We should do our best to keep the conversation going without citing unarguable first principles, either philosophical or religious. If we are sometimes driven to such citation, we should see ourselves as having failed, not as having triumphed.

References

Rorty, Richard
    1994   "Religion as Conversation-Stopper." *Common Knowledge* 3:1 (Spring), 1–6.
    1999   *Philosophy and Social Hope*. London: Penguin Books.

Wolterstorff, Nicholas
    1997a   "Why We Should Reject What Liberalism Tells Us about Speaking and Acting for Religious Reasons." In *Religion and Contemporary Liberalism*, ed. Paul J. Weithman. Notre Dame: University of Notre Dame Press, 162–181.
    1997b   "Audi on Religion, Politics and Liberal Democracy." In *Religion in the Public Square*, by Robert Audi and Nicholas Wolterstorff. Lanham: Rowman & Littlefield.

Is "Cultural Recognition" a Useful Concept for Leftist Politics?

Judith Butler and Nancy Fraser are among the most widely read and discussed philosophers in the USA. I want to discuss a point on which I differ from both of them – the utility of the notion of "cultural recognition." They take for granted that this notion is, or should be, at or near the centre of leftist political thinking. I doubt this, and will use this occasion to say why.

I frequently assign articles by Butler and Fraser to my students. They read those assignments with relish and appreciation, and the ensuing class discussion is often unusually lively. The students typically find the notions of "culture" and "cultural recognition" as important as do Butler and Fraser, and are baffled by my doubts about their utility. They regard my attempts to brush these notions aside, and my scepticism about the recent vogue of "cultural studies" in departments of literature, as symptoms of blindness to the current political situation. When I suggest that the growing "cultural studies" literature does not amount to much as a form of leftist political activity, they sharply disagree. They do the same when I suggest, as I did in my book *Achieving our Country,* that the American academic left overestimates the utility of philosophy, and that terms like "deconstruction," "subject-position" and "power" are of little help in deliberating about what is to be done.[1]

In discussion with students concerning these matters, I often have the feeling of just not getting it. I suspect that I am missing something, and that the rising generation may glimpse something I do not. Even if this is the case, however, it may be useful for me to lay out my persisting doubts in some detail. Setting them down might help clarify the differences between habits of mind characteristic of my generation, whose leftism is a product of the 1940s and 1950s, and those characteristic of people whose leftism took shape in the 1970s and 1980s, and owed a great deal to memories of the 1960s.

A few decades ago, the term "culture" rarely came up in political discussion. The idea that we should assign "positive value" to many different cultures had not yet surfaced,

Richard M. Rorty, "Is 'Cultural Recognition' a Useful Concept for Leftist Politics?" *Critical Horizons*, vol. 1 (1), 2000: 7–20, © 2000 by Critical Horizons. Reprinted by permission of Acumen Publishing Ltd.

1 Richard Rorty, *Achieving our Country: Leftist Thought in Twentieth Century America,* Harvard University Press: Massachusetts, 1998.

except in specifically anthropological contexts. In those days, American leftists talked about the need to overcome prejudice against stigmatised groups rather than about the need to grant recognition to the cultures of these groups. The central leftist idea then was that we all share a common humanity, and that this commonality makes us fit to be citizens of the same nations, to marry each others' brothers and sisters, and so on. The notion of "respect for differences" had not yet made its appearance.

Up through the Sixties, "prejudice" was the word leftists used to signify inability to acknowledge this commonality, and a consequent failure to treat other people fairly. To say that someone is prejudiced, in this sense, is to say that he or she prejudges fellow-humans who are members of despised groups. Prejudiced people assume that membership in such a group trumps everything else – that no feature of intellect or character can redeem such membership, and that the stigma of membership in the despised group makes marriage, friendship, and other cherished forms of association very difficult. Such people are reluctant to think of members of despised groups as fellow-citizens. They assume that people who bear a certain ineradicable stigma are not worth knowing, much less talking with about public affairs.

Many people – especially poor people – gain great benefits from being prejudiced. For they can maintain their own sense of worth by contrasting themselves with purported natural inferiors. Their prejudices are integral to their self-respect. In America, the paradigm of this phenomenon was the need of poor whites in the post-slavery South to take pride in not being "niggers." This need drove them to maintain and defend a system in which African-Americans were treated as only semi-human.

People like these poor whites think of the members of stigmatised groups as degraded specimens of humanity, people whom they would be disgusted to think of their sister or brother marrying. The blood of such people carries pollution. Similarly, many straight men and women would feel blemished by physical proximity to a homosexual, and would regard themselves as having been permanently damaged should they once take part in a homosexual act. These are a few among many examples of the sort of patterns of exclusion which became institutionalised in the caste systems of India, Japan, and many other places. Whole societies have been organised around ideas of purity and pollution. These are the societies the left has always hoped may someday be replaced by a society in which no human being is regarded as anything less than a full-fledged member of both the species and the local community.

In the old days, American leftists assumed that creating a decent and civilised society was in part a matter of redistributing money and opportunity, and in part a matter of erasing stigma by eliminating prejudice. The two efforts were assumed to go hand in hand. No theoretical problems arose about how to integrate the two, though many practical problems did. In those days, the question of whether blacks, or members of lower castes, or manual workers, or women, or homosexuals, had a culture of their own – one which it behooved their oppressors to understand and appreciate – did not often arise.

All this was before the rise of second-wave feminism. That movement owed a great deal to the example set by Dr. King's Civil Rights Movement, as did the movement for gay and lesbian rights. But though gay and lesbian activists could speak of the need to eliminate prejudice and stigma, that terminology did not work well as a description of the changes for which feminists were working. The humiliation of women by men is not happily described as a result of men's *prejudice* against women. Being a woman is not exactly a matter of bearing a *stigma*. Women as a group are not scapegoated in the way blacks or Jews are. Scapegoats must be driven out or killed, whereas wives are too useful to be dispensed with. A man's connection with a woman is thought to pollute him only in occasional, special, circumstances.

"Recognition," however, is a term which works equally well to describe what blacks need from whites, gays need from straights, and women need from men. They all need to be recognised as full members of the species, sharing in the common humanity that straight white males, within a given local community, typically take for granted in their dealings with one another. When the new social movements, with second-wave feminism in the vanguard, tried to bring their struggles under a common rubric, "the need for recognition" seemed more apposite than "the need to eliminate prejudice."

It is less clear, however, why "recognition" came to be thought of as recognition of *culture* or of "cultural differences," rather than as recognition of a common humanity. One reason may be that a claim frequently made about stigmatised people has been that they lacked, and would forever be unable to acquire, culture – culture in the older, Arnoldian, sense. A similar inability was, until very recently, attributed to women by men: they might acquire a kind of lightweight culture (centred around piano-playing and novel-reading) but not the sort of heavyweight culture required to become, for example, professors or legislators. So one part of granting recognition to black Americans, manual labourers, and women, was to concede that they too had the kind of dense, comforting, web of associations, memories, and traditions which the ruling males had thought unique to themselves (and which they sometimes thought could be had only by people with an old fashioned classical education). Raymond Williams' work was particularly important in changing the intellectuals' way of using the term "culture" to mean something less Arnoldian and more anthropological.

It helps, when trying to recognise a common humanity in a person of another gender, class, or ethnicity, to think of them as having as rich an inner life as one does oneself. To picture such an inner life, it helps to know something about the web of memories and associations which make it up. So one way to help eliminate prejudice and erase stigma is to point out that, for example, women have a history, that homosexuals take pride in belonging to the same stigmatised group as Proust, and that African-Americans have detailed memories of the battles which make up what Russell Banks calls "the three hundred year War Between The Races in America" – the sort of memories whites are currently learning about from Toni Morrison's novels. It helps to realise that all such groups wrap a comforting blanket of memories and traditions, customs and institutions, around themselves, just as do classical scholars, old Etonians, or members of the Benevolent and Protective Order of Elks.

Yet drawing attention to this fact is hardly the only way to eliminate prejudice. Another way is to get the prejudiced to see the stigmatised as having the same tendency to bleed when pricked as they themselves: they too worry about their children and parents; they are possessed by the same self-doubts, and lose self-confidence when humiliated; their difficulties in moving from one stage of life to another are much like everyone else's, despite the fact that their life-chances may be minimal. These ways of emphasising commonality rather than difference have little to do with "cultural recognition." They have to do with experiences shared by members of all cultures and all historical epochs, and which remain pretty much the same despite cultural change.

So we still need an explanation of why cultural recognition is thought so important. I think one reason it has become so important in the discourse of the American academic left may be the result of a specifically academic set of circumstances. The only thing we academics can do, in our specifically professional capacities, to eliminate prejudice is to write women's history, celebrate black artistic achievements, and the like. This is what academics who work in such programs as Women's Studies, African-American Studies, and Gay Studies do best. These programs are the academic arms of the new social movements – the movements which, as Judith Butler rightly says, have kept the left alive in the United States in recent years, years during which the rich have consistently had the best of it in the class struggle.

When these academic programs were set up, their founders could not describe themselves as attempting to use the tax-supported resources of the higher education system to pursue political goals – the description preferred by rightist opponents of these programs. Yet the rightists' description was, as far as it went, accurate enough. These programs are, among other things, attempts to continue doing what colleges and universities have, thank God, been doing more and more in recent times: helping the societies which they serve become more generous and tolerant. Still, you cannot persuade a university faculty to institute a new academic program by pointing out that such a program will help change the manners and morals of the citizenry for the better – that it will correct the opinions of the students, and cause them to be less prejudiced than their parents. You need to describe the projected new program as pursuing some apolitical, purely academic, purpose. So those who set up such programs often said that they would devote themselves to studying the *culture* of one or another stigmatised group, an area which previous scholarship had neglected.

I suspect that this pragmatic accommodation to the customs of academic life did a lot to insure that "cultural recognition" would replace "eliminating prejudice" as a leftist political goal. It may help explain why American leftists now talk about recognition of difference rather than about recognition of a common humanity. For the vast majority of leftists in the US now are, we must sadly admit, academics. It is tempting for any group to think that the means they have found to promote a decent and civilised society are essential means to that goal – that any program for reaching that goal must feature their own speciality.

The generation of academics whose political views were formed in the Sixties became, after McGovern's defeat in 1972, distrustful of the idea of reform, and of appeals to the good judgement of an electorate which had re-elected Nixon by a landslide. Because all the campaigning for McGovern had come to nothing, it seemed unlikely that envelope-licking, leafleting, picketing, demonstrating, and similar modes of participating in the political progress would do much good. So it was tempting for this generation to think that perhaps they could promote a cultural, rather than a political revolution – one which would eventually do some political good.

As I said in *Achieving Our Country,* a kind of cultural revolution actually took place. Between 1972 and the present the treatment of women, African-Americans and gays by American institutions and American straight white males improved enormously, thanks in large measure to the generation of teachers that entered the schools, colleges and universities between 1975 and 1990. But, as I also said in that book, nothing much has been done by that generation to help underpaid straight white males make more money. Culture pushed economics aside, in part because the maturing Sixties leftists had a lot of ideas about cultural change, but few ideas about how to counter Reagan's soak-the-poor policies, what to do for the unemployed in the Rust Belt, or how to make sure that a global economy did not pauperise American wage-earners. Because culture pushed economics aside, the straight white male working class in America may find it tempting to think that the leftist academy is uninterested in its problems.

Nowadays, as Nancy Fraser says, "demands for 'recognition of difference' fuel struggles of groups mobilised under the banners of nationality, ethnicity, 'race,' gender, and sexuality."[2] But I am not sure that such demands add anything useful to the old demand that these groups not be (in Fraser's words) "routinely maligned or disparaged in stereotypic public cultural representations and/or in everyday life interactions."[3] The difference between the old and the new demands is the difference between asking not to be singled out for ill-treatment and asking for attention to, and respect for, one's distinctive features. The new demand is harder to meet than the older, and I am not sure that there is any good reason for the change from the easier to the more stringent demand.

The only plausible explanation I can give for this change is that the post-Sixties academic left knows a lot about these differences, and thinks that the public as a whole ought to take an interest in them. This phenomenon strikes me as analogous to the Marxist students of the Thirties knowing a lot about dialectical materialism, and concluding that the members of the UAW ought to take an interest in this subject, lest they succumb to the temptations of bourgeois, non-revolutionary, trade unionism. Those students, like the present generation of leftist academics, desperately wanted to be of use to those who were getting the dirty end of the stick. So they overestimated the importance of their own expertise. The attempt to put "cultural recognition" on a par with redistribution seems to me the result of a similar overestimation: the academics are desperately eager to assure themselves that what they are doing is central, rather than marginal, to leftist politics.

Like Fraser, I quite agree with Charles Taylor that disrespect dictated by prejudice, or by the age-old assumption that women are second-rate members of the species, can "inflict a grievous wound, saddling people with crippling self-hatred."[4] I also agree with Axel Honneth's Hegelian claim that "we owe our integrity ... to the receipt of approval or recognition from other persons."[5] We are crippled unless most of the people we encounter treat us as conversable and as trustworthy partners in co-operative projects. But the idea that we need recognition *as members of a particular community, rather than as individuals* is not prominent in Hegel, and is not intuitively evident. The Hegelian dialectic of master and slave, a dialectic easily rewritten as that of husband and wife, does not take place between cultures but between individuals.

David Bromwich, in his *Politics by Other Means,* has pointed out that the change from "eliminating prejudice" to "recognising cultural differences" has produced confusion on the left because it runs athwart everything individualistic in recent Western ways of thinking – everything that suggests that we want, and should want, to be recognised

2   Nancy Fraser, "From Redistribution to Recognition? Dilemmas of Justice in a 'Postsocialist' Age," *New Left Review,* July/August 1995, no. 212, p. 68.
3   Ibid., p. 71.
4   Charles Taylor, *Multiculturalism and "The Politics of Recognition,"* Princeton University Press: Princeton, 1992, p. 25.
5   Axel Honneth, "Integrity and Disrespect: Principles of a Conception of Morality Based on a Theory of Recognition," *Political Theory,* May 1992, vol. 20. no. 2, p. 188.

either simply as human, or else for our individual traits and achievements.[6] This suggestion has been central to most of the left's rhetoric since the French Revolution. It is hard to integrate this rhetoric with an insistence on the importance of cultural differences.

The old individualistic – and, at the limit, existentialist – ways of thinking suggest that a young person should not focus on what she owes to her ancestors, her parents, or the community from which she comes, but rather on how she might break free of all those, and become who she is. We think well of someone who refuses to be stereotyped as an X, resents being thought of as an X, and tries to create a self-image for herself which escapes all the classificatory terminologies employed by those around her. If someone chooses *not* to break free from her roots, and instead tries to develop a self-image to which group membership is central, we think it important that this decision be fully conscious and entirely free, rather than being treated as the recognition of an evident duty.

This admiration for self-creating independence has nothing to do with a belief in the Cartesian ego, and is entirely compatible with the claim that our selves are social constructions – with the realisation that our selves are contingent products of interactions with other people, and that these interactions are largely governed by what Foucault calls "power." One can agree with Foucault that all choices among alternative beliefs are made within the limits of the truth-candidates available at the time, and that these truth-candidates are available only because somebody had the power to suppress other candidates, while still retaining the individualistic, quasi-Nietzschean, ways of thinking that make us prize self-creation. (Foucault was himself, and knew himself to be, an admirable example of such self-creation.)

Nor does the recognition of our common humanity have anything to do with Kantian or Habermasian universalism. Such recognition is not a matter of believing that our consciences can be relied upon to give us the same instructions, or that moral and political discussion will converge to agreement, thanks to what Habermas and Apel call "the force of the better argument." As I said above, it is much more a matter of coming to think of previously despised people as like oneself in specific, concrete, banal ways: as bleeding when pricked, and crippled when shunned.

I think that if the left had continued to try to eliminate prejudice by emphasising such commonalities, rather than emphasising cultural differences, it might have been able to effect the same cultural revolution as in fact occurred. I doubt that the term "culture" added much weight or force to efforts to get people to treat previously despised groups as fellow-humans. So I would rephrase Fraser's statement that "The remedy for cultural injustice is some sort of cultural or symbolic change" in old-fashioned terms as "The remedy for thinking of people as, first and foremost, members of traditionally despised groups is to emphasise what these people share with those who despise them."[7]

Fraser goes on to say "This [remedy] could involve upwardly revaluing disrespected identities and the cultural products of maligned groups. It could also involve recognising and positively valorising cultural diversity."[8] I agree that it *could,* but it could also involve raising kids not to think much about whether people are black or female or gay or Navajo – to raise them so that they will see little point in questions like "What must it

---

6   David Bromwich, *Politics by Other Means: Higher Education and Group Thinking,* Yale University Press: New Haven, 1992.
7   Fraser, "From Redistribution to Recognition?," p. 73.
8   Ibid.

be like [to be a woman (or to be gay)]?" or "In what does black (or Navajo) identity consist?" or "Which cultural products are pre-eminently associated with being African-American? Vietnamese-American? Mexican-American?"

While reading Fraser's article, I kept asking myself what would be lost if one crossed out the word "cultural" in such contexts as "[homosexuals'] mode of collectivity is that of a despised sexuality, rooted in the cultural-valuational structure of society" or "homophobia: the cultural devaluation of homosexuality."[9] I kept wondering why in order to overcome homophobia we had to "accord positive recognition to gay and lesbian sexual specificity" rather than just raising children to think that being gay or lesbian is no big deal.[10] I wondered why, in order to overcome ethnic prejudice against recent immigrants, we had to try to interest people in these immigrants' native cultures.

Such doubts made me sceptical about the need for what Fraser calls "deconstruction," thought of as "deep restructuring of relations of recognition ... blurring group differentiation."[11] I am not sure that in order to eliminate prejudice we need a "transformative recognition politics of deconstruction."[12] Do we really need to replace "hierarchical racial dichotomies" by "demassified and shifting networks of multiple intersecting differences" rather than just, for example, trying to bring up white kids to think less about differences in skin colour and more about shared pains and pleasures?[13] Doing the latter would accomplish what Fraser calls weaning white people "from their attachment to current cultural constructions of their interests and identities" insofar as it would make it unimportant for white kids to think of themselves as white.[14] Granted that white kids badly need to learn the history of the War Between the Races, that is not the same thing as learning to appreciate the merits of a distinctively black culture.

I find much to admire in Fraser's analyses of the problems confronting the contemporary left, and I am more or less on her side in her disagreements with Iris Marion Young and with Judith Butler.[15] Still, I think that "deconstruction" is a fancier, more sophisticated weapon than the left needs. Fraser's suggestion that "deconstruction" be elevated to a par with "socialism" among leftist aims seems to me to smell of the lamp. Spotting latent incoherence in ideas, identities, and institutions, in the Derridean manner, is something people trained in various recently founded academic programs are often good at. But I doubt that this additional skill makes them any better equipped to help our society eliminate prejudice and increase fairness than, for example, training in battered women's shelters, AIDS support groups, or Head Start programs for black kids in the ghettos.

Fraser says that "the intersection of class, 'race,' gender, and sexuality intensifies the need for transformative solutions, making the combination of socialism and deconstruction

---

9   Ibid., p. 77.
10 Ibid., p. 78.
11 Ibid., p. 87.
12 Ibid., p. 88.
13 Ibid., p. 91.
14 Ibid., p. 91.
15 See Fraser's two chapters "Culture, Political Economy and Difference: On Iris Young's *Justice and the Politics of Difference*" and "False Antitheses: A Response to Seyla Benhabib and Judith Butler" in *Justice Interruptus: Critical Reflections on the 'Postsocialist' Condition,* Routledge: New York, 1996. See also, N. Fraser, "Heterosexism, Misrecognition, and Capitalism: A Response to Judith Butler," *Social Text,* 52/3, vol. 15, nos. 3 & 4, Fall/Winter, 1997, pp. 279–89.

more attractive still."[16] I cannot see the relevance of this intersection to anything as philosophically sophisticated as deconstruction. The intersection seems to amount merely to such facts as that someone may be humiliated or discriminated against for being a woman in the morning, for being black in the afternoon, and for being a lesbian in the evening, and low-paid for any or all of these three reasons. The remedies for this situation do not seem to me to have anything to do with questions about her "identity" as any of these. I am not sure that she will be helped by attending to the construction of such an identity, or that her persecutors will be helped by recognising it once it has been constructed.

Nor does it help to think about possible remedies when Judith Butler, describing the differences between social movements which may attempt alliances, reminds us of the "the self-difference of movement itself, a constitutive rupture that makes movements possible on nonidentitarian grounds, that installs a certain mobilising conflict as the basis of politicisation."[17] As a fellow student of Hegel and Derrida, I can see what she means when she says that "difference is the condition of the possibility of identity, or, rather its constitutive limit" but I do not see the relevance of this philosophical point to the problems encountered in getting movements to relieve the situation of African-Americans together with, for example, movements to relieve that of lesbians. It strikes me as about as *merely* philosophical as a point can get.

Butler says a bit later that:

> When new social movements are cast as so many "particularisms" in search of an overriding universal, it will be necessary to ask how the rubric of a universal itself only became possible through the erasure of the prior workings of social power. This is not to say that universals are impossible, but only that one abstracted from its location in power will always be falsifying and territorialising, and calls to be resisted at every level.[18]

I doubt the "always," and I do not see the relevance of the claim. In what sense does anybody want to bring the various new social movements under "a universal"? Negotiating local and provisional alliances between these movements (as when one movement offers votes, or money, or live bodies, to another) does not require finding a relevant "universal." Urging, as I have, that these new social movements need to get themselves hitched up, in the present American situation, to attempts to improve the lot of unemployed or ludicrously ill-paid straight white males, is not a matter of subsuming them under a universal. It is more like urging that taking several different medicines at once will have a desirable synergistic effect.

In the pages from which I have quoted, Butler is concerned to respond to people who claim that, as she puts it, "the cultural focus of leftist politics has splintered the Left into identitarian sects," with the result that we have "lost a set of common ideals and goals."[19] Todd Gitlin, Arthur Schlesinger and I have indeed said things of this sort. But I cannot see the relevance of Butler's philosophical points to our complaints, which are about the dangerous consequences of developing a left that neglects class and money by focusing

---

16   Fraser, "From Redistribution to Recognition?," p. 91.
17   Judith Butler, "Merely Cultural," *Social Text,* 52/3, vol. 15, nos. 3 & 4, Fall/Winter, 1997, p. 269.
18   Ibid., pp. 269–70.
19   Ibid., p. 265.

on the elimination of prejudice and sexism. I, and probably Gitlin and Schlesinger as well, would never dream of calling the new social movements "a self-centred and trivial form of politics."[20] Nor do we have an interest in exchanging these movements for "a more robust, serious and comprehensive vision of the systematic interrelatedness of social and economic conditions."[21] Doubtless there are such interrelations, but getting them mapped out is not a prerequisite for undertaking leftist initiatives which would serve the purposes of both the newer social movements and the older ones.

Fraser thinks it important to work out such a vision. Although I admire the philosophical acuity she brings to the production of analytical categories, I do not share her sense of priorities. Nor do I think that there is any way to put Fraser in the same box with Gitlin, Schlesinger and myself, as Butler seems to do. All that the three of us share with Fraser is that, like her, we should like to figure out a way to produce a stronger American left, a left which might become a voting majority of citizens. We all want to facilitate alliances between the victims of the Republicans' soak-the-poor legislation and people who are stigmatised, or deprived, for reasons other than poverty. The two groups overlap, but are not identical, and the Republicans are getting good at playing them off against each other.

Though I take it Butler too would like to help create a leftist majority among American voters, I doubt that the philosophical sophistication she brings to bear on questions of identity and difference will be of much use to the left in its attempt to pursue majoritarian politics. I am happy to agree that this sort of philosophical sophistication has been put to good use in the process of building up the academic wings of the new movements. But I see Butler as running together problems of academic politics with larger problems, and of trying to squeeze more political utility out of philosophical sophistication than she is likely to get. Butler says that:

> Within the academy, the effort to separate race studies from sexuality studies from gender studies marks various needs for autonomous articulation, but it also produces a set of important, painful, and promising confrontations that expose the ultimate limits to any such autonomy: the politics of sexuality within African American studies; the politics of race within queer studies, within the study of class, within feminism; the question of misogyny within any of the above, the question of homophobia within feminism - to name a few. This may seem to be precisely the tedium of identitarian struggles that a new, more inclusive left hopes to transcend.[22]

As I see it, however, it is not a matter of transcending these struggles, but of broadening the horizons of those who engage in them – of producing leftist students who spend less time thinking about efforts to separate, or not to separate, these various studies from one another. My own hunch is that they need to spend more time thinking about what will happen if American wages continue to sink toward the level of the global wage market. But whether I am right in this hunch or not, the question of what our students should be thinking about if the American Left is to grow stronger is a purely practical, and presently quite urgent, question. It is a question to which Derrida and Foucault are no more relevant than are Aquinas and Leibniz.

20 Ibid.
21 Ibid.
22 Ibid., p. 269.

The philosophers who seem to me most useful for leftist students are the old standbys - Mill and Dewey. Mill was right to urge that the aim of social institutions should be the encouragement of the greatest possible human diversity. But we should think of this diversity as he did, as a diversity of self-creating individuals, rather than a diversity of cultures. Our utopian dreams should be of a world in which cultures are seen as transitory comings-together of individuals – expedients for increasing human happiness rather than as the principal source of a person's sense of self-worth.

30

Philosophy as a
Transitional Genre

1 Introduction

Richard Bernstein and I are almost exact contemporaries, were educated in mostly the same places by mostly the same people, have been exalted by many of the same hopes, and have been talking to one another about how to fulfill those hopes for more than fifty years. We share not only many enthusiasms, but the vast majority of our convictions, both philosophical and political.

Though Bernstein has been much more politically active than I, I doubt that we have ever seriously disagreed about what measures to support, whom to vote for, or in what direction we want history to go. So what disagreements remain might be called "merely philosophical." This essay is one more attempt to restate my philosophical views in a form that may be a bit less vulnerable to Bernstein's objections.

This attempt is made easier because Bernstein's are among the most careful, detailed, and searching criticisms of my writings. He always understands my motives and intentions perfectly, never distorts or mocks what I say, yet often concludes that the view I am offering is largely wrong. I have been grateful for Bernstein's willingness to spend time reading my stuff ever since he gave me some invaluable advice about how to revise my *Philosophy and the Mirror of Nature*. That book owes a great deal to his comments, as does much that I have written since.

Bernstein has remarked, accurately, that the "aesthetic strain in [my] writings has become more and more pronounced over the years."[1] He has also pointed out that I spend a lot of time reiterating "a version of the narrative of the history of philosophy that has its origin in Nietzsche, has been refined and perpetuated by Heidegger and Derrida, and has been disseminated by many of those who identify themselves as poststructuralist, postmodern or deconstructionist writers" (*NC*, p. 251). In this essay

"Philosophy as a Transitional Genre," from Benhabib, Seyla, and Nancy Fraser (eds.), *Pragmatism, Critique, Judgment: Essays for Richard J. Bernstein*, pp. 3–28, © 2004 Massachusetts Institute of Technology, by permission of The MIT Press.

1 Richard Bernstein, *The New Constellation: The Ethical-Political Horizons of Modernity/Postmodernity* (Cambridge: Polity Press, 1991), pp. 233–234. Page references to this edition in the text are preceded by *NC*.

I rehearse this narrative yet again, and argue that its outcome should indeed be seen as the triumph, if not exactly [of] the aesthetic (a Kantian notion for which I have little use), of what I call the "literary." Once again, I am telling the old Nietzschean story about how "Truth" took the place of "God" in a secular culture, and why we should get rid of this God-surrogate in order to become more self-reliant. I am a hedgehog who, despite showering my reader with allusions and dropping lots of names, has really only one idea: the need to get beyond representationalism, and thus into an intellectual world in which human beings are responsible only to each other.

Bernstein is right to suspect that Dewey would have been unwilling to tell this story, and might have emphatically refused to endorse it. He has always had doubts about my attempts to fabricate a Nietzscheanized James, a Wittgensteinian Derrida, and a Heideggerianized Dewey. But what he calls my "ruthless and violent" readings of these authors are not eliminable extravangances. A way of getting Nietzsche, James, Wittgenstein, Derrida, Heidegger, and Dewey under the same antirepresentationalist tent, and a focus on the overlap between their views rather than on their disagreements, is pretty much all I have to offer. I want us to see all six of them as heralds of a new dawn − not just a new stage in the history of philosophy, but a new self-image for humanity. I think of them all as assisting in the takeover by what I call a "literary culture," a culture unlike anything that has existed in the past. Help in spelling out how they (and various other philosophers, such as Sellars, Davidson, and Brandom) do this is the only contribution I have to make.

Bernstein thinks that we need to move away from such visions of a new intellectual world and get back to the rough ground: to continue discussing the questions that Dewey took seriously and that I do not − questions, for example, about how "the structural dynamics of bourgeois society systematically undermine and belie liberal ideals" (*NC*, p. 245). He believes philosophers can serve good political causes by studying topics that I find relatively fruitless. He wants theoretical arguments for political stances, whereas I think such stances can be justified only by pointing to the results of actual or imagined social experiments. I doubt that he and I will ever break this deadlock, since our disagreement is not about the truth of propositions but about the fruitfulness of topics. All of us, by neglecting some issues and focusing on others, place our bets on what will and what will not seem worth discussing to future generations. Bernstein and I have made slightly different wagers.

I see discussing the structural dynamics of bourgeois society as a distraction from questions about how to use the tools of political reform available in the actually existing constitutional democracies to keep the rich from controlling the government. The gap between the level at which political theorists operate and the political alternatives we presently face seems to me just too great. Although I admire the skill with which Dewey and Habermas weave abstractions together in their writings on political theory, I cannot connect these abstractions with the political decisions we need to make. That is why I greatly prefer *geistesgeschichtlich* books like *Reconstruction in Philosophy* and *The Philosophical Discourse of Modernity* to such books as *The Public and Its Problems* and *Between Facts and Norms*.[2]

2   John Dewey, *Reconstruction in Philosophy* (Boston, Mass.: Beacon Press, 1948), and *The Public and Its Problems* (Chicago, Ill.: Gateway Books, 1946); Jürgen Habermas, *Philosophical Discourse of Modernity: Twelve Lectures*, trans. Frederick Lawrence (Cambridge, Mass.: The MIT Press, 1987), and *Between Facts and Norms*, trans. William Rehg (Cambridge, Mass.: The MIT Press, 1996).

Although the bulk of this essay is, as I have said, just one more retelling of my tediously familiar up-from-representationalism story, its last two sections were written in an attempt to deal with the sorts of doubts that Bernstein has expressed about my philosophical project. In these pages, Bernstein is the reader over my shoulder. I hope they may persuade him to see my use of the private–public distinction in a somewhat more favorable light. But whether they do or not, I am glad to have this occasion to express my gratitude for the stimulation that his criticisms have provided.

2 The Existence of Truth

Questions such as "Does truth exist?" or "Do you believe in truth?" seem fatuous and pointless. Everybody knows that the difference between true and false beliefs is as important as that between nourishing and poisonous foods. Moreover, one of the principal achievements of recent analytic philosophy is to have shown that the ability to wield the concept of "true belief" is a necessary condition for being a user of language, and thus for being a rational agent.

Nevertheless, the question "Do you believe in truth or are you one of those frivolous postmodernists?" is often the first one that journalists ask intellectuals whom they are assigned to interview. That question now plays the role once played by the question "Do you believe in God, or are you one of those dangerous atheists?" Literary types are frequently told that they do not love truth sufficiently. Such admonitions are delivered in the same tones in which their predecessors were reminded that the fear of the Lord is the beginning of wisdom.

Obviously, the sense of the word "truth" invoked by that question is not the everyday one. Nobody is worried about a mere nominalization of the adjective "true." The question "Do you believe that truth exists?" is shorthand for something like "Do you think that there is a natural terminus to inquiry, a way things really are, and that understanding what that way is will tell us what to do with ourselves?"

Those who, like myself, find themselves accused of postmodernist frivolity do not think that there is such a terminus. We think that inquiry is just another name for problem solving, and we cannot imagine inquiry into how human beings should live, into what we should make of ourselves, coming to an end. For solutions to old problems will produce fresh problems, and so on forever. As with the individual, so with both the society and the species: each stage of maturation will overcome previous dilemmas only by creating new ones.

Problems about what to do with ourselves, what purposes to serve, differ, in this respect, from scientific problems. A complete and final unified science, a harmoniously orchestrated assemblage of scientific theories none of which will ever need to be revised, is, perhaps, an intelligible goal. Maybe scientific inquiry could terminate, simply because anomalies stopped turning up. So if a unified account of the causal relations between all spatiotemporal events were all that were meant by "truth," even the farthest-out postmodernists would have no reason to doubt truth's existence. The existence of truth only becomes an issue when another sort of truth is in question.

I shall use the term "redemptive truth" for a set of beliefs that would end, once and for all, the process of reflection on what to do with ourselves. Redemptive truth would not consist in theories about how things interact causally, but instead would fulfill the need that religion and philosophy have attempted to satisfy. This is the need to fit everything – every thing, person, event, idea, and poem – into a single context, a context that will somehow reveal itself as natural, destined, and unique. It would be the only context that would matter for purposes of shaping our lives, because it would be the only one in which those lives appear as they truly are. To believe in redemptive truth is to believe that there is something that stands to human life as elementary physical particles stand to the four elements – something that is the reality behind the appearance, the one true description of what is going on, the final secret.

Hope that such a context can be found is one species of a larger genus. The larger genus is what Heidegger called the hope for authenticity – the hope to become one's own person rather than merely the creation of one's education or one's environment. As Heidegger emphasized, to achieve authenticity in this sense is not necessarily to *reject* one's past. It may instead be a matter of reinterpreting that past so as to make it more suitable for one's own purposes. What matters is to have seen one or more alternatives to the purposes that most people take for granted, and to have chosen among these alternatives – thereby, in some measure, creating yourself. As Harold Bloom has recently reminded us, the point of reading a great many books is to become aware of a great number of alternative purposes, and the point of *that* is to become an autonomous self.[3] Autonomy, in this un-Kantian and distinctively Bloomian sense, is pretty much the same thing as Heideggerian authenticity.

I shall define an intellectual as someone who yearns for Bloomian autonomy, and is lucky enough to have the money and leisure to do something about it: to visit different churches or gurus, go to different theatres or museums, and, above all, to read a lot of different books. Most human beings, even those who have the requisite money and leisure, are not intellectuals. If they read books it is not because they seek redemption but either because they wish to be entertained or distracted, or because they want to become better able to carry out some antecedent purpose. They do not read books to find out what purposes to have. The intellectuals do.

3 From Religion through Philosophy to Literature

Given these definitions of the terms "redemptive truth" and "intellectual," I can now state my thesis. It is that the intellectuals of the West have, since the Renaissance, progressed through three stages: they have hoped for redemption first from God, then from philosophy, and now from literature. Monotheistic religion offers hope for redemption through entering into a new relation to a supremely powerful nonhuman person. Belief in the articles of a creed may be only incidental to such a relationship. For philosophy, however, beliefs are of the essence. Redemption by philosophy is through the acquisition of a set of beliefs that represent things in the one way they really are. Literature, finally, offers redemption through making the acquaintance of as great a variety of human beings as possible. Here again, as in religion, true belief may be of little importance.

From within a literary culture, religion and philosophy appear as literary genres. As such, they are optional. Just as an intellectual may opt to read many poems but few novels, or many novels but few poems, so he or she may read much philosophy, or much

3 Harold Bloom, *How to Read and Why* (New York: Scribner, 2000).

religious writing, but relatively few poems or novels. The difference between the literary intellectuals' readings of *all* these books and other readings of them is that the inhabitant of a literary culture treats books as human attempts to meet human needs, rather than as acknowledgements of the power of a being that is what it is apart from any such needs. God and Truth are, respectively, the religious and the philosophical names for that sort of being.

The transition from religion to philosophy began with the revival of Platonism in the Renaissance, the period in which humanists began asking the same questions about Christian monotheism that Socrates had asked about Hesiod's pantheon. Socrates had suggested to Euthyphro that the real question was not whether one's actions were pleasing to the gods, but rather which gods held the correct views about what actions ought to be done. When that latter question was once again taken seriously, the road lay open to Kant's conclusion that even the Holy One of the Gospels must be judged in the light of one's own conscience.

The transition from a philosophical to a literary culture began shortly after Kant, about the time that Hegel warned us that philosophy paints its gray on gray only when a form of life has grown old. That remark helped the generation of Kierkegaard and Marx realize that philosophy was never going to fill the redemptive role that Hegel himself had claimed for it. Hegel's supremely ambitious claims for philosophy almost instantly flip-flopped into their dialectical opposite. His system was no sooner published than it began to be treated as a self-consuming artifact, the *reductio ad absurdum* of a form of intellectual life that suddenly seemed to be on its last legs.

Since Hegel's time, the intellectuals have been losing faith in philosophy. This amounts to losing faith in the idea that redemption can come in the form of true beliefs. In the literary culture that has been emerging during the last two hundred years, the question "Is it true?" has yielded to the question "What's new?" Heidegger thought that that change was a decline, a shift from serious thinking to mere gossipy curiosity.[4] Many fans of natural science, people who otherwise have no use for Heidegger, would agree with him on this point. On the account I am offering, however, this change is an advance. It represents a desirable replacement of bad questions like "What is Being?" "What is really real?" and "What is man?" with the sensible question "Does anybody have any new ideas about what we human beings might manage to make of ourselves?"

In its pure form, undiluted by philosophy, religion is a relation to a nonhuman person. This relation may be one of adoring obedience, or ecstatic communion, or quiet confidence, or some combination of these. But it is only when religion has become mingled with philosophy that this noncognitive, redemptive relation to a person begins to be mediated by a creed. Only when the God of the philosophers has begun to replace the God of Abraham, Isaac, and Jacob is correct belief thought to be essential to salvation.

For religion in its uncontaminated form, argument is no more in point than is belief. To become a New Being in Christ is, Kierkegaard insisted, not the same sort of thing as being forced to grant the truth of a proposition in the course of Socratic reflection, or as the outcome of Hegelian dialectic. Insofar as religion requires belief in a proposition, it is, as Locke said, belief based on the credit of the proposer rather than belief backed by argument. But beliefs are irrelevant to the special devotion of the illiterate believer to

---

4 Martin Heidegger, *Sein und Zeit* (Tübingen: Max Niemeyer Verlag, 1967), pp. 167–173. See the discussions of *das Gerede* and *die Neugier* in sections 35–36.

Demeter, or to the Virgin of Guadelupe, or to the little fat god on the third altar from the left at the temple down the street. It is this irrelevance that intellectuals like Saint Paul, Kierkegaard, and Karl Barth – spiritual athletes who relish the thought that their faith is a folly to the Greeks – hope to recapture.

To take seriously the idea that redemption can come in the form of true beliefs, one must believe both that the life that cannot be successfully argued for is not worth living, and that persistent argument will lead all inquirers to the same set of beliefs. Religion and literature, insofar as they are uncontaminated by philosophy, share neither of these convictions. Uncontaminated religion may be monotheistic in the sense that a community may think it essential to worship only one particular god. But the idea that there can *be* only one god, that polytheism is contrary to reason, is one that can take hold only after philosophy has convinced us that every human being's reflections must lead to the same outcome.

As I am using the terms "literature" and "literary culture," a culture that has substituted literature for both religion and philosophy finds redemption neither in a noncognitive relation to a nonhuman person nor in a cognitive relation to propositions, but in non-cognitive relations to other human beings, relations mediated by human artifacts such as books and buildings, paintings and songs. These artifacts provide a sense of alternative ways of being human. This sort of culture drops a presupposition common to religion and philosophy – that redemption must come from one's relation to something that is not just one more human creation.

Kierkegaard rightly said that philosophy began to set itself up as a rival to religion when Socrates suggested that our self-knowledge was a knowledge of God – that we had no need of help from a nonhuman person, because the truth was already within us. But literature began to set itself up as a rival to philosophy when people like Cervantes and Shakespeare began to suspect that human beings were, and ought to be, so diverse that there is no point in pretending that they all carry a single truth deep in their bosoms. Santayana pointed to this seismic cultural shift in his essay "The Absence of Religion in Shakespeare."[5] That essay might equally well have been called "The Absence of Either Religion or Philosophy in Shakespeare" or simply "The Absence of Truth in Shakespeare."

I suggested earlier that "Do you believe in truth?" can be given both sense and urgency if it is reformulated as "Do you think that there is a single set of beliefs that can serve a redemptive role in the lives of all human beings, that can be rationally justified to all human beings under optimal communicative conditions, and that will thus form the natural terminus of inquiry?" To answer "yes" to this reformulated question is to take philosophy as the guide of life. It is to agree with Socrates that there is a set of beliefs that is both susceptible of rational justification and such as to take rightful precedence over every other consideration in determining what to do with one's life. The premise of philosophy is that there is a way things really are – a way humanity and the rest of the universe are and always will be, independent of any merely contingent human needs and interests. Knowledge of this way is redemptive. It can therefore replace religion. The striving for Truth can take place of the search for God.

---

5   George Santayana, "The Absence of Religion in Shakespeare" (1900) in *Interpretations of Poetry and Religion*, ed. William G. Holzberger and Herman J. Saatkamp Jr. (Cambridge, Mass.: The MIT Press, 1990), pp. 91–101.

It is not clear that Homer, or even Sophocles, could have made sense of this suggestion. Before Plato dreamt them up, the constellation of ideas necessary to make sense of it were not available. Cervantes and Shakespeare understood Plato's suggestion, but they distrusted his motives. Their distrust led them to play up diversity and downplay commonality – to underline the differences between human beings rather than looking for a common human nature. This change of emphasis weakens the grip of the Platonic assumption that all these different sorts of people should be arranged in a hierarchy, judged on the basis of their relative success at attaining a single goal. Initiatives like Cervantes's and Shakespeare's helped create a new sort of intellectual – one who does not take the availability of redemptive truth for granted, and is not much interested in whether either God or Truth exist.

This change helped create today's high culture, one to which religion and philosophy have become marginal. To be sure, there are still numerous religious intellectuals, and even more philosophical ones. But bookish youngsters in search of redemption nowadays look first to novels, plays, and poems. The sort of books which the eighteenth century thought of as marginal have become central. The authors of *Rasselas* and of *Candide* helped bring about, but could hardly have foreseen, a culture in which the most revered writers neither write nor read either sermons or treatises on the nature of man and the universe.

For members of the literary culture, redemption is to be achieved by getting in touch with the present limits of the human imagination. That is why a literary culture is always in search of novelty, always hoping to spot what Shelley called "the gigantic shadows which futurity casts upon the present,"[6] rather than trying to escape from the temporal to the eternal. It is a premise of this culture that though the imagination has present limits, these limits are capable of being extended forever. The imagination endlessly consumes its own artifacts. It is an ever-living, ever-expanding, fire. It is as subject to time and chance as are the flies and the worms, but although it endures and preserves the memory of its past, it will continue to transcend its previous limits. Though the fear of belatedness is ever present within the literary culture, this very fear makes for a more intense blaze.

The sort of person I am calling a "literary intellectual" thinks that a life that is not lived close to the present limits of the human imagination is not worth living. For the Socratic idea of self-examination and self-knowledge, the literary intellectual substitutes the idea of enlarging the self by becoming acquainted with still more ways of being human. For the religious idea that a certain book or tradition might connect you up with a supremely powerful or supremely lovable nonhuman person, the literary intellectual substitutes the Bloomian thought that the more books you read, the more ways of being human you have considered, the more human you become – the less tempted by dreams of an escape from time and chance, the more convinced that we humans have nothing to rely on save one another. The great virtue of the literary culture that is gradually coming into being is that it tells young intellectuals that the only source of redemption is the human imagination, and that this fact should occasion pride rather than despair.

From the point of view of this culture, philosophy was a transitional stage in a process of gradually increasing self-reliance. Philosophy's attempt to replace God with Truth requires the conviction that a set of beliefs that can be justified to all human beings will

6 Percy Bysshe Shelley, "A Defense of Poetry" (1821) in *The Major Works*, ed. Zachary Leader and Michael O'Neill (Oxford: Oxford University Press, 2003), p. 701.

also fill all the needs of all human beings. But that idea was an inherently unstable compromise between the masochistic urge to submit to the nonhuman and the need to take proper pride in our humanity. Redemptive truth is an attempt to find something that is not made by human beings but to which human beings have a special, privileged relation not shared by the animals. The intrinsic nature of things is like a god in its independence of us, and yet – so Socrates and Hegel tell us – self-knowledge will suffice to get us in touch with it. One way to see the quest for knowledge of such a quasi-divinity is as Sartre saw it: it is a futile passion, a foredoomed attempt to become a for-itself-in-itself. But it would be better to see philosophy as one our greatest imaginative achievements, on a par with the invention of the gods.

Philosophers have often described religion as a primitive and insufficiently reflective attempt to philosophize. But, as I said earlier, a fully self-conscious literary culture would think of both religion and philosophy as relatively primitive, yet glorious, literary genres. They are genres in which it is now becoming increasingly difficult to write, but the genres that are replacing them might never have emerged had they not been read as swerves away from religion, and later as swerves away from philosophy. Religion and philosophy are not merely, from this point of view, ladders to be thrown away. Rather, they are stages in a process of maturation, a process that we should continually look back to, and recapitulate, in the hope of attaining still greater self-reliance.

4 The Culmination of Philosophy: Idealist and Materialist Metaphysics

In the hope of making this account of philosophy as a transitional genre more plausible, I shall say something about the two great movements in which philosophy culminated. Philosophy began to come into its own when the thinkers of the Enlightenment no longer had to hide themselves behind the sort of masks worn by Descartes, Hobbes, and Spinoza, and were able to be openly atheistic. These masks could be dropped after the French Revolution. That event, by making it plausible that human beings might build a new heaven and a new earth, made God seem far less necessary than before.

That newfound self-reliance produced two great metaphysical systems. First came the metaphysics of German idealism, and second, the reaction against idealism which was materialist metaphysics, the apotheosis of the results of natural science. The first movement belongs to the past. Materialist metaphysics, however, is still with us. It is, in fact, pretty much the only version of redemptive truth presently on offer. It is philosophy's last hurrah, its last attempt to provide redemptive truth and thereby avoid being demoted to the status of a literary genre.

This is not the place to recapitulate the rise and fall of German idealism, nor to eulogize what Heidegger called "the greatness, breadth, and originality of that spiritual world." It suffices for my present purposes to say that Hegel, the most original of the idealists, believed himself to have been given the first satisfactory proof of the existence of God, and the first satisfactory solution to the traditional theological problem of evil. He was, in his own eyes, the first fully successful natural theologian – the first to reconcile Socrates with Christ by showing that the Incarnation was not an act of grace on God's part but rather a necessity. "God," Hegel said, "had to have a Son" because eternity is nothing without time, God nothing without man, Truth nothing without its historical emergence.

In Hegel's eyes, the Platonic hope of escape from the temporal to the eternal was a primitive, albeit necessary, stage of philosophical thinking – a stage that the Christian doctrine of Incarnation has helped us outgrow. Now that Kant has opened the way to seeing mind and world as interdependent, Hegel believed, we are in a position to see that philosophy can bridge the Kantian distinction between the phenomenal and the noumenal, just as Christ's stay on earth overcame the distinction between God and man.

Idealist metaphysics seemed both true and demonstrable to some of the best minds of the nineteenth century. Josiah Royce, for example, wrote book after book arguing that Hegel was right: simple armchair reflection on the presuppositions of common sense, exactly the sort of philosophizing that Socrates practiced and commended, will lead you to recognize the truth of pantheism as surely as reflection on geometrical diagrams will lead you to the Pythagorean theorem. But the verdict of the literary culture on this metaphysics was nicely formulated by Kierkegaard when he said that if Hegel had written at the end of his books that "this was all just a thought experiment" he would have been the greatest thinker who ever lived, but that, as it was, he was merely a buffoon.[7]

I would rephrase Kierkegaard's point as follows: if Hegel had been able to stop thinking that he had given us redemptive truth, and claimed instead to have given us something *better* than redemptive truth – namely, a way of holding all the previous products of the human imagination together in a single vision – he would have been the first philosopher to admit that a better cultural product than philosophy had come on the market. He would have been the first philosopher to self-consciously replace philosophy with literature, just as Socrates and Plato were the first self-consciously to replace religion with philosophy. But instead Hegel presented himself (at least part of the time) as having discovered Absolute Truth, and men like Royce took him with a seriousness that now strikes us as both endearing and ludicrous. So it was left to Nietzsche, in *The Birth of Tragedy*, to tell us that the premise common to Socrates and Hegel should be rejected, and that the invention of the idea of self-knowledge was a great imaginative achievement that has outlived its usefulness.

Between Hegel's time and Nietzsche's, however, there arose the second of the great philosophical movements. It bore the same relation to Democritus and Lucretius that German idealism had borne to Parmenides and Plotinus. This was the attempt to put natural science in the place of both religion and Socratic reflection, to see empirical inquiry as providing exactly what Socrates thought it could never give us – redemptive truth.

By the middle of the nineteenth century, it had become clear that mathematics and empirical science were going to be the only areas of culture in which one might conceivably hope to get unanimous, rational agreement – the only disciplines able to provide beliefs that would not be overturned as history rolls along. They were the only sources of cumulative results – of propositions that were plausible candidates for the status of insight into the way things are in themselves. Unified natural science still seems to many intellectuals to be the answer to Socrates' prayers.

On the other hand, pretty much everybody in the nineteenth century had come to agree with Hume that Plato's model of cognitive success – mathematics – was never going to offer us anything redemptive. Only a few flaky neo-Pythagoreans still saw mathematics as having more than practical and aesthetic interest. So nineteenth century

7   Søren Kierkegaard, *Papers and Journals: A Selection*, trans. Alastair Hannay (London: Penguin, 1996). p. 182.

positivists drew the moral that the only other source of rational agreement and unshakable truth, empirical science, just *had* to have a redemptive function. Since philosophy had always taught that an account that bound everything together into a coherent whole would have redemptive value, and since the collapse of idealist metaphysics had left materialism as the only possible candidate for such an account, the positivists concluded that natural science was all the philosophy we would ever need.

This project of giving redemptive status to empirical science still appeals to two sorts of present-day intellectuals. The first is the kind of philosopher who insists that natural science attains objective truth in a way that no other portion of culture does. These philosophers usually go on to claim that the natural scientist is the paradigmatic posses-sor of intellectual virtues, notably the love of truth, that are rarely sought among literary critics. The second sort of intellectual who continues along the lines laid down by the nineteenth century positivists is the kind of scientist who announces that the latest work is in his discipline has deep philosophical implications: that advances in evolutionary biology or cognitive science, for example, do more than tell us how things work and what they are made of. They also tell us, these scientists say, something about how to live, about human nature, about what we really are. They provide, if not redemption, at least wisdom – not merely instructions on how to produce more effective tools for getting what we want but wise counsel about what we should want.

I shall take up these two groups of people separately. The problem about the attempt by philosophers to treat the empirical scientist as a paradigm of intellectual virtue is that the astrophysicist's love of truth seems no different from that of the classical philologist or the archive-oriented historian. All these people are trying hard to get something right. So, when it comes to that, are the master carpenter, the skilled accountant, and the careful surgeon. The need to get it right is central to all these people's sense of who they are, of what makes their lives worthwhile.

It is certainly the case that without people whose lives are centered around this need we should never have had much in the way of civilization. The free play of the imagina-tion is possible only because of the substructure literal-minded people have built. No artisans, no poets. No theoretical scientists to provide the technology of an industrialized world, few people with sufficient money to send their children off to be initiated into a literary culture. But there is no reason to take the contributions of the natural scientist to this substructure as having a moral or philosophical significance that is lacking in those of the carpenter, the accountant, and the surgeon.

John Dewey thought that the fact that the mathematical physicist enjoys greater pres-tige than the skilled artisan is an unfortunate legacy of the Platonic–Aristotelian distinc-tion between eternal truths and empirical truth, the elevation of leisured contemplation above sweaty practicality. His point might be restated by saying that the prestige of the scientific theorist is an unfortunate legacy of the Socratic idea that what we might all agree to be true is, as a result of rational debate, a reflection of something more than the fact of agreement – the idea that intersubjective agreement under ideal communicative conditions is a token of correspondence to the way things really are.

The current debate among analytic philosophers about whether truth is a matter of correspondence to reality, and the parallel debate over Kuhn's denial that science is asymptotically approaching the really real, are disputes between those who see empirical science as fulfilling at least some of Plato's hopes and those who think that those hopes should be abandoned. The former philosophers take it as a matter of unquestionable common sense that adding a brick to the edifice of knowledge is a matter of more accurately aligning thought and language with the way things really are. Their philosophical opponents take this so-called common sense to be merely what Dewey thought it: a relic of the religious hope that redemption can come from contact with something non-human and supremely powerful. To abandon the latter idea, the idea that links philosophy with religion, would mean acknowledging both the ability of scientists to add bricks to the edifice of knowledge and the practical utility of scientific theories for prediction while insisting on the irrelevance of both achievements to searches for redemption.

These debates among the analytic philosophers have little to do with the activities of the second sort of people whom I have labeled "materialist metaphysicians." These are the scientists who think that the public at large should take an interest in the latest discoveries about the genome, or cerebral localization, or child development, or quantum mechanics. Such scientists are good at dramatizing the contrast between the old scientific theories and the shiny new ones, but they are bad at explaining why we should care about the difference. They are like critics of art and literature who are good at pointing to the differences between the paintings and poems of a few years ago and those being produced now, but bad at explaining why these changes are important.

There is, however, a difference between such critics and the sort of scientists I am talking about. The former usually have the sense to avoid the mistake Clement Greenberg made – the mistake of claiming that what fills the art galleries this year is what all the ages have been leading up to, and that there is an inner logic to the history of the products of the imagination that has now reached its destined outcome. But the scientists still retain the idea that the latest product of the scientific imagination is not just an improvement on what was previously imagined, but is also closer to the intrinsic nature of things. That is why they found Kuhn's suggestion that they think of themselves as problem solvers so insulting. Their rhetoric remains "We have substituted reality for appearance!" rather than "We have solved some long-standing problems!" or "We have made it new!"

The trouble with this rhetoric is that it puts a glossy metaphysical varnish on a useful scientific product. It suggests that we have not only learned more about how to predict and control our environment and ourselves but have also done something more – something of redemptive significance. But the successive achievements of modern science exhausted their philosophical significance when they made clear that there are no spooks – that a causal account of the relations between spatiotemporal events did not require the operation of nonphysical forces.

Modern science, in short, has helped us see that if you want a metaphysics, then a materialistic metaphysics is the only one to have. But it has not given us any reason to think that we need a metaphysics. The need for metaphysics lasted only as long as the hope for redemptive truth lasted. But by the time that materialism triumphed over idealism, this hope had waned. So the reaction of most contemporary intellectuals to gee-whiz announcements of new scientific discoveries is "So what?" This reaction is not, as C. P. Snow thought, a matter of pretentious and ignorant litterateurs condescending to honest, hardworking empirical inquirers. It is the perfectly sensible reaction of someone who is thinking about ends and is offered information about means.

The literary culture's attitude toward materialist metaphysics is, and should be, something like this: whereas both Plato's and Hegel's attempts to give us something more interesting than physics were laudable attempts to find a redemptive discipline to put in the place of religion, a materialist metaphysics is just physics getting above itself. Modern science is a gloriously imaginative way of describing things, brilliantly successful for the purpose for which it was developed – namely, predicting and controlling phenomena. But it should not pretend to have the sort of redemptive power claimed by its defeated rival, idealist metaphysics.

Questions of the "So what?" sort began to be posed to scientists by intellectuals of the nineteenth century who were gradually learning, as Nietzsche was to put it, to see science through the optic of art, and art through that of life. Nietzsche's master Emerson was one such figure, and Baudelaire another. Although many of the literary intellectuals of this period thought of themselves as having transcended romanticism, they nevertheless could agree with Schiller that the further maturation of mankind will be achieved through what Kant called "the aesthetic" rather than through what he called "the ethical." They could also endorse Shelley's claim that the great task of human emancipation from priests and tyrants could have been accomplished without "Locke, Hume, Gibbon, Voltaire and Rousseau" but that "it exceeds all imagination to conceive what would have been the moral condition of the world if neither Dante, Petrarch, Boccaccio, Chaucer, Shakespeare, Calderon, Lord Bacon nor Milton, had ever existed; if Raphael and Michael Angelo had never been born; if the Hebrew poetry had never been translated, if a revival of the study of Greek literature had never taken place, if no monuments of ancient sculpture had been handed down to us, and if the poetry and the religion of the ancient world had been extinguished together with its belief."[8]

What Shelley said of Locke and Hume he might also have said of Galileo, Newton, and Lavoisier. What each of them said was well argued, useful, and true. But the sort of truth that is the product of successful argument cannot, Shelley thought, improve our moral condition. Of Galileo's and Locke's productions we may reasonably ask "Yes, but is it true?" But there is little point, Shelley rightly thought, in asking this question about Milton. "Objectively true," in the sense of "such as to gain permanent assent from all future members of the relevant expert culture," is not a notion that will ever be useful to literary intellectuals, for the progress of the literary imagination is not a matter of accumulating *results*.

We philosophers who are accused of not having sufficient respect for objective truth – the ones whom the materialist metaphysicians like to call "postmodern relativists" – think of objectivity as inter-subjectivity. So we can happily agree that scientists achieve objective truth in a way that litterateurs do not. But we explain this phenomenon sociologically rather than philosophically – by pointing out that natural scientists are organized into expert cultures in a way that literary intellectuals should not try to organize themselves. You can have an expert culture if you agree on what you want to get, but not if you are wondering what sort of life you ought to desire. We know what purposes scientific theories are supposed to serve. But we are not now, and never will be, in a position to say what purposes novels, poems, and plays are supposed to serve. For such books continually redefine our purposes.

5 The Literary Culture and Democratic Politics

So far I have said nothing about the relation of the literary culture to politics. I shall close by turning to that topic. For the quarrel between those who see the rise of the literary culture as a good thing and those who see it as a bad thing is largely a quarrel about what

8   Shelley, *Major Works*, p. 695.

sort of high culture will do the most to create and sustain the climate of tolerance that flourishes best in democratic societies.

Those who argue that a science-centered culture is best for this purpose, set the love of truth against hatred, passion, prejudice, superstition, and all the other forces of unreason from which Socrates and Plato claimed that philosophy could save us. But those on the other side of the argument are dubious about the Platonic opposition between reason and unreason. They see no need to relate the difference between tolerant conversability and stiff-necked unwillingness to hear the other side to a distinction between a higher part of ourselves that enables us to achieve redemption by getting in touch with nonhuman reality and another part that is merely animal.

The strong point of those who think that a proper respect for objective truth, and thus for science, is important for sustaining a climate of tolerance and good will is that argument is essential to both science and democracy. Both when choosing between alternative scientific theories and when choosing between alternative pieces of legislation, we want people to base their decisions on arguments – arguments that start from premises that can be made plausible to anyone who cares to look into the matter.

The priests rarely provided such arguments, nor do the literary intellectuals. So it is tempting to think of a preference for literature over science as a rejection of argument in favor of oracular pronouncements – a regression to something uncomfortably like the prephilosophical, religious, stage of Western intellectual life. Seen from this perspective, the rise of a literary culture looks like the treason of the clerks.

But those of us who rejoice in the emergence of the literary culture can counter this charge by saying that although argumentation is essential for projects of social cooperation, redemption is an individual, private, matter. Just as the rise of religious toleration depended on making a distinction between the needs of society and the needs of the individual, and on saying that religion was not necessary for the former, so the literary culture asks us to disjoin political deliberation from projects of redemption. This means acknowledging that private hopes for authenticity and autonomy should be left at home when the citizens of a democratic society foregather to deliberate about what is to be done.

Making this move amounts to saying: the only way in which science is relevant to politics is that the natural scientists provide a good example of social cooperation, of an expert culture in which argumentation flourishes. They thereby provide a model for political deliberation – a model of honesty, tolerance, and trust. This ability is a matter of procedure rather than results, which is why gangs of carpenters or teams of engineers can provide as good a model as do departments of astrophysics. The difference between reasoned agreement on how to solve a problem that has arisen in the course of constructing a house or a bridge, and reasoned agreement on what physicists sometimes call "a theory of everything" is, in this context, irrelevant. For whatever the last theory of everything tells us, it will do nothing to provide either political guidance or individual redemption.

The claim I have just made may seem arrogant and dogmatic, for it is certainly the case that some results of empirical inquiry have, in the past, made a difference to our self-image. Galileo and Darwin expelled various varieties of spooks by showing the sufficiency of a materialist account. They thereby made it much easier for us to move from a religious high culture to a secular, merely philosophical one. So my argument on behalf of the literary culture depends on the claim that getting rid of spooks, of causal agency that does not supervene on the behavior of elementary particles, has exhausted the utility of natural science for either redemptive or political purposes.

I do not put this claim forward as a result of philosophical reasoning or insight, but merely as a prediction about what the future holds in store. A similar prediction led the philosophers of the eighteenth century to think that the Christian religion had done about all that it could for the moral condition of humanity, and that it was time to put religion behind us and to put metaphysics, either idealist or materialist, in its place. When literary intellectuals assume that natural science has nothing to offer us except an edifying example of tolerant conversability, they are doing something analogous to what the *philosophes* did when they said that even the best of the priests had nothing to offer us save edifying examples of charity and decency. Reducing science from a possible source of redemptive truth to a model of rational cooperation is the contemporary analogue of the reduction of the Gospels from a recipe for attaining eternal happiness to a compendium of sound moral advice. That was the sort of reduction that Kant and Jefferson recommended, and that liberal Protestants of the last two centuries have gradually achieved.

To put this last point another way: both the Christian religion and materialist metaphysics turned out to be self-consuming artifacts. The need for religious orthodoxy was undermined by Saint Paul's insistence on the primacy of love, and by the gradual realization that a religion of love could not ask everyone to recite the same creed. The need for a metaphysics was undermined by the ability of modern science to see the human mind as an exceptionally complex nervous system and thus to see itself in pragmatic rather than metaphysical terms. Science showed us how to see empirical inquiry as the use of this extra physiological equipment to gain steadily greater mastery over the environment, rather than as a way of replacing appearance with reality. Just as the eighteenth century became able to see Christianity not as a revelation from on high but as continuous with Socratic reflection, so the twentieth century became able to see natural science not as revealing the intrinsic nature of reality but as continuous with the sort of practical problem solving that both beavers and carpenters are good at.

To give up the idea that there is an intrinsic nature of reality to be discovered either by the priests, or the philosophers, or the scientists, is to disjoin the need for redemption from the search for universal agreement. It is to give up the search for an accurate account of human nature, and thus for a recipe for leading the good life for man. Once these searches are given up, expanding the limits of the human imagination steps forward to assume the role that obedience to the divine will played in a religious culture, and the role that the discovery of what is really real played in a philosophical culture. But this substitution is no reason to give up the search for a single utopian form of political life – the good global society.

6 The "Decadence" of a Literary Culture

I have now said all I can to counter the claim that the rise of the literary culture is a relapse into irrationality, and that a proper respect for the ability of science to achieve objective truth is essential to the morale of a democratic society. But a related claim, much vaguer and harder to pin down, has been even more influential. This is that a literary culture is *decadent* – that it lacks the healthy-mindedness and vigor common to proselytizing Christians, science-worshipping positivists, and Marxist revolutionaries. A high culture centered around literature, one that wishes not to get things right but to make things new, will, it is often said, be a culture of languid and self-involved aesthetes.

The best rebuttal to this suggestion is Oscar Wilde's "The Soul of Man Under Socialism." The message of that essay parallels those of Mill's *On Liberty* and of Rawls's *A Theory of Justice*. It is that the only point of getting rid of the priests and the kings, of setting up democratic governments, of taking from each according to her abilities and giving to each according to her needs, and of thereby creating the Good Global Society, is to make it possible for people to lead the sort of lives they prefer, as long as their doing so does not diminish the opportunities of other humans to do the same thing. As Wilde put it "Socialism itself will be of value simply because it will lead to Individualism."[9] Part of Wilde's point is that there can be no objection to self-involved aesthetes – that is to say, people whose passion is to explore the present limits of the human imagination – as long as they do not use more than their fair share of the social product.

This claim itself, however, strikes many people as decadent. We were not, they would urge, put on this earth to enjoy ourselves, but to do the right thing. Socialism, they think, would not stir our hearts were it no more than a means to individualism, or if the goal of proletarian revolution were merely to make it possible for everybody to become a bourgeois intellectual. This sense that human existence has some point other than pleasure is what keeps the battle between Mill and Kant alive in courses on moral philosophy, just as the sense that natural science must have some point other than practical problem solving keeps the struggle between Kuhn and his opponents alive in courses in philosophy of science. Mill and Kuhn – and, more generally, utilitarians and pragmatists – are still suspected of letting down the side, diminishing human dignity, reducing our noblest aspirations to self-indulgent stimulation of our favorite clusters of neurons.

The antagonism between those who think, with Schiller and Wilde, that human beings are at their best when at play, and those who think that they are at their best when they strive, seems to me at the bottom of the conflicts that have marked the rise of the literary culture. Once again, I would urge that these conflicts be seen as recapitulating those that marked the transition from religion to philosophy. In that earlier transition, the people who thought that a human life that did not strive for perfect obedience to the divine will was a relapse into animality faced off against those who thought that the ideal of such submission was unworthy of beings who could think for themselves. In the current transition, the people who think that we need to hang onto Kantian ideas like "the moral law" and "things as they are in themselves" are facing off against people who think that these ideas are symptoms of insufficient self-reliance, of a self-deluding attempt to find dignity in the acceptance of bondage and freedom in the recognition of constraint.

The only way to resolve this sort of quarrel, it seems to me, is to say that the kinds of people to whom a utopian society would give the resources and the leisure to do their individualistic thing will include Kantian strivers as well as self-involved aesthetes, people who cannot live without religion and people who despise it, nature's metaphysicians as well as nature's pragmatists. For in this utopia, as Rawls has said, there will be no need for people to agree on the point of human existence, the good life for man, or any other topic of similar generality.

If people who heartily disagree about such issues can agree to cooperate in the functioning of the practices and institutions that have, in Wilde's words, "substituted cooperation

9 Oscar Wilde, "The Soul of Man Under Socialism" (1891) in *The Complete Works of Oscar Wilde* (London: Collins, 1966), p. 1080.

for competition,"[10] that will suffice. The Kant versus Mill issue, like the issue between metaphysicians and pragmatists, will seem as little worth quarreling about as will the issue between the believers and the atheists. For we humans need not agree about the nature or the end of man in order to help facilitate our neighbor's ability to act on her own convictions on these matters, just so long as those actions do not interfere with our freedom to act on our own convictions.

In short, just as we have, in the past few centuries, learned that the difference of opinion between the believer and the atheist does not have to be settled before the two can cooperate on communal projects, so we may learn to set aside all the differences between all the various searches for redemption when we cooperate to build Wilde's utopia. In that utopia, the literary culture will not be the only, or even the dominant, form of high culture.

That is because there will be *no* dominant form. High culture will no longer be thought of as the place where the aim of the society as a whole is debated and decided, and where it is a matter of social concern which sort of intellectual is ruling the roost. Nor will there be much concern about the gap that yawns between popular culture, the culture of people who have never felt the need for redemption, and the high culture of the intellectuals – the people who are always wanting to be something more or different than they presently are. In utopia, the religious or philosophical need to live up to the nonhuman, and the need of the literary intellectuals to explore the present limits of the human imagination will be viewed as matters of taste. They will be viewed by nonintellectuals in the same relaxed, tolerant, and uncomprehending way that we presently regard our neighbor's obsession with bird watching, or collecting hubcaps, or discovering the secrets of the great pyramids.

To get along in utopia, however, the literary intellectuals will have to tone down their rhetoric. Certain passages in Wilde will not bear repeating, as when he speaks of "the poets, the philosophers, the men of science, the men of culture – in a word, the real men, the men who have realized themselves, and in whom all humanity gains a partial realization."[11] The idea that some men are more really men than others contradicts Wilde's own better wisdom, as when he says "There is no one type for man. There are as many perfections as there are imperfect men."[12] The same words might have been written by Nietzsche, but to take them seriously we must actively forget Zarathustra's contempt for the "last men," the men who feel no need for redemption. In utopia, the literary culture will have learned not to give itself airs. It will no longer feel the temptation to make invidious and quasi-metaphysical distinctions between real and less real men.

To sum up, I am suggesting that we see the literary culture as itself a self-consuming artifact, and perhaps the last of its kind. For in utopia the intellectuals will have given up the idea that there is a standard against which the products of the human imagination can be measured other than their social utility, as this utility is judged by a maximally free, leisured, and tolerant global community. They will have stopped thinking that the human imagination is getting somewhere, that there is one far off cultural event toward which all cultural creation moves. They will have given up the identification of redemption with the attainment of perfection. They will have taken fully to heart the maxim that it is the journey that matters.

10   Ibid.
11   Ibid.
12   Ibid., p. 1087.

Part VI
Autobiographical

Introduction

The pieces in this final section offer Rorty in his own words on various aspects of his life and work. The most significant is the 1992 quasi-autobiographical essay, "Trotsky and the Wild Orchids." Also included here are two revealing interviews from different points in his career. The volume closes with "The Fire of Life," a brief reflection on poetry and the sources of meaning in human existence that Rorty composed after having been diagnosed with terminal cancer.

"From Philosophy to Post-Philosophy" (1982) is an interview conducted shortly after the publication of *Philosophy and the Mirror of Nature*. Already Rorty has a sense that *Mirror* is being received by nonphilosophers in a way he did not intend, as "blowing the whistle on analytic philosophy and all it stands for," when his own take, at least at this time, is that it is "an attempt to carry out the positivists' original program" (p. 494, this volume). The number of Rorty's later stances that are evident throughout the interview is striking: his notion of making "a transition from philosophy as a discipline to a larger and looser activity"; his sense of the importance of "the human ability to change character by redescribing oneself"; his interest in utopianism and future possible visions as the basis for social criticism; and the idea of "philosophy as a free-floating criticism of culture," to name just a few.

The wide-ranging, later interview "Biography and Philosophy" (2003) delves into Rorty's thoughts on the two decades of work he had authored in the interim, following some retelling of his autobiographical narrative, especially his views as they relate to various political and social issues. The note of pessimism on which he ends may seem surprising, given the spirit of Deweyan optimism that pervades his work more generally. However, this is a good indication of Rorty's disposition in the period after September 11 amid his growing concerns about the threats to democracy emanating from the national security state.[1] In another interview given around the same time, he appended to a similar pessimism the more characteristically Rortyan coda: "If I had to lay bets, my bet would be that everything is going to go to hell, but, you know, what else have we got except hope?"[2]

1 For Rorty's work on this issue, see the General Introduction above, n.155.
2 Interview by Gideon Lewis-Kraus, "Richard Rorty," *The Believer* (June 2003): http://www.believermag.com/issues/200306/?read=interview_rorty, accessed July 31, 2009.

"Trotsky and the Wild Orchids" is one of Rorty's most revealing essays, at least in part because of his recourse to a "bit of autobiography" as a way to respond to criticisms of his views, particularly those expressed in *Contingency, Irony, and Solidarity,* as "so weird as to be merely frivolous," as he puts it.[3] His primary concern is elucidating his views about the relation of philosophy and politics, which he traces to his early attempt to reconcile "Trotsky," his metaphor for the committed political activism he inherits from his parents, with the wild orchids that represent "the Wordsworthian moments" he experienced in the woods around his Flatbrookville, New Jersey home, when in searching for the elusive flower he felt "touched by something numinous, something of ineffable importance" (p. 503, this volume). Finding an intellectual or aesthetic framework to unite these two commitments in a single vision becomes the quest that leads him to philosophy. It is also the quest that, once he abandons Platonism for pragmatism, he ultimately concludes is fundamentally misguided. He describes *Contingency,* which was written forty years after his time in those New Jersey woods, as "a book about what intellectual life might be like if one could manage to give up the Platonic attempt to hold reality [his wild orchids] and justice [his Trotsky] in a single vision." Establishing one of his most enduring stances, the book argues that "there is no need to weave one's personal equivalent of Trotsky and one's personal equivalent of my wild orchids together" (p. 506, this volume). The attempt to do so for Rorty is a function of the desire for a "guarantee" that "whatever idiosyncratic things or persons one loves with all one's heart and soul and mind" are justified in some larger sense beyond our contingent selves and the historical communities and traditions that shape us, justified "in the nature of things, or in the human soul, or in the structure of language, or *somewhere*" – precisely the kind of guarantee that puts those commitments outside the reach of democratic consensus (pp. 506, 509, this volume). The procurement of such a "self-justifying, self-sufficient synoptic vision" risks letting one think that one has "something more to rely on than the tolerance and decency of your fellow human beings." In the "democratic community of Dewey's dreams" that Rorty hopes to realize, nobody thinks that (p. 510, this volume).

It seems best to let "The Fire of Life" speak for itself.

---

3   For a more critical interpretation of this essay, see Christopher J. Voparil, *Richard Rorty: Politics and Vision* (Lanham, MD: Rowman & Littlefield Press, 2006), pp. 18–25.

31

From Philosophy to Post-Philosophy: An Interview with Richard Rorty

Conducted by Wayne Hudson and Wim van Reijen

Q. Professor Rorty, you have recently written a book, *Philosophy and the Mirror of Nature*, which has aroused comment throughout the English speaking world. In it you argue that the analytical movement in philosophy has run its course and that a more hermeneutical kind of philosophy is now required. Could you perhaps say something about your way into philosophy, the main stages in your development, and the tendencies in your own thinking which you have had to struggle against most?

A. As an undergraduate I went to the University of Chicago, to a university with a curriculum devised by a philosopher where you were given the impression that anyone worth anything would study philosophy. I stayed on for graduate work at Chicago. My teachers there were Rudolf Carnap the logical positivist, Charles Hartshorne a disciple of Whitehead and Richard McKeon an historian of philosophy. I worked with Hartshorne on speculative metaphysics and wrote a lot about Whitehead. After getting my Master's degree I went to Yale, where there were the same alternatives: Carl Hempel in place of Carnap, Paul Weiss in place of Hartshorne, and Robert Brumbaugh in place of McKeon. There I wrote a thesis comparing Aristotle on *dunamis* with the seventeenth century rationalists on the notion of possibility. It was a very McKeonite, comparative, piece. My interests until 1960 were historical and metaphysical. Then I got a job at Wellesley, a small college near New York. My colleagues there explained to me that I was behind the times and ought to find out what was going on in the world of philosophy. So I read the then fashionable Oxford philosophers (Austin, Ryle, Strawson). Earlier I had read the logical positivists but not liked them much. I also read Wittgenstein's *Investigations* for the first time and that made a great difference. So I changed from being

"Perspectives on Richard Rorty, I: From Philosophy to Post-Philosophy: An Interview with Richard M. Rorty", conducted by Wayne Hudson and Wim van Reijen, *Radical Philosophy* 32, Autumn 1982: 1–4,© 1982 by Radical Philosophy. Reprinted by permission of the journal, *Radical Philosophy*.

an old-fashioned philosopher to being an up-to-date analytical philosopher partly as a result of pressure from my peers. When I got a job at Princeton after having been at Wellesley for three years, even more pressure was applied. There were certain things one had to know. I then spent about ten years trying to do things with Sellars and Wittgenstein within the framework of contemporary analytical philosophy. In the early seventies I got sick of that and tried to do something larger in *Philosophy and the Mirror of Nature*, which was very much the old McKeonite trick of taking the larger historical view. The tendencies which I have had to struggle against most have been, on the one hand, the temptation to avoid contact with contemporary discussion and just be historical, and, on the other, the temptation to become so immersed in contemporary discussion that I just write journal articles.

Q.   Have your views changed since you wrote *Philosophy and the Mirror of Nature?*

A.   The main change I'm aware of is getting considerably more respect for the late Heidegger. I used to think of Heidegger as having a brilliant grasp of the historical tendencies which led to what he thought of as the late Nietzsche, and what I think of as pragmatism. But I thought that his view of the Greeks was merely nostalgic. I now think I was wrong and that the late Heidegger had a much subtler view. I am now trying to write a book called *Heidegger Against the Pragmatists* to give an account of how Heidegger managed to see Nietzsche's quasi-pragmatism as dialectically correct (in the sense that if you were in the Western tradition Nietzsche was where you were going to end up) but nonetheless as a *reductio ad absurdum* of that tradition.

Q.   What faults do you now detect in *Philosophy and the Mirror of Nature?*

A.   I think that what may be wrong with the book is that I take the positivistic therapeutic enterprise of clearing away pseudo-problems terribly seriously. Sometimes I think I've overdone it. The book has been read by non-philosophers as blowing the whistle on analytic philosophy and all it stands for, whereas it seems to me to be an attempt to carry out the positivists' original programme.

Q.   Are you worried that the effect of your book may be different from that which you intended?

A.   Yes I am. The book should not be read as an attack on analytical philosophy. What I was trying to say was that there is a dialectical strand within analytical philosophy which fulfils itself in the American philosophers Quine and Sellars in a way which leads back to Dewey and the American Pragmatists. Of course, Quine and Sellars don't like what I make of their work. They don't want to see analytical philosophy as veering back to Dewey.

Q.   Many people will want to ask you why Dewey? What can we still learn from him?

A.   I think Dewey and James are the best guides to understanding the modern world that we've got, and that it's a question of putting pragmatism into better shape after thirty years of super-professionalism.

Q.   But such a reformulated pragmatism might differ considerably from your own views. What, for example, do you make of Dewey's theory of experience?

A.   I regard that as the worst part of Dewey. I'd be glad if he had never written *Experience and Nature*.

Q.   But if, as you suggest, philosophers give up the idea of truth as accurate representation, then might not a theory of experience be important for philosophy which had abandoned both the attempt to find foundations and the search for a theory of knowledge?

A.   I'd prefer 'discourse' to 'experience'.

Q.   How far are you worried by the charge that at the end of *Philosophy and the Mirror of Nature* you fail to provide an adequate account of the form which future philosophy should take?

A.   The sense that people have at the end of the book that I should have answered the question 'What should philosophy do *now*?' is probably my fault. The way I hoped they would react was to say that maybe the notion of philosophy as a discipline or a distinct sector of culture had run its course. Philosophy as we understand it was something invented by the German Idealists between about 1780 and 1830 as a candidate for the leadership of culture. After that, no one believed in it anymore. Since then it's just become another academic discipline, but with pretentions. I agree with the late Heidegger that the science/poetry/philosophy distinctions we have lived with are outmoded, and, in particular, the notion of philosophers as the people who can provide the rest of culture with a framework. It seems to me that the demand that there be something for philosophy to be is unfounded. It assumes that there is some normal, necessary, human activity called philosophy.

Q.   Nonetheless, isn't the sense of intellectual parsimony which pervades the book to some extent a legacy from ideas which imply that there is something for philosophy to be?

A.   In *Philosophy and the Mirror of Nature* I was perhaps in transit. I now think that what I should have tried to do at the end of the book was to make a transition from philosophy as a discipline to a larger and looser activity.

Q.   One could question whether that would have been enough if, as you suggest, philosophy is now coming to an end and we are entering a period of post-philosophy. You say in one of your articles that pragmatism is the philosophical equivalent of literary modernism. Isn't modernism a rather old trick to bring out at this stage?

A.   Not in philosophy, which in this respect has lagged behind. I agree that in the culture as a whole it looks a little stale.

Q.   You are conspicuous among contemporary analytical philosophers in your positive reassertion of the post-philosophical significance of creative imagination. To what extent do you think that we need a greater awareness in philosophy of the effectivity of stories?

A.   Surely what the French philosophers and the Yale literary critics are doing is helping us to see how we live in story after story after story. Perhaps the Yale literary critic Harold Bloom does it best. He's currently writing a huge book on Freud which just might provide us with a way of reading Freud as a figure in the Romantic tradition.

People like Derrida and De Man [another Yale literary critic], on the other hand, still seem to me to have too much respect for philosophy.

Q.   Have you particular criticisms of contemporary French philosophy?

A.   What I find disturbing about the fashionable French is that they aren't utopian. They hold out no hope. I think that their position is an over-reaction. I have written a comparison between Dewey and Foucault in which I argue that Foucault's stuff on truth as only being available as a product of power is simply saying what Dewey said: that discourse and truth are made possible by community life. Of course, calling it power sounds more pejorative. But Dewey was a utopian thinker who tried to create a culture in which setting up heroes was a natural form of cultural advance. Whereas Foucault doesn't want any heroes. Almost as though philosophers have no right to have heroes.

Q.   Did Heidegger have any heroes?

A.   Hölderlin. The poets of the past.

Q.   If you recognise the need for a degree of utopianism in philosophy, shouldn't you make more methodological provision for it? Isn't there a contradiction in your work between the tough-minded eliminative side, which is largely continuous with the old analytical philosophy, and the more tender-minded side where you want philosophy to do things for which you don't provide adequate methods?

A.   I don't see that.

Q.   Perhaps it's another way of asking you if your position is not really too conservative? If you are really not still too close to old style analytical philosophy? Take the philosophy of psychology. In *Philosophy and the Mirror of Nature* you attack the Cartesian understanding of human beings which implies that we have minds as well as bodies. You speak instead of persons without minds. That's in the old negative tendency of analytical philosophy. But couldn't you approach it differently. Couldn't you ask how far persons can change what they can become by ascribing to themselves counter-factual properties?

A.   But the human ability to change character by redescribing oneself is not an attempt to discover the nature of the mind. It's an attempt to create something for human beings to be that they have never been before.

Q.   But then isn't the distinction which you draw in your work between empirical description and moral deliberation too dualistic? Doesn't it perhaps reflect the influence of the *Geisteswissenschaften* tradition which you yourself criticise Charles Taylor for advocating?

A.   I agree that you could read some passages in my writings without ever realising that most moral deliberation does take the form of finding new forms of self-description. So I guess that I made too much of that dichotomy.

Q.   One of the most interesting things in your work may be that you suggest that analytical philosophy is watered down Kantianism which should now abandon its transcendental project or the attempt, to construct a single neutral matrix in terms of which all questions can be judged. Could you expand on this?

A.   The fundamental mistake of transcendental philosophy, it seems to me, is to take one form of discourse and to say that it has been so successful that there must be something in it through which we can discover the secret of rationality. I think that analytical philosophy is a recent variation on this transcendental theme, which, in so far as it is a Kantian transcendental enterprise, has the faults of all such enterprises.

Q. But you don't see this as going to the methods used by analytical philosophy?

A. No. I think that analytical philosophy can keep its highly professional methods, the insistence on detail and mechanics, and just drop its transcendental project. I'm not out to criticise analytical philosophy as a style. It's a good style. I think the years of super-professionalism were beneficial.

Q. Aren't there passages in your work which suggest that you yearn for another style? That philosophy should acquire a new vocabulary?

A. In philosophy as therapy, as in psychoanalysis, no special vocabulary is useful. Philosophy as a free-floating criticism of culture does not require a special vocabulary. It's continuous with the kind of writing you get throughout the academy. If you think of Skinner and Dunn in England, Foucault in France and Clifford Geertz and Lionel Trilling in the United States, they are or were really in the same business. Although some of them are philosophers and some of them are not.

Q. If you think that philosophy should be social and cultural criticism because the more ambitious tasks which it has set itself simply cannot be performed, would you want to argue this, not simply in terms of the competence of philosophy as a discipline, but in terms of a doctrine of the radical finitude of man? Are you, after all, influenced by Kant?

A. Certainly by Heidegger's book on Kant. The late Heidegger finds words to express this finitude. I think it's a question of conserving the realisation of it, rather than of attempting to turn it into another theory.

Q. As a pragmatist you tend to evaluate doctrines in terms of their historical success. Doesn't that make it difficult for you to maintain a rationally justifiable critical approach to the way things turn out? To the path which historical tendencies take?

A. I agree that there is something conservative about pragmatism. Nonetheless, it seems to me that devotion to concrete historical contents is something one loses at one's peril. One then falls into utopianism in the bad sense when people begin to kill each other for abstract principles.

Q. But you don't have a stronger notion of utility than simply historical tendency, how things worked out?

A. No, I don't. I think it's a trap to be avoided. It leads to setting up entities above history.

Q. But does that leave you with an adequate position in moral philosophy? How, for example, can one know who acts well or badly?

A. As Kantian individual selves we could not do it. As members of a community we do it all the time. Those who act badly are those who behave contrary to the project which makes us the community we are.

Q. If, however, you take the pragmatist approach here, in what terms would you develop a moral criticism of current social rules?

A. The only way we can criticise current social rules is by reference to utopian notions which proceed by taking elements in the tradition and showing how unfulfilled they are.

Q. Would you think that the only way one could criticise a Nazi guard in a concentration camp was by reference to utopian notions?

A. By reference to what to him would seem utopian notions. Given his education, it would be a question of saying that there is a picture of Europe very different from yours in which all this wasn't necessary. Moral criticism is too easy here. It's as easy to say that someone is doing wrong as it is to kill him. What is difficult is to say why we aren't doing it too.

Q. You once edited a very influential anthology called *The Linguistic Turn*. Do you now think that in some areas the turn to language in analytical philosophy made the real philosophical issues more difficult to see? For example, in the philosophy of psychology?

A. I see what you mean in the case of Gilbert Ryle or Norman Malcolm. But do you think it affects a philosopher like Daniel Dennett? At the moment I'm trying to persuade the people in Heidelberg that in the philosophy of psychology Dennett is all anyone needs.

Q. Despite your enthusiasm for pragmatism, your own approach to psychological questions is neo-behaviourist rather than pragmatist. What do you make of the psychological doctrines of William James?

A. I confess that I never finished his book on psychology. I think that in his philosophical books he was defending his father's religious views against nineteenth century positivism.

Q. There is a lot of interest currently among philosophers in the essentialist logical doctrines of Saul Kripke, who is also at Princeton. What is your attitude to Kripke?

A. I find his views arguable. He seems to me to be saying: take all the intuitions you can think of which are anti-pragmatic and I'll give you a philosophy of language which matches those intuitions. But how one could argue whether one *wanted* these concepts I can't imagine. I have the same reaction to Thomas Nagel, who was at Princeton until recently. Nagel has a deep sense of the problems of philosophical realism as being the problems to work on, and his work is getting more and more interesting – especially towards the end of his new book, *Mortal Questions*, where he emphasises that the traditional philosophical problems are not just historical, but still relevant. He and Kripke fit together beautifully. But I don't think either of them has much in the way of arguments.

Q. What do you make of Donald Davidson and the contemporary philosophy of action, which has been taken very seriously on the continent?

A. I never found it very interesting. It seems to me to be a hangover from the problem of free will. I'm afraid that after reading Hume on the compatibility of free will and determinism I never looked back. Unlike some German writers, I don't see it as having much to do with moral philosophy.

Q. And the work of the Oxford philosopher Michael Dummett? Are you worried by the problem of intuitionism? Some philosophers might say that, as a matter of fact, the giving of grounds often comes to an end with an appeal to intuitions, such as when we say 'I see that' or 'It's not clear'.

A.   I don't see a problem. Either one refers to what we all intuit or to what we all normally do. It doesn't make much difference.

Q.   Are you worried by the charge that there is a contradiction between the idealism of your meta-philosophical views and the materialism of your psychological views?

A.   Idealism as a metaphysical view is pointless: the old idealist attempt to find some phenomena which the materialist cannot explain fails. But I think, as Sellars shows, that you can have all the advantages of both materialism and idealism if you just make a few distinctions. So be a materialist if you want to, but realise that being a materialist is simply putting a bet on what the vocabulary of the predictive disciplines will turn out to be.

Q.   So the doctrine which creates the impression of tough-mindedness doesn't have much tough content. Would you take the same approach to scientism? Do you think that the only reliable, valid knowledge we have is scientific knowledge?

A.   That way of putting it presupposes that knowledge is a natural kind. I think it's better to say that there are lots of different justifiable assertions, including not only scientific assertions but aesthetic and social judgements. One end of the spectrum has an elaborate machinery for establishing the norms behind it, just as there are experts at one end of the spectrum, the other not. But the two kinds of enterprise are one. So there is really no need to worry where knowledge stops because the distinction between where you go to explain something and where not is not a distinction between knowledge and opinion. It's a sociological distinction.

Q.   Nonetheless, you do cling to a form of scientism?

A.   I think of myself as stealing the point from Sellars that one's categories in metaphysics should be the categories of the sciences of one's day. But that's simply to say what a boring subject metaphysics is.

Q.   Can we end on the problem of your approach to history. You began as a McKeonite comparativist taking the larger historical view, and have now returned to it. Yet your philosophical training does not really help you all that much with the problem of how to influence future historical developments. It does train you in the art of destruction and you could be seen as attempting to destroy philosophy as the theory of knowledge just as Adorno attempted to destroy social philosophy. But such destructions often have unintended effects. How can you envisage them, let alone take responsibility for them? In sum, you don't have a theory of history?

A.   No, I don't. I'm not a historicist in Popper's sense.

Q.   But you are perhaps an historicist in the sense of one who holds that history is all-important and that it is usually helpful to take careful account of changing historical circumstances and exact processes of historical genesis. Could you perhaps say something about your relationship to the British philosopher of history, R. G. Collingwood?

A.   I read Collingwood a long time ago in my twenties and forgot most of it. I now realise that I may have recently taken up things which I originally read in Collingwood. We have to take history seriously. I see post-philosophy continuing the conversation of mankind in that context.

32

Trotsky and the Wild Orchids

If there is anything to the idea that the best intellectual position is one which is attacked with equal vigor from the political right and the political left, then I am in good shape. I am often cited by conservative culture warriors as one of the relativistic, irrationalist, deconstructing, sneering, smirking intellectuals whose writings are weakening the moral fiber of the young. Neal Kozody, writing in the monthly bulletin of the Committee for the Free World, an organization known for its vigilance against symptoms of moral weakness, denounces my "cynical and nihilistic view" and says "it is not enough for him [Rorty] that American students should be merely mindless; he would have them positively mobilized for mindlessness." Richard Neuhaus, a theologian who doubts that atheists can be good American citizens, says that the "ironist vocabulary" I advocate "can neither provide a public language for the citizens of a democracy, nor contend intellectually against the enemies of democracy, nor transmit the reasons for democracy to the next generation." My criticisms of Allan Bloom's *The Closing of the American Mind* led Harvey Mansfield – recently appointed by President Bush to the National Council for the Humanities – to say that I have "given up on America" and that I "manage to diminish even Dewey." (Mansfield recently described Dewey as a "medium-sized malefactor.") His colleague on the Council, my fellow philosopher John Searle, thinks that standards can only be restored to American higher education if people abandon the views on truth, knowledge, and objectivity that I do my best to inculcate.

Yet Sheldon Wolin, speaking from the left, sees a lot of similarity between me and Allan Bloom: both of us, he says, are intellectual snobs who care only about the leisured, cultured elite to which we belong. Neither of us has anything to say to blacks, or to other groups who have been shunted aside by American society. Wolin's view is echoed by Terry Eagleton, Britain's leading Marxist thinker. Eagleton says that "in [Rorty's] ideal society the intellectuals will be 'ironists,' practicing a suitably cavalier, laid-back attitude to their own belief, while the masses, for whom such self-ironizing might prove too subversive a weapon, will continue to salute the flag and take life seriously." *Der Spiegel* said that I "attempt to make the yuppie regression look good." Jonathan Culler, one of Derrida's chief disciples and expositors, says that my version of pragmatism "seems

Richard M. Rorty, "Trotsky and the Wild Orchids," *Common Knowledge*, vol. 1 (3), 1992: 140–53, altogether appropriate to the age of Reagan." Richard Bernstein says that my views are "little more than an ideological *apologia* for an old-fashioned version of cold war liberalism dressed up in fashionable 'postmodern' discourse." The left's favorite word for me is "complacent," just as the right's is "irresponsible."

The left's hostility is partially explained by the fact that most people who admire Nietzsche, Heidegger, and Derrida as much as I do – most of the people who either classify themselves as "postmodernist" or (like me) find themselves thus classified willy-nilly – participate in what Jonathan Yardley has called the "America Sucks Sweepstakes." Participants in this event compete to find better, bitterer ways of describing the United States. They see our country as embodying everything that is wrong with the rich post-Enlightenment West. They see ours as what Foucault called a "disciplinary society," dominated by an odious ethos of "liberal individualism," an ethos which produces racism, sexism, consumerism, and Republican presidents. By contrast, I see America pretty much as Whitman and Dewey did, as opening a prospect on illimitable democratic vistas. I think that our country – despite its past and present atrocities and vices, and despite its continuing eagerness to elect fools and knaves to high office – is a good example of the best kind of society so far invented.

The right's hostility is largely explained by the fact that rightist thinkers don't think that it is enough just to *prefer* democratic societies. One also has to believe that they are Objectively Good, that the institutions of such societies are grounded in Rational First Principles. Especially if one teaches philosophy, as I do, one is expected to tell the young that their society is not just one of the better ones so far contrived, but one which embodies Truth and Reason. Refusal to say this sort of thing counts as "the treason of the clerks" – as an abdication of professional and moral responsibility. My own philosophical views – views I share with Nietzsche and Dewey – forbid me to say this kind of thing. I do not have much use for notions like "objective value" and "objective truth." I think that the so-called postmodernists are right in most of their criticisms of traditional philosophical talk about "reason." So my philosophical views offend the right as much as my political preferences offend the left.

I am sometimes told, by critics from both ends of the political spectrum, that my views are so weird as to be merely frivolous. They suspect that I will say anything to get a gasp, that I am just amusing myself by contradicting everybody else. This hurts. So I have tried, in what follows, to say something about how I got into my present position – how I got into philosophy, and then found myself unable to use philosophy for the purpose I had originally had in mind. Perhaps this bit of autobiography will make clear that, even if my views about the relation of philosophy and politics are odd, they were not adopted for frivolous reasons.

When I was twelve, the most salient books on my parents' shelves were two red-bound volumes – *The Case of Leon Trotsky* and *Not Guilty*. These made up the report of the Dewey Commission of Inquiry into the Moscow Trials. I never read them with the wide-eyed fascination I brought to books like Kraft-Ebbing's *Psychopathia Sexualis*, but I thought of them in the way in which other children thought of their family's Bible: they were books that radiated redemptive truth and moral splendor. If I were a really *good* boy, I would say to myself, I should have read not only the Dewey Commission reports, but also Trotsky's *History of the Russian Revolution*, a book I started many times but never managed to finish. For in the 1940's, the Russian Revolution and its betrayal by Stalin were, for me, what the Incarnation and its betrayal by the Catholics had been to precocious little Lutherans four hundred years before.

My father had almost, but not quite, accompanied John Dewey to Mexico as 'PR' man for the Commission of Inquiry which Dewey chaired. Having broken with the American Communist Party in 1932, my parents had been classified by the *Daily Worker* as "Trotskyites," and they more or less accepted the description. When Trotsky was assassinated in 1940, one of his secretaries, John Frank, hoped that the GPU would not think to look for him in the remote little village on the Delaware River where we were living. Using a pseudonym, he was our guest in Flatbrookville for some months. I was warned not to disclose his real identity, though it is doubtful that my schoolmates at Walpack Elementary would have been interested in my indiscretions.

I grew up knowing that all decent people were, if not Trotskyites, at least socialists. I also knew that Stalin had ordered not only Trotsky's assassination but also Kirov's, Ehrlich's, Alter's, and Carlo Tresca's. (Tresca, gunned down on the streets of New York, had been a family friend.) I knew that poor people would always be oppressed until capitalism was overcome. Working as an unpaid office boy during my twelfth winter, I carried drafts of press releases from the Worker's Defense League office off Gramercy Park (where my parents worked) to Norman Thomas' (the Socialist Party's candidate for president) house around the corner, and also to A. Philip Randolph's office at the Brotherhood of Pullman Car Porters on 125th Street. On the subway, I would read the documents I was carrying. They told me a lot about what factory owners did to union organizers, plantation owners to sharecroppers, and the white locomotive engineers' union to the colored firemen (whose jobs white men wanted, now that diesel engines were replacing coal-fired steam engines). So, at twelve, I knew that the point of being human was to spend one's life fighting social injustice.

But I also had private, weird, snobbish, incommunicable interests. In earlier years these had been in Tibet. I had sent the newly enthroned Dalai Lama a present, accompanied by warm congratulations to a fellow eight-year-old who had made good. A few years later, when my parents began dividing their time between the Chelsea Hotel and the mountains of northwest New Jersey, these interests switched to orchids. Some forty species of wild orchids occur in those mountains, and I eventually found seventeen of them. Wild orchids are uncommon, and rather hard to spot. I prided myself enormously on being the only person around who knew where they grew, their Latin names, and their blooming times. When in New York, I would go to the 42nd Street Public Library to reread a nineteenth-century volume on the botany of the orchids of the eastern U.S.

I was not quite sure why those orchids were so important, but I was convinced that they were. I was sure that our noble, pure, chaste, North American wild orchids were morally superior to the showy, hybridized, tropical orchids displayed in florists' shops. I was also convinced that there was a deep significance in the fact that the orchids are the latest and most complex plants to have been developed in the course of evolution. Looking back, I suspect that there was a lot of sublimated sexuality involved (orchids being a notoriously sexy sort of flower), and that my desire to learn all there was to know about orchids was linked to my desire to understand all the hard words in Kraft-Ebbing.

I was uneasily aware, however, that there was something a bit dubious about this esotericism – this interest in socially useless flowers. I had read (in the vast amount of spare time given to a clever, snotty, nerdy, only child) bits of *Marius the Epicurean* and also bits of Marxist criticisms of Pater's aestheticism. I was afraid that Trotsky (whose *Literature and Revolution* I had nibbled at) would not have approved of my interest in orchids.

At fifteen I escaped from the bullies who regularly beat me up on the playground of my high school (bullies who, I assumed, would somehow wither away once capitalism had been overcome) by going off to the so-called Hutchins College of the University of Chicago. (This was the institution immortalized by A. J. Liebling as "the biggest collection of juvenile neurotics since the Childrens' Crusade.") Insofar as I had any project in mind, it was to reconcile Trotsky and the orchids. I wanted to find some intellectual or aesthetic framework which would let me – in a thrilling phrase which I came across in Yeats – "hold reality and justice in a single vision." By *reality* I meant, more or less, the Wordsworthian moments in which, in the woods around Flatbrookville (and especially in the presence of certain coralroot orchids, and of the smaller yellow lady slipper), I had felt touched by something numinous, something of ineffable importance. By *justice* I meant what Norman Thomas and Trotsky both stood for, the liberation of the weak from the strong. I wanted a way to be both an intellectual and spiritual snob and a friend of humanity – a nerdy recluse and a fighter for justice. I was very confused, but reasonably sure that at Chicago I would find out how grownups managed to work the trick I had in mind.

When I got to Chicago (in 1946), I found that Hutchins, together with his friends Mortimer Adler and Richard McKeon (the villain of Pirsig's *Zen and the Art of Motorcycle Maintenance*), had enveloped much of the University of Chicago in a neo-Aristotelian mystique. The most frequent target of their sneers was John Dewey's pragmatism. That pragmatism was the philosophy of my parents' friend Sidney Hook, as well as the unofficial philosophy of most of the other New York intellectuals who had given up on dialectical materialism. But according to Hutchins and Adler, pragmatism was vulgar, "relativistic," and self-refuting. As they pointed out over and over again, Dewey had no absolutes. To say, as Dewey did, that "growth itself is the only moral end," left one without a criterion for growth, and thus with no way to refute Hitler's suggestion that Germany had "grown" under his rule. To say that truth is what works is to reduce the quest for truth to the quest for power. Only an appeal to something eternal, absolute, and good – like the God of St. Thomas or the "nature of human beings" described by Aristotle – would permit one to answer the Nazis, to justify one's choice of social democracy over fascism.

This quest for stable absolutes was common to the neo-Thomists and to Leo Strauss, the teacher who attracted the best of the Chicago students (including my classmate Allan Bloom). The Chicago faculty was dotted with awesomely learned refugees from Hitler, of whom Strauss was the most revered. All of them seemed to agree that something deeper and weightier than Dewey was needed if one was to explain why it would be better to be dead than to be a Nazi. This sounded pretty good to my fifteen-year-old ears. For moral and philosophical absolutes sounded a bit like my beloved orchids – numinous, hard to find, known only to a chosen few. Further, since Dewey was a hero to all the people among whom I had grown up, scorning Dewey was a convenient form of adolescent revolt. The only question was whether this scorn should take a religious or a philosophical form, and how it might be combined with striving for social justice.

Like many of my classmates at Chicago, I knew lots of T. S. Eliot by heart. I was attracted by Eliot's suggestions that only committed Christians (and perhaps only Anglo-Catholics) could overcome their unhealthy preoccupation with their private obsessions, and so serve their fellow humans with proper humility. But a prideful inability to believe what I was saying when I recited the General Confession gradually led me to give up on my awkward attempts to get religion. So I fell back on absolutist philosophy.

I read through Plato during my fifteenth summer, and convinced myself that Socrates was right – virtue *was* knowledge. That claim was music to my ears, for I had doubts about my own moral character and a suspicion that my only gifts were intellectual ones. Besides, Socrates *had* to be right, for only then could one hold reality and justice in a single vision. Only if he were right could one hope to be both as good as the best Christians (such as Alyosha in *The Brothers Karamazov*, whom I could not – and still cannot – decide whether to envy or despise) and as learned and clever as Strauss and his students. So I decided to major in philosophy. I figured that if I became a philosopher I might get to the top of Plato's "divided line" – the place "beyond hypotheses" where the full sunshine of Truth irradiates the purified soul of the wise and good: an Elysian field dotted with immaterial orchids. It seemed obvious to me that getting to such a place was what everybody with any brains really wanted. It also seemed clear that Platonism had all the advantages of religion, without requiring the humility which Christianity demanded, and of which I was apparently incapable.

For all these reasons, I wanted very much to be some kind of Platonist, and from fifteen to twenty I did my best. But it didn't pan out. I could never figure out whether the Platonic philosopher was aiming at the ability to offer irrefutable argument – argument which rendered him able to convince anyone he encountered of what he believed (the sort of thing Ivan Karamazov was good at) – or instead was aiming at a sort of incommunicable, private bliss (the sort of thing his brother Alyosha seemed to possess). The first goal is to achieve argumentative power over others – e.g., to become able to convince bullies that they should not beat one up, or to convince rich capitalists that they must cede their power to a cooperative, egalitarian commonwealth. The second goal is to enter a state in which all your own doubts are stilled, but in which you no longer wish to argue. Both goals seemed desirable, but I could not see how they could be fitted together.

At the same time as I was worrying about this tension within Platonism – and within any form of what Dewey had called "the quest for certainty" – I was also worrying about the familiar problem of how one could possibly get a noncircular justification of any debatable stand on any important issue. The more philosophers I read, the clearer it seemed that each of them could carry their views back to first principles which were incompatible with the first principles of their opponents, and that none of them ever got to that fabled place "beyond hypotheses." There seemed to be nothing like a neutral standpoint from which these alternative first principles could be evaluated. But if there were no such standpoint, then the whole idea of "rational certainty," and the whole Socratic–Platonic idea of replacing passion by reason, seemed not to make much sense.

Eventually I got over the worry about circular argumentation by deciding that the test of philosophical truth was overall coherence, rather than deducibility from unquestioned first principles. But this didn't help much. For coherence is a matter of avoiding contradictions, and St. Thomas' advice, "When you meet a contradiction, make a distinction," makes that pretty easy. As far as I could see, philosophical talent was largely a matter of proliferating as many distinctions as were needed to wriggle out of a dialectical corner. More generally, it was a matter, when trapped in such a corner, of redescribing the nearby intellectual terrain in such a way that the terms used by one's opponent would seem irrelevant, or question-begging, or jejune. I turned out to have a flair for such redescription. But I became less and less certain that developing this skill was going to make me either wise or virtuous.

Since that initial disillusion (which climaxed about the time I left Chicago to get a Ph.D. in philosophy at Yale), I have spent forty years looking for a coherent and convincing way of formulating my worries about what, if anything, philosophy is good for. My starting point was the discovery of Hegel's *Phenomenology of Spirit,* a book which I read as saying: granted that philosophy is just a matter of out-redescribing the last philosopher, the cunning of reason can make use even of this sort of competition. It can use it to weave the conceptual fabric of a freer, better, more just society. If philosophy can be, at best, only what Hegel called "its time held in thought," still, that might be enough. For by thus holding one's time, one might do what Marx wanted done – change the world. So even if there were no such thing as "understanding the world" in the Platonic sense – an understanding from a position outside of time and history – perhaps there was still a social use for my talents, and for the study of philosophy.

For quite a while after I read Hegel, I thought that the two greatest achievements of the species to which I belonged were *The Phenomenology of Spirit* and *Remembrance of Things Past* (the book which took the place of the wild orchids once I left Flat-brookville for Chicago). Proust's ability to weave intellectual and social snobbery together with the hawthorns around Combray, his grandmother's selfless love, Odette's orchidaceous embraces of Swann and Jupien's of Charlus, and with everything else he encountered – to give each of these its due without feeling the need to bundle them together with the help of a religious faith or a philosophical theory – seemed to me as astonishing as Hegel's ability to throw himself successively into empiricism, Greek tragedy, Stoicism, Christianity, and Newtonian physics and to emerge from each, ready and eager for something completely different. It was the cheerful commitment to irreducible temporality which Hegel and Proust shared – the specifically anti-Platonic element in their work – that seemed so wonderful. They both seemed able to weave everything they encountered into a narrative without asking that that narrative have a moral, and without asking how that narrative would appear under the aspect of eternity.

About twenty years or so after I decided that the young Hegel's willingness to stop trying for eternity, and just be the child of his time, was the appropriate response to disillusionment with Plato, I found myself being led back to Dewey. Dewey now seemed to me a philosopher who had learned all that Hegel had to teach about how to eschew certainty and eternity, while immunizing himself against pantheism by taking Darwin seriously. This rediscovery of Dewey coincided with my first encounter with Derrida (which I owe to Jonathan Arac, my colleague at Princeton). Derrida led me back to Heidegger, and I was struck by the resemblances between Dewey's, Wittgenstein's, and Heidegger's criticisms of Cartesianism. Suddenly things began to come together. I thought I saw a way to blend a criticism of the Cartesian tradition with the quasi-Hegelian historicism of Michel Foucault, Ian Hacking, and Alasdair MacIntyre. I thought that I could fit all these into a quasi-Heideggerian story about the tensions within Platonism.

The result of this small epiphany was a book called *Philosophy and the Mirror of Nature.* Though disliked by most of my fellow philosophy professors, this book had enough success among nonphilosophers to give me a self-confidence I had previously lacked. But *Philosophy and the Mirror of Nature* did not do much for my adolescent ambitions. The topics it treated – the mind–body problem, controversies in the philosophy of language about truth and meaning, Kuhnian philosophy of science – were pretty remote from both Trotsky and the orchids. I had gotten back on good terms with Dewey; I had articulated my historicist anti-Platonism; I had finally figured out what I thought about the direction and value of current movements in analytic philosophy. I had sorted out most of the philosophers whom I had read. But I had not spoken to any of the questions which got me started reading philosophers in the first place. I was no closer to the single vision which, thirty years back, I had gone to college to get.

As I tried to figure out what had gone wrong, I gradually decided that the whole idea of holding reality and justice in a single vision had been a mistake – that a pursuit of such a vision had been precisely what led Plato astray. More specifically, I decided that only religion – only a nonargumentative faith in a surrogate parent who, unlike any real parent, embodied love, power, and justice in equal measure – could do the trick Plato wanted done. Since I couldn't imagine becoming religious, and indeed had gotten more and more raucously secularist, I decided that the hope of getting a single vision by becoming a philosopher had been a self-deceptive atheist's way out. So I decided to write a book about what intellectual life might be like if one could manage to give up the Platonic attempt to hold reality and justice in a single vision.

That book – *Contingency, Irony, and Solidarity* – argues that there is no need to weave one's personal equivalent of Trotsky and one's personal equivalent of my wild orchids together. Rather, one should try to abjure the temptation to tie in one's moral responsibilities to other people with one's relation to whatever idiosyncratic things or persons one loves with all one's heart and soul and mind (or, if you like, the things or persons one is obsessed with). The two will, for some people, coincide – as they do in those lucky Christians for whom the love of God and of other human beings are inseparable, or revolutionaries who are moved by nothing save the thought of social justice. But they need not coincide, and one should not try too hard to make them do so. So, for example, Jean-Paul Sartre seemed to me right when he denounced Kant's self-deceptive quest for certainty, but wrong when he denounced Proust as a useless bourgeois wimp, a man whose life and writings were equally irrelevant to the only thing that really mattered, the struggle to overthrow capitalism.

Proust's life and work were, in fact, irrelevant to that struggle. But that is a silly reason to despise Proust. It is as wrongheaded as Savanarola's contempt for the works of art he called "vanities." Single-mindedness of this Sartrean or Savanarolan sort is the quest for purity of heart – the attempt to will one thing – gone rancid. It is the attempt to see yourself as an incarnation of something larger than yourself (the Movement, Reason, the Good, the Holy) rather than accepting your finitude. The latter means, among other things, accepting that what matters most to you may well be something that may never matter much to most people. Your equivalent of my orchids may always seem merely weird, merely idiosyncratic, to practically everybody else. But that is no reason to be ashamed of, or downgrade, or try to slough off, your Wordsworthian moments, your lover, your family, your pet, your favorite lines of verse, or your quaint religious faith. There is nothing sacred about universality which makes the shared automatically better than the unshared. There is no automatic privilege of what you can get everybody to agree to (the universal) over what you cannot (the idiosyncratic).

This means that the fact that you have obligations to other people (not to bully them, to join them in overthrowing tyrants, to feed them when they are hungry) does not entail that what you share with other people is more important than anything else. What you share with them, when you are aware of such moral obligations, is not, I argued in *Contingency*, "rationality" or "human nature" or "the fatherhood of God" or "a knowledge of the Moral Law," or anything other than ability to sympathize with the pain of others. There is no particular reason to expect that your sensitivity to that pain, and your idiosyncratic loves, are going to fit within one big overall account of how everything hangs together. There is, in short, not much reason to hope for the sort of single vision that I went to college hoping to get.

So much for how I came to the views I currently hold. As I said earlier, most people find these views repellent. My *Contingency* book got a couple of good reviews, but these were vastly outnumbered by reviews which said that the book was frivolous, confused, and irresponsible. The gist of the criticisms I get from both left and right is pretty much the same as the gist of the criticisms aimed at Dewey by the Thomists, the Straussians, and the Marxists, back in the thirties and forties. Dewey thought, as I now do, that there was nothing bigger, more permanent and more reliable, behind our sense of moral obligation to those in pain than a certain contingent historical phenomenon – the gradual spread of the sense that the pain of others matters, regardless of whether they are of the same family, tribe, color, religion, nation, or intelligence as oneself. This idea, Dewey thought, cannot be shown to be true by science, or religion, or philosophy – at least if "shown to be true" means "capable of being made evident to anyone, regardless of background." It can only be made evident to people whom it is not too late to acculturate into our own particular, late-blooming, historically contingent form of life.

This Deweyan claim entails a picture of human beings as children of their time and place, without any significant metaphysical or biological limits on their plasticity. It means that a sense of moral obligation is a matter of conditioning rather than of insight. It also entails that the notion of insight (in any area, physics as well as ethics) as a glimpse of what is *there*, apart from any human needs and desires, cannot be made coherent. As William James put it, "The trail of the human serpent is over all." More specifically, our conscience and our aesthetic taste are, equally, products of the cultural environment in which we grew up. We decent, liberal humanitarian types (representatives of the moral community to which both my reviewers and I belong) are just luckier, not more insightful, than the bullies with whom we struggle.

This view is often referred to dismissively as "cultural relativism." But it is not relativistic, if that means saying that every moral view is as good as every other. *Our* moral view is, I firmly believe, much better than any competing view, even though there are a lot of people whom you will never be able to convert to it. It is one thing to say, falsely, that there is nothing to choose between us and the Nazis. It is another thing to say, correctly, that there is no neutral, common ground to which an experienced Nazi philosopher and I can repair in order to argue out our differences. That Nazi and I will always strike one another as begging all the crucial questions, arguing in circles.

Socrates and Plato suggested that if we tried hard enough we should find beliefs which *everybody* found intuitively plausible, and that among these would be moral beliefs whose implications, when clearly realized, would make us virtuous as well as knowledgeable. To thinkers like Allan Bloom (on the Straussian side) and Terry Eagleton (on the Marxist side), there just *must* be such beliefs – unwobbling pivots that determine the answer to the question "which moral or political alternative is *objectively* valid?" For Deweyan pragmatists like me, history and anthropology are enough to show that there are no unwobbling pivots, and that seeking objectivity is just a matter of getting as much intersubjective agreement as you can manage.

Nothing much has changed in philosophical debates about whether objectivity is more than intersubjectivity since the time I went to college – or, for that matter, since the time Hegel went to seminary. Nowadays we philosophers talk about "moral language" instead of "moral experience," and about "contextualist theories of reference" rather than about "the relation between subject and object." But this is just froth on the surface. My reasons for turning away from the anti-Deweyan views I imbibed at Chicago are pretty much the same reasons Dewey had for turning away from evangelical Christianity and from the neo-Hegelian pantheism which he embraced in his twenties. They are also pretty much the reasons which led Hegel to turn away from Kant, and to decide that both God and the Moral Law had to be temporalized and historicized to be believable. I do not think that I have more insight into the debates about our need for "absolutes" than I had when I was twenty, despite all the books I have read and arguments I have had in the intervening forty years. All those years of reading and arguing did was to let me spell out my disillusionment with Plato – my conviction that philosophy was no help in dealing with Nazis and other bullies – in more detail, and to a variety of different audiences.

At the moment there are two cultural wars being waged in the United States. The first is the one described in detail by my colleague James Davison Hunter in his comprehensive and informative *Culture Wars: The Struggle to Define America*. This war – between the people Hunter calls "progressivists" and those he calls "orthodox" – is important. It will decide whether our country continues along the trajectory defined by the Bill of Rights, the Reconstruction Amendments, the building of the land-grant colleges, female suffrage, the New Deal, *Brown vs. Board of Education*, the building of the community colleges, Lyndon Johnson's civil rights legislation, the feminist movement, and the gay rights movement. Continuing along this trajectory would mean that America might continue to set an example of increasing tolerance and increasing equality. But it may be that this trajectory could be continued only while Americans' average real income continued to rise. So 1973 may have been the beginning of the end: the end both of rising economic expectations and of the political consensus that emerged from the New Deal. The future of American politics may be just a series of increasingly blatant and increasingly successful variations on the Willie Horton spots. Sinclair Lewis' *It Can't Happen Here* may become an increasingly plausible scenario. Unlike Hunter, I feel no need to be judicious and balanced in my attitude toward the two sides in this first sort of culture war. I see the "orthodox" (the people who think that hounding gays out of the military promotes traditional family values) as the same honest, decent, blinkered, disastrous people who voted for Hitler in 1933. I see the "progressivists" as defining the only America I care about.

The second cultural war is being waged in magazines like *Critical Inquiry* and *Salmagundi*, magazines with high subscription rates and low circulations. It is between those who see modern liberal society as fatally flawed (the people handily lumped together as "postmodernists") and typical left-wing Democrat professors like myself, people who see ours as a society in which technology and democratic institutions can, with luck, collaborate to increase equality and decrease suffering. This war is not very important. Despite the conservative columnists who pretend to view with alarm a vast conspiracy (encompassing both the postmodernists and the pragmatists) to politicize the humanities and corrupt the youth, this war is just a tiny little dispute within what Hunter calls the "progressivist" ranks.

People on the postmodernist side of this dispute tend to share Noam Chomsky's view of the United States as run by a corrupt elite which aims at enriching itself by immiserating the Third World. From that perspective, our country is not so much in danger of slipping into fascism as it is a country which has always been quasi-fascist. These people typically think that nothing will change unless we get rid of "humanism," "liberal individualism," and "technologism." People like me see nothing wrong with any of these isms, nor with the political and moral heritage of the Enlightenment – with the least common denominator of Mill and Marx, Trotsky and Whitman, William James and Václav Havel. Typically, we Deweyans are sentimentally patriotic about America – willing to grant that it could slide into fascism at any time, but proud of its past and guardedly hopeful about its future.

Most people on my side of this second, tiny, up-market, cultural war have, in the light of the history of nationalized enterprises and central planning in Central and Eastern Europe, given up on socialism. We are willing to grant that welfare-state capitalism is the best we can hope for. Most of us who were brought up Trotskyite now feel forced to admit that Lenin and Trotsky did more harm than good, and that Kerensky has gotten a bum rap for the past seventy years. But we see ourselves as still faithful to everything that was good in the socialist movement. Those on the other side, however, still insist that nothing will change unless there is some sort of total revolution. Postmodernists who consider themselves post-Marxists still want to preserve the sort of purity of heart which Lenin feared he might lose if he listened to too much Beethoven.

I am distrusted by both the "orthodox" side in the important war and the "postmodern" side in the unimportant one, because I think that the "postmoderns" are philosophically right though politically silly, and that the "orthodox" are philosophically wrong as well as politically dangerous. Unlike both the orthodox and the postmoderns, I do not think that you can tell much about the worth of a philosopher's views on topics such as truth, objectivity, and the possibility of a single vision by discovering his politics, or his irrelevance to politics. So I do not think it counts in favor of Dewey's pragmatic view of truth that he was a fervent social democrat, nor against Heidegger's criticism of Platonic notions of objectivity that he was a Nazi, nor against Derrida's view of linguistic meaning that his most influential American ally, Paul de Man, wrote a couple of anti-Semitic articles when he was young. The idea that you can evaluate a writer's philosophical views by reference to their political utility seems to me a version of the bad Platonic–Straussian idea that we cannot have justice until philosophers become kings or kings philosophers.

Both the orthodox and the postmoderns still want a tight connection between people's politics and their views on large theoretical (theological, metaphysical, epistemological, metaphilosophical) matters. Some postmodernists who initially took my enthusiasm for Derrida to mean that I must be on their political side decided, after discovering that my politics were pretty much those of Hubert Humphrey, that I must have sold out. The orthodox tend to think that people who, like the postmodernists and me, believe neither in God nor in some suitable substitute, should think that everything is permitted, that everybody can do what they like. So they tell us that we are either inconsistent or self-deceptive in putting forward our moral or political views.

I take this near unanimity among my critics to show that most people – even a lot of purportedly liberated postmodernists – still hanker for something like what I wanted when I was fifteen – a way of holding reality and justice in a single vision. More specifically, they want to unite their sense of moral and political responsibility with a grasp of the ultimate determinants of our fate. They want to see love, power, and justice as coming together deep down in the nature of things, or in the human soul, or in the structure of language, or *somewhere*. They want some sort of guarantee that their intellectual acuity, and those special ecstatic moments which that acuity sometimes affords, are of some relevance to their moral convictions. They still think that virtue and knowledge are somehow linked – that being right about philosophical matters is important for right action. I think this is important only occasionally and incidentally.

I do not, however, want to argue that philosophy is socially useless. Had there been no Plato, the Christians would have had a harder time selling the idea that all God really wanted from us was fraternal love. Had there been no Kant, the nineteenth century would have had a harder time reconciling Christian ethics with Darwin's story about the descent of man. Had there been no Darwin, it would have been harder for Whitman and Dewey to detach the Americans from their belief that they were God's chosen people, to get them to start standing on their own feet. Had there been no Dewey and no Sidney Hook, American intellectual leftists of the thirties would have been as buffaloed by the Marxists as were their counterparts in France and in Latin America. Ideas do, indeed, have consequences.

But the fact that ideas have consequences does not mean that we philosophers, we specialists in ideas, are in a key position. We are not here to provide principles or foundations or deep theoretical diagnoses, or a synoptic vision. When I am asked (as, alas, I often am) what I take contemporary philosophy's "mission" or "task" to be, I get tongue-tied. The best I can do is to stammer that we philosophy professors are people who have a certain familiarity with a certain intellectual tradition, as chemists have a certain familiarity with what happens when you mix various substances together. We can offer some advice about what will happen when you try to combine or to separate certain ideas, on the basis of our knowledge of the results of past experiments. By doing so, we may be able to help you hold your time in thought. But we are not the people to come to if you want confirmation that the things you love with all your heart are central to the structure of the universe, or that your sense of moral responsibility is "rational and objective" rather than "just" a result of how you were brought up.

There are still, as C. S. Peirce put it, "philosophical slop-shops on every corner" which *will* provide such confirmation. But there is a price. To pay the price you have to turn your back on intellectual history and on what Milan Kundera calls "the fascinating imaginative realm where no one owns the truth and everyone has the right to be understood … the wisdom of the novel." You risk losing the sense of finitude, and the tolerance, which result from realizing how very many synoptic visions there have been, and how little argument can do to help you choose among them. Despite my relatively early disillusionment with Platonism, I am very glad that I spent all those years reading philosophy books. For I learned something that still seems very important: to distrust the intellectual snobbery which originally led me to read them. If I had not read all those books, I might never have been able to stop looking for what Derrida calls "a full presence beyond the reach of play," for a luminous, self-justifying, self-sufficient synoptic vision.

By now I am pretty sure that looking for such a presence and such a vision is a bad idea. The main trouble is that you might succeed, and your success might let you imagine that you have something more to rely on than the tolerance and decency of your fellow human beings. The democratic community of Dewey's dreams is a community in which nobody imagines that. It is a community in which everybody thinks that it is human solidarity, rather than knowledge of something not merely human, that really matters. The actually existing approximations to such a fully democratic, fully secular community now seem to me the greatest achievements of our species. In comparison, even Hegel's and Proust's books seem optional, orchidaceous extras.

33

Biography and Philosophy

Interview Conducted by Andrzej Szahaj

Question: You were born in a leftist family. Many years ago you mentioned to me that some Polish trade-union activists were sometimes guests at the home of your parents. Do you remember them? What did the political activity of your parents consist of?

Richard Rorty: Many of my parents' friends were connected with the U.S. trade union movement, particularly the Amalgamated Clothing Workers. Most of them were Polish Jews, who kept up connections with Poland insofar as they could, and particularly with the trade union movement there. These friends, and their Polish visitors, were around a lot in my childhood, but I cannot remember any particular names or dates. I do remember that my parents and I were informed about the Katyn Forest massacre shortly after it occurred, and that my father tried to publicize the fact that it was done by the Russians rather than the Germans. I also remember that my parents (and I, on their recommendation) read Milosz's book *The Captive Mind* when it first appeared (in, I think, 1948 – simultaneously with Orwell's *1984*).

My father had edited one of the American Communist Party's magazines in the mid-twenties. By the early thirties, my parents had become what the Stalinists called "Trotskyites" – nominally believers in revolution, but drifting toward more conventional social democratic views. By the forties and fifties they had become militant anticommunists – warning the U.S. against putting any faith in Stalin. They were, simultaneously, active in movements in support of relieving the condition of poor un-unionized agricultural workers, and of blacks. For a time during the forties they were employed as publicists and lobbyists by one of the black unions – the Brotherhood of Pullman Car Porters.

Q: Did you have any personal contact with Dewey during your youth? Was it connected with your family, with the work of your parents? You mentioned to me once that there were some Polish accents in Dewey's life? What was it?

RR: My mother told me that I passed sandwiches around at a party which Dewey attended when I was seven years old. That was the only time I was in his presence.

"Biography and Philosophy," interview with Richard Rorty by Andrzej Szahaj, pp. 148–60 in Eduardo Mendieta (ed.), *Take Care of Freedom and Truth Will Take Care of Itself* (Stanford: Stanford University Press, 2006), © 2006 by Andrezej Szahaj. Reprinted by kind permission of the author.

Dewey spent a year in Philadelphia gathering information about the Polish immigrant community there. There are accounts of what he did during that year in the various biographies. He was also very active in the discussions concerning the post–First World War government of Poland, and intervened, unsuccessfully, with Woodrow Wilson on behalf of one of the groups that claimed to represent Poland. I don't know the details, but you can find them in the various biographies of Dewey.

Q: You studied at the University of Chicago. Who was the most influential teacher during the time of your studies, in terms of your personal development? Did Carnap or Sellars exert an influence on you? What was Sellars like as a teacher and as a man? Who was the most important person you ever met in terms of your own philosophical and political development, and why?

RR: I was impressed by several teachers at Chicago – Leo Strauss, Charles Hartshorne (a student of Whitehead's), Richard McKeon, and Carnap.

I learned my first lessons in analytic philosophy from Carnap (who assigned Ayer's *Language, Truth, and Logic*, which I initially found very persuasive). Eventually, however, I was persuaded by Quine and Sellars to reject some of Carnap's best-known views. Sellars was never my teacher; I just read his writings with admiration.

Q: I know that Allan Bloom was one of your colleagues during your studies at Chicago. I know also that you were in touch with him later as well. Could you tell me something about the University of Chicago at the time of your and Bloom's studies, about the Leo Strauss circle, and about Bloom himself? In one of your interviews you said that the University of Chicago had been very leftist during the time of your studies. I was a bit surprised, because the University of Chicago has been seen mostly as a den of conservatism, so to speak.

RR: Chicago was still leftist when I was there (1946–52). The conservatives only came along later. Strauss was a mysterious, charismatic figure. Bloom believed what Strauss said about the need to go back to Plato and Aristotle when thinking about political matters, but I was never convinced. Strauss's students were the brightest people in the university, so I was glad to be part of his circle, even though I never really grasped his point of view.

Q: What was your relation to the so-called counterculture movement?

RR: I smoked a little pot and let my hair grow long, but that was about all. I soon decided that the radical students who wanted to trash the university were people with whom I would never have much sympathy. I never took seriously the idea that American culture was "sick" and needed to be replaced by an alternative culture.

Q: You worked for many years at Princeton. Why did you leave Princeton? What was the reason for your dissident attitude toward analytic philosophy, visible in your essays written while still at Princeton? For the past twenty years you always wanted to work outside any philosophical department. Why?

RR: After I began to think that analytic philosophy, of the sort practiced by my Princeton colleagues, was not as wonderful as I had first imagined, I began to teach Nietzsche and Heidegger. But I felt that graduate students in philosophy who wanted to work with me on authors such as these, and who shared my doubts about analytic philosophy, were in danger of not having proper academic careers. So I thought it best to find a job outside of a philosophy department, one in which I did not have to worry about advising doctoral candidates, and therefore stood in no danger of wrecking their careers by luring them into areas of interest which would make them unpopular with departmental colleagues.

Q: You are one of the Great Four of American philosophy: Davidson, Putnam, Quine, Rorty (in alphabetical order). All of you can be situated (maybe except Davidson) some-where between analytic philosophy and some other traditions, mostly pragmatism, and it seems to me that that is why they are so interesting and inspiring. It seems to me that philosophical heterodoxy is always more interesting than any kind of orthodoxy. What do you think of that? What is your opinion about the role of Quine, Davidson, and Putnam in the process of changing American philosophy, analytic philosophy and philosophy as such? Have they been successful in doing that? Have you been successful in doing that? It seems to me that most American philosophy departments are still fortresses of a very traditional version of analytic philosophy. Stanford seems to be a good example of that. Why is that?

RR: I agree about heterodoxy. But I think that the Big Four in postwar analytic phi-losophy are Quine, Sellars, Davidson, and Brandom. Putnam's and my own contribu-tions are less important. Davidson radicalized Quine, and Brandom radicalized Sellars, and both of them ended up with quite similar views. The conjunction of their views seems to me pragmatist treatment of mind and language that is more perspicuous than that offered by the classical pragmatists.

Davidson and Brandom are, alas, marginal to contemporary American analytic phi-losophy. They are respected, and have many admirers, but they are not "mainstream." This is because they offer no research programs of the sort that other analytic philosophers of mind and language do: they dissolve a lot of old problems without putting forward new ones for the graduate students to work on.

Q: Why is it that only you among those Great Four have reached out so openly to the so-called Continental tradition in philosophy? Even Putnam, who de facto repeats some elements of neo-Kantianism in his philosophy, does not seem to be fully aware of the presence and richness of this tradition. Why this separateness of analytic philosophy? What was the impulse to overcome it in your case?

RR: I do not think there are any very deep reasons why Putnam and I took divergent paths in this respect. I just happened to get on a certain course of reading while he got on another. I had the advantage, however, of having had a better training in the history of philosophy than Putnam had had, for such training was one of Chicago's specialties. Putnam has never, as far as I know, shown much interest in Hegel, whereas I had already read some Hegel when I was in my teens. Putnam swerved briefly in the direction of Hegelian historicism in his book *Reason, Truth, and History*, but historicism has never attracted him as much as it attracts me. (By *historicism* I do not mean claims about his-torical inevitability, of the sort Popper rightly criticized in *The Poverty of Historicism*, but rather the idea that our philosophical vocabularies and problematics are attempts to deal with contingent historical circumstances rather than "perennial" or "basic" ones.)

Q: What is really new and interesting in American philosophy today?

RR: The figure from whom I have learned most is Brandom. I think that his oeuvre may prove to be the upshot of the last fifty years of work in analytic philosophy of mind and language. Nobody else combines an ability to expound a full-fledged systematic account of mind and language with the ability to spin a dramatic narrative of the history of philosophy. He seems to me in a different class from practically every other American philosopher of his generation. Nobody else would even have dreamed of synthesizing Frege and Hegel, but Brandom has managed to do so, brilliantly.

Politics

Q: As far as I know you have always been leftist and anticommunist at the same time (I know for example that as a student you were an author of resolution of sympathy with the students of Charles University in Prague who did not want to accept communism in 1948). Was it easy in the U.S.? You are often treated as a neoliberal thinker. Is there any difference between being leftist and being liberal?

RR: In the U.S., *liberal* means what *social democrat* means in Europe. In the early years of the Cold War there were still American leftists who were apologists for Stalin, but they disappeared fairly quickly in the fifties, as did Marxism. There was a revival of interest in Marxism in the U.S. in the mid-sixties, but it was short-lived. The students who read Marx in the sixties, and who wanted to "overthrow the system," called themselves radicals as opposed to liberals. They tried to deny the title of "leftist" to people who favored working within the system. Some of these people are still around, working as professors in American universities, and they still use "mere liberal" as a term of contempt.

Q: The great Polish poet Czeslaw Milosz wrote that people of good will became spokesmen of communism because of "Hegel bite," the conviction that history must necessarily head in a good direction and that communists need only realize its plan. This "Hegel bite" was typical not only for Polish intellectuals but, for example, for French ones too. I think that the scale of this phenomenon in the U.S. was much less than in Europe. What was the reason for that?

RR: The idea of "the inevitable movement of history" was never very popular among American intellectuals, except in the rather short period between the beginning of the Great Depression in 1929 (when it did indeed seem that capitalism might collapse) and the revelations of Stalin's crimes in the middle and late thirties. Dewey, who was then the most influential American philosopher, had no patience with the idea of historical inevitability. Philosophy has never had the interest or the prestige among American intellectuals that it has had among European ones, and very few American intellectuals in the twentieth century ever read a word of Hegel.

Q: You are known for your friendly attitude toward Eastern Europe. You have visited probably all East European countries, and some, like Poland, several times. What has been the meaning of the Eastern Europe experience for leftist political thought, in your opinion?

RR: I think the main impact of the liberation of Eastern Europe is to permit American intellectuals to look back on the Cold War and think of it as a good, successful war. If one adopts the point of view of people in Guatemala, Vietnam, or Chile, by contrast, it is very difficult to see the long struggle against the Soviet Union as a good, much less an heroic one. But people in Eastern Europe do seem grateful to the U.S. for having kept up the pressure on the Soviet Union for all those decades, and this makes Americans feel that what their country was doing between 1949 and 1989 had some redeeming features, despite the tragedy of Vietnam and the guilt they feel over replacing Allende with Pinochet.

Q: In *Achieving Our Country* you try to show the importance and value of the so-called old left, interested mostly in economical issues, as compared with so-called new left or cultural left, interested mostly in problems of multiculturalism, politics of difference, and politics of recognition. You are very much in favor of the old left. Don't you think that interests of the new left in cultural issues result from the silent conviction that nothing can be changed in the area of the economy? It can be treated as an expression of helplessness in the face of a new stage of evolution of world economy; I mean the transition from regulated, national markets to a deregulated global market. It seems that this kind of politics, typical for the old left, was efficient when the economy was mainly a national one, simply because one could easily find the possible target of political intervention: the state. Today it is much harder because the fight with global capital is in a sense a fight with a shadow: one never knows for sure where the enemy is (some people are not convinced that a global capital and its operations are any threat at all, by the way). Global capital would have to be taken under control, but nobody knows how to do it. Sometimes it is also said that the old left is over because a classical working class is over. What do you think about that?

It seems to me that it lacks any plausible alternative for today's economical system. We are witnessing something like Fukuyama's prophecy being fulfilled, not at the level of politics (global triumph of liberal democracy) but at the level of economy (global triumph of neoliberal economics of the Chicago boys' style). Nobody knows what an alternative economic system could be. Perhaps this is the most visible triumph of the right: success in persuading people that there is no alternative for the status quo. By the way, is there any?

RR: I entirely agree. I have no idea how to arrange the global economy so as to produce global social justice. I don't want the Chicago school economists to run the world, and yet the people who demonstrate against the IMF and the World Bank also, it seem to me, have no positive proposals to offer. The old left has no proposals to make other than to recommend the usual social-democratic welfare-state measures that worked in the rich democracies, but may never be feasible in really poor countries. Neither does the new left. Nobody does. That may indeed be why leftists are turning away from economics to culture. But I do not think that this turn will do anybody much good.

Q: Are the classical analyses by C. W. Mills still valid in the case of the U.S.? I mean his analyses of elites of power, oligarchies, and so on.

RR: I read Mills so long ago that I have, I'm afraid, forgotten what his analyses were. I was not greatly impressed by his work, which did not strike me as particularly original.

Q: You said in your discussion with Angela Davis held at Stanford several months ago that Europe was ahead of America. What did you mean by that?

RR: I meant that the welfare state was better developed in Europe than in America, and that secularism was more advanced in Western Europe than in the U.S. I think that the development of a secularist culture is very important for social progress, and I very much regret the recent rise of evangelical Protestantism, particularly of the fundamentalist variety, in the U.S.

Q: During the same debate you recalled the notion of the West as something very precious, which should be defended or even spread. This is an attitude rather rare among leftist or liberal scholars, in an epoch of the influential ideology of multiculturalism.

Reading a lot about these issues lately, I was astonished by the verve and popularity of anti-Western attitudes among scholars in America. Sometimes they are very anti-American too. Frankly, it seems to me to be a little funny, because while reading them one can have impression that Western culture is the most oppressive culture of all and the U.S. is the most oppressive state of all. Coming from such a country as Poland and remembering quite well the communist times, I am a little bit irritated by such announcements, frankly. To tell the truth, I am under the impression that some of those radical critics do not know what real oppression is. What is your opinion about these issues?

RR: I agree that they have little sense of what real oppression is, and they seem unable to appreciate the immense strides toward freedom and justice that have been made in the West in the course of the last two hundred years. There is a line in one of the Gilbert and Sullivan operettas that comes to mind: "The idiot who praises, in enthusiastic tone/ Every century but this, and every country but his own."

Q: Don't you think that recent interest in group consciousness, community, and so on can be connected with the sense of uncertainty and fear so typical of what Ulrich Beck has called the "risk society"? In one interview you emphasized the need to put communities behind us in the process of self-creation. Don't you think that this is a good scenario only for strong people, for Nietzschean *Übermensch*? People try to find safety and support for themselves as human beings in a world of sharp competition and fight for survival so typical for deregulated capitalism. As individuals they feel helpless and powerless. Group solidarity, especially ethnic or racial solidarity, is probably the easiest and cheapest medicine for lack of certainty and safety. So it seems to me that multiculturalism is a typical Western way of inventing cultures and communities in order to fight the fear present in today's society (in Europe it is probably nationalism instead of multiculturalism). Apart from that, it also seems to be a tool used in a political fight for power. What do you think of that?

RR: We all need communities to belong to, but the best communities are the ones that are flexible enough to allow their members a lot of room for self-creation. I see what you mean about the need for solidarity in risky situations, but I don't think that the multiculturalist movement is to be explained in those terms. I think it is a very parochial phenomenon of contemporary Western (especially U.S.) academic life, and has little resonance or appeal outside the academy.

Q: What is your opinion about political correctness? Is this really a new type of McCarthyism, as is sometimes said?

RR: Most of the things the right calls "politically correct" and makes fun of are very good things – for example, ceasing to tell women humiliating sexist jokes, ceasing to discriminate against gays and lesbians, and so on. Occasionally there are people who carry their watchfulness against sexism and homophobia and racism to absurd extremes, and they sometimes behave in ways for which the term "McCarthyism" is appropriate. But they remain rare exceptions.

Q: You live in a very religious society, and so do I. Can religion still play a significant role in changing society for the better, in pragmatist progress?

RR: Sometimes it has been useful. "Liberation theology" was useful in Latin America until the present pope decided to stamp it out. The black churches in the U.S. were indispensable in the civil rights movement of the fifties and sixties. But on the whole I think religion still does more political harm than good. Certainly in the U.S. the "born-again Christians" who support Bush make up a reactionary, and very dangerous, movement.

Q: You are very much in favor of patriotism (I remember well your article "The Unpatriotic Academy") and individualism at the same time. You do not like all this talk about group consciousness, multiculturalism, community, and so on. But how can one be patriotic without being communal? To put it another way: what should be an object of patriotism in the case of a country like the U.S.? Nation? Political system? Democracy? Constitution? In Europe, we don't have trouble identifying the object: the nation is always seen mostly in terms of ethnicity, like in Germany, or in terms of a common culture, like in France. But it seems that in the U.S. such an idea of nation has no appeal.

RR: French culture is a different thing for French rightists than for French leftists, and a different thing for American rightists than for American leftists. For the latter, it is a matter of taking pride in the heritage of figures like Jefferson, Lincoln, Wilson, Roosevelt, Martin Luther King, and so on. I think it is important for political movements within a country to identify the events and figures in whom citizens of that country can take pride, to use this pride as a means of generating sympathy for its political aims. My article "The Unpatriotic Academy" was a rebuke to the American "cultural left" for not being willing to try to build an electoral majority. One cannot build such a majority if one proclaims that one's country is no good.

Q: In your works (*Achieving Our Country* and others) you postulate a world democratic government as an element of the future political order. How can one be patriotic and a partisan of a democratic world government at the same time? Doesn't one need to be cosmopolitan in order to postulate the government in question?

RR: One can be an American patriot and a cosmopolitan at the same time by taking pride in America's role, since the time of Woodrow Wilson, in constructing an international order, and especially in giving some credibility to the United Nations. This order is the one that President Bush is in the process of destroying, but U.S. presidents from FDR to Clinton did much to build it up. Should the internationalist momentum that American presidents have given to world affairs be resumed after Bush leaves office, it may become possible for Americans to view the gradual turnover of national sovereignty to international authority as the natural outcome of pride in their country's history. Surrender of American sovereignty can be viewed as the ideological Americanization of the world – as having persuaded the nations to come together in the way that the thirteen original American colonies came together in the eighteenth century.

Q: Such a government would demand a certain kind of surrender of the dominant position of the U.S. in today's world. Do you think that it would be possible? If so, what would have to be changed in the U.S. in order to be ready to accept such a government? Is America still an unfinished project? If so, what should be done to finish it?

RR: It is very unlikely to happen, but such a surrender seems the only way to avoid nuclear war between the U.S. and China at some point in the present century. Unless the U.S., Russia, China, and the European Union agree on international peace-keeping measures, and unless they cooperate in setting up a world police force, we are probably doomed. To accomplish what is necessary to avoid an eventual nuclear war, an American president would have to persuade the country that there was more safety in multilateral-ism than in U.S. unilateralism. This would be a hard, but not impossible, sell. Gore might well have attempted it.

Q: What is the future of the U.S.? What kind of concrete social reforms should be implemented in the U.S. in order to improve this country economically and socially? Some people are very afraid of the balkanization of America, which is supposed to take place as a result of uncontrolled immigration; changes in demographics (white people are already the minority in California and in many huge cities like New York, Los Angeles, Detroit, and Chicago, and they will be the minority in the entire country in about 2050); and the potential resistance of some groups against assimilation (Cubans in Florida are probably the best example of successful refusal of assimilation, successful in terms of economical and cultural independence from the majority). Do you think that all of this is a real threat for this country?

RR: The Cubans are indeed setting a very bad example. But the U.S. has been success-ful in incorporating immigrants so far, and I don't think that there is any reason why we should suddenly become much worse. The alarm about nonwhite majorities is no more realistic than the worry, a hundred years ago, that the newly arrived immigrants from Europe would somehow submerge the "real" Americans whose ancestors had arrived earlier. A lot, of course, depends on the willingness of children of previous immigrants to marry children of recent immigrants. Such intermarriage has been essential in the past, and remains essential in the future. Mexican Americans and Vietnamese Americans, for example, are now viewed by people who would call themselves "white" as "mar-riageable," even though black Americans are not.

Q: I remember that you told me once the history of your own family as an example of successful assimilation. How was that done?

RR: My grandfather came over from Ireland around 1850, at a time when Irish immi-grants were treated like dirt by most Americans – as badly as Polish and Italian and Jewish immigrants were treated somewhat later in the nineteenth century. He married above his station, into a family that had emigrated from England in the eighteenth cen-tury. It took another couple of generations for Irish immigrants as a group to win com-plete social acceptance, but it was complete by 1950. By that date, it was almost, if not quite, complete for the Poles and Italians. By now, Americans don't usually ask questions about the ancestry of the people their children marry, except in the case of black – white intermarriage, which is still very rare. (Marriage between Jews and non-Jews, by con-trast, is very common. My mother, for example, was the daughter of a German-American Protestant clergyman, but two of her brothers, as well as her son, married Jewish women.)

Q: To tell the truth I was shocked when I read that separation between black and white people is now nearly the same as it was at the beginning of the civil rights move-ment (this was the conclusion of research done at Harvard University, published several months ago). I do not want to believe it, but it seems as though this problem has not been solved so far. Why is this? It seems to me that it might be the expression of failed expectations on the part of blacks: because you white people do not accept them fully, they separate themselves from you to demonstrate that they do not need you.

RR: I would not blame the blacks for the continuing separation. It is not their choice, it is still being forced upon them. The problem is that the heritage of slavery has produced the so-called black underclass – millions of uneducated, unemployed, and almost unemployable black people living in the big American cities. This underclass contains, naturally, a lot of criminals. So whites are scared of poor black men, and try to stay as far away from them as possible. The problem of the black underclass could be gradually solved by the government, but only by means of a huge increase in public spending. The whites remain too selfish to pay the taxes that would be necessary to rescue black children from misery.

It would also help, of course, if the whites would stop thinking that one drop of black blood (unlike one drop of Irish or Polish or Jewish blood) "pollutes." That belief is why black–white marriage is so rare. It is not a belief shared by the blacks.

Q: Are you optimistic or pessimistic about the future of your own country and the world as such?

RR: Very pessimistic indeed, for the reasons given above. I do not see how nuclear war is to be avoided or how the poor nations are to be raised to the level of the rich ones.

34

The Fire of Life

In an essay called "Pragmatism and Romanticism" I tried to restate the argument of Shelley's "Defense of Poetry." At the heart of Romanticism, I said, was the claim that reason can only follow paths that the imagination has first broken. No words, no reasoning. No imagination, no new words. No such words, no moral or intellectual progress.

I ended that essay by contrasting the poet's ability to give us a richer language with the philosopher's attempt to acquire non-linguistic access to the really real. Plato's dream of such access was itself a great poetic achievement. But by Shelley's time, I argued, it had been dreamt out. We are now more able than Plato was to acknowledge our finitude – to admit that we shall never be in touch with something greater than ourselves. We hope instead that human life here on earth will become richer as the centuries go by because the language used by our remote descendants will have more resources than ours did. Our vocabulary will stand to theirs as that of our primitive ancestors stands to ours.

In that essay, as in previous writings, I used "poetry" in an extended sense. I stretched Harold Bloom's term "strong poet" to cover prose writers who had invented new language games for us to play – people like Plato, Newton, Marx, Darwin, and Freud as well as versifiers like Milton and Blake. These games might involve mathematical equations, or inductive arguments, or dramatic narratives, or (in the case of the versifiers) prosodic innovation. But the distinction between prose and verse was irrelevant to my philosophical purposes.

Shortly after finishing "Pragmatism and Romanticism," I was diagnosed with inoperable pancreatic cancer. Some months after I learned the bad news, I was sitting around having coffee with my elder son and a visiting cousin. My cousin (who is a Baptist minister) asked me whether I had found my thoughts turning toward religious topics, and I said no. "Well, what about philosophy?" my son asked. "No," I replied, neither the philosophy I had written nor that which I had read seemed to have any particular bearing on my situation. I had no quarrel with Epicurus's argument that it is irrational to fear death, nor with Heidegger's suggestion that ontotheology originates in an attempt to evade our mortality. But neither *ataraxia* (freedom from disturbance) nor *Sein zum Tode* (being toward death) seemed in point.

Richard M. Rorty, "The Fire of Life," *Poetry*, November 2007: 129–31, © Richard Rorty. Reprinted with permission from the Estate of Richard Rorty.

"Hasn't *anything* you've read been of any use?" my son persisted. "Yes," I found myself blurting out, "poetry." "Which poems?" he asked. I quoted two old chestnuts that I had recently dredged up from memory and been oddly cheered by, the most quoted lines of Swinburne's "Garden of Proserpine":

> We thank with brief thanksgiving
>   Whatever gods may be
> That no life lives for ever;
> That dead men rise up never;
> That even the weariest river
>   Winds somewhere safe to sea.

and Landor's "On His Seventy-Fifth Birthday":

> Nature I loved, and next to Nature, Art;
> I warmed both hands before the fire of life,
> It sinks, and I am ready to depart.

I found comfort in those slow meanders and those stuttering embers. I suspect that no comparable effect could have been produced by prose. Not just imagery, but also rhyme and rhythm were needed to do the job. In lines such as these, all three conspire to produce a degree of compression, and thus of impact, that only verse can achieve. Compared to the shaped charges contrived by versifiers, even the best prose is scattershot.

Though various bits of verse have meant a great deal to me at particular moments in my life, I have never been able to write any myself (except for scribbling sonnets during dull faculty meetings – a form of doodling). Nor do I keep up with the work of contemporary poets. When I do read verse, it is mostly favorites from adolescence. I suspect that my ambivalent relation to poetry, in this narrower sense, is a result of Oedipal complications produced by having had a poet for a father. (See James Rorty, *Children of the Sun* [Macmillan, 1926].)

However that may be, I now wish that I had spent somewhat more of my life with verse. This is not because I fear having missed out on truths that are incapable of statement in prose. There are no such truths; there is nothing about death that Swinburne and Landor knew but Epicurus and Heidegger failed to grasp. Rather, it is because I would have lived more fully if I had been able to rattle off more old chestnuts – just as I would have if I had made more close friends. Cultures with richer vocabularies are more fully human – farther removed from the beasts – than those with poorer ones; individual men and women are more fully human when their memories are amply stocked with verses.

Guide to Further Reading

Primary Works

For a complete bibliography of Rorty's writings through 2005, see Eduardo Mendieta (ed.), *Take Care of Freedom and Truth Will Take Care of Itself: Interviews with Richard Rorty* (Stanford, CA: Stanford University Press, 2006), pp. 161–205. A version is maintained online as well at: http://www.stanford.edu/~mvr2j/rr/biblio_2007.html.

Additional works that contain primary material by Rorty:

Balslev, Anindita Niyogi, *Cultural Otherness: Correspondence with Richard Rorty* (Atlanta: Scholars Press,1999).

Brandom, Robert (ed.), *Rorty and His Critics* (Oxford: Blackwell, 2000).

Eco, Umberto and Stefan Collini (ed.), *Interpretation and Overinterpretation* (New York: Cambridge University Press, 1992).

Huang, Yong (ed.), *Rorty, Pragmatism, and Confucianism: With Responses by Richard Rorty* (Albany, NY: State University of New York Press, 2009).

Mouffe, Chantal (ed.), *Deconstruction and Pragmatism* (New York: Routledge, 1996).

Niżnik, Józef and John T. Sanders (eds.), *Debating the State of Philosophy: Habermas, Rorty, and Kolakowski* (Westport, CT: Praeger Publishers, 1996).

Nystrom, Derek and Kent Puckett, *Against Oligarchies, Against Bosses: A Conversation with Richard Rorty* (Charlottesville, VA: Prickly Pear Pamphlets, 1998).

Rorty, Richard and Pascal Engel, *What's the Use of Truth?*, trans. William McCuaig (New York: Columbia University Press, 2007).

Saatkamp, Herman J. (ed.), *Rorty and Pragmatism* (Nashville, TN: Vanderbilt University Press, 1995).

Secondary Works

The secondary literature on Rorty is massive. The annotated bibliography compiled by Richard Rumana in 2002, whose over 1,200 entries are helpfully cross-referenced and indexed by subject, provides a good overview:

Richard Rumana (ed.), *Richard Rorty: An Annotated Bibliography of Secondary Literature* (New York: Rodopi, 2002).

Some of the best work on Rorty has been collected in a four-volume reference edition that spans his career, with volumes dedicated to "Philosophy," "Post-Analytic Philosophy," "Politics, Irony and Solidarity," and "Culture, Interpretation and Conversations":

Alan Malachowski (ed.), *Richard Rorty: Sage Masters of Modern Thought*, 4 Vols. (London: Sage Publications, 2002).

Critical anthologies on Rorty

Brandom, Robert (ed.), *Rorty and His Critics* (Oxford: Blackwell, 2000).

Casey, M.A., *Meaninglessness: The Solutions of Nietzsche, Freud, and Rorty* (Lanham, MD: Lexington Books, 2002).

Festenstein, Matthew and Simon Thompson (eds.), *Richard Rorty: Critical Dialogues* (Cambridge: Polity Press, 2001).

Guignon, Charles and David Hiley (eds.), *Richard Rorty* (Cambridge: Cambridge University Press, 2003).

Jenkins, Keith, *On "What is History?": From Carr and Elton to Rorty and White* (New York: Routledge, 1995).

Malachowski, Alan (ed.), *Reading Rorty* (Oxford: Blackwell, 1990).

Peters, Michael A. and Paulo Ghiraldelli, Jr. (eds.), *Richard Rorty: Education, Philosophy, and Politics* (Lanham, MD: Rowman & Littlefield, 2002).

Pettegrew, John (ed.), *A Pragmatist's Progress?: Richard Rorty and American Intellectual History* (Lanham, MD: Rowman & Littlefield, 2000).

Saatkamp, Herman J. (ed.), *Rorty and Pragmatism* (Nashville, TN: Vanderbilt University Press, 1995).

Selected books on Rorty

Arcilla, Rene, *For the Love of Perfection: Richard Rorty and Liberal Education* (New York: Routledge, 1995).

Auxier, Randall E. and Lewis E. Hahn (eds.), *The Philosophy of Richard Rorty*, Library of Living Philosophers, vol. 32 (Chicago: Open Court, 2009).

Bacon, Michael, *Richard Rorty: Pragmatism and Political Liberalism* (Lanham, MD: Lexington Books, 2007).

Calder, Gideon, *Rorty's Politics of Redescription* (Cardiff: University of Wales Press, 2007).

Dann, Elijah G. *After Rorty: The Possibilities for Ethics and Religious Belief* (New York: Continuum, 2006).

Dussel, Enrique, *The Underside of Modernity: Apel, Ricoeur, Rorty, Taylor, and the Philosophy of Liberation*, trans. Eduardo Mendieta (Atlantic Highlands, NJ: Humanities Press, 1996).

Festenstein, Matthew, *Pragmatism and Political Theory: From Dewey to Rorty* (Chicago: University of Chicago Press, 1997).

Frazier, Brad, *Rorty and Kierkegaard on Irony and Moral Commitment: Philosophical and Theological Connections* (New York: Palgrave Macmillan, 2006).

Gander, Eric M., *The Last Conceptual Revolution: A Critique of Richard Rorty's Political Philosophy* (Albany: State University of New York Press, 1999).

Gascoigne, Neil, *Richard Rorty* (Cambridge: Polity Press, 2008).

Geras, Norman, *Solidarity in the Conversation of Mankind: The Ungroundable Liberalism of Richard Rorty* (London: Verso, 1995).

Green, Judith, *Pragmatism and Social Hope: Deepening Democracy in Global Contexts* (New York: Columbia University Press, 2008).

Hall, David L. *Richard Rorty: Prophet and Poet of the New Pragmatism* (Albany: State University of New York Press, 1994).

Hayfa, Tarek. *The Problem of Public Justification in Political Philosophy: Rawls, Rorty, and Habermas* (Saarbrücken: VDM Verlag, 2008).

Heineman, Robert A. *Authority and the Liberal Tradition: From Hobbes to Rorty* (New Brunswick, NJ: Transaction Publishers, 1994 [1984]).

Hollinger, Robert and David Depew, *Pragmatism: From Progressivism to Postmodernism* (Westport, CT: Praeger Publishers, 1995).

Johnson, Peter, *Moral Philosophers and the Novel: A Study of Winch, Nussbaum, and Rorty* (New York: Palgrave Macmillan, 2004).

Kolenda, Konstantin, *Rorty's Humanistic Pragmatism: Philosophy Democratized* (Tampa: University of South Florida Press, 1990).

Koopman, Colin, *Pragmatism as Transition: Historicity and Hope in James, Dewey, and Rorty* (New York: Columbia University Press, 2009).

Kuipers, Ronald A., *Solidarity and the Stranger: Themes in the Social Philosophy of Richard Rorty* (Lanham, MD: University Press of America, 1997).

Langsdorf, Lenore and Andrew R. Smith, *Recovering Pragmatism's Voice: The Classical Tradition, Rorty, and the Philosophy of Communication* (Albany: State University Press of New York, 1995).

Malachowski, Alan, *Richard Rorty* (Princeton, NJ: Princeton University Press, 2002).

Melkonian, Markar, *Richard Rorty's Politics: Liberalism at the End of the American Century* (Amherst, NY: Humanity Books, 1999).

Mosteller, Timothy, *Relativism in Contemporary Philosophy: MacIntyre, Putnam, and Rorty* (New York: Continuum, 2006).

Mounce, Howard, *The Two Pragmatisms: From Peirce to Rorty* (New York: Routledge, 1997).

Nielsen, Kai, *After the Demise of the Tradition: Rorty, Critical Theory, and the Fate of Philosophy* (Boulder, CO: Westview Press, 1991).

Rothleder, Dianne, *The Work of Friendship: Rorty, His Critics, and The Project of Solidarity* (Albany: State University of New York Press, 1999).

Rumana, Richard, *On Rorty* (Belmont, CA: Wadsworth, 2000).

Tartaglia, James, *Routledge Philosophy Guidebook to Rorty and the Mirror of Nature* (New York: Routledge, 2007).

Tolland, Anders, *Epistemological Relativism and Realistic Epistemology: Richard Rorty and the Possibility of a Philosophical Theory of Knowledge* (Goteborg: Acta Universitatis Gothoburgensis, 1991).

Vaden House, D., *Without God or His Double: Realism, Relativism, and Rorty* (Leiden: E.J. Brill, 1994).

Voparil, Christopher J., *Richard Rorty: Politics and Vision* (Lanham, MD: Rowman & Littlefield, 2006).

Zhang, Wei, *Heidegger, Rorty, and the Eastern Thinkers: A Hermeneutics of Cross-Cultural Understanding* (Albany: State University of New York Press, 2006).

Index

Page numbers followed by 'n' indicate footnotes. Abbreviations used in the index are: PMN = *Philosophy and the Mirror of Nature*; RR = Richard Rorty; in cross-references, a comma is used to indicate a sub-entry, e.g. analytic philosophy/philosophers, conversations with